Mike Holt's Illustrated Guide to

CHANGES TO THE
NATIONAL ELECTRICAL CODE®

BASED ON THE

2020 NEC®

D0904039

Mike Holt Enterprises
888.NEC.CODE (632.2633) • www.MikeHolt.com

NOTICE TO THE READER

Mike Holt's Illustrated Guide to Changes to the National Electrical Code®*, based on the 2020 NEC*®
First Printing: November 2019

Author: Mike Holt
Technical Illustrator: Mike Culbreath
Cover Design: Bryan Burch
Layout Design and Typesetting: Cathleen Kwas

COPYRIGHT © 2019 Charles Michael Holt
ISBN 978-1-950431-01-4

Produced and Printed in the USA

 This logo is a registered trademark of Mike Holt Enterprises, Inc.

If you are an instructor and would like to request an examination copy of this or other Mike Holt Publications:

Call: 888.NEC.CODE (632.2633) • Fax: 352.360.0983

E-mail: Info@MikeHolt.com • Visit: www.MikeHolt.com/Instructors

You can download a sample PDF of all our publications by visiting www.MikeHolt.com/products.

I dedicate this book to the
Lord Jesus Christ, *my mentor and teacher.*
Proverbs 16:3

We Care...

Since the day we started our business over 40 years ago, we have been working hard to produce products that get results, and to help individuals in their pursuit of learning how to be successful in this exciting industry. I have built my business on the idea that customers come first, and that everyone on my team will do everything they possibly can to take care of you. I want you to know that we value you, and are honored that you have chosen us to be your partner in electrical training.

I believe that you are the future of this industry and that it is you who will make the difference in years to come. My goal is to share with you everything that I know and to encourage you to pursue your education on a continuous basis. I hope that not only will you learn theory, code, calculations or how to pass an exam, but that in the process you will become the expert in the field and the person who others know to trust.

We are dedicated to providing quality electrical training that will help you take your skills to the next level and we genuinely care about you. Thanks for choosing Mike Holt Enterprises for your electrical training needs.

God bless and much success,

Mike Holt

Exam Preparation | Continuing Education | Apprenticeship Products | In-House Training | & more

"...as for me and my house, we will serve the Lord." [Joshua 24:15]

Table of Contents

About This Textbook

Mike Holt's Illustrated Guide to Changes to the National Electrical Code®, based on the 2020 NEC®

This textbook provides insight, clarification, and a review of the 2020 *NEC* and how to apply those revisions in the field.

There were thousands of Public Inputs in the "First Revision" recommending changes to the 2017 *NEC*, and perhaps just as many Public Comments about those recommendations in the "Second Revision". As a result of all this input, there were hundreds of updates and a few new articles added to the 2020 *NEC*.

There were also a few "global" changes in style, major overhauls of some articles, and still other articles were deleted altogether!

The goal of this textbook is to review the significant changes and provide explanations and analyses to help you understand the modifications made to the rules, their impact, and their practical application in the field.

Mike's writing style is informative, practical, easy to comprehend, and applicable for today's electrical professional. Just like all of Mike Holt's textbooks, this one is built around hundreds of full-color illustrations and photographs that show the requirements of the *National Electrical Code* in practical use, helping you visualize *Code* rules as they're applied to electrical installations and maintain safe and compliant installations.

This textbook also contains possible conflicts or confusing *NEC* requirements, tips on proper electrical installations, and warnings of dangers related to improper electrical installations. It's possible that some rules may still seem unclear and may even sometimes leave us all scratching our heads wondering why a rule was changed in the first place! We can't eliminate confusing, conflicting, or controversial *Code* requirements, but our goal is to put them into perspective and provide fair and focused assessment to help you understand their intended purpose so that you can remain compliant in the field. Sometimes a requirement seems confusing and it might be hard to understand its actual application. When this occurs, this textbook will point the situation out in an upfront and straightforward manner. We apologize in advance if that ever seems disrespectful, but our intention is to help the industry by helping you to understand the current

NEC as best as possible, point out areas that need refinement, and encourage *Code* users to be a part of the change process that creates a better *NEC* for the future.

Keeping up with the ever-changing requirements of the *Code* is a must. Whether you're an installer, contractor, inspector, engineer, or instructor, understanding these changes is essential, regardless of your particular application of the *Code* rules, and this textbook is the perfect tool to help you do that.

The Scope of This Textbook

This textbook, *Mike Holt's Illustrated Guide to Changes to the National Electrical Code, based on the 2020 NEC*, covers those installation requirements that we consider to be of critical importance and is based on the following conditions:

1. Power Systems and Voltage. All power-supply systems are assumed to be one of the following nominal voltages or "voltage class", unless identified otherwise:

- ▸ 2-wire, single-phase, 120V
- ▸ 3-wire, single-phase, 120/240V
- ▸ 4-wire, three-phase, 120/240V Delta
- ▸ 4-wire, three-phase, 120/208V or 277/480V Wye

2. Electrical Calculations. Unless the question or example specifies three-phase, they're based on a single-phase power supply. In addition, all amperage calculations are rounded to the nearest ampere in accordance with Section 220.5(B).

3. Conductor Material. Conductors are considered copper, unless aluminum is identified or specified.

4. Conductor Sizing. Conductors are sized based on a THHN/THWN copper conductor terminating on a 75°C terminal in accordance with 110.14(C), unless the question or example indicates otherwise.

5. Overcurrent Device. The term "overcurrent device" refers to a molded-case circuit breaker, unless specified otherwise. Where a fuse is specified, it's a single-element type fuse, also known as a "onetime fuse," unless the text specifies otherwise.

How to Use this Textbook

This textbook is to be used along with the *NEC* and not as a replacement for it. Be sure to have a copy of the *2020 National Electrical Code* handy. Compare what's being explained in this textbook to what the *Code* book says and get with others who are knowledgeable about the *NEC* to discuss any topics that you find difficult to understand.

This textbook follows the *Code* format, but it doesn't cover every change or requirement. For example, it doesn't include every article, section, subsection, exception, or Informational Note. So, don't be concerned if you see that the textbook contains Exception 1 and Exception 3, but not Exception 2. Also, some rules are included that did not change but they lend context or were provided for convenience.

Cross-References. *NEC* cross-references to other related *Code* requirements are included to help you develop a better understanding of how the *NEC* rules relate to one another. These cross-references are indicated by *Code* section numbers in brackets, an example of which is "[90.4]."

Informational Notes. Informational Notes contained in the *NEC* will be identified in this textbook as "Note."

Exceptions. Exceptions contained in this textbook will be identified as "Ex" and not spelled out.

As you read through this textbook, allow yourself sufficient time to review the text along with the outstanding graphics and examples, which will be invaluable to your understanding of the *NEC*.

Technical Questions

As you progress through this textbook, you might find that you don't understand every explanation, example, calculation, or comment. Don't become frustrated, and don't get down on yourself. Remember, this is the *National Electrical Code*, and sometimes the best attempt to explain a concept isn't enough to make it perfectly clear. If you're still confused, visit www.MikeHolt.com/forum and post your question on our free Code Forum. The forum is a moderated community of electrical professionals.

Textbook Corrections

We're committed to providing you with the finest product with the fewest errors and take great care to ensure our textbooks are correct. But we're realistic and know that errors might be found after printing. The last thing we want is for you to have problems finding, communicating, or accessing this information, so we list it on our website.

To check for known errors, visit www.MikeHolt.com/corrections.

If you believe that there's an error of any kind (typographical, grammatical, technical, etc.) in this textbook or in the Answer Key, and it's not listed on the website, send an e-mail and be sure to include the textbook title, page number, and any other pertinent information.

To report an error, email corrections@MikeHolt.com.

Textbook Format

The layout of this textbook incorporates special features and symbols designed not only to help you navigate easily through the material, but to also enhance your understanding.

 A **QR Code** under the article number can be scanned with a smartphone app to take you to a sample video clip to see Mike and the video panel discuss this rule.

Caution, Warning, and Danger Icons

These icons highlight areas of concern.

 Caution
Caution: An explanation of possible damage to property or equipment.

 Warning
Warning: An explanation of possible severe property damage or personal injury.

 Danger
Danger: An explanation of possible severe injury or death.

Formulas

$$P = I \times E$$

Formulas are easily identifiable in green text on a gray bar.

Key Features

A summary of the *NEC* change is indicated in a gray box immediately under a black bar with the *Code* rule title.

Analysis of the rule in the yellow box provides the explanation and context for the change.

Underlined text denotes changes to the *Code* for the 2020 *NEC*.

Author's comments provide additional information to help you understand the context.

Detailed full-color educational graphics illustrate the change in a real-world application.

Examples and practical application questions and answers are contained in framed yellow boxes.

If you see an ellipsis (● ● ●) at the bottom of the example, it is continued on the following page.

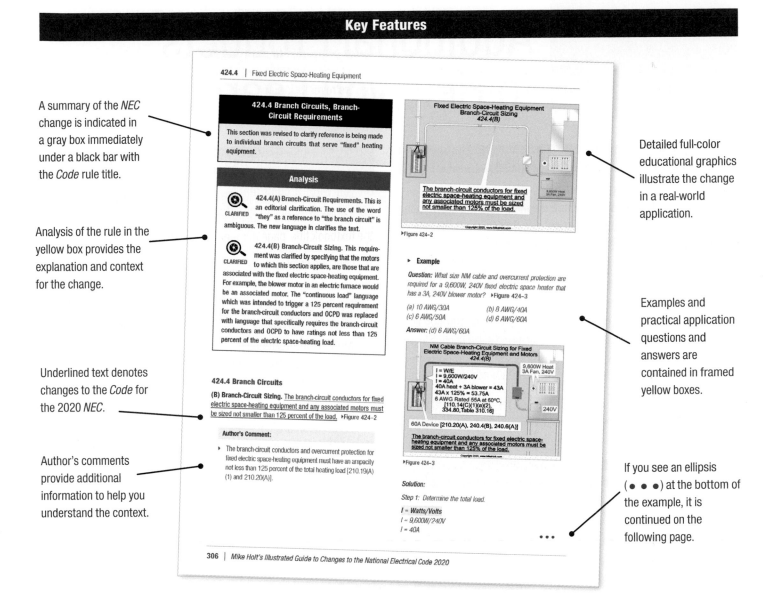

Code Change Icons

A *Code* Change icon signifies whether the rule is new, deleted, edited, reduced, clarified, expanded, reorganized, or moved.

CLARIFIED — A change that clarifies the requirements of a rule that wasn't clear in the previous *Code* cycle.

EDITED — An editorial revision that doesn't change the requirement; but it gives us the opportunity to review the rule.

EXPANDED — A change where a previous requirement(s) was expanded to cover additional applications.

NEW — A new requirement which could be an entirely new section, subsection, exception, table, and/or Informational Note.

REDUCED — A change that's reduced the requirements from the previous edition of the *NEC*.

RELOCATED — This identifies a rule that was relocated from one section of the *Code* to another without a change in the requirement(s).

REORGANIZED — A change made to place the existing requirements in a more logical order or list.

Additional Products to Help you Learn

How to Use the *National Electrical Code*

The original *NEC* document was developed in 1897 as a result of the united efforts of various insurance, electrical, architectural, and other cooperative interests. The National Fire Protection Association (NFPA) has sponsored the *National Electrical Code* since 1911.

The purpose of the *Code* is the practical safeguarding of persons and property from hazards arising from the use of electricity. It isn't intended as a design specification or an instruction manual for untrained persons. It is, in fact, a standard that contains the minimum requirements for an electrical installation that's essentially free from hazard. Learning to understand and use the *Code* is critical to you working safely; whether you're training to become an electrician, or are already an electrician, electrical contractor, inspector, engineer, designer, or instructor.

The *NEC* was written for qualified persons; those who understand electrical terms, theory, safety procedures, and electrical trade practices. Learning to use the *Code* is a lengthy process and can be frustrating if you don't approach it the right way. First, you'll need to understand electrical theory and if you don't have theory as a background when you get into the *NEC*, you're going to struggle. Take one step back if necessary and learn electrical theory. You must also understand the concepts and terms in the *Code* and know grammar and punctuation in order to understand the complex structure of the rules and their intended purpose(s). The *NEC* is written in a formal outline which many of us haven't seen or used since high school or college so it's important for you to pay particular attention to this format. Our goal for the next few pages is to give you some guidelines and suggestions on using your *Code* book to help you understand that standard, and assist you in what you're trying to accomplish and, ultimately, your personal success as an electrical professional!

Language Considerations for the *NEC*

Terms and Concepts

The *NEC* contains many technical terms, and it's crucial for *Code* users to understand their meanings and applications. If you don't understand a term used in a rule, it will be impossible to properly apply the *NEC* requirement. Article 100 defines those that are used generally in two or more articles throughout the *Code*; for example, the term "Dwelling Unit" is found in many articles. If you don't know the *NEC* definition for a "dwelling unit" you can't properly identify its *Code* requirements. Another example worth mentioning is the term "Outlet." For many people it has always meant a receptacle—not so in the *NEC*!

Many *Code* articles use terms unique to that specific article, and the definitions of those terms only apply to that given article. Definitions for them are usually found in the beginning of the article. For example, Section 250.2 contains the definitions of terms that only apply to Article 250—Grounding and Bonding. Whether definitions are unique to a specific article, or apply throughout the *NEC*, is indicated at the beginning of the definitions (xxx.2) section of the article. For example,

Article 690 contains definitions (in 690.2) that apply ONLY to that article while Article 705 introduces definitions (in 705.2) that apply throughout the entire *Code*.

Small Words, Grammar, and Punctuation

Technical words aren't the only ones that require close attention. Even simple words can make a big difference to the application of a rule. Is there a comma? Does it use "or," "and," "other than," "greater than," or "smaller than"? The word "or" can imply alternate choices for wiring methods. A word like "or" gives us choices while the word "and" can mean an additional requirement must be met.

An example of the important role small words play in the *NEC* is found in 110.26(C)(2), where it says equipment containing overcurrent, switching, "or" control devices that are 1,200A or more "and" over 6 ft wide require a means of egress at each end of the working space. In this section, the word "or" clarifies that equipment containing any of the three types of devices listed must follow this rule. The word "and" clarifies that 110.26(C)(2) only applies if the equipment is both 1,200A or more and over 6 ft wide.

Grammar and punctuation play an important role in establishing the meaning of a rule. The location of a comma can dramatically change the requirement of a rule such as in 250.28(A), where it says a main bonding jumper shall be a wire, bus, screw, or similar suitable conductor. If the comma between "bus" and "screw" was removed, only a "bus screw" could be used. That comma makes a big change in the requirements of the rule.

Slang Terms or Technical Jargon

Trade-related professionals in different areas of the country often use local "slang" terms that aren't shared by all. This can make it difficult to communicate if it isn't clear what the meaning of those slang terms are. Use the proper terms by finding out what their definitions and applications are before you use them. For example, the term "pigtail" is often used to describe the short piece of conductor used to connect a device to a splice, but a "pigtail" is also used for a rubberized light socket with pre-terminated conductors. Although the term is the same, the meaning is very different and could cause confusion. The words "splice" and "tap" are examples of terms often interchanged in the field but are two entirely different things! The uniformity and consistency of the terminology used in the *Code*, makes it so everyone says and means the same thing regardless of geographical location.

NEC Style and Layout

It's important to understand the structure and writing style of the *Code* if you want to use it effectively. The *National Electrical Code* is organized using twelve major components.

1. Table of Contents
2. Chapters—Chapters 1 through 9 (major categories)
3. Articles—Chapter subdivisions that cover specific subjects
4. Parts—Divisions used to organize article subject matter
5. Sections—Divisions used to further organize article subject matter
6. Tables and Figures—Represent the mandatory requirements of a rule
7. Exceptions—Alternatives to the main *Code* rule
8. Informational Notes—Explanatory material for a specific rule (not a requirement)
9. Tables—Applicable as referenced in the *NEC*
10. Annexes—Additional explanatory information such as tables and references (not a requirement)
11. Index
12. Changes to the *Code* from the previous edition

1. Table of Contents. The Table of Contents displays the layout of the chapters, articles, and parts as well as the page numbers. It's an excellent resource and should be referred to periodically to observe the interrelationship of the various *NEC* components. When attempting to locate the rules for a specific situation, knowledgeable *Code* users often go first to the Table of Contents to quickly find the specific *NEC* rule that applies.

2. Chapters. There are nine chapters, each of which is divided into articles. The articles fall into one of four groupings: General Requirements (Chapters 1 through 4), Specific Requirements (Chapters 5 through 7), Communications Systems (Chapter 8), and Tables (Chapter 9).

Chapter 1—General
Chapter 2—Wiring and Protection
Chapter 3—Wiring Methods and Materials
Chapter 4—Equipment for General Use
Chapter 5—Special Occupancies
Chapter 6—Special Equipment
Chapter 7—Special Conditions
Chapter 8—Communications Systems (Telephone, Data, Satellite, Cable TV, and Broadband)
Chapter 9—Tables–Conductor and Raceway Specifications

3. Articles. The *NEC* contains approximately 140 articles, each of which covers a specific subject. It begins with Article 90, the introduction to the *Code* which contains the purpose of the *NEC*, what is covered and isn't covered, along with how the *Code* is arranged. It also gives information on enforcement, how mandatory and permissive rules are written, and how explanatory material is included. Article 90 also includes information on formal interpretations, examination of equipment for safety, wiring planning, and information about formatting units of measurement. Here are some other examples of articles you'll find in the *NEC*:

Article 110—Requirements for Electrical Installations
Article 250—Grounding and Bonding
Article 300—General Requirements for Wiring Methods and Materials
Article 430—Motors, Motor Circuits, and Motor Controllers
Article 500—Hazardous (Classified) Locations
Article 680—Swimming Pools, Fountains, and Similar Installations
Article 725—Remote-Control, Signaling, and Power-Limited Circuits
Article 800—General Requirements for Communications Systems

4. Parts. Larger articles are subdivided into parts. Because the parts of a *Code* article aren't included in the section numbers, we tend to forget to what "part" an *NEC* rule is relating. For example, Table 110.34(A) contains working space clearances for electrical equipment. If we aren't careful, we might think this table applies to all electrical installations, but Table 110.34(A) is in Part III, which only contains requirements for "Over 1,000 Volts, Nominal" installations. The rules for working clearances for electrical equipment for systems 1,000V, nominal, or less are contained in Table 110.26(A)(1), which is in Part II—1,000 Volts, Nominal, or Less.

5. Sections. Each *NEC* rule is called a "*Code* Section." A *Code* section may be broken down into subdivisions; first level subdivision will be in parentheses like (A), (B),..., the next will be second level subdivisions in parentheses like (1), (2),..., and third level subdivisions in lowercase letters such as (a), (b), and so on.

For example, the rule requiring all receptacles in a dwelling unit bathroom to be GFCI protected is contained in Section 210.8(A)(1) which is in Chapter 2, Article 210, Section 8, first level subdivision (A), and second level subdivision (1).

Note: According to the *NEC Style Manual*, first and second level subdivisions are required to have titles. A title for a third level subdivision is permitted but not required.

Many in the industry incorrectly use the term "Article" when referring to a *Code* section. For example, they say "Article 210.8," when they should say "Section 210.8." Section numbers in this textbook are shown without the word "Section," unless they're at the beginning of a sentence. For example, Section 210.8(A) is shown as simply 210.8(A).

6. Tables and Figures. Many *NEC* requirements are contained within tables, which are lists of *Code* rules placed in a systematic arrangement. The titles of the tables are extremely important; you must read them carefully in order to understand the contents, applications, and limitations of each one. Notes are often provided in or below a table; be sure to read them as well since they're also part of the requirement. For example, Note 1 for Table 300.5 explains how to measure the cover when burying cables and raceways and Note 5 explains what to do if solid rock is encountered.

7. Exceptions. Exceptions are *NEC* requirements or permissions that provide an alternative method to a specific rule. There are two types of exceptions—mandatory and permissive. When a rule has several exceptions, those exceptions with mandatory requirements are listed before the permissive exceptions.

Mandatory Exceptions. A mandatory exception uses the words "shall" or "shall not." The word "shall" in an exception means that if you're using the exception, you're required to do it in a specific way. The phrase "shall not" means it isn't permitted.

Permissive Exceptions. A permissive exception uses words such as "shall be permitted," which means it's acceptable (but not mandatory) to do it in this way.

8. Informational Notes. An Informational Note contains explanatory material intended to clarify a rule or give assistance, but it isn't a *Code* requirement.

9. Tables. Chapter 9 consists of tables applicable as referenced in the *NEC*. They're used to calculate raceway sizing, conductor fill, the radius of raceway bends, and conductor voltage drop.

10. Informative Annexes. Annexes aren't a part of the *Code* requirements and are included for informational purposes only.

Annex A. Product Safety Standards
Annex B. Application Information for Ampacity Calculation
Annex C. Raceway Fill Tables for Conductors and Fixture Wires of the Same Size
Annex D. Examples
Annex E. Types of Construction
Annex F. Critical Operations Power Systems (COPS)
Annex G. Supervisory Control and Data Acquisition (SCADA)
Annex H. Administration and Enforcement
Annex I. Recommended Tightening Torques
Annex J. ADA Standards for Accessible Design

11. Index. The Index at the back of the *NEC* is helpful in locating a specific rule using pertinent keywords to assist in your search.

12. Changes to the *Code*. Changes in the *NEC* are indicated as follows:

▶ Rules that were changed since the previous edition are identified by shading the revised text.

▶ New rules aren't shaded like a change, instead they have a shaded "N" in the margin to the left of the section number.

▶ Relocated rules are treated like new rules with a shaded "N" in the left margin by the section number.

▶ Deleted rules are indicated by a bullet symbol " • " located in the left margin where the rule was in the previous edition. Unlike older editions the bullet symbol is only used where one or more complete paragraphs have been deleted. There's no indication used where a word, group of words, or a sentence was deleted.

▶ A Δ represents text deletions and figure/table revisions.

How to Locate a Specific Requirement

How to go about finding what you're looking for in the *Code* book depends, to some degree, on your experience with the *NEC*. Experts typically know the requirements so well that they just go to the correct rule. Very experienced people might only need the Table of Contents to locate the requirement for which they're looking. On the other hand, average users should use all the tools at their disposal, including the Table of Contents, the Index, and the search feature on electronic versions of the *Code* book.

Let's work through a simple example: What *NEC* rule specifies the maximum number of disconnects permitted for a service?

Using the Table of Contents. If you're an experienced *Code* user, you might use the Table of Contents. You'll know Article 230 applies to "Services," and because this article is so large, it's divided up into multiple parts (eight parts to be exact). With this knowledge, you can quickly go to the Table of Contents and see it lists the Service Equipment Disconnecting Means requirements in Part VI.

> **Author's Comment:**
>
> ▸ The number "70" precedes all page numbers in this standard because the *NEC* is NFPA Standard Number 70.

Using the Index. If you use the Index (which lists subjects in alphabetical order) to look up the term "service disconnect," you'll see there's no listing. If you try "disconnecting means," then "services," you'll find that the Index indicates the rule is in Article 230, Part VI. Because the *NEC* doesn't give a page number in the Index, you'll need to use the Table of Contents to find it, or flip through the *Code* book to Article 230, then continue to flip through pages until you find Part VI.

Many people complain that the *NEC* only confuses them by taking them in circles. Once you gain experience in using the *Code* and deepen your understanding of words, terms, principles, and practices, you'll find it much easier to understand and use than you originally thought.

With enough exposure in the use of the *NEC*, you'll discover that some words and terms are often specific to certain articles. The word "solar" for example will immediately send experienced *Code* book users to Article 690—Solar Photovoltaic (PV) Systems. The word "marina" suggests what you seek might be in Article 555. There are times when a main article will send you to a specific requirement in another one in which compliance is required in which case it will say (for example), "in accordance with 230.xx." Don't think of these situations as a "circle," but rather a map directing you to exactly where you need to be.

Customizing Your *Code* Book

One way to increase your comfort level with your *Code* book is to customize it to meet your needs. You can do this by highlighting and underlining important *NEC* requirements. Preprinted adhesive tabs are also an excellent aid to quickly find important articles and sections that are regularly referenced. However, understand that if you're using your *Code* book to prepare to take an exam, some exam centers don't allow markings of any type. For more information about tabs for your *Code* book, visit www.MikeHolt.com/tabs.

Highlighting. As you read through or find answers to your questions, be sure you highlight those requirements in the *NEC* that are the most important or relevant to you. Use one color, like yellow, for general interest and a different one for important requirements you want to find quickly. Be sure to highlight terms in the Index and the Table of Contents as you use them.

Underlining. Underline or circle key words and phrases in the *Code* with a red or blue pen (not a lead pencil) using a short ruler or other straightedge to keep lines straight and neat. This is a very handy way to make important requirements stand out. A short ruler or other straightedge also comes in handy for locating the correct information in a table.

Interpretations

Industry professionals often enjoy the challenge of discussing, and at times debating, the *Code* requirements. These types of discussions are important to the process of better understanding the *NEC* requirements and applications. However, if you decide you're going to participate in one of these discussions, don't spout out what you think without having the actual *Code* book in your hand. The professional way of discussing a requirement is by referring to a specific section rather than talking in vague generalities. This will help everyone involved clearly understand the point and become better educated. In fact, you may become so well educated about the *NEC* that you might even decide to participate in the change process and help to make it even better!

Become Involved in the *NEC* Process

The actual process of changing the *Code* takes about two years and involves hundreds of individuals trying to make the *NEC* as current and accurate as possible. As you advance in your studies and understanding of the *Code*, you might begin to find it very interesting, enjoy it more, and realize that you can also be a part of the process. Rather than sitting back and allowing others to take the lead, you can participate by making proposals and being a part of its development. For the 2020 cycle, there were 3,730 Public Inputs and 1,930 comments. Hundreds of updates and five new articles were added to keep the *NEC* up to date with new technologies and pave the way to a safer and more efficient electrical future.

Here's how the process works:

STEP 1—Public Input Stage

Public Input. The revision cycle begins with the acceptance of Public Input (PI) which is the public notice asking for anyone interested to submit input on an existing standard or a committee-approved new draft standard. Following the closing date, the committee conducts a First Draft Meeting to respond to all Public Inputs.

First Draft Meeting. At the First Draft (FD) Meeting, the Technical Committee considers and provides a response to all Public Input. The Technical Committee may use the input to develop First Revisions to the standard. The First Draft documents consist of the initial meeting consensus of the committee by simple majority. However, the final position of the Technical Committee must be established by a ballot which follows.

Committee Ballot on First Draft. The First Draft developed at the First Draft Meeting is balloted. In order to appear in the First Draft, a revision must be approved by at least two-thirds of the Technical Committee.

First Draft Report Posted. First revisions which pass ballot are ultimately compiled and published as the First Draft Report on the document's NFPA web page. This report serves as documentation for the Input Stage and is published for review and comment. The public may review the First Draft Report to determine whether to submit Public Comments on the First Draft.

STEP 2—Public Comment Stage

Public Comment. Once the First Draft Report becomes available, there's a Public Comment period during which anyone can submit a Public Comment on the First Draft. After the Public Comment closing date, the Technical Committee conducts/holds their Second Draft Meeting.

Second Draft Meeting. After the Public Comment closing date, if Public Comments are received or the committee has additional proposed revisions, a Second Draft Meeting is held. At the Second Draft Meeting, the Technical Committee reviews the First Draft and may make additional revisions to the draft Standard. All Public Comments are considered, and the Technical Committee provides an action and response to each Public Comment. These actions result in the Second Draft.

Committee Ballot on Second Draft. The Second Revisions developed at the Second Draft Meeting are balloted. To appear in the Second Draft, a revision must be approved by at least two-thirds of the Technical Committee.

Second Draft Report Posted. Second Revisions which pass ballot are ultimately compiled and published as the Second Draft Report on the document's NFPA website. This report serves as documentation of the Comment Stage and is published for public review.

Once published, the public can review the Second Draft Report to decide whether to submit a Notice of Intent to Make a Motion (NITMAM) for further consideration.

STEP 3—NFPA Technical Meeting (Tech Session)

Following completion of the Public Input and Public Comment stages, there's further opportunity for debate and discussion of issues through the NFPA Technical Meeting that takes place at the NFPA Conference & Expo®. These motions are attempts to change the resulting final Standard from the committee's recommendations published as the Second Draft.

STEP 4—Council Appeals and Issuance of Standard

Issuance of Standards. When the Standards Council convenes to issue an NFPA standard, it also hears any related appeals. Appeals are an important part of assuring that all NFPA rules have been followed and that due process and fairness have continued throughout the standards development process. The Standards Council considers appeals based on the written record and by conducting live hearings during which all interested parties can participate. Appeals are decided on the entire record of the process, as well as all submissions and statements presented.

After deciding all appeals related to a standard, the Standards Council, if appropriate, proceeds to issue the Standard as an official NFPA Standard. The decision of the Standards Council is final subject only to limited review by the NFPA Board of Directors. The new NFPA standard becomes effective twenty days following the Standards Council's action of issuance.

Temporary Interim Amendment—(TIA)

Sometimes, a change to the *NEC* is of an emergency nature. Perhaps an editing mistake was made that can affect an electrical installation to the extent it may create a hazard. Maybe an occurrence in the field created a condition that needs to be addressed immediately and can't wait for the normal *Code* cycle and next edition of the standard. When these circumstances warrant it, a TIA or "Temporary Interim Amendment" can be submitted for consideration.

The NFPA defines a TIA as, "tentative because it has not been processed through the entire standards-making procedures. It is interim because it is effective only between editions of the standard. A TIA automatically becomes a Public Input of the proponent for the next edition of the standard; as such, it then is subject to all of the procedures of the standards-making process."

Author's Comment:

▸ Proposals, comments, and TIAs can be submitted for consideration online at the NFPA website, www.nfpa.org. From the homepage, look for "Codes & Standards," then find "Standards Development," and click on "How the Process Works." If you'd like to see something changed in the *Code*, you're encouraged to participate in the process.

GLOBAL CHANGES IN THE 2020 *NATIONAL ELECTRICAL CODE*

Introduction to Global Changes in the 2020 *National Electrical Code*

If you have been in the electrical profession long enough, you know that learning and training (and sometimes re-training) are never-ending processes that follow you through your entire career. Perhaps the most common of these processes is navigating the changes and revisions made to the *National Electrical Code* every three years. Over the years there have been many changes, clarifications and additions introduced and applied to the *Code*. Some may seem to have had little substantiation but are in keeping with the intention and mission of the NFPA which is to minimize the risks and hazards involved with the use of electricity.

Definitions

With that mission in mind, many substantial changes were made for the 2020 *NEC* with one of the most significant being the global reorganization of the "Definitions" used throughout the *Code*.

To globally analyze how the definitions in Article 100 and the "xxx.2" sections of each Article apply to the associated rules, a task group was created to review definitions globally. They compared the current location of each definition with the *NEC Style Manual* requirements and relocated many terms that appeared in two or more articles to Article 100. The *NEC Style Manual* does not prohibit a definition located in an "xxx.2" section from applying elsewhere in the *Code*, however, it states that "in general, Article 100 shall contain definitions of terms that appear in two or more articles of the *NEC*."

During this process the task group identified that there are some cases in the (xxx.2) of an Article, where definitions apply only in that Article and others where they apply throughout the *Code*.

The task group report stated that, where the definitions in an "xxx.2" section only apply within that article the following parent text should be added:

"The definitions in this section shall only apply within this article."

The task group report also acknowledged that some "xxx.2" definitions apply outside the article in which they appear. In those cases, the following parent text should be added:

"The definitions in this section shall apply within this article and throughout the *Code*."

By adding this new text and creating new "xxx.2" subsections where they were needed, the application and usability of the definitions was greatly increased, and the text now better complies with the *NEC Style Manual*.

Specific Terms

"Global Changes" as such, are generalized changes that apply throughout the *Code*. Sometimes the change might be an *NEC Style Manual* change, and other times, as is the case here, the change might just apply to a specific term or terms used throughout the *Code*.

Global Changes

The word "allowable" as applied to ampacity was removed from the *Code* and the phrases "provisions of" and "the provisions of this" were also removed as they were deemed to be redundant.

Analysis

The word "allowable," as applied to the ampacity of conductors, was removed from the *NEC* in all locations. The definition of ampacity says that the ampacity of a conductor is the ampacity "under the conditions of use" making the word allowable unnecessary.

An example of the removal of "the provisions of" is in section 110.3(A)(1) of the 2017 *NEC* where it said, "Suitability for installation and use in conformity with the provisions of this *Code*." It now says, "Suitability for installation and use in conformity with this *Code*." The redundancy is obvious.

Revisions, Edits and Reorganizations

With every *Code* cycle revision, it seems there is at least one article that receives extensive editing and/or reorganization. The 2020 *NEC* is no exception! A few articles were extensively revised, and others were deleted altogether!

A few Articles where significant changes occurred were:

- **Chapter 2.** A new article (Article 242) was added containing relocated text from Articles 280 and 285.
- **Chapter 3.** Article 310 was significantly revised.
- **Chapter 6.** Articles 690 and 691 were almost completely revised and reorganized.
- **Chapter 7.** Extensive changes were made in Articles 705 and 710.
- **Chapter 8.** Was reorganized and a new Article 805 was added.

INTRODUCTION TO THE
NATIONAL ELECTRICAL CODE

Introduction to Article 90—Introduction to the *National Electrical Code*

Article 90 opens by saying the *National Electrical Code (NEC/Code)* is not intended as a design specification or instruction manual. It has one purpose only, and that is the "practical safeguarding of persons and property from hazards arising from the use of electricity." That does not necessarily mean the installation will be efficient, convenient, or able to accommodate future expansion. The necessity of carefully studying the *Code* rules cannot be overemphasized, and the step-by-step explanatory format of a textbook such as this is designed to help in that undertaking. Understanding where to find the rules in the *NEC* that apply to each installation is invaluable. Rules in several different articles often apply to even a simple installation. Face it, you are not going to remember every section of every article of the *Code* but you will know where to look!

Article 90 then goes on to describe the scope and arrangement of the *NEC*. The balance of this article provides the reader with information essential to understanding the *Code* rules.

Most electrical installations require you to understand the first four chapters of the *NEC* which apply generally, plus have a working knowledge of the Chapter 9 tables. That understanding begins with Article 90. Chapters 5, 6, and 7 make up a large portion of the *Code* book, but they apply to special occupancies, special equipment, or special conditions. They build on, modify, or amend the rules in the first four chapters. Chapter 8 contains the requirements for communications systems, such as radio and television equipment, satellite receivers, antenna systems, twisted pair conductors, and coaxial cable wiring. Communications systems are not subject to the general requirements of Chapters 1 through 4, or the special requirements of Chapters 5 through 7, unless there is a specific reference to a rule in the previous chapters.

90.2 Scope of the *NEC*

There are two changes to this section. List item 90.2(A)(5) expands the type of installations where the *NEC* is intended to apply and includes the shore power connection to watercraft at marinas or boatyards. This means that the cords running from the source of power are now part of the *Code*. List item 90.2(A)(6) expands the *NEC's* intended application to the bidirectional power export from electric vehicles. Energy stored in the batteries of electric vehicles can be a source of electrical power and backfed into to an occupancy if needed.

Analysis

CLARIFIED **NEW**

90.2(A)(5) Covered. While 90.2(B)(1) says the *Code* does not cover electrical installations in ships or watercraft, this new list item (5) to 90.2(A) clarifies that it does cover connections between ships or watercraft and the power supply on the shore in marinas and boatyards. This addition to the scope of the *NEC* is intended to address the serious hazard of leakage current in the water surrounding ships or watercraft that are connected to shore power. Prior to the 2020 *Code* there was some question as to the applicability of the *NEC* to these types of installations.

CLARIFIED EXPANDED

90.2(A)(6) Covered. The scope expansion in list item (6) clarifies that the connection between an electric vehicle and a premises wiring system for the export of power and bidirectional power flow is covered by the *Code*. Some electric vehicles can be used as an alternate source of electrical power to the premises. The rules for this application are found in Article 625.

90.2 Scope of the *NEC*

(A) What Is Covered by the *NEC*. The *NEC* covers the installation and removal of electrical conductors, equipment, and raceways; signaling and communications conductors, equipment, and raceways; and optical fiber cables and raceways for the following: ▶Figure 90–1 and ▶Figure 90–2

(5) Installations supplying shore power to watercraft in marinas and boatyards, including monitoring of leakage current. ▶Figure 90–3

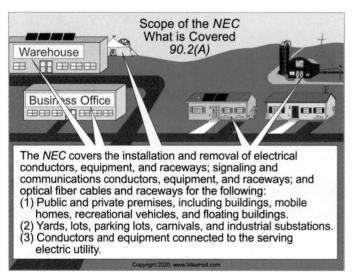

Scope of the *NEC*
What is Covered
90.2(A)

Warehouse

Business Office

The *NEC* covers the installation and removal of electrical conductors, equipment, and raceways; signaling and communications conductors, equipment, and raceways; and optical fiber cables and raceways for the following:
(1) Public and private premises, including buildings, mobile homes, recreational vehicles, and floating buildings.
(2) Yards, lots, parking lots, carnivals, and industrial substations.
(3) Conductors and equipment connected to the serving electric utility.

Copyright 2020, www.MikeHolt.com

▶Figure 90–1

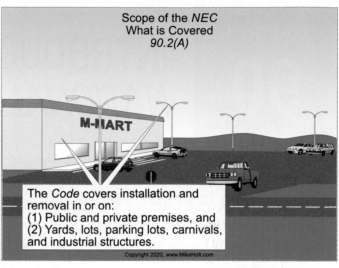

Scope of the *NEC*
What is Covered
90.2(A)

M-MART

The *Code* covers installation and removal in or on:
(1) Public and private premises, and
(2) Yards, lots, parking lots, carnivals, and industrial structures.

Copyright 2020, www.MikeHolt.com

▶Figure 90–2

Scope of the *NEC*
Shore Power to Watercraft
90.2(A)(5)

The *NEC* covers installations supplying shore power to watercraft in marinas and boatyards, including monitoring of leakage current.

Copyright 2020, www.MikeHolt.com

▶Figure 90–3

Author's Comment:

▸ It is no secret there is a serious issue with electric shock drowning (especially around docks and marinas) that the current standards have not been able to stem. This change in scope clarifies that the authority having jurisdiction may now address this issue and enforce rules that try to protect against this serious life safety hazard. Some of the changes this addition to the scope permit are addressed later in this textbook where the changes to Article 555 are covered.

▸ There are two important points here; "shore power" refers to a boat or other watercraft's access to a land-based power source such as that from the electric utility. The other is that many times the source of leakage current may be the watercraft itself, so the "monitoring of leakage current" allows for periodic testing of individual shore power circuits at boat slips and docks. Doing so will either confirm or eliminate the craft as a possible source. More information on these changes is covered in Article 555.

▸ The new item in the scope, 90.2(A)(5) appears to include the power cable between the pedestal and the boat in the scope of the *NEC*, but there are no specific rules in Article 555 that apply to that power supply cord.

▸ The text in 555.35(B) requires leakage detection equipment to detect leakage from the boat and that requirement applies to the load side of the supplying receptacle.

(6) Installations used to export electric power from vehicles to premises wiring or for bidirectional current flow. ▸Figure 90–4

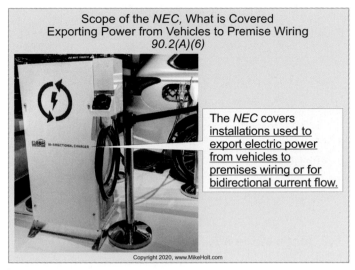

Scope of the *NEC*, What is Covered
Exporting Power from Vehicles to Premise Wiring
90.2(A)(6)

The *NEC* covers installations used to export electric power from vehicles to premises wiring or for bidirectional current flow.

Copyright 2020, www.MikeHolt.com

▸Figure 90–4

Author's Comment:

▸ The battery power supply of an electrical vehicle can be used "bidirectionally" which means it can be used as a backup or alternate power source to supply premises wiring circuits in the event of a power failure. The rules for this application can be found in Article 625.

GENERAL RULES

Introduction to Chapter 1—General Rules

Before you can make sense of the *NEC*, you must become familiar with its general rules, concepts, definitions, and requirements. Chapter 1 consists of two topics, Article 100 which provides definitions that help ensure consistency when *Code*-related matters are the topic of discussion, and Article 110, which supplies the general requirements needed to correctly apply the *NEC*.

After gaining an understanding of Chapter 1, some of the *Code* requirements that might be confusing to many, will become increasingly clear to you. *NEC* requirements will make more sense to you because you will have the foundation from which to build upon your understanding and application of the rules.

- **Article 100—Definitions.** Article 100 is organized into three parts. Part I contains the definitions of terms used throughout the *Code* for systems that operate at 1,000V, nominal, or less. The definitions of terms in Part II apply to systems that operate at over 1,000V, nominal, and are not within the scope of this textbook. Part III contains definitions applicable to the "Hazardous (Classified) Locations" found in Chapter 5 of the *NEC*.

  This article only contains terms used in more than one article. Definitions of standard terms, such as volt, voltage drop, ampere, impedance, and resistance, are not contained in Article 100. If the *Code* does not define a term, then a dictionary or a building code standard that is acceptable to the authority having jurisdiction should be consulted.

  Definitions are sometimes located at the beginning of an article. When this occurs, guidance is now provided that those terms might only apply to that given article or both, that article and throughout the *Code*. There is uniformity in the location of the definitions specific to an article in that the article number will be followed by ".2." For example, definitions specific to solar photovoltaic (PV) systems are found in 690.2.

- **Article 110—Requirements for Electrical Installations.** This article contains general requirements applicable to all electrical installations.

ARTICLE
100

DEFINITIONS

Introduction to Article 100—Definitions

Have you ever had a conversation with someone, only to discover that what you said and what he or she heard were completely different? This often happens when people in a conversation have different definitions or interpretations of the words being used, and that is why the definitions of key *NEC* terms are located at the beginning of the *Code* (Article 100), or at the beginning of each article. If we can all agree on important definitions, then we speak the same language and avoid misunderstandings. Words taken out of context have created more than their fair share of problems. Because the *NEC* exists to protect people and property, it is very important for you to be able to convey and comprehend the language used. Review and study Article 100 until you are confident you know the definitions of the terms presented.

100 Definitions

Not a *Code* cycle goes by without changes and/or additions to Article 100 and this one is no exception! Wherein definitions are concerned, this cycle's revisions may just be some of the most complex. Many of the definitions that appeared in individual articles were moved to Article 100. This is mainly due to certain terminology being used in more than one article making the term(s) more common. Some of the definition sections in individual articles were deleted altogether because their terms were relocated to Article 100 (250.2 for example). In fact, only a few definitions remain in all of Chapter 8! The definitions in Article 100 are now divided into Parts I, II, and III.

The overall scope of the changes to definitions also includes guidance for those that remain in individual articles and clearly states whether the definition is specific to only that article, or applicable throughout the *NEC*. There are a few new definitions and some clarification was added to some of the existing ones.

Analysis

EXPANDED Article 100 now contains three parts. Part I General, contains definitions that apply throughout the *Code*; Part II Over 1,000V, Nominal includes the definitions specific to systems operating over 1,000V (which are beyond the scope of this textbook); and now Part III Hazardous (Classified) Locations contains definitions identified by the title and is new for the 2020 edition.

In the 2017 *NEC*, many of the definitions used in the hazardous location articles were moved from those articles to Part I of Article 100 and placed in alphabetical order. That seemed to make finding them more difficult. Placing all the previously relocated hazardous location definitions in the new Part III, Hazardous (Classified) Locations of the 2020 *Code* book should make them easier to locate. In addition, the definitions that remained in the "xxx.2" sections of Articles 500, 501, 502, 503, 504, 505, 506, 511, 513, 514, 515, and 516 in the 2017 *NEC* were moved to this new Part III of Article 100. Having all the hazardous location definitions in a single place should improve the usability of the *Code*.

Accessible (as Applied to Equipment). This editorial change removes language about what makes something inaccessible, such as "locked doors" or "elevation" and clarifies that equipment which can be "reached for operation, renewal and inspection" is accessible.

CLARIFIED

Attachment Fitting. This new definition identifies the name of the device that makes both the electrical connection and provides support for the utilization equipment the fitting is connecting to power.

NEW

Bathroom. The previous language used the term "basin" which has been replaced with "sink (basin)."

CLARIFIED

Bonding Jumper, Supply-Side. This definition was relocated here from 250.2 because it is used in multiple articles. The *NEC Style Manual* says that definitions used in two or more *Code* articles should appear in Article 100. This relocation resulted in the deletion of Section 250.2 altogether.

RELOCATED

RELOCATED **CLARIFIED**

DC-to-DC Converter. This definition was moved from 690.2 to Article 100 and revised. When the definition was in 690.2 it only applied to a dc-to-dc converter that was used with PV equipment. A more general definition of the term makes it easier to apply to other *Code* rules.

Dormitory Unit. This new definition was added because there were requirements for "dormitory units," such as AFCI protection, but the term was not defined. If the *NEC* requires a device in specific location, we need to understand what those locations are. If you look back to the definitions of bathroom and kitchen, they were added to the *Code* after GFCI protection was required in those areas.

NEW

RELOCATED

Electrical Datum Plane. The term "Electrical Datum Plane" was relocated to Article 100 because it is used in more than one article. In addition, the *NEC Style Manual* does not permit a definition to contain actual installation requirements, so they were removed from the definition and relocated to 682.5 and remain unchanged from the 2017 *Code*.

Author's Comment:

▸ This definition previously specified the actual elevations of the electrical datum plane and those acted as requirements. The detailed requirements in 682.5 appear as though they would only apply within that article, and not to the other articles that also use this term.

Electric Power Production and Distribution Network. This definition was clarified to include the associated equipment, facilities, and wiring as parts of an electrical power distribution network.

CLARIFIED

RELOCATED

Electric Vehicle (EV). This definition was used in multiple articles, so it was relocated here from Article 625 and now clarifies that Plug-in hybrid electric vehicles (PHEVs) have a second source of power.

CLARIFIED **NEW**

Fault Current. This new definition is used in several articles and is based on language in NFPA 70E, *Standard for Electrical Safety in the Workplace*. It identifies that "fault current" is the current delivered into a given point in the system during a short circuit or ground-fault.

Fault Current, Available (Available Fault Current). This new definition and accompanying figure were brought in from NFPA 70E, *Standard for Electrical Safety in the Workplace* to replace the terms "available short-circuit current" and "short-circuit current" throughout the *NEC* and serves to improve coordination between installation and safety requirements.

NEW

Free Air (as applied to conductors). The term "Free Air" is used in conjunction with many wiring methods. Whether a conductor or cable is in free air or not effects its ampacity, but the term was previously undefined in the *Code*.

NEW

Generating Capacity, Inverter. The word "Inverter" was added to the title and "watts" was added to the definition to clear up any ambiguity as to the naturally arising question, "What if it is less than one kilowatt?"

CLARIFIED

 Ground-Fault Current Path. This definition was revised to include the neutral conductor as part of the ground-fault current path. The previous definition only included normally noncurrent-carrying conductors, and the neutral conductor is normally a current-carrying conductor. While it is not common for a neutral conductor, other than the one between the utility supply and the service equipment, to carry ground-fault current there are applications (such as those in 250.142) where the neutral conductor is called on to do so.

EDITED

 Grounded Conductor. A new Informational Note clarifies that the definition for a "Grounded Conductor" refers to a neutral or an intentionally grounded phase conductor but never to an equipment grounding conductor EGC).

CLARIFIED

 Grounding Conductor, Equipment (EGC). This definition now clarifies that the EGC "is a part of" an effective ground-fault current path and not just a ground-fault current path as previously stated. The addition of the words "is a part of" clarifies that the EGC is not the only part of the path to carry the fault current back to the source.

CLARIFIED

 Habitable Room. The term "Habitable Room" is used in at least six locations in the *NEC* but was not defined. A new definition of this term was added so the rules pertaining to habitable rooms can be correctly applied. It is also consistent with the definitions in other building codes. This is a much-needed improvement in the usability of the *Code*.

NEW

 Interactive Inverter. This revision identifies that interactive inverters may be connected to any appropriate alternating-current source, not just to utilities.

CLARIFIED

 Interactive System. This definition was relocated as part of the global reorganization of definitions throughout the *NEC*.

RELOCATED

  Inverter. This definition was relocated here from 690.2 and greatly simplified because inverters are used with applications other than just PV systems; such as wind generation (694), energy storage systems (706), fuel cells (602), or interconnected power production sources (705).

RELOCATED   CLARIFIED

 Inverter Input Circuit. This definition was relocated here from 690.2 and now clarifies that the conductors connected to the direct-current input are the input circuit. The reference to energy storage systems (ESS) was deleted as this definition is intended to be suitable for use with inverters in all types of systems such as with PV systems, wind systems, fuel cells, and others.

RELOCATED   CLARIFIED

  Inverter Output Circuit. As with the input circuit, this definition was relocated here from 690.2 and revised so it applies to all inverters, no matter the type of system with which they are associated. This circuit consists of the conductors connected to the alternating-current output of an inverter.

RELOCATED   EDITED

 **Inverter, Multimode.** This definition was relocated here from 690.2 and edited from "Multimode Inverter" to "Inverter, Multimode" for consistency with other definitions and ease of use. Since the definitions are arranged in alphabetical order in Article 100, this change places the multimode inverter definition next to the others associated with the term "inverter." There was no change to the actual definition; it is equipment that has the capabilities of both the interactive inverter and the stand-alone inverter.

RELOCATED   EDITED

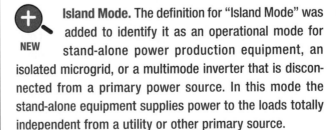 **Island Mode.** The definition for "Island Mode" was added to identify it as an operational mode for stand-alone power production equipment, an isolated microgrid, or a multimode inverter that is disconnected from a primary power source. In this mode the stand-alone equipment supplies power to the loads totally independent from a utility or other primary source.

NEW

• • •

A new Informational Note was also added to call attention to the fact that an isolated microgrid is not the same as the interconnected microgrids addressed in Article 705.

 CLARIFIED **Labeled.** Labeled products typically have a label with information related to their listing. Some products are too small to display one and the listing agencies permit the complete label to appear on the smallest container in which the product is packaged. In these cases, the product itself will almost always show the symbol of the listing agency. An Informational Note was added to give notice to *Code* users to look to the product container for the complete label.

 EDITED **Laundry Area.** This definition was relocated here from 550.2. Although there are various requirements for the laundry area, the only previous definition of one was found in Article 550. If the area is designed for laundry equipment, then it is a laundry area with or without the laundry equipment.

 NEW **Messenger or Messenger Wire.** Some wiring methods have an internal or external messenger wire attached to the wiring method to support it. This new definition addresses the support wire itself.

  CLARIFIED **RELOCATED** **Power Production Equipment.** This definition was relocated here from the "xxx.2" section of Article 705, Interconnected Electric Power Production Sources and now clarifies that the source disconnecting means is what makes the distinction between power production equipment and other electrical equipment.

  CLARIFIED **RELOCATED** **Prime Mover.** Defining "Prime Mover" adds overall clarity in the application of the *NEC*. Since the term is used in several articles, it is now located in the general definitions section of Article 100.

 CLARIFIED **PV (Photovoltaic) System.** Language about utilization loads was removed from this definition since a PV system might not have any direct loads. The purpose of all electricity is to eventually supply a load, so the definition should be for a PV system and not what electricity is used for.

 EXPANDED **Raceway, Communications.** The purpose of this identification revision was to group the definitions of the various cables together in the same manner as the various types of "dwelling units" are grouped together.

 CLARIFIED **Receptacle.** This revision adds the words "or strap" making this definition consistent with other *Code* sections as shown in the new Informational Note.

 NEW **Reconditioned.** This new definition identifies the equipment suitable to be reconditioned and indicates that reconditioning differs from maintenance. The new Informational Note lists other terms used to identify reconditioned equipment.

▸ Electromechanical protective relays and current transformers

▸ High-voltage circuit breakers

▸ Industrial and commercial panelboards

▸ Low- and medium-voltage power circuit breakers

▸ Low- and medium-voltage replaceable link fuses

▸ Low-voltage switchgear

▸ Manual and magnetic controllers

▸ Medium-voltage switchgear

▸ Metallic conduit, tubing, raceways, and fittings

▸ Motor control centers

▸ Motors

▸ Switchboards

▸ Uninterruptible power supply equipment

 CLARIFIED **Service.** This definition was changed from "delivering electric energy from" to "connecting" because of the bidirectional current flow that may be present when alternative energy sources are interconnected with a utility source of electricity.

CLARIFIED **Service Equipment.** This definition was clarified by removing the term "conductors" because in some cases service equipment is not connected with wire type service "conductors."

The word "cutoff" was replaced with "disconnect" for clarity. The previous definition said the service equipment cut off the supply, implying that it would disconnect the power to the building or structure. The new wording says that it disconnects the serving utility from the premises wiring. This change was required because the building or structure may have other sources of supply such as generators, wind, or PV systems that the service disconnect does not open.

Part III—Definitions, Hazardous (Classified) Locations

NEW Article 100 was given a Part III for the 2020 edition; previous editions only had two. In the 2017 *NEC*, many of the definitions used in the hazardous (classified) location articles were relocated from those articles to Part I of Article 100 and placed in alphabetical order. This, according to some *Code* users, made accessing those definitions more difficult; therefore, they were placed in a new Part III, Hazardous (Classified) Locations with no technical changes for 2020. In addition, all the definitions that remained in the "xxx.2" sections of Articles 500, 501, 502, 503, 504, 505, 506, 511, 513, 514, 515, and 516 were moved to this new Part III of Article 100.

Accessible (as it applies to equipment). Capable of being reached for operation, renewal, and inspection.

Author's Comment:

▸ This new definition is intended to be clear and concise. It now appears as though anything you can access without damaging the building's finishes or structure is considered "accessible."

Accessible (as it applies to wiring methods). Not permanently closed in by the building structure or finish and capable of being removed or exposed without damaging the building structure or finish. ▸Figure 100–1

Accessible, (As it Applies to Wiring Methods)
Article 100 Definition

Not permanently closed in by the building structure or finish and capable of being removed or exposed without damaging the building structure or finish.

Copyright 2020, www.MikeHolt.com

▸Figure 100–1

Attachment Fitting. A device that, by insertion into a locking support and mounting receptacle, establishes a connection between the conductors of the attached utilization equipment and the branch-circuit conductors connected to the locking support and mounting receptacle.

Note: An attachment fitting is different from an attachment plug because no cord is associated with the fitting. An attachment fitting in combination with a locking support and mounting receptacle secures the associated utilization equipment in place and supports its weight.

Bathroom. A bathroom area is an area that includes a sink (basin) as well as one or more of the following: a toilet, urinal, tub, shower, bidet, or similar plumbing fixture. ▸Figure 100–2

Bonding Jumper, Supply-Side. The conductor installed on the supply side of the service or for a separately derived system that ensures electrical conductivity between metal parts and the grounded-neutral conductor or grounded-phase conductor. ▸Figure 100–3, ▸Figure 100–4, and ▸Figure 100–5

DC-to-DC Converter. A device that can provide an output dc voltage and current at a higher or lower value than the input dc voltage and current.

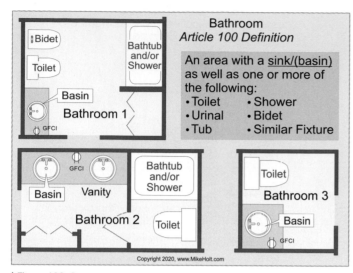

▶Figure 100–2

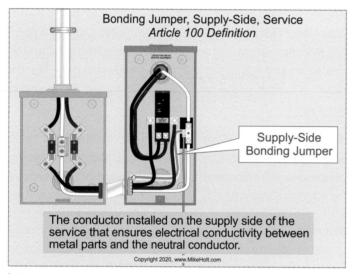

▶Figure 100–3

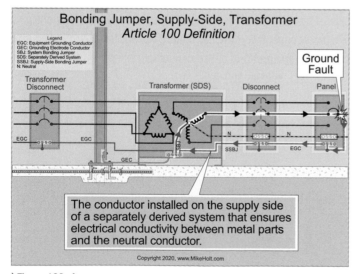

▶Figure 100–4

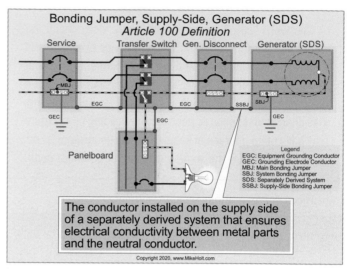

▶Figure 100–5

Author's Comment:

▸ DC-to-DC converters are intended to maximize the output of independent power source modules and reduce losses due to variances between modules' outputs. They are directly wired to each module and are bolted to the module frame or rack.

▸ A dc-to-dc converter enables the power source inverter to automatically maintain a fixed circuit voltage, at the optimal point for dc/ac conversion by the inverter, regardless of circuit length and individual module performance.

Dormitory Unit. A building, or a space in a building, in which group sleeping accommodations are provided for more than 16 persons who are not members of the same family in one room, or a series of closely associated rooms, under joint occupancy and single management, with or without meals, but without individual cooking facilities. ▶Figure 100–6

Electrical Datum Plane. A specified distance above a water level above which electrical equipment can be installed and electrical connections can be made.

Author's Comment:

▸ This definition previously specified the actual elevations of the electrical datum plane and those acted as requirements. The detailed requirements in 682.5 appear as though they would only apply within that article, and not to the other articles that also use the term.

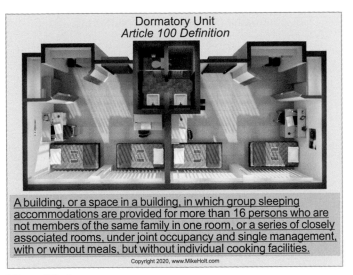

▶Figure 100–6

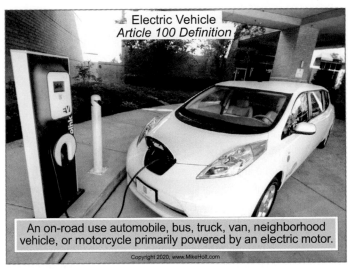

An on-road use automobile, bus, truck, van, neighborhood vehicle, or motorcycle primarily powered by an electric motor.

▶Figure 100–8

Electric Power Production and Distribution Network. A serving electric utility that is connected to premises wiring and is not controlled by an interactive system. ▶Figure 100–7

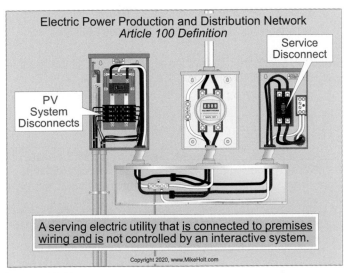

A serving electric utility that is connected to premises wiring and is not controlled by an interactive system.

▶Figure 100–7

Author's Comment:

▶ An interactive system is an electric power production system that operates in parallel with, and may deliver power to, the serving electric utility. An example of an interactive system is a PV system interactively connected in parallel to the utility by an interactive inverter.

Electric Vehicle. An on-road use automobile, bus, truck, van, neighborhood electric vehicle, or motorcycle primarily powered by an electric motor. ▶Figure 100–8

Author's Comment:

▶ Plug-in hybrid type vehicles containing both an electric motor and a combustion engine that portion of which pertains to the re-charging of the electric motor is covered by Article 625.

Fault Current. The current delivered at a point on the system during a short-circuit condition. ▶Figure 100–9

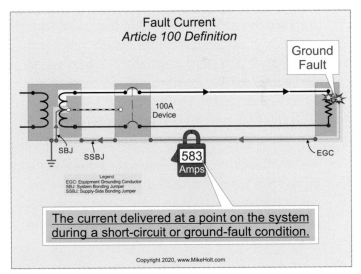

The current delivered at a point on the system during a short-circuit or ground-fault condition.

▶Figure 100–9

Fault Current, Available (Available Fault Current). The largest amount of current capable of being delivered at a point on the system during a short-circuit condition.

Note: A short circuit can occur during abnormal conditions such as a fault between circuit conductors or a ground fault.(See Informational Note Figure 100.1 in the *NEC.*)

Author's Comment:

▸ Fault current is current outside the usual circuit path and with a magnitude that exceeds the normal circuit current. A fault can be line-to-line, line-to-neutral, or line-to-ground. The new *NEC* Informational Note, Figure 100.1, helps explain the differences between "Available Fault Current," "Short-Circuit Current Rating" (SCCR), and "Interrupting Rating" (AIC). The available fault current is the largest amount of current available at that point on the circuit. It is important to note that the fault current value is not the same throughout the circuit; it becomes smaller as the impedance is increased between the point of the fault and the source of the power.

▸ The SCCR is the maximum amount of current that equipment, other than overcurrent protective devices (OCPDs), can safely withstand. Much of the equipment supplied by the electrical system is required to be marked with this rating. The designer and installer need to make sure the fault current available at the equipment is less than what the equipment can withstand. This often needs to be addressed at the design stage of a project so specified equipment can have a suitable SCCR. Correcting an installation where the available fault current exceeds the SCCR of the equipment after it has been installed can be costly and time consuming. One very common issue is with large air conditioning equipment which often has an SCCR of 5,000A, unless a higher rating was specified at the time the equipment was purchased.

▸ The interrupting rating of an overcurrent protective device is the maximum amount of current that an OCPD can safely interrupt. OCPDs that are subjected to currents exceeding their AIC (or KAIC) rating may fail violently. Applying equipment within their SCCR or AIC ratings is critical for a safe installation.

Free Air (as applied to conductors). An open or ventilated environment that allows for heat dissipation and air flow around a conductor. ▸Figure 100–10

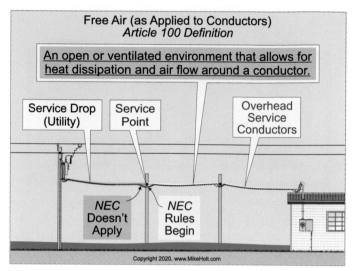
▸Figure 100–10

Author's Comment:

▸ This is, and will remain, a subjective rule as there is no clear guidance as to how much air flow is required or how to determine that the installation allows for heat dissipation.

Grounded Conductor. The system or circuit conductor that is intentionally connected to the earth (ground). ▸Figure 100–11

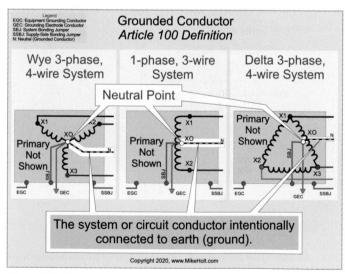
▸Figure 100–11

Note: Although an equipment grounding conductor is grounded, it is not considered a grounded conductor.

▸ There are two types of grounded conductors; a grounded-neutral conductor and a grounded-phase conductor. A system where the transformer secondary is wye-connected with the neutral point grounded will have a neutral. ▸**Figure 100–12**

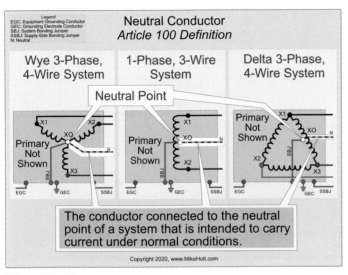

▸Figure 100–12

▸ A system where the transformer secondary is delta-connected with one corner winding grounded will have a grounded-phase conductor. ▸**Figure 100–13**

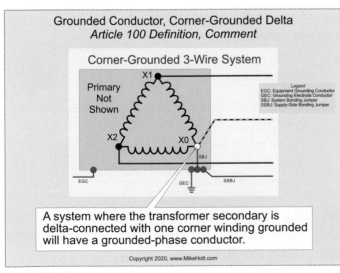

▸Figure 100–13

Grounding Conductor, Equipment (Equipment Grounding Conductor). The conductive path(s) that is part of an effective ground-fault current path and connects metal parts of equipment to the system neutral conductor or grounded-phase conductor to the grounding electrode conductor, or both [250.110 through 250.126]. ▸**Figure 100–14**

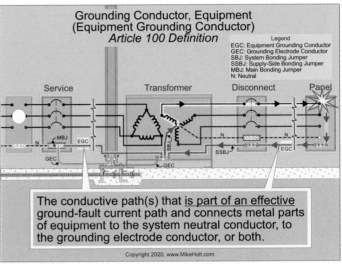

▸Figure 100–14

Note 1: The circuit equipment grounding conductor also performs bonding.

▸ To quickly remove dangerous touch voltage on metal parts from a ground fault, the equipment grounding conductor (EGC), must be connected to the system grounded-neutral conductor or grounded-phase conductor at the source and have low enough impedance so fault current will quickly rise to a level that will open the circuit's overcurrent protective device [250.4(A)(3)]. ▸**Figure 100–15**

Note 2: An equipment grounding conductor can be any one or a combination of the types listed in 250.118. ▸**Figure 100–16**

Ground-Fault Current Path. An electrically conductive path from the point of a ground fault on a wiring system through normally noncurrent-carrying conductors, neutral conductors, equipment, or the earth to the electrical supply source. ▸**Figure 100–17**

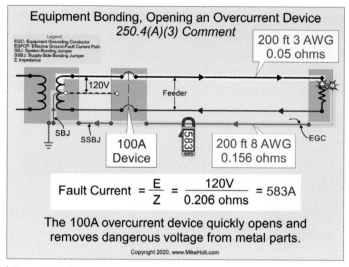

Figure 100–15

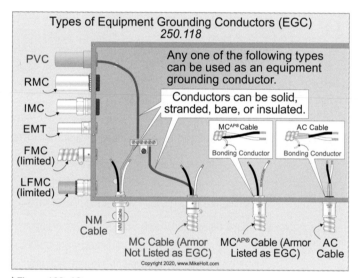

Figure 100–16

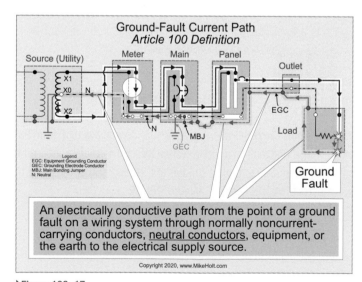

Figure 100–17

Note: Examples of ground-fault current paths are any combination of equipment grounding conductors, metallic raceways, metallic cable sheaths, electrical equipment, and any other electrically conductive material such as metal, water, and gas piping; steel framing members; stucco mesh; metal ducting; reinforcing steel; shields of communications cables; neutral conductors; and the earth itself.

Habitable Room. A room in a building for living, sleeping, eating, or cooking, but excluding bathrooms, toilet rooms, closets, hallways, storage or utility spaces, and similar areas. ▸Figure 100–18

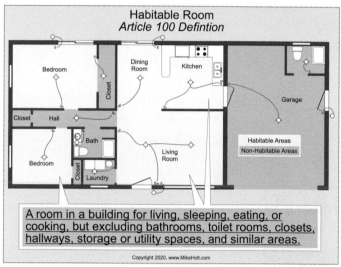

Figure 100–18

Interactive Inverter. An inverter intended to be used in parallel with a power source(s) such as the serving electric utility to supply common loads, and capable of delivering power to the serving electric utility. ▸Figure 100–19

Author's Comment:

▸ A listed interactive inverter automatically ceases exporting power upon loss of utility voltage and cannot be reconnected until the voltage has been restored. Interactive inverters can automatically or manually resume exporting power to the utility once the utility source is restored.

Interactive System. An electric power production system that operates in parallel with, and may deliver power to, the serving electric utility. ▸Figure 100–20

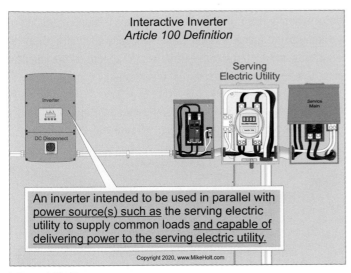

▶Figure 100–19

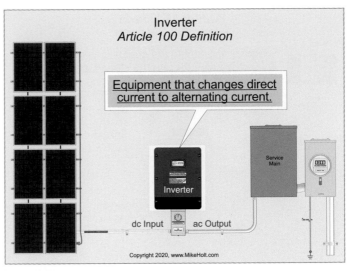

▶Figure 100–21

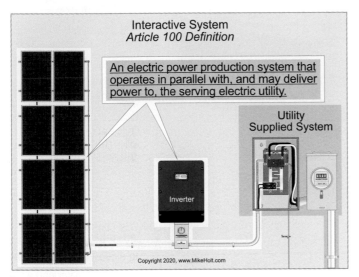

▶Figure 100–20

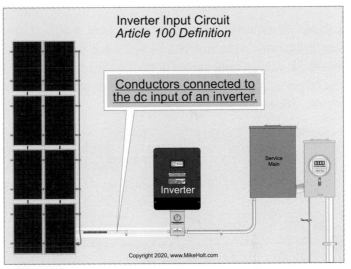

▶Figure 100–22

Inverter. Equipment that changes direct current to alternating current. ▶Figure 100–21

Inverter Input Circuit. Conductors connected to the direct-current input of an inverter. ▶Figure 100–22

Inverter Output Circuit. The circuit conductors connected to the alternating-current output of an inverter. ▶Figure 100–23

Inverter, Multimode. Equipment having the capabilities of both the interactive inverter and the stand-alone inverter. ▶Figure 100–24

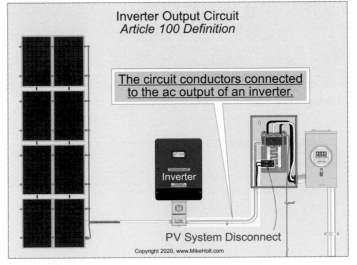

▶Figure 100–23

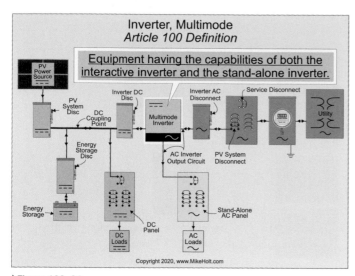

▶Figure 100–24

Labeled. Equipment or materials that have a label, symbol, or other identifying mark in the form of a sticker, decal, printed label, or with the identifying mark molded or stamped into the product by a recognized testing laboratory acceptable to the authority having jurisdiction. ▶Figure 100–25

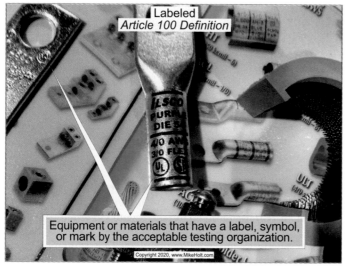

▶Figure 100–25

Author's Comment:

▶ Labeling and listing of equipment typically provides the basis for equipment approval by the authority having jurisdiction [90.4, 90.7, 110.2, and 110.3].

Note: When a listed product is of such a size, shape, material, or surface texture that it is not possible to legibly apply the complete label to the product, the complete label may appear on the smallest unit container in which the product is packaged.

Laundry Area. An area containing, or designed to contain, a laundry tray, clothes washer, or clothes dryer. ▶Figure 100–26

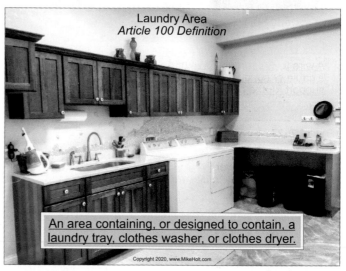

▶Figure 100–26

Author's Comment:

▶ A "laundry tray" is basically a fixed laundry or utility sink with necessary plumbing connections and most commonly installed close to the washer and dryer. A "laundry area" is such by design regardless if the laundry equipment is in place or not.

Messenger or Messenger Wire. A wire that is run along with, or integral to, a cable or conductor to provide mechanical support for the cable or conductor. ▶Figure 100–27

Power Production Equipment. Electrical generating equipment supplied by any source other than a utility service, up to the source system's disconnecting means. ▶Figure 100–28

Note: Examples of power production equipment include such items as generators, solar photovoltaic systems, and fuel cell systems.

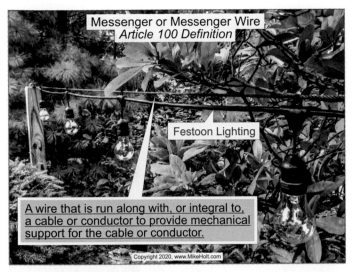

▶Figure 100–27

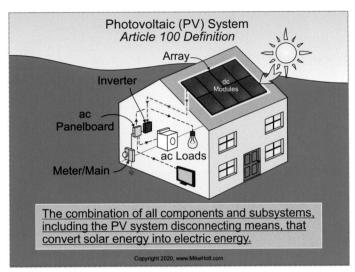

▶Figure 100–29

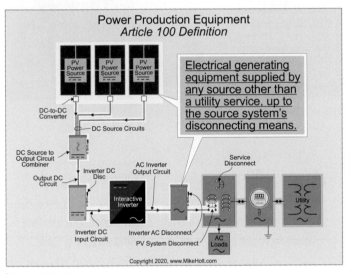

▶Figure 100–28

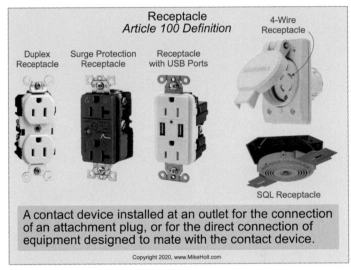

▶Figure 100–30

PV System. The combination of all components and subsystems, including the PV system disconnecting means, that convert solar energy into electric energy for utilization loads. ▶Figure 100–29

Receptacle. A contact device installed at an outlet for the connection of an attachment plug, or for the direct connection of equipment designed to mate with the contact device (SQL receptacle). ▶Figure 100–30

Author's Comment:

▶ For additional information about listed locking, support and mounting receptacles, visit www.safetyquicklight.com.

A single receptacle contains one contact device on a yoke or strap; a multiple receptacle has more than one contact device on the same yoke or strap. ▶Figure 100–31

Author's Comment:

▶ A yoke, also called a "strap," is the metal mounting structure for such items as receptacles, switches, switches with pilot lights, and switch-receptacles to name a few. ▶Figure 100–32 and ▶Figure 100–33

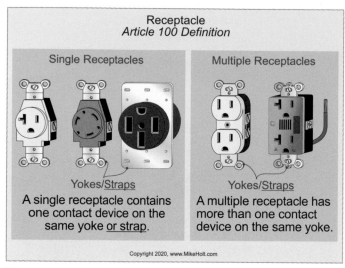

Receptacle
Article 100 Definition

Single Receptacles

Multiple Receptacles

Yokes/Straps

Yokes/Straps

A single receptacle contains one contact device on the same yoke or strap.

A multiple receptacle has more than one contact device on the same yoke.

Copyright 2020, www.MikeHolt.com

▶Figure 100–31

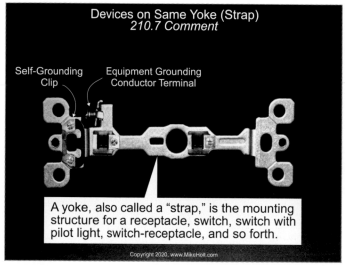

Devices on Same Yoke (Strap)
210.7 Comment

Self-Grounding Clip

Equipment Grounding Conductor Terminal

A yoke, also called a "strap," is the mounting structure for a receptacle, switch, switch with pilot light, switch-receptacle, and so forth.

Copyright 2020, www.MikeHolt.com

▶Figure 100–32

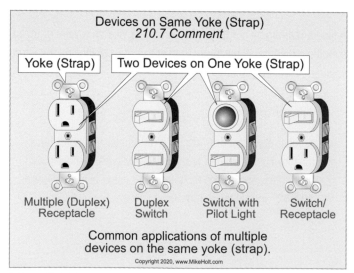

Devices on Same Yoke (Strap)
210.7 Comment

Yoke (Strap)

Two Devices on One Yoke (Strap)

Multiple (Duplex) Receptacle

Duplex Switch

Switch with Pilot Light

Switch/ Receptacle

Common applications of multiple devices on the same yoke (strap).

Copyright 2020, www.MikeHolt.com

▶Figure 100–33

Note: A duplex receptacle is an example of a multiple receptacle that has two receptacles on the same yoke or strap.

Service [Article 230]. The conductors and equipment connecting the serving electric utility to the wiring system of the premises served. ▶Figure 100–34

Service
Article 100 Definition

The conductors and equipment connecting the serving electric utility to the wiring system of the premises.

Copyright 2020, www.MikeHolt.com

▶Figure 100–34

> **Author's Comment:**

> ▶ A service can only be supplied by the serving electric utility. A service is not covered by the *NEC*. If power is supplied by other than the serving electric utility, the conductors and equipment are part of a feeder and covered by the *Code*.

> ▶ Conductors from a UPS system, solar PV system, generator, or transformer are not service conductors. See the definitions of "Feeder" and "Service Conductors" in this article.

Service Equipment (Service Disconnect). Disconnects such as circuit breakers or switches connected to the serving electric utility, intended to control and disconnect the power from the serving electric utility. ▶Figure 100–35

> **Author's Comment:**

> ▶ It's important to know where a service begins and where it ends in order to properly apply the *Code* requirements. Sometimes the service ends before the metering equipment. ▶**Figure 100–36** and ▶**Figure 100–37**

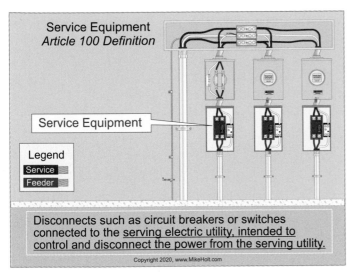

Service Equipment
Article 100 Definition

Service Equipment

Legend
Service
Feeder

Disconnects such as circuit breakers or switches connected to the serving electric utility, intended to control and disconnect the power from the serving utility.

Copyright 2020, www.MikeHolt.com

▶Figure 100–35

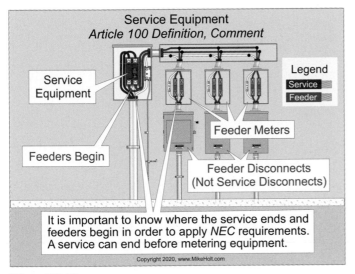

Service Equipment
Article 100 Definition, Comment

Service Equipment

Feeders Begin

Feeder Meters

Feeder Disconnects (Not Service Disconnects)

Legend
Service
Feeder

It is important to know where the service ends and feeders begin in order to apply *NEC* requirements. A service can end before metering equipment.

Copyright 2020, www.MikeHolt.com

▶Figure 100–36

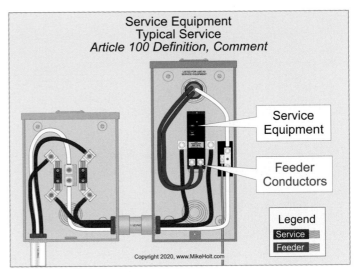

Service Equipment
Typical Service
Article 100 Definition, Comment

Service Equipment

Feeder Conductors

Legend
Service
Feeder

Copyright 2020, www.MikeHolt.com

▶Figure 100–37

Author's Comment:

▶ Service equipment is often referred to as the "service disconnect" or "service main."

▶ Meter socket enclosures are not considered service equipment [230.66].

REQUIREMENTS FOR ELECTRICAL INSTALLATIONS

Introduction to Article 110—Requirements for Electrical Installations

Article 110 sets the stage for how the rest of the *NEC* is implemented. It is critical for you to completely understand all aspects of this article since it is the foundation for much of the *Code*. As you read and master Article 110, you are building your own essential foundation for correctly applying the *NEC*. The purpose of the *National Electrical Code* is to provide a safe installation, but this article is perhaps focused a little more on providing an installation that is safe for the installer and maintenance electrician, so time spent here is time well spent.

110.3 Examination, Identification, Installation, Use, and Product Listing (Certification) of Equipment

The revision clarifies that equipment that is listed, labeled, or both be installed in accordance with the instructions included in the listing or labeling. How the product might be used or installed is still ultimately at the discretion of the authority having jurisdiction (AHJ).

Analysis

CLARIFIED Nationally recognized listing standards (UL and CSA for example) require a product to be listed and the product itself to be marked (labeled) to indicate it is listed. Listed products are often installed and used in applications that are outside of their listing. The information on the equipment label helps the installer and the authority having jurisdiction (AHJ) avoid potentially dangerous misuse of equipment.

110.3 Examination, Identification, Installation, Use, and Product Listing (Certification) of Equipment

(B) Installation and Use. Equipment that is listed and/or labeled must be installed and used in accordance with instructions included in the listing or labeling requirements. ▶Figure 110–1

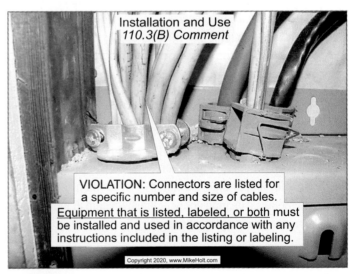

Installation and Use
110.3(B) Comment

VIOLATION: Connectors are listed for a specific number and size of cables. Equipment that is listed, labeled, or both must be installed and used in accordance with any instructions included in the listing or labeling.

Copyright 2020, www.MikeHolt.com

▶Figure 110–1

Author's Comment:

▶ Connectors are listed for a specific number and size of cables. ▶Figure 110–2

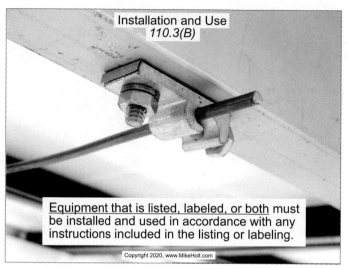

Installation and Use
110.3(B)

Equipment that is listed, labeled, or both must be installed and used in accordance with any instructions included in the listing or labeling.

Copyright 2020, www.MikeHolt.com

▶Figure 110–2

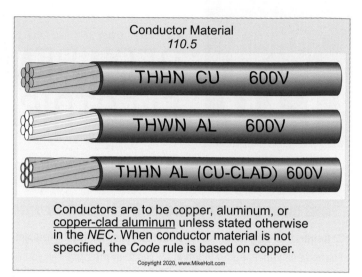

Conductor Material
110.5

THHN CU 600V

THWN AL 600V

THHN AL (CU-CLAD) 600V

Conductors are to be copper, aluminum, or copper-clad aluminum unless stated otherwise in the *NEC*. When conductor material is not specified, the *Code* rule is based on copper.

Copyright 2020, www.MikeHolt.com

▶Figure 110–3

110.5 Conductor Material

Copper-clad aluminum conductors seem to have been neglected for a very long time and for no reason other than perhaps limited availability due to lack of demand. Since most of the electrical current travels on the outside of the conductor, copper-cladded aluminum is just as reliable as copper by itself. This section was revised to delete the Informational Note regarding a copper-clad aluminum conductor and place it into the rule text.

Analysis

CLARIFIED The *NEC* permits the use of copper-clad aluminum conductors just as it does copper and aluminum conductors and there was no good reason not to include copper-clad aluminum in the main text. The ampacity tables include copper-clad aluminum in the same column as aluminum conductors.

110.5 Conductor Material

Conductors are to be copper, aluminum, or copper-clad aluminum unless otherwise provided in this *Code*; and when the conductor material isn't specified in a rule, the sizes given in the *NEC* are based on a copper conductor. ▶Figure 110–3

110.12 Mechanical Execution of Work

This is perhaps one of the most contentious and practically unenforceable rules in the entire *NEC* because it is entirely subjective since there is no solid definition of "installed in a neat and workmanlike manner." This rule, that appeared in the "xxx.24" sections of some Chapter 7 and 8 articles, was relocated to Article 110 where it applies generally throughout the *Code*.

Analysis

NEW **RELOCATED** **110.12(C) Cables and Conductors.** A new subsection (C) was added using text relocated from the "xxx.24" section of some Chapter 7 and 8 articles to apply generally throughout the *NEC*. It provides guidance for the installation of exposed alarm, communications and data cables, and conductors. While this rule was intended to only apply to Chapter 7 and 8 installations, its placement in Article 110 now makes it apply generally—except for Chapter 8 installations.

The overall scope of these changes still does not provide the guidance specific to distances between supports such as those found in the Chapter 3 cable articles.

NEW Informational Notes are also a part of this new first level subsection. One refers to accepted industry practices and another advises that contaminants such as paint, plaster, abrasives, corrosive residues, or others may have an undetermined effect on the properties of optical fiber cables.

110.12 Mechanical Execution of Work

<u>(C) Cables and Conductors.</u> Equipment and cabling must be installed in a neat and workmanlike manner. ▶Figure 110–4

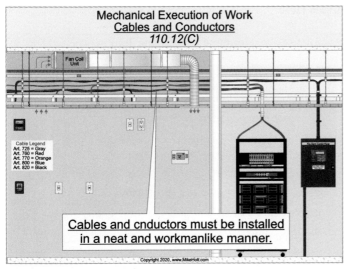

Mechanical Execution of Work
Cables and Conductors
110.12(C)

Cable Legend
Art. 725 = Gray
Art. 760 = Red
Art. 770 = Orange
Art. 800 = Blue
Art. 820 = Black

Cables and cnductors must be installed in a neat and workmanlike manner.

▶Figure 110–4

Exposed cables must be supported by the structural components of the building so the cable will not be damaged by normal building use. Support must be by straps, staples, hangers, cable ties, or similar fittings designed and installed in a manner that will not damage the cable. ▶Figure 110–5 and ▶Figure 110–6

Cables installed through or parallel to framing members or furring strips must be protected, where they are likely to be penetrated by nails or screws, by installing the wiring method so it is not less than 1¼ in. from the nearest edge of the framing member or furring strips, or by protecting it with a ¹⁄₁₆ in. thick steel plate or equivalent [300.4(A)(1) and (D)]. ▶Figure 110–7

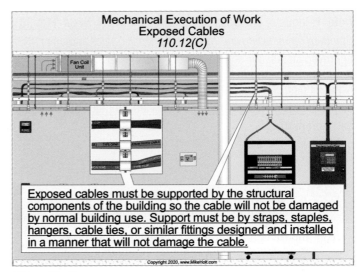

Mechanical Execution of Work
Exposed Cables
110.12(C)

Exposed cables must be supported by the structural components of the building so the cable will not be damaged by normal building use. Support must be by straps, staples, hangers, cable ties, or similar fittings designed and installed in a manner that will not damage the cable.

▶Figure 110–5

Mechanical Execution of Work
Cable Support
110.12(C)

Equipment and cabling must be installed in a neat and workmanlike manner.

▶Figure 110–6

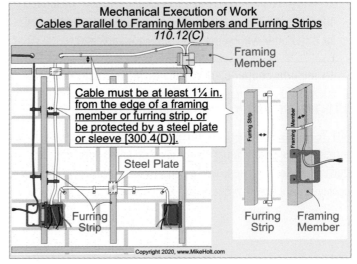

Mechanical Execution of Work
Cables Parallel to Framing Members and Furring Strips
110.12(C)

Framing Member

Cable must be at least 1¼ in. from the edge of a framing member or furring strip, or be protected by a steel plate or sleeve [300.4(D)].

Steel Plate

Furring Strip

Furring Strip

Framing Member

▶Figure 110–7

Note 1: Industry practices are described in ANSI/NECA/FOA 301, *Standard for Installing and Testing Fiber Optic Cables* and other ANSI-approved installation standards.

Note 3: Paint, plaster, cleaners, abrasives, corrosive residues, or other contaminants can result in an undetermined alteration of optical fiber cable properties.

110.14 Conductor Termination and Splicing

The importance of properly tightened electrical terminations cannot be stressed enough. Loose connections are the cause of far too many service calls, equipment damage, and (worse yet) electrical fires. This rule addressing the torqueing of connections first appeared in the 2017 *NEC*. It was revised to require the use of an approved means (not just a calibrated torque tool) to achieve the required torque value. Three new Informational Notes provide guidance for the *Code* user.

Analysis

EDITED **CLARIFIED**

110.14(D) Terminal Connection Torque. The title of the subsection was changed to make the *NEC* easier to use. Finding termination torque requirements in a rule that is titled "Terminal Connection Torque" is easier than finding the same information in a rule called "Installation."

The previous requirement was for the use of a "calibrated torque tool," but an approved means could be a torque tool or a fastener with some type of torque indicator.

110.14 Conductor Termination and Splicing

(D) Terminal Connection Torque. Tightening torque values for terminal connections must be as indicated on equipment or installation instructions. An approved means, (torque tool), must be used to achieve the indicated torque value. ▶Figure 110–8 and ▶Figure 110–9

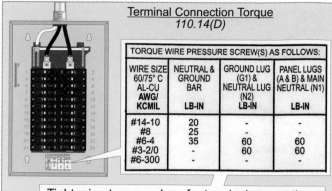

Terminal Connection Torque
110.14(D)

TORQUE WIRE PRESSURE SCREW(S) AS FOLLOWS:			
WIRE SIZE 60/75° C AL-CU AWG/ KCMIL	NEUTRAL & GROUND BAR	GROUND LUG (G1) & NEUTRAL LUG (N2)	PANEL LUGS (A & B) & MAIN NEUTRAL (N1)
	LB-IN	LB-IN	LB-IN
#14-10	20	-	-
#8	25	-	-
#6-4	35	60	60
#3-2/0	-	60	60
#6-300	-	-	-

Tightening torque values for terminal connections must be as indicated on equipment or installation instructions. An approved means must be used to achieve the indicated torque value.

Copyright 2020, www.MikeHolt.com

▶Figure 110–8

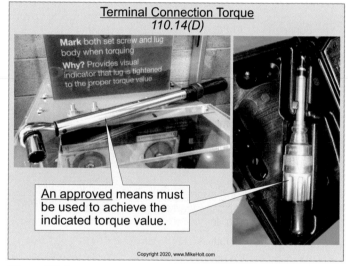

Terminal Connection Torque
110.14(D)

Mark both set screw and lug body when torquing

Why? Provides visual indicator that lug is tightened to the proper torque value

An approved means must be used to achieve the indicated torque value.

Copyright 2020, www.MikeHolt.com

▶Figure 110–9

Author's Comment:

▸ Conductors must terminate in devices that have been properly tightened in accordance with the manufacturer's torque specifications included with equipment instructions. Failure to torque terminals properly can result in excessive heating of terminals or splicing devices due to a loose connection. A loose connection can also lead to arcing which increases the heating effect and may also lead to a short circuit or ground fault. Any of these can result in a fire or other failure, including an arc flash event. In addition, this is a violation of 110.3(B), which requires all equipment to be installed in accordance with listing or labeling instructions.

Note 1: Examples of approved means of achieving the indicated torque values include torque tools or devices such as shear bolts or breakaway-style devices with visual indicators that demonstrate the proper torque has been applied.

Note 2: The equipment manufacturer can be contacted if numeric torque values are not indicated on the equipment or if the installation instructions are not available. Annex I of UL Standard 486A-486B, *Standard for Safety-Wire Connectors*, provides torque values in the absence of manufacturer's recommendations.

Note 3: Additional information for torqueing threaded connections and terminations can be found in Section 8.11 of NFPA 70B, *Recommended Practice for Electrical Equipment Maintenance.*

Author's Comment:

▸ Connections are arguably one of the most common points of electrical failure and properly making those connections properly is critical in preventing connection failures. Either too tight or too loose can result in connection failures and it is difficult to manually find the optimal intersect of mechanical strength and the most desirable performance.

▸ There is still no guidance as to how often a torqueing tool must be calibrated or who is to do so. The revised rule just requires an approved means to achieve the required torque value. This approved means could be a torque tool or a fastener with some type of torque indicator. One such indicator is a double head bolt found on some electrical equipment, where the outer head snaps off at the required torque.

▸ This rule is still difficult from an enforcement point of view. You may need to try to verify what the AHJ requires. Some may want to be present to watch the torqueing of the connection, others may just want to see the tool, and some want to see a "sign off" sheet with the equipment location, the torque value, the date, and the name of the person who torqued the connection. New Informational Notes provide some additional guidance. (See Notes: 1, 2, and 3.)

110.21 Markings

Reconditioning, and when it is permitted, was addressed globally throughout the *Code* during this 2020 revision cycle. This section was clarified to require that, in addition to the equipment being identified as "reconditioned," the original listing marking must be removed.

Analysis

NEW   DELETED

110.21(A)(2) Reconditioned Equipment. This change requires the original listing mark to be removed because it no longer applies to the reconditioned equipment. Even if it was reconditioned to meet (or even exceed) current safety and other standards, it is not the same as the original listing. A new Informational Note 3 was added to indicate that only the original listing mark, and not the entire label, is to be removed. The original manufacturer's label often includes information that needs to be retained.

110.21 Markings

(A) Equipment Markings

(1) General. The manufacturer's name, trademark, or other descriptive marking by which the organization responsible for the product can be identified must be placed on all electrical equipment. Other markings that indicate voltage, current, wattage, or other ratings must be provided as specified elsewhere in this *Code*. The marking or label must be of sufficient durability to withstand the environment involved.

(2) Reconditioned Equipment

Reconditioned equipment must be marked with the name, trademark, or other descriptive marking by which the organization responsible for reconditioning the electrical equipment can be identified, along with the date of the reconditioning.

Reconditioned equipment must be identified as "reconditioned" and the original listing mark removed. Approval of the reconditioned equipment must not be based solely on the equipment's original listing.

Ex.: In industrial occupancies, where conditions of maintenance and supervision ensure that only qualified persons service the equipment, the markings indicated in 110.21(A)(2) are not required <u>for equipment that is reconditioned by the owner or operator as part of a regular equipment maintenance program.</u>

Note 1: Industry standards are available for the application of reconditioned and refurbished equipment.

Note 2: <u>The term "reconditioned" may be interchangeable with terms such as "rebuilt," "refurbished," or "remanufactured."</u>

Note No. 3: <u>The original listing mark may include the mark of the certifying body and not the entire equipment label.</u>

Author's Comment:

▸ One might assume that removing the original listing mark is to be completed during the reconditioning process, but the *Code* provides no guidance on just who is responsible for its removal, the removal criteria, or verification that it was done!

110.22 Identification of Disconnecting Means

All electrical circuits large or small require a means to turn off the power and those means are required to be clearly identified. Turning off the wrong circuit(s) can sometimes create havoc! The requirement to identify the disconnecting means in this rule was expanded to include a requirement to identify the source of the circuit that supplies the disconnecting means.

Analysis

EXPANDED This rule was expanded to require that the power source, as well as the equipment served, be marked on the disconnect that is being served. This requirement doesn't apply to one- or two-family dwellings.

110.22 Identification of Disconnecting Means

(A) General. Each disconnect must be legibly marked to indicate its purpose unless located and arranged so the purpose is evident. <u>In other than one- or two-family dwellings, the marking must include the identification of the circuit source that supplies the disconnecting means.</u> The marking must be of sufficient durability to withstand the environment involved. ▸Figure 110–10

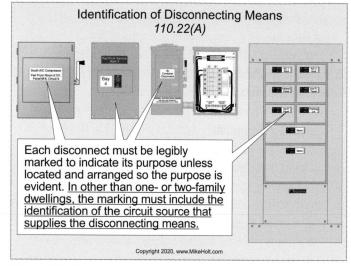

Identification of Disconnecting Means
110.22(A)

Each disconnect must be legibly marked to indicate its purpose unless located and arranged so the purpose is evident. <u>In other than one- or two-family dwellings, the marking must include the identification of the circuit source that supplies the disconnecting means.</u>

Copyright 2020, www.MikeHolt.com

▸Figure 110–10

Author's Comment:

▸ See 408.4 for additional requirements for identification markings on circuit directories for switchboards and panelboards.

▸ These rules are intended to make it safer to work on electrical equipment. The premise is that if the worker knows the location of the power source, he or she is much more likely than not to lockout and tagout the power source.

110.24 Available Fault Current

Fault current far exceeds that of rated current and as such is far more dangerous. The sheer power behind an electrical fault can vaporize metal and justifies the critical attention it receives. The word "maximum" that preceded "available fault current" was deleted because the new definition of "Fault Current, Available (Available Fault Current)" specifies that current is the largest amount that can be delivered into a short circuit at that point on the system. A new Informational Note was also added.

Analysis

EDITED **CLARIFIED**

110.24(A) Field Marking. The change here is an example of revisions made throughout the *NEC* as a result of the new "Fault Current, Available (Available Fault Current)" definition in Article 100. The definition says that the available fault current is the maximum current available at that location, and the word "maximum" is being removed from *Code* sections where it was applied to the term "Fault Current."

A second Informational Note was added to say that values of available fault current for use in determining the appropriate minimum short-circuit current and interrupting ratings of service equipment are available from the electric utilities. This information, which is required to be provided, aids a worker in the ability to recognize hazards and identify safety-related work practices located in NFPA 70E, *Standard for Electrical Safety in the Workplace.*

110.24 Available Fault Current

(A) Field Marking. In other than dwelling units, service disconnects must be field marked with the available fault current on the line side of the service disconnect, the date the fault current calculation was performed, and the marking must be of sufficient durability to withstand the environment present.

The available fault current calculation must be documented and be available to those who are authorized to design, install, inspect, maintain, or operate the system. ▶Figure 110–11

Note 1: The available fault current markings required by this section are related to the short-circuit current and interrupting ratings of equipment required by 110.9 and 110.10. They are not intended to be used for arc flash analysis. Arc flash hazard information is available in NFPA 70E, *Standard for Electrical Safety in the Workplace.*

Note 2: Values of available fault current for use in determining short-circuit current and interrupting ratings of service equipment are available from electric utilities in published or other forms.

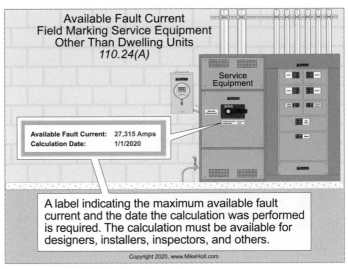

Available Fault Current Field Marking Service Equipment Other Than Dwelling Units *110.24(A)*

Service Equipment

800A

| Available Fault Current: | 27,315 Amps |
| Calculation Date: | 1/1/2020 |

A label indicating the maximum available fault current and the date the calculation was performed is required. The calculation must be available for designers, installers, inspectors, and others.

Copyright 2020, www.MikeHolt.com

▶Figure 110–11

110.26 Spaces About Electrical Equipment

There just cannot be enough emphasis placed upon the importance of clear and accessible working space around electrical equipment. The *NEC* goes to great lengths to help ensure the safety of electrical workers. It is sad, but sometimes a change to this section is the result of an unforeseeable incident that results in injury, property damage, and even fatalities. This is not the case for all changes to the *Code*, but some changes and clarifications during the 2020 revision cycle were made to require even safer workspaces. When equipment is installed on concrete pads it affects the equipment, but the pad itself is not equipment so it could extend out past the 6 in. permitted for electrical equipment. This change clarifies this. Clarifications were also made to entrances and egresses to and from working spaces (C) as well as the illumination (D) of these areas.

Analysis

CLARIFIED

110.26(A)(3) Height of Working Space. Large electrical equipment is often installed on a raised concrete pad that extends a few inches in front of the face of the equipment. The use of such pads was unclear in the 2017 *Code* language which permitted "other equipment" associated with the electrical installation to project not more than 6 in. in front of the equipment. ● ● ●

Public Comment (PC) indicated that it would be a real stretch of the Article 100 definition of "Equipment" to see the "housekeeping pad" as equipment. The revision permits "other equipment or support structures, such as concrete pads, associated with the electrical equipment to extend not more than 6 in. beyond the front of the electrical equipment." The revised wording now very clearly permits this commonly used installation method.

EDITED

110.26(C)(2) Large Equipment. This section was revised to prevent a worker from being trapped because an open equipment door protrudes into the means of egress thereby impeding or even blocking the worker's escape from the area in the event of an emergency.

CLARIFIED

110.26(C)(3) Personnel Doors. This is another large equipment rule; however, the current must be 800A or more for the rule to apply. This rule requires the exit doors from the working space to swing in the direction of egress and have listed panic hardware or listed fire exit hardware. Permitting listed fire exit hardware was added because it is required where the electrical equipment is in a room with fire-rated walls.

CLARIFIED

110.26(D) Illumination. Having the working space go completely dark because an automatic control turns off the lights creates a serious safety hazard to someone who may be working on energized equipment. This change requires that at least some of the working space lighting be controlled only by manual means.

110.26 Spaces About Electrical Equipment

For the purpose of safe operation and maintenance of equipment, access and working space must be provided about all electrical equipment. ▶Figure 110–12

> **Author's Comment:**
>
> ▸ Spaces about electrical equipment (width, depth, and height) consist of working space for worker protection [110.26(A)] and dedicated space to provide access to, and protection of, equipment [110.26(E)].

Spaces About Electrical Equipment
110.26

AREA IN FRONT OF THIS ELECTRICAL PANEL MUST BE KEPT CLEAR FOR 36 INCHES OSHA-NEC REGULATIONS

For the purposes of safe operation and maintenance of equipment, access and working space must be provided about all electrical equipment.

Copyright 2020, www.MikeHolt.com

▶Figure 110–12

(A) Working Space. Equipment that may need examination, adjustment, servicing, or maintenance while energized must have a working space provided in accordance with 110.26(A)(1), (2), (3), and (4).

> **Author's Comment:**
>
> ▸ The phrase "while energized" is the root of many debates. As always, check with the authority having jurisdiction to see what equipment he or she believes needs a clear working space.

Note: NFPA 70E, *Standard for Electrical Safety in the Workplace*, provides guidance in determining the severity of potential exposure, planning safe work practices including establishing an electrically safe work condition, arc flash labeling, and selecting personal protective equipment.

(1) Depth of Working Space. The depth of working space, which is measured from the enclosure front, is not permitted to be less than the distances contained in Table 110.26(A)(1), which is dependent on voltage and three different conditions. ▶Figure 110–13

> **Author's Comment:**
>
> ▸ Depth of working space must be measured from the enclosure front, not the live parts. ▶Figure 110–14

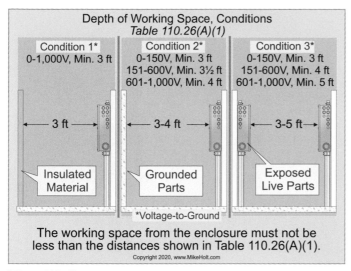

Depth of Working Space, Conditions
Table 110.26(A)(1)

Condition 1*	Condition 2*	Condition 3*
0-1,000V, Min. 3 ft	0-150V, Min. 3 ft	0-150V, Min. 3 ft
	151-600V, Min. 3½ ft	151-600V, Min. 4 ft
	601-1,000V, Min. 4 ft	601-1,000V, Min. 5 ft

3 ft — Insulated Material

3-4 ft — Grounded Parts

3-5 ft — Exposed Live Parts

*Voltage-to-Ground

The working space from the enclosure must not be less than the distances shown in Table 110.26(A)(1).

Copyright 2020, www.MikeHolt.com

▶Figure 110–13

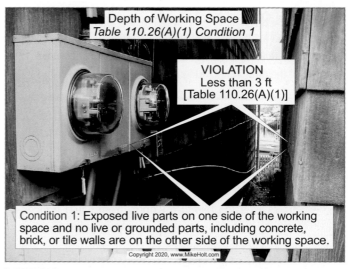

Depth of Working Space
Table 110.26(A)(1) Condition 1

VIOLATION
Less than 3 ft
[Table 110.26(A)(1)]

Condition 1: Exposed live parts on one side of the working space and no live or grounded parts, including concrete, brick, or tile walls are on the other side of the working space.

Copyright 2020, www.MikeHolt.com

▶Figure 110–15

Depth of Working Space
110.26(A)(1) Comment

Correct

Improper

Depth of working space must be measured from the enclosure front, not from the live parts.

Copyright 2020, www.MikeHolt.com

▶Figure 110–14

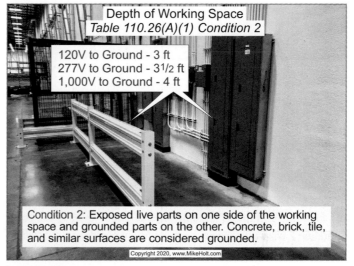

Depth of Working Space
Table 110.26(A)(1) Condition 2

120V to Ground - 3 ft
277V to Ground - 3½ ft
1,000V to Ground - 4 ft

Condition 2: Exposed live parts on one side of the working space and grounded parts on the other. Concrete, brick, tile, and similar surfaces are considered grounded.

Copyright 2020, www.MikeHolt.com

▶Figure 110–16

Table 110.26(A)(1) Working Space			
Voltage–to–Ground	Condition 1	Condition 2	Condition 3
0–150V	3 ft	3 ft	3 ft
151–600V	3 ft	3½ ft	4 ft
601–1,000V	3 ft	4 ft	5 ft

▶Figure 110–15, ▶Figure 110–16, and ▶Figure 110–17

Depth of Working Space
Table 110.26(A)(1) Condition 3

120V to Ground - 3 ft
277V to Ground - 4 ft
1,000V to Ground - 5 ft

Condition 3: Exposed live parts on both sides of the working space.

Copyright 2020, www.MikeHolt.com

▶Figure 110–17

(a) Rear and Sides of Dead-Front Equipment. Working space is not required at the back or sides of equipment where all connections and all renewable, adjustable, or serviceable parts are accessible from the front of the equipment. ▸Figure 110–18

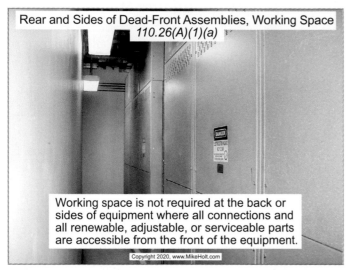

▸Figure 110–18

Author's Comment:

▸ Sections of equipment that require rear or side access to make field connections are to be marked by the manufacturer on the front of the equipment, see 408.8(C).

(c) Existing Buildings. If electrical equipment is being replaced, Condition 2 working space is permitted between dead-front switchboards, switchgear, panelboards, or motor control centers located across the aisle from each other where conditions of maintenance and supervision ensure that written procedures have been adopted to prohibit equipment on both sides of the aisle from being open at the same time, and only authorized, qualified persons will service the installation.

(2) Width of Working Space. The width of the working space must be a minimum of 30 in., but in no case less than the width of the equipment. ▸Figure 110–19

Author's Comment:

▸ The width of the working space can be measured from left-to-right, from right-to-left, or simply centered on the equipment, and can overlap the working space for other electrical equipment. ▸Figure 110–20 and ▸Figure 110–21

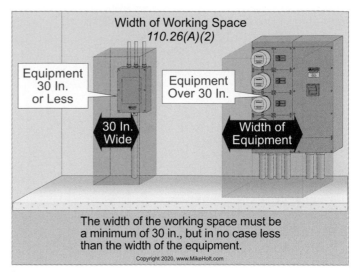

▸Figure 110–19

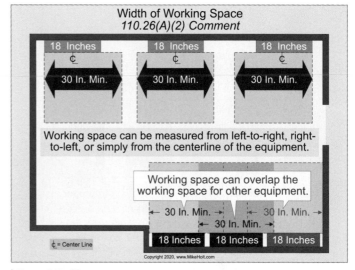

▸Figure 110–20

▸Figure 110–21

The working space must be of sufficient width, depth, and height to permit equipment doors to open at least 90 degrees. ▶Figure 110–22

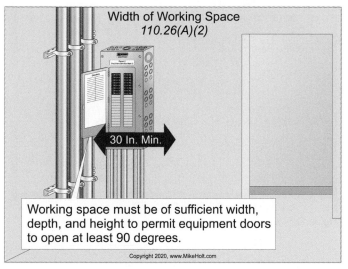

▶Figure 110–22

Author's Comment:

▶ If the working space is a platform, it must be sized to the working space requirement, in this example the working platform is not 30 in. deep. ▶Figure 110–23

▶Figure 110–23

(3) Height of Working Space. The height of the working space must be clear and extend from the grade, floor, or platform to a height of 6½ ft or the height of the equipment. ▶Figure 110–24

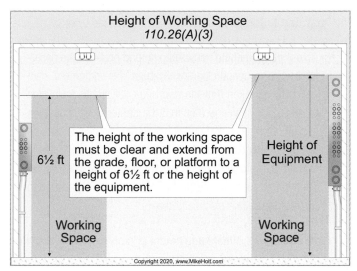

▶Figure 110–24

Electrical equipment such as raceways, cables, wireways, or panelboards or support structures, such as concrete pads are permitted to extend not more than 6 in. beyond the front of the electrical equipment. ▶Figure 110–25

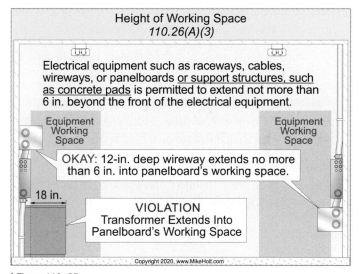

▶Figure 110–25

Ex. 1: The minimum height of working space does not apply to a service disconnect or panelboards rated 200A or less located in an existing dwelling unit.

Ex. 2: Meters are permitted in the working space.

Author's Comment:

▸ Unless the size of the housekeeping pad provides the necessary working space clearances about the equipment, care needs to be taken that the pad does not create a violation of 404.8(A) which specifies that the center of the operating handle of switches and circuit breakers used as switches be not more than 6 ft 7 in. above the floor or work surface and that the pad provides the necessary depth of working space. The workspace is the surface on which the worker stands to operate the switch or circuit breaker.

(4) Limited Access. Where equipment is likely to require examination, adjustment, servicing, or maintenance while energized is located above a suspended ceiling or crawl space, all of the following conditions apply:

(1) Equipment installed above a suspended ceiling must have an access opening not smaller than 22 in. × 22 in., and equipment installed in a crawl space must have an accessible opening not smaller than 22 in. × 30 in.

(2) The width of the working space must be a minimum of 30 in., but in no case less than the width of the equipment.

(3) The working space must permit equipment doors to open 90 degrees.

(4) The working space in front of the equipment must comply with the depth requirements of Table 110.26(A)(1), and horizontal ceiling structural members are permitted in this space.

(B) Clear Working Space. The working space required by this section must be clear at all times; therefore, this space is not permitted for storage. ▸Figure 110–26

Caution

⚠ It is very dangerous to service energized parts in the first place, and it is unacceptable to be subjected to additional dangers by working around bicycles, boxes, crates, appliances, and other impediments.

When live parts are exposed for inspection or servicing, the working space, if in a passageway or open space, must be suitably guarded.

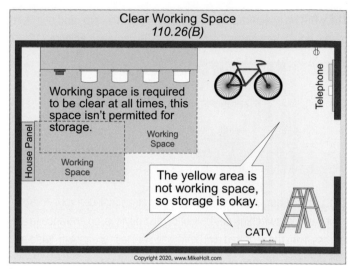

▸Figure 110–26

Author's Comment:

▸ When working in a passageway, the working space should be guarded from use by occupants. When working on electrical equipment in a passageway one must be mindful of a fire alarm evacuation with many people congregating and moving through the area.

▸ Signaling and communications equipment are not permitted to be installed in a manner that encroaches on the working space of the electrical equipment. ▸Figure 110–27

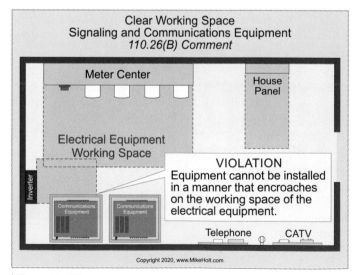

▸Figure 110–27

(C) Access to and Egress from Working Space

(1) Minimum Required. At least one entrance of sufficient area must provide access to and egress from the working space.

> **Author's Comment:**
>
> ▸ Check to see what the authority having jurisdiction considers "sufficient area." Building codes contain minimum dimensions for doors and openings for personnel travel.

(2) Large Equipment. For large equipment that contains overcurrent devices, switching devices, or control devices, an entrance to and egress from the required working space not less than 24 in. wide and 6½ ft high is required at each end of the working space. This requirement applies for either of the following conditions:

(1) Where equipment is over 6 ft wide rated 1,200A or more ▸Figure 110–28

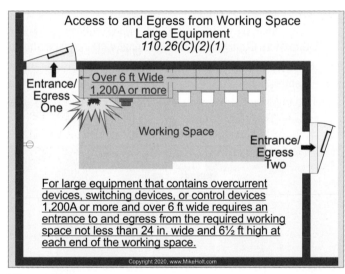

▸Figure 110–28

(2) Where the service disconnect is over 6 ft wide and where the combined ampere rating is 1,200A ▸Figure 110–29

Open equipment doors must not impede the entry to or egress from the working space.

A single entrance for access to, and egress from, the required working space is permitted where either of the following conditions are met:

(a) Unobstructed Egress. Where the location permits a continuous and unobstructed way of egress travel. ▸Figure 110–30

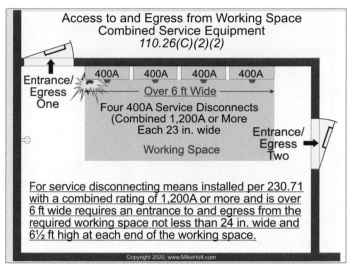

▸Figure 110–29

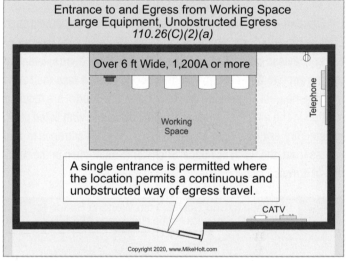

▸Figure 110–30

(b) Double Working Space. Where the required working space depth is doubled, and the equipment is located so the edge of the entrance is no closer than the required working space distance. ▸Figure 110–31

> **Author's Comment:**
>
> ▸ The requirement for a path of egress with the door open may require wider aisle space. The *Code* does not give specific guidance as to the required width of the egress path, but the egress door must be at least 24 in. wide. It would be reasonable to ensure the aisle has a width equal to the door plus 24 in. Doors that open more than 90 degrees would be ideal for providing more space for egress.

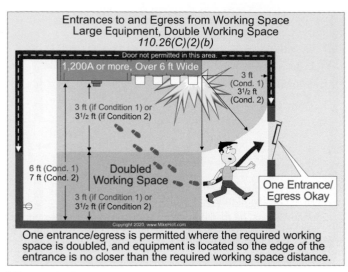

▶Figure 110-31

(3) Fire Exit Hardware on Personnel Doors. Where equipment rated 800A or more that contains overcurrent devices, switching devices, or control devices is installed and there is a personnel door(s) intended for entrance to and egress from the working space less than 25 ft from the nearest edge of the working space, the door(s) are required to open in the direction of egress and be equipped with listed panic or listed fire exit hardware on personnel door(s) for entrance to, and egress from, the working space. Such doors must open in the direction of egress. ▶Figure 110-32

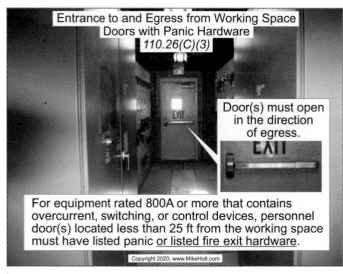

▶Figure 110-32

Author's Comment:

▸ History has shown that electricians who suffer burns on their hands in electrical arc flash or arc blast events often cannot open doors equipped with knobs that must be turned or those that must be pulled open.

▸ Since this requirement is in the *NEC*, the electrical contractor is responsible for ensuring that panic hardware is installed where required. Some are offended at being held liable for nonelectrical responsibilities, but this rule is designed to save the lives of electricians. For this and other reasons, many construction professionals routinely hold "pre-construction" or "pre-con" meetings to review potential opportunities for miscommunication—before the work begins.

▸ The minimum requirement to provide listed panic hardware at or above 800A shouldn't overshadow the importance to perform a risk assessment to incorporate specific room design, equipment layout, and egress accessibility.

(D) Illumination. Illumination is required for all working spaces about service equipment, switchboards, switchgear, panelboards, or motor control centers installed indoors. Control by automatic means is not permitted to control illumination within the working space. ▶Figure 110-33 and ▶Figure 110-34

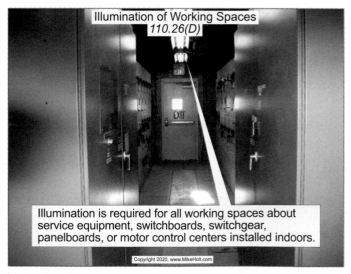

▶Figure 110-33

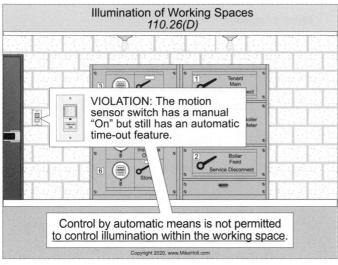

Illumination of Working Spaces
110.26(D)

VIOLATION: The motion sensor switch has a manual "On" but still has an automatic time-out feature.

Control by automatic means is not permitted to control illumination within the working space.

Copyright 2020, www.MikeHolt.com

▶Figure 110–34

Additional lighting outlets are not required where the working space is illuminated by an adjacent light source or as permitted by 210.70(A)(1) Ex 1, for switched receptacles.

Author's Comment:

▸ The *Code* does not identify the minimum foot-candles required to provide proper illumination even though proper illumination of electrical equipment rooms is essential for the safety of those qualified to work on such equipment.

110.28 Enclosure Types

Two new Informational Notes were added to the enclosure selection rule to advise the reader that dusttight-rated enclosures are suitable for use in Class II, Division 2 dust hazard areas.

Analysis

NEW **CLARIFIED**

The two new Informational Notes were added and tell us that dusttight enclosures are suitable for use in Class II, Division 2; Class III; and Zone 22 locations as well as per the permissions in 502.10(B)(4), 503.10(A)(2), and 506.15(C)(8). Before these notes, some AHJs may have been inclined to reject dusttight enclosures in hazardous areas where ignitible dust or ignitible fibers/flyings were present.

110.28 Enclosure Types

Enclosures must be marked with an enclosure-type number and be suitable for the location in accordance with Table 110.28. Enclosures are not intended to protect against condensation, icing, corrosion, or contamination that might occur within the enclosure or that enters via a raceway or unsealed openings. ▶Figure 110–35 and ▶Figure 110–36

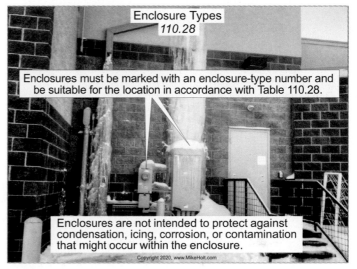

Enclosure Types
110.28

Enclosures must be marked with an enclosure-type number and be suitable for the location in accordance with Table 110.28.

Enclosures are not intended to protect against condensation, icing, corrosion, or contamination that might occur within the enclosure.

Copyright 2020, www.MikeHolt.com

▶Figure 110–35

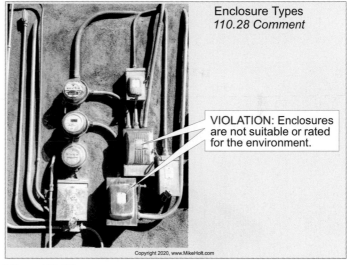

Enclosure Types
110.28 Comment

VIOLATION: Enclosures are not suitable or rated for the environment.

Copyright 2020, www.MikeHolt.com

▶Figure 110–36

Note: Raintight enclosures include Types 3, 3S, 3SX, 3X, 4, 4X, 6, and 6P; rainproof enclosures are Types 3R and 3RX; watertight enclosures are Types 4, 4X, 6, and 6P; driptight enclosures are Types 2, 5, 12, 12K, and 13; and dusttight enclosures are Types 3, 3S, 3SX, 3X, 5, 12, 12K, and 13.

Note 3: Dusttight enclosures are suitable for use in hazardous locations in accordance with 502.10(B)(4), 503.10(A)(2), and 506.15()9).

Note 4: Dusttight enclosures are suitable for use in unclassified locations and in Class II, Division 2; Class III; and Zone 22 hazardous (classified) locations.

Author's Comment:

▸ Remember that with these hazards, we are only trying to keep the ignitable materials out of the electrical equipment as opposed to Class I locations where the enclosures may be called on to physically contain an explosion within the enclosure.

CHAPTER 2

WIRING AND PROTECTION

Introduction to Chapter 2—Wiring and Protection

Chapter 2 provides the general rules for wiring and sizing services, feeders, and branch circuits, and for the overcurrent protection of conductors as well as the proper grounding and bonding of electrical circuits and systems. The rules in this chapter apply to all electrical installations covered by the *NEC*—except as modified in Chapters 5, 6, and 7 [90.3].

Communications Systems [Chapter 8] (twisted-pair conductors, antennas, and coaxial cable) are not subject to the general requirements of Chapters 1 through 4, or the special requirements of Chapters 5 through 7, unless there is a specific reference in Chapter 8 to a rule in Chapters 1 through 7 [90.3].

As you go through Chapter 2, remember that it is primarily focused on correctly sizing and protecting circuits. Every article in this chapter deals with a different aspect of providing a safe installation.

- **Article 200—Use and Identification of Neutral and Grounded-Phase Conductors.** This article contains the requirements for the use and identification of the grounded conductor, which (in most cases) is the neutral conductor.

- **Article 210—Branch Circuits.** Article 210 contains the requirements for branch circuits; such as conductor sizing, identification, AFCI and GFCI protection, and receptacle and lighting outlet requirements.

- **Article 215—Feeders.** This article covers the requirements for the installation and ampacity of feeders.

- **Article 220—Branch-Circuit, Feeder, and Service Calculations.** Article 220 provides the requirements for calculating the sizes required for branch circuits, feeders, and services. It also provides guidance in determining such things as the mandatory number of branch circuits and the number of receptacles on each.

- **Article 225—Outside Feeders.** This article covers the requirements for wiring methods located outside (both overhead and underground). It includes feeders that run on or between buildings, poles, and other structures which may be present on the premises and used to feed equipment.

- **Article 230—Services.** Article 230 covers the installation requirements for service conductors and equipment. It is very important to know where the service begins and ends when applying Article 230.

- **Article 240—Overcurrent Protection.** This article provides the requirements for overcurrent protection and overcurrent protective devices. Overcurrent protection for conductors and equipment is provided to open the circuit if the current reaches a value that will cause an excessive or dangerous temperature on the conductors or conductor insulation.

- **Article 242—Overvoltage Protection.** Part I of this article covers the general installation and connection requirements for surge-protective devices (SPDs) permanently installed on both the line side and load side of service disconnects. Part II covers SPDs permanently installed on wiring systems 1,000V and less. Part III covers surge arresters for systems over 1,000V which are beyond the scope of this textbook.

- **Article 250—Grounding and Bonding.** Article 250 covers the grounding requirements for providing a path to the Earth to reduce overvoltage from lightning, and the bonding requirements for the low-impedance fault current path necessary to facilitate the operation of overcurrent protective devices in the event of a ground fault.

USE AND IDENTIFICATION OF GROUNDED CONDUCTORS

Introduction to Article 200—Use and Identification of Grounded Conductors

This article contains the requirements for the identification of the grounded conductor and its terminals.

Author's Comment:

▸ There are two types of grounded conductors; neutral conductors and grounded-phase conductors. A system where the transformer secondary is wye-connected with the neutral point grounded will have a neutral. ▸Figure 200–1

▸ A system where the transformer secondary is delta-connected with one winding or coil grounded at its midpoint will have a neutral but will also produce one phase with a higher voltage-to-ground known as a "high-leg." ▸Figure 200–2

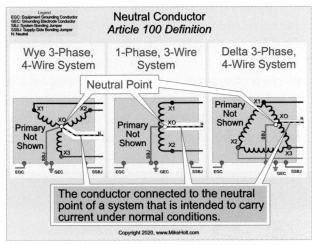

▸Figure 200–1

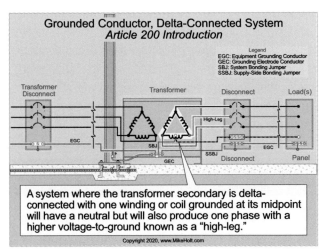

▸Figure 200–2

Author's Comment:

▸ A system where the transformer secondary is delta-connected with one corner winding grounded will have a grounded-phase conductor. ▸Figure 200–3

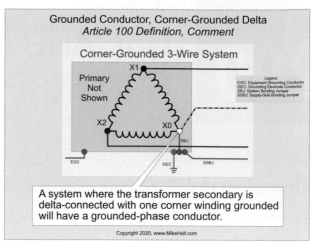

Grounded Conductor, Corner-Grounded Delta
Article 100 Definition, Comment

Corner-Grounded 3-Wire System

Primary Not Shown

Legend
EGC: Equipment Grounding Conductor
GEC: Grounding Electrode Conductor
SBJ: System Bonding Jumper
SSBJ: Supply-Side Bonding Jumper

A system where the transformer secondary is delta-connected with one corner winding grounded will have a grounded-phase conductor.

Copyright 2020, www.MikeHolt.com

▸Figure 200–3

200.3 Connections to Grounded System

Even though there are both neutral conductors and grounded-phase conductors, this section focuses primarily on distinguishing neutral conductors from phase conductors and grounded-phase conductors. The rule ensuring that neutral conductors are properly connected was revised to make it clear it applies to all premises wiring systems—both indoor and outdoor.

Analysis

CLARIFIED

This rule requires that where the premises wiring system has a neutral conductor, it must be connected to the supply system neutral conductor. The word "interior" implied that a neutral conductor was only required in the supply system if the premises wiring was located inside a building or structure. Replacing "interior" with "premises wiring" clarifies that this rule applies to wiring other than just "interior wiring."

200.6 Identification of Grounded Conductors

Subsection (A) was revised to clarify the fact that it is talking about the identification of insulated conductors. Exception 1 to 200.6(E), which previously only permitted the re-identification of conductors in multiconductor cables as neutral or grounded-phase conductors where the conditions of maintenance and supervision ensure that only qualified persons service the installation, was reduced and moved to the latter part of this rule.

Analysis

CLARIFIED **NEW**

200.6(A) Sizes 6 AWG or Smaller. The term "insulated conductor" was added to list items (1) through (4) to clarify that these rules apply to the identification of insulated neutral conductors.

REDUCED

200.6(E) Grounded Conductors of Multiconductor Cables, Ex 1. This revision removes the restriction on the use of multiconductor cables that often do not have a conductor that is identifiable as a neutral conductor by the color of the conductor insulation within the cable. This change clearly permits the re-identification of conductors used as neutral conductors at the time of their installation, no matter in what location they were installed.

200.6 Identification of Grounded Conductors

(A) 6 AWG or Smaller. Neutral and grounded-phase conductors 6 AWG and smaller must be identified by any of the following means: ▶Figure 200–4

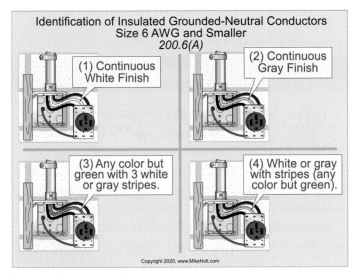

Identification of Insulated Grounded-Neutral Conductors
Size 6 AWG and Smaller
200.6(A)

(1) Continuous White Finish

(2) Continuous Gray Finish

(3) Any color but green with 3 white or gray stripes.

(4) White or gray with stripes (any color but green).

Copyright 2020, www.MikeHolt.com

▶Figure 200–4

(1) Insulated conductors with a continuous white outer finish.

(2) Insulated conductors with a continuous gray outer finish.

(3) Insulated conductors with three continuous white or gray stripes along its entire length on other than green insulation.

(4) Insulated conductors with their outer covering finished to show a white or gray color but have colored tracer threads in the braid identifying the source of manufacture.

Author's Comment:

▸ The use of white tape, paint, or other methods of identification is not permitted for neutral conductors 6 AWG and smaller. ▶Figure 200–5

(E) Grounded Conductors of Multiconductor Cables. Insulated neutral conductor(s) sized 6 AWG and smaller in multiconductor cables must be identified by a continuous white or gray outer finish, or by three continuous white or gray stripes. Conductors in multiconductor cables sized 4 AWG or larger can have the neutral conductor identified in accordance with 200.6(B).

Ex 1: Conductors within multiconductor cables are permitted to be re-identified at their terminations at the time of installation by a distinctive white or gray marking.

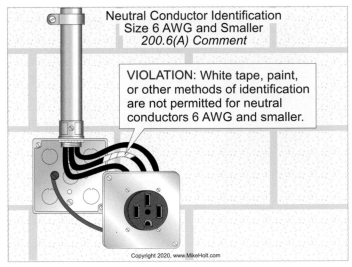

Neutral Conductor Identification
Size 6 AWG and Smaller
200.6(A) Comment

VIOLATION: White tape, paint, or other methods of identification are not permitted for neutral conductors 6 AWG and smaller.

Copyright 2020, www.MikeHolt.com

▶Figure 200–5

200.9 Means of Identification

This rule requiring a substantially white color terminal for neutral conductor connections was revised to only apply to devices or equipment with polarized connections. It was also modified to recognize that neutral termination points may be identified by a silver color.

Analysis

CLARIFIED

This rule was revised so it only applies to the terminals of devices or equipment having "polarized" connections. Taken literally, the previous language could have been applied to equipment such as panelboards, switchgear, and switchboards which typically do not differentiate the neutral conductor terminations with a substantially white color.

200.9 Means of Identification

In devices or utilization equipment with polarized connections, identification of terminals to which a neutral conductor is to be connected must be substantially white or silver in color. The identification of other terminals must be of a readily distinguishable different color. ▶Figure 200–6

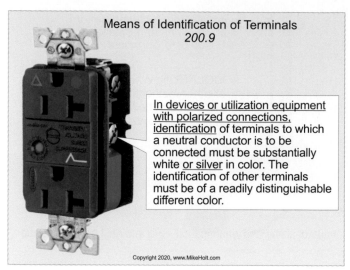

Means of Identification of Terminals
200.9

In devices or utilization equipment with polarized connections, identification of terminals to which a neutral conductor is to be connected must be substantially white or silver in color. The identification of other terminals must be of a readily distinguishable different color.

Copyright 2020, www.MikeHolt.com

▶Figure 200–6

Author's Comment:

▸ It was never the intent of the *Code* to require that panelboards and switchgear have the neutral conductor termination points be "substantially white in color." Neutral conductor termination screws are typically silver in color so the words "or silver" were added for clarification.

200.10 Identification of Terminals

The color used to identify the neutral conductor connection on most wiring devices (duplex receptacles for example) is silver rather than "substantially white," so the language was revised to reflect that fact.

Analysis

CLARIFIED   NEW

200.10(B) Receptacles, Plugs, and Connectors. This is the same change as we saw in 200.9 with the addition of the words "or silver." The rule for the identification of the neutral conductor terminals on receptacles, plugs, and connectors was modified to reflect the fact that terminals on such devices are not "substantially white in color."

200.10 Identification of Terminals

(B) Receptacles. Receptacles must have the neutral terminal identified by:

(1) A metal terminal or metal coating terminal that is substantially white or silver in color or marked by the word "white" or the letter "W."

(2) If the terminal is not visible, the conductor entrance hole must be marked with the word "white" or the letter "W."

ARTICLE
210

BRANCH CIRCUITS

Introduction to Article 210—Branch Circuits

This article contains branch-circuit requirements such as those for conductor sizing and identification, GFCI and AFCI protection, and receptacle and lighting outlet requirements. It consists of three parts:

- Part I. General Provisions
- Part II. Branch-Circuit Ratings
- Part III. Required Outlets

Table 210.3 of this article identifies specific-purpose branch circuits. The provisions for branch circuits that supply equipment listed in Table 210.3 amend or supplement the provisions given in Article 210 for branch circuits, so it is important to be aware of the contents of this table.

210.5 Identification for Branch Circuits

We have all become accustomed to using the term "nominal" when referring to different voltages, but the *NEC* now uses the term "voltage classes." This may take some getting used to as there are much higher "voltage classes" throughout the electrical industry. For example, we refer to 240/120 as a low nominal voltage but outside of the *NEC*, a lower-class voltage might be anything below 5,000V and a medium-class voltage can be as high as 35,000V. With that in mind, this rule was revised to clarify that where there are multiple systems of the same system "voltage class," all systems of the same voltage class are permitted to use the same identification. So, for all intents and purposes, if you have 480/277V and 208Y/120V within the same facility, this rule requires them to be marked to distinguish the different voltage classes, and the marking style must remain consistent.

Analysis

 CLARIFIED **210.5(C)(1) Branch Circuits Supplied from More Than One Nominal Voltage System.** This addresses the issue where there are multiple separately derived systems having the same secondary voltage in a single building. The previous language could be read as requiring each of them to be identified differently.

210.5 Identification for Branch Circuits

(C) Identification of Phase Conductors. Circuit phase conductors must be identified as follows:

(1) More Than One Voltage Distribution System. Where premises wiring is supplied from more than one nominal voltage system, the phase conductors of branch circuits must be identified by phase or line and by voltage class at all termination, connection, and splice points in accordance with 210.5(C)(1)(a) and (b). Different systems within the premises with the same system voltage class can use the same method of identification. ▶Figure 210–1

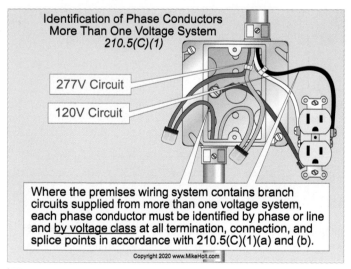

▶Figure 210–1

Author's Comment:

▶ "Voltage class" should be read as "nominal" voltage as used here. For example, a premises with two sources of 120/208V nominal such as a separately derived system, can use the same conductor identification scheme (which in this case would typically be black, red, blue, and white) because the "voltage class" (nominal voltage) is the same.

(a) Means of Identification. Identification of the phase conductors can be by color coding, marking tape, tagging, or other means approved by the authority having jurisdiction. ▶Figure 210–2

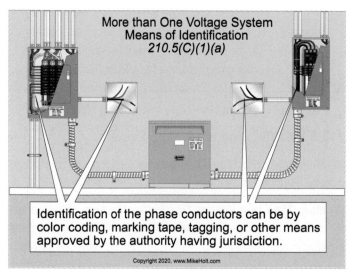

▶Figure 210–2

(b) Posting of Identification. The method of identification must be readily available or permanently posted at each branch-circuit panelboard, not be handwritten, and be sufficiently durable to withstand the environment involved. ▶Figure 210–3

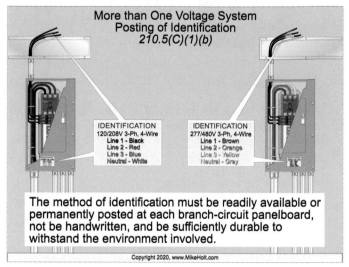

▶Figure 210–3

Ex: Where a different voltage system is added to an existing installation, branch-circuit identification is only required for the new voltage system. The existing voltage system distribution equipment must have a label with the words "other unidentified systems exist on the premises." ▶Figure 210–4

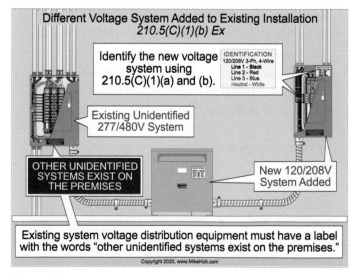

▶Figure 210–4

Author's Comment:

▸ When a premises has more than one voltage system supplying branch circuits, the phase conductors must be identified by phase and system. This can be done by permanently posting an identification legend that describes the method used, such as color-coded marking tape or color-coded insulation.

▸ Although the *NEC* does not require a specific color code for phase conductors, electricians often use the following color system: ▸Figure 210–5

  ◆ 120/240V, single-phase—black, red, and white

  ◆ 120/208V, three-phase—black, red, blue, and white

  ◆ 120/240V, three-phase—black, orange, blue, and white

  ◆ 277/480V, three-phase—brown, orange, yellow, and gray; or, brown, purple, yellow, and gray

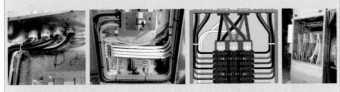

Common Phase Conductor Identification Methods
210.5, 215.12, 310.6(C) Comment

Although the *NEC* does not require a specific color code for phase conductors, electricians often use the following color system for power and lighting conductor identification:
• 120/240V, single-phase—black, red, and white
• 120/208V, three-phase—black, red, blue, and white
• 120/240V, three-phase—black, orange, blue, and white
• 277/480V, three-phase—brown, orange, yellow, and gray; or, brown, purple, yellow, and gray

Copyright 2020, www.MikeHolt.com

▸Figure 210–5

Author's Comment:

▸ Whichever color scheme is used, it is important for it to remain consistent wherever terminated or accessible throughout the entire premises, especially when identifying different system voltages and neutrals.

210.6 Branch-Circuit Voltage Limitations

There are voltage limitations for dwelling occupancies where circuits are terminated. The rules of where circuits having a voltage that exceeds 120V between conductors but does not exceed 277V to ground were editorially revised without technical change.

Analysis

EDITED   **RELOCATED**

210.6(C) 277V to Ground. The permission for equipment to be supplied by circuits exceeding 120V and not 277V between conductors has been relocated from the list and placed into the text preceding the subsections (the "parent text"). This leaves the list to cover various types of luminaries.

RELOCATED

All references to "listed" as applied to luminaries were removed from this section. All luminaries are required to be listed in accordance with 410.6 so the word "listed" is no longer required.

RELOCATED

List items (1) through (8) were reorganized and a few were re-designated.

210.8 GFCI Protection

There is absolutely no doubt that ground-fault circuit-interrupter protection has done more than its fair share of protecting people from the hazards involved with the use of electricity. Each *Code* cycle increases the emphasis on GFCI protection and the locations in which such protection is required. With so much attention given to this section, it is inevitable that all circuits in dwelling units will eventually require this protection. The 2020 changes and revisions to this section are numerous and include clarifications, expansions to existing rules, and a few new additional items. Some items were relocated and placed in their appropriate articles as indicated in the Informational Notes.

So much revision requires the extensive analysis that follows.

Analysis

210.8 GFCI Protection. The method of determining the distance from a receptacle was revised. It is now the shortest path an appliance's supply cord will follow without piercing a floor, wall, ceiling, fixed barrier, or passing through a window. This change was made to address the question as to whether a cabinet door is a door or doorway. With the elimination of any reference to doors, the path through a cabinet door is included in the measurement. In most cases this means that receptacles installed in a cabinet under sink must have GFCI protection.

CLARIFIED

210.8(A) Dwelling Units. This was expanded to require GFCI protection for all receptacles rated 125V through 250V rated 150V or less to ground in the areas specified in list items (1) through (11). The hazards are related to the location of the receptacle and exists for the higher voltage and higher current receptacles. Things like cord-and-plug-connected shop equipment in a dwelling unit garage that operate above 120V, or require circuits having an ampacity greater than 20A, will now be required to have GFCI protection.

EXPANDED

The GFCI requirements for protection in dwelling unit basements has been expanded to include both finished and unfinished basements.

210.8(A)(5). List item (5) for basements was expanded to require all basement receptacles to have GFCI protection. Previous editions of the *NEC* did not require GFCI protection for the finished areas of a basement. Floor surfaces in finished and unfinished basements are prone to moisture and possible flooding creating a potential hazard.

EXPANDED

210.8(A)(11). A new list item (11) was added to require all receptacles in an indoor damp or wet location to have GFCI protection. Indoor dog washing areas were cited in the substantiation for this new requirement.

NEW

210.8(B) Other Than Dwelling Units. The intent of this rule was corrected for this *Code* cycle. The 2017 *NEC* specified the GFCI protection rule applied to receptacles having a rating of 150V or less to ground. Receptacles are listed and identified as having nominal or maximum voltage ratings, but their voltage-to-ground ratings are not identified. This rule was clarified to indicate that all 125V through 250V receptacles supplied by single-phase supply circuits rated 50A or less, or three-phase supply circuits rated 100A or less with a voltage of 150V or less to ground, must have GFCI protection. The locations where GFCI protection is required are found in the twelve list items, two of which are new to the 2020 *Code*.

CLARIFIED

210.8(B)(2). This list item now applies to "kitchens or areas with a sink and permanent provisions for either food preparation or cooking." Places like ice cream parlors, coffee shops, and similar areas present the same shock hazard as areas with kitchens. These places typically do not have stoves or ovens for cooking and so the receptacles were not required to have GFCI protection unless they were located within 6 ft of a sink.

EXPANDED

210.8(B)(6). The fact that dampness increases the conductivity of things and results in an increased shock hazard has been recognized, and correlates with the new item (11) for dwelling occupancies that also requires GFCI protection for indoor receptacles in damp or wet locations.

EXPANDED

210.8(B)(8). List item 8 previously covered garages, service bays, and similar areas. It was expanded to include accessory buildings. Nondwelling occupancies may have accessory buildings and the shock hazard in an accessory building is essentially the same as in a garage.

EXPANDED

210.8(B)(10). This rule was editorially revised to apply to unfinished areas of basements. It previously applied to unfinished "portions." The wording "not intended as a habitable room" was deleted. The deleted language does not make a technical change in the requirement and, unlike the change made in 210.8(A)(5) for dwelling unit basements, it was not expanded to include finished areas of nondwelling unit basements.

EDITED

210.8(B)(11). The requirement to provide GFCI protection for receptacles installed in laundry areas in nondwelling occupancies is more closely related to the type of equipment than it is to the type of occupancy. This rule will require GFCI protection for receptacles that service laundry equipment.

NEW

210.8(B)(12). List item 12 is new and was added to cover receptacles installed within 6 ft of bathtubs or shower stalls that are not covered by one of the other list items. In nondwelling occupancies, there may be tubs and showers installed in other than bathrooms and locker rooms.

NEW

210.8(C) Crawl Space Lighting Outlets. With the scope change in Article 555 to include dwelling unit boat docks, the GFCI protection requirement for boat hoists for all occupancies is now found in 555.9, and 210.8(C) is now "Crawl Space Lighting." The crawl space lighting GFCI requirement was reassigned from (E) to (C) without change and (E) is now dedicated to a new section, "Equipment Requiring Servicing."

RELOCATED

210.8(D) Specific Appliances. The requirement for outlets that supply dwelling unit dishwashers to have GFCI protection was moved to 422.5(A)(7), and 210.8(D) was repurposed to cover "Specific Appliances."

RELOCATED

210.8(E) Equipment Requiring Servicing. Not all receptacles installed for servicing heating, air-conditioning, and refrigeration equipment are installed in locations where other rules would require them to have GFCI protection. This change requires GFCI protection for those receptacles that otherwise would not have such protection. The shock hazard concern is more closely related to the use of portable electric hand tools and cords while servicing the equipment rather than the physical location of the receptacle.

RELOCATED

210.8(F) Outdoor Outlets. This change requires outlets supplying equipment such as HVAC to have GFCI protection at dwelling units. The revision is the result of a fatality where a person contacted a faulty air-conditioning unit with a compromised equipment grounding conductor (EGC).

RELOCATED

The rules in 210.8(A) address GFCI protection for receptacles. This one addresses GFCI protection for outlets which include hard-wired equipment and was added to address fatalities that have been caused by faulty hard-wired equipment installed at outdoor dwelling unit locations.

There is also an exception that says this new rule does not require GFCI protection for lighting outlets other than lighting outlets covered by 210.8(C).

210.8 GFCI Protection

 Scan this QR code for a video of Mike explaining this topic; it's a sample from the videos that accompany this textbook.

Ground-fault circuit interruption protection, located in a readily accessible location, must be provided in accordance with 210.8(A) through (F). ▶Figure 210–6

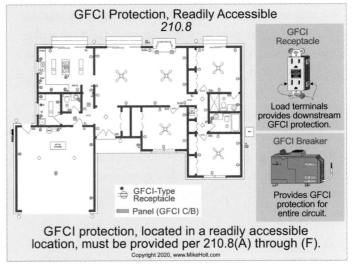

GFCI Protection, Readily Accessible
210.8

GFCI Receptacle

Load terminals provides downstream GFCI protection.

GFCI Breaker

Provides GFCI protection for entire circuit.

✳ GFCI-Type Receptacle
▨ Panel (GFCI C/B)

GFCI protection, located in a readily accessible location, must be provided per 210.8(A) through (F).
Copyright 2020, www.MikeHolt.com

▶Figure 210–6

Author's Comment:

▶ According to Article 100, a "Ground-Fault Circuit Interrupter" (GFCI) is a device intended to protect people by de-energizing a circuit when a current imbalance has a value of 6 mA or higher and does not trip when the current to ground is less than 4 mA. ▶Figure 210–7

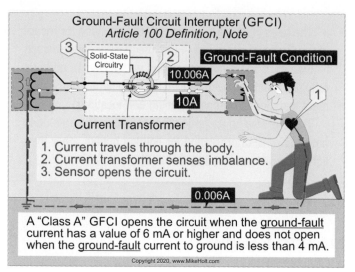

▶Figure 210–7

▶Figure 210–8

Author's Comment:

▶ The GFCI circuit breaker provides ground-fault protection starting at the breaker, so the entire circuit has ground-fault protection. A GFCI receptacle provides ground-fault protection for whatever is plugged into it, but also has load-side terminals that provide downstream protection for any other receptacle(s) or device(s) on the circuit.

▶ According to Article 100, "Readily Accessible" means capable of being reached quickly without having to climb over or remove obstacles, or resort to the use of portable ladders.

Note 2: See 422.5 for GFCI requirements for specific equipment such as automotive vacuum machines, drinking water coolers, high-pressure spray washing machines, tire inflation machines provided for public use, and vending machines.

Note 3: See 555.9 for GFCI requirements for boat hoists.

Note 4: Additional GFCI requirements for specific circuits and equipment are contained in Chapters 4, 5, and 6.

For the application of 210.8(A)(7), 210.8(A)(9), 210.8(B)(5), and 210.8(B)(12), the distance is measured as the shortest path an appliance's supply cord will follow without piercing a floor, wall, ceiling, fixed barrier, or passing through a window. ▶Figure 210–8

Author's Comment:

▶ This new language literally serves to require a receptacle in an adjacent room and to have GFCI protection where that receptacle is within 6 ft of a sink. This would be the case in a house with a master suite and a bedroom receptacle outside of the bathroom doorway, but within 6 ft of the sink in the master bath.

(A) Dwelling Units. 125V through 250V receptacles installed in the following dwelling unit locations must be GFCI protected.

Author's Comment:

▶ Note that this expansion applies no matter the ampere rating of the receptacle. It is no longer limited to just 15A and 20A receptacles as it was in the previous edition of the *NEC*.

(1) Bathroom Area. GFCI protection is required for all receptacles located in dwelling unit bathroom areas. ▶Figure 210–9

Author's Comment:

▶ According to Article 100, a "Bathroom Area" is an area that includes a basin as well as one or more of the following: a toilet, urinal, tub, shower, bidet, or similar plumbing fixture.

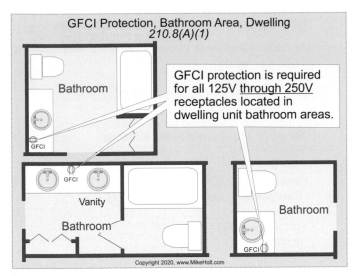

▶Figure 210–9

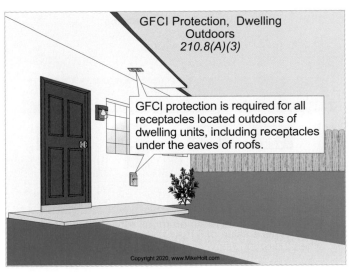

▶Figure 210–11

(2) Garages and Accessory Buildings. GFCI protection is required for all receptacles located in garages of dwelling units and grade-level portions of accessory buildings used for storage or work areas of a dwelling unit. ▶Figure 210–10

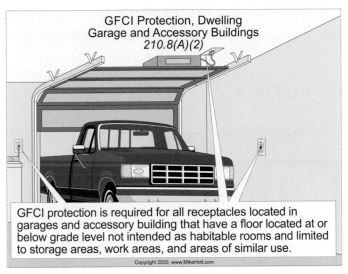

▶Figure 210–10

(3) Outdoors. GFCI protection is required for all receptacles located outdoors of dwelling units, including receptacles under the eaves of roofs. ▶Figure 210–11

Ex: GFCI protection is not required for a receptacle dedicated to fixed electric snow-melting, deicing, or pipeline and vessel heating equipment if the receptacle is not readily accessible and the equipment has internal ground-fault protection of equipment (GFPE) [426.28 and 427.22]. ▶Figure 210–12

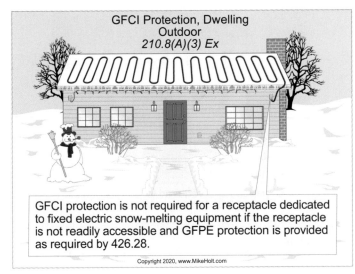

▶Figure 210–12

(4) Crawl Spaces. GFCI protection is required for all receptacles located in dwelling unit crawl spaces at or below grade. ▶Figure 210–13

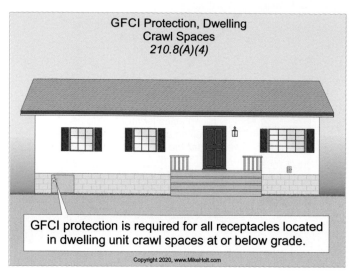

▶Figure 210–13

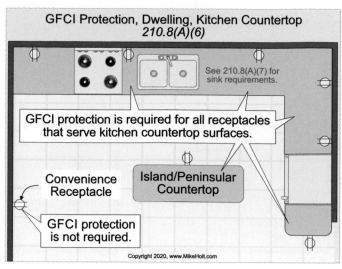

▶Figure 210–15

(5) Basements. GFCI protection is required for all receptacles located in <u>finished and</u> unfinished areas of a dwelling unit basement. ▶Figure 210–14

▶Figure 210–14

Ex: A receptacle supplying only a permanently installed fire alarm or burglar alarm system is not required to have ground-fault circuit-interrupter protection.

(6) Kitchen Countertop. GFCI protection is required for all receptacles that serve kitchen countertop surfaces. ▶Figure 210–15

Author's Comment:

▶ Receptacles located below a countertop for appliances, such as trash compactors or garbage disposals, do not require GFCI protection unless they are located 6 ft or less from the top inside edge of the bowl of the sink [210.8(A)(7)].

▶ A refrigerator is not a countertop appliance so GFCI protection is not required, unless the receptacle is located 6 ft or less from the top inside edge of the bowl of the kitchen sink [210.8(A)(7)]. ▶Figure 210–16

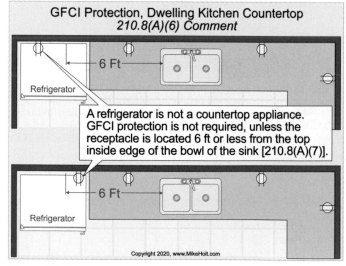

▶Figure 210–16

▸ Outlets supplying dishwashers require GFCI protection [210.8(D)].

(7) Sinks. GFCI protection is required for all receptacles located within 6 ft from the top inside edge of the bowl of a dwelling unit sink. ▸Figure 210–17

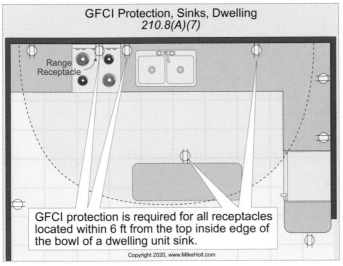

GFCI Protection, Sinks, Dwelling
210.8(A)(7)

GFCI protection is required for all receptacles located within 6 ft from the top inside edge of the bowl of a dwelling unit sink.

Copyright 2020, www.MikeHolt.com

▸Figure 210–17

(8) Boathouses. GFCI protection is required for all receptacles located in a dwelling unit boathouse. ▸Figure 210–18

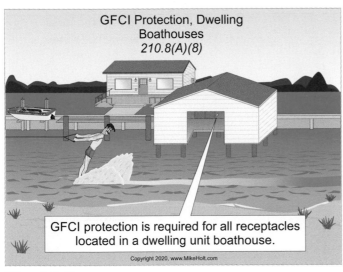

GFCI Protection, Dwelling
Boathouses
210.8(A)(8)

GFCI protection is required for all receptacles located in a dwelling unit boathouse.

Copyright 2020, www.MikeHolt.com

▸Figure 210–18

▸ The *Code* does not require a receptacle to be installed in a boathouse, but if any are installed, they must be GFCI protected.

(9) Bathtubs or Shower Stalls. GFCI protection is required for receptacles located within 6 ft of the outside edge of a bathtub or shower stall not installed within a bathroom as defined in Article 100. ▸Figure 210–19

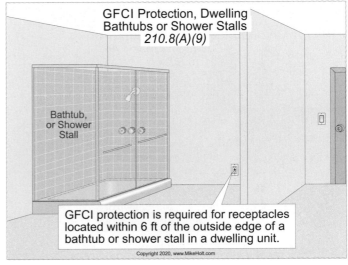

GFCI Protection, Dwelling
Bathtubs or Shower Stalls
210.8(A)(9)

Bathtub, or Shower Stall

GFCI protection is required for receptacles located within 6 ft of the outside edge of a bathtub or shower stall in a dwelling unit.

Copyright 2020, www.MikeHolt.com

▸Figure 210–19

(10) Laundry Areas. GFCI protection is required for all receptacles installed in the laundry area of a dwelling unit. ▸Figure 210–20

GFCI Protection, Dwelling
Laundry Areas
210.8(A)(10)

GFCI protection is required for all receptacles installed in the laundry area of a dwelling unit.

Copyright 2020, www.MikeHolt.com

▸Figure 210–20

(11) Damp and Wet Locations Indoors. GFCI protection is required for all receptacles installed in indoor damp and wet locations.

(B) Other Than Dwellings. GFCI protection is required for all 125V through 250V receptacles supplied by single-phase branch circuits rated 150 volts or less to ground, 50A or less, and all receptacles supplied by three-phase branch circuits rated 150 volts or less to ground, 100A or less, installed in the following locations.

(1) Bathroom Areas. GFCI protection is required for all receptacles located in bathroom areas. ▸Figure 210–21

▸Figure 210–21

Author's Comment:

▸ According to Article 100, a "Bathroom Area" is an area that includes a basin as well as one or more of the following: a toilet, urinal, tub, shower, bidet, or similar plumbing fixture.

(2) Kitchens. GFCI protection is required for all receptacles located in kitchens or areas with a sink and permanent provisions for either food preparation or cooking. ▸Figure 210–22

Author's Comment:

▸ The *NEC* does not give clear guidance, but since list item (5) already covers receptacles within 6 ft of the sink, this rule serves to cover receptacles beyond that distance but still within the "area" containing a sink and provisions for food preparation or cooking.

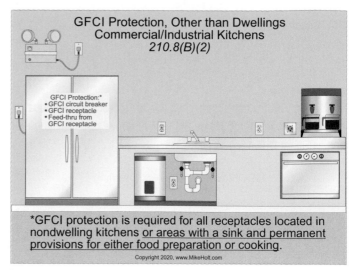

*GFCI protection is required for all receptacles located in nondwelling kitchens or areas with a sink and permanent provisions for either food preparation or cooking.

Copyright 2020, www.MikeHolt.com

▸Figure 210–22

(3) Rooftops. GFCI protection is required for all receptacles located on rooftops. ▸Figure 210–23

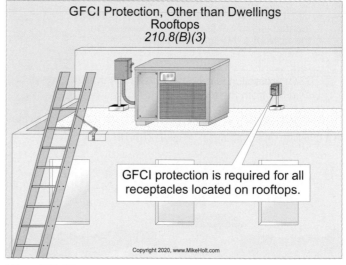

▸Figure 210–23

Author's Comment:

▸ A 15A or 20A, 125V receptacle outlet must be installed within 25 ft of heating, air-conditioning, and refrigeration equipment [210.63(A)].

▸ Roof top GFCI receptacles are only required to be readily accessible from the rooftop itself. [210.8(B)(3) Ex.]

(4) Outdoors. GFCI protection is required for all receptacles located outdoors. ▸Figure 210–24

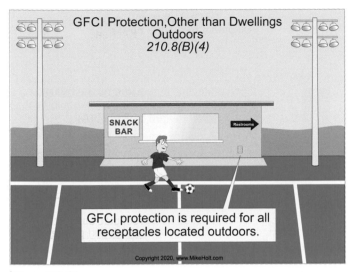

Figure 210–24

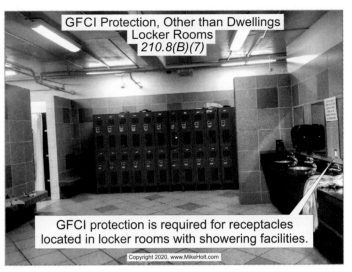

Figure 210–26

(5) Sinks. GFCI protection is required for all receptacles located within 6 ft from the top inside edge of the bowl of a sink. ▸Figure 210–25

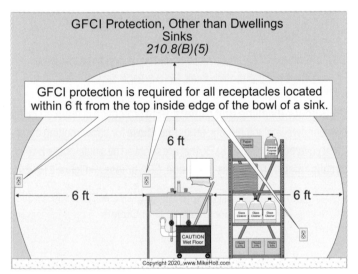

Figure 210–25

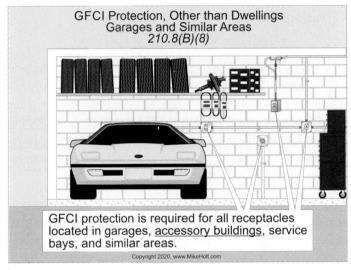

Figure 210–27

(6) Indoor Damp and Wet Locations. GFCI protection is required for all receptacles located in indoor damp and wet locations.

(7) Locker Rooms. GFCI protection is required for receptacles located in locker rooms with showering facilities. ▸Figure 210–26

(8) Garages and Similar Areas. GFCI protection is required for all receptacles located in garages, accessory buildings, service bays, and similar areas. ▸Figure 210–27

Author's Comment:

▸ According to Article 100, a "Garage" is a building or portion of a building in which one or more self-propelled vehicles can be kept for use, sale, storage, rental, repair, exhibition, or demonstration.

(10) Unfinished Areas of Basements. GFCI protection is required for all receptacles located in the unfinished areas of a basement.

(11) Laundry Areas. GFCI protection is required for all receptacles located in the laundry area.

(12) Bathtubs and Shower Stalls. GFCI protection is required for all receptacles installed within 6 ft of the outside edge of the bathtub or shower stall not installed in a bathroom as defined in Article 100.

Author's Comment:

▸ This addition is to cover receptacles installed within 6 ft from bathtubs or shower stalls that are not covered by one of the other list items. In nondwelling occupancies, the hazard is related to the tub and shower, not to where they may be physically located within the building. A hydro-massage unit might be in the corner of a physical therapy room for example.

(C) Crawl Space Lighting Outlets. GFCI protection is required for 120V lighting outlets in crawl spaces.

Author's Comment:

▸ A lighting outlet is not required for a dwelling unit crawl space unless the space is used for storage or has equipment requiring servicing [210.70(A)(3)].

(D) Specific Appliances. Unless GFCI protection is provided in accordance with 422.5(B)(3) through (B)(5), the outlets supplying appliances specified in 422.5(A) must have GFCI protection in accordance with 422.5(B)(1) or (B)(2).

Where the appliance is a vending machine as specified in 422.5(A)(5) and GFCI protection is not provided in accordance with 422.5(B)(3) or (B)(4), the branch circuit supplying the vending machines must have GFCI protection in accordance with 422.5(B)(1) or (B)(2).

Author's Comment:

▸ The product standards and product testing for hard-wired appliances do not specify a maximum permitted leakage current or test for such current. The idea is that hard-wired equipment has a reliable EGC that will eliminate danger from leakage current, unlike a cord and plug connected appliance that is more likely to have a compromised EGC.

(E) Equipment Requiring Servicing. GFCI protection is required for the heating, air-conditioning, and refrigeration equipment receptacles required by 210.63(A). ▸Figure 210–28

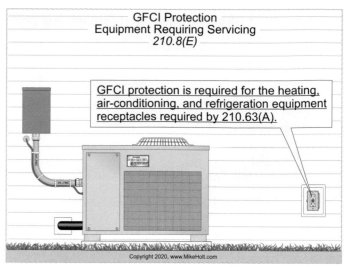

GFCI Protection
Equipment Requiring Servicing
210.8(E)

GFCI protection is required for the heating, air-conditioning, and refrigeration equipment receptacles required by 210.63(A).

Copyright 2020, www.MikeHolt.com

▸Figure 210–28

Author's Comment:

▸ A 15A or 20A, 125V receptacle outlet must be installed within 25 ft of heating, air-conditioning, and refrigeration equipment [210.63(A)].

▸ Rooftop GFCI receptacles are only required to be readily accessible from the rooftop itself. [210.8(B)(3) Ex.]

(F) Outdoor Dwelling Unit Outlets. GFCI protection is required for all outdoor dwelling unit outlets, other than those for snow-melting equipment covered in 210.8(A)(3) Ex, that are supplied by single-phase branch circuits rated 150V or less to ground, 50A or less. ▸Figure 210–29

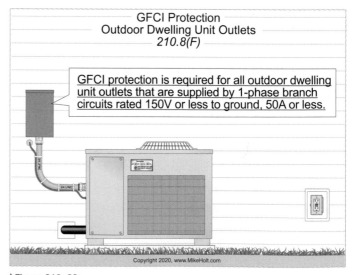

GFCI Protection
Outdoor Dwelling Unit Outlets
210.8(F)

GFCI protection is required for all outdoor dwelling unit outlets that are supplied by 1-phase branch circuits rated 150V or less to ground, 50A or less.

Copyright 2020, www.MikeHolt.com

▸Figure 210–29

Ex: GFCI protection is not required on lighting outlets other than those covered in 210.8(C).

Author's Comment:

▸ Here is an example of why it is important to understand the terminology used in the *Code*. This rule overall mentions, "outlets," "receptacle outlets," but only "lighting outlets" in the exception, all of which are outlets but take on different characteristics when defined. (See Article 100 Definitions.)

210.11 Branch Circuits Required

The rule in 210.11(C)(3) was revised to make it clear that the receptacle outlets required by 210.52(D), and any additional receptacle outlets installed to serve any countertop or similar work surface, must be supplied by one or more 20A branch circuits. Section 210.11(C)(4) was also revised and permits receptacle outlets, other than the ones required by 210.52(G)(1), to be supplied by branch circuits with a rating of other than 20A.

Analysis

CLARIFIED

210.11(C)(3) Bathroom Branch Circuits. This section was modified to make it clear that the 20A branch circuit is only required to supply the receptacles mandated by 210.52(D) or located to serve a bathroom countertop or work surface. Some inspection authorities have been reading this section as requiring all receptacles installed in a bathroom to be served by the required one or more 20A branch circuit. Equipment such as towel warmers may require a 15A branch circuit. This change makes it clear that receptacles installed to serve such equipment are not required to be supplied by the one or more 20A bathroom branch circuits.

CLARIFIED

210.11(C)(4) Garage Branch Circuits. This revision is much the same as the one in 210.11(C)(3). The added reference to the receptacle outlet(s) required by 210.52(G)(1) makes it clear that only those receptacles must be supplied by one or more 20A branch circuits.

The requirement in 210.52(G)(1) is for at least one receptacle outlet in each vehicle bay located not more than 5½ ft above the floor. This change leaves the rating of any branch circuits suppling receptacle outlets not required by the *Code* up to the designer or owner.

210.11 Branch Circuits Required

(C) Dwelling Unit.

(1) Small-Appliance Circuits. At least two 20A, 120V branch circuits are required to supply receptacle outlets in a dwelling unit kitchen, dining room, breakfast room, pantry, or similar dining areas as required by 210.52(B). ▸Figure 210–30

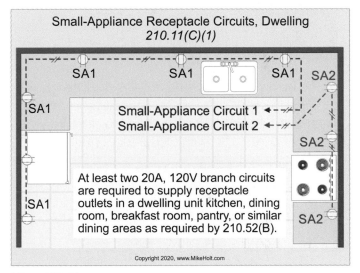

▸Figure 210–30

Author's Comment:

▸ The two 20A small-appliance branch circuits can be supplied by one 3-wire multiwire circuit or by two separate 120V circuits [210.4(A)].

(2) Laundry Area Circuit. At least one 20A, 120V branch circuit is required to supply receptacle outlet(s) in the laundry area as required by 210.52(F). The laundry receptacle circuit is not permitted to supply lighting outlets or receptacle outlets in other rooms. ▸Figure 210–31

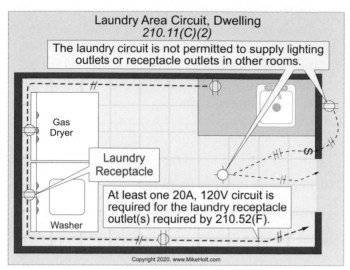

▶Figure 210-31

Author's Comment:

▶ The laundry receptacle circuit can supply more than one receptacle outlet in the laundry area.

▶ The laundry receptacle circuit is required even if the laundry appliance is a 30A, 240V combination washer/dryer. ▶Figure 210-32

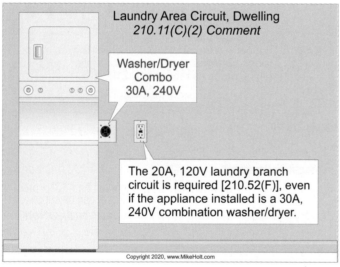

▶Figure 210-32

(3) Bathroom Area Circuit. At least one 20A, 120V branch circuit is required to supply the receptacle outlet(s) in the bathroom(s) as required by 210.52(D), and any countertop and similar work surface receptacle outlets. This bathroom area receptacle circuit is not permitted to supply lighting outlets or receptacle outlets in other rooms. ▶Figure 210-33

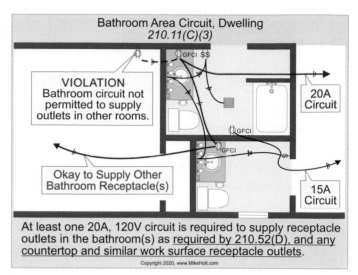

▶Figure 210-33

Ex: A single 20A, 120V branch circuit can supply all the outlets in a single bathroom area, as long as no load fastened in place is rated more than 10A [210.23(A)]. ▶**Figure 210-34**

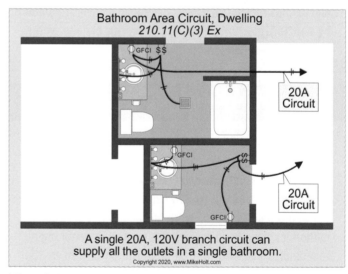

▶Figure 210-34

Author's Comment:

▶ This implies that the additional bathroom branch circuits identified in 210.52 (B)(1) Ex 2 can be installed.

(4) Garage Circuits. At least one 20A, 120V branch circuit is required to supply receptacle outlet(s) in garages with electric power [210.52(G)(1)]. This garage receptacle circuit is not permitted to supply lighting outlets or receptacle outlets in other rooms. ▶**Figure 210-35**

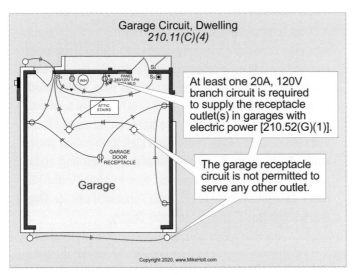

▶Figure 210–35

Ex: Outdoor receptacle outlets are permitted to be supplied by the 20A, 120V garage receptacle circuit. ▶Figure 210–36

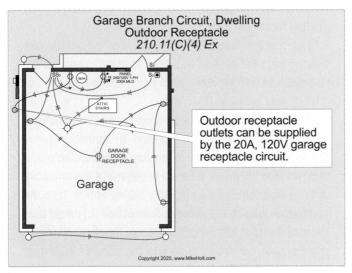

▶Figure 210–36

Author's Comment:

▶ Shop equipment branch circuits rated higher than 20A are often used in dwelling unit garages, and the previous *Code* language could be read as prohibiting higher rated receptacle branch circuits such as might be needed for an arc welder.

210.12 Arc-Fault Circuit-Interrupter Protection

The requirement to provide AFCI protection where the branch circuit is extended or modified was expanded to include guest rooms and guest suites. In addition, the exception to this branch circuit extension and modified rule was revised to say that any conductors inside an enclosure do not count as part of the 6-ft limit and to say that the addition of a splicing device does not trigger the AFCI requirement.

Analysis

EXPANDED **210.12(D) Branch Circuit Extensions or Modifications, Dwelling Units, Dormitory Units, Guest Rooms, and Guest Suites.** AFCI requirements for modified, replaced, or extended branch-circuit wiring was expanded to include guest rooms and guest suites.

The exception to this rule was revised to say that conductors inside an enclosure do not count as part of the 6-ft limit and that the addition of a splicing device is not a violation.

210.12 Arc-Fault Circuit-Interrupter Protection

Arc-fault circuit-interrupter protection, located in a readily accessible location, must be provided in accordance with 210.12(A), (B), (C), and (D).

(D) Branch Circuit Extensions or Modifications—Dwelling Units, Dormitory Units, Guest Rooms, and Guest Suites. Where 15A or 20A, 120V branch-circuit wiring is modified, replaced, or extended in any of the areas specified in 210.12(A), (B), or (C), the modified, replaced, or extended branch-circuit wiring must be AFCI protected.

Ex: AFCI protection is not required for extension wiring that is less than 6 ft in length (raceway or cable) if no outlets or devices are added, other than splicing devices. This measurement does not include the conductors inside an enclosure, cabinet, or junction box.

‣ The *Code* previously implied that the total length of the conductor, including that portion within an enclosure, cabinet, or junction box was included in this measurement. This exception is intended to permit the installation of a new panel in a location close to the original panel without requiring AFCI protection.

210.15 Reconditioned Equipment

Here is another instance of the *Code* globally addressing reconditioning of electrical equipment. A new rule was added prohibiting some protective devices required by Article 210 from being reconditioned. It is just not worth the risk of trying to recondition such sensitive lifesaving devices as GFCIs, GFPEs, and AFCIs.

Analysis

NEW
This new section prohibits the reconditioning of various devices. Such equipment provides critical safety protections and just is not worth the risk compromising the intended protection by using reconditioned devices.

210.15 Reconditioned Equipment

The following is not permitted to be reconditioned:

(1) GFCI equipment

(2) AFCI equipment

(3) GFPE equipment

210.19 Conductor Sizing

If you understand the fundamentals of current flow and how electrons move through a circuit, then you will understand that a conductor rating higher than the termination rating can act as a "funnel" with all of these electrons merging into one lane and creating a "traffic-jam" that just generates more and more heat.

This is never a good situation and the branch-circuit minimum conductor ampacity rule in 210.19(A)(1) has been clarified by adding a reference to the termination requirements of 110.14(C). A new exception was also added, which mirrors the one in 215.2(A)(1)(a) for feeders, permitting the use of 90°C conductors between terminal blocks installed outside of the source and load termination enclosures. By the way, if you are interested in learning about some of these fundamentals, be sure to check out *Mike Holt's Illustrated Guide to Electrical Fundamentals*, or *Mike Holt's Illustrated Guide to Electrical Theory*.

Analysis

CLARIFIED
210.19(A)(1) Branch Circuits Not More Than 600V. Text was added which references the termination requirements of 110.14(C). The temperature ratings of the termination will often be the limiting factor for conductor sizing.

The word "allowable" that preceded ampacity was deleted from the section as part of a global change and a reference to 310.14 was added to (a) and a reference to 310.15 was added to (b).

The new wording may be a bit confusing as the defined term "ampacity," used in both (a) and (b), already requires the application of adjustment and/or correction factors. It appears that the intent is for (a) to reference the ampacity directly from one of the ampacity tables and to take the continuous load at 125 percent. Subsection (b) would take the actual load at 100 percent and apply the required adjustment and/or correction factors to the values taken from the ampacity table.

NEW
210.19(A)(1) Ex 2. The new Exception 2 was added to permit the use of higher temperature rated conductors connected to separately installed pressure connections as provided in 110.14(C)(2). This permits conductors to be used at their 90°C ampacity between separately installed pressure connectors installed in a junction box at each end of the circuit and the conductors used at the ampacity of the supply and load terminations extended from the junction boxes to the line and load.

210.19 Conductor Sizing

(A) Branch Circuits

Note 3: To provide reasonable efficiency of operation of electrical equipment, branch-circuit conductors should be sized to prevent a voltage drop not to exceed 3 percent. In addition, the total voltage drop on both feeders and branch circuits should not exceed 5 percent [215.2(A)(1)]. ▸Figure 210–37 and ▸Figure 210–38

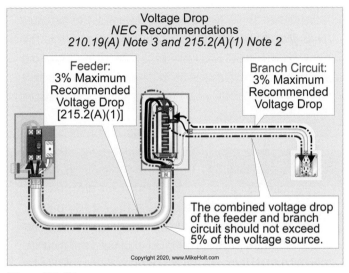

▸Figure 210–37

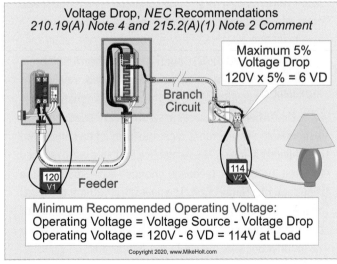

▸Figure 210–38

Author's Comment:

▸ Sizing conductors to accommodate the voltage drop percentages indicated in the *NEC's* Informational Note is not a *Code* requirement because Informational Notes are only advisory [90.5(C)]. ▸Figure 210–39

▸ See 695.7 for fire pump voltage-drop requirements.

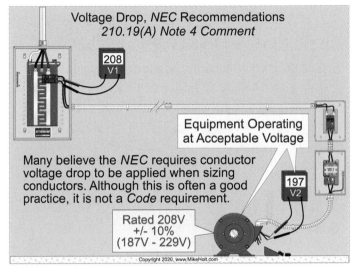

▸Figure 210–39

(1) General. Branch-circuit conductors must be sized to carry at least the largest of the calculations contained in (a) or (b) and comply with the equipment termination provisions of 110.14(C). ▸Figure 210–40

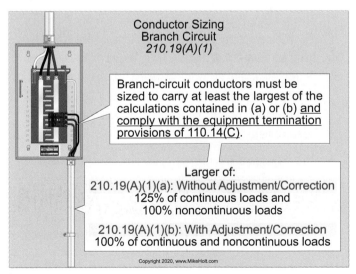

▸Figure 210–40

Ex 2: A section of conductors that terminates in a junction box at both ends to 90°C terminals in accordance with 110.14(C)(2) is permitted to have an ampacity of not less than 100 percent of the continuous and 100 percent of the noncontinuous loads based on the 90°C column of Table 310.16 for 90°C conductor insulation. The 100 percent at 90°C conductors are not permitted to extend into the supply or the load terminations to the circuit. ▶Figure 210–41

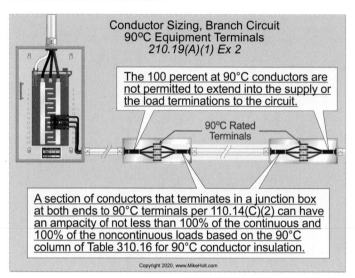

Conductor Sizing, Branch Circuit
90°C Equipment Terminals
210.19(A)(1) Ex 2

The 100 percent at 90°C conductors are not permitted to extend into the supply or the load terminations to the circuit.

90°C Rated Terminals

A section of conductors that terminates in a junction box at both ends to 90°C terminals per 110.14(C)(2) can have an ampacity of not less than 100% of the continuous and 100% of the noncontinuous loads based on the 90°C column of Table 310.16 for 90°C conductor insulation.

Copyright 2020, www.MikeHolt.com

▶Figure 210–41

Author's Comment:

▸ As stated by CMP-2, "Ampacity is the maximum current, in amperes, that a conductor can carry continuously under the conditions of use without exceeding its temperature rating. The term used in this section should be "ampacity" and not "allowable ampacity" as it is the intent for this section to determine the ampacity of the conductor based on its conditions of use. The use of the word "allowable" does not add clarity. "In accordance with 310.15" was added to improve usability and direct the user to the section that governs ampacity of conductors.

▸ The language of this rule has been a problem for some time and this change appears to have done little to refine the language. The rule, when taken as written, in combination with the Article 100 definition of "Ampacity," will always make the determination in 210.19(A)(1)(a) result in the larger conductor.

210.52 Dwelling Unit Receptacle Outlet Requirements

Section 210.52 always seems to bring out some of the most contentious debates. Arguments range from what a countertop is versus a work surface, to where the measurement for the length of a peninsula should begin. The 2020 revision reorganized and clarified much of this section and even provided some guidance when measuring for peninsula receptacles. There was also some expansion to the rules regarding balconies, decks, basements, and garages. The term "wall switch" was replaced by "listed wall-mounted control device" which seems to be part of a general shift in consideration of the new electronic and wireless devices throughout the *Code*.

Analysis

 210.52(2) Dwelling Unit Receptacle Outlets. This clarification in list item (2) applies to receptacles that are controlled by a listed wall-mounted control device since the use of electronic control devices is becoming more common. This rule now requires the receptacles required by 210.52 to be continuously energized and not controlled by some type of device.

 210.52(C) Countertops and Work Surfaces. This section was reorganized, revised for clarification, and has new language specifying that where multioutlet assemblies are used, each 12 in. containing two or more receptacles must be considered one receptacle outlet. The former five list items were reduced to three, and major technical changes were made in the requirements. Subsection (1) was retitled without technical change, and the language that said the requirements for countertop receptacles only apply where the countertop is 12 in. or wider was moved to the parent text.

210.52(C)(2)(a) and (b) Island and Peninsular Countertops and Work Surfaces. Subsection (a) bases the number of receptacles on the area of the island or peninsular countertop or work surface and is a new concept for these receptacles. It requires at least one receptacle outlet to be provided for the first 9 sq ft or fraction thereof of the countertop or work surface, and each additional 18 sq ft of fraction thereof requires an additional receptacle outlet.

EXPANDED

Subsection (b) requires that at least one receptacle outlet is to be located within 2 ft of the outer end of a peninsular countertop or work surface. Additional outlets are permitted to be located as determined by the installer, designer, or building owner.

 210.52(C)(3) Receptacle Outlet Location. A last paragraph says that receptacle outlets rendered not readily accessible by appliances fastened in place, appliance garages, sinks, or range tops cannot be counted as the receptacle outlets required by this section. A new Informational Note was also added referencing 406.5(E) and (G) for receptacles in countertops, 406.5(F) and (G) for installations in work surfaces, and 380.10 for the installation of multioutlet assemblies.

REORGANIZED   NEW

 210.52(E)(3) Balconies, Decks, and Porches. Not all dwelling unit decks are directly attached to the dwelling unit and under the provision of the previous *Code* such a deck did not require a receptacle outlet. This revision requires the deck to have a receptacle where it is within 4 in. horizontally of the dwelling unit.

EXPANDED

 210.52(G) Basements, Garages, and Accessory Buildings. This requirement was expanded to apply to garages for multifamily dwellings as well as the one- and two-family dwellings previously required. The change is meant to apply to multifamily dwelling complexes where the garage is part of the actual dwelling unit. Section 210.52(G)(1) requires a receptacle to be installed in each garage bay, not more than 5½ ft above the floor. The new exception indicates this only applies to multifamily dwellings where the garage is attached to the dwelling.

EXPANDED

210.52 Dwelling Unit Receptacle Outlet Requirements

This section provides the requirements for 15A and 20A, 125V receptacle outlets in dwelling units, and are in addition to those for any receptacle that is:

(1) Part of a luminaire or appliance,

(2) Controlled by a listed wall-mounted control device in accordance with 210.70(A)(1) Ex 1

(3) Located within cabinets or cupboards, or

(4) Located more than 5½ ft above the floor.

> **Author's Comment:**
>
> ▸ Note that this does not imply that the use of split-wired duplex receptacles where one half is switched, and the other half is always on, is prohibited. Receptacle rules do not require duplex receptacles. That makes it permissible to use a split-wired receptacle as the required receptacle as well as being able to provide a controlled receptacle.

(C) Countertops and Work Surfaces. In kitchens, pantries, breakfast rooms, dining rooms, and similar areas of dwelling units, receptacle outlets for countertop and work surfaces that are 12 in. or wider must be installed in accordance with 210.52(C)(1) through (C)(3) and are not permitted to be used to meet the receptacle outlets for wall space as required by 210.52(A). ▸Figure 210–42

In kitchens, pantries, breakfast rooms, dining rooms, and similar areas of dwelling units, receptacle outlets for countertop and work surfaces 12 in. or wider must be installed per 210.52(C)(1) through (C)(3) and are not permitted to be used to meet the receptacle outlets for wall space as required by 210.52(A).

Countertop Surface, Dwelling 210.52(C)

Copyright 2020, www.MikeHolt.com

▸Figure 210–42

Where multioutlet assemblies are used, each 12 in. of multioutlet assembly containing two or more receptacles are considered to be one receptacle outlet.

(1) Wall Spaces. Receptacle Outlets. A receptacle outlet must be installed so that no point along the countertop wall space is more than 2 ft, measured horizontally, from a receptacle outlet. ▸Figure 210–43

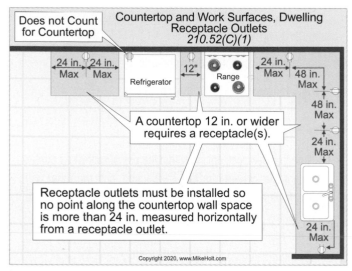

▸Figure 210–43

Ex: A receptacle outlet is not required directly behind a range, counter-mounted cooking unit, or sink, in accordance with Figure 210.52(C)(1) in the NEC. ▸Figure 210–44

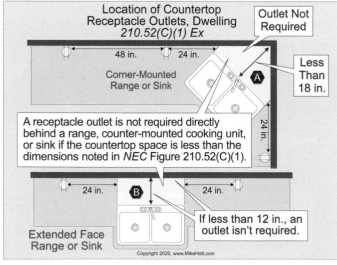

▸Figure 210–44

Author's Comment:

▸ If the countertop space behind a range or sink is larger than the dimensions noted in Figure 210.52(C)(1) of the *Code* book, then a GFCI-protected receptacle must be installed in that space. This is because, for all practical purposes, if there is enough space for an appliance, one will be placed there.

(2) Island and Peninsular Countertops and Work Surfaces. Receptacle outlets must be installed in accordance with the following:

(a) At least one receptacle outlet must be provided for the first 9 sq ft, or fraction thereof, of the countertop or work surface. A receptacle outlet must be provided for every additional 18 sq ft, or fraction thereof, of the countertop or work surface. ▸Figure 210–45

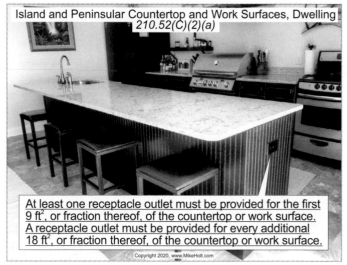

▸Figure 210–45

(b) At least one receptacle outlet must be located within 2 ft of the outer end of a peninsular countertop or work surface. Additional required receptacle outlets are permitted to be located as determined by the installer, designer, or building owner. The location of the receptacle outlets must be in accordance with 210.52(C)(3). ▸Figure 210–46

A peninsular countertop must be measured from the connected perpendicular wall.

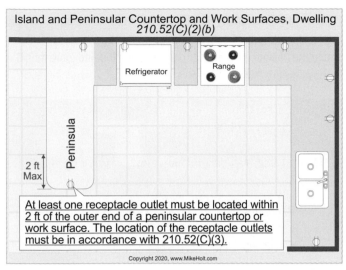

▶Figure 210–46

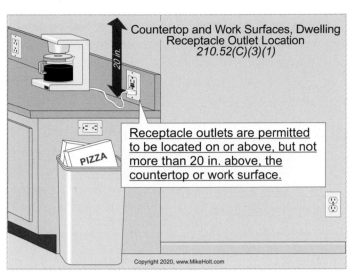

▶Figure 210–47

Author's Comment:

▸ This rule does not address sinks or cooktops installed on islands or peninsulas since they are not considered countertop or work surface space. It would be reasonable to assume that it would be correct to deduct the area of those items from the total area for the purpose of determining total square footage.

▸ No guidance is given as to the location of the receptacles for island countertops or work surfaces. It appears this is left totally to the installer, designer or building owner as long as the location complies with 210.51(C)(3).

▸ This section has always been tricky. It seems this reorganization has provided a much clearer explanation than in previous editions making it easier for the installer, designer, or building owner to apply.

(3) Receptacle outlets must be installed in one or more of the following locations:

(1) On or above, but not more than 20 in. above, the countertop or work surface. ▶Figure 210–47

Author's Comment:

▸ This rule permits multioutlet assemblies to be installed on the bottom of an overhead cabinet and still meet the receptacle outlet placement requirements for countertop surfaces, provided the bottom of the cabinet is no more than 20 in. above the countertop surface.

(2) In countertop or work surfaces: Receptacle outlet assemblies listed for use in countertop or work surfaces are permitted to be installed in countertops or work surfaces. ▶Figure 210–48

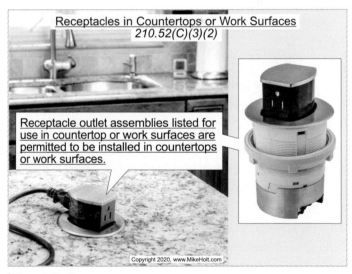

▶Figure 210–48

Author's Comment:

▸ Installing receptacles below the countertop was limited in the previous *Code* because of the increased possibility that a toddler could pull on an appliance cord and pull an appliance down on him or her thereby creating a burn or scalding hazard.

▸ A clearer distinction between a countertop and a work surface is not yet defined for an accurate and effective application of this rule. This is critical if "pop-up" type receptacles are used. There are several products listed for use in work surfaces, but as of this writing, only one is listed for use in a countertop.

(3) Below countertop or work surfaces: Receptacles must not be located more than 12 in. below the countertop or work surface. Receptacles installed below a countertop or work surface must not be located where the countertop or work surface extends more than 6 in. beyond its support base. ▸Figure 210–49

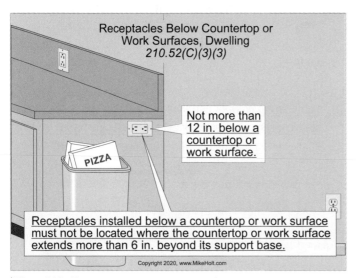

▸Figure 210–49

Receptacle outlets rendered not readily accessible by appliances fastened in place, located in an appliance garage, behind sinks, ranges, or cooktops [210.52(C)(1)(b) Ex], or supplying appliances that occupy assigned spaces, do not count as the required countertop surface receptacle outlets.

Author's Comment:

▸ An "Appliance Garage" is an enclosed area on the countertop where an appliance can be stored and hidden from view when not in use. Receptacles installed inside an appliance garage do not count as a required countertop receptacle outlet.

Note 1: See 406.5(E) and 406.5(G) for installation of receptacles in countertops, 406.5(F) and 406.5(G) for installation of receptacles in work surfaces, and 380.10 for installation of multioutlet assemblies.

(E) Outdoor Receptacle Outlets. Outdoor receptacle outlets must comply with the following:

(1) One- and Two-Family Dwellings. Two outdoor readily accessible from grade receptacle outlets must be installed, one at the front and one at the back of each dwelling unit, and not located more than 6½ ft above grade. ▸Figure 210–50

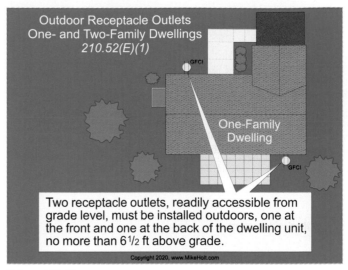

▸Figure 210–50

(2) Multifamily Dwelling. Each dwelling unit of a multifamily dwelling with grade level entry must have at least one outdoor receptacle outlet, readily accessible from grade, and located not more than 6½ ft above grade. ▸Figure 210–51

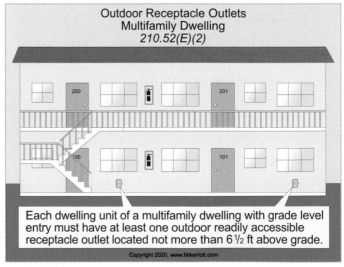

▸Figure 210–51

(3) Balconies, Decks, and Porches. At least one receptacle outlet must be installed not more than 6½ ft above any balcony, deck, or porch surface that is within 4 in. horizontally of the dwelling unit. ▸Figure 210–52

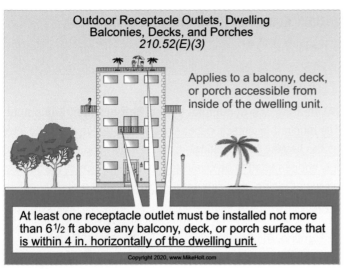

Outdoor Receptacle Outlets, Dwelling Balconies, Decks, and Porches
210.52(E)(3)

Applies to a balcony, deck, or porch accessible from inside of the dwelling unit.

At least one receptacle outlet must be installed not more than 6½ ft above any balcony, deck, or porch surface that is within 4 in. horizontally of the dwelling unit.

Copyright 2020, www.MikeHolt.com

▶Figure 210–52

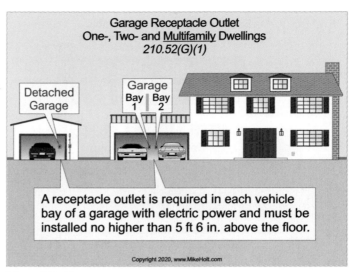

Garage Receptacle Outlet
One-, Two- and Multifamily Dwellings
210.52(G)(1)

Detached Garage

Garage
Bay 1 | Bay 2

A receptacle outlet is required in each vehicle bay of a garage with electric power and must be installed no higher than 5 ft 6 in. above the floor.

Copyright 2020, www.MikeHolt.com

▶Figure 210–53

Author's Comment:

▸ There are various reasons a deck may be detached from the building; one of which may be to provide drainage space between the structure and the deck to prevent water damage.

(G) Garage, Basement, and Accessory Building Receptacle Outlet. For one- and two-family dwellings, and multifamily dwellings, at least one receptacle outlet must be installed in accordance with (1) through (3).

(1) Garages. A receptacle outlet is required in each vehicle bay of a garage with electric power and must be installed no higher than 5 ft 6 in. above the floor. ▶Figure 210–53

Ex: A receptacle outlet is not required in a garage space not attached to an individual dwelling unit of a multifamily dwelling.

Author's Comment:

▸ In the prior *Code* language, multifamily dwelling structures implied the presence of common area parking garages, but no clear distinction was made. Taken literally, this meant that any multifamily dwelling, by virtue of the name, did not require garage receptacles and this was clearly not the intent of the rule.

(2) Accessory Buildings. A receptacle outlet is required in each accessory building with electric power. ▶Figure 210–54

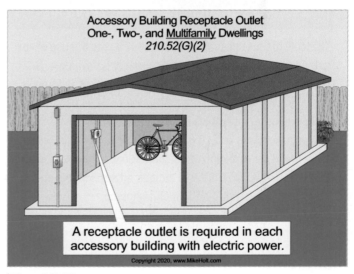

Accessory Building Receptacle Outlet
One-, Two-, and Multifamily Dwellings
210.52(G)(2)

A receptacle outlet is required in each accessory building with electric power.

Copyright 2020, www.MikeHolt.com

▶Figure 210–54

(3) Basements. Each unfinished portion of a basement must have a receptacle outlet. ▶Figure 210–55

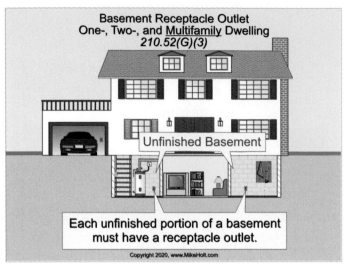

Basement Receptacle Outlet
One-, Two-, and Multifamily Dwelling
210.52(G)(3)

Unfinished Basement

Each unfinished portion of a basement
must have a receptacle outlet.

Copyright 2020, www.MikeHolt.com

▶Figure 210–55

210.63 Equipment Requiring Servicing

This rule makes sense in that it often requires the use of an extension cord to service HVAC equipment for example. That is not to say that using an extension cord that is in good repair is a bad thing, but not having to need one because of a close enough receptacle outlet reduces unnecessary risk. The requirements of 210.63 and 210.64 requiring a receptacle outlet for servicing of equipment have been combined into 210.63 and expanded to include all serviceable equipment, not just heating and air-conditioning.

Analysis

EXPANDED **EDITED**

210.63 Equipment Requiring Servicing. The name of this section was changed from "Heating, Air-Conditioning, and Refrigeration Equipment" to "Equipment Requiring Servicing." The parent text requires a 15A or 20A, 125V receptacle outlet to be installed in an accessible location and within 25 ft of the equipment to be serviced, and (A) and (B) define the areas where the equipment requiring servicing might be located.

210.63 Equipment Requiring Servicing

A 15A or 20A, 125V, single-phase receptacle outlet must be installed at an accessible location within 25 ft of equipment in accordance with the following:

(A) Heating, Air-Conditioning, and Refrigeration Equipment. The required receptacle outlet must be located on the same level as the heating, air-conditioning, and refrigeration equipment and it is not permitted to be connected to the load side of the heating, air-conditioning, and refrigeration equipment's disconnecting means. ▶Figure 210–56

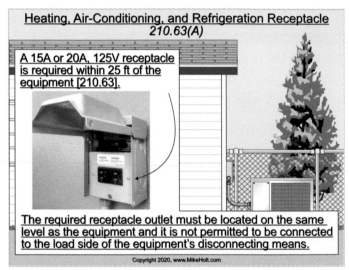

Heating, Air-Conditioning, and Refrigeration Receptacle
210.63(A)

A 15A or 20A, 125V receptacle
is required within 25 ft of the
equipment [210.63].

The required receptacle outlet must be located on the same
level as the equipment and it is not permitted to be connected
to the load side of the equipment's disconnecting means.

Copyright 2020, www.MikeHolt.com

▶Figure 210–56

Author's Comment:

▶ These equipment service receptacles are required to be GFCI protected even if the equipment is installed in areas that would not typically require GFCI protection. [210.8(E)]

▶ The source of power for the receptacle must not be connected to the load side of the equipment's branch-circuit disconnecting means. The intent of this requirement is to ensure that serviceable equipment receptacles remain energized whether or not the equipment itself is energized.

The outdoor 15A or 20A, 125V receptacle outlet required for dwelling units [210.52(E)(1)] can be used to satisfy this requirement. ▶Figure 210–57

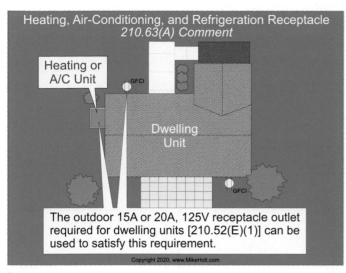

Heating, Air-Conditioning, and Refrigeration Receptacle
210.63(A) Comment

Heating or A/C Unit

GFCI

Dwelling Unit

GFCI

The outdoor 15A or 20A, 125V receptacle outlet required for dwelling units [210.52(E)(1)] can be used to satisfy this requirement.

Copyright 2020, www.MikeHolt.com

▶Figure 210–57

(B) Other Electrical Equipment. In other than one- and two-family dwellings, a receptacle outlet must be installed in locations as follows:

(1) Indoor Service Equipment. A 15A or 20A, 125V, single-phase receptacle outlet must be installed at an accessible location within the same room or area as the service equipment. ▶Figure 210–58

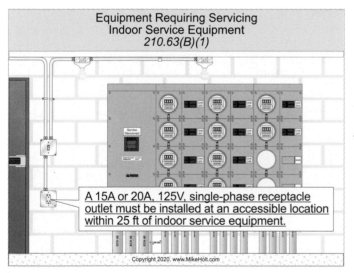

Equipment Requiring Servicing
Indoor Service Equipment
210.63(B)(1)

Service Disconnect

A 15A or 20A, 125V, single-phase receptacle outlet must be installed at an accessible location within 25 ft of indoor service equipment.

Copyright 2020, www.MikeHolt.com

▶Figure 210–58

(2) Indoor Switchboards, Switchgear, Panelboards, and Motor Control Centers. A 15A or 20A, 125V, single-phase receptacle outlet must be installed at an accessible location within the same room or area of switchboards, switchgear, panelboards, and motor control centers and may not be connected to the load side of the equipment disconnecting means.

Ex: A receptacle outlet is not required at one- and two-family dwellings for the service of evaporative coolers.

210.65 Meeting Rooms

This section was relocated from 210.71 because it is better suited to follow the receptacle rules. The meeting room receptacle outlet rule was clarified to more clearly indicate the number and location of the required receptacle outlets. Section 210.65(B)(1) clarifies that covers the required receptacles in fixed walls of meeting rooms.

Analysis

CLARIFIED **EDITED**

210.65(B)(1) Receptacles Outlets Required, Receptacle Outlets in Fixed Walls. The 2017 *Code* required receptacles to be installed in accordance with 210.52(A)(1); however, the language in that subsection didn't clearly require specific placement of the receptacles. The new language makes it clear that the number of receptacles is calculated as required by 210.52(A)(1), but their placement is up to the installer, designer, or building owner.

CLARIFIED

210.65(B)(2) Floor Outlets. Where the room is 12 ft or greater in any dimension and is at least 215 sq ft, a floor receptacle or a floor receptacle outlet is required. The floor outlet or floor receptacle must be at least 6 ft from any fixed wall.

210.65 Meeting Rooms

(A) General. Meeting rooms not larger than 1,000 sq ft must have receptacle outlets for 15A or 20A, 125V receptacles in accordance with 210.71(B) through (E). ▶Figure 210–59

▶Figure 210–59

Where a room or space is provided with a movable partition(s), the room size must be determined with the partition(s) in the position that results in the smallest size meeting room.

Note 1: Meeting rooms are typically designed or intended for the gathering of seated occupants for conferences, deliberations, or similar purposes, where portable electronic equipment such as computers, projectors, or similar equipment is likely to be used.

Note 2: Examples of rooms that are not meeting rooms within the scope of 210.65 include auditoriums, school rooms, and coffee shops. ▶Figure 210–60

▶Figure 210–60

(B) Number of Receptacle Outlets Required. The total number of receptacle outlets, including floor outlets and receptacle outlets in fixed furniture, must not be less than as determined in (1) and (2).

(1) The required number of receptacle outlets must be determined in accordance with 210.52(A)(1) through (A)(4). The location of these receptacle outlets can be determined by the installer, designer, or building owner. ▶Figure 210–61

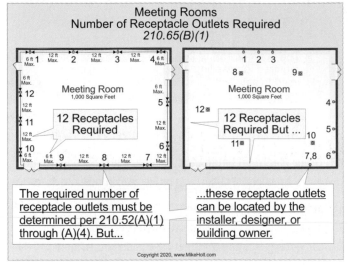

▶Figure 210–61

(2) A meeting room with any floor dimension that is 12 ft or greater in any direction and has a floor area of at least 215 sq ft must have at least one floor receptacle outlet or floor outlet to serve a receptacle(s) located not less than 6 ft from any fixed wall for each 215 sq ft or major portion of floor space. ▶Figure 210–62

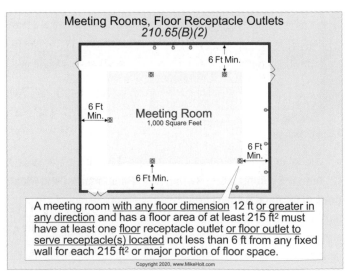

▶Figure 210–62

Note 1: See 314.27(B) for floor boxes used for receptacles located in the floor.

Author's Comment:

▸ The requirement for the floor receptacle to be at least 6 ft from the fixed walls is to provide clear egress passage in an emergency.

▸ The wording "12 feet or greater in any dimension" will permit a dimension less than 12 ft. How can the floor receptacle be at least 6 ft from any wall where the space has a dimension of less than 12 ft in one direction?

210.70 Lighting Outlet Requirements

The control method of the required lighting outlets was changed from "wall switch" to "listed wall-mounted control device." The storage and equipment space lighting outlet rule in 210.70(C) was modified to require control devices at each point of entry and to permit the use of listed wall-mounted control devices.

Analysis

CLARIFIED **210.70(A) Dwelling Units, and (B) Guest Rooms or Guest Suites.** The rules in 210.70(A)(1) and (2), as well as those in 210.70(B), all required lighting outlets to be controlled by a wall switch. This revision permits the control to be by a "listed wall-mounted control device."

EXPANDED **210.70(C) All Occupancies.** This section applies to all occupancies and requires that attics, under-floor spaces, utility rooms, and basements have at least one lighting outlet that is controlled by a listed wall-mounted lighting control device where those spaces are used for storage or contain equipment that requires servicing. A control device must now be installed at each point of entry—the 2017 *NEC* only required the lighting control at the "usual" point of entry.

210.70 Lighting Outlet Requirements

(A) Dwelling Unit Lighting Outlets. Lighting outlets must be installed in:

(1) Habitable Rooms. At least one lighting outlet controlled by a listed wall-mounted control device must be installed in every habitable room, kitchen, and bathroom area of a dwelling unit. The wall-mounted control device must be located near an entrance to the room on a wall. ▸Figure 210–63

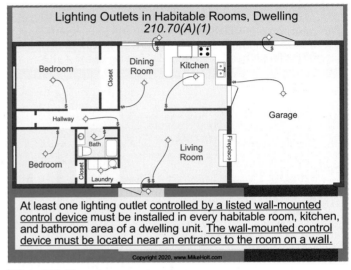

▸Figure 210–63

Author's Comment:

▸ See the definition of "Lighting Outlet" in Article 100.

▸ See the definition of "Habitable Room" in Article 100.

Ex 1: In other than dwelling unit kitchens and bathroom areas, a receptacle controlled by a listed wall-mounted control device can be used instead of a lighting outlet. ▸Figure 210–64

Ex 2: Lighting outlets can be controlled by occupancy sensors that are in addition to a wall-mounted control device or located in a customary wall switch location and are capable of manual override. ▸Figure 210–65

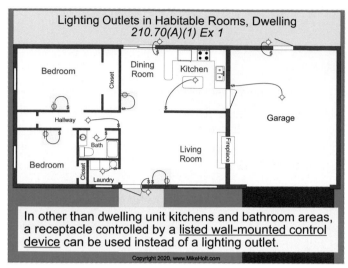

Lighting Outlets in Habitable Rooms, Dwelling
210.70(A)(1) Ex 1

In other than dwelling unit kitchens and bathroom areas, a receptacle controlled by a <u>listed wall-mounted control device</u> can be used instead of a lighting outlet.

▶Figure 210–64

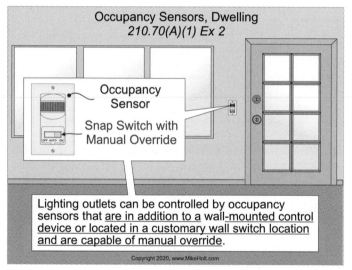

Occupancy Sensors, Dwelling
210.70(A)(1) Ex 2

Occupancy Sensor

Snap Switch with Manual Override

Lighting outlets can be controlled by occupancy sensors that <u>are in addition to a wall-mounted control device or located in a customary wall switch location and are capable of manual override</u>.

▶Figure 210–65

Author's Comment:

▶ The *Code* specifies the location of the lighting outlet, but it does not specify the switch location. Naturally, you would not want to install a switch behind a door or other inconvenient location, but the *NEC* does not require you to relocate the switch to suit the swing of the door. When in doubt as to the best location to place a light switch, consult the job plans or ask the customer. ▶Figure 210–66

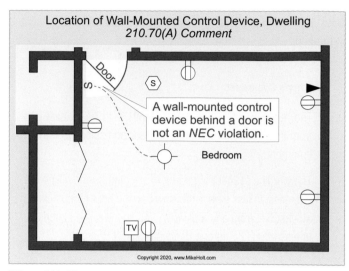

Location of Wall-Mounted Control Device, Dwelling
210.70(A) Comment

A wall-mounted control device behind a door is not an *NEC* violation.

Bedroom

▶Figure 210–66

(2) Other Than Habitable Rooms

(1) Hallways, Stairways, and Garages. At least one wall switch-controlled lighting outlet must be installed in hallways, stairways, and garages with electric power. ▶Figure 210–67

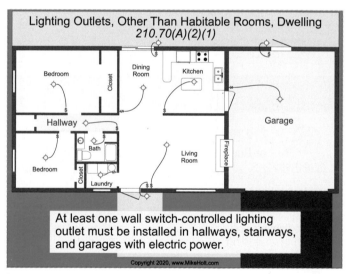

Lighting Outlets, Other Than Habitable Rooms, Dwelling
210.70(A)(2)(1)

At least one wall switch-controlled lighting outlet must be installed in hallways, stairways, and garages with electric power.

▶Figure 210–67

(2) Exterior Entrances. For dwelling units, attached garages, and detached garages with electric power, at least one lighting outlet <u>controlled by a listed wall-mounted control device</u> must provide illumination on the exterior side of outdoor entrances or exits with grade-level access. A garage vehicle door is not considered an outdoor entrance or exit. ▶Figure 210–68

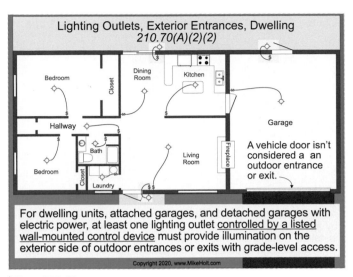

▶Figure 210–68

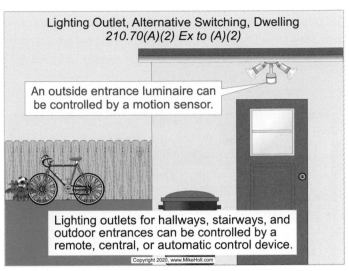

▶Figure 210–70

(3) Stairway. Where a lighting outlet(s) is installed in interior stairways having six risers or more, a <u>listed wall-mounted control device</u> for the lighting outlet(s) must be located at each floor level and at each landing level that includes an entryway. ▶Figure 210–69

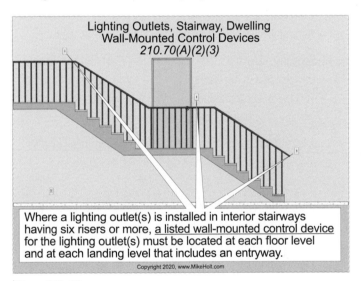

▶Figure 210–69

Ex to (A)(2(1), (2), and (3): Lighting outlets for hallways, stairways, and outdoor entrances can be controlled by a remote, central, or automatic control device. ▶Figure 210–70

(4) Dimmer Control. Lighting outlets located in stairways [210.70(A)(2)(3)] can be controlled by <u>a listed wall-mounted control device</u> where there is a full range of dimming control at each switch location in accordance with 210.70(A)(2)(3).

(B) Guest Rooms or Guest Suites. At least one <u>lighting outlet controlled by a listed wall-mounted control device</u> must be installed in every habitable room and bathroom area of a guest room or guest suite of hotels, motels, and similar occupancies.

Ex 1: In other than bathroom areas and kitchens, a receptacle controlled by a <u>listed wall-mounted control device</u> is permitted. ▶Figure 210–71

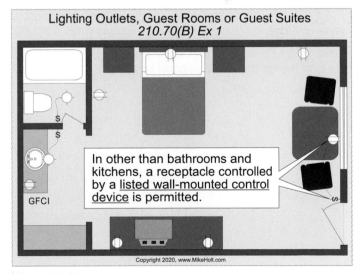

▶Figure 210–71

Ex 2: Lighting outlets can be controlled by occupancy sensors that <u>are in addition to a wall-mounted control device or located in a customary wall switch location and are capable of manual override.</u> ▶Figure 210–72

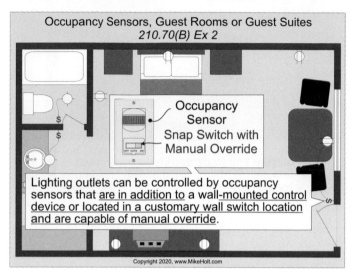

▶Figure 210–72

(C) All Occupancies. At least one lighting outlet that contains a switch or is controlled by a wall switch <u>or listed wall-mounted control device</u> must be installed in attics, underfloor spaces, utility rooms, and basements used for storage or containing equipment that requires servicing. ▶Figure 210–73

The switch <u>or wall-mounted control device</u> must be located at the usual point of entrance to these spaces, and the lighting outlet must be located at <u>each entry that permits access to the attic and underfloor space, utility room, or basement. Where a lighting outlet is installed for equipment requiring service, the lighting outlet</u> must <u>be installed at</u> or near the equipment that requires servicing.

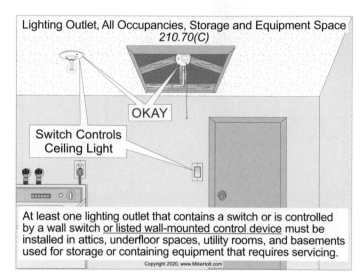

▶Figure 210–73

Author's Comment:

▶ The use of electronic wireless control devices is becoming more common and such devices are available from several manufacturers. In keeping up with technology, many of the electronic switches are addressable via "WiFi" as well.

▶ Section 210.70 introduced a new term, "Wall-Mounted Control Device," that is not defined in either this article or in Article 100 but is implied to include both the traditional wall switch and the newer electronic control devices.

▶ It is also important to note that the lighting in these spaces may require GFCI protection as specified in 210.8.

ARTICLE
215

FEEDERS

Introduction to Article 215—Feeders

Article 215 covers the rules for the installation and ampacity of feeders. The requirements for feeders have some similarities to those for branch circuits, and in some ways, feeders bear a resemblance to service conductors. It is important to understand the distinct differences between these three types of circuits in order to correctly apply the *Code* requirements.

Feeders are the conductors between the service disconnect, the separately derived system, or other supply source, and the final branch-circuit overcurrent protective device. Conductors past the final overcurrent protective device protecting the circuit and the outlet are branch-circuit conductors and fall within the scope of Article 210 [Article 100 Definitions].

Service conductors are the conductors from the service point to the service disconnect. [Article 100 Definitions]. If there is no serving utility, and the electrical power is derived from a generator or other on-site electric power source, then the conductors from the supply source are defined as feeders and there are no service conductors.

It is easy to be confused between feeder, branch circuit, and service conductors, so it is important to evaluate each installation carefully using the Article 100 Definitions to be sure the correct *NEC* rules are followed.

Author's Comment:

▶ The high-end feeder voltage has been increased from 600V to 1,000V. This change is to correlate with an ongoing global change from 600V to 1,000V that began with the 2014 Code cycle, and to recognize that there are some systems that operate over 600V but not over 1,000V. Without such a change, feeders operating above 600V but not exceeding 1,000V would be covered by the "high-voltage rules." As part of this voltage increase change, 215.2(B) was changed from over 600V to over 1,000V.

215.2 Conductor Sizing

As has been the trend, the *Code* has been modifying the "not more than 600V" limitation to "not more than 1,000V." The feeder minimum conductor ampacity rule has been clarified and a reference to the termination requirements of 110.14(C) was added effectively "catching up" to this trend. With PV systems sometimes generating more than 600V (for example), it is good that voltage ratings across the board have been increased including manufacturer's listing of hand tools and test equipment at the same 1,000V.

Analysis

215.2(A)(1) Feeders Not More Than 1,000V. There's a bit of confusion surrounding the application of this rule since "Ampacity" is defined as the maximum current a conductor can carry under the conditions of use. Those conditions of use include any ampacity corrections and/or adjustments that may be required.

CLARIFIED

• • •

Section 215.2(A)(1)(a) says that the conductor ampacity must be equal to, or greater than, the sum of the noncontinuous load plus 125 percent of the continuous load; but, (A)(1)(b) says that the conductor ampacity must be equal to, or greater than, the total load after the application of any required ampacity adjustments and/or corrections.

The issue here is the definition of the term "Ampacity," which is determined by the actual conditions of use. The conditions of use stipulate the application of any required adjustments and/or corrections. It appears that the intent of the *Code* is that you use the "Table" ampacity for (A)(1)(a) and the ampacity as it is defined for (A)(1)(b).

Author's Comment:

▶ There may be a few cases where the termination requirements in 110.14(C) have an impact, but such cases are rare as most, if not all, new equipment has terminations that are suitable for use with 75°C conductor ampacities.

215.2 Conductor Sizing

(A) Feeders—Sizing

(1) General. Feeder conductors must be sized to carry not less than the largest of the calculations contained in (a) or (b) as follows <u>and meet the equipment termination provisions of 110.14(C)</u>. ▶Figure 215–1

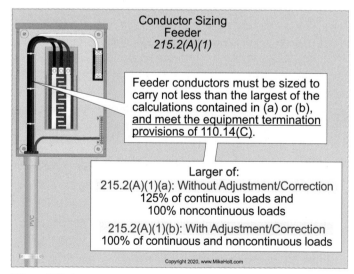

Conductor Sizing
Feeder
215.2(A)(1)

Feeder conductors must be sized to carry not less than the largest of the calculations contained in (a) or (b), <u>and meet the equipment termination provisions of 110.14(C).</u>

Larger of:
215.2(A)(1)(a): Without Adjustment/Correction
125% of continuous loads and
100% noncontinuous loads

215.2(A)(1)(b): With Adjustment/Correction
100% of continuous and noncontinuous loads

Copyright 2020, www.MikeHolt.com

▶Figure 215–1

215.9 Ground-Fault Circuit-Interrupter Protection for Personnel

GFCI devices for feeders are permitted to provide the protection required by 210.8 for circuits of any ampacity. The GFCI protection requirements have been expanding to include circuits rated higher than 15A and 20A. Feeders that have GFCI protection can now protect these higher rated circuits when such protection is required.

Analysis

EXPANDED

215.9 Ground-Fault Circuit-Interrupter Protection for Personnel. Feeders having GFCI protection are permitted to protect downstream branch circuits or outlets where such protection is required by 210.8 or 590.6(A). The previous *Code* only permitted this where the feeder supplied 15A or 20 branch circuits, which has now been deleted from the language. The revision recognizes the expansion of the GFCI requirements in this, and the previous *NEC*, to circuits of higher ampacities. A single larger feeder GFCI breaker may be used to protect a panelboard, and the branch circuits served from that panelboard would not require individual GFCI protection.

Author's Comment:

▶ The installer will have to be careful that the sum of the cumulative normal leakage current for all the circuits and outlets supplied by the feeder GFCI breaker do not approach the ground-fault trip point. Even though the GFCI breaker has a much higher overcurrent trip point, it still provides the 5 mA ground-fault protection for personnel. All circuits and equipment have a small amount of leakage to ground as no insulator is perfect.

▶ The product standard for appliances permits a maximum leakage current of ½ mA, so if you have 10 appliances protected by the feeder GFCI breaker, you are at the trip point of the breaker. Of course, not all appliances have leakage current that high, but it is possible.

BRANCH-CIRCUIT, FEEDER, AND SERVICE LOAD CALCULATIONS

Introduction to Article 220—Branch-Circuit, Feeder, and Service Load Calculations

This article focuses on the requirements for calculating demand loads (including demand factors) in order to size branch circuits [210.19(A)(1)], feeders [215.2(A)(1)], and service conductors [230.42(A)].

Part I describes the layout of Article 220 and provides a table showing where other types of load calculations can be found in the *NEC*. Part II provides requirements for branch-circuit calculations and for specific types of branch circuits. Part III covers the requirements for feeder and service calculations, using what is commonly called the "Standard Method of Calculation." Part IV provides optional calculations that can be used in place of the standard calculations provided in Parts II and III—if your installation meets certain requirements. "Farm Load Calculations" are discussed in Part V of the article.

In some cases, the *Code* provides an optional method (Part IV) for feeder and service calculations in addition to the standard method (Part III); however, these two methods do not yield identical results. In fact, the optional method of calculation will often result in a smaller feeder or service. When taking an exam, read the instructions carefully to be sure which method the test question wants you to use. As you work through Article 220, be sure to study the illustrations to help you fully understand this article. Also, be sure to review the examples in Annex D of the *NEC* to gain more practice with these calculations. The *Code* recognizes that not all demand for power will occur at the same time and it is because of this varying demand that certain demand factors are able to be applied.

220.11 Floor Area

If you have ever sat in an electrical classroom or studied for an exam, one thing that might resonate is that the total floor area of a structure is based on the outside footprint of the building. The requirement for this method of measurement was moved from 220.12 into its own standalone section.

Analysis

CLARIFIED This change makes it so the rule may be used with all the load calculations that are based on floor area making it usable anytime "floor area" is referenced in Article 220.

220.11 Floor Area

The floor area is calculated from the outside dimensions of the building, dwelling unit, or other area involved. For dwelling units, the calculated floor area does not include open porches, garages, or unused or unfinished spaces not adaptable for future use. ▶Figure 220–1

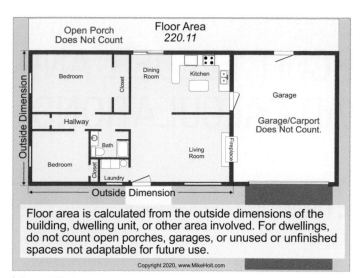

Open Porch
Does Not Count

Floor Area
220.11

Bedroom

Closet

Dining Room

Kitchen

Garage

Hallway

Garage/Carport
Does Not Count.

Bath

Living Room

Fireplace

Bedroom

Closet

Laundry

Outside Dimension

Floor area is calculated from the outside dimensions of the building, dwelling unit, or other area involved. For dwellings, do not count open porches, garages, or unused or unfinished spaces not adaptable for future use.

Copyright 2020, www.MikeHolt.com

▶Figure 220–1

220.12 Lighting Load for Non-Dwelling Occupancies

This section now only applies to nondwelling occupancies and the lighting load table was revised to more closely conform to the maximum permitted lighting loads as specified in the energy codes.

The energy code lighting loads are much less than those found in the *NEC*, but the *Code* wants to make sure the services and feeders can still support loads that are not in compliance with the energy codes.

The scope of this section was changed to only include lighting loads for nondwelling occupancies and was reorganized from a single paragraph with exceptions into subsections with the previous Ex 1 becoming positive text in (B). The new language in (B) made Ex 2 unnecessary and it was deleted.

Analysis

CLARIFIED

220.12(A) General. This says that loads not less than those specified in Table 220.12, along with the floor area determination in 220.11, must be used to calculate the minimum nondwelling occupancy lighting load. New language was added to specify that motors rated ⅛ HP or less are considered a general lighting load, and no additional load needs to be added for those motors.

NEW

220.12(B) Energy Code. Subsection (B) is new and recognizes there are other codes that apply to electrical installations. It also specifically addresses energy codes. Energy codes have been adopted in all 50 states and they often limit the lighting load to a value much less than what is required by the *NEC*'s load calculations. This subsection recognizes those codes and permits the unit values in them to be used in lieu of those found in Table 220.12 provided the conditions as stated are met.

DELETED

220.12(B) Ex 2. Exception No. 2 was deleted because it only permitted a reduction from the lighting loads shown in Table 220.12 of 1 VA per sq ft where the building was designed and constructed in accordance with an adopted energy code for bank and office occupancies. The new language permits the use of the lighting load values from the energy code itself to be used if all four conditions in 220.12(B) are met.

EDITED

Table 220.12. Some of the occupancies that were included in the previous version of this table are not in the new one. There is a note that cross references the occupancies that do not appear in the new table to those that do. That note also indicates that the 125 percent multiplier specified in 210.20(A) is included in the unit loads found in Table 220.12. You do not add the 125 percent to loads calculated using the values in this table, but you must do so if you are using the values from the energy codes as permitted in 220.12(B). The new unit loads are less than the previously required loads but are still in excess of those required by the energy codes.

220.12 Lighting Load for Non-Dwelling Occupancies

(A) General. The general lighting load specified in Table 220.12 for non-dwelling occupancies, and the floor area determined in accordance with 220.11, must be used to calculate the minimum lighting load. ▶Figure 220–2

(B) Energy Code. Where the building is designed and constructed to comply with an energy code adopted by the local authority, the lighting load is permitted to be calculated using the unit values specified in the energy code where the following conditions are met:

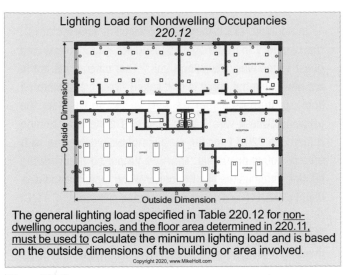

Lighting Load for Nondwelling Occupancies
220.12

Outside Dimension

The general lighting load specified in Table 220.12 for non-dwelling occupancies, and the floor area determined in 220.11, must be used to calculate the minimum lighting load and is based on the outside dimensions of the building or area involved.

Copyright 2020, www.MikeHolt.com

▶Figure 220–2

(1) A power monitoring system is installed that will provide continuous information regarding the total general lighting load of the building.

(2) The power monitoring system will be set with alarm values to alert the building owner or manager if the lighting load exceeds the values set by the energy code. Automatic means to act to reduce the connected load is permitted.

(3) The demand factors specified in 220.42 are not applied to the general lighting load.

(4) The continuous load multiplier of 125 percent is to be applied.

Table 220.12 General Lighting Loads by Nondwelling Occupancy

Type of Occupancy	VA/ft²
Automotive facilities	1.50
Convention centers	1.40
Courthouses	1.40
Dormitories	1.50
Exercise centers	1.40
Fire stations	1.30
Gymnasiums[a]	1.70
Health care clinics	1.60
Hospitals	1.60

Table 220.12 General Lighting Loads by Nondwelling Occupancy (continued)

Type of Occupancy	VA/ft²
Hotels and motels, including apartment houses without provisions for cooking by tenants[b]	1.70
Libraries	1.50
Manufacturing facilities[c]	2.20
Motion picture theaters	1.60
Museums	1.60
Offices[d]	1.30
Parking garages[e]	0.30
Penitentiaries	1.20
Performing arts theaters	1.50
Police stations	1.30
Post offices	1.60
Religious facilities	2.20
Restaurants	1.50
Retail[g,h]	1.90
Schools/universities	3.00
Sports arenas	3.00
Town halls	1.40
Transportation occupancies	1.20
Warehouses	1.20
Workshops	1.70

Note: The 125 percent multiplier for a continuous load as specified in 210.20(A) is included when using the unit loads in this table for calculating the minimum lighting load for a specified occupancy.

[a] *Armories and auditoriums are considered gymnasium-type occupancies.*

[b] *Lodge rooms are similar to hotels and motels.*

[c] *Industrial commercial loft buildings are considered manufacturing-type occupancies.*

[d] *Banks are office-type occupancies.*

[e] *Garages—commercial (storage) are considered parking garage occupancies.*

[f] *Clubs are considered restaurant occupancies.*

[g] *Barber shops and beauty parlors are considered retail occupancies.*

[h] *Stores are considered retail occupancies.*

Author's Comment:

▸ While there are federal requirements that direct states to adopt energy codes within two years of their publication, not all states do so; some are a decade or more behind and not all of them actively enforce the energy codes they have adopted.

220.14 Other Loads—Occupancies

This section, for service and feeder calculation(s) purposes, has seen some clarification made to (J) and (K). In addition, a new subsection (M) was added to address the lighting and receptacle loads for hotel and motel occupancies.

Analysis

CLARIFIED

220.14(J) Dwelling Units. This subsection now only applies to one- and two-family, and multi-family dwelling units. Guest rooms and guest suites were previously included in (J) but were moved to the new 220.14(M). While the *Code* is somewhat deferring to the energy codes for nondwelling unit loads, that is not the case for dwelling unit lighting and receptacle loads. The energy codes specify 1W per sq ft for lighting loads, but the *NEC* has retained the long standing 3 VA per sq ft as it also includes the general-purpose receptacle loads and lowering this value could have unintended consequences.

As with the nondwelling occupancy lighting calculations, motor loads of ⅛ horsepower or less are included in the lighting load.

CLARIFIED

220.14(K) Office Buildings. This subsection has two changes. It was titled "Banks and Office Buildings" but since banks were deleted from Table 220.12, and the note tells us they are treated as office buildings for the purpose of load calculations, its title is now "Office Buildings."

NEW

220.14(M) Hotel and Motel Occupancies. This is new and covers the lighting load calculations for guest rooms and guest suites in hotels or motels. These calculations were previously included in 220.14(J) with dwelling units but are no longer covered there.

In addition, since they were previously covered in (J), the category in Table 220.12 used for guest rooms and guest suites was "Dwelling Units." That category is not in the new table but there is one called "Hotels and Motels." The load in that category is 1.70 VA per sq ft; under the previous *Code* it was 3 VA per sq ft. The new subsection references 220.11 for the purpose of calculating the sq ft area of hotels or motels. The 1.70 VA per sq ft covers the lighting loads as well as the general-use receptacles specified in 210.11(C)(3); bathroom branch circuits [210.11(C)(4)], garage branch circuits [210.52(E)(3)], receptacles on balconies, decks, and porches; the lighting loads in 210.70(A) dwelling unit lighting loads, and (B) guest rooms and guest suites lighting loads.

220.14 Other Loads—Occupancies

(J) Dwelling Units. In one- and two-family, and multifamily dwellings, the lighting and receptacle outlets specified in 220.14(J)(1), (J)(2), and (J)(3) are included in the 3 VA per sq ft unit load in Table 220.12. No additional load calculations are required for such outlets. The minimum lighting load is to be determined using the 3 VA per sq ft unit load and the floor area as determined in 220.11. ▸Figure 220–3

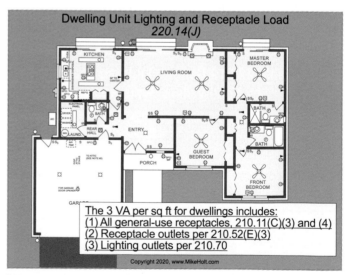

Dwelling Unit Lighting and Receptacle Load
220.14(J)

The 3 VA per sq ft for dwellings includes:
(1) All general-use receptacles, 210.11(C)(3) and (4)
(2) Receptacle outlets per 210.52(E)(3)
(3) Lighting outlets per 210.70

Copyright 2020, www.MikeHolt.com

▸Figure 220–3

(1) General-use receptacle outlets of 20A rating or less, including receptacles connected to the bathroom or garage circuits in accordance with 210.11(C)(3) and 210.11(C)(4).

(2) Receptacle outlets specified in 210.52(E) and (G) for outdoors, garages, and basements.

(3) Lighting outlets specified in 210.70.

Author's Comment:

▶ There is no VA load for 15A and 20A, 125V general-use receptacle outlets because the loads for those devices are part of the 3 VA per sq foot for general lighting contained in Table 220.12 for dwelling units.

▶ The *Code* does not limit the number of receptacle outlets on a general-purpose branch circuit in a dwelling unit. See the *NEC* Handbook for more information.

▶ **Example**

Question: What are the maximum number of 15A or 20A, 125V receptacles permitted on a 15A or 20A, 120V general-purpose branch circuit in a dwelling unit?

(a) 10 receptacles
(b) 11 receptacles
(c) 12 receptacles
(d) There is no limit.

Answer: (d) There is no limit.

Author's Comment:

▶ Although there is no limit on the number of receptacles on dwelling unit general-purpose branch circuits, the *Code* does require a minimum number of circuits to be installed for general-purpose receptacle and lighting outlets [210.11(A)]. In addition, the receptacle and lighting loads must be evenly distributed among the appropriate number of circuits [210.11(B)].

(K) Office Buildings. The calculated load for receptacle outlets in office buildings is based on the largest calculation of (1) or (2).

(1) The receptacle outlet load at 180 VA per receptacle yoke [220.14(I)], after all demand factors have been applied.

(2) The receptacle outlet load at 1 VA per sq ft.

▶ **Office General Receptacle—Example**

Question: What is the calculated receptacle load for an 18,000 sq ft office space with one hundred sixty 15A, 125V receptacles? ▶Figure 220–4

(a) 18,200 VA
(b) 19,400 VA
(c) 20,100 VA
(d) 22,200 VA

Answer: (b) 19,400 VA [220.14(K)(1) and 220.14(I)]

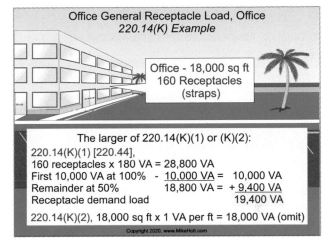

Office General Receptacle Load, Office
220.14(K) Example

Office - 18,000 sq ft
160 Receptacles
(straps)

The larger of 220.14(K)(1) or (K)(2):
220.14(K)(1) [220.44],
160 receptacles × 180 VA = 28,800 VA
First 10,000 VA at 100% - 10,000 VA = 10,000 VA
Remainder at 50% 18,800 VA = + 9,400 VA
Receptacle demand load 19,400 VA
220.14(K)(2), 18,000 sq ft × 1 VA per ft = 18,000 VA (omit)
Copyright 2020, www.MikeHolt.com

▶Figure 220–4

Solution:

160 Receptacles × 180 VA = 28,800 VA
First 10,000 VA at 100% = –10,000 VA × 100% = 10,000 VA
Remainder at 50% = 18,800 VA × 50% = + 9,400 VA
Receptacle Calculated Load = 19,400 VA

[220.14(K)(2)
18,000 × 1 VA per sq ft = 18,000 VA (omit)

▶ **Office General Lighting and Receptacle—Example**

Question: What is the lighting and receptacle demand load for an 18,000 sq ft office space with one hundred forty 15A, 125V receptacles? ▶Figure 220–5

(a) 41,400 VA
(b) 51,000 VA
(c) 68,200 VA
(d) 70,000 VA

Answer: (a) 41,400 VA [220.12, 220.42, 220.14(K)(1), and 220.14(I)]
● ● ●

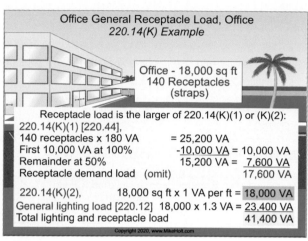

▶Figure 220–5

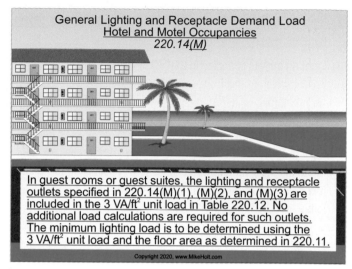

In guest rooms or guest suites, the lighting and receptacle outlets specified in 220.14(M)(1), (M)(2), and (M)(3) are included in the 3 VA/ft² unit load in Table 220.12. No additional load calculations are required for such outlets. The minimum lighting load is to be determined using the 3 VA/ft² unit load and the floor area as determined in 220.11.

▶Figure 220–6

Solution:

Step 1: Determine general lighting [220.12].

18,000 sq ft × 1.30 VA = 23,400 VA

Step 2: Determine receptacles [220.44].

Based on Actual:

140 Receptacles × 180 VA = 25,200 VA

First 10,000 VA at 100% = −10,000 VA × 100% =10,000 VA

Remainder at 50% = 15,200 VA × 50% = + 7,600 VA

Receptacle Calculated Load = 17,600 VA

(omit)

Based on the NEC [220.14(K)(2)]:

18,000 × 1 VA per sq ft = 18,000 VA

Step 3: Determine total demand load.

General Lighting   23,400 VA

Receptacles   +18,000 VA

Total   41,400 VA

(M) Hotel and Motel Occupancies. In guest rooms or guest suites of hotels and motels, the lighting and receptacle outlets specified in 220.14(M)(1), (M)(2), and (M)(3) are included in the 3 VA per sq ft unit load in Table 220.12. No additional load calculations are required for such outlets. The minimum lighting load is to be determined using the 3 VA per sq ft unit load and the floor area as determined in 220.11. ▶Figure 220–6

(1) General-use receptacle outlets of 20A rating or less, including receptacles connected to the bathroom or garage circuits in accordance with 210.11(C)(3) and 210.11(C)(4).

(2) Receptacle outlets specified in 210.52(E)(3) for balconies, decks, and porches.

(3) Lighting outlets specified in 210.70.

220.16 Loads for Additions to Existing Installations

Loads added to an existing dwelling unit must be calculated for an expansion of any size.

Analysis

EXPANDED   **DELETED**

220.16(A) Dwelling Units. The 2017 *Code* excluded requiring additional loads for dwelling units where the structural addition or previously unwired area of the dwelling unit did not exceed 500 sq ft. That exclusion has been deleted, requiring the additional loads be accounted for regardless of the size of the addition or previously unwired area of the dwelling.

220.42 General Lighting Demand Factors

Hospitals require a lot of light and all this light requires significant electrical power. Subject to the previous demand factors, the demand load for hospitals has been grossly underestimated and this change compensates for that. On the other hand, lighting demands in the hospitality sector have greatly decreased in the past few years and that fact has also been taken into consideration. With all that said, the demand factors for hospital lighting loads were eliminated and those for hotels and motels have decreased.

Analysis

EDITED   DELETED

Table 220.42 Lighting Demand Factors. The demand factor for hospital lighting was removed as a result of not being able to confirm the actual required VA per sq ft. Data from energy metering in hospitals indicates the actual lighting load is 0.94 VA per sq ft. That would result in an actual load for a 500,000 sq ft hospital of 470 kVA which is well above the demand factor load of 170 kVA when calculated applying the prior demand factors. With this in mind, the derating factors for hospital lighting were removed from the 2020 *Code*.

The lighting load values for hotels and motels were decreased from 2 VA per sq ft to 1.70 VA per sq ft [Table 220.12]. The decrease in the demand factors is to account for the unit lighting load reduction. With the load reduction, it is expected the actual loads will be much closer to the calculated loads than they have been in the past.

220.42 General Lighting Demand Factors

The *Code* recognizes that not all luminaires will be on at the same time, and it permits the following demand factors to be applied to the general lighting load as determined in accordance with Table 220.42.

Author's Comment:

▸ For dwelling units, the demand factors of Table 220.42 apply to the two small-appliance circuits of 1,500 VA [220.5(A)]. A laundry circuit of 1,500 VA [220.52(B)] is included as part of the general lighting load calculation, along with the required lighting and general-use receptacle load of 3 VA per sq ft [Table 220.12 Note a].

Table 220.42 General Lighting Demand Factors

Type of Occupancy	Lighting VA Load	Demand Factor
Dwelling units	First 3,000 VA	100%
	3,001 VA to 120,000VA	35%
	Remainder over 120,000 VA	25%
Hotels/motels/apartment houses without provision for cooking*	First 20,000 VA	60%
	20,001 VA to 100,000 VA	50%
	Remainder over 100,000	35%
Warehouses (storage)	First 12,500 VA	100%
	Remainder over 12,500	50%
Others	Total VA	100%

*The demand factors of this table do not apply to the calculated load of feeders or services supplying areas in hotels and motels where the entire lighting is likely to be used at one time, such as in ballrooms or dining rooms.

▸ **Example**

Question: What is the general lighting and receptacle load, after demand factors, for a 40 ft × 50 ft dwelling unit? ▸Figure 220–7

(a) 4,500 VA   (b) 5,625 VA   (c) 5,825 VA   (d) 6,225 VA

Answer: (b) 5,625 VA

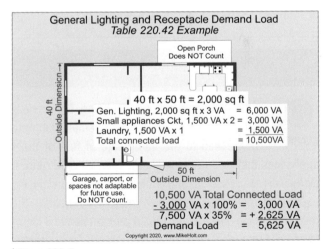

General Lighting and Receptacle Demand Load
Table 220.42 Example

Open Porch
Does NOT Count

40 ft × 50 ft = 2,000 sq ft
Gen. Lighting, 2,000 sq ft x 3 VA   = 6,000 VA
Small appliances Ckt, 1,500 VA x 2 = 3,000 VA
Laundry, 1,500 VA x 1   = 1,500 VA
Total connected load   = 10,500VA

Garage, carport, or spaces not adaptable for future use. Do NOT Count.

10,500 VA Total Connected Load
- 3,000 VA x 100% =   3,000 VA
  7,500 VA x 35% = + 2,625 VA
Demand Load   =   5,625 VA

Copyright 2020, www.MikeHolt.com

▸Figure 220–7

• • •

Solution:

General Lighting and Receptacles = 40 ft × 50 ft

General Lighting and Receptacles = 2,000 sq ft × 3 VA per sq ft

General Lighting and Receptacles = 6,000 VA

General Lighting and Receptacles = 6,000 VA

Small-Appliance Circuit

[210.52(A)] =	*1,500 VA × 2 circuits =*	*3,000 VA*
Laundry Circuit [210.52(B)] =	*1,500 VA × 1 circuit =*	*+1,500 VA*
Total General Lighting =		*10,500 VA*
First 3,000 VA at 100%	*3,000 VA × 100% =*	*3,000 VA*
Next 117,000* VA at 35%	*7,500 VA × 35% =*	*+2,625 VA*

General Lighting and General-Use Receptacles Calculated Load =   5,625 VA

*Note: Remember to subtract 3,000 VA from 120,000 VA when using Table 220.42 since the 35% only applies to the 3,001 VA to 120,000 VA range.

220.53 Appliance Load, Dwelling

The demand factor of 75 percent for four or more appliances fastened in place when calculating a service or feeder is now limited to appliances rated ¼ hp or greater, or 500W or greater.

Analysis

CLARIFIED

220.53 Appliance Load—Dwelling. The previous *Code* permitted a 75 percent demand factor to be applied to the nameplate of four or more appliances fastened in place (other than electric ranges, clothes dryers, space-heating equipment, or air-conditioning equipment) no matter what size load they required. The revised wording only permits the 75 percent demand factor to be used where the appliances are rated ¼ hp or greater, and to appliances rated 500W or greater. For clarity and ease of use, appliances not included in this permission were moved to be shown in a list format.

220.53 Appliance Load, Dwelling

A demand factor of 75 percent can be applied to the total connected load of four or more appliances <u>rated ¼ hp or greater, or 500W or greater, that are fastened in place</u>.

This demand factor does not apply to:

(1) Household electric cooking equipment that is fastened in place [220.55]

(2) Clothes dryers [220.54]

(3) Space-heating equipment [220.51]

(4) Air-conditioning equipment [220.50] ▸Figure 220–8

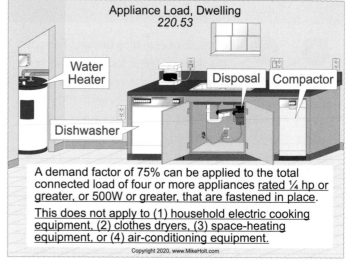

Appliance Load, Dwelling
220.53

A demand factor of 75% can be applied to the total connected load of four or more appliances <u>rated ¼ hp or greater, or 500W or greater, that are fastened in place.</u>

<u>This does not apply to (1) household electric cooking equipment, (2) clothes dryers, (3) space-heating equipment, or (4) air-conditioning equipment.</u>

Copyright 2020, www.MikeHolt.com

▸Figure 220–8

▸ **Example 1**

Question: *What is the demand load for a dwelling unit that contains a 1,000 VA garbage disposal, a 1,500 VA dishwasher, and a 4,500 VA water heater?* ▸Figure 220–9

(a) 6,000 VA   (b) 7,000 VA   (c) 8,000 VA   (d) 9,000 VA

Answer: *(b) 7,000 VA*

Solution:

1,000 VA + 1,500 VA + 4,500 VA = 7,000 VA

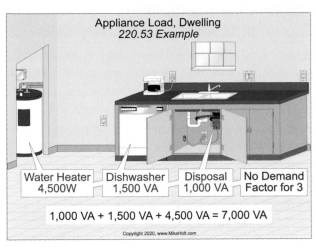

Water Heater 4,500W | Dishwasher 1,500 VA | Disposal 1,000 VA | No Demand Factor for 3

1,000 VA + 1,500 VA + 4,500 VA = 7,000 VA

Copyright 2020, www.MikeHolt.com

▶Figure 220–9

▶ **Example 2**

Question: What is the demand load for a 12-unit multifamily dwelling if each unit contains a 1,000 VA garbage disposal, a 1,500 VA dishwasher, and a 4,500 VA water heater? ▶Figure 220–10

(a) 63,000 VA
(b) 71,000 VA
(c) 82,000 VA
(d) 93,000 VA

Answer: (a) 63,000 VA

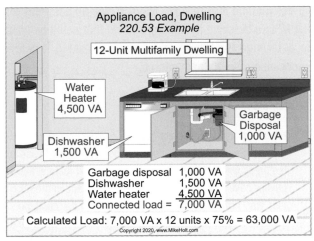

▶Figure 220–10

Solution:

Calculated Load = (1,000 VA + 1,500 VA + 4,500 VA) × 12 units × 75%*
Calculated Load = 63,000 VA

*Each dwelling unit has only three appliances, but the feeder/ service supplies a total of 36 appliances (12 units × 3 appliances).

220.60 Noncoincident Loads

When determining demand loads that are not likely to all place a burden on the service at the same time, the lesser of these loads can be disregarded for the purposes of sizing a service. This rule was clarified to say that where a motor is one of the noncoincident loads 125 percent of the motor load must be used in the calculation.

Analysis

CLARIFIED This rule permits you to omit the smaller of two loads that will not be in use simultaneously from the load calculation. This revision requires that where a motor is one of the loads it must be rated at 125 percent for the calculation.

220.60 Noncoincident Loads

If it is unlikely that two or more loads will be used at the same time, only the largest load is used for load calculations. Where a motor is part of the noncoincident load, and is not the largest of the noncoincident loads, 125 percent of the motor load must be used in the calculation if it is the largest motor. ▶Figure 220–11

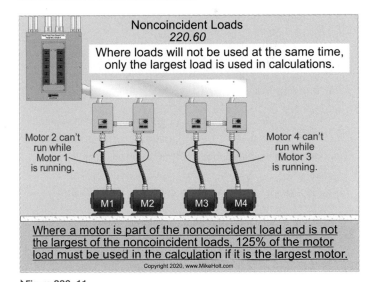

▶Figure 220–11

▶ **Example**

Question: *What is the feeder/service calculated load for a dwelling air conditioner having a rated load current of 14A at 240V as compared to a 9.60 kW electric space heater with a 3A air-handling unit (AHU) fan at 240V?* ▶Figure 220–12

(a) 10,320 VA (b) 12,320 VA   (c) 14,320 VA   (d) 16,320 VA

Answer: *(a) 10,320 VA*

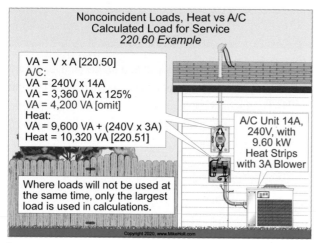

Noncoincident Loads, Heat vs A/C
Calculated Load for Service
220.60 Example

VA = V x A [220.50]
A/C:
VA = 240V x 14A
VA = 3,360 VA x 125%
VA = 4,200 VA [omit]
Heat:
VA = 9,600 VA + (240V x 3A)
Heat = 10,320 VA [220.51]

A/C Unit 14A, 240V, with 9.60 kW Heat Strips with 3A Blower

Where loads will not be used at the same time, only the largest load is used in calculations.

Copyright 2020, www.MikeHolt.com

▶Figure 220–12

Solution:

Air-Conditioning VA = Volts × Amperes

Air-Conditioning VA = 240V × 14A

Air-Conditioning VA = 3,360 VA × 125% [220.50]

Air-Conditioning VA = 4,200 VA (omit)

Electric Space-Heating Load = 9,600 VA [220.51]

Air-Handling Unit Fan (AHU) = Volts × Amperes

Air Handling Unit Fan (AHU) = 240V × 3A

Air Handling Unit Fan (AHU) = 720 VA

Electric Space-Heating Load with AHU Fan = 9,600 VA + 720 VA

Electric Space-Heating Load with AHU Fan = 10,320 VA

220.87 Determining Existing Loads

A new exception was added prohibiting the use of demand load data from being used where the system is also supplied by a renewable energy system. There is just no way to easily determine the contribution from a renewable energy source such as a PV system, or the reduction from the peak shaving when the PV system is under load, making this method virtually unreliable.

Analysis

NEW

220.87 Determining Existing Loads, Exception. This section permits the use of actual maximum demand to determine the existing load. A new exception was added specifying that you cannot use the maximum demand method of determining the existing load where the feeder or service has any renewable energy system or employs any form of peak load shaving. Either of these things will distort the actual load and make this method unsuitable for determining the existing load. There is no way to easily determine the contribution from a renewable energy source or the reduction from the peak shaving so this method is unreliable. There is also no easy way for the *NEC* to describe a metering system that could be used to determine the actual peak demand making it nearly impossible to verify and enforce.

Author's Comment:

▶ Where the service does not have renewable energy or peak shaving equipment, this method has become easier to use in the areas where the utility has installed smart meters. Many utilities have online access to the meter demand information that was not previously available to residential customers as prior analog meters typically did not include a demand register.

220.87 Determining Existing Loads

The calculation of a feeder or service load for an existing dwelling unit must be in accordance with all of the following:

(1) The maximum demand data for a 1-year period.

Ex: The highest average kW for a 15-minute period, over a period of 30 days. ▶Figure 220–13

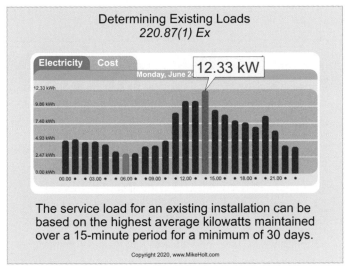

The service load for an existing installation can be based on the highest average kilowatts maintained over a 15-minute period for a minimum of 30 days.

Copyright 2020, www.MikeHolt.com

▶Figure 220–13

(2) The maximum peak demand at 125 percent plus the new load does not exceed the ampacity of the feeder or rating of the service.

(3) The feeder has overcurrent protection in accordance with 240.4, and the service has overload protection in accordance with 230.90.

Ex: If the feeder or service has any renewable energy system such as solar photovoltaic systems or wind electric systems, or employs any form of peak load shaving, this calculation method is not permitted.

OUTSIDE BRANCH CIRCUITS AND FEEDERS

Introduction to Article 225—Outside Branch Circuits and Feeders

This article covers the installation requirements for equipment, including overhead and underground branch-circuit and feeder conductors located outdoors on or between buildings, poles, and other structures on the premises. Conductors installed outdoors can serve many purposes such as area lighting, power for outdoor equipment, or for providing power to separate buildings or structures. It is important to remember that the power supply for buildings is not always a service conductor but may be feeder or branch-circuit conductors originating in another building. Never just assume that the conductors supplying power to a building are service conductors until you have identified where the service point is [Article 100 Definitions] and reviewed the Article 100 definitions for feeders, branch circuits, and service conductors. If you have correctly determined the conductors are service conductors, then use Article 230.

Part II of this article limits the number of feeders plus branch-circuits to a building and provides rules regarding the disconnects. These rules include the disconnect rating, construction characteristics, labeling, where to locate the disconnect, and the grouping of multiple disconnects.

225.4 Conductor Covering

Conductors run on the exterior of buildings and structures are obviously going to be exposed to direct sunlight, a warmer environment, and subsequently more heat overall. "Thermoplastic" (rubber) coverings do not hold up to heat as well as "Thermoset," so "Rubber Covered" was replaced with "Thermoset" as that term includes rubber-covered conductors.

Analysis

CLARIFIED The term "rubber covered" was replaced with the more technically correct term of "thermoset." Thermoset was formerly referred to as rubber covered. The most commonly used thermoset insulation type is XHHW and the most commonly used thermoplastic type is THHN. Where subjected to heat, the thermoplastic type softens and can be displaced by pressure against the insulation; thermoset does not. This difference between the two types of insulation is one of the reasons the rooftop temperature adder found in 310.15(B)(3)(c) Ex does not apply to XHHW-2.

225.10 Wiring on Buildings (or Other Structures)

The list item for multiconductor cable was deleted and new list items for SE and TC-ER cables were added as the term "Multiconductor" was too broad.

Analysis

DELETED "Multiconductor Cable" was deleted as that term is too general. Type NM cable is a multiconductor cable, but it is not permitted to be used in wet locations. Article 225 is for outside installations and they are, by definition, wet locations. Section 300.9 makes it clear that the interior of a raceway installed in a wet location is also a wet location. Since there would be no permitted use of Type NM cable, the list item "multiconductor cable" was deleted.

• • •

Type TC-ER cable was added based on its jacket being thicker than that of Type SE cable and is suitable for use in outside and wet locations. Many types of Type TC cable are also listed and marked for direct burial use.

Type SE cable was added as a specific list item because the deletion of the term "multiconductor cable" acts to prohibit any multiconductor cable that does not have its own list item.

225.15 Supports over Buildings

The requirement for outside branch circuits or feeders that pass over a building in accordance with 230.29 was replaced with one requiring them to be securely supported. This corrects the mistakenly referenced 230.29 (which required the bonding of metal structures that support service conductors) since bonding metal support structures is only appropriate ahead of the service disconnect.

Analysis

CLARIFIED   DELETED   This section was revised to delete the reference to 230.29; the requirements were changed in the 2017 *Code* cycle to require the neutral conductor to be bonded to the supports where such supports are metal. That revision was not correlated with this rule at that time. While connecting the neutral conductor to the metal supports is acceptable on the line side of the service disconnect, it is not acceptable for the branch circuit and feeder conductors covered by Article 225. The revised language requires these Article 225 conductors that pass over a building to be securely supported.

In 225.17, Masts as Supports, the term "Guy" was replaced with "Guy Wires" for clarification.

225.19 Clearances from Buildings

This section was revised to clarify that it only applies to overhead spans of open conductors and open multiconductor cables, not to cable assemblies with an outer jacket such as Type SE cable.

Analysis

CLARIFIED   NEW   New parent text makes it clear that the rules in this section only apply to overhead spans of "open conductors" and "open multiconductor cables." Without the new parent text, 225.19(C) made very little sense. Using just the title and the text in (C) you could read it as saying that no wiring method could be installed within 3 ft horizontally from the building, which is certainly not the intent of the rules in this section. The parent text limits the application of all the subsections of this rule to overhead installations of open conductors or open multiconductor cables.

225.19 Clearances from Buildings

Overhead spans of conductors must comply with 225.19(A), (B), (C), and (D).

(A) Above Roofs. Overhead conductors must maintain a vertical clearance of 8 ft 6 in. above the surface of a roof and must be maintained for a distance of at least 3 ft from the edge of the roof. ▶Figure 225–1

Ex 2: The overhead conductor clearances from the roof can be reduced to 3 ft if the slope of the roof meets or exceeds 4 in. of vertical rise for every 12 in. of horizontal run.

Ex 3: For 120/208V or 120/240V circuits, the conductor clearance over the roof overhang can be reduced to 18 in., if no more than 6 ft of conductor passes over no more than 4 ft of roof. ▶Figure 225–2

Ex 4: The 3-ft clearance from the roof edge does not apply when the point of attachment is on the side of the building below the roof. ▶Figure 225–3

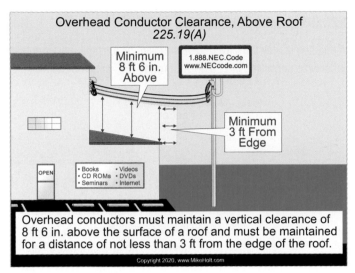

Overhead Conductor Clearance, Above Roof
225.19(A)

Minimum 8 ft 6 in. Above

1.888.NEC.Code
www.NECcode.com

Minimum 3 ft From Edge

OPEN

• Books   • Videos
• CD ROMs   • DVDs
• Seminars   • Internet

Overhead conductors must maintain a vertical clearance of 8 ft 6 in. above the surface of a roof and must be maintained for a distance of not less than 3 ft from the edge of the roof.

Copyright 2020, www.MikeHolt.com

▶Figure 225-1

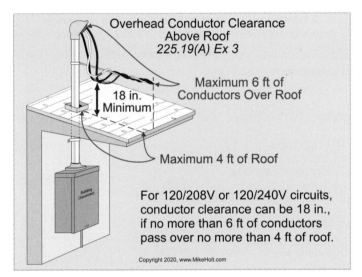

Overhead Conductor Clearance
Above Roof
225.19(A) Ex 3

18 in. Minimum

Maximum 6 ft of Conductors Over Roof

Building Disconnect

Maximum 4 ft of Roof

For 120/208V or 120/240V circuits, conductor clearance can be 18 in., if no more than 6 ft of conductors pass over no more than 4 ft of roof.

Copyright 2020, www.MikeHolt.com

▶Figure 225-2

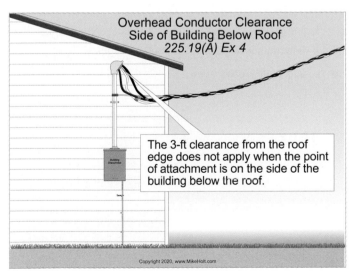

Overhead Conductor Clearance
Side of Building Below Roof
225.19(A) Ex 4

Building Disconnect

The 3-ft clearance from the roof edge does not apply when the point of attachment is on the side of the building below the roof.

Copyright 2020, www.MikeHolt.com

▶Figure 225-3

(B) From Other Structures. Overhead conductors must maintain a clearance of at least 3 ft from signs, chimneys, radio and television antennas, tanks, and other nonbuilding structures.

(D) Final Span Clearance

(1) Clearance from Windows. Overhead conductors must maintain a clearance of 3 ft from windows that open, doors, porches, balconies, ladders, stairs, fire escapes, or similar locations. ▶Figure 225-4

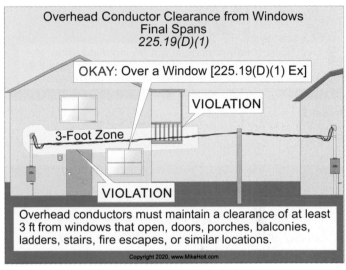

Overhead Conductor Clearance from Windows
Final Spans
225.19(D)(1)

OKAY: Over a Window [225.19(D)(1) Ex]

VIOLATION

3-Foot Zone

VIOLATION

Overhead conductors must maintain a clearance of at least 3 ft from windows that open, doors, porches, balconies, ladders, stairs, fire escapes, or similar locations.

Copyright 2020, www.MikeHolt.com

▶Figure 225-4

Ex: Overhead conductors installed above a window are not required to maintain the 3 ft distance from the window.

(2) Vertical Clearance. Overhead conductors must maintain a vertical clearance of at least 10 ft above platforms, projections, or surfaces that permit personal contact in accordance with 225.18. This vertical clearance must be maintained for 3 ft, measured horizontally from the platforms, projections, or surfaces from which they might be reached.

(3) Below Openings. Overhead conductors are not permitted to be installed under an opening through which materials might pass, and they are not permitted to be installed where they will obstruct an entrance to these openings. ▶Figure 225-5

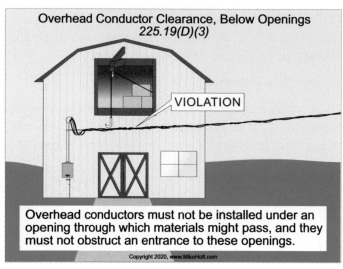

Overhead Conductor Clearance, Below Openings
225.19(D)(3)

VIOLATION

Overhead conductors must not be installed under an opening through which materials might pass, and they must not obstruct an entrance to these openings.

Copyright 2020, www.MikeHolt.com

▶Figure 225–5

225.30 Number of Supplies

A new list item (A) was added to permit docking facilities and piers to be supplied by multiple feeders or branch circuits. Much like services, the general rule is to permit only one supply source per building. Revised language in (B) permits up to six feeders to a second building or structure under limited circumstances.

Analysis

EXPANDED

225.30(A) Special Conditions. As with services, the general rule is that only a single source of supply to a second building or structure is permitted. Section 225.30(A) listed seven special conditions where more than one supply to a second building or structure would be permitted. This change adds an eighth list item to permit multiple sources of supply to feed docking facilities or piers.

NEW

225.30(B) Common Supply Equipment. This new subsection permits up to six feeders to supply a second building or structure where they originate in the same panelboard, switchboard, or other distribution equipment. Each feeder must terminate at the second building in a single disconnecting means and those disconnecting means are required to be grouped together.

225.30 Number of Supplies

A building is only permitted to be supplied by a single feeder unless otherwise permitted in 225.30(A) through (E). ▶Figure 225–6

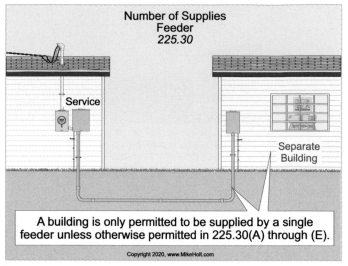

Number of Supplies
Feeder
225.30

Service

Separate Building

A building is only permitted to be supplied by a single feeder unless otherwise permitted in 225.30(A) through (E).

Copyright 2020, www.MikeHolt.com

▶Figure 225–6

(A) Special Conditions. Additional feeders are permitted to supply:

(1) Fire pumps.

(2) Emergency systems.

(3) Legally required standby systems.

(4) Optional standby systems.

(5) Parallel power production sources.

(6) Systems designed for connection to multiple sources of supply for the purpose of enhanced reliability.

(7) Electric vehicle charging systems listed, labeled, and identified for more than a single branch circuit or feeder.

(8) Docking facilities and piers.

(B) Common Supply Equipment. Where feeder conductors originate in the same panelboard, switchboard, or other distribution equipment, and each feeder terminates in a single disconnecting means, not more than six feeders are permitted. ▸Figure 225-7

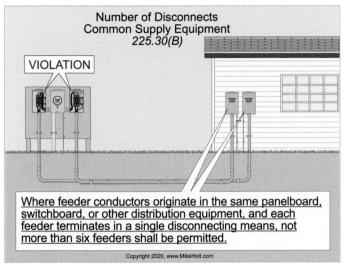

Number of Disconnects
Common Supply Equipment
225.30(B)

VIOLATION

Where feeder conductors originate in the same panelboard, switchboard, or other distribution equipment, and each feeder terminates in a single disconnecting means, not more than six feeders shall be permitted.

Copyright 2020, www.MikeHolt.com

▸Figure 225-7

Where more than one feeder is installed, all feeder disconnects supplying the building must be grouped in the same location. Each disconnect must be marked to indicate the load served.

Author's Comment:

▸ This new rule simply permits up to six feeders with individual disconnects to be used instead of a single large feeder and six disconnects at the second building. It also increases safety because multiple smaller feeders will act to reduce the arc flash hazard by reducing the incident energy.

ARTICLE
230

SERVICES

Introduction to Article 230—Services

This article covers the installation requirements for service conductors and the first means of disconnect. The requirements for service conductors differ from those for other conductors. For one thing, service conductors for one building cannot pass through the interior of another [230.3], and different rules are applied depending on whether a service conductor is inside or outside a building. When are they "outside" as opposed to "inside"? The answer may seem obvious, but 230.6 will help you determine when (and if) service conductors are considered to be outside.

Article 230 consists of seven parts:

- Part I. General
- Part II. Overhead Service Conductors
- Part III. Underground Service Conductors
- Part IV. Service-Entrance Conductors
- Part V. Service Disconnect
- Part VI. Disconnecting Means
- Part VIII. Overcurrent Protection

230.31 Underground Service Conductor Size and Ampacity

The last word of this section title was editorially changed from "Rating" to "Ampacity." The same revisions were made throughout to correlate with this global effort since "ampacity" is the more correct term. There are no technical changes to this rule about underground service conductors.

Analysis

EDITED The word "Rating" alone, is too broad a term to be associated with conductors. Rating can mean many things without being prefaced with another word such as "temperature rating."

When used by itself it can even mean tensile strength! "Ampacity" is more precise and leaves no doubt. The redundant term "Allowable" was removed as well. The Informational Note added to (A) references a UL Standard, and a reference to the temperature limitations of conductors is made in the parent text.

Author's Comment:

▸ There is a general shift toward replacing the word "rating" (as it pertains to conductors) throughout the *Code* with the more precise term "ampacity," as demonstrated here and again in 230.23 and 230.42.

230.31 Underground Service Conductor Size and Ampacity

(A) General. Underground service conductors must have sufficient ampacity to carry the load as calculated in accordance with Article 220. ▶Figure 230–1

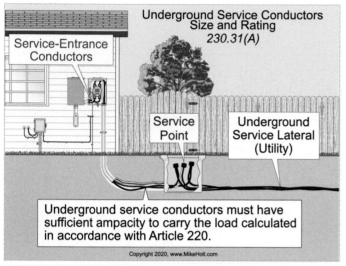

▶Figure 230–1

230.42 Conductor Sizing

(A) General. Conductors must be sized to carry not less than the largest of the calculations contained in 230.42(A)(1) or (2).

Conductor ampacity must be determined in accordance with 310.14 and the conductors must be sized to the terminal temperature rating in accordance with 110.14(C)(1). ▶Figure 230–2

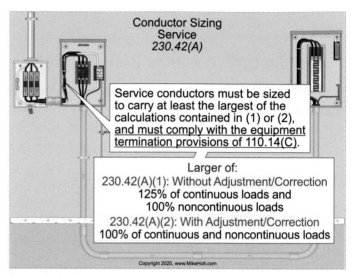

▶Figure 230–2

230.42 Minimum Size and Ampacity

This section, regarding the minimum sizing of service-entrance conductors, has the same editorial title change (from "Rating" to "Ampacity") as 230.31. The same revisions were made throughout to correlate with the global effort to use the more correct terminology. A new Informational Note concerning busways was also added.

Analysis

EDITED The word "Rating" alone, is too broad a term to be associated with conductors. Rating can mean many things without being prefaced with another word such as "temperature." When used by itself it can even mean tensile strength! "Ampacity" is more precise and leaves no doubt. The redundant term "Allowable" was removed, the Informational Note added to (A) references a UL Standard, and a reference to the temperature limitations of conductors was made in the parent text.

230.43 Wiring Methods

An additional wiring method, Type TC-ER cable, was added to the permitted wiring methods for service-entrance conductors.

Analysis

EXPANDED This section listed 19 wiring methods permitted to be used for service-entrance conductors. Added to this list is number 20, Type TC-ER cable which is mechanically equivalent to Type SE cable. The testing required for TC-ER cable by the product standards is at least equal to, and in some case more stringent than, what is required for Type SE cable.

230.43 Wiring Methods

Service-entrance conductors can be installed with any of the following wiring methods:

(1) Open wiring on insulators.

(3) Rigid metal conduit (RMC).

(4) Intermediate metal conduit (IMC).

(5) Electrical metallic tubing (EMT).

(6) Electrical nonmetallic tubing (ENT).

(7) Service-entrance cables.

(8) Wireways.

(11) PVC conduit.

(13) Type MC cable.

(15) Flexible metal conduit (FMC) or liquidtight flexible metal conduit (LFMC) in lengths not longer than 6 ft.

(16) Liquidtight flexible nonmetallic conduit (LFNC). ▸Figure 230–3

(17) High-density polyethylene conduit (HDPE).

(18) Nonmetallic underground conduit with conductors (NUCC).

(19) Reinforced thermosetting resin conduit (RTRC).

(20) Type TC-ER cable.

Wiring Methods, Service-Entrance Conductors
230.43(16)

Service-entrance conductors can be installed in LFNC.

Copyright 2020, www.MikeHolt.com

▸Figure 230–3

Author's Comment:

▸ The outer jacket of Type TC-ER cable is 50 percent thicker than the jacket on Type SE cable, and the inner conductors are constructed to the same standards as the inner connectors of Type SE cable. It stands to reason that the use of Type TC-ER cable should be permitted.

230.44 Cable Trays

There are a variety of wiring methods suitable to be used for service entrances. Type TC-ER cable was added to the five other types of service-entrance cables that are permitted to be installed in cable tray.

Analysis

EXPANDED

As a part of the previous section being changed to permit the use of Type TC-ER cable as service conductors, that wiring method was added to the list of service conductor wiring methods permitted to be installed in cable tray.

The other wiring methods that are permitted to be supported by cable trays are Type SE, Type MC, Type MI, Type IGS, and single conductors 1/0 and larger that are listed for use in cable tray.

230.46 Spliced Conductors

Using power distribution blocks with higher termination temperature limitations allowing for the use of smaller conductors has become a cost-effective way of installing larger services. When used ahead of the service disconnect, these power distribution blocks must be marked suitable for this purpose; however, the *NEC* has extended enforcement of this rule until the next *Code* cycle giving manufacturer's ample time to comply with this new requirement. This section was expanded to include requirements for the devices used to splice or tap service conductors.

Analysis

EXPANDED This change requires power distribution blocks, pressure connectors, and devices for splices and taps to be listed. It also requires power distribution blocks installed on service conductors to be marked as suitable for that use. Power distribution blocks marked as "suitable for use on the line side of the service equipment" are evaluated without an overcurrent protective device and are subjected to short-circuit current for a duration of no less than three electrical cycles.

230.46 Spliced Conductors

Service-entrance conductors can be spliced or tapped in accordance with 110.14, 300.5(E), 300.13, and 300.15.

Pressure connectors and devices for splices and taps must be listed. Power distribution blocks installed on service conductors must be listed and marked "suitable for use on the line side of the service equipment" or equivalent. ▶Figure 230–4

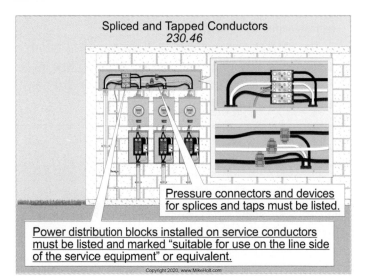

Spliced and Tapped Conductors
230.46

Pressure connectors and devices for splices and taps must be listed.

Power distribution blocks installed on service conductors must be listed and marked "suitable for use on the line side of the service equipment" or equivalent.

Copyright 2020, www.MikeHolt.com

▶Figure 230–4

Note: Effective January 1, 2023, pressure connectors and devices for splices and taps installed on service conductors must be marked "suitable for use on the line side of the service equipment" or equivalent.

Author's Comment:

▸ Because power distribution blocks are secured to the enclosure, they must have the ability to withstand opposing forces so that conductors do not pull out of the terminals and potentially short circuit to each other or to ground during a short-circuit condition.

▸ The same opposing forces are in effect for devices used for splicing and tapping service conductors. The current product standards and testing do not evaluate for these forces and as a result, a new requirement effective (January 1, 2023) states that pressure connectors and devices for splices and taps installed on service conductors must be marked "suitable for use on the line side of the service equipment" or the equivalent.

▸ It is important to note that when the *Code* sites a future effective date it gives the industry manufacturers, designers, installers, and building owners an opportunity to adjust and be prepared for the anticipated change.

230.62 Service Equipment— Enclosed or Guarded

No matter how many times we are told to de-energize and never work on "hot" electrical equipment, there are times where shutting down is not an option. This new rule requires uninsulated service-phase busbars or terminals to be protected from inadvertent contact by barriers. This, along with the proper personal protective equipment (PPE), will help protect service technicians.

Analysis

NEW **230.62(C) Barriers.** A new subsection (C) was added to require barriers to be placed in service equipment so no uninsulated, phase busbar, or terminal is exposed to inadvertent contact while servicing load side terminations. The same hazard exists in enclosed circuit breakers, transfer switches suitable for use as service equipment, enclosed switches, MCCs marked as suitable for service equipment, and industrial control panels marked as suitable for use as service equipment. This revision requires all types of service equipment to have the energized parts protected from accidental contact.

230.62 Service Equipment—Enclosed or Guarded

(C) Barriers. Barriers must be placed in service equipment so that no uninsulated, ungrounded service busbar or service terminal is exposed to inadvertent contact by persons or maintenance equipment while servicing load terminations. ▶Figure 230–5

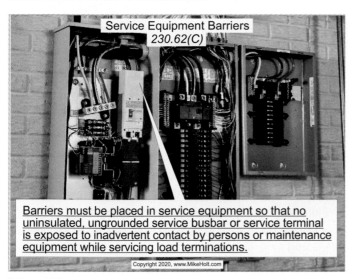

Service Equipment Barriers
230.62(C)

Barriers must be placed in service equipment so that no uninsulated, ungrounded service busbar or service terminal is exposed to inadvertent contact by persons or maintenance equipment while servicing load terminations.

Copyright 2020, www.MikeHolt.com

▶Figure 230–5

Author's Comment:

▶ This new rule expands on the (now deleted) requirement that was found in 408.3(A) requiring barriers over service busbars or terminals in panelboards, switchboards, and switchgear.

230.66 Marking for Service Disconnect

Service equipment must be listed or field evaluated. It has pretty much always been required to be listed; but, on occasions when service equipment is assembled or constructed in the field listing is not possible. The components may be listed for the purpose but once assembled it becomes a single unlisted item. This is where the FEB or "Field Evaluation Body" comes in. A field evaluation can be conducted and that documented field evaluation result will suffice.

Analysis

CLARIFIED   REORGANIZED

This section has been separated into two subsections and editorially revised.

The text in (A) clarifies that the service equipment must either be listed, or field evaluated. The 2017 *NEC* said listed or "field labeled." Field labeling is just part of the process of a field evaluation. A field evaluation requires several steps, the last of which is the labeling.

The text in (B) clarifies that meter sockets are not service equipment but must be listed for the voltage and ampacity of the service. Separating this section into two subsections adds clarity and ease of use to the *Code*.

230.66 Marking for Service Disconnect

(A) General. The service disconnect must be marked to identify it as being suitable as service equipment and be listed or field evaluated. ▶Figure 230–6

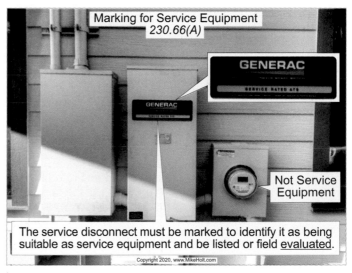

Marking for Service Equipment
230.66(A)

GENERAC

Not Service Equipment

The service disconnect must be marked to identify it as being suitable as service equipment and be listed or field evaluated.

Copyright 2020, www.MikeHolt.com

▶Figure 230–6

Author's Comment:

▸ A proper field evaluation is completed by a Field Evaluation Body (FEB). These procedures include selection of the correct nationally recognized standard, conducting a complete evaluation of construction, performing applicable field testing, and completing documentation in formal engineering reports to both the client and the authority having jurisdiction. When the process is completed with satisfactory results, then the "field label" of the FEB may be applied.

▸ An FEB is an organization or part of an organization complying with NFPA 790 *Standard for Competency of Third-Party Field Evaluation Bodies* and NFPA 791 *Recommended Practice and Procedures for Unlabeled Electrical Equipment Evaluation*. Each FEB may be uniquely qualified in one or more electrical fields of expertise. It is important to remember the certifications of said FEB's must cover the specific type of evaluation solicited.

(B) Meter Sockets. Meter sockets must be listed and rated for the voltage and current rating of the service. ▸Figure 230–7

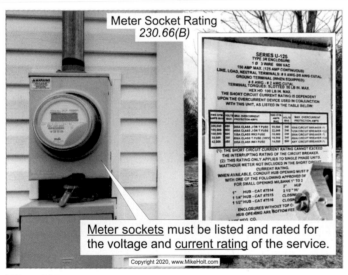

Meter Socket Rating
230.66(B)

Meter sockets must be listed and rated for the voltage and current rating of the service.

Copyright 2020, www.MikeHolt.com

▸Figure 230–7

Ex: Meter socket enclosures supplied by and under the exclusive control of a serving electric utility are not required to be listed.

230.67 Surge Protection

This new section requiring the installation of a surge-protective device (SPD) for all dwelling unit services has been a long time coming. Up until now, dwelling unit surge protection has been optional and usually an "extra" for the electrician.

Analysis

NEW This requirement is being driven by the increasing amount of sensitive electronic equipment found in dwelling units. Electronic life safety equipment such as fire alarm systems, AFCIs, GFCIs, and smoke alarms, as well as consumer electronic devices such as computers and televisions can all be damaged by voltage surges. Studies by NEMA, IEEE, and UL all show that surges cause a significant amount of damage. The text in (B) requires the SPD to be an integral part of the service equipment or located immediately adjacent to that equipment. There is an exception that permits the SPD to be located at the next level downstream distribution equipment.

230.67 Surge Protection

Scan this QR code for a video of Mike explaining this topic; it's a sample from the videos that accompany this textbook.

(A) Surge-protective Device. All services supplying dwelling units must be provided with a surge-protective device.

(B) Location. The surge-protective device must be an integral part of the service disconnect or be located immediately adjacent to the service disconnect. ▸Figure 230–8

Ex: The surge-protective device is permitted to be located in the downstream panelboard.

Author's Comment:

▸ An example of where the exception could be applied is where there is an exterior meter main that feeds an interior panel. The SPD could be installed at the interior panel using the exception.

▸ See Parts I and II of Article 242 for the installation requirements that apply to SPDs.

Required Dwelling Unit Surge Protective Device Location
230.67(B)

The required surge protective device for a dwelling unit must be an integral part of the service equipment or be located immediately adjacent to the service equipment.

Copyright 2020, www.MikeHolt.com

▶Figure 230–8

(C) Type. The surge-protective device must be a Type 1 or Type 2 SPD.

(D) Replacement. Where service equipment is replaced, surge protection must be installed.

230.70 Service Disconnect Requirements

This rule was revised to clarify that only the phase conductors need to be disconnected from the service conductors, thereby prohibiting the neutral conductor from being part of this disconnection.

Analysis

CLARIFIED The language of this section was revised to clarify that the service disconnect is only required to disconnect the building's phase conductors from the service conductors. While never the intent of the rule, the previous language required all the building's conductors to be disconnected from the service conductors—including the neutral conductor.

The word "entrance" was deleted as some types of services, such as a meter main, do not have service-entrance conductors.

230.70 Service Disconnect Requirements

The service disconnect must open all phase conductors.

230.71 Number of Service Disconnects

A service is permitted to have only one disconnecting means; however, the number of service disconnects can vary based on the number of disconnects, the grouping, and special circumstances which permit more than one service disconnect.

Analysis

EXPANDED This is a major change. The new parent language says that each service must have only one disconnecting means unless the requirements of 230.71(B) are met. All the language in (A) that related to the permission to have up to six service disconnects was deleted. It now just lists the four equipment disconnecting means that are part of listed service equipment but not considered to be service disconnects; this part of the rule is unchanged.

Subsection (B) specifies the conditions under which you are permitted to have more than one service disconnect. The use of two or three single-pole devices with identified handle ties to serve as service disconnects was previously permitted. Each set of single-pole devices that could be operated with a single operation of the hand was considered a single service discontent. All that language was removed. There are no longer any provisions permitting single-pole devices with handle ties to be used as service disconnects.

The new text of (B) allows the use of two to six service disconnects for each service permitted by 230.2, or for each set of service-entrance conductors as permitted by 230.40 Ex 1, 3, 4, or 5.

230.71 Number of Service Disconnects

 Scan this QR code for a video of Mike explaining this topic; it's a sample from the videos that accompany this textbook.

Each service must have only one disconnecting means except as permitted in 230.71(B).

(A) General. For the purpose of this section, a disconnecting means installed as part of listed equipment and used solely for the following is not considered a service disconnecting means:

(1) Power monitoring equipment.

(2) Surge-protective device(s).

(3) Control circuit of the ground-fault protection system.

(4) Power-operable service disconnect.

(B) Two to Six Service Disconnecting Means. Up to six service disconnects are permitted for each service allowed by 230.2, or for each set of service-entrance conductors permitted by 230.40 Ex 1, 3, 4, or 5.

The two to six service disconnecting means may consist of a combination of any of the following:

(1) Separate enclosures with a main service disconnecting means in each enclosure

(2) Panelboards with a main service disconnecting means in each panelboard

(3) Switchboard(s) where there is only one service disconnect in each separate vertical section where there are barriers separating each vertical section

(4) Service disconnects in switchgear or metering centers where each disconnect is located in a separate compartment

Note 2: Examples of separate enclosures with main service disconnecting means in each enclosure include but are not limited to, motor control centers, fused disconnects, circuit breaker enclosures, and transfer switches that are suitable for use as service equipment.

Author's Comment:

▶ The rule is six disconnects for each service, not for each building. If the building has two services, then there can be a total of 12 service disconnects (six disconnects per service). ▶Figure 230–9

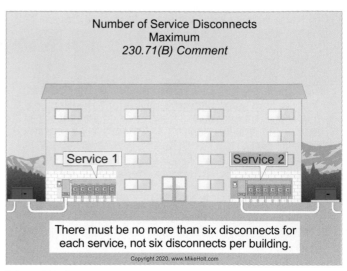

▶Figure 230–9

Author's Comment:

▶ This revision retains the previous permission to have 2 to 6 service disconnects for each service or each set of service-entrance conductors but provides the increase in safety that a single service disconnect provides. The previous six main disconnect rule for a single enclosure made it impossible to work in service equipment when applying electrical safe work practices in accordance with NFPA 70E, unless the line side of the multi-disconnect enclosure was disconnected by the utility.

▶ This revision also reflects the electrical hazards inherent while working on service equipment where there is more than one service disconnect in a single enclosure. This, combined with the rule in 230.62(C) that requires line side barriers, is a significant safety improvement towards reducing the risk to electricians by limiting their exposure to energized parts.

230.82 Connected on Supply Side of the Service Disconnect

Emergency disconnect switches, as required by 230.85, and meter-mounted transfer switches were added to the list of equipment that can be connected on the supply side of the service disconnect. When this is done ahead of metering equipment it is called "cold sequencing."

Many utility companies are not particularly fond of this practice because it allows the consumer to de-energize the electrical service before the metering equipment. This obviously creates security concerns because, while these disconnects are designed to be used in case of emergency, not everyone's intent may be so noble.

Analysis

CLARIFIED Modifications were made to four of the previous nine list items, and two new ones were added. There were minor editorial changes to item (3) for meter disconnects and item (5) for conductors. Item (6) was modified to the extent of suitability of disconnects for electric power production sources. The new list item (10) permits an emergency disconnect switch to be installed on the line side of the actual service disconnect, provided that all metal housings and service enclosures are bonded and grounded in accordance with Parts V and VII of Article 250.

The new list item (11) was added to permit the installation of meter-mounted transfer switches, provided they have a short-circuit current rating equal to or greater than the available fault current.

230.82 Connected on Supply Side of the Service Disconnect

Only the following electrical equipment is permitted to be connected to the supply side of the service disconnect:

(3) Meter disconnect switches are permitted to be connected to the supply side of the service disconnect, and they must be legibly field marked on the exterior in a manner suitable for the environment as follows: **METER DISCONNECT—NOT SERVICE EQUIPMENT** ▶Figure 230–10

Author's Comment:

▸ Some electric utilities require a disconnect switch ahead of the meter enclosure for 277/480V services for the purpose of enhancing safety for serving electric utility personnel when they install or remove a meter socket.

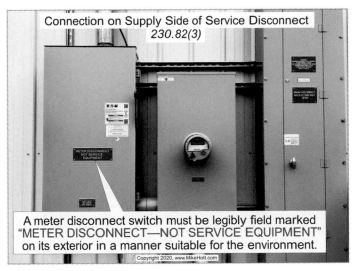

Connection on Supply Side of Service Disconnect
230.82(3)

A meter disconnect switch must be legibly field marked "METER DISCONNECT—NOT SERVICE EQUIPMENT" on its exterior in a manner suitable for the environment.

Copyright 2020, www.MikeHolt.com

▶Figure 230–10

(5) Conductors for legally required and optional standby power systems, fire pump equipment, fire and sprinkler alarms, and load (energy) management devices can be connected to the supply side of the service disconnect enclosure. ▶Figure 230–11

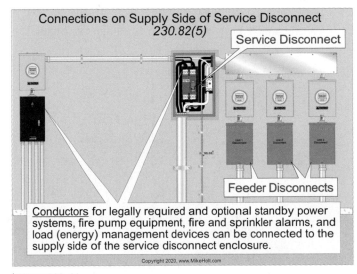

Connections on Supply Side of Service Disconnect
230.82(5)

Service Disconnect

Feeder Disconnects

Conductors for legally required and optional standby power systems, fire pump equipment, fire and sprinkler alarms, and load (energy) management devices can be connected to the supply side of the service disconnect enclosure.

Copyright 2020, www.MikeHolt.com

▶Figure 230–11

(6) Solar PV systems, wind electric systems, energy storage systems, or interconnected power production sources can be connected to the supply side of the service disconnect enclosure if provided with a disconnecting means listed as suitable for use as service equipment, and overcurrent protection as specified in Part VII of Article 230. ▶Figure 230–12

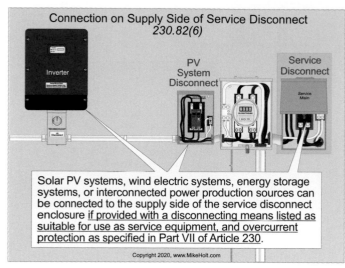

Connection on Supply Side of Service Disconnect
230.82(6)

Inverter

PV System Disconnect

Service Disconnect

Solar PV systems, wind electric systems, energy storage systems, or interconnected power production sources can be connected to the supply side of the service disconnect enclosure if provided with a disconnecting means listed as suitable for use as service equipment, and overcurrent protection as specified in Part VII of Article 230.

Copyright 2020, www.MikeHolt.com

▶Figure 230–12

(10)   Emergency disconnects in accordance with 230.85.

(11)   Meter-mounted transfer switches that have a short-circuit current rating equal to or greater than the available fault current. A meter-mounted transfer switch must be listed and be capable of transferring the load served. A meter-mounted transfer switch must be marked on its exterior the following manner: ▶Figure 230–13

(a) Meter-mounted transfer switch

(b) Not service equipment

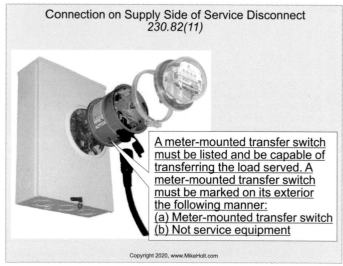

Connection on Supply Side of Service Disconnect
230.82(11)

A meter-mounted transfer switch must be listed and be capable of transferring the load served. A meter-mounted transfer switch must be marked on its exterior the following manner:
(a) Meter-mounted transfer switch
(b) Not service equipment

Copyright 2020, www.MikeHolt.com

▶Figure 230–13

230.85 Emergency Disconnects

One- and two-family dwelling units are now required to have an "emergency disconnect" installed in a readily accessible exterior location in accordance with 230.85. Finally! Firefighters can respond to a fully engulfed residence and turn the electric supply to the building off without potentially standing in a pool of electrified water!

Analysis

NEW   This new section requires that an "emergency disconnect" be installed at a readily accessible outdoor location at all one- and two-family dwelling units. The rule is driven by the needs of first responders to have a safe and effective way of removing power from the dwelling unit in the event of an emergency.

The parent text requires the disconnect to have a short-circuit rating equal to or greater than the available fault current and, where there are multiple disconnects, they must be grouped together.

230.85 Emergency Disconnects

For one- and two-family dwelling units, all service conductors must terminate in a disconnecting means having a short-circuit current rating equal to or greater than the available fault current and installed in a readily accessible outdoor location. If more than one disconnect is provided, they must be grouped. Each disconnect must be one of the following:

(1) Service disconnects marked: **EMERGENCY DISCONNECT, SERVICE DISCONNECT**

(2) Meter disconnects installed in accordance with 230.82(3) must be marked: **EMERGENCY DISCONNECT, METER DISCONNECT, NOT SERVICE EQUIPMENT**

(3) Other listed disconnect switches or circuit breakers on the load side of the meter and supply side of each service disconnect marked: **EMERGENCY DISCONNECT, NOT SERVICE EQUIPMENT**

Markings must be permanently affixed and have sufficient durability to withstand the environment involved in accordance with 110.21(B).

Author's Comment:

▸ Option (1) permits an outside service disconnect to be both the service disconnect and the emergency disconnect. In some areas it is already common to locate the service disconnect on the exterior and the only thing that changes in those cases is the new marking that is required.

▸ Option (2) permits a meter disconnect to serve as the required emergency disconnect. This is useful where the utility has required the installation of a meter disconnect. The meter disconnect must be installed in accordance with the requirements of 230.83(3) and must be marked.

▸ Option (3) provides for the installation of other listed disconnect switches or circuit breakers that are suitable for use as service disconnects and are marked as such.

OVERCURRENT PROTECTION

Introduction to Article 240—Overcurrent Protection

This article provides the requirements for overcurrent protection and selecting and installing overcurrent protective devices—typically circuit breakers or fuses. Overcurrent exists when current exceeds the rating of equipment or the ampacity of a conductor due to an overload, short circuit, or ground fault [Article 100 Definitions].

▸ **Overload.** An overload is a condition where equipment or conductors carry current exceeding their current rating [Article 100 Definitions]. A fault, such as a short circuit or ground fault, is not an overload. An example of an overload is plugging two 12.50A (1,500W) hair dryers into a 20A branch circuit.

▸ **Short Circuit.** A short circuit is the unintentional electrical connection between any two normally current-carrying conductors of an electrical circuit, either line-to-line or line-to-neutral.

▸ **Ground Fault.** A ground fault is an unintentional, electrically conducting connection between a phase conductor of an electrical circuit and the normally noncurrent-carrying conductors, metal enclosures, metal raceways, metal equipment, or the Earth [Article 100 Definitions]. During the period of a ground fault, dangerous voltages will be present on metal parts until the circuit overcurrent protective device opens.

Overcurrent protective devices protect conductors and equipment. Selecting the proper overcurrent protection for a specific circuit can be more complicated than it sounds. The general rule for overcurrent protection is that conductors must be protected in accordance with their ampacities at the point where they receive their supply [240.4 and 240.21]. The asterisks next to the small conductor sizes in Table 310.16 refer to a footnote directing you to 240.4(D). That section contains the general rules for small conductors which limit the rating of the overcurrent devices protecting them. There are quite a few circumstances that deviate from this and seem to "break" those rules for small conductors. Table 240.4(G) lists articles in the *Code* that modify the basic requirements of 240.4(D). There are also several rules allowing tap conductors (with much lower ampacities more than the overcurrent device protecting them seems to allow) in specific situations [240.21(B)].

Author's Comment:

▸ The tripping action of an overcurrent protective device during an overload is based on a "time curve," which essentially means that the higher the current, the faster the device will trip. Because of this time curve, conductors with lower ampacities than the overcurrent protective device protecting them, may seem to break the rules, but they will only see the overcurrent condition for a very short and safe amount of time.

An overcurrent protective device must be capable of opening a circuit when an overcurrent situation occurs and must also have an interrupting rating sufficient to avoid damage in fault conditions [110.9]. Carefully study this article to be sure you provide enough overcurrent protection in the correct location(s).

240.2 Definitions

As a part of the global reorganization of the definitions this *Code* cycle, new parent text was added to say that the definitions in this section apply only within Article 240. Also, in order to ensure clarity and consistent enforcement, the term "Reconditioned" is defined here as well as in Article 100.

Analysis

CLARIFIED This revision is part of the efforts of a global task group that was assigned to look at how definitions in Article 100 and the "xxx.2" sections apply. The *NEC Style Manual* requires that, in general, where terms appear in two or more articles the definitions must be in Article 100. The task group says it is extremely important to understand that the style manual does not prohibit a definition located in an "xxx.2" section from applying elsewhere in the *Code*.

NEW **Reconditioned.** This definition was added to Article 100 and 240.2 as it is critical with respect to the application of the requirements within Article 240 for the reconditioning of overcurrent protective devices.

This term appears in numerous locations and must be defined and its definition was taken from the NEMA document which, as written, is unacceptable because it contains requirements. This wording retains the essential elements from the NEMA definition without including requirements that may need to be developed in future *Code* editions. The wording also clearly distinguishes routine maintenance and also one-for-one part replacements from reconditioning. For additional clarity this also incorporates an adaptation of the Informational Note that CMP-1 added to 110.21(B)(2) relative to other terminology that is often used interchangeably.

240.5 Protection of Flexible Cords, Flexible Cables, and Fixture Wires

The conductors in most fixtures are usually smaller than those of ordinary branch circuits which are protected by 15A and 20A overcurrent devices. The language highlighted that 16AWG and 18 AWG fixture wire can be protected with a 15A overcurrent protective device (OCPD) in addition to the previously permitted 20A OCPD. This makes sense but as we all know, if it is not permitted by the *Code* it cannot be done!

Analysis

CLARIFIED **240.5(B)(2) Fixture Wire.** In the 2017 *NEC*, the use of 18 AWG up to 50 ft and 16 AWG up to 100 ft was only permitted where the branch-circuit OCPD was rated 20A. The language did not permit this where the branch-circuit OCPD was rated at 15A. Two list items were modified to apply to either 15A or 20A branch circuits. It made no sense to permit these small conductors to be protected by a 20A OCPD but not by one rated 15A.

240.5 Protection of Flexible Cords, Flexible Cables and Fixture Wires

Flexible cord and flexible cable, including tinsel cord and extension cords, and fixture wires must be protected against overcurrent by either 240.5(A) or (B).

(A) Ampacities. Flexible cord and flexible cable must be protected by an overcurrent device in accordance with their ampacity as specified in Table 400.5(A)(1) and Table 400.5(A)(2). Fixture wire must be protected against overcurrent in accordance with its ampacity as specified in Table 402.5. Supplementary overcurrent protection, as covered in 240.10, is permitted to be an acceptable means for providing this protection.

(B) Branch-Circuit Overcurrent Device. Flexible cord must be protected, where supplied by a branch circuit, in accordance with one of the methods described in 240.5(B)(1), (B)(3), or (B)(4). Fixture wire must be protected, where supplied by a branch circuit, in accordance with 240.5(B)(2).

(1) Supply Cord of Listed Appliance or Luminaire. Where flexible cord or tinsel cord is approved for and used with a specific listed appliance or luminaire, it is considered to be protected when applied within the appliance or luminaire listing requirements. For the purposes of this section, a luminaire may be either portable or permanent.

(2) Fixture Wire. Fixture wire is permitted to be tapped to the branch-circuit conductor of a branch circuit in accordance with the following:

(1) 15- or 20-ampere circuits — <u>18 AWG</u>, up to 15 m (50 ft) of run length

(2) 15- or 20-ampere circuits — <u>16 AWG</u>, up to 30 m (100 ft) of run length

> **Author's Comment:**
>
> ▸ This section is often overlooked, but it is what permits us to make fixture whips using conductors with an ampacity that is less than the rating of the branch-circuit OCPD. However, it only applies where you are using fixture wire.

240.6 Standard Ampere Ratings

Adjustable circuit breakers require a high level of expertise when determining their settings. In order to keep unqualified personnel from making inaccurate and possibly dangerous adjustments, preventative measures need to be in place. A fourth method of restricting access (password protection) was added for these adjustable trip circuit breakers.

Analysis

CLARIFIED **240.6(C) Restricted Access Adjustable Trip Circuit Breakers.** This section permits the use of adjustable trip circuit breakers at their adjusted set point where the access to the adjustment is restricted. There were three types of restriction in the 2017 *NEC*, and the 2020 *Code* is adding a fourth. The original three were all physical restrictions and required the adjusting means to be "located behind" removable and sealable covers, bolted equipment enclosure doors, or locked doors accessible only to qualified persons. The "located behind" was in the parent text, but since the newly added restriction is not a physical one, the "located behind" had to be removed from the parent text and was added in each of the first three list items. This part of the change is just editorial.

240.6 Standard Ampere Ratings

(C) Adjustable Trip Circuit Breakers, Restricted Access. The ampere rating of adjustable trip circuit breakers with restricted access to the adjusting means is equal to the adjusted long-time pickup current settings. Restricted access is <u>achieved by</u> one of the following <u>methods</u>:

(1) <u>Locating behind removable</u> and sealable covers over the adjusting means

(2) <u>Locating behind bolted</u> equipment enclosure doors

(3) <u>Locating behind locked</u> doors accessible only to qualified personnel

(4) Being <u>password protected with the password only accessible to qualified personnel</u>

> **Author's Comment:**
>
> ▸ The new list item (4) recognizes that modern electronic trip circuit breakers may have the ability to set a password to restrict access to the adjusting means. It in turn permits a password to serve the purpose of preventing unauthorized users from changing the trip settings.

240.21 Location in Circuit

Feeder circuits are permitted to be protected at a much higher rated current than the individual loads they might serve, but the loads and the smaller conductors feeding them still need to be protected as well. This protection is provided by a suitably rated overcurrent device for the smaller demand load. This rule was revised to clarify that these types of taps are permitted at any point on the load side of the feeder OCPD.

Analysis

CLARIFIED **240.21(B) Feeder Taps.** This should clear up any confusion as to originating a feeder tap on the load termination of the feeder OCPD. The change is intended clarify that the tap can originate on the breaker termination point.

240.21 Location in Circuit

(B) Feeder Taps. Conductors are permitted to be tapped, without overcurrent protection at the tap, to a feeder as specified in 240.21(B)(1) through (B)(5). The tap is permitted at any point on the load side of the feeder overcurrent protective device. ▸Figure 240–1 and ▸Figure 240–2

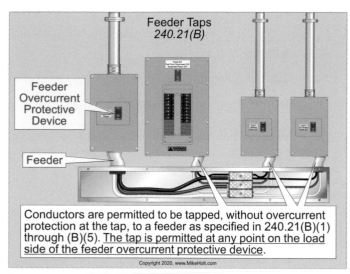

Feeder Taps
240.21(B)

Conductors are permitted to be tapped, without overcurrent protection at the tap, to a feeder as specified in 240.21(B)(1) through (B)(5). The tap is permitted at any point on the load side of the feeder overcurrent protective device.

Copyright 2020, www.MikeHolt.com

▸Figure 240–1

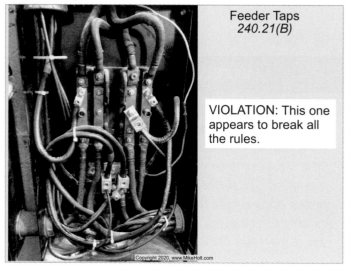

Feeder Taps
240.21(B)

VIOLATION: This one appears to break all the rules.

Copyright 2020, www.MikeHolt.com

▸Figure 240–2

(1) Feeder Tap Not Over 10 Feet. Tap conductors up to 10 ft long are permitted when they comply with the following:

(1) Tap conductors have an ampacity equal to or greater than: ▸Figure 240–3

   a. The calculated load in accordance with Article 220, and

   b. The rating of the overcurrent device or the equipment supplied by the tap conductors.

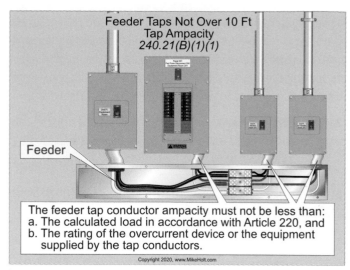

Feeder Taps Not Over 10 Ft
Tap Ampacity
240.21(B)(1)(1)

Feeder

The feeder tap conductor ampacity must not be less than:
a. The calculated load in accordance with Article 220, and
b. The rating of the overcurrent device or the equipment supplied by the tap conductors.

Copyright 2020, www.MikeHolt.com

▸Figure 240–3

(2) The tap conductors are not permitted to extend beyond the equipment they supply.

(3) The tap conductors are installed within a raceway.

(4) Tap conductors that leave the enclosure where the tap is made must have an ampacity not less than 10 percent of the rating of the overcurrent device that protects the feeder. ▸Figure 240–4

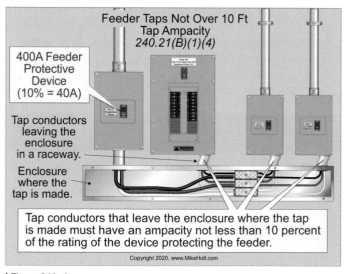

Feeder Taps Not Over 10 Ft
Tap Ampacity
240.21(B)(1)(4)

400A Feeder Protective Device (10% = 40A)

Tap conductors leaving the enclosure in a raceway.

Enclosure where the tap is made.

Tap conductors that leave the enclosure where the tap is made must have an ampacity not less than 10 percent of the rating of the device protecting the feeder.

Copyright 2020, www.MikeHolt.com

▸Figure 240–4

Note: If a tap supplies a panelboard, the tap conductors must terminate into an overcurrent device in accordance with 408.36.

10-Foot Tap Rule

▸ **10-Foot Tap Rule Example 1**

Question: What size 10-ft tap is needed from a 400A circuit breaker to supply a 200A panelboard if the terminals are rated 75°C? ▸**Figure 240–5**

(a) 1/0 AWG   (b) 2/0 AWG   (c) 3/0 AWG   (d) 4/0 AWG

Answer: (c) 3/0 AWG

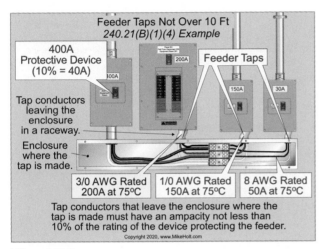

▸Figure 240–5

Solution:

3/0 AWG is rated 200A at 75°C [110.14(C)(1) and Table 310.16] which is greater than 10 percent of the rating of the 400A over-current protective device.

▸ **10-Foot Tap Rule Example 2**

Question: What size 10-ft tap is needed from a 400A circuit breaker to supply a 150A feeder disconnect if the terminals are rated 75°C? ▸**Figure 240–6**

(a) 1/0 AWG   (b) 2/0 AWG   (c) 3/0 AWG   (d) 4/0 AWG

Answer: (a) 1/0 AWG

Solution:

Ten Percent of 400A = 40A minimum conductor ampacity permitted.

1/0 AWG is rated 150A at 75°C [110.14(C)(1) and Table 310.16] which is greater than 10 percent of the rating of the 400A over-current protective device.

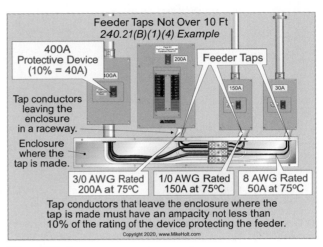

▸Figure 240–6

▸ **10-Foot Tap Rule Example 3**

Question: What size 10-ft tap is needed from a 400A circuit breaker to supply a 30A feeder disconnect if the terminals are rated 75°C? ▸**Figure 240–7**

(a) 8 AWG   (b) 6 AWG   (c) 4 AWG   (d) 3 AWG

Answer: (a) 8 AWG

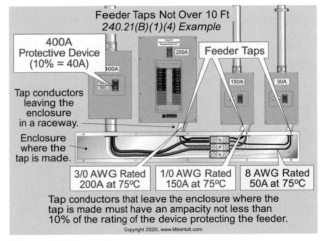

▸Figure 240–7

Solution:

8 AWG is rated 50A at 75°C [110.14(C)(1) and Table 310.16] which is greater than 10 percent of the rating of the 400A over-current device.

(2) Feeder Tap Not Over 25 Feet. Tap conductors up to 25 ft long are permitted when they comply with the following: ▸**Figure 240–8**

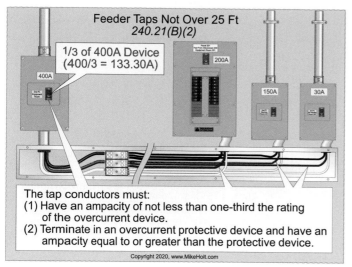

▶Figure 240–8

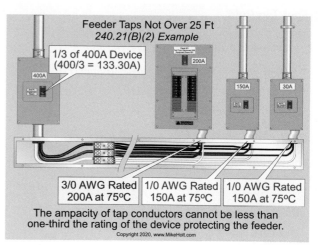

▶Figure 240–9

(1) The tap has an ampacity not less than ⅓ the rating of the overcurrent protective device that protects the feeder.

(2) The tap conductors terminate in an overcurrent protective device, and the tap conductors have an ampacity equal to or greater than the rating of the overcurrent protective device.

25-Foot Tap Rule

▶ **25-Foot Tap Example 1**

Question: *What size 25-ft tap is needed from a 400A circuit breaker to supply a 200A panelboard if the terminals are rated 75°C?* ▶Figure 240–9

(a) 1/0 AWG   (b) 2/0 AWG   (c) 3/0 AWG   (d) 4/0 AWG

Answer: (c) 3/0 AWG

Solution:

The tap conductor must have a minimum rating of no less than 133A (⅓ the rating of the 400A overcurrent device). 3/0 AWG is rated 200A at 75°C [110.14(C)(1) and Table 310.16] which is greater than 133A (⅓ the rating of the 400A overcurrent device) and equal to the 200A disconnect.

▶ **25-Foot Tap Example 2**

Question: *What size 25-ft tap is needed from a 400A circuit breaker to supply a 150A feeder disconnect if the terminals are rated 75°C?* ▶Figure 240–10

(a) 1/0 AWG   (b) 2/0 AWG   (c) 3/0 AWG   (d) 4/0 AWG

Answer: (a) 1/0 AWG

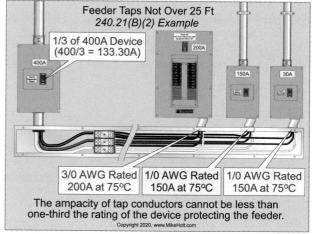

▶Figure 240–10

Solution:

The tap conductor must have a minimum rating of no less than 133A (⅓ the rating of the 400A overcurrent device).

1/0 AWG is rated 150A at 75°C [110.14(C)(1) and Table 310.16] which is greater than 133A (⅓ the rating of the 400A overcurrent device) and equal to the 150A disconnect.

▶ 25-Foot Tap Example 3

Question: What size 25-ft tap is needed from a 400A circuit breaker to supply a 30A feeder disconnect if the terminals are rated 75°C? ▶Figure 240–11

(a) 3 AWG   (b) 2 AWG   (c) 1 AWG   (d) 1/0 AWG

Answer: (d) 1/0 AWG

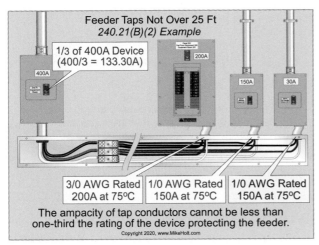

▶Figure 240–11

Solution:

The tap conductor must have a minimum rating of no less than 133A (⅓ the rating of the 400A overcurrent protective device). 1/0 AWG is rated 150A at 75°C [110.14(C)(1) and Table 310.16] which is greater than 133A (⅓ the rating of the 400A overcurrent device) and greater than the 100A panelboard main breaker.

(3) Taps Supplying a Transformer (Primary Plus Secondary Not Over 25 Feet).
Primary tap conductors are permitted to supply a transformer if the installation complies with all the following conditions:

(1) The primary tap conductors to the transformer have an ampacity at least one-third the rating of the overcurrent device that protects the primary of the transformer.

(2) The secondary conductors have an ampacity of no less than the value of the primary-to-secondary voltage ratio multiplied by one-third the rating of the overcurrent device protecting the primary of the transformer.

(3) The total length of the primary tap conductor and the secondary conductor does not exceed 25 ft.

(4) The primary and secondary conductors are protected from physical damage by being enclosed in a raceway or other approved means.

(5) The secondary conductors terminate in an overcurrent device, and the secondary conductors have an ampacity rating equal to or greater than the rating of the overcurrent protective device.

(5) Outside Feeder Taps. Outside tap conductors can be of unlimited length if they comply with all of the following: ▶Figure 240–12

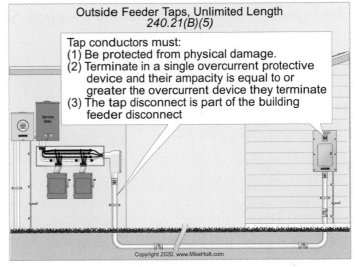

▶Figure 240–12

(1) The outside tap conductors are protected from physical damage.

(2) The outside tap conductors terminate in a single overcurrent protective device and their ampacity is equal to or greater than the overcurrent device into which they terminate.

(3) The tap overcurrent device is part of the building feeder disconnect.

240.24 Location of Overcurrent Protective Devices at Premises

Whether circuit breakers or fuses are used, overcurrent protective devices must be readily accessible. The word "switches" previously used in this rule was edited to read "switches that contain fuses."

Analysis

CLARIFIED

240.24(A) Accessibility. The language was revised for grammatical correctness without any technical change.

240.24 Location of Overcurrent Protective Devices at Premises

(A) Readily Accessible. Circuit breakers and switches containing fuses must be readily accessible and be installed so the center of the grip of the operating handle of the circuit breaker or switch, when in its highest position, is not more than 6 ft 7 in. above the floor or working platform, except for the following: ▶Figure 240–13 and ▶Figure 240–14

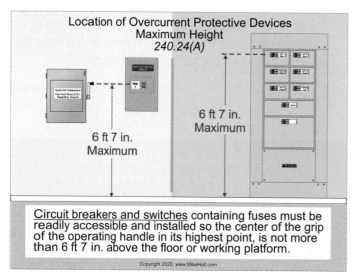

Location of Overcurrent Protective Devices Readily Accessible
240.24(A)

Circuit breakers and switches containing fuses must be readily accessible.

Copyright 2020, www.MikeHolt.com

▶Figure 240–13

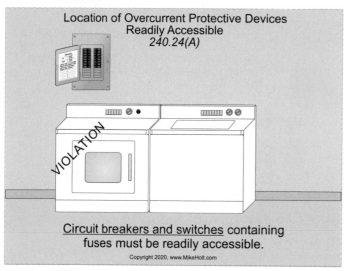

Location of Overcurrent Protective Devices Maximum Height
240.24(A)

6 ft 7 in. Maximum

6 ft 7 in. Maximum

Circuit breakers and switches containing fuses must be readily accessible and installed so the center of the grip of the operating handle in its highest point, is not more than 6 ft 7 in. above the floor or working platform.

Copyright 2020, www.MikeHolt.com

▶Figure 240–14

(2) Supplementary overcurrent protection, as described in 240.10. ▶Figure 240–15

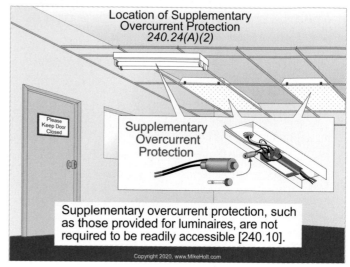

Location of Supplementary Overcurrent Protection
240.24(A)(2)

Please Keep Door Closed

Supplementary Overcurrent Protection

Supplementary overcurrent protection, such as those provided for luminaires, are not required to be readily accessible [240.10].

Copyright 2020, www.MikeHolt.com

▶Figure 240–15

(4) Overcurrent devices are permitted to be above 6 ft 7 in. where located next to equipment they supply if accessible by portable means. ▶Figure 240–16

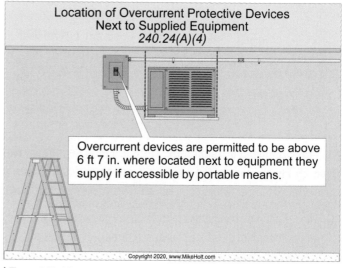

Location of Overcurrent Protective Devices Next to Supplied Equipment
240.24(A)(4)

Overcurrent devices are permitted to be above 6 ft 7 in. where located next to equipment they supply if accessible by portable means.

Copyright 2020, www.MikeHolt.com

▶Figure 240–16

240.33 Vertical Position

Circuit-breaker enclosures (panelboards) need to be oriented in a vertical position. They can be mounted horizontally so long as, when operating the device, on is up and off is down. This seems impractical since half of the breakers in a typical panel will be in violation of this rule. There was an editorial change here about mounting a panel vertically, that deleted a blanket exemption by saying, "unless that is impracticable." Mounting panels vertically may orient the circuit breakers horizontally, left to right, and right to left but operation of circuit breakers in these directions is permitted. The language was revised in an attempt to prohibit circuit breaker enclosures from being installed in the face up position.

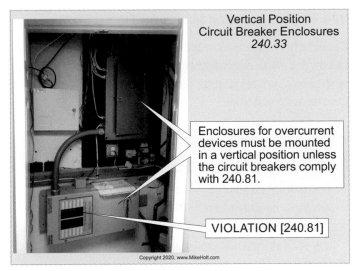

▶Figure 240–17

Analysis

EXPANDED The language previously said that the enclosure must be mounted in a vertical position unless that is shown to be impracticable. The phrase "unless that is shown to be impractical" was deleted. The intent was to prohibit the enclosure from being installed in a face-up position and to address the potential for debris falling into a face-up installation. In addition, the workspace and equipment space requirements of 110.26 do not address a panel that is installed in that position.

240.33 Vertical Position

Enclosures containing overcurrent devices must be mounted in a vertical position. Circuit-breaker enclosures can be mounted horizontally if the circuit breaker is installed in accordance with 240.81. ▶Figure 240–17

Author's Comment:

▸ Section 240.81 specifies that where circuit-breaker handles are operated vertically, the "up" position of the handle must be in the "on" position. So, in effect, an enclosure that contains one row of circuit breakers can be mounted horizontally, but one that contains a panelboard with multiple circuit breakers on opposite sides of each other must be mounted vertically.

240.40 Disconnecting Means for Fuses

Most fused disconnects are designed so the blades of the knife switch are above the fuse cartridge which automatically de-energizes the fuse when the disconnect is turned to the off position. Cartridge fuses must now have a line-side disconnect even where they are only accessible to qualified persons.

Analysis

CLARIFIED **NEW** There are both revisions and new information in this change. In the previous *Code*, fuses that were accessible only to qualified persons were not required to have a line-side disconnect. All fuses are now required to have a line-side disconnect as the language addressing "qualified persons" was deleted. This change reflects the fact that even qualified persons must not be subjected to replacing fuses in energized circuits since doing so presents both a serious shock and arc flash hazard to the worker.

240.40 Disconnecting Means for Fuses

Cartridge fuses and fuses in circuits over 150 volts-to-ground, must be provided with a disconnecting means on their supply side so that each circuit containing fuses can be independently disconnected from the source of power.

240.62 Reconditioned Equipment

The global introduction of the rules for reconditioning electrical equipment are throughout the entire 2020 revision of the *NEC*. A new section was added here to prohibit low-voltage fuseholders and low-voltage nonrenewable fuses from being reconditioned.

Analysis

NEW Low-voltage fuseholders and low-voltage nonrenewable fuses are not suitable to be reconditioned and language was added to prohibit such reconditioning.

240.67 Arc Energy Reduction--Fuses

Anytime arc fault or arc blast risks can be reduced to further protect electricians and service technicians it's a good thing. A new sentence was added to subsection (A) requiring that the method chosen to reduce the clearing time of a fuse must operate at a value below the available arcing current, and a new list item (4) adds another permitted method; "current limiting, electronically actuated fuses." Subsection (C) was added and requires the arc energy reduction system to be performance tested when first installed.

Analysis

EXPANDED **240.67(A) Documentation.** For the arc energy reduction to function quickly enough to help protect a worker, the fuse must be set low enough so it will function to open the circuit. A setting above the available arcing current does not reduce the risk of an arc flash hazard to a worker. The new wording in (A) only addresses the documentation of the setting.

New language was added to the parent text in (B) to require that arc energy reduction devices be set to operate at less than the available arcing current and there was a new arc energy reduction method added to the list items.

This new item permits current-limiting electronically actuated fuses to be used as an arc energy reduction method.

NEW **240.67(C) Performance Testing.** Testing of arc energy reduction systems must be completed at the time of installation by qualified persons, according to the manufacturer's instructions, to verify the correct installation and connection of the arc energy reduction system. This rule is modeled after the required performance testing of the ground-fault protection equipment (GFPE) required by 210.13, 215.10, and 230.95. The substantiation indicates that it is practical and feasible to require this testing and also states that these new technologies may not lend themselves well to traditional testing, which makes following the manufacturer's instructions very important. A written record of this testing must be available to the AHJ. An Informational Note was added indicating some energy reduction protection systems cannot be tested using primary current injection. Some types of arc energy reduction systems do not use current as the method of arc reduction. One example is a system that detects the visible light from the arc and causes the current to be interrupted. Systems that use fuses for arc energy reduction cannot be tested with primary current injection since the fuses will open when the current is applied.

240.67 Arc Energy Reduction—Fuses

Where fuses rated 1,200A or greater are installed, 240.67(A) and (B) must be applied.

(A) Documentation. Documentation must be available to those authorized to design, install, operate, or inspect the installation as to the location of the fuses. <u>Documentation must be provided to demonstrate that the method chosen to reduce clearing time is set to operate at a value below the available arcing current.</u>

(B) Method to Reduce Clearing Time. A fuse must have a clearing time of 0.07 seconds or less at the available arcing current, or one of the following means must be provided <u>and be set to operate at less than the available arcing current:</u>

(1) Differential relaying.

(2) Energy-reducing maintenance switching with local status indicator.

(3) Energy-reducing active arc flash mitigation system.

(4) Current-limiting, electronically actuated fuses.

(5) An approved equivalent means.

Note 1: An energy-reducing maintenance switch allows a worker to set a disconnect switch to reduce the clearing time while working within an arc flash boundary as defined in NFPA 70E, *Standard for Electrical Safety in the Workplace*, and then to set the disconnect switch back to a normal setting after the potentially hazardous work is complete.

Note 2: An energy-reducing active arc flash mitigation system helps in reducing arcing duration in the electrical distribution system. No change in the disconnect switch or the settings of other devices is required during maintenance when a worker is working within an arc flash boundary as defined in NFPA 70E *Standard for Electrical Safety in the Workplace*.

Note 3: IEEE 1584, IEEE *Guide for Performing Arc Flash Hazard Calculations*, is one of the available methods that provides guidance in determining arcing current.

(C) Performance Testing. Where a method to reduce clearing time is required in 240.67(B), the arc energy reduction system must be performance tested when installed. The testing must be conducted by a qualified person in accordance with the manufacturer's instructions.

Performance testing of an instantaneous element of the protective device must be conducted by a qualified person using a test process of primary current injection and the manufacturer's recommended test procedures.

A written record of testing must be made available to the authority having jurisdiction.

Note: Some energy-reduction protection systems cannot be tested using a test process of primary current injection due to either the protection method being damaged such as with the use of fuse technology or because current is not the primary method of arc detection.

240.86 Series Ratings

Series rating of electrical service and distribution equipment is a specialized skill. In fact, the *Code* requires it to be performed only by qualified persons, and on larger jobs its usually engineered and included in the drawing specifications. Editorial revisions were made to the series rating rule to replace "acceptable" with "approved," and the motor contribution in subsection (C) was revised for clarity; but there was no actual change to the requirements.

Analysis

 EDITED This section permits the use of a circuit breaker at a location where the fault current exceeds the interrupting rating of the breaker, provided there is an approved upstream device that will act in combination with the downstream breaker to clear the fault and protect the lower rated breaker. On loss of power, motors continue to spin as a result of their mechanical inertia, and act as generators supplying additional energy into the fault for a short period of time.

240.86 Series Ratings

Where a circuit breaker is used on a circuit having an available fault current higher than the marked interrupting rating by being connected on the load side of an approved overcurrent protective device having a higher rating, the circuit breaker must meet the requirements specified in 240.86 (A) or (B), and (C).

(A) Selected Under Engineering Supervision in Existing Installations. The series rated combination devices must be selected by a licensed professional engineer engaged primarily in the design or maintenance of electrical installations. The selection must be documented and stamped by the professional engineer. This documentation must be available to those authorized to design, install, inspect, maintain, and operate the system. This series combination rating, including identification of the upstream overcurrent protective device(s), must be field marked on the end use equipment. For calculated applications, the engineer must ensure that the downstream circuit breakers that are part of the series combination remain passive during the interruption period of the line side fully rated, current-limiting device.

(B) Tested Combinations. The combination of the line-side overcurrent device and the load-side circuit breaker(s) is tested and marked on the end use equipment, such as switchboards and panelboards.

Note to (A) and (B): See 110.22 for marking of series combination systems.

(C) Motor Contribution. Series ratings cannot be used where:

(1) Motor circuits are connected between the load side of the higher-rated overcurrent device of a series rated combination device and on the lower-rated circuit breaker, and

(2) The sum of the motor full-load currents exceeds one percent of the interrupting rating of the lower-rated circuit breaker.

240.87 Arc Energy Reduction— Circuit Breakers

The changes here are the same as those in 240.67 for fuses; anytime the dangers surrounding arc faults or arc blasts can be reduced to further protect electricians and service technicians it's a good thing. The change here applies to circuit breakers and the change in (B) clarifies that temporary adjustment of the breaker's instantaneous trip setting is not a permitted method of arc energy reduction.

Analysis

EXPANDED The previous *Code* required the instantaneous trip or override settings of arc energy circuit breakers to be below the available arcing current. This change expands that requirement to all the permitted methods of arc energy reduction. As with fuses, the revision in (A) adds a documentation requirement for this setting and the one in (B) requires the actual device to be set below the available arcing fault current. This change is intended to prohibit a worker from turning down the instantaneous trip setting on the breaker while working on the equipment and then setting it back to the design setting when the work is finished. The new subsection (C) mirrors that of 240.67(C) for fuses, but it pertains to circuit breakers here.

240.87 Arc Energy Reduction—Circuit Breakers

Where the highest continuous current trip setting for which the overcurrent device in a circuit breaker is rated or can be adjusted to 1,200A or higher, 240.87(A) and (B) apply.

(A) Documentation. Documentation must be available to those authorized to design, install, operate, or inspect the installation as to the location of the arc energy reduction circuit breaker(s). Documentation must be provided to demonstrate that the method chosen to reduce clearing time is set to operate at a value below the available arcing current.

(B) Method to Reduce Clearing Time. One of the following means must be provided and set to operate at less than the available arcing current:

(1) Zone-selective interlocking

(2) Differential relaying

(3) Energy-reducing maintenance switching with local status indicator

(4) Energy-reducing active arc flash mitigation system

(5) An instantaneous trip setting. Temporary adjustment of the instantaneous trip setting to achieve arc energy reduction is not permitted.

(6) An instantaneous override

(7) An approved equivalent means

Note 1: An energy-reducing maintenance switch [240.87(B)(3)] allows a worker to set a circuit breaker trip unit to "no intentional delay" to reduce the clearing time while working within an arc flash boundary as defined in NFPA 70E, *Standard for Electrical Safety in the Workplace*, and then to set the trip unit back to a normal setting after the potentially hazardous work is complete.

Note 2: An energy-reducing active arc flash mitigation system [240.87(B)(4)] helps in reducing arcing duration in the electrical distribution system. No change in the circuit breaker or the settings of other devices is required during maintenance when a worker is working within an arc flash boundary as defined in NFPA 70E, *Standard for Electrical Safety in the Workplace*.

Note 3: An instantaneous trip [240.87(B)(5)] is a function that causes a circuit breaker to trip with no intentional delay when currents exceed the instantaneous trip setting or current level. If arcing currents are above the instantaneous trip level, the circuit breaker will trip in the minimum possible time.

Note 4: IEEE 1584, IEEE *Guide for Performing Arc Flash Hazard Calculations*, is one of the available methods that provides guidance in determining arcing current.

(C) Performance Testing. The arc energy reduction protection system must be performance tested by primary current injection testing or another approved method when first installed on site. This testing must be conducted by a qualified person(s) in accordance with the manufacturer's instructions.

Performance testing of an instantaneous element of the protective device must be conducted by a qualified person using a test process of primary current injection and the manufacturer's recommended test procedures.

A written record of this testing must be made and must be available to the authority having jurisdiction.

Note: Some energy reduction protection systems cannot be tested using a test process of primary current injection due to either the protection method being damaged such as with the use of fuse technology or because current is not the primary method of arc detection.

240.88 Reconditioned Equipment

The global introduction of the rules for reconditioning electrical equipment are throughout the entire 2020 revision of the *NEC*. This new section was added to specify the types of equipment involved with circuit breakers that are permitted to be reconditioned.

Analysis

NEW This section has parent text and two subsections, all of which contain list items. The parent text says that reconditioned equipment must be listed as "reconditioned" and the original listing mark must be removed.

240.88 Reconditioned Equipment

Reconditioned equipment must be listed as "reconditioned" and the original listing mark removed.

(A) Circuit Breakers. The use of reconditioned circuit breakers must comply with the following:

(1) Molded-case circuit breakers are not permitted to be reconditioned.

(2) Low- and medium-voltage power circuit breakers are permitted to be reconditioned.

(3) High-voltage circuit breakers are be permitted to be reconditioned.

(B) Components. The use of reconditioned trip units, protective relays, and current transformers must comply with the following:

(1) Low-voltage power circuit breaker electronic trip units are not permitted to be reconditioned.

(3) Electromechanical protective relays and current transformers are permitted to be reconditioned.

Author's Comment:

▸ The requirement that reconditioned breakers be "listed" as such is not exactly correct. Reconditioned equipment is not listed equipment. Perhaps the intent here is that reconditioned equipment is to be "marked" and/or "labeled" as such.

240.91 Protection of Conductors

Subsection (B) was clarified to permit the OCPD to have a rating other than a standard rating as found in 240.6, and to provide a reference to Table 240.92(B).

Analysis

CLARIFIED

240.91(B) Devices Rated Over 800A. This rule is in Part VIII, Supervised Industrial Installations, and only applies to those locations. It is like the "round-up" rule in 240.4(B), but applies to OCPDs having a rating greater than 800A. It permits the use of a conductor with an ampacity of at least 95 percent of the OCPD that protects the conductors.

The conductors must be protected within recognized time vs. current limits for short-circuit current. To assist the *Code* user, a new Informational Note was added directing the reader to Table 240.92(B) for formulas that will determine the time vs. current limits for copper and aluminum conductors.

The previous language had a reference to 240.6 and that was deleted. While 240.6 permits the use of OCPDs with non-standard ratings, removing the reference is intended to clarify that permission. The only requirement is that the conductor have an ampacity of not less than 95 percent of the rating of the OCPD.

Author's Comment:

▸ Non-standard ratings are often the result of using adjustable trip circuit breakers. If the adjusting method of an adjustable trip circuit breaker does not have its access limited by one of the methods in 240.6(C), the rating of that device is the maximum possible setting of the adjustable trip circuit breaker.

ARTICLE
242

OVERVOLTAGE PROTECTION

Introduction to Article 242—Overvoltage Protection

Part I of this article provides the general requirements, installation requirements, and connection requirements for overvoltage protection and overvoltage protective devices, (surge-protective devices or SPDs). Part II covers SPDs rated 1kV or less that are permanently installed on premises wiring systems.

Surge-protective devices are designed to reduce transient voltages present on premises power distribution wiring and load-side equipment, particularly electronic equipment such as computers, telecommunications equipment, security systems, and electronic appliances.

These transient voltages can originate from several sources, including anything from lightning to laser printers. Voltage spikes and transients caused by the switching of utility power lines, power factor correction capacitors, or lightning can reach thousands of volts and amperes. ▶Figure 242–1

Voltage spikes and transients produced by premises equipment such as photocopiers, laser printers, and other high reactive loads cycling off can be in the hundreds of volts. ▶Figure 242–2

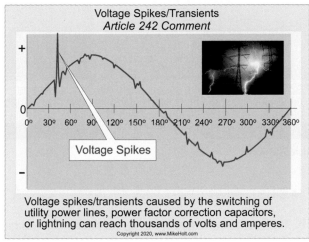

▶Figure 242–1

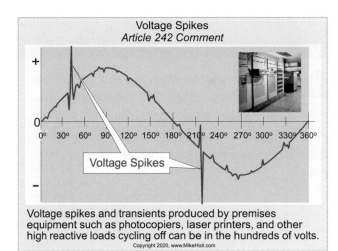

▶Figure 242–2

The best line of defense for all types of electronic equipment may be the installation of surge-protective devices at the electrical service and source of power, as well as at the location of the utilization equipment.

The intent of a surge-protective device is to limit transient voltages by diverting or limiting surge current and preventing continued flow of current while remaining capable of repeating these functions [Article 100 Definitions]. ▶Figure 242–3

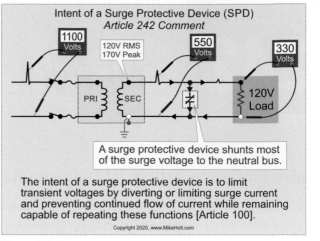

▶Figure 242–3

Article 242 Overvoltage Protection

This new article replaces Articles 280, Surge Arresters, Over 1,000V, and Article 285, Surge-Protective Devices (SPDs), 1,000V or Less.

Analysis

RELOCATED These requirements are more appropriately located after Article 240 since they apply to equipment protection. Article 240 provides rules for protection from overcurrent and this new Article 242 contains requirements to provide protection from overvoltage.

Part I. General

242.1 Scope

This article provides the general requirements, installation requirements, and connection requirements for overvoltage protection and overvoltage protective devices. Part II covers surge-protective devices (SPDs) permanently installed on premises wiring systems of not more than 1,000V, nominal. Part III covers surge arresters permanently installed on premises wiring systems over 1,000V, nominal. ▶Figure 242–4

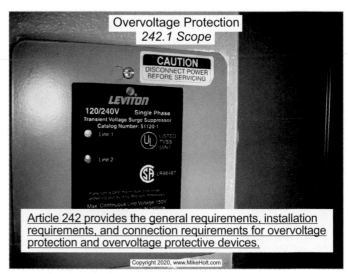

▶Figure 242–4

Author's Comment:

▸ This textbook only addresses the requirements for surge-protective devices in Parts I and II, not the surge arresters in Part III.

Part II. Surge-Protective Devices (SPDs), 1,000V or Less

242.6 Uses Not Permitted

A surge-protective device is not permitted to be used:

(1) In circuits that exceed 1,000V.

(2) In ungrounded systems, impedance grounded systems, or corner-grounded delta systems, unless listed specifically for use on these systems.

(3) If the voltage rating of the surge-protective device is less than the maximum continuous phase-to-ground voltage available at the point of connection.

242.8 Listing

Surge-protective devices must be listed.

Author's Comment:

▶ According to UL 1449, Standard for Surge-protective Devices, these units are intended to limit the maximum amplitude of transient voltage surges on power lines to specified values. They are not intended to function as lightning arresters. The adequacy of the voltage suppression level to protect connected equipment from voltage surges has not been evaluated.

242.10 Short-Circuit Current Rating

Surge-protective devices must be marked with their short-circuit current rating, and they are not permitted to be installed if the available fault current exceeds that rating. This short-circuit current marking requirement does not apply to receptacles containing surge-protective device protection.

Warning

⚠ Surge-protective devices are susceptible to failure at high fault currents. A hazardous condition is present if the short-circuit current rating of a surge-protective device is less than the available fault current. See 110.10 in the *NEC*.

242.12 Type 1 SPD—Line Side of Service Disconnect

(A) Installation. Type 1 surge-protective devices can be connected as follows:

(1) On the supply side of the service disconnect [230.82(4)]. ▶Figure 242–5

(2) On the load side of the service disconnect in accordance with 242.14.

(B) Service Disconnect. When installed at the service disconnect, Type 1 surge-protective devices must be connected to any one of the following: ▶Figure 242–6

Type 1 SPD Installation
Line Side of Service Disconnect
242.12(A)(1)

A Type 1 SPD can be connected on the supply side of service equipment [230.82(4)].
Copyright 2020, www.MikeHolt.com

▶Figure 242–5

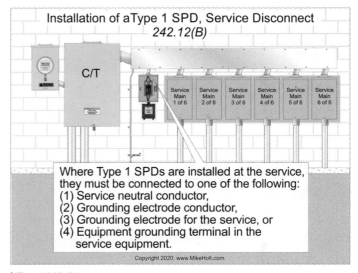

Installation of a Type 1 SPD, Service Disconnect
242.12(B)

C/T

Service Main 1 of 6 | Service Main 2 of 6 | Service Main 3 of 6 | Service Main 4 of 6 | Service Main 5 of 6 | Service Main 6 of 6

Where Type 1 SPDs are installed at the service, they must be connected to one of the following:
(1) Service neutral conductor,
(2) Grounding electrode conductor,
(3) Grounding electrode for the service, or
(4) Equipment grounding terminal in the service equipment.
Copyright 2020, www.MikeHolt.com

▶Figure 242–6

(1) Service neutral conductor,

(2) Grounding electrode conductor,

(3) Grounding electrode for the service, or

(4) Equipment grounding terminal in the service equipment.

Author's Comment:

▶ Only one conductor can be connected to a terminal, unless the terminal is identified for multiple conductors [110.14(A)].

▶ According to Article 100, a Type 1 "Surge-protective Device" is a permanently connected surge-protective device listed for installation on the line side of the service disconnect.

242.14 Type 2 SPD—Feeder Circuits

(A) Load Side of Service Disconnect. Type 2 surge-protective devices must be connected to the load side of the service disconnect. ▸Figure 242–7

▸Figure 242–7

▸ Only one conductor can be connected to a terminal, unless the terminal is identified for multiple conductors [110.14(A)]. ▸Figure 242–8

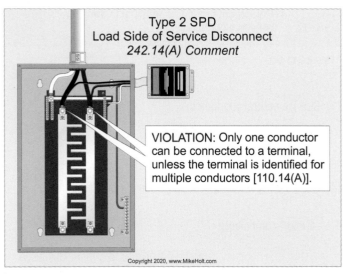

▸Figure 242–8

▸ According to Article 100, a Type 2 "Surge-protective Device" is a permanently connected surge-protective device listed for installation on the load side of the service disconnect.

(B) Feeder-Supplied Buildings. Type 2 surge-protective devices must be connected anywhere on the load side of the building overcurrent device.

(C) Separately Derived Systems. Type 2 surge-protective devices can be connected anywhere on the premises wiring of the separately derived system.

242.16 Type 3 SPDs—Branch Circuits

Type 3 surge-protective devices can be installed on the load side of a branch-circuit overcurrent protective device. If included in the manufacturer's instructions, the Type 3 SPD connection must be a minimum 30 ft of conductor distance from the service or transformer disconnect. ▸Figure 242–9

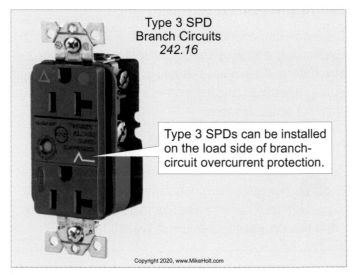

▸Figure 242–9

▸ The definition of a Type 3 "Surge-protective Device" in Article 100 is a surge-protective device listed for installation on branch circuits.

242.20 Number Required

If used, the surge-protective device must be connected to each phase conductor of the circuit. ▶Figure 242–10

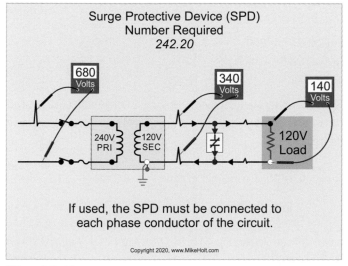

▶Figure 242–10

242.22 Location

Surge-protective devices can be located indoors or outdoors and be made inaccessible to unqualified persons, unless listed for installation in accessible locations.

242.24 Routing of Surge-Protective Device Conductors

Surge-protective device conductors must not be any longer than necessary, and unnecessary bends must be avoided. ▶Figure 242–11

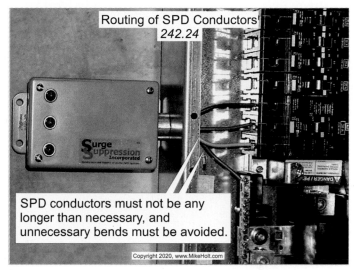

▶Figure 242–11

Author's Comment:

▶ Shorter conductors and minimal bends will improve the performance of the surge-protective device by helping to reduce conductor impedance during high-frequency transient events.

ARTICLE
250

GROUNDING AND BONDING

Introduction to Article 250—Grounding and Bonding

No other article can match Article 250 for misapplication, violation, and misinterpretation. Terminology used in this article has been a source of much confusion, but that has been improved during the last few *NEC* revisions. It is very important to understand the difference between grounding and bonding in order to correctly apply the provisions of this article. Pay careful attention to the definitions of important terms located in Article 100 that apply to grounding and bonding. Article 250 covers the grounding requirements for providing a path to the earth to reduce overvoltage from lightning, and the bonding requirements that establish a low-impedance fault current path back to the source of the electrical supply to facilitate the operation of overcurrent protective devices in the event of a ground fault.

This article is arranged in a logical manner, so it's a good idea to just read through Article 250 to get a big picture view—after you review the definitions. Next, study the article closely so you understand the details. Although not all of Article 250 is included in this textbook, those necessary to lend context to the 2020 *Code* are covered.

250.6 Objectionable Current

The change here clarifies that electronic equipment must be connected to an equipment grounding conductor, even if doing so results in "objectionable current" that interferes with the operation of the equipment. This is especially annoying for equipment sensitive to the alternating-current frequency (or "60 cycle") humming or buzzing that often occurs with audio equipment.

Analysis

CLARIFIED

250.6(D) Limitations to Permissible Alterations. This section was clarified without a technical change. The intention was to make it clear that electronic equipment must be connected to an equipment grounding conductor (EGC), even where such a connection results in "objectionable current" that interferes with the equipment's operation. The term "noise" was replaced with "electromagnetic interference." The rule states that such interference is not considered objectionable current.

250.12 Clean Surfaces

This rule was revised to require clean surfaces for bonding connections as well as grounding connections. This means that it is necessary to ensure metal-to-metal contact. Paint and/or other types of coatings can create a nonconductive coating and interfere with (or prevent) electrical continuity.

Analysis

CLARIFIED

The language requiring nonconductive coatings (such as paint, lacquer, and enamel) to be removed from equipment to be grounded so good electrical continuity is ensured was expanded to include bonding connections. This change recognizes that many of the field connections required by Article 250 are bonding connections and a solid electrical connection is required to permit the bonding connection to do its job. This also permits the use of fittings that are designed to make the removal of such coatings unnecessary.

250.12 Clean Surfaces

Nonconductive coatings, such as paint, must be removed <u>on equipment to be grounded or bonded</u> to ensure good electrical continuity, or the termination fittings must be designed so as to make such removal unnecessary [250.53(A) and 250.96(A)].

Author's Comment:

▸ Fittings such as locknuts are designed to cut through the nonconductive coating and establish the intended electrical continuity when they are properly tightened.

▸ Tarnish on copper water pipe need not be removed before making a termination.

250.20 Systems Required to be Grounded

An Informational Note was added to the end of subsection (B), Alternating-Current Systems 50V to 1,000V, referencing high-impedance grounding as an effective tool to reduce arc flash hazards. This information was extracted from *Annex "O"* of NFPA 70E, *Standard for Electrical Safety in the Workplace*.

Analysis

EXPANDED

250.20(B)(3) Alternating-Current Systems of 50V to 1,000V. An Informational Note referencing Annex O of NFPA 70E, *Standard for Electrical Safety in the Workplace* was added to emphasize that high-impedance grounding is an effective tool to reduce arc flash levels and highlights the safety aspects of such systems.

250.20 Systems Required to be Grounded

(B) Alternating-Current Systems 50V to 1,000V. The following systems must be grounded (connected to a grounding electrode) where the neutral conductor is used as a circuit conductor for:

(1) Single-phase systems. ▸Figure 250–1

(2) Three-phase, wye-connected systems. ▸Figure 250–2

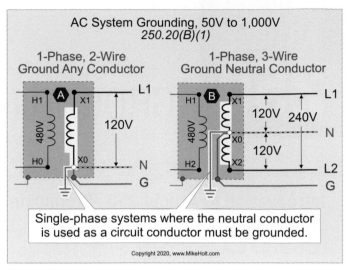

AC System Grounding, 50V to 1,000V
250.20(B)(1)

Single-phase systems where the neutral conductor is used as a circuit conductor must be grounded.

Copyright 2020, www.MikeHolt.com

▸Figure 250–1

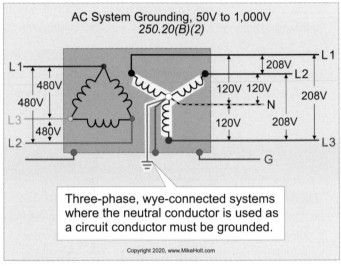

AC System Grounding, 50V to 1,000V
250.20(B)(2)

Three-phase, wye-connected systems where the neutral conductor is used as a circuit conductor must be grounded.

Copyright 2020, www.MikeHolt.com

▸Figure 250–2

(3) Three-phase, high-leg delta-connected systems. ▸Figure 250–3

Note: According to Annex O of NFPA 70E, *Standard for Electrical Safety in the Workplace,* high-impedance grounding is an effective tool to reduce arc flash hazards.

Author's Comment:

▸ It is important to note that high-impedance grounding does not reduce the level of PPE required of the incident energy shown on the hazard label. It only reduces the incident energy from a ground fault, and while that is by far the most common fault, it has no effect on the arc flash hazard from a short circuit.

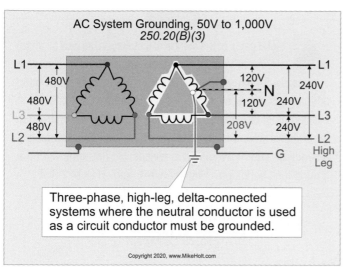

AC System Grounding, 50V to 1,000V
250.20(B)(3)

Three-phase, high-leg, delta-connected systems where the neutral conductor is used as a circuit conductor must be grounded.

Copyright 2020, www.MikeHolt.com

▶Figure 250–3

250.25 Grounding for Supply Side of the Service Disconnect

The redundant text in 250.25 was removed since not all equipment connected to the utility is considered a service. PV system power production equipment is connected in parallel with a service and may even be connected to the utility (if only for power production to the utility) with no service equipment in parallel. By referencing parts of 250.24, this rule requires that supply-side equipment is connected to a grounding electrode system, has an effective ground-fault current path, and is bonded with the more stringent requirements of 250.92 and 250.102(C).

Analysis

NEW

250.25(A) Grounded System. This subsection applies where the utility supply system is a grounded system and requires the systems connected on the supply side of the service disconnect to comply with the rules of 250.24(A) though (D). This results in the system being connected to the supply side of the service disconnect being installed, exactly like service equipment is installed.

NEW

250.25(B) Ungrounded Systems. Subsection (B) applies where the service is supplied by an ungrounded system and requires the supply-side system installation to comply with the requirements of 240.24(E). Again, this makes the installation of the supply-side system equipment identical to the installation of service equipment.

250.25 Grounding for Supply Side of the Service Disconnect

Electrical systems permitted on the supply side of the service disconnect, in accordance with 230.82, must be grounded in accordance with 250.24(A) through (D).

(A) Grounded System. If the utility supply system is grounded, the grounding of systems permitted to be connected on the supply side of the service disconnect and are installed in one or more separate enclosures from the service equipment enclosure must comply with the requirements of 250.24(A) through (D).

(B) Ungrounded Systems. If the utility supply system is ungrounded, the grounding of systems permitted to be connected on the supply side of the service disconnect and are installed in one or more separate enclosures from the service equipment enclosure must comply with the requirements of 250.24(E).

250.26 Conductor to Be Grounded-Alternating-Current Systems

This section was revised to clarify which conductor of various grounded systems is to be grounded and is now presented in a list format containing items (1) through (5). For example, the neutral conductor of a 3-wire system is to be grounded.

Analysis

CLARIFIED

The revision to this section clarifies it only applies to grounded systems. The first sentence was changed from "For ac premises wiring systems,…" to "For grounded ac premises wiring systems,…"

• • •

These revisions are intended to ensure no one is interpreting this section as requiring an alternating-current system to be a grounded system. The rules that tell *Code* users what ac systems are required to be grounded, permitted to be grounded, and not permitted to be grounded are found in 250.20 through 250.22. This section just specifies which conductor is to be grounded where 250.20 through 250.22 either require or permit a grounded system.

250.28 Main Bonding Jumper and System Bonding Jumper

The change in this section helps to avoid any confusion as it aligns with the requirements in 250.102(C)(1) which is used to size wire type bonding jumpers and permits the use of aluminum and copper-clad aluminum for main bonding jumpers.

Analysis

EXPANDED

250.28(A) Material. The text was revised to add aluminum and copper-clad aluminum, in addition to copper, as materials that are specifically permitted to be used as main or system bonding jumpers. This was already reflected in Table 250.102(C)(1) (which is used to size these jumpers where they are of the wire type) and adding the same language to this section avoids confusion. The phrase "or other corrosion-resistant material" remains to permit the use of main and system bonding jumpers of the screw type that are not copper, aluminum, or copper-clad aluminum.

250.28 Main Bonding Jumper and System Bonding Jumper

Author's Comment:

▸ The primary purpose of the main bonding jumper and system bonding jumper is to create a path for fault current to flow from a fault to the power supply to facilitate the opening of the circuit overcurrent protective device.

Danger

⚠ Metal parts of the electrical installation, as well as metal piping and structural steel, will become and remain energized with dangerous voltage from a ground fault if a main bonding jumper or system bonding jumper is not installed. A missing main or system bonding jumper causes an opening in the effective ground-fault current path back to the source creating a condition where overcurrent devices will not open during a ground-fault condition. ▸Figure 250–4 and ▸Figure 250–5

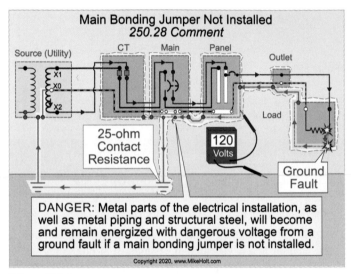

Main Bonding Jumper Not Installed
250.28 Comment

DANGER: Metal parts of the electrical installation, as well as metal piping and structural steel, will become and remain energized with dangerous voltage from a ground fault if a main bonding jumper is not installed.

Copyright 2020, www.MikeHolt.com

▸Figure 250–4

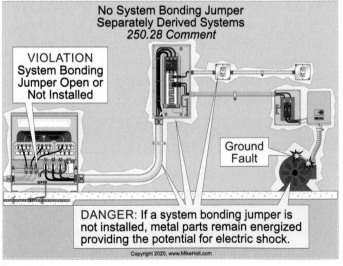

No System Bonding Jumper
Separately Derived Systems
250.28 Comment

VIOLATION
System Bonding Jumper Open or Not Installed

Ground Fault

DANGER: If a system bonding jumper is not installed, metal parts remain energized providing the potential for electric shock.

Copyright 2020, www.MikeHolt.com

▸Figure 250–5

Main and system bonding jumpers must be installed as follows:

(A) Material. The bonding jumper can be a wire, bus, or screw and can be made of copper, copper-clad aluminum, or aluminum. ▸Figure 250–6

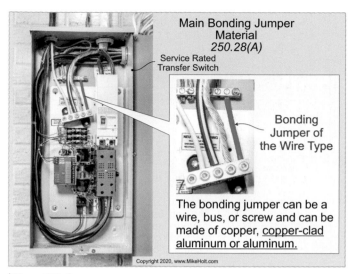

Main Bonding Jumper
Material
250.28(A)

Service Rated
Transfer Switch

Bonding
Jumper of
the Wire Type

The bonding jumper can be a wire, bus, or screw and can be made of copper, <u>copper-clad aluminum or aluminum.</u>

Copyright 2020, www.MikeHolt.com

▶Figure 250–6

250.30 Separately Derived Systems

The phrase "separately derived systems" was replaced with "power sources of the same type" for clarification. Several list items were also clarified, and a new exception was added to (A)(1)(b) that describes how the system bonding jumper (SBJ) is required to be connected when multisource separately derived systems are involved. Emphasis has been placed on the fact that the neutral conductor need not be larger than the phase conductors, and clarification as to sizing the tap conductor from a common <u>grounding electrode conductor was made by the addition of an exception to 250.30(A)(6)(b).</u>

Analysis

CLARIFIED The parent text of this section was revised for the connection of multiple separately derived systems in parallel. This change was required because where you connect a separately derived system to another separately derived system, you no longer have separately derived systems. Where two or more separately derived systems are connected in parallel, they have connections to circuit conductors of another system.

Such parallel connections are common for generators, fuel cells, and solar photovoltaic (PV) systems, and wind inverter systems. The revised language provides that where power sources of the same type are connected in parallel to form one system supplying premises wiring, the connected systems must be considered a single separately derived system. Other changes in the subsections include a new exception to (A)(1)(b) and further clarifications.

NEW **250.30(A)(1)(b) Ex, Grounded Systems, System Bonding Jumper.** A new exception was added to permit separately derived systems that consist of multiple sources connected in parallel to form a single system allowing the system bonding jumper to be installed at the paralleling switchgear, switchboard, or other paralleling connection instead of at the disconnect located at each separate source. The substantiation for this change was that the requirement to have a system bonding jumper at each power source connected in parallel may result in undesirable circulating current between the individual power sources that can cause heating issues and interference with the operation of the automatic paralleling equipment. The new exception will permit a single system bonding jumper at the paralleling equipment to eliminate these issues. The installation of a system bonding jumper at the paralleling equipment will require supply-side bonding jumpers between the source disconnects and the paralleling equipment.

CLARIFIED **250.30(A)(2) Supply-Side Bonding Jumper.** The word "enclosure" was added following "disconnecting means" to clarify that the supply-side bonding jumper does not connect to the disconnecting means (switch) itself, but to the disconnecting means enclosure.

CLARIFIED **250.30(A)(3) Neutral Conductor.** Additional wording was added to clarify that the neutral conductor installed between the source and the location of the system bonding jumper would never be required to be larger than the derived phase conductors.

250.30(A)(6)(b) Ex, Multiple Separately Derived Systems, Tap Conductor Size. A new exception was added saying that where the only electrodes present are of the types in 250.66(A) ground rods, (B) concrete encased electrodes, or (C) ground rings, the common grounding electrode conductor is not required to be larger than what is required by those subsections for the type of electrode that is present.

CLARIFIED   NEW

250.30 Separately Derived Systems

In addition to complying with 250.30(A) for grounded systems, or as provided in 250.30(B) for ungrounded systems, separately derived systems must comply with 250.20, 250.21, 250.22, or 250.26, as applicable.

Note 1: An alternate alternating-current power source, such as an on-site generator, is not a separately derived system if the neutral conductor is solidly interconnected to a service-supplied system neutral conductor. An example of such a situation is where alternate source transfer equipment does not include a switching action in the neutral conductor and allows it to remain solidly connected to the service-supplied neutral conductor when the alternate source is operational and supplying the load served. ▶Figure 250–7 and ▶Figure 250–8

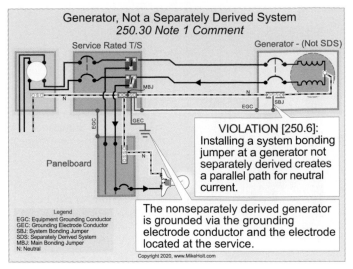

Generator, Not a Separately Derived System
250.30 Note 1 Comment

VIOLATION [250.6]: Installing a system bonding jumper at a generator not separately derived creates a parallel path for neutral current.

The nonseparately derived generator is grounded via the grounding electrode conductor and the electrode located at the service.

Legend
EGC: Equipment Grounding Conductor
GEC: Grounding Electrode Conductor
SBJ: System Bonding Jumper
SDS: Separately Derived System
MBJ: Main Bonding Jumper
N: Neutral

Copyright 2020, www.MikeHolt.com

▶Figure 250–8

Author's Comment:

▸ According to Article 100, a "Separately Derived System" is a wiring system whose power is derived from a source, other than the serving electric utility, and where there is no direct electrical connection to the supply conductors of another system other than through grounding and bonding connections. ▶Figure 250–9

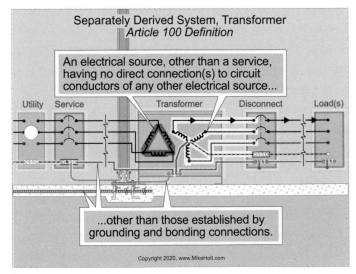

Separately Derived System, Transformer
Article 100 Definition

An electrical source, other than a service, having no direct connection(s) to circuit conductors of any other electrical source...

...other than those established by grounding and bonding connections.

Copyright 2020, www.MikeHolt.com

▶Figure 250–9

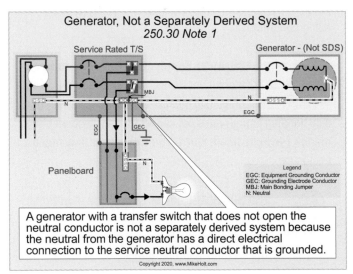

Generator, Not a Separately Derived System
250.30 Note 1

A generator with a transfer switch that does not open the neutral conductor is not a separately derived system because the neutral from the generator has a direct electrical connection to the service neutral conductor that is grounded.

Legend
EGC: Equipment Grounding Conductor
GEC: Grounding Electrode Conductor
MBJ: Main Bonding Jumper
N: Neutral

Copyright 2020, www.MikeHolt.com

▶Figure 250–7

Author's Comment:

▶ Transformers are separately derived because the primary conductors have no direct electrical connection from the circuit conductors of one system to the circuit conductors of another system. ▶**Figure 250–10**

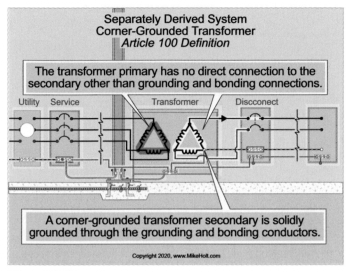

Separately Derived System
Corner-Grounded Transformer
Article 100 Definition

The transformer primary has no direct connection to the secondary other than grounding and bonding connections.

Utility Service   Transformer   Disconnect

A corner-grounded transformer secondary is solidly grounded through the grounding and bonding conductors.

Copyright 2020, www.MikeHolt.com

▶Figure 250–10

(A) Grounded Systems. Separately derived systems must be grounded and bonded in accordance with (A)(1) through (A)(8). A neutral-to-case connection is not permitted to be made on the load side of the system bonding jumper.

(1) System Bonding Jumper. A system bonding jumper must be installed at the same location where the grounding electrode conductor terminates to the neutral terminal of the separately derived system; either at the separately derived system or the secondary separately derived system disconnect, but not at both locations. ▶**Figure 250–11** and ▶**Figure 250–12**

Author's Comment:

▶ Section 250.30(A)(5) requires the connection of the grounding electrode conductor to be made at the same point where the neutral conductor is connected to the system bonding jumper in order to avoid parallel paths for neutral current.

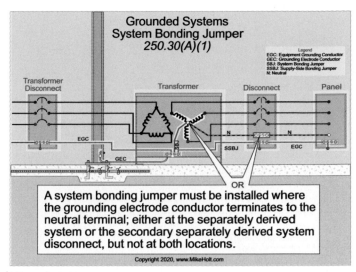

Grounded Systems
System Bonding Jumper
250.30(A)(1)

Legend
EGC: Equipment Grounding Conductor
GEC: Grounding Electrode Conductor
SBJ: System Bonding Jumper
SSBJ: Supply-Side Bonding Jumper
N: Neutral

Transformer Disconnect   Transformer   Disconnect   Panel

OR

A system bonding jumper must be installed where the grounding electrode conductor terminates to the neutral terminal; either at the separately derived system or the secondary separately derived system disconnect, but not at both locations.

Copyright 2020, www.MikeHolt.com

▶Figure 250–11

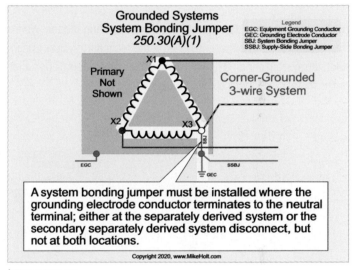

Grounded Systems
System Bonding Jumper
250.30(A)(1)

Legend
EGC: Equipment Grounding Conductor
GEC: Grounding Electrode Conductor
SBJ: System Bonding Jumper
SSBJ: Supply-Side Bonding Jumper

Primary Not Shown

Corner-Grounded 3-wire System

A system bonding jumper must be installed where the grounding electrode conductor terminates to the neutral terminal; either at the separately derived system or the secondary separately derived system disconnect, but not at both locations.

Copyright 2020, www.MikeHolt.com

▶Figure 250–12

Ex 2: If a building or structure is supplied by a feeder from an outdoor separately derived system, a system bonding jumper at both the source and the first disconnecting means is permitted if doing so does not establish a parallel path for the neutral current. The neutral conductor is not permitted to be smaller than the size specified for the system bonding jumper, but it is not required to be larger than the phase conductor(s).

(a) System Bonding Jumper at Source. Where the system bonding jumper is installed at the separately derived system, the system bonding jumper must connect the neutral conductor to the metal enclosure of the separately derived system. ▶**Figure 250–13**

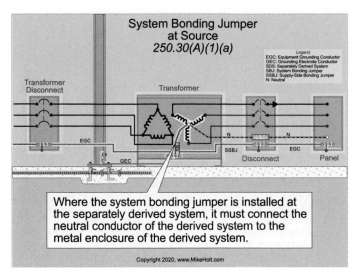

▶Figure 250-13

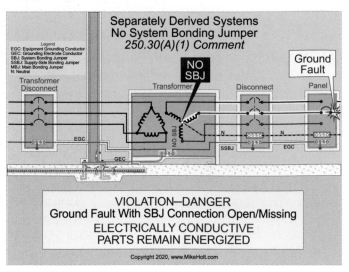

▶Figure 250-15

(b) System Bonding Jumper at First Disconnecting Means. Where the system bonding jumper is installed at the secondary system disconnect, the system bonding jumper must connect the neutral conductor to the metal disconnect enclosure. ▶Figure 250-14

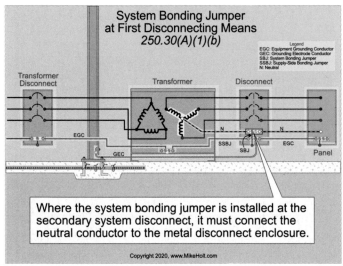

▶Figure 250-14

Danger

⚠ During a ground fault, metal parts of electrical equipment, as well as metal piping and structural steel, will become and remain energized providing the potential for electric shock and fire if the system bonding jumper is not installed. ▶Figure 250-15

Caution

⚠ Dangerous objectionable neutral current will flow on conductive metal parts of electrical equipment as well as metal piping and structural steel, in violation of 250.6(A), if more than one system bonding jumper is installed, or if it is not located where the grounding electrode conductor terminates to the neutral conductor. ▶Figure 250-16

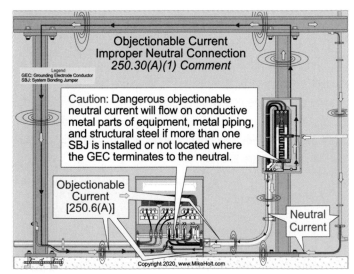

▶Figure 250-16

(2) Supply-Side Bonding Jumper to Disconnect. A supply-side bonding jumper must be installed to the first disconnecting means enclosure and it is not be required to be larger than the derived phase conductors. The supply-side bonding jumper can be of a nonflexible metal raceway type or of the wire type.

▸ The supply-side bonding jumper can be RMC, IMC, or EMT run between the separately derived system enclosure and the secondary system disconnect enclosure. A nonmetallic or flexible raceway must have a supply-side bonding jumper of the wire type.

(1) A supply-side bonding jumper of the wire type must be sized in accordance with 250.102(C) based on the size/area of the secondary phase conductor in the raceway or cable.

▸ **Example**

Question: What size supply-side bonding jumper is required for flexible metal conduit containing 300 kcmil secondary conductors? ▸**Figure 250–17**

(a) 4 AWG   (b) 2 AWG   (c) 1/0 AWG   (d) 3/0 AWG

Answer: (b) 2 AWG [Table 250.102(C)(1)]

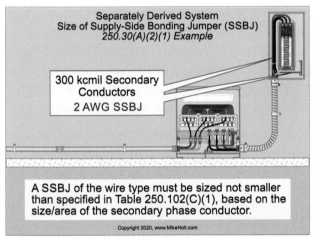

▸Figure 250–17

(3) Neutral Conductor Size. The neutral conductor between the separately derived system to the secondary system disconnect is not required to be larger than the derived phase conductors. If the system bonding jumper is installed at the secondary system disconnect instead of at the separately derived system, the following apply:

(a) Sizing for Single Raceway. A secondary neutral conductor must be run from the separately derived system to the secondary system disconnect and the secondary neutral conductor must be sized not smaller than specified in Table 250.102(C)(1), based on the size/area of the secondary phase conductor.

▸ **Example**

Question: What size neutral conductor is required for a 75 kVA transformer with 250 kcmil secondary conductors? ▸**Figure 250–18**

(a) 2 AWG   (b) 1/0 AWG   (c) 4/0 AWG   (d) 250 kcmil

Answer: (a) 2 AWG [Table 250.102(C)(1)]

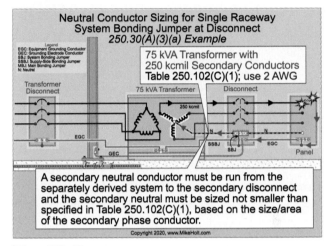

▸Figure 250–18

▸ Given that the neutral conductor size is based on the size of the phase conductors and Table 250.102(C)(1), or by the load calculation, it does not seem possible that the neutral conductor would ever be larger than the phase conductors making this change redundant.

(b) Parallel Conductors in Two or More Raceways. If the conductors from the separately derived system are installed in parallel in two or more raceways, the secondary neutral conductor must be installed in each raceway. The size of the secondary neutral conductor in each raceway or cable must not be smaller than specified in Table 250.102(C)(1), based on the size/area of the secondary phase conductor contained in the raceway or cable. ▸Figure 250–19

In no case is the parallel secondary neutral conductor permitted to be smaller than 1/0 AWG [310.12(F)].

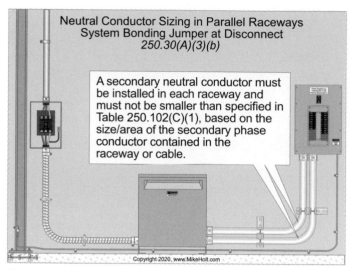

▶Figure 250–19

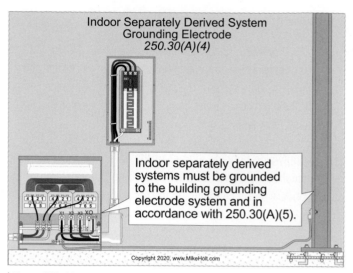

▶Figure 250–20

▶ **Example**

Question: What size neutral conductor is required for a 112.50 kVA transformer with two sets of 3/0 AWG secondary conductors?

(a) 4 AWG in each raceway   (b) 2 AWG in each raceway
(c) 1/0 AWG in each raceway   (d) 3/0 AWG in each raceway

Answer: (c) 1/0 AWG in each raceway

Solution:

Table 250.102(C)(1) requires a minimum of a 4 AWG conductor based on the 3/0 AWG phase conductors but 1/0 AWG is the minimum neutral conductor size permitted if run in parallel [310.10(G)(1)].

(4) Grounding Electrode. Separately derived systems located indoors must be grounded to the building grounding electrode system and in accordance with 250.30(A)(5). ▶Figure 250–20

Separately derived systems located outdoors must be grounded in accordance with 250.30(C).

Author's Comment:

▶ The metal structural frame of a building is not a grounding electrode but when it is properly connected to the grounding electrodes [250.68(C)(2)], it can be used as a grounding electrode conductor.

Note 1: Interior metal water piping in the area served by separately derived systems must be bonded to the separately derived system in accordance with 250.104(D).

(5) Grounding Electrode Conductor, Single Separately Derived System. The grounding electrode conductor for a separately derived system must be sized in accordance with 250.66 based on the area of the largest secondary phase conductor and it must terminate to the building grounding electrode in accordance with 250.30(A)(4), or to the building structural steel as permitted in 250.68(C).

The grounding electrode conductor is required to terminate to the neutral conductor at the same point on the separately derived system where the system bonding jumper is connected. ▶Figure 250–21

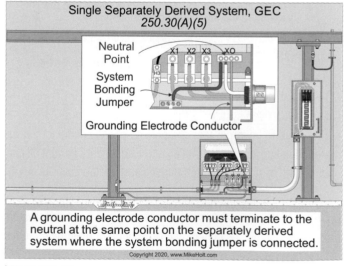

▶Figure 250–21

▸ System grounding is intended to reduce overvoltage caused by induction from multiple indirect lightning strikes or intermittent ground faults. System grounding helps reduce fires in buildings as well as voltage stress on electrical insulation, thereby ensuring longer insulation life for motors, separately derived systems, and other system components. ▸Figure 250–22

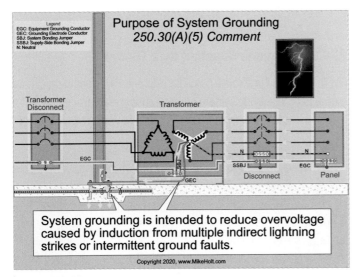

▸Figure 250–22

Author's Comment:

▸ To prevent objectionable neutral current from flowing onto metal parts [250.6], the grounding electrode conductor must originate at the same point on the separately derived system as where the system bonding jumper is connected [250.30(A)(1)].

Ex 1: If the system bonding jumper is a wire or busbar [250.30(A)(1)], the grounding electrode conductor is permitted to terminate to the equipment grounding terminal, bar, or bus. ▸Figure 250–23

(6) Common Grounding Electrode Conductor, Multiple Separately Derived Systems. Where there are multiple separately derived systems, a grounding electrode conductor tap from each separately derived system to a common grounding electrode conductor is permitted. This connection must be made at the same point on the separately derived system secondary as where the system bonding jumper is connected [250.30(A)(1)]. ▸Figure 250–24

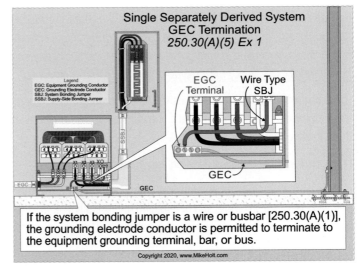

▸Figure 250–23

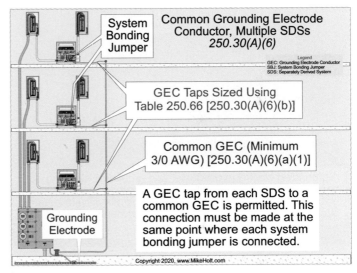

▸Figure 250–24

(a) Common Grounding Electrode Conductor. The common grounding electrode conductor can be any of the following:

(1) An unspliced conductor not smaller than 3/0 AWG copper or 250 kcmil aluminum.

(2) Interior metal water pipe located not more than 5 ft from the point of entrance to the building [250.68(C)(1)].

(3) The metal frame of the building that complies with 250.68(C)(2) or is connected to the grounding electrode system by a conductor not smaller than 3/0 AWG copper or 250 kcmil aluminum.

(b) Tap Conductor Size. Grounding electrode conductor taps must be sized in accordance with Table 250.66, based on the area of the largest secondary phase conductor.

Ex: If the only electrodes that are present are of the types specified in 250.66(A), (B), or (C), the size of the common grounding electrode conductor is not required to be larger than the largest conductor required by 250.66(A), (B), or (C) for the type of electrode that is present.

(c) Connections. Tap connections to the common grounding electrode conductor must be made at an accessible location by any of the following methods:

(1) A connector listed as grounding and bonding equipment.

(2) Listed connections to aluminum or copper busbars not less than ¼ in. thick × 2 in. wide, and of sufficient length to accommodate the terminations necessary for the installation. ▶Figure 250–25

(3) Exothermic welding.

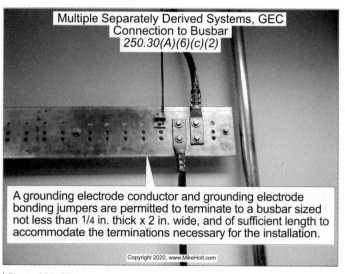

Multiple Separately Derived Systems, GEC Connection to Busbar
250.30(A)(6)(c)(2)

A grounding electrode conductor and grounding electrode bonding jumpers are permitted to terminate to a busbar sized not less than 1/4 in. thick x 2 in. wide, and of sufficient length to accommodate the terminations necessary for the installation.

Copyright 2020, www.MikeHolt.com

▶Figure 250–25

250.32 Buildings Supplied by a Feeder

The text was clarified to require a grounding electrode system and a grounding electrode conductor to be installed at a building supplied by feeders. This means that a grounding electrode and a grounding electrode conductor are required at a detached garage with electrical power.

Analysis

CLARIFIED

250.32(A) Grounding Electrode. The previous text did not actually require the installation of a grounding electrode conductor. It only required a grounding electrode or grounding electrode system. The revised language requires both.

250.32 Buildings Supplied by a Feeder

(A) Grounding Electrode. A building supplied by a feeder must have a grounding electrode system and a grounding electrode conductor installed in accordance with Part III of Article 250. ▶Figure 250–26

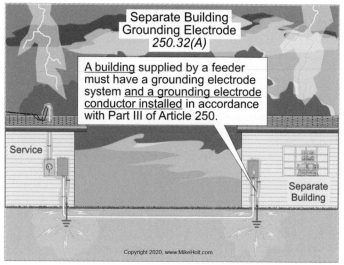

Separate Building Grounding Electrode
250.32(A)

A building supplied by a feeder must have a grounding electrode system and a grounding electrode conductor installed in accordance with Part III of Article 250.

Service

Separate Building

Copyright 2020, www.MikeHolt.com

▶Figure 250–26

Ex: A grounding electrode is not required for a building if it is supplied by a single branch circuit or multiwire branch circuit. ▶Figure 250–27

Caution

To prevent dangerous objectionable neutral current from flowing on metal parts [250.6(A)], the supply circuit neutral conductor is not permitted to be connected to the remote building disconnect [250.142(B)]. ▶Figure 250–28

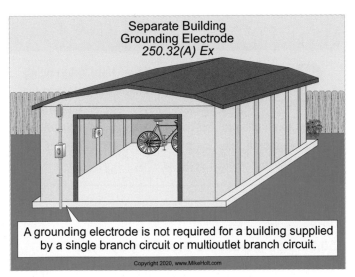

Separate Building
Grounding Electrode
250.32(A) Ex

A grounding electrode is not required for a building supplied by a single branch circuit or multioutlet branch circuit.

Copyright 2020, www.MikeHolt.com

▶Figure 250–27

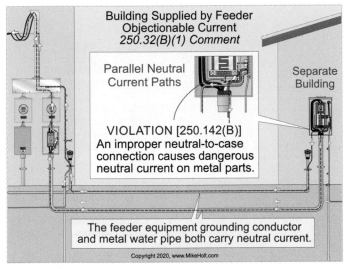

Building Supplied by Feeder
Objectionable Current
250.32(B)(1) Comment

Parallel Neutral
Current Paths

Separate Building

VIOLATION [250.142(B)]
An improper neutral-to-case connection causes dangerous neutral current on metal parts.

The feeder equipment grounding conductor and metal water pipe both carry neutral current.

Copyright 2020, www.MikeHolt.com

▶Figure 250–28

250.34 Generators—Portable and Vehicle- or Trailer-Mounted

This section, for portable and vehicle-mounted generators was expanded to include trailer-mounted generators. There is really no difference between a vehicle- or trailer-mounted generator but they are different in name. This revision clears up any ambiguity and applies the same requirements to the now distinguishable "trailer-mounted" generator.

Analysis

EXPANDED **250.34(B) Vehicle- and Trailer-Mounted Generators.** There is no difference between vehicle-mounted and trailer-mounted generators when it comes to producing electricity, however they are not the same things and the term "vehicle-mounted" does not include "trailer-mounted." Section 250.34(B) now applies to both vehicle-mounted and trailer-mounted generators; there are no technical changes to the requirements.

250.34 Generators—Portable and Vehicle- or Trailer-Mounted

(A) Portable Generators. A portable generator is not required to be connected to a grounding electrode (grounded) if both:

(1) The generator only supplies equipment and/or receptacles mounted on the generator. ▶Figure 250–29

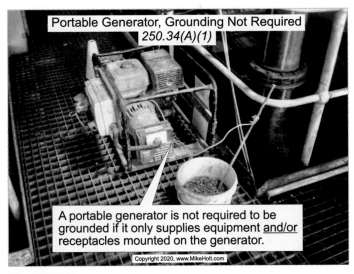

Portable Generator, Grounding Not Required
250.34(A)(1)

A portable generator is not required to be grounded if it only supplies equipment and/or receptacles mounted on the generator.

Copyright 2020, www.MikeHolt.com

▶Figure 250–29

(2) The normally noncurrent-carrying metal parts of equipment and the equipment grounding conductor terminals of the receptacles are connected to the generator frame.

(B) Vehicle- or Trailer-Mounted Generators. A vehicle- or trailer-mounted generator is not required to be connected to a grounding electrode (grounded) if:

(1) The generator frame is bonded to the vehicle or trailer frame

(2) The generator only supplies equipment or receptacles mounted on the vehicle, <u>trailer,</u> or generator ▶Figure 250–30

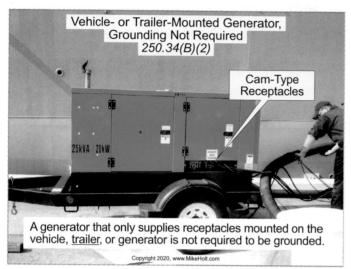

Vehicle- or Trailer-Mounted Generator,
Grounding Not Required
250.34(B)(2)

Cam-Type
Receptacles

25kVA 20kW

A generator that only supplies receptacles mounted on the vehicle, <u>trailer,</u> or generator is not required to be grounded.

Copyright 2020, www.MikeHolt.com

▶Figure 250–30

(3) The normally noncurrent-carrying metal parts of equipment and the equipment grounding conductor terminals of the receptacles are connected to the generator frame.

(C) Neutral Conductor Bonding. <u>The generator manufacturer is required to bond the neutral conductor to the generator frame under all of the following conditions:</u>

(1) <u>The generator is a component of a separately derived system.</u>

(2) <u>A grounding-type receptacle(s) is mounted on the generator or is supplied by the generator.</u>

(3) <u>A receptacle on the generator is supplied by the generator with GFCI protection.</u>

Author's Comment:

▶ This expansion is long overdue. The increased use of trailer-mounted generators adds confusion for installers and perhaps blurs the lines between separately derived systems and temporary wiring methods depending on the application, where vehicle-mounted generators do not.

250.36 High-Impedance Grounded Systems

An Informational Note was added to the end of the section.

250.36 High-Impedance Grounded Systems

High-impedance grounded three-phase systems up to 1,000V are permitted where all the following conditions are met: ▶Figure 250–31

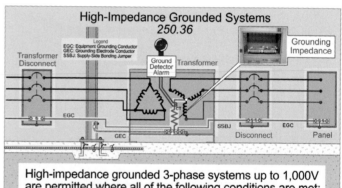

High-Impedance Grounded Systems
250.36

Legend
EGC: Equipment Grounding Conductor
GEC: Grounding Electrode Conductor
SSBJ: Supply-Side Bonding Jumper

Transformer
Disconnect

Ground
Detector
Alarm

Transformer

Grounding
Impedance

EGC

GEC

SSBJ

EGC

Disconnect

Panel

High-impedance grounded 3-phase systems up to 1,000V are permitted where all of the following conditions are met:
(1) Conditions of maintenance and supervision ensure that only qualified persons service the installation.
(2) Ground detectors are installed on the system.
(3) Only line-to-line loads are served.

Copyright 2020, www.MikeHolt.com

▶Figure 250–31

(1) Conditions of maintenance and supervision ensure that only qualified persons service the installation.

(2) Ground detectors are installed on the system.

(3) Only line-to-line loads are served.

Author's Comment:

▶ High-impedance grounded systems are generally referred to as "High-Resistance Grounded Systems" in the industry. These systems are generally used where sudden interruption of power will create increased hazards and where a reduction of incident energy is needed for worker safety.

(A) Grounding Impedance Location. To limit fault current to a very low value, high-impedance grounded systems must have a resistor installed between the neutral point of the separately derived system and the equipment grounding conductor. ▸Figure 250–32

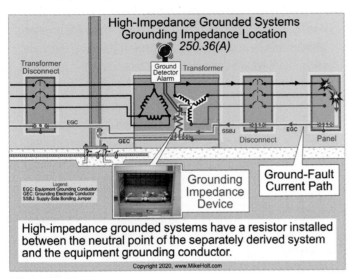

High-impedance grounded systems have a resistor installed between the neutral point of the separately derived system and the equipment grounding conductor.

▸Figure 250–32

Note: According to Annex O of NFPA 70E, *Standard for Electrical Safety in the Workplace*, high-impedance grounding is an effective tool to reduce arc flash hazards.

250.53 Grounding Electrode Installation Requirements

A new last sentence was added to this section to prohibit using rebar as a conductor to interconnect the electrodes of a grounding electrode system. Steel reinforcing rod, better known as "rebar," has been used as a "Ufer" ground for many years and has proven its reliability as an effective ground-fault current path. Even so, rebar cannot be used as a bonding jumper to interconnect grounding electrodes, but it can be used to extend a grounding electrode itself as defined in 250.68.

Analysis

CLARIFIED

250.53(C) Bonding Jumper. This new language makes it clear that rebar cannot be used as a bonding jumper to interconnect the various electrodes of a grounding electrode system. The substantiation indicates that a bonding jumper could be required to be a minimum of 3/0 copper and that ½ in. rebar has not been demonstrated to be equivalent to 3/0 copper.

250.53 Grounding Electrode Installation Requirements

(C) Grounding Electrode Bonding Jumper. Grounding electrode bonding jumpers must be copper when within 18 in. of the earth [250.64(A)]. Exposed grounding electrode bonding jumpers must be securely fastened to the surface and protected from physical damage [250.64(B)]. The bonding jumper to each electrode must be sized in accordance with 250.66 based on the area of the largest phase conductor. ▸Figure 250–33

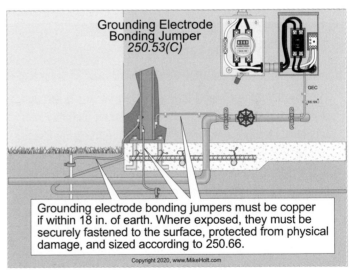

Grounding electrode bonding jumpers must be copper if within 18 in. of earth. Where exposed, they must be securely fastened to the surface, protected from physical damage, and sized according to 250.66.

▸Figure 250–33

▸ Grounding electrode bonding jumpers must terminate by any of the following means in accordance with 250.8(A):

- ◆ Listed pressure connectors
- ◆ Terminal bars
- ◆ Pressure connectors listed as grounding and bonding equipment
- ◆ Exothermic welding
- ◆ Machine screw-type fasteners that engage not less than two threads or are secured with a nut
- ◆ Thread-forming machine screws that engage not less than two threads in the enclosure
- ◆ Connections that are part of a listed assembly
- ◆ Other listed means

When the grounding electrode conductor termination is encased in concrete or buried, the termination fittings must be listed for this purpose [250.70].

Rebar is not permitted to be used to interconnect the electrodes of grounding electrode systems.

250.64 Grounding Electrode Conductor Installation

This section was revised into a list format of (A) through (F) as indicated in the parent text for greater usability with technical changes only in subsection (A) and clarifications throughout. The only technical change as mentioned is that bare, covered, or insulated aluminum or copper-clad aluminum grounding electrode conductors, where the installation complies with one of the three list items, is permitted. That means that bare conductors cannot be exposed to corrosive environments so terminations to outdoor enclosures must be approved for the environment. Last, but certainly not least, anything aluminum cannot be terminated within 18 in. of the earth.

Analysis

EXPANDED The locations where aluminum or copper-clad aluminum grounding electrode conductors are permitted to be installed was expanded. This new language permits the use of bare, covered, or insulated aluminum or copper-clad aluminum grounding electrode conductors where the installation complies with one of the three list items.

CLARIFIED **250.64(A) Aluminum or Copper-Clad Aluminum Conductors.** Requirements were added to this section for bare, covered, or insulated aluminum or copper-clad aluminum grounding electrode conductors.

CLARIFIED **250.64(B)(2) and (3) Exposed to Physical Damage.** According to UL, "Schedule 40 conduit is also suitable for aboveground use indoors or outdoors exposed to sunlight and weather where not subject to physical damage." It was decided that a product that is not suitable for installation where subject to physical damage could not be used to protect a GEC from physical damage. This will be a change in the installation practices of many electricians as Schedule 40 PVC is often used to protect the GEC. List item (2) requires protection for GECs sized 6 AWG and larger where subject to physical damage, and list item (3) requires protection for GECs smaller than 6 AWG no matter where they might be installed.

EXPANDED **250.64(E) Raceways and Enclosures for Grounding Electrode Conductors.** List item (1) requires that where ferrous metal raceways, enclosures, and cable armor are used for the protection of the GEC, those items must be bonded to the GEC at each end.

List item **(3)** was revised to address the case where there are multiple GECs in a single raceway or enclosure. The change requires the bonding jumper between the GEC and the ferrous material to be the same size or larger than the largest GEC contained in that enclosure. While the language does not specifically say each GEC must be bonded, it is required in 250.64(E)(1) and the use of the plural "conductors(s)" in 250.64(E)(3) suggests the requirement.

250.64 Grounding Electrode Conductor Installation

Grounding electrode conductors must be installed as specified in (A) through (F).

(A) Aluminum Conductors. Bare, covered, or insulated aluminum grounding electrode conductors must comply with the following:

(1) Bare or covered conductors without an extruded polymeric covering are not permitted to be installed where subject to corrosive conditions or to be installed in direct contact with concrete.

(2) Terminations made within listed enclosures identified for outdoor use are permitted within 18 in. of the earth. If open-bottom enclosures are installed on a concrete pad, the concrete is not considered earth.

(3) Aluminum conductors external to buildings or equipment enclosures are not permitted to be terminated within 18 in. of the earth.

(B) Conductor Protection. Where exposed, a grounding electrode conductor must be securely fastened to the surface on which it is carried.

(1) Not Exposed to Physical Damage. Grounding electrode conductors 6 AWG and larger can be installed exposed along the surface of the building if securely fastened and not exposed to physical damage. ▶Figure 250–34

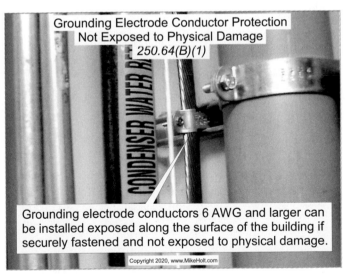

Grounding electrode conductors 6 AWG and larger can be installed exposed along the surface of the building if securely fastened and not exposed to physical damage.

▶Figure 250–34

(2) Exposed to Physical Damage. Grounding electrode conductors subject to physical damage must be protected in rigid metal conduit (RMC), intermediate metal conduit (IMC), Schedule 80 rigid poly-vinyl chloride conduit (PVC), reinforced thermosetting resin conduit Type XW (RTRC-XW), electrical metallic tubing (EMT), or cable armor. ▶Figure 250–35

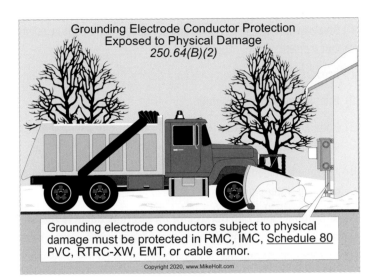

Grounding electrode conductors subject to physical damage must be protected in RMC, IMC, Schedule 80 PVC, RTRC-XW, EMT, or cable armor.

▶Figure 250–35

(3) Smaller Than 6 AWG. Grounding electrode conductors smaller than 6 AWG must be protected in RMC, IMC, Schedule 80 PVC, RTRC-XW, EMT, or cable armor.

Author's Comment:

▶ While Table 250.66 permits the use of 8 AWG copper as the grounding electrode conductor for the phase conductor sizes typically used for a 100A service, use of a GEC smaller than 6 AWG is not common.

(4) In Contact with the Earth. Grounding electrode conductors and bonding jumpers in contact with the earth are not required to comply with the cover requirements of 300.5 but must be protected where subject to physical damage. ▶Figure 250–36

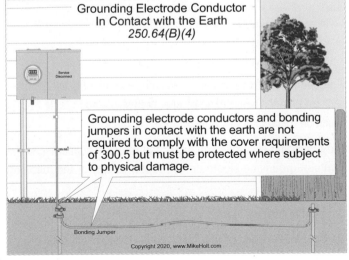

Grounding electrode conductors and bonding jumpers in contact with the earth are not required to comply with the cover requirements of 300.5 but must be protected where subject to physical damage.

▶Figure 250–36

(C) Continuous. Grounding electrode conductor(s) must be installed without a splice or joint except by:

(1) Irreversible compression-type connectors or exothermic welding.

(2) Busbars connected together.

(3) Bolted, riveted, or welded connections of structural metal frames of buildings.

(4) Threaded, welded, brazed, soldered, or bolted-flange connections of metal water piping.

(D) Grounding Electrode Conductor for Multiple Building Disconnects. If a building contains two or more service or building disconnects in separate enclosures, the grounding electrode connections must be made by any of the following methods:

(1) Common Grounding Electrode Conductor and Taps. The unspliced common grounding electrode conductor must be sized in accordance with 250.66 based on the sum of the circular mil area of the largest phase conductor supplying the equipment. ▶Figure 250–37

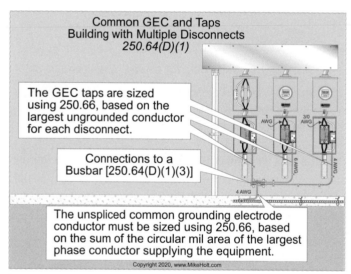

▶Figure 250–37

A grounding electrode conductor tap must extend from each disconnect, and it must be sized no smaller than specified in Table 250.66 based on the area of the largest phase conductor.

The grounding electrode conductor tap must be connected to the common grounding electrode conductor by any of the following methods:

(1) Exothermic welding.

(2) Connectors listed as grounding and bonding equipment.

(3) Connections to a busbar of sufficient length and not less than ¼ in. thick × 2 in. wide that is securely fastened and installed in an accessible location. ▶Figure 250–38

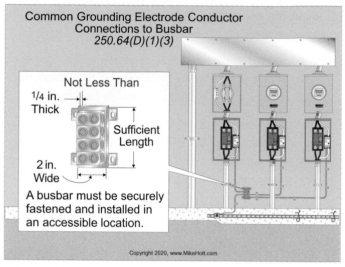

▶Figure 250–38

(2) Individual Grounding Electrode Conductors. An individual grounding electrode conductor from each disconnect, sized in accordance with 250.66 based on the phase conductor(s) supplying the individual disconnect, must connect the grounding electrode system to one of the following:

(1) The service neutral conductor ▶Figure 250–39

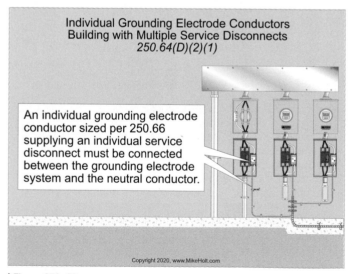

▶Figure 250–39

(2) The equipment grounding conductor of the feeder circuit

(3) The service supply-side bonding jumper

(3) Supply Side of Disconnects. A grounding electrode conductor from an accessible enclosure on the supply side of the disconnects, sized in accordance with 250.66 and based on the phase conductor(s) supplying the disconnect, must connect the grounding electrode system to one of the following:

(1) The service neutral conductor ▶Figure 250–40

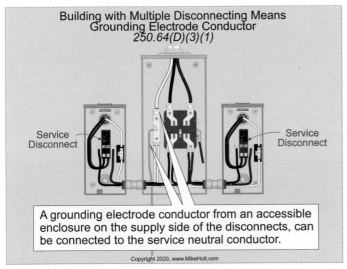

Building with Multiple Disconnecting Means
Grounding Electrode Conductor
250.64(D)(3)(1)

Service
Disconnect

Service
Disconnect

A grounding electrode conductor from an accessible enclosure on the supply side of the disconnects, can be connected to the service neutral conductor.

Copyright 2020, www.MikeHolt.com

▶Figure 250–40

(2) The equipment grounding conductor of the feeder circuit

(3) The service supply-side bonding jumper

(E) Ferrous Raceways Containing Grounding Electrode Conductors

(1) General. To prevent inductive choking of grounding electrode conductors, ferrous metal raceways, enclosures, and cable armor containing grounding electrode conductors must have each end of the raceway or enclosure bonded to the grounding electrode conductor. ▶Figure 250–41

(2) Methods. Raceway bonding must be done in accordance with 250.92(B)(2) through (B)(4).

(3) Size. Bonding jumpers must be the same size or larger than the largest grounding electrode conductor in the raceway or other enclosure.

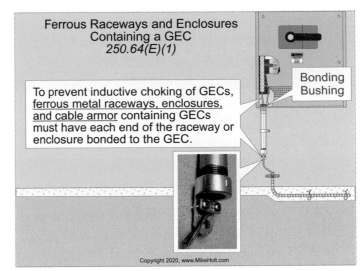

Ferrous Raceways and Enclosures
Containing a GEC
250.64(E)(1)

Bonding
Bushing

To prevent inductive choking of GECs, ferrous metal raceways, enclosures, and cable armor containing GECs must have each end of the raceway or enclosure bonded to the GEC.

Copyright 2020, www.MikeHolt.com

▶Figure 250–41

Author's Comment:

▶ Nonferrous metal raceways, such as aluminum rigid metal conduit, enclosing the grounding electrode conductor are not required to meet the "bonding each end of the raceway to the grounding electrode conductor" provisions of this section.

▶ To save a lot of time and effort, install the grounding electrode conductor in a nonmetallic raceway suitable for the application [352.10(F)]. ▶Figure 250–42

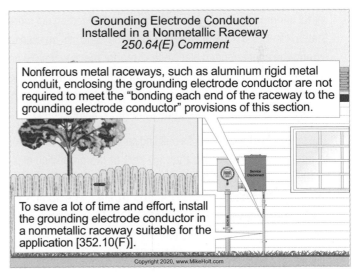

Grounding Electrode Conductor
Installed in a Nonmetallic Raceway
250.64(E) Comment

Nonferrous metal raceways, such as aluminum rigid metal conduit, enclosing the grounding electrode conductor are not required to meet the "bonding each end of the raceway to the grounding electrode conductor" provisions of this section.

Service
Disconnect

To save a lot of time and effort, install the grounding electrode conductor in a nonmetallic raceway suitable for the application [352.10(F)].

Copyright 2020, www.MikeHolt.com

▶Figure 250–42

250.68 Grounding Electrode Conductor and Bonding Jumper Connection to Grounding Electrodes

The requirements for using rebar to extend a grounding electrode were clarified in list items (C)(3)(a), (b), and (c).

Analysis

CLARIFIED **250.68(C)(3) Rebar Type Electrodes.** Rebar must either be continuous or extended using approved connection methods. An extension must be protected from direct contact with the earth and rebar cannot be used to interconnect grounding electrodes.

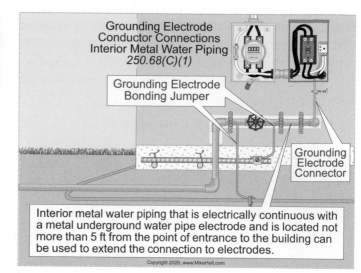

Interior metal water piping that is electrically continuous with a metal underground water pipe electrode and is located not more than 5 ft from the point of entrance to the building can be used to extend the connection to electrodes.

Copyright 2020, www.MikeHolt.com

▸Figure 250–43

250.68 Grounding Electrode Conductor and Bonding Jumper Connection to Grounding Electrodes

(C) Grounding Electrode Conductor Connections. Grounding electrode conductors and bonding jumpers are permitted to terminate at the following locations and be used to extend the connection to an electrode(s):

(1) Interior metal water piping that is electrically continuous with a metal underground water pipe electrode and is located not more than 5 ft from the point of entrance to the building can be used to extend the connection to electrodes. Interior metal water piping located more than 5 ft from the point of entrance to the building is not permitted to be used as a conductor to interconnect electrodes of the grounding electrode system. ▸**Figure 250–43**

(2) The metal structural frame of a building can be used as a conductor to interconnect electrodes that are part of the grounding electrode system, or as a grounding electrode conductor where the hold-down bolts secure the structural steel column to a concrete-encased electrode [250.52(A)(3)]. The hold-down bolts must be connected to the concrete-encased electrode by welding, exothermic welding, the usual steel tie wires, or other approved means. ▸**Figure 250–44** and ▸**Figure 250–45**

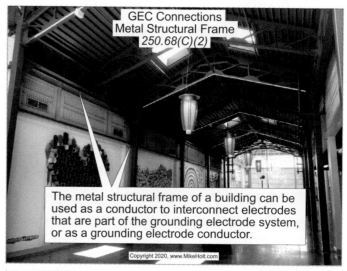

The metal structural frame of a building can be used as a conductor to interconnect electrodes that are part of the grounding electrode system, or as a grounding electrode conductor.

Copyright 2020, www.MikeHolt.com

▸Figure 250–44

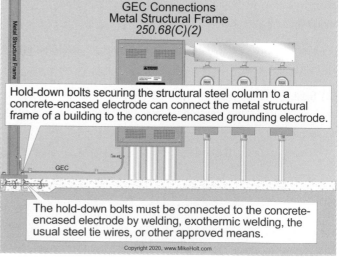

Hold-down bolts securing the structural steel column to a concrete-encased electrode can connect the metal structural frame of a building to the concrete-encased grounding electrode.

The hold-down bolts must be connected to the concrete-encased electrode by welding, exothermic welding, the usual steel tie wires, or other approved means.

Copyright 2020, www.MikeHolt.com

▸Figure 250–45

(3) A rebar-type concrete-encased electrode [250.52(A)(3)] with rebar extended to an accessible location above the concrete foundation or footing is permitted under the following conditions:

(a) The additional rebar section must be continuous with the grounding electrode rebar or must be connected to the grounding electrode rebar and connected together by the usual steel tie wires, exothermic welding, welding, or other effective means. ▶Figure 250–46

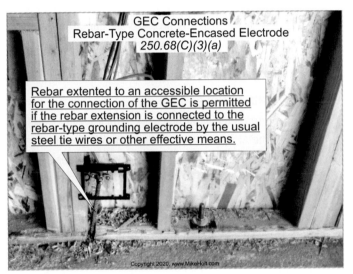

GEC Connections
Rebar-Type Concrete-Encased Electrode
250.68(C)(3)(a)

Rebar extented to an accessible location for the connection of the GEC is permitted if the rebar extension is connected to the rebar-type grounding electrode by the usual steel tie wires or other effective means.

▶Figure 250–46

(b) The rebar extension is not permitted to be in contact with the earth ▶Figure 250–47

(c) The rebar extension is not permitted to be used as a conductor to interconnect the electrodes of grounding electrode systems.

Author's Comment:

▸ The most commonly specified type of rebar becomes very brittle where subjected to heat. Welding or exothermic welding to that type of rebar may not be identified for such use. Check with the structural engineer before making a connection with that type to rebar.

▸ Rebar located outdoors could be subject to corrosion.

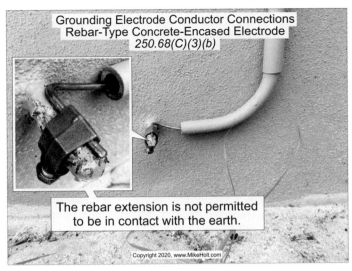

Grounding Electrode Conductor Connections
Rebar-Type Concrete-Encased Electrode
250.68(C)(3)(b)

The rebar extension is not permitted to be in contact with the earth.

▶Figure 250–47

250.98 Bonding Loosely Jointed Metal Raceways

This section was expanded to cover "expansion-deflection, or deflection" fittings as well as the previously covered expansion fittings. This is almost self-explanatory in that whenever metal-to-metal connections are required to be able to move or slide, a bonding jumper must be installed to compensate for this movement and maintain electrical continuity.

Analysis

CLARIFIED Some types of expansion fittings are not suitable for bonding a metal raceway without a bonding jumper. Other types are listed as suitable for that purpose. As always, look at the manufacturer's instructions to determine the installation requirements.

250.98 Bonding Loosely Jointed Metal Raceways

Expansion, expansion-deflection, or deflection fittings and telescoping sections of metal raceways must be made electrically continuous by the use of equipment bonding jumpers. ▶Figure 250–48

Bonding Loosely Jointed Metal Raceways
250.98

Expansion, <u>expansion-deflection, or deflection</u> fittings and telescoping sections of metal raceways must be made electrically continuous by the use of equipment bonding jumpers.

Copyright 2020, www.MikeHolt.com

▶Figure 250–48

250.104 Bonding of Piping Systems and Exposed Structural Metal

This rule was revised to clarify that the bonding jumper to a metal water piping system is never required to be larger than 3/0 copper or 250 kcmil aluminum. The sizing requirements for bonding jumpers to a metal water pipe in a building or structure supplied by a feeder were moved from 250.102(C)(1) to 250.102(D).

Analysis

CLARIFIED

250.104(A) Metal Water Piping. This section addresses the bonding of metal water piping systems in or attached to a building or structure. If there is a metal underground water pipe used as a grounding electrode and an interior metal water piping system, nothing additional is required by this rule as the GEC will provide the required bonding. However, there are cases where the building has a metal interior water piping system supplied by a nonmetallic underground system. In that case, the interior water piping must be bonded by the requirements found here.

The bonding conductor requirements found in (1) now indicate the maximum conductor size is limited to 3/0 copper or 250 kcmil aluminum.

Subsection (3) addresses bonding requirements where the building or structure is served by other than a service. The ending text changed the rule for the size of the bonding jumper. The previous reference to Table 250.102(C)(1), and the size of the feeder or branch-circuit conductors that supply the building or structure, was deleted and replaced by a reference to the requirements of 250.102(D). That section is for sizing a bonding jumper on the load side of an overcurrent protective device. In that case, the sizing of the bonding jumper is in accordance with 250.122 and the rating of the OCPD. There is no need for the larger sized bonding conductors that were required by the reference to 250.102(C)(1) in the previous *Code*.

CLARIFIED

250.104(C) Structural Metal. As with the interior metal water piping system, if the structural metal is not part of the grounding electrode system it must be bonded to the electrical system. The change made in the 2017 cycle of the *NEC* to reference Table 250.102(C)(1) resulted in an inadvertent increase in the size of the bonding jumper as that table includes a 12.50 percent rule. This change makes the maximum required size of the bonding jumper no larger than the maximum required size of the grounding electrode conductor.

CLARIFIED

250.104(D) Separately Derived Systems. As in the other changes in this section, subsections (1) for metal water piping and (2) for structural steel were both revised to say the size of the bonding jumper is based on the largest derived phase conductor and Table 250.102(C)(1), and is not required to be larger than 3/0 copper or 250 kcmil aluminum.

250.104 Bonding of Piping Systems and Exposed Structural Metal

(A) Metal Water Piping System. Electrically continuous metal water piping systems, including sprinkler piping, must be bonded in accordance with 250.104(A)(1), (A)(2), or (A)(3).

(1) Buildings Supplied by a Service. Electrically continuous metal water piping must be bonded to any one of the following: ▶Figure 250–49

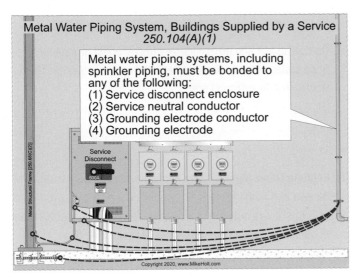

▶Figure 250–49

The metal water piping system bonding jumper must be sized in accordance with Table 250.102(C)(1), based on the size/area of the ungrounded service conductors <u>and it is not required to be larger than 3/0 copper or 250 kcmil aluminum or copper-clad aluminum and except</u> as permitted in 250.104(A)(2) and (A)(3).

▶ **Example**

Question: *What size bonding jumper is required for a metal water piping system if the 300 kcmil service conductors are paralleled in two raceways?* ▶**Figure 250–50**

(a) 1/0 AWG   (b) 2/0 AWG   (c) 3/0 AWG   (d) 4/0 AWG

Answer: *(a) 1/0 AWG*

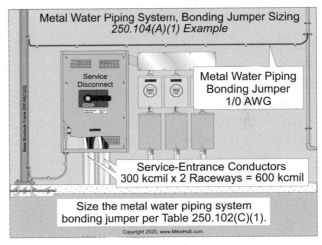

▶Figure 250–50

(1) Service disconnect enclosure,

(2) Service neutral conductor,

(3) Grounding electrode conductor if of sufficient size, or

(4) One of the grounding electrodes of the grounding electrode system if the grounding electrode conductor or bonding jumper to the electrode is of sufficient size.

Author's Comment:

▸ To remove dangerous voltage on metal parts from a ground fault, electrically conductive metal water piping systems, metal sprinkler piping, metal gas piping, as well as exposed structural metal members likely to become energized, must be connected to an effective ground-fault current path [250.4(A)(4)].

The metal-piping system bonding jumper must be copper where within 18 in. of the surface of earth [250.64(A)], must be adequately protected if exposed to physical damage [250.64(B)], and points of attachment must be accessible. A ferrous metal raceway containing a grounding electrode conductor must be made electrically continuous by bonding each end of the raceway to the grounding electrode conductor [250.64(E)].

Author's Comment:

▸ In the 2017 *Code* revision cycle, the reference to Table 250.66 was changed to Table 250.102(C)(1). This resulted in the possibility of the size of the bonding jumper for the interior water piping being larger than 3/0. This was an unintentional consequence of that change and has now been corrected.

Solution:

A 1/0 AWG bonding jumper is required based on 600 kcmil conductors (300 kcmil × 2 raceways) [250.102(C)(1)].

Author's Comment:

▸ If hot and cold metal water pipes are electrically connected, only one bonding jumper is required, either to the cold or hot water pipe.

▸ Bonding is not required for isolated sections of metal water piping connected to a nonmetallic water piping system. In fact, these isolated sections of metal piping should not be bonded because they could become a shock hazard under certain conditions. ▶**Figure 250–51**

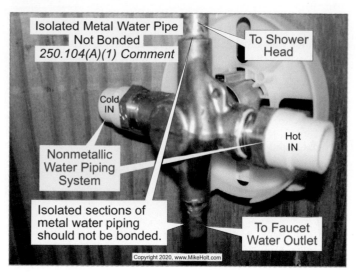

▶Figure 250–51

(2) Bonding Multiple Occupancy Buildings. When an electrically continuous metal water piping system in an individual occupancy is metallically isolated from other occupancies in a building, the metal water piping system for that occupancy can be bonded to the equipment grounding terminal of the occupancy's switchgear, switchboard, or panelboard. The bonding jumper must be sized based on the rating of the circuit overcurrent protective device in accordance with 250.122 [250.102(D)]. ▶Figure 250–52

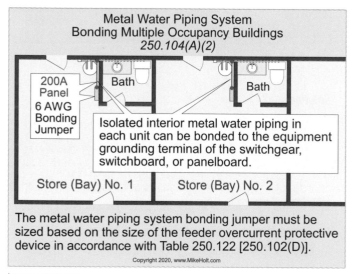

▶Figure 250–52

(3) Buildings Supplied by a Feeder. The metal water piping system of a building that is supplied by a feeder must be bonded to one of the following:

(1) The equipment grounding terminal of the building disconnect enclosure,

(2) The feeder equipment grounding conductor, or

(3) One of the building grounding electrodes of the grounding electrode system if the grounding electrode or bonding jumper to the electrode is of sufficient size.

The bonding jumper is sized in accordance with 250.102(D) and it is not required to be larger than the largest feeder phase or branch-circuit conductor supplying the building.

(B) Bonding Other Metal-Piping Systems. Metal-piping systems in or attached to a building must be bonded. The piping is considered bonded when it is connected to an appliance that is connected to the circuit equipment grounding conductor. ▶Figure 250–53

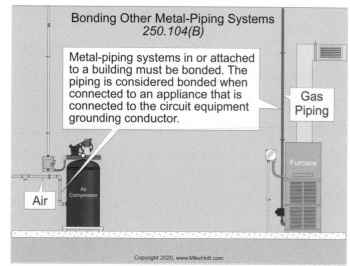

▶Figure 250–53

Note 1: Bonding piping and metal air ducts within the premises will provide additional safety, but this is not required by the *National Electrical Code*.

Note 2: Additional information for gas piping systems can be found in NFPA 54, *National Fuel Gas Code* and NFPA 780, *Standard for the Installation of Lightning Protection Systems.*

(C) Bonding Exposed Structural Metal. Exposed structural metal that is interconnected to form a metal building frame must be bonded to any of the following: ▶Figure 250–54

(1) The service disconnect enclosure,

(2) The neutral at the service disconnect,

(3) The building disconnect enclosure for buildings supplied by a feeder,

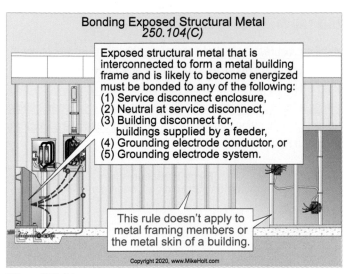

▶Figure 250–54

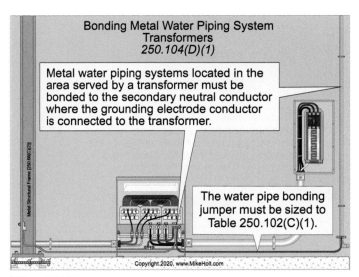

▶Figure 250–55

(4) The grounding electrode conductor where of sufficient size, or

(5) One of the grounding electrodes of the grounding electrode system if the grounding electrode conductor or bonding jumper to the electrode is of sufficient size.

The structural metal bonding conductor must be sized in accordance with Table 250.102(C)(1), based on the size/area of the supply phase conductors and is not be required to be larger than 3/0 copper or 250 kcmil aluminum or copper-clad aluminum. The bonding jumper must be copper where within 18 in. of the surface of the earth [250.64(A)], be securely fastened to the surface on which it is carried [250.64(B)] and be adequately protected if exposed to physical damage [250.64(B)]. In addition, all points of attachment must be accessible, except as permitted in 250.68(A) Ex 1 and 2.

(D) Transformers. Metal water piping systems and structural metal that is interconnected to form a building frame must be bonded to the transformer secondary winding in accordance with 250.104(D)(1) through (D)(3).

(1) Bonding Metal Water Pipe. Metal water piping systems located in the area served by a transformer must be bonded to the secondary neutral conductor where the grounding electrode conductor is connected at the transformer. ▶Figure 250–55

The bonding jumper must be sized in accordance with Table 250.102(C)(1), based on the size/area of the secondary phase conductors and is not be required to be larger than 3/0 copper or 250 kcmil aluminum or copper-clad aluminum.

Ex 2: The metal water piping system can be bonded to the metal structural building frame if it serves as the grounding electrode [250.52(A)(1)] for the transformer. ▶Figure 250–56

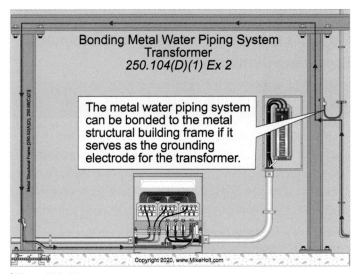

▶Figure 250–56

(2) Bonding Exposed Structural Metal. Exposed structural metal that is interconnected to form the building frame located in the area served by a transformer must be bonded to the secondary neutral conductor where the grounding electrode conductor is connected at the transformer.

The bonding jumper must be sized in accordance with Table 250.102(C)(1), based on the size/area of the secondary phase conductors and is not be required to be larger than 3/0 copper or 250 kcmil aluminum or copper-clad aluminum.

Ex 1: Bonding to the transformer is not required if the metal structural frame serves as the grounding electrode [250.52(A)(2)] for the transformer. ▶Figure 250–57

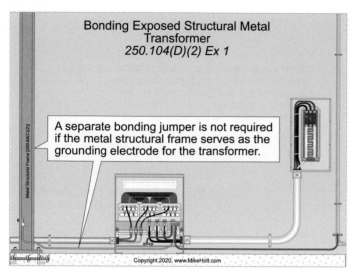

Bonding Exposed Structural Metal
Transformer
250.104(D)(2) Ex 1

Metal Structural Frame [250.68(C)(2)]

A separate bonding jumper is not required if the metal structural frame serves as the grounding electrode for the transformer.

Copyright 2020, www.MikeHolt.com

▶Figure 250–57

Part VI. Equipment Grounding and Equipment Grounding Conductors

250.109 Metal Enclosures

This new section specifically permits metal enclosures to be used to connect bonding jumpers or equipment grounding conductors as a part of the effective ground-fault current path. This has been a long-standing practice; like an unwritten rule. The rule is now written, and the practice is officially permitted!

Analysis

NEW Metal enclosures have been successfully used for many years as part of the equipment bonding path, but there was never *Code* language that specifically permitted them to be used as such. There were multiple Public Inputs (PIs) and Public Comments (PCs) suggesting that these metal enclosures be added as an additional list item in 250.118. All PIs were rejected, but CMP-5 (in response to the PCs) created this new section stating,

"Presently metal items such as cabinets, boxes, wireways and their covers are required to be connected to equipment grounding conductors by 250.110" and, "that these metal items can be used to establish an effective ground-fault current path solves the problem better than just adding those items to the list in 250.118 as suggested by the Public Comments."

250.109 Metal Enclosures

Metal enclosures can be used to connect bonding jumpers or equipment grounding conductors, or both, together to become a part of an effective ground-fault current path. Metal covers and metal fittings attached to these metal enclosures are considered as being connected to bonding jumpers or equipment grounding conductors, or both. ▶Figure 250–58

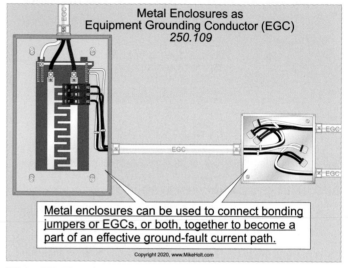

Metal Enclosures as
Equipment Grounding Conductor (EGC)
250.109

EGC

Metal enclosures can be used to connect bonding jumpers or EGCs, or both, together to become a part of an effective ground-fault current path.

Copyright 2020, www.MikeHolt.com

▶Figure 250–58

250.112 Specific Equipment Fastened in Place (Fixed) or Connected by Permanent Wiring Methods

Skid-mounted systems are prominent in industrial processes because they are extremely efficient for storage and distribution of any machinery or equipment used in the process. They include electrical wiring and control systems as well and are a cost-effective means of providing electrical distribution throughout the system. This revision clarifies that for permanently skid-mounted equipment, only EGCs of the wire type are sized by the rules in 250.122.

Analysis

CLARIFIED

250.112(K) Skid-Mounted Equipment. This section requires skid-mounted equipment to be connected to an EGC. The previous *Code* required it to be sized in accordance with the rules in 250.122. The change addresses the fact that only one of the 14 types of EGCs found in 250.118 is sized per 250.122. The revised wording says that "Wire-type equipment grounding conductors must be sized as required by 250.122."

250.114 Equipment Connected by Cord and Plug

Portable luminaires? Handlamps? There are just too many slang terms for these items for many to know exactly what this type of equipment is based on in the *Code* language. Suffice it to say, whatever you are calling your construction lights today, they are required to be connected to an equipment grounding conductor (a three-prong plug). Non-technical edits were made in the parent text regarding the aforementioned, and list items (3)e and (4)e were revised to include the term "portable luminaires" to ensure that the grounding needs for these products is included and applies to both residential and non-residential occupancies.

Analysis

CLARIFIED

Portable handlamps were originally covered by UL 298, *Portable Electric Hand Lamps*. That standard was withdrawn in 2004 and superseded by UL 153, *Portable Electric Luminaires*. Devices that were once called "Portable Handlamps" on their label are now being labeled as "Portable Luminaires," but are the same product. The term "portable handlamps" was retained as there are products that still use that term.

250.114 Equipment Connected by Cord and Plug

Exposed, normally noncurrent-carrying metal parts of cord-and-plug connected equipment must be connected to the equipment grounding conductor of the circuit suppling the equipment under any of the following conditions:

Ex: Listed tools, listed appliances, and listed equipment covered in 250.114(2) through (4) is not be required to be connected to an equipment grounding conductor where protected by a system of double insulation or its equivalent. Double insulated equipment must be distinctively marked.

(1) In hazardous (classified) locations [Articles 500 through 517].

(2) Where operated at over 150V to ground.

Ex 1 to (2): Motors that are guarded.

Ex 2 to (2): Metal frames of exempted electrically heated appliances.

(3) In residential occupancies:

    a. Refrigerators, freezers, and air conditioners.

    b. Clothes-washing, clothes-drying, and dish-washing machines, ranges, kitchen waste disposers, IT equipment, sump pumps, and electrical aquarium equipment.

Author's Comment:

▸ Electric ranges and clothes dryers are shipped from the factory with a bonding strap that bonds the metal frame of the appliance to the neutral termination of the cord connection terminal block. This bonding strap may or may not have to be removed! The *Code* requires an insulated neutral for these appliances using a 4-wire branch circuit and the bonding strap should be removed—that is not always the case. If an existing 3-wire branch circuit is to supply a replacement appliance, the factory-installed bonding strap is to remain in place [250.140 Ex]. ▸Figure 250–59

    c. Hand-held, stationary or fixed, and light industrial motor-operated tools.

    d. Motor-operated hedge clippers, lawn mowers, snow-blowers, and wet scrubbers.

    e. Portable handlamps and portable luminaires.

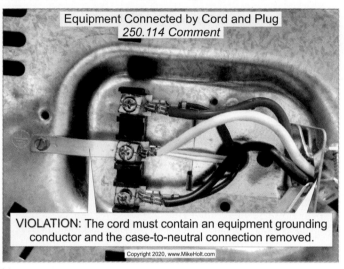

VIOLATION: The cord must contain an equipment grounding conductor and the case-to-neutral connection removed.

Copyright 2020, www.MikeHolt.com

▶Figure 250–59

(4) In other than residential occupancies:

   a. Refrigerators, freezers, and air conditioners.

   b. Clothes-washing, clothes-drying, and dish-washing machines, IT equipment, sump pumps, and electrical aquarium equipment.

   c. Hand-held, stationary or fixed, and light industrial motor-operated tools.

   d. Motor-operated hedge clippers, lawn mowers, snow-blowers, and wet scrubbers.

   e. Portable handlamps and portable luminaires.

   f. Appliances used in damp or wet locations or by persons standing on the ground, standing on metal floors, or working inside of metal tanks or boilers.

   g. Tools likely to be used in wet or conductive locations

Ex: Tools and portable handlamps and portable luminaires likely to be used in wet or conductive locations are not required to be connected to an equipment grounding conductor where supplied through an isolating transformer with an ungrounded secondary not over 50V.

250.119 Identification of Equipment Grounding Conductors

The revision to this section permits an insulted conductor of a multiconductor cable to be re-identified as an EGC, no matter what the occupancy or conditions of maintenance and supervision are.

Analysis

CLARIFIED   EDITED

250.119(B) Multiconductor Cable. This subsection was revised. In the previous *Code*, you were only permitted to re-identify one or more insulated conductors in a multi-conductor cable as an EGC where the "conditions of maintenance and supervision ensure that only qualified persons service the installation." This was one of two re-identification rules in the *NEC* that had such a restrictive requirement. The panel agreed with the submitter of the PI that there is no logical reason for that requirement. The re-identification of one or more insulated conductors as an EGC is now permitted regardless of the conditions of main-tenance and supervision. The second change was in 200.6(E) Ex 1 which was revised in the same manner.

250.119 Identification of Equipment Grounding Conductors

Unless required to be insulated in this *Code*, equipment grounding conductors can be bare or covered.

Insulated equipment grounding conductors 6 AWG and smaller must have a continuous outer finish that is either green or green with one or more yellow stripes. ▶Figure 250–60

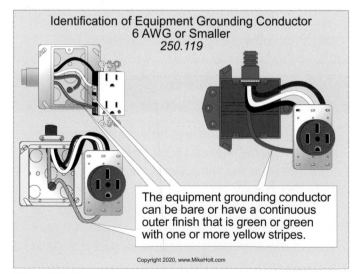

Identification of Equipment Grounding Conductor 6 AWG or Smaller
250.119

The equipment grounding conductor can be bare or have a continuous outer finish that is green or green with one or more yellow stripes.

Copyright 2020, www.MikeHolt.com

▶Figure 250–60

Conductors with insulation that is green, or green with one or more yellow stripes, are not permitted to be used for a phase or neutral conductor.

▸ The *NEC* neither requires nor prohibits the use of the color green for the identification of grounding electrode conductors. ▸Figure 250–61

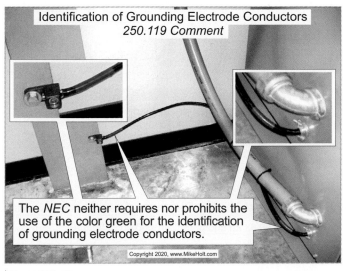

Identification of Grounding Electrode Conductors
250.119 Comment

The *NEC* neither requires nor prohibits the use of the color green for the identification of grounding electrode conductors.

Copyright 2020, www.MikeHolt.com

▸Figure 250–61

(B) Multiconductor Cable

One or more insulated conductors in a multiconductor cable, at the time of installation, are permitted to be permanently identified as equipment grounding conductors at each end and at every point where the conductors are accessible by one of the following means:

(1) Stripping the insulation from the entire exposed length.

(2) Coloring the exposed insulation green.

(3) Marking the exposed insulation with green tape or green adhesive labels. Identification must encircle the conductor.

250.120 Equipment Grounding Conductor Installation

The permitted uses of aluminum and copper-clad aluminum EGCs has been expanded. The only technical change in this section is that bare, covered, or insulated aluminum or copper-clad aluminum grounding electrode conductors (where the installation complies with one of the three list items) are permitted. Bare conductors cannot be exposed to corrosive environments and terminations to outdoor enclosures must be approved for the environment. Last but certainly not least, anything aluminum cannot be terminated within 18 in. of the earth.

Analysis

  250.120(B) Aluminum and Copper-Clad Aluminum Conductors. There **EXPANDED EDITED** are both technical and editorial changes in this section. The editorial changes were conversions to a list format for the rules. The text was revised to include "covered" as well as bare and insulated conductors. Section 250.118(1) says that EGCs may be bare, covered, or insulated; 250.120(B) previously only addressed bare and insulated conductors.

250.120 Equipment Grounding Conductor Installation

An equipment grounding conductor must be installed as follows:

(B) Aluminum Conductors. Equipment grounding conductors of bare, covered, or insulated aluminum must be installed as follows:

(1) Unless part of a Chapter 3 wiring method, bare or covered conductors are not permitted to be installed where subject to corrosive conditions or in direct contact with concrete, masonry, or the earth.

(2) Terminations made within outdoor enclosures that are listed and identified for the environment are permitted within 18 in. of the bottom of the enclosure.

(3) Aluminum conductors external to buildings or enclosures are not permitted to be terminated within 18 in. of the earth, unless terminated within a listed wire connector system.

250.121 Restricted Use of Equipment Grounding Conductors

Where the metal structure of a building is permitted to be used as a grounding electrode conductor (GEC), and in fact is required to be part of the grounding system, such is not the case when it comes to equipment grounding conductors (EGCs). A new subsection was added to prohibit using the structural metal frame of a building or structure as an EGC. That rule was moved from 250.136(A) to this section.

Analysis

EDITED The title of this section was changed from "Use of Equipment Grounding Conductors" to "Restricted Use of Equipment Grounding Conductors" as it only covers restrictions and not uses of EGCs. It was also divided into two subsections.

EDITED Subsection (A) was the previous rule prohibiting using an EGC as a GEC. The only change here is the addition of the subsection's title. The existing exception permits the use of a single conductor as both an EGC and a GEC provided all the requirements for both remain met.

NEW Subsection (B) is new and prohibits using the metal frame of a building or structure as an EGC. This was relocated from 250.136(A) to clarify this prohibition on the use of a metal building structure as an EGC applies throughout the *Code*.

250.121 <u>Restricted</u> Use of Equipment Grounding Conductors

(A) <u>Grounding Electrode Conductor.</u> An equipment grounding conductor is not permitted to be used as a grounding electrode conductor. ▸Figure 250–62

Ex: An equipment grounding conductor meeting the requirements for an equipment grounding conductor and grounding electrode conductor can be used as a grounding electrode conductor.

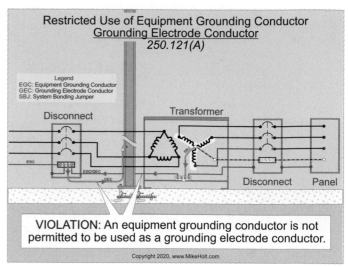

▸Figure 250–62

(B) <u>Metal Frame of Building.</u> The structural metal frame of a building is not to be used as an equipment grounding conductor.

Author's Comment:

▸ Here is an example of why it is so important for you to understand the terminology used throughout the *NEC*. While the structural metal frame of a building is not permitted to be used as an "equipment grounding conductor," the metal structure of a building is permitted to be used as a "grounding electrode conductor."

250.122 Sizing Equipment Grounding Conductors

The language here was revised to clarify that the increase in the size of the phase conductors as a result of required ampacity adjustment and/or correction do not require an increase in the size of the EGC and an exception was added. Hopefully this will put to rest the long-standing debates about this proportional increase of the EGC.

Analysis

CLARIFIED

250.122(B) Increased in Size. The new language says the increase in size of the EGC is required anytime the phase conductors are increased in size other than as required by 310.15(B) or 310.15(C). The proportional increase in the EGC is required whenever the phase conductors are larger than the minimum size permitted by the *NEC* rules.

The exception permits EGCs to be sized by a qualified person to provide an effective ground-fault current path, but the *Code* gives no guidance as to the use of this exception.

EXPANDED

250.122(C) Multiple Circuits. Section 300.5 addresses the installation of EGCs in a trench and requires them to be close to the phase and neutral circuit conductors. This expansion permits a single EGC to be used with multiple circuits installed within a trench.

EXPANDED

250.122(F)(1) and (2) Conductors in Parallel. The title of (1)(a) was revised to include auxiliary gutters and subsection (2)(a) was added to clarify that the where multiconductor cables are installed in parallel, the EGC in each cable must be sized in accordance with 250.122, except as provided in 250.122(F)(2) (c) for raceway, auxiliary gutter, or cable tray installations.

As for 250.122(F)(2)(a), the general rule is that each multiconductor cable of a set of cables connected in parallel, must have a full sized EGC within the cable. This is the same as the rule for paralleled circuits in raceways. In both cases the EGCs in the cables or raceways must be sized based on Table 250.122.

The provisions of 250.122(F)(2)(c) permit a single external equipment grounding conductor to be used with cables that are installed in parallel within a raceway, auxiliary gutters, or cable trays. This EGC is sized based on the upstream OCPD and Table 250.122 and is required to be connected in parallel with the internal cable's EGCs.

250.122 Sizing Equipment Grounding Conductors

(A) General. Equipment grounding conductors must be sized not smaller than shown in Table 250.122, based on the rating of the circuit overcurrent protective device; however, the equipment grounding conductor is not required to be larger than the phase conductors. ▶Figure 250–63

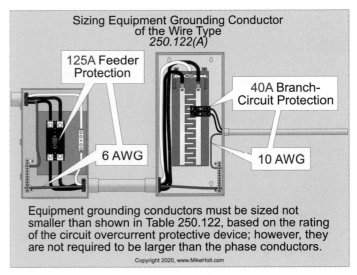

Equipment grounding conductors must be sized not smaller than shown in Table 250.122, based on the rating of the circuit overcurrent protective device; however, they are not required to be larger than the phase conductors.

Copyright 2020, www.MikeHolt.com

▶Figure 250–63

Table 250.122 Sizing Equipment Grounding Conductor

Overcurrent Protective Device Rating	Copper Conductor
15A	14 AWG
20A	12 AWG
25A–60A	10 AWG
70A–100A	8 AWG
110A–200A	6 AWG
225A–300A	4 AWG
350A–400A	3 AWG
450A–500A	2 AWG
600A	1 AWG
700A–800A	1/0 AWG
1,000A	2/0 AWG
1,200A	3/0 AWG

Note: Where necessary to comply with 250.4(A)(5) or (B)(4), the equipment grounding conductor might be required to be sized larger than given in this table.

(B) Increased in Size. If phase conductors are increased in size for any reason other than as required in 310.15(B) or 310.15(C), wire-type equipment grounding conductors, if installed, must be increased in size proportionately to the increase in the circular mil area of the phase conductors. ▸Figure 250–64

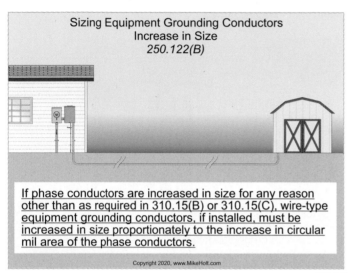

▸Figure 250–64

Ex: Equipment grounding conductors can be sized by a qualified person to provide an effective ground-fault current path in accordance with 250.4(A)(5) or (B)(4).

Author's Comment:

▸ Phase conductors are sometimes increased in size to accommodate conductor voltage drop, short-circuit rating, or simply for future capacity.

▸ **Example**

Question: If the phase conductors for a 40A circuit (with 75°C terminals) are increased in size from 8 AWG to 6 AWG due to voltage drop, the circuit equipment grounding conductor must be increased in size from 10 AWG to _____. ▸Figure 250–65

(a) 8 AWG   (b) 6 AWG   (c) 4 AWG   (d) 3 AWG

Answer: (a) 8 AWG

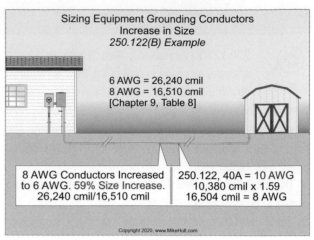

▸Figure 250–65

Solution:

The circular mil area of 6 AWG is 59 percent more than 8 AWG (26,240 cmil/16,510 cmil) [Chapter 9, Table 8]. According to Table 250.122, the circuit equipment grounding conductor for a 40A overcurrent protective device will be 10 AWG (10,380 cmil), but the circuit equipment grounding conductor for this circuit must be increased in size by a multiplier of 159%.

Conductor Size = 10,380 cmil × 159%
Conductor Size = 16,504 cmil

The circuit equipment grounding conductor must be increased to 8 AWG [Chapter 9, Table 8].

Author's Comment:

▸ One example that may fit under the exception is where the branch-circuit conductors for an air conditioner are larger than the minimum circuit ampacity shown on the unit's nameplate. Take for example where the nameplate gives a minimum circuit ampacity of 27A and a maximum OCPD of 45A. The *Code* permits the use of 10 AWG conductors on the 45A breaker. If 8 AWG conductors are installed because of a voltage-drop concern that would normally require an increase in size of the EGC.

▸ In this instance, the case could be made that the EGC is still an effective ground-fault current path where it is sized based on 250.122 and the 45A OCPD, without having to increase its size because of the larger phase conductors.

(C) Multiple Circuits. When multiple circuits are installed in the same raceway, cable, trench, or cable tray, a single equipment grounding conductor sized in accordance with Table 250.122, based on the rating of the largest overcurrent device protecting the circuit conductors may be installed. ▸Figure 250–66

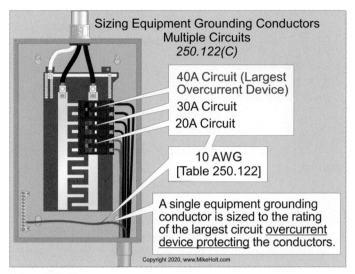

Sizing Equipment Grounding Conductors Multiple Circuits 250.122(C)

40A Circuit (Largest Overcurrent Device)

30A Circuit

20A Circuit

10 AWG [Table 250.122]

A single equipment grounding conductor is sized to the rating of the largest circuit overcurrent device protecting the conductors.

Copyright 2020, www.MikeHolt.com

▸Figure 250–66

(D) Motor Branch Circuits. Equipment grounding conductors for motor circuits must be sized in accordance with 250.122(D)(1) or (D)(2).

(1) General. The equipment grounding conductor must not be smaller than determined by 250.122(A), based on the rating of the motor circuit branch-circuit short-circuit and ground-fault protective device sized in accordance with 430.52(C)(1) Ex 1.

Author's Comment:

▸ The equipment grounding conductor is not required to be larger than the motor circuit conductors; see 250.122(A).

▸ **Example**

Question: What size equipment grounding conductor of the wire type is required for a 14 AWG motor branch circuit [430.22], protected with a 2-pole, 40A circuit breaker in accordance with 430.22 and 430.52(C)(1)? ▸**Figure 250–67**

(a) 14 AWG   (b) 12 AWG   (c) 10 AWG   (d) 8 AWG

Answer: *(a) 14 AWG*

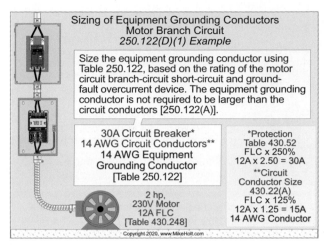

Sizing of Equipment Grounding Conductors Motor Branch Circuit 250.122(D)(1) Example

Size the equipment grounding conductor using Table 250.122, based on the rating of the motor circuit branch-circuit short-circuit and ground-fault overcurrent device. The equipment grounding conductor is not required to be larger than the circuit conductors [250.122(A)].

30A Circuit Breaker*
14 AWG Circuit Conductors**
14 AWG Equipment Grounding Conductor
[Table 250.122]

*Protection
Table 430.52
FLC x 250%
12A x 2.50 = 30A

**Circuit Conductor Size
430.22(A)
FLC x 125%
12A x 1.25 = 15A
14 AWG Conductor

2 hp, 230V Motor
12A FLC
[Table 430.248]

Copyright 2020, www.MikeHolt.com

▸Figure 250–67

Solution:

The equipment grounding conductor is not required to be larger than the 14 AWG motor branch circuit conductors [250.122(D)(1) and 250.122(A)].

(F) Parallel Conductors. Where circuit conductors are installed in parallel in accordance with 310.10(G), an equipment grounding conductor of the wire type must be installed in accordance with the following:

(1) Nonmetallic Raceways or Cable Trays

(a) Parallel Conductors in a Single Nonmetallic Raceway or Cable Tray. If parallel circuit conductors are installed in a single nonmetallic raceway or cable tray, a single wire-type equipment grounding conductor, sized in accordance with Table 250.122 based on the rating of the circuit overcurrent protective device, must be installed with the parallel circuit conductors.

(b) Parallel Conductor in Multiple Nonmetallic Raceways. If parallel circuit conductors are installed in multiple nonmetallic raceways, a wire-type equipment grounding conductor is required in each nonmetallic raceway. The parallel equipment grounding conductors must be connected in parallel in accordance with 310.10(G) and each parallel equipment grounding conductor must be sized in accordance with Table 250.122, based on the rating of the circuit overcurrent protective device. ▸Figure 250–68

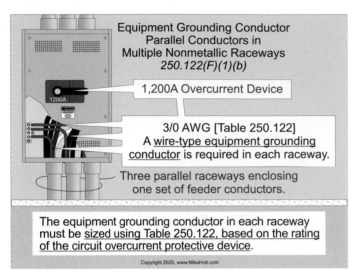

▶Figure 250–68

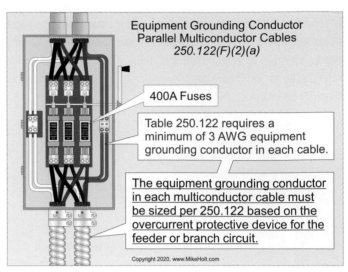

▶Figure 250–69

▶ **Example**

Question: What size equipment grounding conductor of the wire type is required for a 4,000A feeder containing thirteen parallel sets of 500 kcmil per phase in PVC conduit?

(a) 250 kcmil   (b) 300 kcmil   (c) 400 kcmil   (d) 500 kcmil

Answer: (d) 500 kcmil

Solution:

According to Table 250.122, the equipment grounding conductor in each raceway must not be smaller than 750 kcmil aluminum.

(c) Wire-Type Equipment Grounding Conductors in Cable Trays. Wire-type equipment grounding conductors installed in cable trays must meet the minimum requirements of 392.10(B)(1)(c).

(d) Metal Raceways or Cable Trays. Metal raceways can serve as the required equipment grounding conductor in accordance with 250.118 and cable trays complying with 392.60(B) can serve as the required equipment grounding conductor.

(2) Parallel Multiconductor Cables

(a) Except as provided in 250.122(F)(2)(c) for raceway or cable tray installations, the equipment grounding conductor in each multiconductor cable must be sized in accordance with 250.122 based on the overcurrent protective device for the feeder or branch circuit. ▶Figure 250–69

(b) If circuit conductors of multiconductor cables are connected in parallel, the equipment grounding conductor(s) in each cable must be connected in parallel.

(c) If multiconductor cables are paralleled in the same raceway or cable tray, a single equipment grounding conductor that is sized in accordance with 250.122 is permitted in combination with the equipment grounding conductors provided within the multiconductor cables and all equipment grounding conductors must be connected together.

(d) Equipment grounding conductors installed in cable trays must meet the requirements of 392.10(B)(1)(c).

Cable trays complying with 392.60(B) and metal raceways in accordance with 250.118 can be used as the required equipment grounding conductor.

250.132 Short Sections of Raceway

This rule was revised to clarify that if short sections of raceways or cable armor are required to be "grounded" they must be connected to an EGC. Short sections of metal raceways used to sleeve and protect a wiring method and effectively connected to a metal box which is connected to the equipment grounding conductor, comply with this provision. A similar sleeve that is mid-span and not connected at either end is not compliant and electrical continuity to ground must be established by another means.

Analysis

CLARIFIED
This change is part of the ongoing process to use the correct grounding and bonding terms throughout the *NEC*. The previous language requiring the raceway or cable armor to be "grounded" was replaced with a requirement that they be connected to an EGC.

Author's Comment:

▸ This rule uses the term "if required." I am not sure exactly what short isolated sections of raceway or cable armor are required by other sections of the *Code* to be connected to an EGC.

250.136 Equipment Secured to Grounded Metal Supports

This rule was relocated here from 250.121 and clarifies that equipment is considered connected to the equipment grounding conductor where a metal rack or structure is connected to an equipment grounding conductor and in electrical contact with the equipment. The reappearance of this rule in this location makes it apparent it applies throughout the *NEC*.

Analysis

RELOCATED
This section was revised for clarity and the rule prohibiting the use of the structural metal frame of a building as an equipment grounding conductor was moved to 250.121(B). The relocation was to clarify that the prohibition on using the metal structure of a building as an EGC applies throughout the *Code*.

The rule provides that equipment secured to, and in electrical contact with, a metal rack or structure is considered as being connected to an EGC if the metal rack or structure is connected to an EGC by one of the means identified 250.134.

250.136 Equipment Secured to Grounded Metal Supports

Metal equipment and enclosures secured to and in electrical contact with a metal rack <u>or structure are considered</u> connected to an equipment grounding conductor <u>if the metal rack or structure is connected to an equipment grounding conductor</u> in accordance with 250.134. ▸Figure 250–70

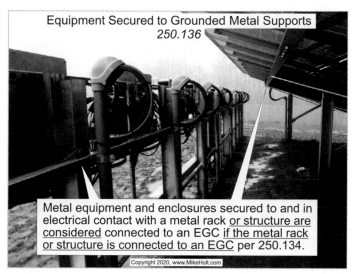

Equipment Secured to Grounded Metal Supports
250.136

Metal equipment and enclosures secured to and in electrical contact with a metal rack <u>or structure are considered</u> connected to an EGC <u>if the metal rack or structure is connected to an EGC</u> per 250.134.

Copyright 2020, www.MikeHolt.com

▸Figure 250–70

Author's Comment:

▸ This would be an unusual application as the EGC is run with the wiring method that supplies or connects to the equipment and is connected within the equipment. An EGC connected to the metal rack or structure that supports the equipment and is not connected to the equipment itself is rare.

250.138 Cord-and-Plug-Connected Equipment

The incorrect term of "grounded" was removed from this section to avoid confusion. Grounded means exactly that, connected to the ground or the Earth and even though an equipment grounding conductor does eventually make its way to the Earth when terminated at the main disconnecting means, it serves a different purpose and must make its way back to the source of the electrical power to maintain an effective ground-fault current path.

Analysis

CLARIFIED EDITED

This section required that if cord-and-plug-connected equipment was grounded it must be connected to an equipment grounding conductor. That language was confusing and was revised for clarity. It now says that if such equipment is required to be connected to an EGC, it must be connected by one of the methods in 250.136(A) or (B). Section 250.136(A) provides for a connection to an EGC that is part of the power-supply cord or cable that is terminated with a grounding type attachment plug. Subsection (B) permits a separate flexible wire or strap, that is connected to an EGC and protected against physical damage, to be the EGC connection to the equipment. This is permitted only where the flexible wire or strap is part of the equipment.

Analysis

CLARIFIED EDITED

The edits made in the terminology of this entire section were intended to provide consistency with other parts of the *NEC* and to account for nonmetallic boxes. The previous *Code* used the term "grounded" which is defined in Article 100 as "connected to ground or to a conductive body that extends the ground connection." "Grounded" was never the intent here. A receptacle requires a connection to an EGC so there is an effective ground-fault current path and "connection to ground (earth)" does not provide one. Everything having to do with any receptacle, its yoke or strap, the metal box on which it is mounted, the raised metal coved to which it is mounted, and the metal faceplate that covers the receptacle, must be connected to an equipment grounding conductor. Anything less that that makes that third prong useless!!

250.138 Cord-and-Plug-Connected

(A) Equipment Grounding Conductor. Metal parts of cord-and-plug-connected equipment must be connected to an equipment grounding conductor that terminates to a grounding-type attachment plug but only when required.

250.146 Connecting Receptacle Grounding Terminal to an Equipment Grounding Conductor

The section's title and its parent text were revised to clarify that a receptacle must be connected to an EGC. In keeping with the intent, the language in (A), (C), and (D) was also revised to clarify that a receptacle grounding terminal must be connected to an equipment grounding conductor.

250.146 Connecting Receptacle Grounding Terminal to an <u>Equipment Grounding Conductor</u>

An equipment bonding conductor is required to connect the grounding contacts of a receptacle to a <u>metal box that is connected to an equipment grounding conductor,</u> except as permitted in (A) through (D). ▶Figure 250–71

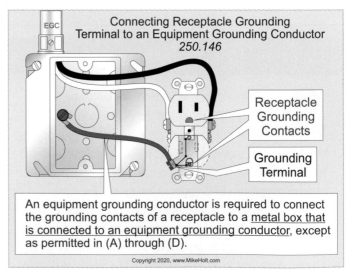

Connecting Receptacle Grounding Terminal to an Equipment Grounding Conductor
250.146

Receptacle Grounding Contacts

Grounding Terminal

An equipment grounding conductor is required to connect the grounding contacts of a receptacle to a <u>metal box that is connected to an equipment grounding conductor</u>, except as permitted in (A) through (D).

Copyright 2020, www.MikeHolt.com

▶Figure 250–71

Author's Comment:

▸ The *NEC* does not restrict the position of the receptacle grounding terminal; it can be up, down, or sideways. *Code* proposals to specify the mounting position of receptacles have always been rejected. ▸Figure 250–72

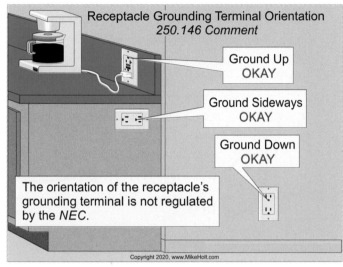

▸Figure 250–72

(A) Surface-Mounted Box. A receptacle having direct metal-to-metal contact between the receptacle <u>strap or</u> yoke and a surface metal box is considered to be connected to the required effective ground-fault current path. To ensure sufficient metal-to-metal contact, at least one of the insulating retaining washers on the yoke screw must be removed. ▸Figure 250–73

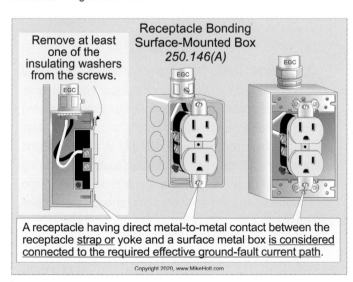

▸Figure 250–73

A receptacle installed on a cover is considered to be connected to the required effective ground-fault current path <u>under both of the following conditions</u>:

(1) The receptacle is attached to the metal cover with at least two fasteners that have a thread locking, or screw or nut locking means.

(2) The cover mounting holes are located on a flat non-raised portion of the cover. ▸Figure 250–74

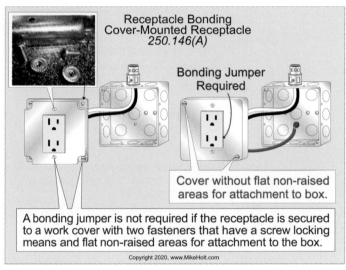

▸Figure 250–74

(B) Self-Grounding Receptacles. Receptacle yokes listed as self-grounding establish the equipment bonding between the receptacle yoke and a metal box. ▸Figure 250–75

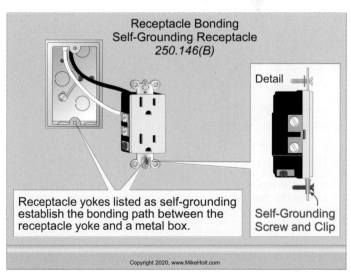

▸Figure 250–75

(C) Floor Boxes. Listed metal floor boxes must establish the bonding path between the receptacle yoke and a metal box.

(D) Isolated Ground Receptacles. The grounding terminal of an isolated ground receptacle must be connected to an insulated equipment grounding conductor. ▸Figure 250–76

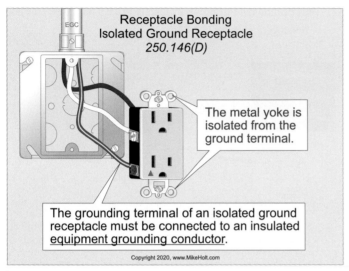

**Receptacle Bonding
Isolated Ground Receptacle
250.146(D)**

The metal yoke is isolated from the ground terminal.

The grounding terminal of an isolated ground receptacle must be connected to an insulated equipment grounding conductor.

Copyright 2020, www.MikeHolt.com

▸Figure 250–76

Note: Use of an isolated equipment grounding conductor does not relieve the requirement for connecting the raceway system and outlet box to an equipment grounding conductor. ▸Figure 250–77

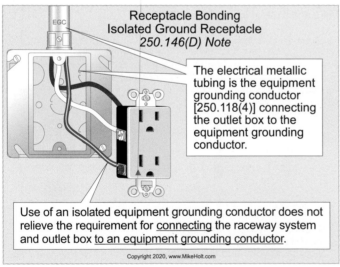

**Receptacle Bonding
Isolated Ground Receptacle
250.146(D) Note**

The electrical metallic tubing is the equipment grounding conductor [250.118(4)] connecting the outlet box to the equipment grounding conductor.

Use of an isolated equipment grounding conductor does not relieve the requirement for connecting the raceway system and outlet box to an equipment grounding conductor.

Copyright 2020, www.MikeHolt.com

▸Figure 250–77

Author's Comment:

▸ Type AC cable containing an insulated equipment grounding conductor can be used to supply isolated ground receptacles because the metal armor of the cable is listed as an equipment grounding conductor [250.118(8)]. ▸Figure 250–78

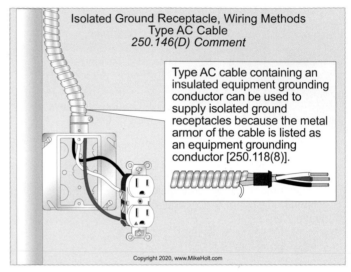

**Isolated Ground Receptacle, Wiring Methods
Type AC Cable
250.146(D) Comment**

Type AC cable containing an insulated equipment grounding conductor can be used to supply isolated ground receptacles because the metal armor of the cable is listed as an equipment grounding conductor [250.118(8)].

Copyright 2020, www.MikeHolt.com

▸Figure 250–78

Author's Comment:

▸ Interlocked Type MC[AP®] cable with a 10 AWG bare aluminum grounding/bonding conductor can be used to supply isolated ground receptacles because the combination of the metal armor and the 10 AWG bare aluminum conductor is listed as an equipment grounding conductor [250.118(10)(b)]. ▸Figure 250–79

Caution

⚡ *Type MC Cable.* The metal armor sheath of traditional interlocked Type MC cable containing an insulated equipment grounding conductor is not listed as an equipment grounding conductor. Therefore, this wiring method with a single equipment grounding conductor cannot supply an isolated ground receptacle. Type MC cable with two insulated equipment grounding conductors is acceptable, since one bonds to the metal box and the other one connects to the isolated ground receptacle. ▸Figure 250–80

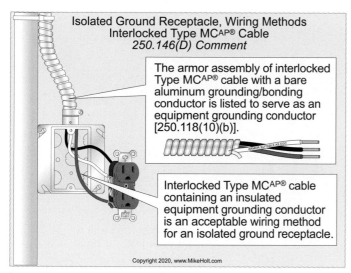

Isolated Ground Receptacle, Wiring Methods
Interlocked Type MC^{AP®} Cable
250.146(D) Comment

The armor assembly of interlocked Type MC^{AP®} cable with a bare aluminum grounding/bonding conductor is listed to serve as an equipment grounding conductor [250.118(10)(b)].

ARMOR SUITABLE AS EGC

Interlocked Type MC^{AP®} cable containing an insulated equipment grounding conductor is an acceptable wiring method for an isolated ground receptacle.

Copyright 2020, www.MikeHolt.com

▶Figure 250–79

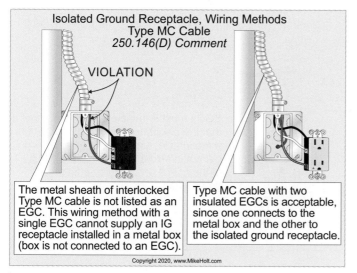

Isolated Ground Receptacle, Wiring Methods
Type MC Cable
250.146(D) Comment

VIOLATION

The metal sheath of interlocked Type MC cable is not listed as an EGC. This wiring method with a single EGC cannot supply an IG receptacle installed in a metal box (box is not connected to an EGC).

Type MC cable with two insulated EGCs is acceptable, since one connects to the metal box and the other to the isolated ground receptacle.

Copyright 2020, www.MikeHolt.com

▶Figure 250–80

Author's Comment:

▶ When should an isolated ground receptacle be installed and how should the isolated ground system be designed? These questions are design issues and are not answered based on the *NEC* alone [90.1(A)]. In most cases, using isolated ground receptacles is a waste of money. For example, IEEE 1100, Powering and Grounding Electronic Equipment (Emerald Book) states, "The results from the use of the isolated ground method range from no observable effects, the desired effects, or worse noise conditions than when standard equipment bonding configurations are used to serve electronic load equipment [8.5.3.2]."

▶ Few electrical installations truly require an isolated ground system. For those systems that can benefit from one, engineering opinions differ as to what is a proper design. Making matters worse—of those properly designed, few are correctly installed, and even fewer are properly maintained.

250.148 Continuity of Equipment Grounding Conductors in Boxes

Another attempt is being made to write a rule that reflects the Code-Making Panel's intent as to the connection of EGCs at metal boxes. There is one universal rule when it comes to metal electrical equipment, it must be bonded! Be sure it has a connection to an effective ground-fault current path via the equipment grounding conductor (EGC) when that is the requirement, or to the grounding electrode conductor (GEC) at the first means of disconnect. While the rules here in 250.148 do not change any of this, there has been much misunderstanding of just what needs to be bonded in metal boxes and when special provisions for them are needed. Hopefully the revisions, though minor, may be enough to provide proper clarification.

Analysis

CLARIFIED   EDITED

The title was revised to indicate that the rule applies to both the continuity of the EGCs and their attachment in a box. The parent text was revised during the last *Code* cycle and has been restored to what it was in the 2014 *NEC*. The rule now only requires that EGCs associated with circuit conductors, that are spliced within the box or terminated on equipment within or supported by the box, to be connected within the box or to the box. These connections are to be in accordance with 250.8 and 250.148(A) through (D). Where the box is metallic, the EGCs associated with the circuit conductors must be connected to each other and to the box. Where the box is nonmetallic, they are only connected to each other. In both cases they must connect to any box-mounted or supported equipment that requires an EGC.

250.148 Continuity and Attachment of Equipment Grounding Conductors in Boxes

Equipment grounding conductors associated with circuit conductors that are spliced or terminated on equipment within a box must be connected within the box or to the box in accordance with 250.8 and 250.148(A) through (D).

Ex: The circuit equipment grounding conductor for an isolated ground receptacle [250.146(D)] is not required to be connected to the other equipment grounding conductors or to the metal box. ▶Figure 250–81

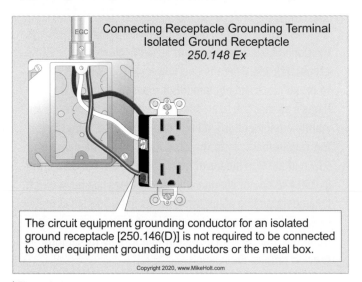

Connecting Receptacle Grounding Terminal
Isolated Ground Receptacle
250.148 Ex

The circuit equipment grounding conductor for an isolated ground receptacle [250.146(D)] is not required to be connected to other equipment grounding conductors or the metal box.

Copyright 2020, www.MikeHolt.com

▶Figure 250–81

(A) Connections and Splices. Equipment grounding conductors must be connected and spliced with a device identified for the purpose in accordance with 110.14(B). ▶Figure 250–82

(B) Continuity of Equipment Grounding Conductors. Equipment grounding conductors must terminate in such a manner that the disconnection or the removal of a receptacle, luminaire, or other device will not interrupt the electrical continuity of the equipment grounding conductor(s) providing an effective ground-fault current path. ▶Figure 250–83

(C) Metal Boxes. Equipment grounding conductors for circuit conductors that are spliced or terminated on equipment within a metal box must be spliced together [250.148] and have a connection to the metal box in accordance with 250.8. ▶Figure 250–84

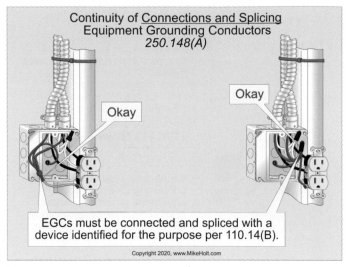

Continuity of Connections and Splicing
Equipment Grounding Conductors
250.148(A)

Okay

Okay

EGCs must be connected and spliced with a device identified for the purpose per 110.14(B).

Copyright 2020, www.MikeHolt.com

▶Figure 250–82

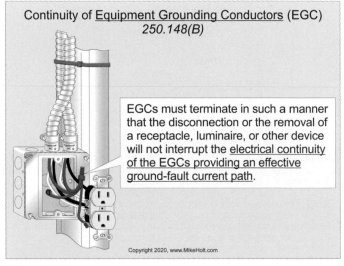

Continuity of Equipment Grounding Conductors (EGC)
250.148(B)

EGCs must terminate in such a manner that the disconnection or the removal of a receptacle, luminaire, or other device will not interrupt the electrical continuity of the EGCs providing an effective ground-fault current path.

Copyright 2020, www.MikeHolt.com

▶Figure 250–83

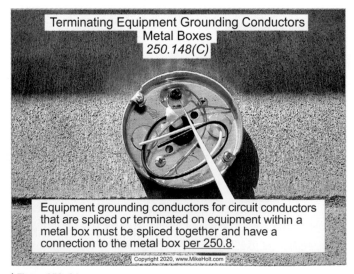

Terminating Equipment Grounding Conductors
Metal Boxes
250.148(C)

Equipment grounding conductors for circuit conductors that are spliced or terminated on equipment within a metal box must be spliced together and have a connection to the metal box per 250.8.

Copyright 2020, www.MikeHolt.com

▶Figure 250–84

▸ Equipment grounding conductors are not permitted to terminate to a screw that secures a plaster ring. ▸**Figure 250–85**

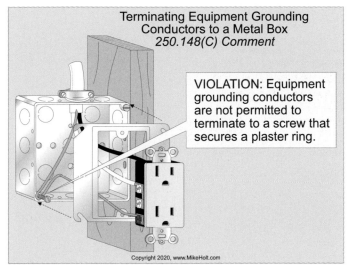

Terminating Equipment Grounding Conductors to a Metal Box
250.148(C) Comment

VIOLATION: Equipment grounding conductors are not permitted to terminate to a screw that secures a plaster ring.

Copyright 2020, www.MikeHolt.com

▸Figure 250–85

(D) Nonmetallic Boxes. Equipment grounding conductors in a nonmetallic outlet box must be arranged such that a connection can be made to any fitting or device in that box requiring connection to an equipment grounding conductor.

WIRING METHODS AND MATERIALS

Introduction to Chapter 3—Wiring Methods and Materials

Chapter 3 focuses on wiring methods and materials, and provides some very specific installation requirements for conductors, cables, boxes, raceways, and fittings. This chapter includes detailed information about the installations and restrictions involved with wiring methods.

Not fully understanding the information in this chapter may be the reason many people incorrectly apply these rules. Pay careful attention to each and every detail to be sure your installations comply with these requirements. Disregarding the rules for the wiring methods found in Chapter 3 can result in problems with power quality and can lead to fire, shock, and overall poor installations. The type of wiring method you will use depends on several factors; job specifications, *Code* requirements, the environment, need, the type of building construction, and cost effectiveness just to name a few.

Chapter 3 begins with rules that are common to most wiring methods [Article 300]. It then covers conductors [Article 310], boxes [Article 312], and enclosures [Article 314]. The articles that follow become more specific and deal more in-depth with individual wiring methods such as specific types of cables [Articles 320 through 340] and various raceways [Articles 342 through 390]. The chapter winds up with Article 392, a support system.

Notice as you read through the various wiring methods that the *Code* attempts to use similar section numbering for similar topics from one article to the next, using the same digits after the decimal point in the section number for the same topic. This makes it easier to locate the specific requirements of a particular article. For example, the rules for securing and supporting can be found in the section that ends with ".30" of each article.

Wiring Method Articles

- **Article 300—General Requirements for Wiring Methods and Materials.** Article 300 contains the general requirements for all wiring methods included in the *NEC*, except for signaling and communications systems (communications, antennas, and coaxial cable), which are covered in Chapters 7 and 8.

- **Article 310—Conductors for General Wiring.** This article contains the general requirements for conductors, such as insulation markings, ampacity ratings, and conductor use. There is also a section that addresses single family dwelling service and feeder conductors exclusively. Article 310 does not apply to conductors that are part of flexible cords, fixture wires, or conductors that are an integral part of equipment [90.6 and 300.1(B)].

- **Article 312—Cabinets and Meter Socket Enclosures.** Article 312 covers the installation and construction specifications for cabinets and meter socket enclosures.

- **Article 314—Outlet, Device, Pull, and Junction Boxes; Conduit Bodies; Fittings; and Handhole Enclosures.** Installation requirements for outlet boxes, pull and junction boxes, as well as conduit bodies and handhole enclosures are contained in this article.

Cable Articles

Articles 320 through 340 address specific types of cables. If you take the time to become familiar with the various types of cables, you will be able to:

▸ Understand what is available for doing the work.

▸ Recognize cable types that have special *NEC* requirements.

▸ Avoid buying cable you cannot install due to *Code* requirements you cannot meet with that particular wiring method.

Here is a brief overview of those included in this book:

- **Article 320—Armored Cable (Type AC).** Armored cable is an assembly of insulated conductors, 14 AWG through 1 AWG, individually wrapped with wax paper. The conductors are contained within a flexible metal (steel or aluminum) spiral sheath that interlocks at the edges. Armored cable looks like flexible metal conduit. Many electricians call this metal cable "BX®."

- **Article 330—Metal-Clad Cable (Type MC).** Metal-clad cable encloses insulated conductors in a metal sheath of either corrugated or smooth copper or aluminum tubing, or spiral interlocked steel or aluminum. The physical characteristics of Type MC cable make it a versatile wiring method permitted in almost any location and for almost any application. The most commonly used Type MC cable is the interlocking kind, which looks similar to armored cable or flexible metal conduit.

- **Article 334—Nonmetallic-Sheathed Cable (Type NM).** Nonmetallic-sheathed cable is commonly referred to by its trade name "Romex®." It encloses two, three, or four insulated conductors, 14 AWG through 2 AWG, within a nonmetallic outer jacket. Because this cable is manufactured in this manner, it contains a separate (usually bare) equipment grounding conductor. Nonmetallic-sheathed cable is most commonly used for residential wiring applications but may sometimes be permitted for use in commercial occupancies.

- **Article 336—Power and Control Tray Cable (Type TC).** Power and control tray cable is flexible, inexpensive, and easily installed. It provides very limited physical protection for the conductors, so the installation restrictions are rigorous. Its low cost and relative ease of installation make it a common wiring method for industrial applications.

- **Article 338—Service-Entrance Cable (Types SE and USE).** Service-entrance and underground service-entrance cables can be a single conductor or a multiconductor assembly within an overall nonmetallic outer jacket or covering. These cables are most often used for services not over 1,000V, but are also permitted for feeders and branch circuits. When used as a service conductor(s) or a service-entrance conductor(s), pre-manufactured Type "SE" cable assemblies will typically contain two insulated phase conductors and a bare neutral conductor. When permitted for use as a feeder or branch circuit, Type SE cable is usually designated as Type "SER" and will contain the same three conductors as Type SE but a fourth conductor (which is insulated) will be added to serve as the neutral conductor.

- **Article 340—Underground Feeder and Branch-Circuit Cable (Type UF).** Underground feeder cable is a moisture-, fungus-, and corrosion-resistant cable suitable for direct burial in the earth, and it comes in sizes 14 AWG through 4/0 AWG [340.104]. Multiconductor UF cable is covered in molded plastic that surrounds the insulated conductors.

Raceway Articles

Articles 342 through 390 address specific types of raceways. Refer to Article 100 for the definition of a raceway. If you take the time to become familiar with the various types of raceways, you will be able to:

▸ Understand what is available for doing the work.

▸ Recognize raceway types that have special *Code* requirements.

▸ Avoid buying a raceway you cannot install due to *NEC* requirements you cannot meet with that particular wiring method.

Here is a brief overview of each those included in this book:

- **Article 342—Intermediate Metal Conduit (Type IMC).** Intermediate metal conduit is a circular metal raceway with the same outside diameter as rigid metal conduit. The wall thickness of intermediate metal conduit is less than that of rigid metal conduit, so it has a larger interior cross-sectional area for holding conductors. Intermediate metal conduit is lighter and less expensive than rigid metal conduit and is approved by the *NEC* for use in the same applications as rigid metal conduit. Intermediate metal conduit also uses a different steel alloy, which makes it stronger than rigid metal conduit, even though the walls are thinner.

- **Article 344—Rigid Metal Conduit (Type RMC).** Rigid metal conduit is similar to intermediate metal conduit, except the wall thickness is greater, so it has a smaller interior cross-sectional area. Rigid metal conduit is heavier than intermediate metal conduit and is permitted for use in the same applications as intermediate metal conduit (Type IMC).

- **Article 350—Liquidtight Flexible Metal Conduit (Type LFMC).** Liquidtight flexible metal conduit is a raceway of circular cross section with an outer liquidtight, nonmetallic, sunlight-resistant jacket over an inner flexible metal core, with associated couplings, connectors, and fittings. It is listed for the installation of electrical conductors. Liquidtight flexible metal conduit is commonly called "Sealtite®" or simply "liquidtight." Liquidtight flexible metal conduit is similar in construction to flexible metal conduit, but it has an outer thermoplastic covering.

- **Article 356—Liquidtight Flexible Nonmetallic Conduit (Type LFNC).** Liquidtight flexible nonmetallic conduit (most commonly referred to as "Carflex®") is a raceway of circular cross section with an outer liquidtight, nonmetallic, sunlight-resistant jacket over an inner flexible core, with associated couplings, connectors, and fittings.

- **Article 358—Electrical Metallic Tubing (EMT).** Electrical metallic tubing is a nonthreaded thinwall raceway of circular cross section designed for the physical protection and routing of conductors and cables. Compared to rigid metal conduit and intermediate metal conduit, electrical metallic tubing is relatively easy to bend, cut, and ream. EMT is not threaded, so all connectors and couplings are of the threadless type. It is available in a range of colors, such as red and blue.

- **Article 380—Multioutlet Assemblies.** A multioutlet assembly is a surface, flush, or freestanding raceway designed to hold conductors and receptacles. It is assembled in the field or at the factory.

Cable Tray

- **Article 392—Cable Trays.** A cable tray system is a unit or assembly of units or sections with associated fittings that form a structural system used to securely fasten or support cables and raceways. A cable tray is not a raceway; it is a support system for raceways, cables, and enclosures.

Introduction to the 2020 <u>Changes</u> in Chapter 3

To say that Chapter 3 has seen a major overhaul this *NEC* cycle might be considered an understatement by those who have been in the field for a while. Article 310 has probably received the most revision it has seen in a long time as it has been completely reorganized. The scope of this article was changed to limit its application to the general requirements for conductors rated up to and including 2,000V. In the previous *Code* it covered conductors of all voltages. Table header information was removed from the actual Table(s) and is now listed in the article subsections and our old friend 310.16 (2008 *NEC* and prior) is back to reclaim, the now former, Table 310.15(B)(16). A new Article 311 was created for conductors with a voltage rating over 2,000V. The requirements and tables that were in Article 310 along with the requirements of Article 328, Medium Voltage Cable (Type MV) are now combined into this new article. Some may also remember when finding Table 310.15(B)(7) for single family dwelling service conductor sizes seemed like a wild-goose chase going from Article 310 to the Annex in (D7). Well a new section, 310.12 is now home to "Single-Phase Dwelling Services and Feeders." There were many more changes within Chapter 3, but we wanted to highlight a few in this introduction.

GENERAL REQUIREMENTS FOR WIRING METHODS AND MATERIALS

Introduction to Article 300—General Requirements for Wiring Methods and Materials

This article contains the general requirements for all wiring methods included in the *NEC*. However, it does not apply to twisted-pair cable and coaxial cable, which are covered in Chapters 7 and 8 unless, Article 300 is specifically referenced.

This article is primarily concerned with how to install, route, splice, protect, and secure conductors and raceways. How well you understand and apply the requirements of Article 300 will usually be evident in the finished work. Many of these requirements will affect the appearance, longevity, and even the safety of the installation. Imagine your surprise if you are shoveling some soil onto a plant in the garden and your shovel hits an electrical service cable! After studying and learning the rules in this article, you will immediately realize that the burial depth requirements of 300.5 were possibly overlooked or ignored. Even worse, they might not even have been known at the time of installation.

A good understanding of this article will start you on the path to correctly and safely installing the wiring methods included in Chapter 3. Be sure to carefully consider the accompanying illustrations and refer to the definitions in Article 100 as needed.

300.3 Conductors

Additional language was added in section (B)(1) to ensure that when connections, taps, or extensions are made from paralleled conductors, each connection involves all the paralleled conductors of each phase and/or neutral.

Analysis

CLARIFIED **300.3(B) Conductors.** This is required by the rules in 310.10(H), but the substantiation indicates that many installers and some inspectors may not fully understand those requirements. The panel stated that this change to 300.3(B)(1) was made to make it totally clear, that where connections are made to a parallel set of conductors, the connection must include all conductors of that phase of the paralleled set.

300.3 Conductors

(B) Circuit Conductors Grouped Together. All conductors of a circuit, including the neutral and equipment grounding conductors must be installed together in the same raceway, cable, trench, cord, or cable tray, except as permitted by (1) through (4).

Author's Comment:

▸ Keeping all circuit conductors together helps minimize induction since the individual electromagnetic fields will cancel each other and help maintain the low-impedance ground-fault current path. See 300.5(I). ▸Figure 300–1

(1) Paralleled Installations. Conductors installed in parallel in accordance with 310.10(G) must have all circuit conductor sets grouped together within the same raceway, cable tray, trench, or cable. ▸Figure 300–2

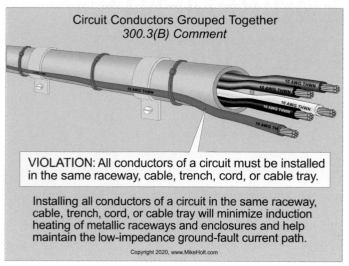

Circuit Conductors Grouped Together
300.3(B) Comment

VIOLATION: All conductors of a circuit must be installed in the same raceway, cable, trench, cord, or cable tray.

Installing all conductors of a circuit in the same raceway, cable, trench, cord, or cable tray will minimize induction heating of metallic raceways and enclosures and help maintain the low-impedance ground-fault current path.

Copyright 2020, www.MikeHolt.com

▶Figure 300–1

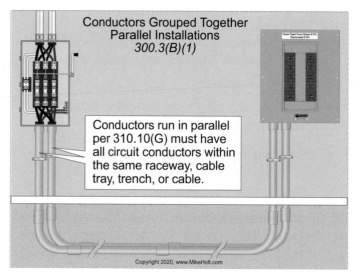

Conductors Grouped Together
Parallel Installations
300.3(B)(1)

Conductors run in parallel per 310.10(G) must have all circuit conductors within the same raceway, cable tray, trench, or cable.

Copyright 2020, www.MikeHolt.com

▶Figure 300–2

▶ Grouping in sets when paralleling circuits helps minimize the inductive heating of ferrous metal raceways and ferrous metal enclosures for alternating-current circuits. See 250.102(E), 300.3(B), 300.5(I), 300.20(A), 376.20, 378.20, and 392.8(D) for similar requirements. ▶Figure 300–3

Connections, taps, or extensions made from paralleled conductors must connect to all conductors of the paralleled set.

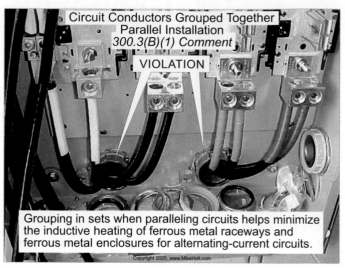

Circuit Conductors Grouped Together
Parallel Installation
300.3(B)(1) Comment

VIOLATION

Grouping in sets when paralleling circuits helps minimize the inductive heating of ferrous metal raceways and ferrous metal enclosures for alternating-current circuits.

Copyright 2020, www.MikeHolt.com

▶Figure 300–3

Ex: Parallel phase and neutral conductors can be installed in individual underground nonmetallic raceways (Phase A in raceway 1, Phase B in raceway 2, and so forth) as permitted by 300.5(I) Ex 2 if the installation complies with 300.20(B). ▶Figure 300–4

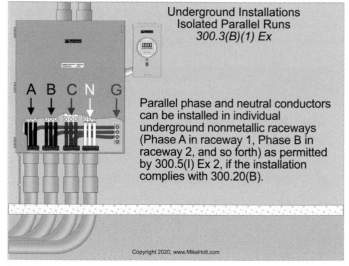

Underground Installations
Isolated Parallel Runs
300.3(B)(1) Ex

A B C N G

Parallel phase and neutral conductors can be installed in individual underground nonmetallic raceways (Phase A in raceway 1, Phase B in raceway 2, and so forth) as permitted by 300.5(I) Ex 2, if the installation complies with 300.20(B).

Copyright 2020, www.MikeHolt.com

▶Figure 300–4

▶ This means that when you tap to just "A" phase and the neutral conductor, that the tap connection must include all of the conductors of "A" phase and all of the conductors of the neutral conductor. Tapping or connecting to less than all of the conductors of a paralleled set can result in a current imbalance within that set that may overload one of more of the conductors of the set.

300.4 Protection Against Physical Damage

Subsection (G) was expanded and reorganized into a list format (1) through (4) encompassing the use of listed metal fittings with smoothly rounded edges as well as insulated fittings and threaded hubs.

Analysis

EXPANDED

300.4(G) Fittings. The title and text of this subsection was revised to reflect the availability of noninsulated fittings that provide the required protection for conductors. The word "insulated" was dropped from the title, making it just "Fittings." The rule was reorganized into a list format for ease of use and the former exception for threaded hubs or bosses that are part of an enclosure has become one of the 4 list items.

300.4 Protection Against Physical Damage

Where subject to physical damage, conductors, raceways, and cables must be protected in accordance with (A) through (H).

(G) Fittings. Raceways containing insulated circuit conductors 4 AWG and larger that enter a cabinet, box, enclosure, or raceway, must have the conductors protected as follows:

(1) A fitting providing a smoothly rounded insulating surface ▶Figure 300-5

(2) A listed metal fitting that has smoothly rounded edges. ▶Figure 300-6

(3) Separation from the fitting or raceway using an identified insulating material that is securely fastened in place

(4) Threaded hubs or bosses that are an integral part of a cabinet, box, enclosure, or raceway that provide a smoothly rounded or flared entry for conductors. ▶Figure 300-7

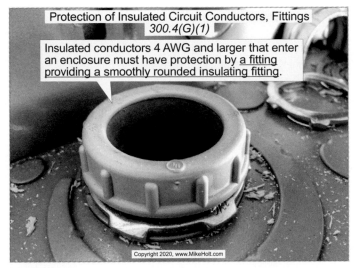

Protection of Insulated Circuit Conductors, Fittings
300.4(G)(1)

Insulated conductors 4 AWG and larger that enter an enclosure must have protection by a fitting providing a smoothly rounded insulating fitting.

Copyright 2020, www.MikeHolt.com

▶Figure 300-5

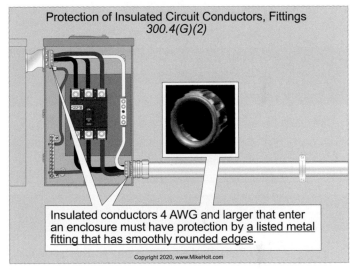

Protection of Insulated Circuit Conductors, Fittings
300.4(G)(2)

Insulated conductors 4 AWG and larger that enter an enclosure must have protection by a listed metal fitting that has smoothly rounded edges.

Copyright 2020, www.MikeHolt.com

▶Figure 300-6

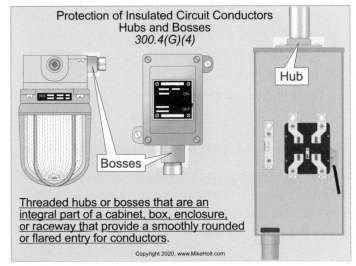

Protection of Insulated Circuit Conductors
Hubs and Bosses
300.4(G)(4)

Hub

Bosses

Threaded hubs or bosses that are an integral part of a cabinet, box, enclosure, or raceway that provide a smoothly rounded or flared entry for conductors.

Copyright 2020, www.MikeHolt.com

▶Figure 300-7

▸ If IMC or RMC enters an enclosure without a connector, a bushing must be provided, regardless of the conductor size [342.46 and 344.46].

▸ A bushing or adapter for PVC is required if the box or fitting does not provide equivalent protection [352.46 and Note]. A conduit bushing that is constructed wholly of insulating material is not permitted to be used to secure a fitting or a raceway. This would seem to imply, (but stops short of saying it outright), that an insulated throat metal bushing is permitted to be used to secure a raceway or fitting.

▸ There is at least one listed all metal bushing on the market that can be used for the protection of conductors 4 AWG and larger, where those conductors enter a cabinet, box, enclosure, or a raceway. (www.slicknut.com).

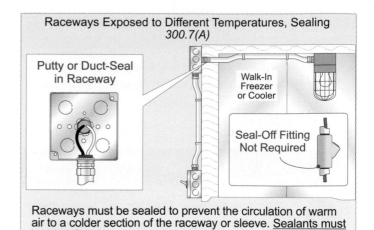

Raceways Exposed to Different Temperatures, Sealing
300.7(A)

Putty or Duct-Seal in Raceway

Walk-In Freezer or Cooler

Seal-Off Fitting Not Required

Raceways must be sealed to prevent the circulation of warm air to a colder section of the raceway or sleeve. Sealants must be identified for use with cable insulation, conductor insulation, a bare conductor, a shield, or other components.

Copyright 2020, www.MikeHolt.com

▸Figure 300–8

300.7 Raceways Exposed to Different Temperatures

The rule in the subsection (A) was revised to require the use of an "identified" sealant that is safe for the conductors and the raceway itself, and to correlate with the language in 225.27.

Analysis

CLARIFIED **300.7(A) Sealing.** Revisions in this section require that a raceway or sleeve be sealed to prevent the mixing of warm and cool air. New text also requires that the sealant used be identified for use with the insulated or bare cable or conductors. The intent here is for the sealing product not to damage the conductor, its jacket, or insulation.

300.7 Raceways Exposed to Different Temperatures

(A) Sealing. If a raceway is subjected to different temperatures, and where condensation is known to be a problem, the raceway must be filled with a material approved by the authority having jurisdiction that will prevent the circulation of warm air to a colder section of the raceway. Sealants must be identified for use with cable insulation, conductor insulation, a bare conductor, a shield, or other components. ▸Figure 300–8

▸ One common product used for this is electrical duct seal and it is so identified. There are other identified products such as Polywater's "FST Duct Sealant." Typical expanding foams used to seal buildings are not identified for this application.

300.22 Wiring in Ducts and Plenum Spaces

A conflict with the *NEC Style Manual* created the need for this revision in subsection (D) with no technical change. The conflict was that any reference to an article as a whole is prohibited; this was corrected by identifying the *Code* references by section.

Analysis

EDITED **300.22(D) Information Technology Equipment.** The *NEC Style Manual* does not permit references to an entire article as was the case in the 2017 *Code*. This type of installation, which is based on Article 645, must first comply with 645.4 so that 645.5(E) can permit the different requirements than would normally be required in 300.22(C) for wiring under raised floors.

300.22 Wiring in Ducts and Plenum Spaces

This section applies to the installation and uses of electrical wiring and equipment in ducts used for dust, loose stock, or vapor removal; ducts specifically fabricated for environmental air; and plenum spaces used for environmental air.

(D) Information Technology Equipment. Where the installation complies with the special requirements in 645.4, wiring methods installed below raised floors or above suspended ceilings used for environmental air are permitted to be installed in accordance with 645.5(E). ▶Figure 300–9

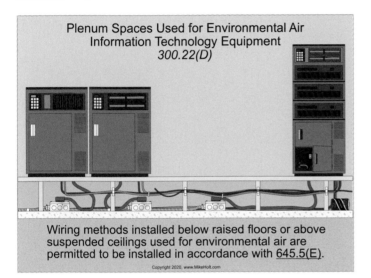

Plenum Spaces Used for Environmental Air
Information Technology Equipment
300.22(D)

Wiring methods installed below raised floors or above suspended ceilings used for environmental air are permitted to be installed in accordance with 645.5(E).

Copyright 2020, www.MikeHolt.com

▶Figure 300–9

300.25 Exit Enclosures (Stair Towers)

This rule requires electrical wiring or equipment serving areas other than the emergency exit enclosure to be installed outside of the exit structure.

300.25 Exit Enclosures (Stair Towers)

Where an exit enclosure is required to be separated from the building, only electrical wiring methods serving equipment permitted by the authority having jurisdiction in the exit enclosure are permitted to be installed within the exit enclosure.

Author's Comment:

▶ As used here, "separated from the building" does not necessarily mean detached. Article 100 defines a 'building' as "a structure that stands alone or that is separated from adjoining structures by fire walls." The fire rating rules for walls surrounding a star tower are much more stringent and serve to 'separate' it from the main building. Typically, only lighting and heat are necessary to serve a stair tower. If the need should arise that a stair tower landing was the only place for a sub-panel, (for example), to be installed, it would require documented special permission from the authority having jurisdiction.

Note: For more information, refer to NFPA 101, *Life Safety Code*, *7.1.3.2(10)(b)*.

ARTICLE 310

CONDUCTORS FOR GENERAL WIRING

Introduction to Article 310—Conductors for General Wiring

This article contains the general requirements for conductors, such as insulation markings, ampacity ratings, and conditions of use. Article 310 does not apply to conductors that are part of flexible cords, fixture wires, or to conductors that are an integral part of equipment [90.7 and 300.1(B)].

Why does this article contain so many tables? Why does Table 310.17 list the ampacity of 6 THHN as 105A, while Table 310.16 lists the same conductor as having an ampacity of only 75A? To answer that, go back to Article 100 and review the definition of "Ampacity." Notice the phrase "conditions of use." These tables set a maximum current value at which premature failure of the conductor insulation should not occur during normal use, under the conditions described in the tables. Tables throughout the *Code* are accompanied by a section of text with information about that table. For example, section 310.16 states that Table 310.16 applies to conductors carrying voltages, "rated 0 volts through 2000 volts." It can be easy to overlook that limitation if you are not careful! It is imperative that you read the *Code* section about each table and any footnotes at the bottom of the actual table before you decide what is necessary for your particular application.

The designations THHN, THHW-2, RHH, and so on, are insulation types. Designations containing a "W" are suitable for use in wet locations. Every type of insulation has a limit as to how much heat it can withstand. When current flows through a conductor, it creates heat. How well the insulation around a conductor can dissipate that heat depends on factors such as whether the conductor is in free air or not. Think about what happens when you put on a sweater, a jacket, and then a coat—all at the same time. You heat up. Your skin cannot dissipate heat with all that clothing on nearly as well as it dissipates heat in free air. The same principle applies to conductors.

Conductor insulation degrades with age and is called "aging." Conductor insulation failure takes decades under normal use and becomes a maintenance issue for the appropriate personnel to manage. However, if a conductor is forced to exceed the ampacity listed in the appropriate table, (and as a result its design temperature is exceeded), insulation failure happens much sooner, and is too often catastrophic. Consequently, exceeding the ampacity of a conductor is a serious safety issue.

310.1 Scope

Article 310 was completely reorganized, and its scope changed to limit its application to conductors with a voltage rating up to and including 2,000V. When compared to the voltage classes for power distribution (which can exceed 35,000V) 2,000V is relatively low. A new Article 311 was created for conductors with a voltage rating over 2,000V so the two voltage classes are now separated.

Analysis

REORGANIZED

The scope of this article was changed to limit its application to the general requirements for conductors rated up to and including 2,000V; in the previous *Code* it covered conductors of all voltages. The requirements and tables for conductors rated 2,001V and higher that were in Article 310 along with the requirements of Article 328, Medium Voltage Cable (Type MV) were combined into the new Article 311.

310.1 Scope

Article 310 contains the general requirements for conductors <u>rated up to and including 2,000V,</u> such as insulation markings, ampacity ratings, and their use. ▶Figure 310–1

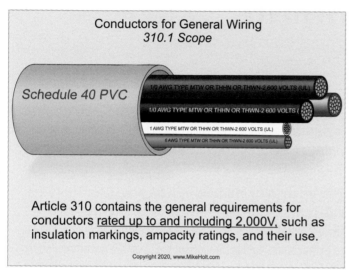

Conductors for General Wiring
310.1 Scope

Schedule 40 PVC

1/0 AWG TYPE MTW OR THHN OR THWN-2 600 VOLTS (UL)

1/0 AWG TYPE MTW OR THHN OR THWN-2 600 VOLTS (UL)

1 AWG TYPE MTW OR THHN OR THWN-2 600 VOLTS (UL)

6 AWG TYPE MTW OR THHN OR THWN-2 600 VOLTS (UL)

Article 310 contains the general requirements for conductors <u>rated up to and including 2,000V,</u> such as insulation markings, ampacity ratings, and their use.

Copyright 2020, www.MikeHolt.com

▶Figure 310–1

Note: For flexible cords and cable, see Article 400. For fixture wires, see Article 402.

310.3 Conductors

Information pertaining to the minimum size of conductors for specific voltage ranges up to and including 2,000V that was in section and Table 310.106(A) of the 2017 *Code* was relocated to 310.3 with revisions in the subsections.

Analysis

RELOCATED **310.3(A) Minimum Size of Conductors.** Minimum conductor size requirements for conductors 2,000V or less have been relocated here from Table 310.106(A) along with conductor material requirements from 310.106(B).

RELOCATED **310.3(B) Conductor Material.** Conductor material requirements were relocated here from 310.106(B) with a revision that adds two insulation types (XHHN and XHWN) that were not in the 2017 *NEC*. These are both thermoset compounds with an outer nylon jacket. These types were not previously available with a nylon jacket.

CLARIFIED **RELOCATED** **310.3(C) Stranded Conductors.** The rule requiring 8 AWG and larger conductors installed in raceways to be stranded, unless specifically permitted or required elsewhere in the *Code* to be solid, was relocated here and revised for clarity without technical changes.

310.3 Conductors

(A) Minimum Size Conductors. The minimum sizes of conductors are <u>14 AWG copper or 12 AWG aluminum or copper-clad aluminum,</u> except as permitted elsewhere in this *Code*.

Author's Comment:

▶ There's a misconception that 12 AWG copper is the smallest conductor permitted for commercial or industrial facilities. Although this isn't true based on *NEC* rules, it might be a job specification or local *Code* requirement.

▶ Conductors smaller than 14 AWG are permitted for Class 1 remote-control circuits [725.43], Fixture wire [402.6], and Motor control circuits [Table 430.72(B)].

(C) Stranded Conductors. Conductors 8 AWG and larger installed in a raceway <u>must be stranded, unless</u> specifically permitted or required elsewhere in this *Code* to be solid. ▶Figure 310–2

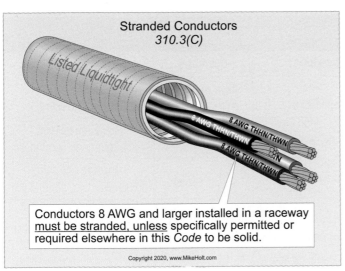

Stranded Conductors
310.3(C)

Conductors 8 AWG and larger installed in a raceway <u>must be stranded, unless</u> specifically permitted or required elsewhere in this *Code* to be solid.

Copyright 2020, www.MikeHolt.com

▶Figure 310–2

Author's Comment:

▶ According to 250.120(C), exposed equipment grounding conductors 8 AWG and smaller for direct-current circuits [250.134(B) Ex.2], such as required by 690.45 for solar PV systems, are permitted to be run separately from the circuit conductors. Where the 8 AWG or smaller exposed equipment grounding conductor is subject to physical damage, it must be installed within a raceway or cable.

▶ A grounding electrode conductor is an instance where an 8 AWG and larger solid conductor is permitted to be installed in a raceway when required to be protected from physical damage [250.64(B)].

310.4 Conductor Construction and Applications

The information about the construction requirements for conductors suitable for carrying up to (and including) 2,000V, was relocated from 310.104 in the 2017 *Code* and the information for those suitable for carrying over 2,000V was moved to the new Article 311.

 Analysis

RELOCATED There are no technical changes in this relocation. There was a correction made to SIS Cable and Table Notes were edited to correlate with the *NEC Style Manual*.

310.4 Conductor Construction and Application

Table 310.4(A) provides information on conductor insulation properties such as letter type, maximum operating temperature, application, insulation, and outer cover properties. Only conductors in Tables 310.4(A) can be installed for the application identified in the tables.

Author's Comment:

▶ The following explains the lettering on conductor insulation [Table 310.4(A)]: ▶Figure 310–3

◆	No H	60°C insulation rating
◆	H	75°C insulation rating
◆	HH	90°C insulation rating in a dry location
◆	-2	90°C insulation rating in wet locations
◆	N	Nylon outer cover
◆	T	Thermoplastic insulation
◆	U	Underground
◆	W	Wet or damp locations

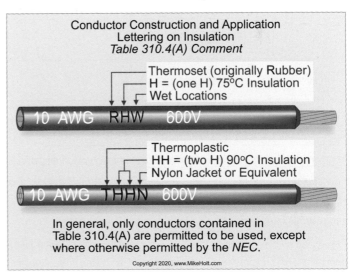

Conductor Construction and Application
Lettering on Insulation
Table 310.4(A) Comment

Thermoset (originally Rubber)
H = (one H) 75°C Insulation
Wet Locations

10 AWG RHW 600V

Thermoplastic
HH = (two H) 90°C Insulation
Nylon Jacket or Equivalent

10 AWG THHN 600V

In general, only conductors contained in Table 310.4(A) are permitted to be used, except where otherwise permitted by the *NEC*.

Copyright 2020, www.MikeHolt.com

▶Figure 310–3

In general, only conductors contained in Tables 310.4(A) are permitted to be used, except where otherwise permitted in the *NEC*. Some examples are PV wire, PV cables, or DG cable [690.31(C)].

	Table 310.4(A) Conductor Applications and Insulations				
Type Letter	**Column 2**	**Column 3**	**Column 4**	**Column 5**	**Column 6**
	Insulation	**Max. Operating Temperature**	**Application**	**Sizes Available AWG or kcmil**	**Outer Covering**
RHH	Flame-retardant thermoset	90°C	Dry and damp locations	14 – 2,000	Moisture-resistant, flame-retardant, nonmetallic
RHW	Flame-retardant, moisture-resistant thermoset	75°C	Dry and wet locations	14 – 2,000	Moisture-resistant, flame-retardant, nonmetallic
RHW-2	Flame-retardant, moisture-resistant thermoset	90°C	Dry and wet locations	14 – 2,000	Moisture-resistant, flame-retardant, nonmetallic
THHN	Flame-retardant, heat-resistant thermoplastic	90°C	Dry and damp locations	14 – 1,000	Nylon jacket or equivalent
THHW	Flame-retardant, moisture- and heat-resistant thermoplastic	75°C / 90°C	Wet locations / Dry locations	14 – 1,000	None
THW	Flame-retardant, moisture- and heat-resistant thermoplastic	75°C	Dry, damp, and wet locations	14 – 2,000	None
THW-2	Flame-retardant, moisture- and heat-resistant thermoplastic	90°C	Dry, damp, and wet locations	14 – 1,000	None
THWN	Flame-retardant, moisture- and heat-resistant thermoplastic	75°C	Dry, damp, and wet locations	14 – 1,000	Nylon jacket or equivalent
THWN-2	Flame-retardant, moisture- and heat-resistant thermoplastic	90°C	Dry, damp, and wet locations	14 – 1,000	Nylon jacket or equivalent
TW	Flame-retardant, moisture-resistant thermoplastic	60°C	Dry, damp, and wet locations	14 – 2,000	None
USE	Heat- and moisture-resistant	75°C	See Article 338	14 – 2,000	Moisture-resistant nonmetallic
USE-2	Heat- and moisture-resistant	90°C	See Article 338	14 – 2,000	Moisture-resistant nonmetallic

[1] *Conductors are permitted to be rated up to 1000 volts if listed and marked.*

[2] *Outer coverings are not required where listed without a covering.*

[3] *Higher temperature rated constructions are permitted where design conditions require maximum conductor operating temperatures above 90°C (194°F).*

[4] *Conductor sizes are permitted for signaling circuits permitting 300-volt insulation.*

[5] *The ampacity of Type UF cable must be limited in accordance with 340.80.*

[6] *Type UF insulation thickness must include the integral jacket.*

[7] *Insulation thickness is permitted to be 2.03 mm (80 mils) for listed Type USE conductors that have been subjected to special investigations. The nonmetallic covering over individual rubber-covered conductors of aluminum-sheathed cable and of lead-sheathed or multiconductor cable is not required to be flame retardant.*

310.6 Conductor Identification

Section 310.110(C), that was in the 2017 *NEC*, was relocated here and states that phase conductors must be clearly distinguishable from neutral and equipment grounding conductors. The term "grounding" was revised to read "equipment grounding" for clarity.

Analysis

CLARIFIED

310.6(C) Ungrounded Conductors. This corrects an issue that prohibited a black insulated cable for a grounding electrode conductor from being used as a phase conductor within that same facility. The panel statement said this should only apply to neutral and equipment grounding conductors since they have specific color requirements in the *Code*, and other grounding conductors do not.

310.6 Conductor Identification

(C) Identification of Phase Conductors. Circuit phase conductors must have a finish that is clearly distinguishable from the neutral and equipment grounding conductors. ▸Figure 310–4

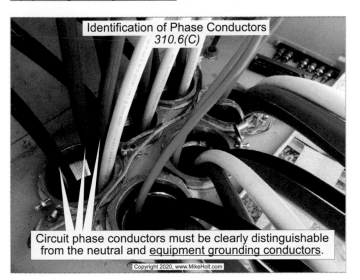

Identification of Phase Conductors
310.6(C)

Circuit phase conductors must be clearly distinguishable from the neutral and equipment grounding conductors.

Copyright 2020, www.MikeHolt.com

▸Figure 310–4

Where premises wiring is supplied from more than one nominal voltage system, the phase conductors of branch-circuit phase conductors must be identified in accordance with 210.5(C) and feeders must be identified in accordance with 215.12(C).

Ex: Conductor identification is permitted in accordance with 200.7.

Author's Comment:

▸ Although the *NEC* does not require a specific color code for phase conductors, electricians often use the following color system: ▸Figure 310–5

- ◆ 120/240V, single-phase—black, red, and white
- ◆ 120/208V, three-phase—black, red, blue, and white
- ◆ 120/240V, three-phase—black, orange, blue, and white
- ◆ 277/480V, three-phase—brown, orange, yellow, and gray; or, brown, purple, yellow, and gray

Common Phase Conductor Identification Methods
210.5, 215.12, 310.6(C) Comment

Although the *NEC* does not require a specific color code for phase conductors, electricians often use the following color system for power and lighting conductor identification:
- 120/240V, single-phase—black, red, and white
- 120/208V, three-phase—black, red, blue, and white
- 120/240V, three-phase—black, orange, blue, and white
- 277/480V, three-phase—brown, orange, yellow, and gray; or, brown, purple, yellow, and gray

Copyright 2020, www.MikeHolt.com

▸Figure 310–5

310.10 Uses Permitted

The only technical changes were that all the items applying to conductors suitable for carrying over 2,000V were moved to the new Article 311.

Analysis

RELOCATED The relocation of requirements for conductors greater than 2,000V resulted in several subsections being renumbered. Direct Burial Conductors is now 310.10(E), Corrosive Conditions is 310.10(F), and Parallel Conductors is 310.10(G). *Code* users will need to familiarize themselves with the renumbered sections.

310.10 Uses Permitted

Conductors described in Table 310.4(A) are permitted for use in any of the wiring methods covered in Chapter 3.

(B) Dry and Damp Locations. Insulated conductors typically used in dry and damp locations include THHN, THHW, THWN, THWN-2, and XHHW.

(C) Wet Locations. Insulated conductors typically used in wet locations include THHW, THWN, THWN-2, XHHW, XHHW-2, <u>XHHN, XHWN,</u> and <u>XHWN-2.</u>

> **Author's Comment:**
>
> ‣ The letter "W" found on the insulation types indicate it is suitable for wet locations.

310.12 Single-Phase Dwelling Services and Feeders

The Table now included in this rule has been literally "bouncing" around the *Code* book (and at one time, even removed) much to the displeasure of all those who had become accustomed to its location in 310.15(B)7. It has now found its way "home" to its own, hopefully permanent, parent section of 310.12 and reformatted with individual subsections. In addition, the table that has been in Annex D since the 2014 *NEC* has been restored as Table 310.12.

Analysis

RELOCATED For services rated 100A through 400A that supply the entire load of a one-family dwelling or of the individual units of multifamily dwellings, service conductors are permitted to have an ampacity of not less than 83 percent of the service rating. The revision itself adds the following, "If no adjustment or correction factors are required," Table 310.12 can be applied.

RELOCATED Table 310.12 Single-Phase Dwelling Services and Feeders was relocated from Annex D without a change except the addition of a new table note. The note reads, "If no adjustment or correction factors are required, this table shall be permitted to be applied."

When the dwelling ampacity table was deleted from the *NEC* text and moved to Annex D, the main reason was to permit the application of any required adjustment and/or correction factors, but moving the table created usability issues for *Code* users. The restoration of the table to the *NEC* proper along with the new language only permitting the use of Table 310.12 where adjustment and/or correction factors are not required addresses both issues.

310.12 Single-Phase Dwelling Services and Feeders

Dwelling unit service and feeder conductors supplied by a single-phase, 120/240V and 120/208V systems can be sized in accordance with the following requirements: ‣Figure 310–6

(A) Services. <u>Service conductors supplying the entire load associated with the dwelling unit can have the conductor sized in accordance with Table 310.12 where there is no conductor ampacity adjustment or correction as required by 310.14.</u>

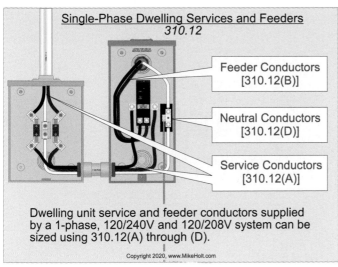

Single-Phase Dwelling Services and Feeders
310.12

Feeder Conductors
[310.12(B)]

Neutral Conductors
[310.12(D)]

Service Conductors
[310.12(A)]

Dwelling unit service and feeder conductors supplied by a 1-phase, 120/240V and 120/208V system can be sized using 310.12(A) through (D).

Copyright 2020, www.MikeHolt.com

▸Figure 310–6

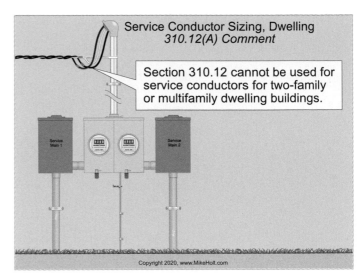

Service Conductor Sizing, Dwelling
310.12(A) Comment

Section 310.12 cannot be used for service conductors for two-family or multifamily dwelling buildings.

Copyright 2020, www.MikeHolt.com

▸Figure 310–8

▸ **Example**

Question: What size service conductors are required if the calculated load for a dwelling unit requires a service disconnect rated 200A? ▸Figure 310–7

(a) 1/0 AWG   (b) 2/0 AWG   (c) 3/0 AWG   (d) 4/0 AWG

Answer: (b) 2/0 AWG [Table 310.12]

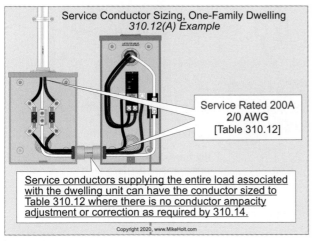

Service Conductor Sizing, One-Family Dwelling
310.12(A) Example

Service Rated 200A
2/0 AWG
[Table 310.12]

Service conductors supplying the entire load associated with the dwelling unit can have the conductor sized to Table 310.12 where there is no conductor ampacity adjustment or correction as required by 310.14.

Copyright 2020, www.MikeHolt.com

▸Figure 310–7

Author's Comment:

▸ Section 310.12 cannot be used for service conductors for two-family or multifamily dwelling buildings. ▸**Figure 310–8**

Service conductors supplying the entire load associated with the dwelling unit can have the conductor sized to 83 percent of the service rating where conductor ampacity adjustment or correction is required by 310.14. ▸Figure 310–9

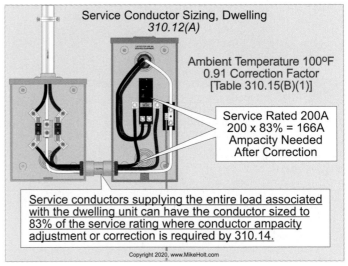

Service Conductor Sizing, Dwelling
310.12(A)

Ambient Temperature 100ºF
0.91 Correction Factor
[Table 310.15(B)(1)]

Service Rated 200A
200 x 83% = 166A
Ampacity Needed
After Correction

Service conductors supplying the entire load associated with the dwelling unit can have the conductor sized to 83% of the service rating where conductor ampacity adjustment or correction is required by 310.14.

Copyright 2020, www.MikeHolt.com

▸Figure 310–9

(B) Feeders. Feeder conductors supplying the entire load associated with the dwelling unit can have the conductor sized in accordance with Table 310.12 where there is no conductor ampacity adjustment or correction as required by 310.14. ▸Figure 310–10 and ▸Figure 310–11

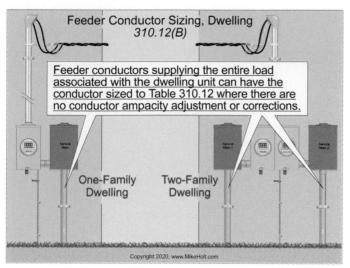

▶Figure 310-10

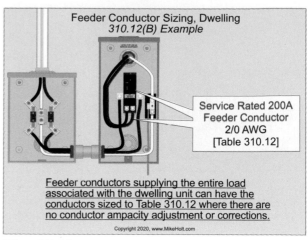

▶Figure 310-12

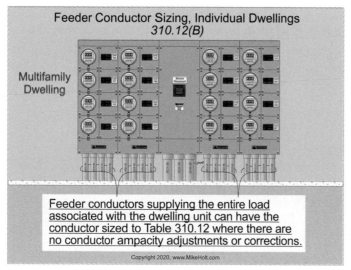

▶Figure 310-11

Author's Comment:

▶ Section 310.12(B) cannot be used to size feeder conductors where a feeder does not carry the entire load of the dwelling unit, except as permitted in 310.12(C). ▶Figure 310-13

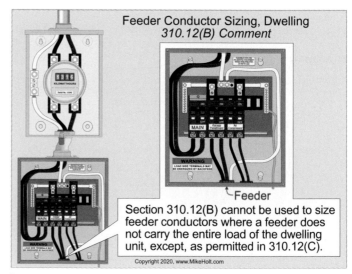

▶Figure 310-13

▶ **Example**

Question: What size feeder conductors are required if the calculated load for a dwelling unit requires a service disconnect rated 200A, and the feeder conductors carry the entire load of the dwelling unit? ▶**Figure 310-12**

(a) 1/0 AWG   (b) 2/0 AWG   (c) 3/0 AWG   (d) 4/0 AWG

Answer: (b) 2/0 AWG [Table 310.12]

Feeder conductors supplying the entire load associated with the dwelling unit can have the conductor sized to 83 percent of the service where there is conductor ampacity adjustment or correction as required by 310.14. ▶Figure 310-14

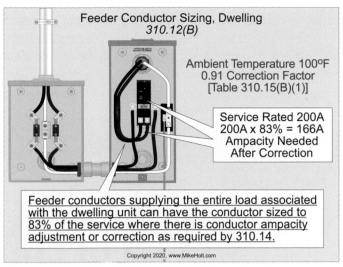

Feeder Conductor Sizing, Dwelling
310.12(B)

Ambient Temperature 100°F
0.91 Correction Factor
[Table 310.15(B)(1)]

Service Rated 200A
200A x 83% = 166A
Ampacity Needed
After Correction

Feeder conductors supplying the entire load associated with the dwelling unit can have the conductor sized to 83% of the service where there is conductor ampacity adjustment or correction as required by 310.14.

Copyright 2020, www.MikeHolt.com

▶Figure 310–14

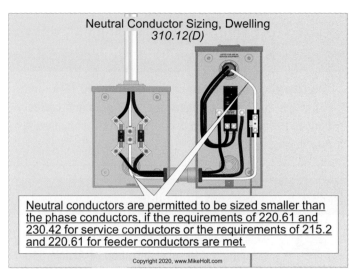

Neutral Conductor Sizing, Dwelling
310.12(D)

Neutral conductors are permitted to be sized smaller than the phase conductors, if the requirements of 220.61 and 230.42 for service conductors or the requirements of 215.2 and 220.61 for feeder conductors are met.

Copyright 2020, www.MikeHolt.com

▶Figure 310–16

(C) Feeder Conductors Not Greater Than Service Conductors.
Feeder conductors for an individual dwelling unit are not required to be larger than the service conductors. ▶Figure 310–15

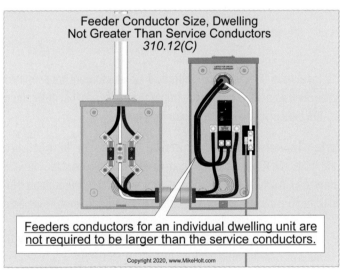

Feeder Conductor Size, Dwelling
Not Greater Than Service Conductors
310.12(C)

Feeders conductors for an individual dwelling unit are not required to be larger than the service conductors.

Copyright 2020, www.MikeHolt.com

▶Figure 310–15

Table 310.12 Single-Phase Dwelling Services and Feeders		
Service or Feeder Rating	Copper	Aluminum or Copper-Clad Aluminum
100A	4 AWG	2 AWG
110A	3 AWG	1 AWG
125A	2 AWG	1/0 AWG
150A	1 AWG	2/0 AWG
175A	1/0 AWG	3/0 AWG
200A	2/0 AWG	4/0 AWG
225A	3/0 AWG	250 kcmil
250A	4/0 AWG	300 kcmil
300A	250 kcmil	350 kcmil
350A	350 kcmil	500 kcmil
400A	400 kcmil	600 kcmil

(D) Neutral Conductors. Neutral conductors are permitted to be sized smaller than the phase conductors, if the requirements of 220.61 and 230.42 for service conductors or the requirements of 215.2 and 220.61 for feeder conductors are met. ▶Figure 310–16

Author's Comment:

▶ It is important to understand the Informative Annexes are just that "informative" and are not part of the enforceable *Code*. Relocating the table with the new clarification gives *Code* users the information in the applicable section essentially making it easier to use.

310.14 Ampacities for Conductors Rated 0V Through 2,000V

The charging text and requirements from 310.15(A) and (C) in the 2017 *NEC* containing adjustments and corrections to the ampacities of conductors 2,000V and below is now in this section.

Analysis

RELOCATED

This relocation is just another part of the overall relocation and reorganization of Article 310 with no technical change.

310.14 Ampacities for Conductors Rated 0V to 2,000V

(A) General Requirements

(1) Tables or Engineering Supervision. The ampacity of a conductor can be determined either by using the tables contained in the *NEC* as corrected and adjusted in accordance with 310.15, or under engineering supervision as provided in 310.14(B).

(2) Conductor Ampacity—Lower Rating. Where more than one ampacity applies for a given circuit length, the lowest ampacity value must be used for the circuit. ▶**Figure 310–17**

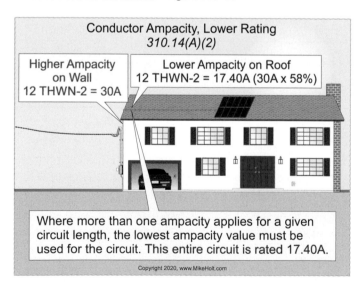

Conductor Ampacity, Lower Rating
310.14(A)(2)

Higher Ampacity on Wall
12 THWN-2 = 30A

Lower Ampacity on Roof
12 THWN-2 = 17.40A (30A x 58%)

Where more than one ampacity applies for a given circuit length, the lowest ampacity value must be used for the circuit. This entire circuit is rated 17.40A.

Copyright 2020, www.MikeHolt.com

▶Figure 310–17

Ex: When different ampacities apply to a length of conductor because of temperature correction [310.15(B)(1)] or conductor bundling [Table 310.15(C)(1)], the higher ampacity can apply for the entire circuit if the length of the portion of the circuit with the corrected or adjusted ampacity does not exceed the lesser of 10 ft or 10 percent of the length of the total circuit. ▶*Figure 310–18*

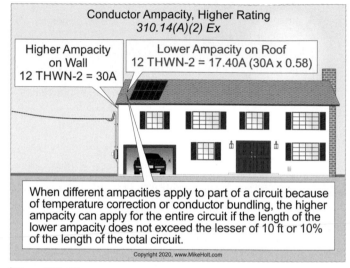

Conductor Ampacity, Higher Rating
310.14(A)(2) Ex

Higher Ampacity on Wall
12 THWN-2 = 30A

Lower Ampacity on Roof
12 THWN-2 = 17.40A (30A x 0.58)

When different ampacities apply to part of a circuit because of temperature correction or conductor bundling, the higher ampacity can apply for the entire circuit if the length of the lower ampacity does not exceed the lesser of 10 ft or 10% of the length of the total circuit.

Copyright 2020, www.MikeHolt.com

▶Figure 310–18

(3) Insulation Temperature Limitation. Conductors are not permitted to be used where the operating temperature exceeds that designated for the type of insulated conductor involved.

Note 1: The insulation temperature rating of a conductor [Table 310.4(A) and Table 311.10(A)] is the maximum temperature a conductor can withstand over a prolonged time period without serious degradation. The main factors to consider for conductor operating temperature include:

(1) Ambient temperature that may vary along the conductor length as well as from time to time [Table 310.15(B)(1)].

(2) Heat generated internally in the conductor as the result of load current flow.

(3) The rate at which generated heat dissipates into the ambient medium.

(4) Adjacent load-carrying conductors that have the effect of raising the ambient temperature and impeding heat dissipation [Table 310.15(C)(1)].

Author's Comment:

▶ The insulation temperature rating of a conductor must be limited to an operating temperature that prevents damage to the conductor's insulation. If the conductor carries excessive current, the I²R heating within the conductor can destroy its insulation. For this reason, elevated conductor operating temperatures created by the current flow in the conductors and conductor bundling might need to be limited.

310.15 Ampacity Tables

This section contains most of the information that was in 310.15(B), except for the dwelling unit service and feeder conductor size rules that are now found in 310.12. Section 310.15 contains the rules that apply to the conductor ampacity tables for conductors rated 0V through 2,000V which were originally part of the table headings. The tables themselves are in 310.16 through 310.21. This move restores the table numbers that were used in the 2008 and earlier *NEC* editions. The parent text in this section provides that the ampacities from the tables are modified by the rules in 310.15(A) though (F) and 310.12.

Analysis

CLARIFIED New language in the parent text provides guidance on the ampacity of conductor sizes not shown in the tables. It specifies that the nonstandard size conductor's ampacity be based on interpolation of the ampacities of the "adjacent" conductors in the ampacity tables and the conductor area of the nonstandard conductor, however this is only permitted under engineering supervision.

CLARIFIED **310.15(B) Ambient Temperature Correction Factors.** This subsection provides that the conductor ampacity must be corrected based on the ambient temperature. This correction can be made using Table 310.15(B)(1) for conductors where the ampacity tables specify 30°C and Table 310.15(B)(2) for those ampacity tables based on 40°C. It also provides that the ampacity can be corrected using Equation 310.15(B).

CLARIFIED **310.15(B)(2) Rooftop.** The language in the 2020 *Code* (like that in the 2017 *NEC*) requires that where raceways or cables are installed less than ⅞ in. above a roof top and exposed to direct sunlight, 33°C (60°F) must be added to the outdoor ambient temperature for the application of the temperature correction factors. The previous exception indicating this temperature adder did not apply to XHHW-2 conductors has been retained.

EDITED **310.15(C) Adjustment Factors.** This requirement was relocated from 310.15(B)(3) and while there are editorial changes, there are none in the technical requirements for ampacity adjustment.

CLARIFIED **310.15(C)(1) More than Three Current-Carrying Conductors.** This text requires that the ampacity of each conductor be reduced by the factor shown in Table 310.15(C)(1) where the number of current-carrying conductors in a raceway or cable exceeds three, or where single conductors or multiconductor cables not installed in raceways are installed without maintaining spacing for a continuous length longer than 24 in. Each current-carrying conductor of a paralleled set of conductors must be counted as a current-carrying conductor.

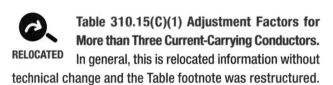
RELOCATED **Table 310.15(C)(1) Adjustment Factors for More than Three Current-Carrying Conductors.** In general, this is relocated information without technical change and the Table footnote was restructured.

RELOCATED **310.15(C)(2) Raceway Spacing.** This requirement was relocated without change from 310.15(B)(3)(b).

CLARIFIED **310.15(E) Neutral Conductors.** The new parent text clarifies that the neutral conductor is to be considered current carrying in accordance with list items (1), (2), and (3)—there was no technical change.

RELOCATED **310.15(F) Grounding or Bonding Conductors.** This subsection was relocated without technical changes as part of the article reorganization and reference to the new adjustments table location.

310.15 Ampacity Tables

(A) General. Ampacities for conductors are contained in Table 310.16.

The temperature ampacity correction of 310.15(B)(1) and adjustment ampacity factors of 310.15(C)(1) are applied to the ampacity listed in Table 310.16 based on the conductor insulation temperature rating.

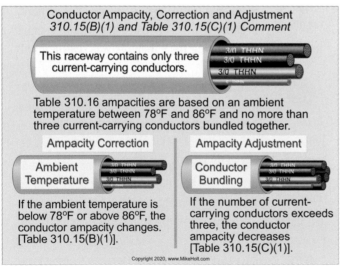

▸Figure 310–19

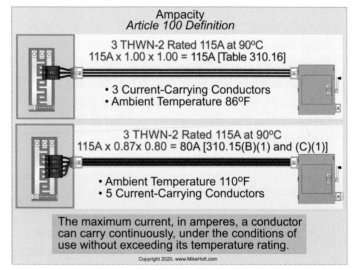

▸Figure 310–20

The neutral conductor might be a current-carrying conductor, but only under the conditions specified in 310.15(E). Equipment grounding conductors are never considered current-carrying [310.15(F)].

(B) Ambient Temperature Correction Factors

(1) General. Ampacities for ambient temperatures other than those shown in the ampacity tables must be corrected in accordance with Table 310.15(B)(1). ▸**Figure 310–21**

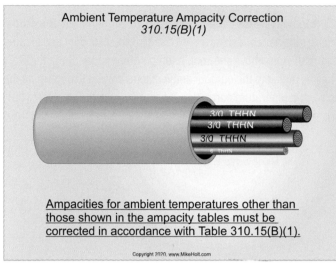

Ambient Temperature Ampacity Correction
310.15(B)(1)

Ampacities for ambient temperatures other than those shown in the ampacity tables must be corrected in accordance with Table 310.15(B)(1).

Copyright 2020, www.MikeHolt.com

▶Figure 310–21

Author's Comment:

▶ The conductor ampacities contained in Table 310.16 are based on the condition where the ambient temperature is between 78ºF and 86ºF, and no more than three current-carrying conductors are bundled together; such ampacity must be corrected in accordance with Table 310.15(B)(1) if the ambient temperature is lower than 78ºC or greater than 86ºC. ▶Figure 310–22

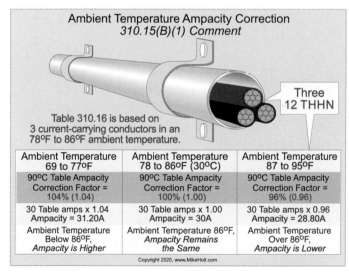

Ambient Temperature Ampacity Correction
310.15(B)(1) Comment

Table 310.16 is based on 3 current-carrying conductors in an 78ºF to 86ºF ambient temperature.

Three 12 THHN

Ambient Temperature 69 to 77ºF	Ambient Temperature 78 to 86ºF (30ºC)	Ambient Temperature 87 to 95ºF
90ºC Table Ampacity Correction Factor = 104% (1.04)	90ºC Table Ampacity Correction Factor = 100% (1.00)	90ºC Table Ampacity Correction Factor = 96% (0.96)
30 Table amps x 1.04 Ampacity = 31.20A	30 Table amps x 1.00 Ampacity = 30A	30 Table amps x 0.96 Ampacity = 28.80A
Ambient Temperature Below 86ºF, *Ampacity is Higher*	Ambient Temperature 86ºF, *Ampacity Remains the Same*	Ambient Temperature Over 86ºF, *Ampacity is Lower*

Copyright 2020, www.MikeHolt.com

▶Figure 310–22

Table 310.15(B)(1) Ambient Temperature Correction Factors Based on 30°C (86°F) and 90°C Insulation

Ambient Temperature °F	Ambient Temperature °C	Correction Factor 90°C Conductors
50°F or less	10°C or less	1.15
51–59°F	11–15°C	1.12
60–68°F	16–20°C	1.08
69–77°F	21–25°C	1.04
78–86°F	26–30°C	1.00
87–95°F	31–35°C	0.96
96–104°F	36–40°C	0.91
105–113°F	41–45°C	0.87
114–122°F	46–50°C	0.82
123–131°F	51–55°C	0.76
132–140°F	56–60°C	0.71
141–149°F	61–65°C	0.65
150–158°F	66–70°C	0.58
159–167°F	71–75°C	0.50

Corrected Conductor Ampacity—Ambient Temperature Correction Formula: **Corrected Ampacity = Table 310.16 Ampacity × Ambient Correction Factor**

▶ **Ambient Temperature Below 30ºC (86ºF) Example**

Question: *What is the ampacity of a 12 THHN conductor when installed in an ambient temperature of 50ºF?* ▶**Figure 310–23**

(a) 20A   (b) 25A   (c) 31A   (d) 35A

Answer: *(d) 35A*

Solution:

The conductor ampacity for 12 THHN is 30A at 90ºC [Table 310.16].

The correction factor for a 90ºC conductor installed in an ambient temperature of 50ºF is 1.15 [Table 310.15(B)(1)].

Corrected Ampacity = 30A × 115%
Corrected Ampacity = 34.50A, round to 35A

Note: Ampacity increases when the ambient temperature is less than 30ºC (86ºF).   •••

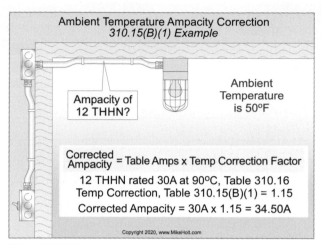

▶Figure 310–23

▶ **Ambient Temperature Above 86°F (30°C) Example**

Question: *What is the ampacity of a 6 THWN-2 conductor installed in an ambient temperature of 50°C?* ▶**Figure 310–24**

(a) 35A   *(b) 53A*   *(c) 62A*   *(d) 75A*

Answer: *(c) 62A*

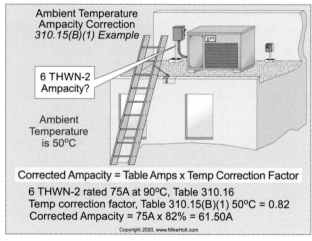

▶Figure 310–24

Solution:

The conductor ampacity for 6 THWN-2 is 75A at 90°C [Table 310.16].

The correction factor for a 90°C conductor installed in an ambient temperature of 50°C is 0.82 [Table 310.15(B)(1)].

Corrected Ampacity = 75A × 82%
Corrected Ampacity = 61.50A; round to 62A

(2) Raceways and Cables Exposed to Sunlight on Rooftops. Where raceways or cables are exposed to direct sunlight and located less than ⅞ in. above the roof, a temperature adder of 60°F (33°C) must be added to the outdoor ambient temperature to determine the ambient temperature correction in accordance with Table 310.15(B)(1). ▶Figure 310–25

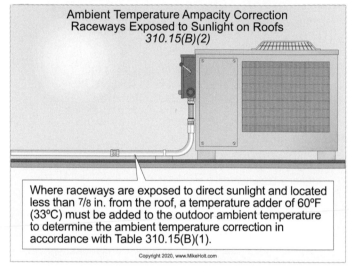

▶Figure 310–25

Author's Comment:

▶ The reason for the temperature adder is because the air inside raceways and cables that are in direct sunlight is significantly hotter than the surrounding air.

▶ **Example**

Question: *What is the ampacity of 6 THWN-2 in a raceway located ½ in. above the roof, where the ambient temperature is 90°F?* ▶Figure 310–26

(a) 40A   *(b) 41A*   *(c) 42A*   *(d) 44A*

Answer: *(d) 44A*
Solution:

Corrected Temperature = 90°F + 60°F adder
Corrected Temperature = 150°F

The temperature correction factor for 150°F = 0.58 [Table 310.15(B)(1)]

6 THWN-2 is rated 75A at 90°C [Table 310.16]

Corrected Ampacity = 75A × 58%
Corrected Ampacity = 43.50A, round to 44A

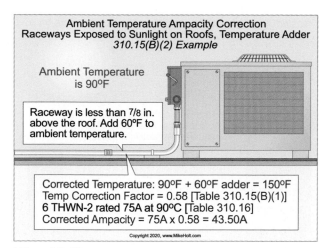

Ambient Temperature Ampacity Correction
Raceways Exposed to Sunlight on Roofs, Temperature Adder
310.15(B)(2) Example

Ambient Temperature
is 90°F

Raceway is less than 7/8 in. above the roof. Add 60°F to ambient temperature.

Corrected Temperature: 90°F + 60°F adder = 150°F
Temp Correction Factor = 0.58 [Table 310.15(B)(1)]
6 THWN-2 rated 75A at 90°C [Table 310.16]
Corrected Ampacity = 75A x 0.58 = 43.50A

Copyright 2020, www.MikeHolt.com

▶Figure 310–26

Ex: Type XHHW-2 insulated conductors are not subject to the rooftop temperature adder.

Note 1: See the ASHRAE Handbook—Fundamentals (www.ashrae.org) as a source for the ambient temperatures in various locations.

(C) Conductor Bundle Adjustment

(1) Four or More Current-Carrying Conductors. Where four or more current-carrying conductors are contained within a raceway that is longer than 24 in., the <u>ampacities contained in Table 310.16 must be reduced in accordance with</u> Table 310.15(C)(1).

Where multiconductor cables are installed without maintaining spacing for a continuous length longer than 24 in., the <u>ampacities contained in Table 310.16 must be reduced in accordance with</u> Table 310.15(C)(1).
▶Figure 310–27

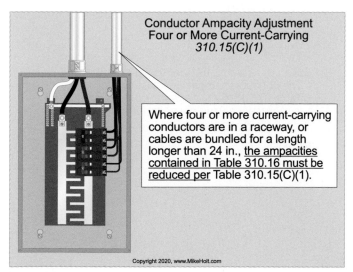

Conductor Ampacity Adjustment
Four or More Current-Carrying
310.15(C)(1)

Where four or more current-carrying conductors are in a raceway, or cables are bundled for a length longer than 24 in., <u>the ampacities contained in Table 310.16 must be reduced per</u> Table 310.15(C)(1).

Copyright 2020, www.MikeHolt.com

▶Figure 310–27

▶ The neutral conductor might be a current-carrying conductor, but only under the conditions specified in 310.15(E). Equipment grounding conductors are never considered current carrying [310.15(F)].

Table 310.15(C)(1) Conductor Ampacity Adjustment for More Than Three Current–Carrying Conductors	
Number of Conductors[1]	**Adjustment**
4–6	80%
7–9	70%
10–20	50%
21–30	45%
31–40	40%
41 and above	35%

[1] *Does not include conductors that cannot be energized at the same time.*

▶ Conductor ampacity reduction is required when four or more current-carrying conductors are bundled together because heat generated by current flow is not able to dissipate as quickly as when there are fewer current-carrying conductors. ▶Figure 310–28

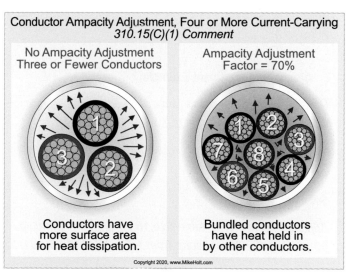

Conductor Ampacity Adjustment, Four or More Current-Carrying
310.15(C)(1) Comment

No Ampacity Adjustment
Three or Fewer Conductors

Ampacity Adjustment
Factor = 70%

Conductors have more surface area for heat dissipation.

Bundled conductors have heat held in by other conductors.

Copyright 2020, www.MikeHolt.com

▶Figure 310–28

▶ **Ampacity Adjustment Example**

Question: *What is the adjusted ampacity of four current-carrying 12 THWN-2 conductors in a raceway?* ▶**Figure 310–29**

(a) 20A   *(b) 24A*   *(c) 29A*   *(d) 32A*

Answer: *(b) 24A*

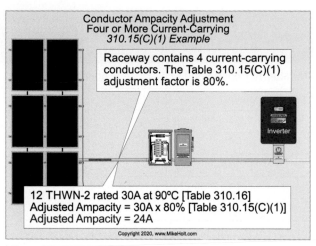

12 THWN-2 rated 30A at 90°C [Table 310.16]
Adjusted Ampacity = 30A x 80% [Table 310.15(C)(1)]
Adjusted Ampacity = 24A

▶Figure 310–29

Solution:

Adjusted Ampacity = Table 310.16 Ampacity × Bundled Ampacity Adjustment Factor from Table 310.310.15(C)(1)

12 THWN-2 is rated 30A at 90°C [Table 310.16].

The adjustment factor for four current-carrying conductors is 80 percent [Table 310.310.15(C)(1)].

Adjusted Ampacity = 30A × 80%
Adjusted Ampacity = 24A

▶ **Ampacity Adjustment Example 2**

Question: *What is the adjusted ampacity of eight current-carrying 12 THWN-2 conductors in a raceway?* ▶**Figure 310–30**

(a) 16A   *(b) 21A*   *(c) 35A*   *(d) 43A*

Answer: *(b) 21A*

Solution:

Adjusted Ampacity = Table 310.16 Ampacity × Bundled Ampacity Adjustment Factor from Table 310.310.15(C)(1)

12 THWN-2 is rated 30A at 90°C [Table 310.16].

The adjustment factor for eight current-carrying conductors is 70 percent [Table 310.310.15(C)(1)].

Adjusted Ampacity = 30A × 70%
Adjusted Ampacity = 21A

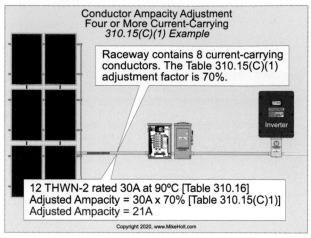

12 THWN-2 rated 30A at 90°C [Table 310.16]
Adjusted Ampacity = 30A x 70% [Table 310.15(C)1)]
Adjusted Ampacity = 21A

▶Figure 310–30

(a) Where conductors are installed in cable trays, the provision of 392.80 applies.

(b) Conductor ampacity adjustment from Table 310.15(C)(1) does not apply to conductors in raceways having a length not exceeding 24 in. ▶Figure 310–31

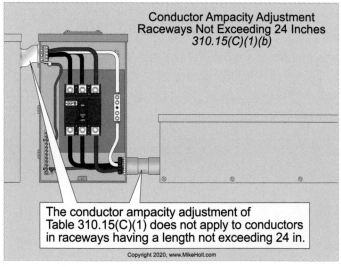

The conductor ampacity adjustment of Table 310.15(C)(1) does not apply to conductors in raceways having a length not exceeding 24 in.

▶Figure 310–31

▶ **Ampacity Adjustment—Raceway Not Exceeding 24 Inches Example**

Question: What is the ampacity of five 3/0 THWN-2 conductors in a raceway that does not exceed 24 in. in length? ▶Figure 310–32

(a) 150A   (b) 195A   (c) 205A   (d) 225A

Answer: (d) 225A

3/0 THWN-2 is rated 225A at 90ºC [Table 310.16].

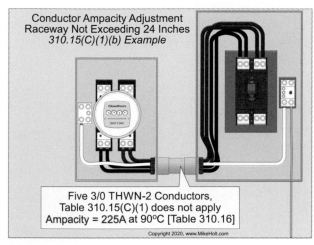

Conductor Ampacity Adjustment
Raceway Not Exceeding 24 Inches
310.15(C)(1)(b) Example

Five 3/0 THWN-2 Conductors,
Table 310.15(C)(1) does not apply
Ampacity = 225A at 90ºC [Table 310.16]

Copyright 2020, www.MikeHolt.com

▶Figure 310–32

(d) The conductor ampacity adjustment of Table 310.15(C)(1) does not apply to conductors within Type AC or Type MC cable under the following conditions: ▶Figure 310–33

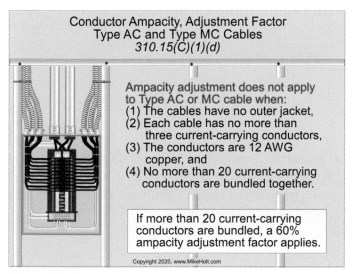

Conductor Ampacity, Adjustment Factor
Type AC and Type MC Cables
310.15(C)(1)(d)

Ampacity adjustment does not apply to Type AC or MC cable when:
(1) The cables have no outer jacket,
(2) Each cable has no more than three current-carrying conductors,
(3) The conductors are 12 AWG copper, and
(4) No more than 20 current-carrying conductors are bundled together.

If more than 20 current-carrying conductors are bundled, a 60% ampacity adjustment factor applies.

Copyright 2020, www.MikeHolt.com

▶Figure 310–33

(1) The cables do not have an outer jacket,

(2) Each cable has no more than three current-carrying conductors,

(3) The conductors are 12 AWG copper, and

(4) No more than twenty current-carrying conductors (ten 2-wire cables or six 3-wire cables) are bundled together.

Ex: A 60 percent adjustment factor can be applied if more than twenty current-carrying conductors in these cables are bundled together.

(E) Neutral Conductor. Neutral conductors must be considered current carrying in accordance with the following:

(1) Not Considered Current Carrying. The neutral conductor of a 3-wire, single-phase, 120/240V system, or 4-wire, three-phase, 120/208V or 277/480V wye-connected system, is not considered a current-carrying conductor for the application of conductor ampacity adjustments in accordance with Table 310.15(C)(1). ▶Figure 310–34

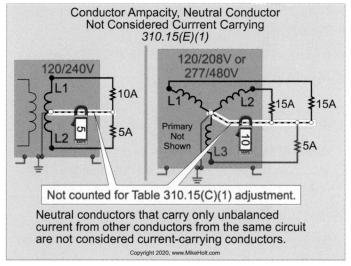

Conductor Ampacity, Neutral Conductor
Not Considered Currrent Carrying
310.15(E)(1)

120/240V

L1   10A
L2   5A

120/208V or 277/480V

L1   L2   15A   15A
Primary Not Shown
L3   5A

Not counted for Table 310.15(C)(1) adjustment.

Neutral conductors that carry only unbalanced current from other conductors from the same circuit are not considered current-carrying conductors.

Copyright 2020, www.MikeHolt.com

▶Figure 310–34

(2) Considered Current Carrying. The neutral conductor of a 3-wire circuit from a 4-wire, three-phase, wye-connected system carries approximately the same current as the line-to-neutral load currents of the other conductors and is considered a current-carrying conductor for conductor ampacity adjustments in accordance with Table 310.15(C)(1). ▶Figure 310–35

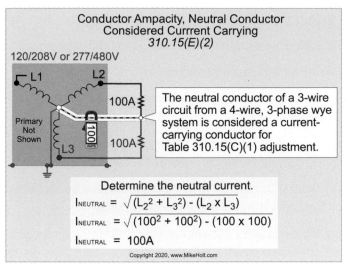

▶Figure 310–35

In such a situation, one of the line-to-neutral currents is not present and can be zeroed out of the neutral current formula, resulting in the following formula:

Unbalanced 3-Wire Wye Secondary Neutral Current Formula:

$$I_{Neutral} = \sqrt{(I_{Line1}^2 + I_{Line2}^2) - (I_{Line1} \times I_{Line2})}$$

▶ **Neutral Conductor Current Example**

Question: What is the neutral current for two 16A, 120V circuits with a common neutral? The system is a 120/208V, three-phase, 4-wire, wye-connected system. ▶**Figure 310–36**

(a) 8A   (b) 16A   (c) 32A   (d) 40A

Answer: (b) 16A

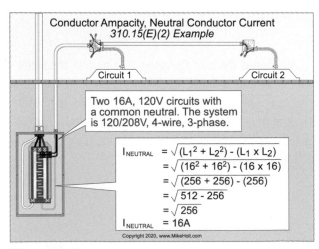

▶Figure 310–36

Solution:

$$I_{Neutral} = \sqrt{(I_{Line1}^2 + I_{Line2}^2) - (I_{Line1} \times I_{Line2})}$$
$$I_{Neutral} = \sqrt{(16^2 + 16^2) - (16 \times 16)}$$
$$I_{Neutral} = \sqrt{(512 - 256)}$$
$$I_{Neutral} = \sqrt{256}$$
$$I_{Neutral} = 16A$$

(3) Considered Current Carrying. On a 4-wire, 3-phase, wye circuit where the major portion of the load consists of nonlinear loads, the neutral conductor is considered a current-carrying conductor for conductor ampacity adjustments in accordance with Table 310.15(C)(1). ▶**Figure 310–37**

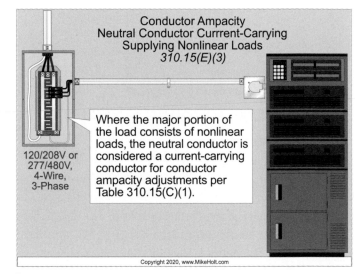

▶Figure 310–37

Author's Comment:

▶ According to Article 100, a "Nonlinear Load" is a load where the current waveform does not follow the applied sinusoidal voltage waveform.

(F) Equipment Grounding and Bonding Conductor. Equipment grounding and bonding conductors are not considered current carrying for conductor ampacity adjustments in accordance with Table 310.15(C)(1). ▶Figure 310–38

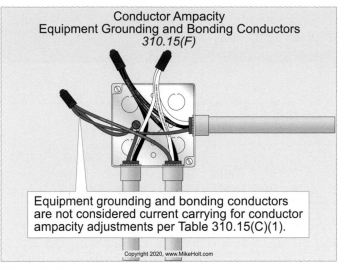

Conductor Ampacity
Equipment Grounding and Bonding Conductors
310.15(F)

Equipment grounding and bonding conductors
are not considered current carrying for conductor
ampacity adjustments per Table 310.15(C)(1).

Copyright 2020, www.MikeHolt.com

▶Figure 310–38

310.16 Ampacities of Insulated Conductors in Raceways, Cables, or Buried

The information that was in the headings of Tables 310.15(B)(16) through 310.15(B)(21) that provided guidance as to the conditions under which the listed ampacities for conductors applied was relocated to this section.

Analysis

NEW This section and its associated table contain the most commonly used ampacities for most electricians. The language tells us that the maximum allowable ampacities are specified in Table 310.16 where all the pre-requisite conditions apply. These requirements were previously found in the heading for Table 310.15(B)(16). The requirements were relocated in a more usable format here in 310.16 and the table number was restored to its original "Table 310.16."

310.16 Ampacities of Insulated Conductors in Raceways, Cables, or Buried

The conductor ampacities specified in Table 310.16 are based on the following conditions: ▶Figure 310–39

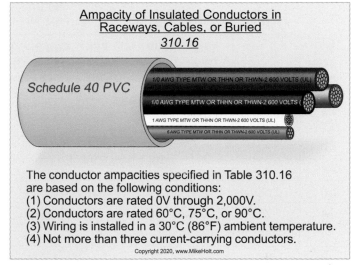

Ampacity of Insulated Conductors in
Raceways, Cables, or Buried
310.16

Schedule 40 PVC

1/0 AWG TYPE MTW OR THHN OR THWN-2 600 VOLTS (UL)
1/0 AWG TYPE MTW OR THHN OR THWN-2 600 VOLTS (
1 AWG TYPE MTW OR THHN OR THWN-2 600 VOLTS (UL)
6 AWG TYPE MTW OR THHN OR THWN-2 600 VOLTS (UL)

The conductor ampacities specified in Table 310.16
are based on the following conditions:
(1) Conductors are rated 0V through 2,000V.
(2) Conductors are rated 60°C, 75°C, or 90°C.
(3) Wiring is installed in a 30°C (86°F) ambient temperature.
(4) Not more than three current-carrying conductors.

Copyright 2020, www.MikeHolt.com

▶Figure 310–39

Author's Comment:

▶ Newer electricians will see this as a change, but for those of us who worked with the 2008 and older *Codes*, this is a reversion back to what we had long been accustomed. For purposes of this book, Table 310.16 will be the only ampacity table covered at length

(1) Conductors are rated 0V through 2,000V.

(2) Conductors are rated 60°C (140°F), 75°C (167°F), or 90°C (194°F).

(3) Wiring is installed in a 30°C (86°F) ambient temperature.

(4) There are not more than three current-carrying conductors.

Table 310.16 Ampacities of Insulated Conductors Not More Than Three Current-Carrying Conductors in Raceway, Cable, or Earth (Directly Buried)							
	Copper	Aluminum	Size AWG kcmil		Copper	Aluminum	
	60°C (140°F)	75°C (167°F)	90°C (194°F)	60°C (140°F)	75°C (167°F)	90°C (194°F)	
Size AWG kcmil	TW UF	RHW THHW THW THWN XHHW USE	RHH RHW-2 THHN THHW THW-2 THWN-2 USE-2 XHHW XHHW-2	TW UF	THHN THW THWN XHHW	THHN THW-2 THWN-2 THHW XHHW XHHW-2	
14**	15	20	25				
12**	20	25	30	15	20	25	12**
10**	30	35	40	25	30	35	10**
8	40	50	55	35	40	45	8
6	55	65	75	40	50	55	6
4	70	85	95	55	65	75	4
3	85	100	115	65	75	85	3
2	95	115	130	75	90	100	2
1	110	130	145	85	100	115	1
1/0	125	150	170	100	120	135	1/0
2/0	145	175	195	115	135	150	2/0
3/0	165	200	225	130	155	175	3/0
4/0	195	230	260	150	180	205	4/0
250	215	255	290	170	205	230	250
300	240	285	320	195	230	260	300
350	260	310	350	210	250	280	350
400	280	335	380	225	270	305	400
500	320	380	430	260	310	350	500

Notes:

1 - Section 310.16 must be referenced for conditions of use.

*2 – Section 310.15(B) must be referenced for the ampacity correction factors where the ambient temperature is other than 30°C (86°F).

*3 – Section 310.15(C)(1) must be referenced for more than three current-carrying conductors.

Section 240.4(D) must be referenced for conductor overcurrent protection limitations except as modified elsewhere in the Code.

Author's Comment:

▸ Remember that, unlike "Informational Notes" "Notes" to Tables throughout the *Code* are a part of that particular rule or requirement and are enforceable.

ARTICLE
312

CABINETS

Introduction to Article 312—Cabinets

Conditions of use effect the selection and application of cabinets. For example, you cannot use just any enclosure in a wet location or in a hazardous location. The conditions of use impose special requirements for these situations.

For all such enclosures, certain requirements apply—regardless of the use. For example, you must cover any openings, protect conductors from abrasion, and allow sufficient bending room for conductors.

Notice that Article 408 covers switchboards, switchgear, and panelboards, with the primary emphasis on the interior, or "guts," while the cabinet that is used to enclose a panelboard is covered here in Article 312. Therefore, you will find that some important considerations such as wire-bending space at the terminals of panelboards are included in this article.

312.5 Enclosures

A new exception was added for cable tray installations in subsection (C) to permit commonly used installation methods for conductors entering enclosures.

Analysis

➕ NEW **312.5(C) Ex 2 Cables.** This rule itself requires that each cable be secured to the enclosure, however the new exception references 392.46(A) and (B) which permit cable tray conductors and cables to leave the tray and enter an enclosure via a bushed conduit, without securing the cable or conductors to the enclosure.

312.5 Enclosures

(C) Cable Termination. Cables must be secured to the cabinet with fittings designed and listed for the cable. See 300.12 and 300.15. ▶Figure 312–1 and ▶Figure 312–2

Author's Comment:

▸ Cable clamps or cable connectors must only be used with one cable, unless that clamp or fitting is identified for more than one cable. Some Type NM cable clamps are listed for two or more Type NM cables within a single fitting (UL White Book, *Guide Information for Electrical Equipment*). ▶Figure 312–3 and ▶Figure 312–4

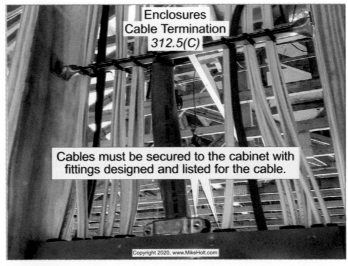

Enclosures
Cable Termination
312.5(C)

Cables must be secured to the cabinet with fittings designed and listed for the cable.

Copyright 2020, www.MikeHolt.com

▶Figure 312–1

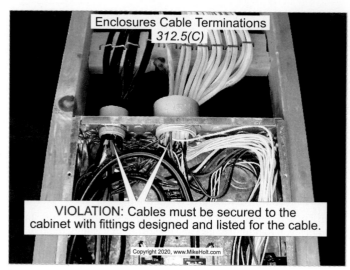

Enclosures Cable Terminations
312.5(C)

VIOLATION: Cables must be secured to the cabinet with fittings designed and listed for the cable.

Copyright 2020, www.MikeHolt.com

▶Figure 312–2

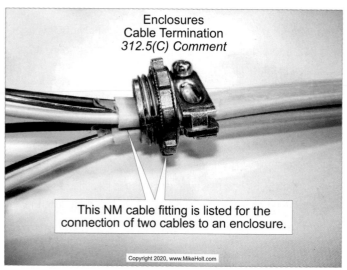

Enclosures
Cable Termination
312.5(C) Comment

This NM cable fitting is listed for the connection of two cables to an enclosure.

Copyright 2020, www.MikeHolt.com

▶Figure 312–3

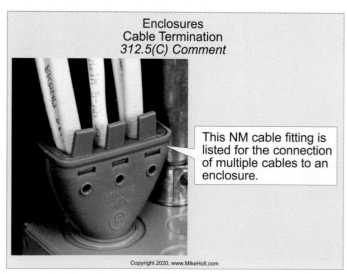

Enclosures
Cable Termination
312.5(C) Comment

This NM cable fitting is listed for the connection of multiple cables to an enclosure.

Copyright 2020, www.MikeHolt.com

▶Figure 312–4

Ex: Cables with nonmetallic sheaths are not required to be secured to the cabinet if the cables enter the top of a surface-mounted cabinet through a nonflexible raceway not less than 18 in. or more than 10 ft long, if all of the following conditions are met: ▶Figure 312–5

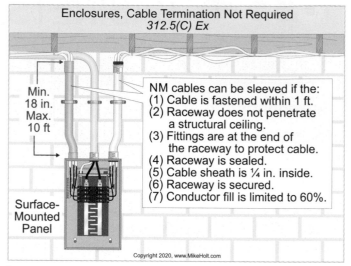

Enclosures, Cable Termination Not Required
312.5(C) Ex

Min. 18 in. Max. 10 ft

NM cables can be sleeved if the:
(1) Cable is fastened within 1 ft.
(2) Raceway does not penetrate a structural ceiling.
(3) Fittings are at the end of the raceway to protect cable.
(4) Raceway is sealed.
(5) Cable sheath is ¼ in. inside.
(6) Raceway is secured.
(7) Conductor fill is limited to 60%.

Surface-Mounted Panel

Copyright 2020, www.MikeHolt.com

▶Figure 312–5

(1) *Each cable is fastened within 12 in. from the raceway.*

(2) *The raceway does not penetrate a structural ceiling.*

(3) *Fittings are provided on the raceway to protect the cables from abrasion.*

(4) *The raceway is sealed.*

(5) *Each cable sheath extends not less than ¼ in. into the panelboard.*

(6) *The raceway is properly secured.*

(7) *Where installed as conduit or tubing so Chapter 9 Table 1 may be used; Note 2 to the tables in Chapter 9 do not apply to this condition.*

Author's Comment:

▶ This rule created a conflict with Article 392 as it does not amend the requirements of 310.15(C). The new exception added here, addresses that conflict with what has been a long-standing installation practice.

312.6 Deflection of Conductors

The rule regarding the deflection of conductors or space necessary for conductors to be bent without damage was revised to clarify that the rule also applies to conductors in meter socket enclosures.

Analysis

CLARIFIED The term "meter socket enclosures" replaces "the like" from the 2017 *Code* to clarify that the deflection of conductor rules apply to meter socket enclosures. It is now consistent with the scope and other sections of this article. A listed meter socket enclosure will comply with the deflection rules as long as the conductors enter through a factory provided knock out (KO).

312.6 Deflection of Conductors

Conductors entering or leaving cabinets and <u>meter socket enclosures</u> must comply with 312.6(A) and 312.6(B).

Author's Comment:

▸ Where field opening(s) are made in locations that differ from the factory KO locations, the deflection space will have to be evaluated by the installer and ultimately approved by the AHJ.

312.8 Overcurrent Device Enclosures

Subsection (B) was expanded to permit both power monitoring and control equipment to be installed in switch or overcurrent device enclosures.

Analysis

EXPANDED 312.8(B) Power Monitoring or Energy Management Equipment. This change recognizes that some such installed equipment both monitors and controls as part of an energy management system.

The actual requirements for the equipment remain as they were in the 2017 *Code*; the equipment must be identified as a field installable accessory for the listed equipment, or a listed kit evaluated for field installation in switch or overcurrent device enclosures.

In addition, the total area of all conductors, splices, taps, and equipment must not exceed 75 percent of the cross-sectional area of the space. One of the concerns is the unknown effect that wireless transmissions from the power monitoring equipment and the energy management equipment may have on live safety equipment such as AFCIs and GFCIs.

312.8 Overcurrent Device Enclosures

(B) Power Monitoring <u>or Energy Management Equipment</u>. The wiring space of enclosures for switches or overcurrent devices are permitted to contain power monitoring <u>or energy management</u> equipment where all of the following conditions are met:

(1) Identification. The power monitoring <u>or energy management</u> equipment is identified as a field installable accessory as part of the listed equipment or is a listed kit evaluated for field installation in switch or overcurrent device enclosures.

(2) Area. The total area of all conductors, splices, taps, and equipment at any cross section of the wiring space does not exceed 75 percent of the cross-sectional area of that space.

(3) Conductors. Conductors used exclusively for control or instrumentation circuits must comply with either 312.8(B)(3) (a) or (b).

    (a) Conductors must comply with 725.49.

    (b) Conductors smaller than 18 AWG, but not smaller than 22 AWG for a single conductor and 26 AWG, or a multiconductor cable is permitted where the conductors and cable assemblies meet all of the following conditions:

(1) Conductors or cables are within raceways or routed along one or more walls of the enclosure and secured at intervals not exceeding 10 in.

(2) Are secured within 10 in. of terminations.

(3) Are secured to prevent contact with current carrying components within the enclosure

(4) Are rated for the system voltage and not less than 600 volts

(5) Have a minimum insulation temperature rating of 90°C

ARTICLE 314

OUTLET, DEVICE, PULL, JUNCTION BOXES; CONDUIT BODIES; AND HANDHOLE ENCLOSURES

Introduction to Article 314—Outlet, Device, Pull, and Junction Boxes; Conduit Bodies; and Handhole Enclosures

Article 314 contains the installation requirements for outlet boxes, pull and junction boxes, conduit bodies, and handhole enclosures. As with the cabinets covered in Article 312, the conditions of use have a bearing on the type of material and equipment selected for a particular installation.

The information contained in this article will help you size an outlet box using the proper cubic-inch capacity as well as calculating the minimum dimensions for pull boxes. There are limits on the amount of weight that can be supported by an outlet box, and rules on how to support a device or outlet box to various surfaces. Article 314 will help you understand these rules so your installation will be compliant with the *NEC*. As always, the clear illustrations in this article will help you visualize the finished installation.

314.16 Number of Conductors

A new sentence was added requiring that, in addition to the volume required for conductors and devices in a box, the box must also comply with the depth requirements of 314.24. More than four equipment grounding conductors can no longer be grouped together as "one of the largest conductors" as evidenced by the new language in subsection (B)(5).

Analysis

EXPANDED The yokes of deep devices such as GFCIs, dimmers, timers, and occupancy sensors are often bent, or the conductors are damaged where these devices are installed in a box of the proper conductor volume.

While there is nothing in 314.16 that says 314.24 does not apply, the panel elected to add a reference to that section in lieu of requiring a volume allowance of four. The parent text in 314.24 requires the box to have enough depth for the conductors and devices to be installed without damage.

EXPANDED **314.16(B)(5) Equipment Grounding Conductor Fill.** The revision to this subsection recognizes that where there are multiple EGCs, there can be a box volume issue where the 2017 *NEC* text is used in that it only requires a single volume, based on the largest EGC in the box, to be used no matter how many EGCs may exist. The revision requires a single volume, still based on the largest EGC, where there are four or less EGCs. It further provides that where there are more than four EGCs, a ¼ volume is required for each additional EGC. The language also does not require any volume for an EGC or bonding jumper that does not leave the box.

314.16 Sizing Outlet Boxes

Boxes containing 6 AWG and smaller conductors must be sized in an approved manner to provide free space for all conductors, devices, and fittings. In no case can the volume of the box, as calculated in 314.16(A) be less than the volume requirement as calculated in 314.16(B). ▶Figure 314–1 and ▶Figure 314–2

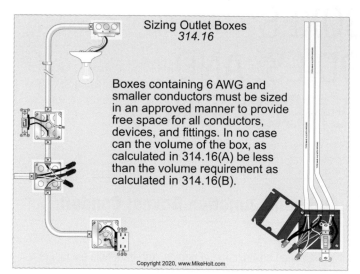

▶Figure 314–1

▶Figure 314–2

Author's Comment:

▶ Requirements for sizing boxes and conduit bodies containing conductors 4 AWG and larger are in 314.28, and those for sizing handhole enclosures are contained in 314.30(A).

An outlet box is generally used for the attachment of devices and luminaires and has a specific amount of space (volume) for conductors, devices, and fittings. The volume taken up by conductors, devices, and fittings in a box must not exceed the box fill capacity.

Boxes and conduit bodies enclosing conductors 4 AWG or larger must also comply with the provisions of 314.28. Outlet and device boxes must also comply with 314.24.

(B) Box Fill Calculations. Table 314.16(A) doesn't consider switches, receptacles, luminaire studs, luminaire hickeys, cable clamps, or equipment grounding conductors. The calculated conductor volumes determined by 314.16(B)(1) through (B)(5) are added together to determine the total volume of the conductors, devices, and fittings. ▶Figure 314–3

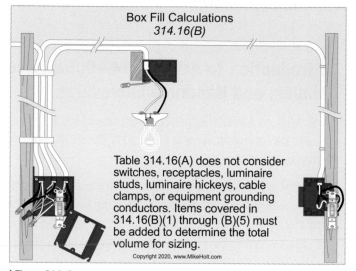

▶Figure 314–3

Raceway and cable fittings, including locknuts and bushings, are not counted for box fill calculations. ▶Figure 314–4

Each space within a box with a barrier must be calculated separately. ▶Figure 314–5

(1) Conductor Volume. Each conductor that originates outside the box and terminates or is spliced inside the box counts as a single conductor volume as shown in Table 314.16(B). ▶Figure 314–6

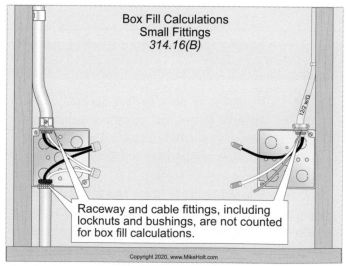

▶Figure 314–4

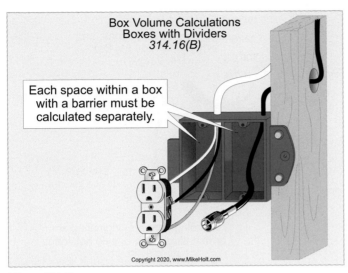

▸Figure 314–5

Table 314.16(B) Volume Allowance Required per Conductor	
Conductor AWG Size	Free Space Required for Each Conductor (cu in.)
18	1.50
16	1.75
14	2.00
12	2.25
10	2.50
8	3.00
6	5.00

Each conductor loop having a total length of less than 12 in. is considered a single conductor volume, and each conductor loop having a length of at least twice 12 in. is considered as two conductor volumes in accordance with Table 314.16(B) [300.14]. ▸Figure 314–7

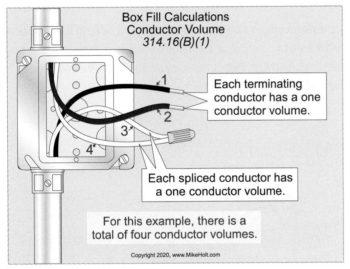

▸Figure 314–6

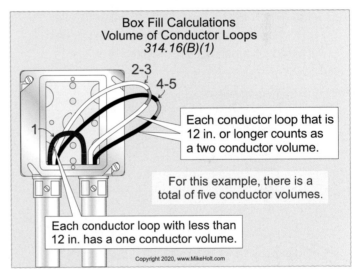

▸Figure 314–7

Author's Comment:

▸ Table 314.16(B) lists the conductor cubic inch volumes for 18 AWG through 6 AWG. For example, one 14 AWG conductor has a volume of 2 cu in. If a box has four 14 AWG conductors, the conductor volume is 8 cu in.

▸ Conductor insulation is not a factor for box fill calculations.

Author's Comment:

▸ At least 6 in. of conductor, measured from the point in the box where the conductor enters the enclosure, must be available at each point for conductor splices or terminations. ▸Figure 314–8

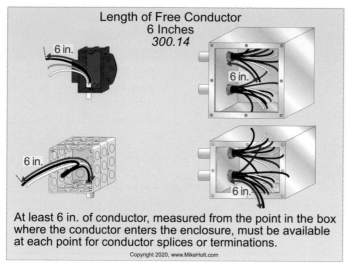

Length of Free Conductor
6 Inches
300.14

At least 6 in. of conductor, measured from the point in the box where the conductor enters the enclosure, must be available at each point for conductor splices or terminations.

▶Figure 314–8

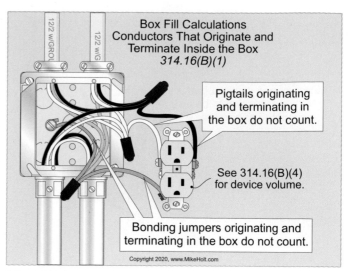

Box Fill Calculations
Conductors That Originate and
Terminate Inside the Box
314.16(B)(1)

Pigtails originating and terminating in the box do not count.

See 314.16(B)(4) for device volume.

Bonding jumpers originating and terminating in the box do not count.

▶Figure 314–10

Author's Comment:

▶ Boxes that have openings of less than 8 in. in any dimension must have at least 6 in. of conductor, measured from the point where the conductor enters the box, and at least 3 in. of conductor outside the box. ▶**Figure 314–9**

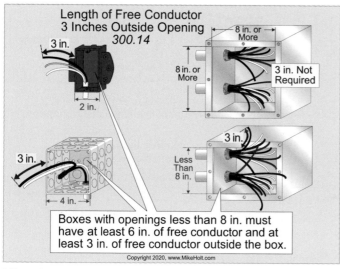

Length of Free Conductor
3 Inches Outside Opening
300.14

Boxes with openings less than 8 in. must have at least 6 in. of free conductor and at least 3 in. of free conductor outside the box.

▶Figure 314–9

Conductors that originate and terminate within the box, such as pigtails and bonding jumpers, are not counted as a conductor volume. ▶Figure 314–10

Ex: Equipment grounding conductors and not more than four fixture wires are not counted as a conductor volume if they enter the box from a domed luminaire or similar canopy, such as a ceiling paddle fan canopy. ▶Figure 314–11

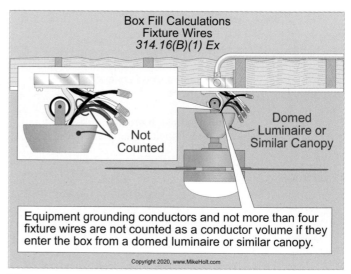

Box Fill Calculations
Fixture Wires
314.16(B)(1) Ex

Not Counted

Domed Luminaire or Similar Canopy

Equipment grounding conductors and not more than four fixture wires are not counted as a conductor volume if they enter the box from a domed luminaire or similar canopy.

▶Figure 314–11

(2) Cable Clamp Volume. Cable clamps that are part of the outlet box are counted as a single conductor volume based on the largest conductor in accordance with Table 314.16(B). ▶Figure 314–12

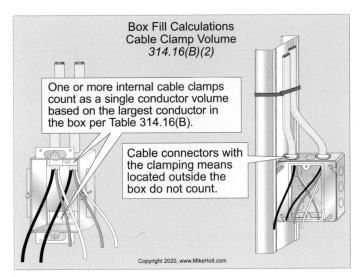

▶Figure 314–12

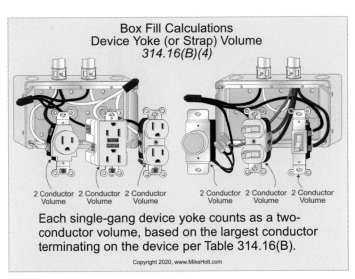

▶Figure 314–14

(3) Support Fitting Volume. Each luminaire stud or luminaire hickey counts as a single conductor volume based on the largest conductor that enters the box in accordance with Table 314.16(B). ▶Figure 314–13

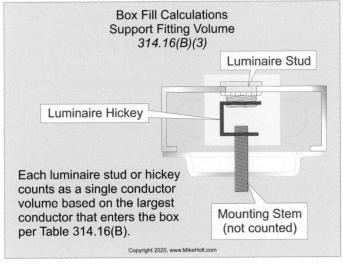

▶Figure 314–13

(4) Device Yoke Volume. Each single-gang device yoke counts as two conductor volumes based on the largest conductor that terminates on the device in accordance with Table 314.16(B). ▶Figure 314–14

Author's Comment:

▶ A device yoke, also called a strap, is the mounting structure for a receptacle, switch, switch with pilot light, switch-receptacle, and so forth. ▶Figure 314–15

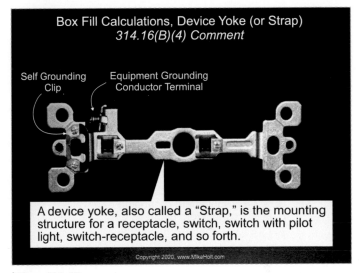

▶Figure 314–15

Each device yoke wider than 2 in. counts as a two-conductor volume for each gang required for mounting, based on the largest conductor that terminates on the device in accordance with Table 314.16(B). ▶Figure 314–16

(5) Equipment Grounding Conductor Volume. Up to four equipment grounding conductors count as a single conductor volume based on the largest equipment grounding conductor that enters the box in accordance with Table 314.16(B).

A ¼ volume allowance applies for each additional equipment grounding conductor or equipment bonding jumper that enters the box, based on the largest equipment grounding or bonding conductor. ▶Figure 314–17

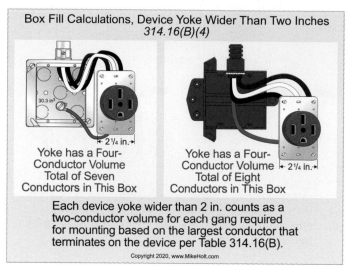

▶Figure 314–16

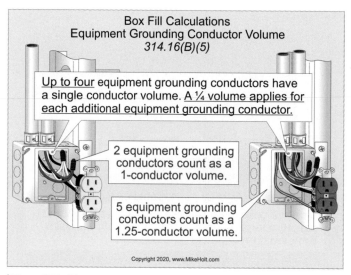

▶Figure 314–17

Equipment grounding conductors for isolated ground receptacles count as an additional single conductor volume in accordance with Table 314.16(B).

▶ **Number of Conductors Example**

Question: What is the total number of conductors used for a box fill calculations in a 2⅛ in. deep box with two internal cable clamps, one single-pole switch, one duplex receptacle, one 14/3 with ground NM cable, and one 14/2 with ground NM cable? ▶Figure 314–18

(a) 5 conductors   (b) 7 conductors
(c) 9 conductors   (d) 11 conductors

Answer: (d) 11 conductors

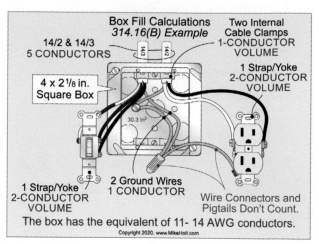

▶Figure 314–18

Solution:

Switch and Conductors	5 – 14 AWG conductors †
Receptacles and Conductors	4 – 14 AWG conductors ††
Equipment Grounding Conductor	1 – 14 AWG conductors
Cable Clamps	+ 1 – 14 AWG conductors
Total	11 – 14 AWG conductors

†Two conductors for the device and three conductors terminating

††Two conductors for the device and two conductors terminating

Each 14 AWG conductor counts as 2 cu in. [Table 314.16(B)]. 11 conductors × 2 cu in. = 22 cu in.

If the cubic-inch volume of the plaster ring is not stamped on it, or given in the problem, we cannot include it in the box volume. Without knowing the plaster ring volume, a 4 in. square by 2⅛ in. deep box is the minimum required for this example.

▶ **Box Fill Example**

Question: How many 14 AWG conductors can be pulled through a 4 in. square × 2⅛ in. deep box with a plaster ring with a marking of 3.60 cu in.? The box contains two receptacles, five 12 AWG conductors, and two 12 AWG equipment grounding conductors. ▶Figure 314–19

(a) 4 conductors   (b) 5 conductors
(c) 6 conductors   (d) 7 conductors

Answer: (b) 5 conductors

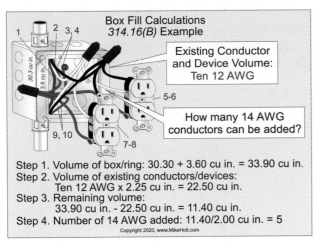

Box Fill Calculations
314.16(B) Example

Existing Conductor and Device Volume: Ten 12 AWG

How many 14 AWG conductors can be added?

Step 1. Volume of box/ring: 30.30 + 3.60 cu in. = 33.90 cu in.
Step 2. Volume of existing conductors/devices:
Ten 12 AWG x 2.25 cu in. = 22.50 cu in.
Step 3. Remaining volume:
33.90 cu in. - 22.50 cu in. = 11.40 cu in.
Step 4. Number of 14 AWG added: 11.40/2.00 cu in. = 5

Copyright 2020, www.MikeHolt.com

▶Figure 314–19

Solution:

Step 1: Determine the volume of the box assembly [314.16(A)].

Box Assembly Volume = Box 30.30 cu in. + 3.60 cu in.
plaster ring
Box Assembly Volume = 33.90 cu in.

Step 2: Determine the volume of the devices and conductors in the box:

Two—receptacles	4–12 AWG
Five–12 AWG conductors	5–12 AWG
Two–12 AWG equipment grounding conductors	1–12 AWG

Total Device Volume and Conductors = Ten–12 AWG × 2.25 cu in.
Total Device Volume and Conductors = 22.50 cu in.

Step 3: Determine the remaining volume permitted for the 14 AWG conductors (volume of the box minus the volume of the conductors).

Remaining Volume = 33.90 cu in. – 22.50 cu in.
Remaining Volume = 11.40 cu in.

Step 4: Determine the number of 14 AWG conductors (at 2.00 cu in. each) permitted in the remaining volume of 11.40 cu in.:

14 AWG = 2.00 cu in. each [Table 314.16(B)]
11.40 cu in./2.00 cu in. = 5 conductors
Five 14 AWG conductors can be pulled through.

Author's Comment:

▶ This makes one wonder how the physical volume of a conductor could be different based on its function. It obviously takes the same amount of physical space regardless.

314.17 Conductors That Enter Boxes or Conduit Bodies

The language in subsection (A) was revised to require openings through which conductors enter to be closed in a manner "identified for the application" in place of the 2017 *Code* rule that required the closing device to be approved. In addition, subsections (B) and (C) were merged and reorganized.

Analysis

CLARIFIED

314.17(A) Openings to Be Closed. The term "Approved" permits the inspection authority to "approve" anything, and to not require the use of an identified product. Note that while the term "identified" stops short of requiring a listed product, the Informational Note that follows the Article 100 definition of "Identified" indicates that listing is one way of identifying a product that is recognized as suitable for the application.

The CMP comment said:

"The word 'approved' means that the manner is acceptable to the Authority Having Jurisdiction. The use of the word 'identified' will increase field consistency of enforcement because the methods used will need to be shown to be 'recognizable as suitable for the specific use'."

The problem with this is that there is nothing in the *NEC* that specifies just who has the authority to "recognize" something as suitable for the specific use. While a listing is one method that identifies a product as suitable for the use, the definition of "identified" stops short of requiring a listed product.

REORGANIZED

314.17(B) Boxes and Conduit Bodies. Subsections 314.17(B) and (C) were combined and reorganized from long paragraphs into second level subsections. The merging of (B) for metal boxes and (C) for nonmetallic boxes results in the deletion of the word "metal" from the title. Parent text was also added specifying that the installation of conductors in boxes and conduit bodies must comply with 314.17(B)(1) through (B)(4). These new subsections replace the long paragraphs in the previous *Code*, resulting in greater usability for the reader.

314.17 Conductors That Enter Boxes or Conduit Bodies

(A) Openings to be Closed. Unused openings through which cables or raceways enter a box must be closed in an approved manner that is identified for the application. ▸Figure 314–20

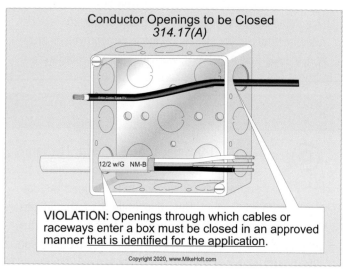

Conductor Openings to be Closed
314.17(A)

12/2 w/G   NM-B

VIOLATION: Openings through which cables or raceways enter a box must be closed in an approved manner that is identified for the application.

Copyright 2020, www.MikeHolt.com

▸Figure 314–20

▸ Unused cable or raceway openings must be effectively closed by fittings that provide protection substantially equivalent to the wall of the equipment [110.12(A)].

(B) Boxes. The installation of the conductors in Boxes must comply with the following:

(2) Conductors Entering Through Cable Clamps. Where cable assemblies (Type NM or UF), are used, the sheath must extend not less than ¼ in. inside the box and beyond any cable clamp. Except as provided in 300.15(C), the wiring method must be secured to the box. ▸Figure 314–21

▸ Two Type NM cables can terminate in a single cable clamp if the clamp is listed for this purpose [UL White Book].

Ex: Type NM cable terminating to a single gang nonmetallic box not larger than 2¼ in. × 4 in. is not required to be secured to the box if the cable is securely fastened within 8 in. of the box and the sheath extends at least ¼ in. inside the box. ▸Figure 314–22

(3) Conductors Entering Through Raceways. Where the raceway is complete between boxes and encloses individual conductors or

nonmetallic cable assemblies or both, the conductors or cable assemblies are not required to be additionally secured. Where raceways enclose cable assemblies as provided in 300.15(C), the cable assembly is not required to be additionally secured within the box or conduit body.

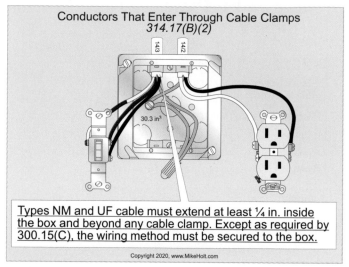

Conductors That Enter Through Cable Clamps
314.17(B)(2)

14/3   14/2

30.3 in³

Types NM and UF cable must extend at least ¼ in. inside the box and beyond any cable clamp. Except as required by 300.15(C), the wiring method must be secured to the box.

Copyright 2020, www.MikeHolt.com

▸Figure 314–21

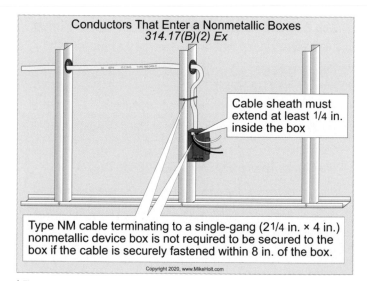

Conductors That Enter a Nonmetallic Boxes
314.17(B)(2) Ex

Cable sheath must extend at least 1/4 in. inside the box

Type NM cable terminating to a single-gang (2 1/4 in. × 4 in.) nonmetallic device box is not required to be secured to the box if the cable is securely fastened within 8 in. of the box.

Copyright 2020, www.MikeHolt.com

▸Figure 314–22

314.27 Outlet Box Requirements

The revised rule in subsection (C) requires ceiling outlet boxes installed in habitable rooms of dwelling units in a location where a ceiling fan may be installed to be ceiling fan rated. An option not to install the fan rated box was added where there is access to structural framing that will support a ceiling fan in the future.

314.27(C) Boxes at Ceiling Suspended (Paddle) Fan Outlets. The general part of the rule requires that a box listed for the support of ceiling fans be used where the box is the sole support of the fan. The 2017 *Code* introduced the requirement that where a spare separately switched conductor was installed to a ceiling box, the box must be listed for the support of a ceiling fan. This is now expanded to require all ceiling-mounted boxes in habitable rooms of dwelling units where a fan could be installed to be listed for the sole support of a fan. This change recognizes that almost all ceiling fans are now available with a remote control and that a fan might be installed at any ceiling outlet that is far enough from a wall to permit its installation.

314.27 Outlet Box Requirements

(C) Ceiling Paddle Fan Box. Outlet boxes for a ceiling paddle fan must be listed and marked as suitable for the purpose and are not permitted to support a fan weighing more than 70 lb. Outlet boxes for a ceiling paddle fan that weighs more than 35 lb must include the maximum weight to be supported in the required marking. ▸Figure 314–23

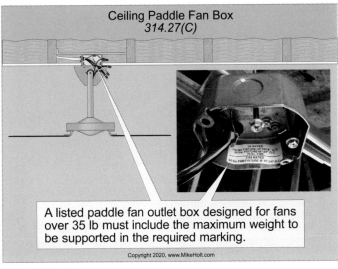

Ceiling Paddle Fan Box
314.27(C)

A listed paddle fan outlet box designed for fans over 35 lb must include the maximum weight to be supported in the required marking.

Copyright 2020, www.MikeHolt.com

▸Figure 314–23

Ceiling-mounted outlet boxes in a habitable room of a dwelling unit where a ceiling-suspended (paddle) fan could be installed must comply with one of the following: ▸Figure 314–24

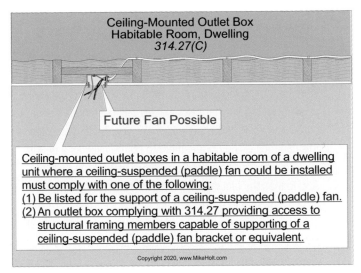

Ceiling-Mounted Outlet Box
Habitable Room, Dwelling
314.27(C)

Future Fan Possible

Ceiling-mounted outlet boxes in a habitable room of a dwelling unit where a ceiling-suspended (paddle) fan could be installed must comply with one of the following:
(1) Be listed for the support of a ceiling-suspended (paddle) fan.
(2) An outlet box complying with 314.27 providing access to structural framing members capable of supporting of a ceiling-suspended (paddle) fan bracket or equivalent.

Copyright 2020, www.MikeHolt.com

▸Figure 314–24

(1) Be listed for the support of a ceiling-suspended (paddle) fan.

(2) An outlet box complying with 314.27 providing access to structural framing members capable of supporting a ceiling-suspended (paddle) fan bracket or equivalent.

(D) Utilization Equipment. Boxes used for the support of utilization equipment must be designed to support equipment that weighs a minimum of 50 lb [314.27(A)].

Ex: Utilization equipment weighing 6 lb or less can be supported by any box or plaster ring secured to a box, provided the equipment is secured with no fewer than two No. 6 or larger screws. ▸Figure 314–25

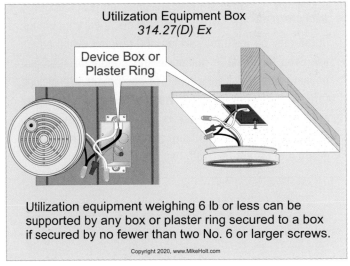

Utilization Equipment Box
314.27(D) Ex

Device Box or
Plaster Ring

Utilization equipment weighing 6 lb or less can be supported by any box or plaster ring secured to a box if secured by no fewer than two No. 6 or larger screws.

Copyright 2020, www.MikeHolt.com

▸Figure 314–25

Author's Comment:

▸ It's understood that this rule recognizes, from a safety perspective, that many ceiling fans are installed by "do it yourselfers" who may not replace a non-fan rated box with the proper box when they install a fan. Nonetheless, it has created some contentious debate among field professionals. Some feel that this contradicts the *Code's* intent to not be used as a design specification or as an instruction manual for untrained persons. Add to that, the fact that this is a prime example of why electrical work should be performed by licensed professionals. There's also the argument that the appropriate box is used for whatever is being installed at the time and that providing accommodations for future installations, deprives contractors of what may have been additional or future work for them.

314.29 Boxes, Conduit Bodies, and Handhole Enclosures to Be Accessible

The revision to this section expanded the original text into two new subsections without technical change.

Analysis

REORGANIZED Boxes, conduit bodies, and handhole enclosures are used for many purposes and they are certain to contain electrical conductors. Some may be used for splicing and tapping, while others are used to assist in pulling longer conductor runs just passing through. These types of equipment will include removable covers that must remain accessible for future access and can't be "buried" or concealed for any reason. The rules in this section were revised from a single paragraph into parent text with two subsections.

314.29 Wiring to be Accessible

(A) Above Ground. Boxes and conduit bodies must be installed so the wiring contained within is accessible without removing any part of the building or structure. ▸Figure 314–26

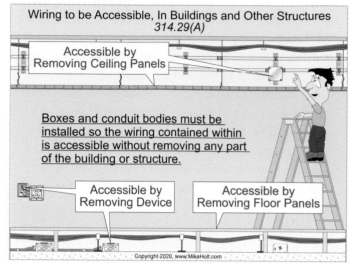

▸Figure 314–26

(B) Underground. Underground boxes and handhole enclosures must be installed so the wiring contained within is accessible without removing any part of the excavating, sidewalks, paving, earth, or other substance that is used to establish the finished grade. ▸Figure 314–27

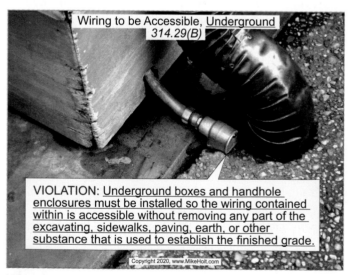

▸Figure 314–27

ARTICLE 320

ARMORED CABLE (TYPE AC)

Introduction to Article 320—Armored Cable (Type AC)

Armored cable (Type AC) is an assembly of insulated conductors, 14 AWG through 1 AWG, individually wrapped within wax paper (jute) and contained within a flexible spiral metal sheath. To the casual observer the outside appearance of armored cable is similar to flexible metal conduit as well as metal-clad cable (Type MC). Type AC cable has been referred to as "BX®" cable over the years.

320.23 In Accessible Attics or Roof Spaces

The intention of the change in subsection (A) was to clarify that this rule does not apply where "pull down" stairs are used, and the cable might be installed exposed.

Analysis

CLARIFIED 320.23(A) Cables Run Across Top of Floor Joists. This rule requires AC cable to be protected where installed on top of joists within 7 ft of an area that is accessible by "permanently installed" stairs. If there are no permanent stairs, the protection is only required within 6 ft of the scuttle hole or attic access.

AC Cable, Cables Run Across the Top of Joists or Rafters
320.23(A)

Where run across the top of floor joists, or across the face of rafters or studding within 7 ft of the floor or floor joists, Type AC cable must be protected by guard strips that are at least as high as the cable.

Guard Strip

If this space is not accessible by permanently installed stairs or ladders, protection is required only within 6 ft of the nearest edge of the scuttle hole or attic entrance.

Copyright 2020, www.MikeHolt.com

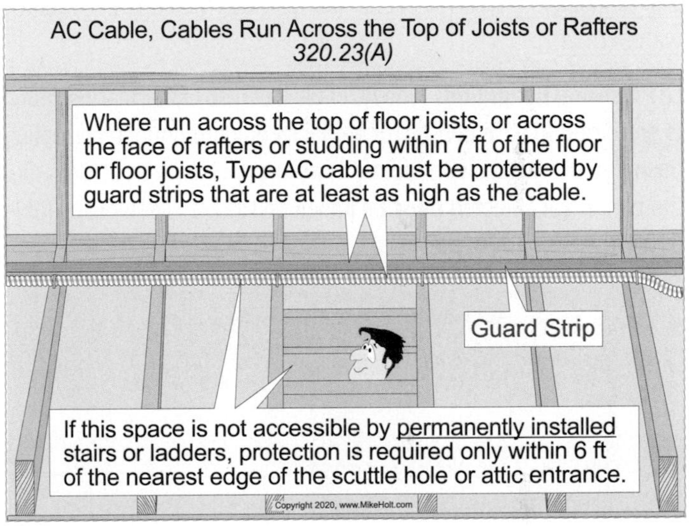

▶Figure 320–1

320.80 Conductor Ampacity

Language was added to subsection (A) that requires ampacity adjustment to be made in accordance with 310.15(C)(1) where more than two Type AC cables containing two or more current-carrying conductors in each cable are installed in contact with thermal installation, caulk, or sealing foam without maintaining spacing between conductors.

320.23 In Accessible Attics or Roof Spaces

(A) Cables Run Across the Top of Floor Joists. Where run across the top of floor joists, or across the face of rafters or studding within 7 ft of the floor or floor joists, Type AC cable must be protected by guard strips that are at least as high as the cable. If this space is not accessible by <u>permanently installed</u> stairs or ladders, protection is required only within 6 ft of the nearest edge of the scuttle hole or attic entrance. ▶Figure 320–1

Author's Comment:

▸ By reference and in their respective articles, this rule also applies to Type(s) MC and NM cables.

320.80 Conductor Ampacity

The ampacity of Type AC cable must be determined in accordance with 310.14.

(A) Thermal Insulation. Type AC cable installed in thermal insulation is permitted to have conductor ampacity adjustment and correction based on 90°C rated conductors in accordance with 310.15(B), but the conductor selected must be based on the 60°C column of Table 310.16. ▸Figure 320–2

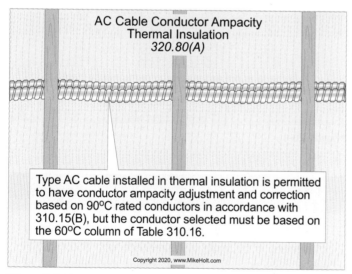

Type AC cable installed in thermal insulation is permitted to have conductor ampacity adjustment and correction based on 90°C rated conductors in accordance with 310.15(B), but the conductor selected must be based on the 60°C column of Table 310.16.

▸Figure 320–2

Where more than two Type AC cables containing two or more current-carrying conductors in each cable are installed in contact with thermal insulation, caulk, or sealing foam without maintaining spacing between cables, the ampacity of each conductor must be adjusted in accordance with Table 310.15(C)(1). ▸Figure 320–3

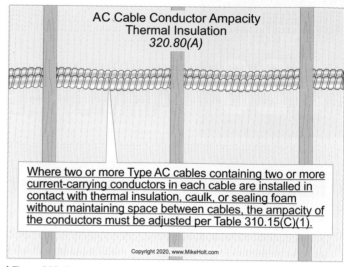

AC Cable Conductor Ampacity
Thermal Insulation
320.80(A)

Where two or more Type AC cables containing two or more current-carrying conductors in each cable are installed in contact with thermal insulation, caulk, or sealing foam without maintaining space between cables, the ampacity of the conductors must be adjusted per Table 310.15(C)(1).

▸Figure 320–3

▸ **Example**

Question: Is Type AC cable containing four 12 AWG current-carrying conductors suitable to be protected by a 20A circuit breaker?

(a) Yes   (b) No

Answer: (a) Yes

Solution:

Step 1: Determine the ampacity of the circuit conductors in accordance with 310.16 and Table 310.15(C)(1).

12 AWG is rated 30A at 90°C [Table 310.16]

Conductor Adjustment = 80% [Table 310.15(C)(1)]

Conductor Adjusted Ampacity = 30A × 80%
Conductor Adjusted Ampacity = 24A

Step 2: Verify that the adjusted conductor ampacity can be protected by the 20A circuit breaker. In this case, 12 AWG is rated 24A after adjustment at 90°C, and 20A at 60°C [240.4(D)].

Author's Comment:

▸ Again, as with multiconductor cable spacing, the *Code* language gives no guidance about how much spacing between the cables is needed to avoid the application of the ampacity adjustments.

METAL-CLAD CABLE (TYPE MC)

Introduction to Article 330—Metal-Clad Cable (Type MC)

Metal-clad cable (Type MC) is probably the most typically used metal protected wiring method. Type MC cable surrounds insulated conductors in a metal sheath of either corrugated or smooth copper or aluminum tubing, or in spiral interlocked steel or aluminum. The physical characteristics of Type MC cable make it a versatile wiring method that can be used in almost any location, and for almost any application. The most commonly used Type MC cable is the interlocking kind, which looks similar to armored cable or flexible metal conduit. Traditional interlocked Type MC cable is not permitted to serve as an equipment grounding conductor; therefore, this cable must contain an equipment grounding conductor in accordance with 250.118(1). Another type of Type MC cable is called interlocked Type MC^{AP®} cable that contains a bare aluminum grounding/bonding conductor running just below the metal armor, which allows the sheath to serve as an equipment grounding conductor [250.118(10)(b)].

330.80 Conductor Ampacities

The language that was added for Armored Cable was also added here to subsection (C) and requires ampacity adjustment where Type MC cable is used in thermal insulation to be in accordance with 310.15(C)(1).

Analysis

330.80(C) Thermal Insulation. Where more than two MC cables containing two or more current-carrying conductors in each cable are installed in contact with thermal installation, caulk, or sealing foam without maintaining spacing between conductors, there is a potential for the cables to heat beyond their temperature rating. This rule requires spacing to be maintained between the cables or that ampacity adjustments be applied.

NEW

(C) Thermal Insulation. Where multiple Type MC cables are installed in contact with thermal insulation or pass through the same wood framing opening that is to be sealed with thermal insulation, caulking, or sealing foam, the ampacity of each conductor must be adjusted in accordance with Table 310.15(C)(1). ▶Figure 330–1

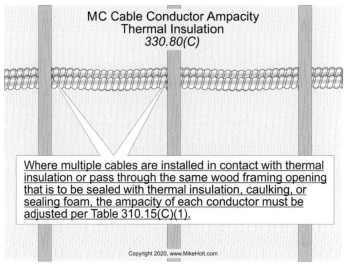

MC Cable Conductor Ampacity
Thermal Insulation
330.80(C)

Where multiple cables are installed in contact with thermal insulation or pass through the same wood framing opening that is to be sealed with thermal insulation, caulking, or sealing foam, the ampacity of each conductor must be adjusted per Table 310.15(C)(1).

Copyright 2020, www.MikeHolt.com

▶Figure 330–1

Author's Comment:

▶ As with Type AC cable spacing, the *Code* language gives no guidance about how much spacing between the cables is needed to avoid the application of the ampacity adjustments.

NONMETALLIC-SHEATHED CABLE (TYPE NM)

Introduction to Article 334—Nonmetallic-Sheathed Cable (Type NM)

Nonmetallic-sheathed cable (Type NM) provides very limited physical protection for the conductors, so the installation restrictions are stringent. Its low cost and relative ease of installation make it a common wiring method for residential and commercial branch circuits.

334.30 Securing and Supporting

The method of measurement from, and length of excess cable between, the last means of cable support and the enclosure is now specified for Type NM cable.

Analysis

CLARIFIED A revision to the parent text of this section specifies the measuring method for the distances between an enclosure entry and the first support. This change is triggered by the fact that, in some areas, leaving a "service loop" at the enclosure entry may be required. It is still necessary to have the securement within 12 in. of the enclosure entry, as measured in a straight line from the entry to the support, but no more than 18 in. as measured along the cable sheath.

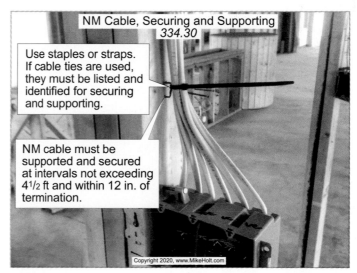

NM Cable, Securing and Supporting
334.30

Use staples or straps. If cable ties are used, they must be listed and identified for securing and supporting.

NM cable must be supported and secured at intervals not exceeding 4½ ft and within 12 in. of termination.

Copyright 2020, www.MikeHolt.com

▶Figure 334–1

Author's Comment:

▶ Many times, there is a tendency to leave a length of sheathed NM cable in a box or enclosure, (such as a panelboard), just to have "extra" cable. While this practice is not prohibited, the length of such sheathed cable cannot exceed 18 in. as measured in a straight line.

Two-wire (flat) Type NM cable is not permitted to be stapled on edge.
▶Figure 334–2

334.30 Securing and Supporting

Type NM cable must be supported and secured by staples or straps; cable ties listed and identified for securing and supporting; hangers, or similar fittings, at intervals not exceeding 4½ ft and within 12 in. of termination. The cable length between the cable entry into cabinets and enclosures, and the closest cable support, may not exceed 18 in. ▶Figure 334–1

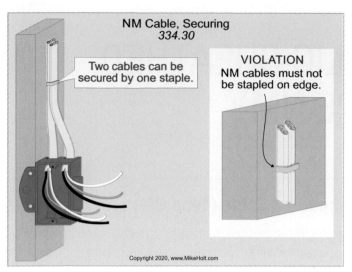

▶Figure 334–2

ARTICLE 336

POWER AND CONTROL TRAY CABLE (TYPE TC)

Introduction to Article 336—Power and Control Tray Cable (Type TC)

Power and control tray cable (Type TC) is flexible, inexpensive, and easily installed. It provides very limited physical protection for the conductors, so the installation restrictions are stringent. Its low cost and relative ease of installation make it a common wiring method for industrial applications.

336.2 Definition

The definition of Type TC cable was revised to specify that it contains an equipment grounding conductor.

Analysis

CLARIFIED **Power and Control Cable, Type TC.** The previous definition just used the undefined term, "grounding conductor" and the addition of the word "equipment" serves to add clarity.

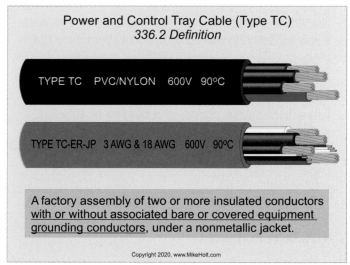

Power and Control Tray Cable (Type TC)
336.2 Definition

TYPE TC   PVC/NYLON   600V   90°C

TYPE TC-ER-JP   3 AWG & 18 AWG   600V   90°C

A factory assembly of two or more insulated conductors with or without associated bare or covered equipment grounding conductors, under a nonmetallic jacket.

Copyright 2020, www.MikeHolt.com

▶Figure 336–1

336.2 Definition

Power and Control Tray Cable (Type TC). A factory assembly of two or more insulated conductors with or without associated bare or covered equipment grounding conductors, under a nonmetallic jacket. ▶Figure 336–1

336.10 Uses Permitted

Because Type TC cable provides limited physical protection for the conductors inside the cable assembly, it was assumed that its use was restricted just because "TC" was in its letter designation. The new language has somewhat alleviated this self-imposed restriction. The rule regarding the use of TC-ER-JP was clarified to permit its use for branch circuits and feeders as well as exterior wiring.

Analysis

EXPANDED

336.10(9). This subsection permits the use of TC-ER-JP cable, containing both power and control conductors in, one- and two-family dwelling units where identified as suitable to be pulled through structural members. The "identified for pulling through structural members" language was deleted and the "-JP" was added to the cable type. The listing standard requires the "-JP" marking to be on all TC-ER cable that is listed as suitable for pulling through structural members. This provides clarity for the installer as well as the inspector as to what cable is acceptable for this installation. The previous Informational Note 1 that addressed the "–JP" was deleted since this information needed to be in the enforceable *Code* text.

The addition of the words "branch circuits and feeders" is intended to prohibit its use for service conductors, however a new list item (20) was added to 230.43 permitting TC-ER cable to be used as service-entrance conductors. Since Type TC cable is a wet location wiring method, it can be used outdoors. New language was added to specify that, where used on the exterior of a building or structure, it be installed in accordance with the requirements of Part II of Article 340, Underground Feeder and Branch-Circuit Cable: Type UF.

336.10 Uses Permitted

Type TC cable is permitted to be used:

(1) For power, lighting, control, and signaling circuits.

(2) In cable trays including those with mechanically discontinuous segments up to 1 ft.

(3) In raceways.

(4) In outdoor locations supported by a messenger wire.

(5) For Class 1 circuits in accordance with Article 725.

(7) Between a cable tray and equipment if it complies with 336(10)(7).

(8) In wet locations where the cable is resistant to moisture and corrosive agents.

(9) In one- and two-family dwellings, Type TC-ER-JP cable is permitted for branch circuit and feeders where installed in accordance with Part II of Article 334 for interior wiring and Part II of Article 340 for exterior wiring. ▶Figure 336–2

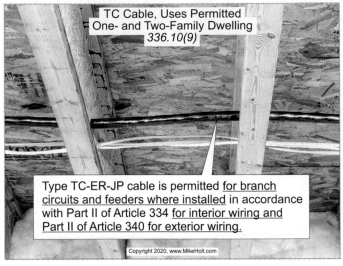

TC Cable, Uses Permitted
One- and Two-Family Dwelling
336.10(9)

Type TC-ER-JP cable is permitted for branch circuits and feeders where installed in accordance with Part II of Article 334 for interior wiring and Part II of Article 340 for exterior wiring.

Copyright 2020, www.MikeHolt.com

▶Figure 336–2

Author's Comment:

▸ The "ER" marking on Type TC-ER cable identifies it as suitable for exposed run use in accordance with UL 1277 and the suffix "-JP" identifies it as being suitable for pulling through framing members.

Ex: Where Type TC cable is used to connect a generator and its associated equipment, the cable ampacity limitations of 334.80 and 340.80 do not apply.

Author's Comment:

▸ You may find it interesting that only TC-ER with both power and control conductors is permitted to be used for feeders and branch circuits. The construction and safety of the cable is the same with or without the control conductors. There was some concern about the availability of the proper fittings but that defies logic as TC-ER without control conductors have been used in other occupancies for some time

(10) Direct buried where identified for direct burial.

SERVICE-ENTRANCE CABLE (TYPES SE AND USE)

Introduction to Article 338—Service-Entrance Cable (Types SE and USE)

Service-entrance (SE) and underground service-entrance (USE) cables, can be a single conductor or a multiconductor assembly within an overall nonmetallic outer jacket or covering. This cable is used primarily for services but is permitted for feeders and branch circuits. When used as a service conductor(s) or service entrance conductor(s), Type SE cable assemblies will contain insulated phase conductors and a bare neutral conductor. For feeders or branch circuits, you must use Type SE cable that contains insulated phase and neutral conductors, with an uninsulated equipment grounding conductor.

338.2 Definitions

The definition of "Service-Entrance Cable" was revised to make it clear that a service-entrance cable has an overall covering. A new definition, "Service-Entrance Conductor Assembly" was also added.

Analysis

CLARIFIED **Service-Entrance Cable.** This change was made in conjunction with the new definition of a service-entrance conductor assembly. A cable has an overall outer covering, and an assembly does not.

NEW **Service-Entrance Conductor Assembly.** A new definition that applies to multiple single insulated conductors twisted together without an overall covering, other than an optional binder intended to keep the conductors together. It appears this is similar to triplex, but without a bare neutral/messenger conductor.

338.2 Definitions

Service-Entrance Cable (Types SE and USE). Service-entrance cable is a single or multiconductor cable <u>with an overall covering</u>. ▶Figure 338–1

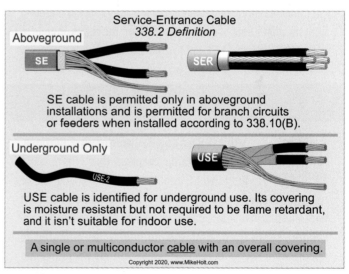

Service-Entrance Cable
338.2 Definition

Aboveground

SE cable is permitted only in aboveground installations and is permitted for branch circuits or feeders when installed according to 338.10(B).

Underground Only

USE cable is identified for underground use. Its covering is moisture resistant but not required to be flame retardant, and it isn't suitable for indoor use.

A single or multiconductor <u>cable</u> with an overall covering.

Copyright 2020, www.MikeHolt.com

▶Figure 338–1

Service-Entrance Conductor Assembly. <u>Multiple single-insulated conductors twisted together without an overall covering, other than an optional binder intended only to keep the conductors together.</u>

▸ "Triplex" and "Quadruplex" that have an outer wire wrapped around them are examples of this type of SE conductor assembly.

Type SE. Type SE cables have a flame-retardant, moisture-resistant covering and are permitted only in aboveground installations. These cables are permitted for branch circuits or feeders when installed in accordance with 338.10(B).

Type USE. USE cable is identified as a wiring method permitted for underground use; its covering is moisture resistant, but not flame retardant.

▸ Type USE cable is not permitted to be installed indoors [338.10(B)].

338.10 Uses Permitted

The installation methods for interior installations in subsection (B) were reorganized into a new list format with a new "in contact with thermal insulation" ampacity rule added to both new list items to assist in explaining the requirements of using Types SE and USE cable as feeders or branch circuits.

Analysis

REORGANIZED

338.10(B)(4)(a)(2) Interior Installations. This subsection requires that where more than two SE cables (each containing two or more current-carrying conductors) are installed in contact with thermal insulation, caulk, or sealing foam without maintaining separation, that the ampacity be adjusted in accordance with 310.15(C)(1). This expands the items that trigger the ampacity adjustment, but also permits single SE cables, not in contact with other SE cables, to be installed in contact with these insulating materials without triggering an ampacity adjustment. This matches the requirement in 334.80 for Type NM cable but had to be repeated here because 338.10(B)(4)(a)(1) tells us that the requirements of 334.80 do not apply to SE cable used as interior branch circuits and feeders.

REORGANIZED

338.10(B)(4)(a)(3) Interior Installations. Where a single SE cable with phase conductors sized 10 AWG and smaller is installed in contact with thermal insulation, the ampacity must be based on the 60°C column. The actual ampacity rating of the conductor is permitted to be used for the purposes of ampacity adjustment and/or correction, as long as the final ampacity does not exceed the 60°C ampacity.

338.10 Uses Permitted

(B) Branch Circuits or Feeders

(2) Insulated Conductor. Type SE service-entrance cable is permitted for branch circuits and feeders where the neutral conductor is insulated, and the uninsulated conductor is only used for equipment grounding. ▸Figure 338–2

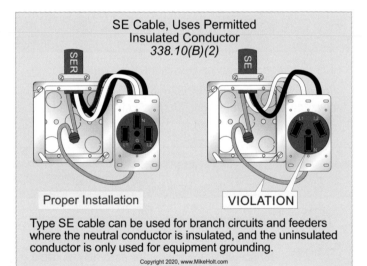

SE Cable, Uses Permitted
Insulated Conductor
338.10(B)(2)

Proper Installation — VIOLATION

Type SE cable can be used for branch circuits and feeders where the neutral conductor is insulated, and the uninsulated conductor is only used for equipment grounding.

Copyright 2020, www.MikeHolt.com

▸Figure 338–2

(3) Temperature Limitations. SE cable is not permitted to be subjected to conductor temperatures exceeding its insulation rating.

(4) Installation Methods for Branch Circuits and Feeders. SE cable used for branch circuits or feeders must comply with (a) and (b).

(a) Interior Installations.

(1) SE cable used for interior branch-circuit or feeder wiring must be installed in accordance with the same requirements as Type NM cable in Part II of Article 334, excluding 334.80. ▸Figure 338–3

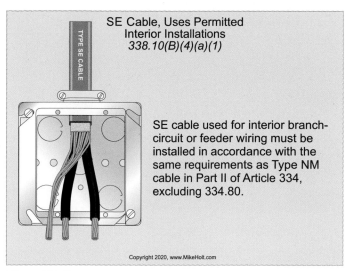

SE Cable, Uses Permitted
Interior Installations
338.10(B)(4)(a)(1)

TYPE SE CABLE

SE cable used for interior branch-circuit or feeder wiring must be installed in accordance with the same requirements as Type NM cable in Part II of Article 334, excluding 334.80.

Copyright 2020, www.MikeHolt.com

▶Figure 338–3

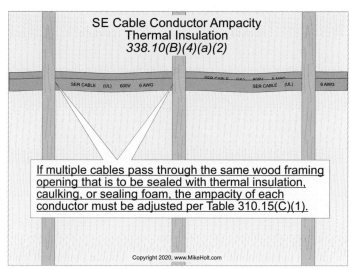

SE Cable Conductor Ampacity
Thermal Insulation
338.10(B)(4)(a)(2)

SER CABLE (UL) 600V 6 AWG SER CABLE (UL) 600V 6 AWG SER CABLE (UL) 6 AWG

If multiple cables pass through the same wood framing opening that is to be sealed with thermal insulation, caulking, or sealing foam, the ampacity of each conductor must be adjusted per Table 310.15(C)(1).

Copyright 2020, www.MikeHolt.com

▶Figure 338–4

(2) If multiple cables pass through the same wood framing opening that is to be sealed with thermal insulation, caulking, or sealing foam, the ampacity of each conductor must be adjusted in accordance with Table 310.15(C)(1). ▶Figure 338–4

(3) The ampacity of conductors 10 AWG and smaller, where installed in contact with thermal insulation, must be sized in accordance with 60°C (140°F) conductor temperature rating. For conductor ampacity correction and/or adjustment, the conductor temperature rating ampacity is to be used.

(b) Exterior Installations.

(1) The cable must be installed in accordance with Part I of Article 225 and supported in accordance with 334.30. Where it is run underground, the cable must comply with Part II of Article 340.

UNDERGROUND FEEDER AND BRANCH-CIRCUIT CABLE (TYPE UF)

Introduction to Article 340—Underground Feeder and Branch-Circuit Cable (Type UF)

UF cable (Type UF) is a moisture-, fungus-, and corrosion-resistant cable suitable for direct burial in the earth. It comes in sizes 14 AWG through 4/0 AWG [340.104]. The covering of multiconductor Type UF cable is molded plastic that encases the insulated conductors. Because the covering of Type UF cable encapsulates the insulated conductors, it is difficult to strip off the outer jacket to gain access to them, but this covering provides excellent corrosion protection. Be careful not to damage the conductor insulation or cut yourself when you remove the outer cover.

340.10 Uses Permitted

There were revisions to the list items regarding the permitted uses of Type UF cable.

Analysis

The following list items were clarified as follows:

CLARIFIED
340.10(1). The rules in 300.5 apply to all underground installations and there is no reason to reference that section here.

CLARIFIED
340.10(2). The previously misplaced words "grounded conductor" that followed "feeder" were removed from this section. The language made no sense and it was confusing to the user.

CLARIFIED
340.10(3). The words "under the recognized wiring methods of this *Code*" were deleted as confusing and misleading. Those words could lead a user to think that Type UF cable is required to be installed in another wiring method. While that is permitted, it is not required. Removing this language clarifies that it can be installed in wet, dry, or corrosive locations unless prohibited by 340.12.

CLARIFIED
340.10(5). This list item permitting Type UF cable to be used for solar photovoltaic systems was deleted as unnecessary. Its permitted by 690.31(A) and 690.31(D) for these applications. The specific permission in this article is not required because 90.3 permits Article 690 to modify 340. The former list items (6) and (7) were renumbered as (5) and (6) without change.

340.10 Uses Permitted

Type UF cable is permitted:

(1) Underground in accordance with 300.5.

(2) As a single conductor in a trench or raceway with circuit conductors.

(3) For wiring in wet, dry, or corrosive locations.

(4) Where installed as nonmetallic-sheathed cable, the installation must comply with Parts II and III of Article 334.

340.12 Uses Not permitted

A new Informational Note following 340.12(9) advises that sunlight-resistant marking on the cable jacket does not apply to the individual conductors contained within the jacket unless they are identified as such.

Analysis

340.12(9). This prohibits Type UF cable to be exposed to the direct rays of the sun unless the cable is identified as sunlight resistant. The new Informational Note informs us that the sunlight-resistant marking on the jacket of the cable does not apply to the conductors within that cable. The outer jacket of the cable may be so identified, but unless the individual internal conductors are identified as sunlight-resistant they are not permitted to be exposed to the sun.

NEW

340.12 Uses Not Permitted

Type UF cable is not permitted to be used:

(1) As services [230.43].

(2) In commercial garages [511.3].

(3) In theaters [520.5].

(4) In motion picture studios [530.11].

(5) In storage battery rooms [Article 480].

(6) In hoistways [Article 620].

(7) In hazardous locations, except as specifically permitted by other articles in the *Code*.

(8) Embedded in concrete.

(9) Exposed to direct sunlight unless identified.

Note: The sunlight-resistant marking on the outer jacket, does not apply to the individual conductors.

(10) Where subject to physical damage. ▶Figure 340–1

(11) As overhead messenger-supported wiring.

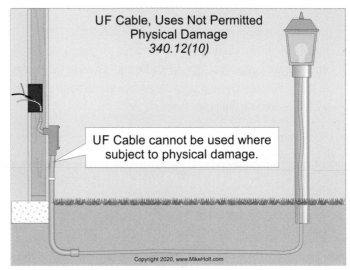

UF Cable, Uses Not Permitted
Physical Damage
340.12(10)

UF Cable cannot be used where subject to physical damage.

Copyright 2020, www.MikeHolt.com

▶Figure 340–1

Author's Comment:

▶ UF cable is not permitted in ducts or plenum spaces [300.22], or in patient care spaces of health care facilities [517.13].

ARTICLE 342

INTERMEDIATE METAL CONDUIT (TYPE IMC)

Introduction to Article 342—Intermediate Metal Conduit (Type IMC)

Intermediate metal conduit is a circular metal raceway with the same outside diameter as rigid metal conduit. The wall thickness of IMC is less than that of rigid metal conduit, so it has a larger interior cross-sectional area for holding conductors. IMC is lighter and less expensive than rigid metal conduit and is approved by the *NEC* for use in the same applications as Type RMC (Rigid Metal Conduit, Article 344). IMC also uses a different steel alloy, which makes it stronger than RMC even though the walls are thinner. Intermediate metal conduit is manufactured in both galvanized steel and aluminum; the steel type is much more common.

342.10 Uses Permitted

New wording in subsection (E) clarifies that IMC is suitable for use where subject to severe physical damage.

342.14 Dissimilar Metals

This section was clarified as to what types of fittings are acceptable for use with stainless and galvanized steel IMC.

Analysis

NEW   **342.10(E) Severe Physical Damage.** This subsection was added to the uses permitted to clarify that IMC is permitted in areas subject to severe physical damage. There was confusion in the field as to the use of this wiring method in areas subject to severe physical damage as that was not specified in the uses permitted. It meets the same requirements as rigid metal conduit and can be used in the same manner.

Analysis

CLARIFIED   **EDITED**   There have been both editorial and technical changes made in this section. The editorial revision clarifies that both stainless steel and aluminum fittings and enclosures are permitted to be used with galvanized IMC in areas not subject to severe corrosive influences that result in galvanic action. The second change revises the rules for the use of stainless steel IMC with fittings made of other materials.

342.10 Uses Permitted

(E) Severe Physical Damage. IMC is permitted where subject to subject to severe physical damage.

342.14 Dissimilar Metals

Where practical, contact of IMC with dissimilar metals should be avoided to prevent the deterioration of the metal because of galvanic action. Aluminum and stainless steel fittings and enclosures are permitted to be used with galvanized steel Type IMC where not subject to severe corrosive influences.

Author's Comment:

▸ Severe corrosive influences may be present in industrial and water treatment applications, pool pump houses, as well as applications near bodies of saltwater. Some soils also have a severe corrosive influence. The use of the term "severe" is a subjective and unquantifiable concept. Severities of effect can vary with the location and environment installed.

▸ Galvanic action occurs between two dissimilar metals in cases where there is metal to metal contact, the connections are subject to relative humidity, or corrosive environmental influences.

RIGID METAL CONDUIT (TYPE RMC)

Introduction to Article 344—Rigid Metal Conduit (Type RMC)

Rigid metal conduit (Type RMC), commonly called "rigid," has long been the standard raceway for providing protection from physical damage and from difficult environments. The outside diameter of rigid metal conduit is the same as intermediate metal conduit. However, the wall thickness is greater than intermediate metal conduit; therefore, the interior cross-sectional area is smaller. Rigid metal conduit is heavier and more expensive than intermediate metal conduit, and it can be used in any location. It is manufactured in both galvanized steel and aluminum; the steel type is much more common.

344.10 Uses Permitted

Specific language in subsection (E) was added to permit RMC to be installed in areas subject to severe physical damage.

Analysis

 NEW **344.10(E) Severe Physical Damage.** The changes here are the same as for IMC and allow rigid metal conduit (RMC) to be installed where subject to severe physical damage.

344.10 Uses Permitted

(E) Severe Physical Damage. RMC is permitted where subject to severe physical damage.

344.14 Dissimilar Metals

This section was clarified as to what types of fittings are acceptable for use with stainless steel RMC.

Analysis

  CLARIFIED **EDITED** There have been both editorial and technical changes made in this section. The first revision clarifies that both stainless steel and aluminum fittings and enclosures are permitted to be used with galvanized RMC in areas not subject to severe corrosive influences.

The second change revises the rules for the use of stainless steel RMC with fittings made of other materials. It was revised into a list format, and the permitted fittings and enclosures were more clearly spelled out. The previous language just used the term "approved" and was not specific.

If practical, contact of RMC with dissimilar metals should be avoided to prevent the deterioration of the metal because of galvanic action. Aluminum and stainless steel fittings and enclosures are permitted to be used with galvanized steel rigid metal conduit where not subject to severe corrosive influences.

LIQUIDTIGHT FLEXIBLE METAL CONDUIT (TYPE LFMC)

Introduction to Article 350—Liquidtight Flexible Metal Conduit (Type LFMC)

Liquidtight flexible metal conduit (Type LFMC), with its associated connectors and fittings, is a flexible raceway commonly used for connections to equipment that vibrates or must be occasionally moved. Liquidtight flexible metal conduit is commonly called "Sealtight®" or "liquidtight." Liquidtight flexible metal conduit is similar in construction to flexible metal conduit, but it has an outer liquidtight thermoplastic covering. It has the same primary purpose as flexible metal conduit, but also provides protection from liquids and some corrosive effects.

350.10 Uses Permitted

The permitted uses for LFMC were expanded to include areas subject to machine oils in list item (1), and a new list item (4) regarding the temperature rating of conductors was added.

Analysis

 EXPANDED **350.10(1).** This now contains a specific reference that LFMC may be used in areas exposed to machine oils. The requirements of UL 360 require that LFMC be tested for exposure to machine oils. The previous language said that LFMC provides protection from liquids, vapors, or solids. That language implied that it could not provide protection from all three at the same time.

 NEW **350.10(4).** This new list item permits higher temperature rated conductors or cables to be used where the conductors are not operated at a temperature higher than the listed temperature rating of the LFMC. If not marked on the jacket, LFMC has a temperature rating of 60°C. Conductors are often used at their 75°C ampacities. The use of unmarked LFMC, or LFMC marked for 60°C, would only permit conductors to be used at their 60°C ampacities. The issue here is the protection of the nonmetallic jacket of LFMC from excessive heat. This is the same concept we will see in 352.10(I) for PVC conduit.

350.10 Uses Permitted

Listed LFMC is permitted, either exposed or concealed, at any of the following locations: ▶Figure 350–1

LFMC, Uses Permitted
Exposed and Concealed
350.10

Listed LFMC is permitted either exposed or concealed.

Copyright 2020, www.MikeHolt.com

▶Figure 350–1

(1) If flexibility or protection from machine oils, liquids, vapors, or solids is required.

(2) In hazardous locations as permitted in Chapter 5.

(3) For direct burial, if listed and marked for this purpose. ▶Figure 350–2

LFMC, Uses Permitted
Direct Burial
350.10(3)

LFMC can be used for direct burial, if listed and marked for this purpose.

Copyright 2020, www.MikeHolt.com

▶Figure 350–2

(4) Conductors or cables rated at a temperature higher than the listed temperature rating of LFMC conduit may be installed in LFMC, provided the conductors or cables are not operated at a temperature higher than the listed temperature rating of the LFMC per 110.14(C).

350.12 Uses Not Permitted

LFMC is not to be used where subject to physical damage. ▶Figure 350–3

LFMC, Uses Not Permitted
Subject to physical Damage
350.12

VIOLATION
LFMC is not permitted to be used where subject to physical damage.

Copyright 2020, www.MikeHolt.com

▶Figure 350–3

350.12 Uses Not Permitted

The parent text was revised into a single sentence prohibiting the use of LFMC where it is subject to physical damage and the list items were removed.

Analysis

CLARIFIED

The parent text was revised to a single sentence. LFMC cannot be used where subject to physical damage which was list item (1) in the previous *Code*. Item (2) that addressed the combination of ambient and conductor temperatures exceeding the listing temperature rating of the LFMC was deleted. The temperature requirement removed from list item (2) is now addressed in a new list item (4) in 350.10 and does not need to appear in this section. This is consistent with how the temperature limitations are addressed in other articles such as 352 for PVC conduit and 362 for electrical nonmetallic tubing (ENT).

350.30 Securing and Supporting

The permission to use the LFMC fittings as a means of support has been limited to installations permitted by the exceptions after subsection (A).

Analysis

CLARIFIED

350.30(A) Ex Securely Fastened. The language was revised to state the actual intent. Exception 4 previously stated that (for the purposes of 350.30) listed LFMC conduit fittings were permitted to be used as a means of securing and supporting the LFMC. This was never intended to be a blanket permission applying to all of 350.30.

350.30 Securing and Supporting

LFMC must be securely fastened in place and supported in accordance with (A) and (B).

(A) Securely Fastened. LFMC must be securely fastened by a means approved by the authority having jurisdiction within 1 ft of termination and must be secured and supported at intervals not exceeding 4½ ft. ▶Figure 350–4

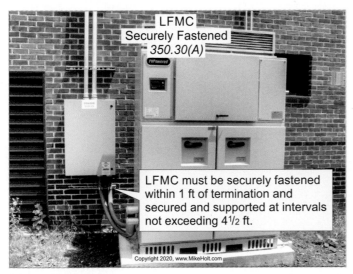

▶Figure 350–4

Where cable ties are used for securing LFMC they must be listed and identified for securement and support.

Ex 1: LFMC is not required to be securely fastened or supported where fished between access points through concealed spaces and supporting is impracticable.

Ex 2: If flexibility is necessary after installation, unsecured lengths from the last point where the raceway is securely fastened are not permitted to exceed: ▶Figure 350–5

(1)   3 ft for trade sizes ½ through 1¼

(2)   4 ft for trade sizes 1½ through 2

(3)   5 ft for trade sizes 2½ and larger

Ex 4: Lengths not exceeding 6 ft from the last point where the raceway is securely fastened can be unsecured within an accessible ceiling for a luminaire(s) or other equipment. Listed fittings are considered a means of securement and support. ▶Figure 350–6

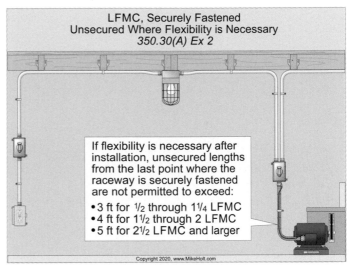

▶Figure 350–5

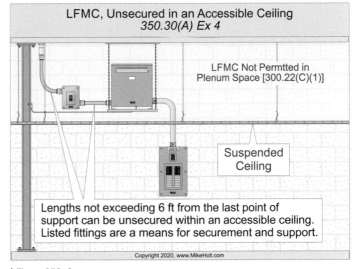

▶Figure 350–6

For the purposes of these exceptions, listed LFMC fittings are permitted as a means of securement and support.

> **Author's Comment:**
>
> ▶ This last sentence following the four exceptions means that, the use of LFMC fittings as the means of securing and supporting, only applies to installations made using one of the four exceptions. It should not be misconstrued as blanket permission to use the fittings to secure and support the LFMC in all applications.
>
> ▶ An exception to a general rule is exactly that, an exception and must meet the intent and requirement or criteria of the exception to apply.

LIQUIDTIGHT FLEXIBLE NONMETALLIC CONDUIT (TYPE LFNC)

Introduction to Article 356—Liquidtight Flexible Nonmetallic Conduit (Type LFNC)

Liquidtight flexible nonmetallic conduit (Type LFNC) is a listed raceway of circular cross section having an outer liquidtight, nonmetallic, sunlight-resistant jacket over an inner flexible core with associated couplings, connectors, and fittings. Liquidtight flexible nonmetallic conduit is commonly referred to as "Carflex®."

356.10 Uses Permitted

The permitted uses for LFNC were expanded to include areas subject to machine oils in list item (2), and a new list item (8) was added regarding the temperature rating of conductors used in LFNC.

Analysis

➕ NEW **356.10(2).** This was modified in the same manner as was done for LFMC (list item (1) in 350.10) and for the same reasons. The product is listed and tested to provide protection from machine oils, and it will provide protection from vapors, liquids, and solids at the same time.

➕ NEW **356.10(8).** The new list item (8) was added to identify that LFNC has a temperature rating of 60° unless otherwise marked on the surface of the raceway.

356.10 Uses Permitted

Listed LFNC is permitted, either exposed or concealed, at any of the following locations:

Note: Extreme cold can cause nonmetallic conduits to become brittle and more susceptible to damage from physical contact.

(1) If flexibility is required.

(2) If protection from liquids, vapors, <u>machine oils, and</u> solids is required.

(3) Outdoors, if listed and marked for this purpose.

(4) Directly buried in the earth, if listed and marked for this purpose.
▶Figure 356–1

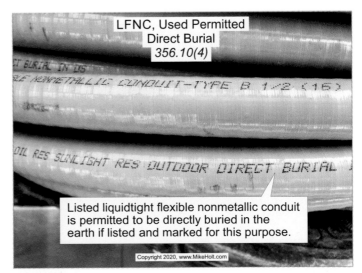

LFNC, Used Permitted
Direct Burial
356.10(4)

Listed liquidtight flexible nonmetallic conduit is permitted to be directly buried in the earth if listed and marked for this purpose.

Copyright 2020, www.MikeHolt.com

▶Figure 356–1

(5) LFNC-B (gray color) is permitted in lengths over 6 ft if secured in accordance with 356.30.

(6) LFNC-C (black color) is permitted as a listed manufactured prewired assembly.

(7) Encasement in concrete if listed for direct burial.

(8) <u>Conductors or cables rated at a temperature rating of LFNC conduit is permitted to be installed in LFNC, provided the conductors or cables are not operated at a temperature higher than the listed temperature rating of the LFNC.</u>

Note: Extreme cold can cause some types of nonmetallic conduits to become brittle and therefore more susceptible to damage from physical contact.

Author's Comment:

▸ When using conductors at their 75°C ampacity, electricians will have to ensure that the LFMC has the correct temperature rating. For instance, one particular brand is marked for 80°C for dry locations and 60°C for wet locations.

ARTICLE 358

ELECTRICAL METALLIC TUBING (TYPE EMT)

Introduction to Article 358—Electrical Metallic Tubing (Type EMT)

Electrical metallic tubing (Type EMT) is perhaps the most commonly used raceway in commercial and industrial installations. EMT is a lightweight raceway that is relatively easy to bend, cut, and ream. Because it is not threaded, all connectors and couplings are of the threadless type, either set-screw or compression, and provide for quick, easy, and inexpensive installations as compared to other metallic raceway systems; all of which make it very popular. Electrical metallic tubing is manufactured in both galvanized steel and aluminum; the steel type is used the most often.

358.10 Uses Permitted

A new subsection (E) was added to permit steel and stainless steel EMT to be installed were subject to physical damage.

Analysis

NEW

358.10(E) Physical Damage. A new subsection was added to the uses permitted specifically permitting the use of steel and stainless steel EMT to be installed where subject to physical damage. While list item (1) in 358.12 prohibits the use in areas subject to "severe" physical damage, there was no language that specifically permitted the use of EMT in areas subject to physical damage. This is intended to address confusion in the field and provide positive language on the use of EMT in areas subject to physical damage.

Author's Comment:

▸ This leaves in question why the use of aluminum EMT where subject to physical damage is not addressed in this new subsection as the new language only specifies steel and stainless steel EMT.

ARTICLE

380

MULTIOUTLET ASSEMBLIES

Introduction to Article 380—Multioutlet Assemblies

A multioutlet assembly is a surface, flush, or freestanding raceway designed to hold conductors and receptacles, and is assembled in the field or at the factory [Article 100]. It is not limited to systems commonly referred to by the trade names "Plugtrak®" or "Plugmold®."

380.12 Uses Not Permitted

A new list item (7) was added.

Analysis

NEW

380.12(7). This section covers multioutlet assemblies that are designed and listed for permanent installation. It does not apply to "relocatable power taps" which are cord-and-plug-connected and not suitable for permanent installation. The new list item (7) prohibits the use of cord-and-plug-connected multioutlet assemblies. Even though multioutlet assemblies are not intended to be cord-and-plug-connected, the relocatable power taps were being called multioutlet assemblies. The language is intended to act to prohibit the permanent installation of "relocatable power taps."

380.12 Uses Not Permitted

A multioutlet assembly may not be installed as follows:

(1) Concealed.

(2) Where subject to severe physical damage.

(3) If the voltage is 300V or more between conductors, unless the metal has a thickness not less than 0.04 in.

(4) Where subject to corrosive vapors.

(5) In hoistways.

(6) In any hazardous location, except as permitted by 501.10(B).

(7) Where cord and plug connected.

Author's Comment:

▸ You may have noticed that the phrase "unless listed" (which usually grants permission to use otherwise), is missing. That is because there are no listed portable multioutlet assemblies by any Nationally Recognized Testing Laboratory (NRTL) for the purpose of permanent installation.

ARTICLE
392

CABLE TRAYS

Introduction to Article 392—Cable Trays

A cable tray system is a unit or an assembly of units or sections with associated fittings that forms a structural system used to securely fasten or support cables and raceways.

Cable tray systems include ladder, ventilated trough, ventilated channel, solid bottom, and other similar structures. They are manufactured in many forms, from a simple hanger or wire mesh to a substantial, rigid, steel support system. Cable trays are designed and manufactured to support specific wiring methods, as identified in 392.10(A).

392.10 Uses Permitted

The language was revised to clarify the use of single insulated conductors in a cable tray.

Analysis

CLARIFIED The ongoing confusion as to the use of single conductors in cable trays may now be resolved with the revised wording in this section. The new language specifies that single insulated conductors may only be installed in a cable tray where installed in accordance with 392.10(B)(1). Section 392.10(B) only applies to industrial establishments, as indicated by the subsection's title of "In Industrial Establishments." Subsection (B)(1) requires that single conductors be not smaller than 1/0 AWG and that they be listed and marked as suitable for use in cable trays. The addition of the words "wiring methods containing" addresses single conductors that are installed in a wiring method such as where they are installed in a raceway or as part of a cable assembly.

392.10 Uses Permitted

Cable trays can be used as a support system for <u>wiring methods containing</u> service, feeder, or branch-circuit conductors, as well as communications circuits, control circuits, and signaling circuits. ▶Figure 392–1

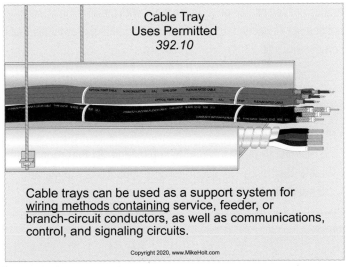

Cable Tray
Uses Permitted
392.10

Cable trays can be used as a support system for <u>wiring methods containing</u> service, feeder, or branch-circuit conductors, as well as communications, control, and signaling circuits.

Copyright 2020, www.MikeHolt.com

▶Figure 392–1

<u>Single insulated conductors are only permitted in cable trays when installed in accordance with 392.10(B)(1).</u>

392.18 Cable Tray Installations

The change to the rule in subsection (H) clarifies that the "over 600V" applies to the operating voltage of the system and not to the voltage rating of the conductors.

Analysis

CLARIFIED

392.18(H) Marking. Cable trays have been required to be marked "**DANGER—HIGH VOLTAGE— KEEP AWAY**" where the tray contained conductors rated over 600V. There are cases where systems are modified and cables that were previously used as part of a medium-voltage system, and rated for that use, were repurposed for use with a system operating at 600V or less. The danger is not with the voltage rating of the conductors but rather with their operating voltage.

392.18 Cable Tray Installations

(H) Marking. Cable trays containing conductors <u>operating over 600V</u> must have a permanent, legible warning notice carrying the wording, "**DANGER—HIGH VOLTAGE—KEEP AWAY**" placed in a readily visible position on all cable trays, with the spacing of warning notices not to exceed 10 ft. The danger marking(s) or labels must comply with 110.21(B).

392.30 Securing and Supporting

A new list item was added to subsection (B) that requires cable ties used for securing and supporting cables and conductors in a cable tray to be listed for the purpose.

Analysis

NEW

392.30(B) Cables and Conductors. A new list item (4) was added to require that where cable ties are used for securing cables and conductors to the tray, that the cable ties be listed and identified for the application, and for securement and support.

The same language was added in the 2017 *Code* cycle for the securing and supporting of cable wiring methods and some of the flexible raceways.

392.30 Securing and Supporting

(A) Cable Trays. Cable trays must be supported in accordance with the installation instructions.

(B) Cables and Conductors. Cables and conductors must be secured to, and supported by, the cable tray system in accordance with 392.30(B)(1), (2), (3), and (4).

(4) Cable ties must be listed and identified as suitable for the application and for securement and support.

> **Author's Comment:**
>
> ▸ Compliance with this rule would require the use of Type 2S or 21S cable ties. Standard cable ties are types 2 and 21. The "S" in the type number indicates that they are suitable securing and supporting.

392.44 Expansion Splice Plates

This change requires expansion splice plates be used where necessary to compensate for expansion and contraction.

Analysis

NEW

Cable trays are often installed as long straight runs and thermal expansion and contraction can cause issues if provisions are not made to address them. The new section requires that a cable tray be provided with expansion splice plates where necessary to compensate for thermal expansion and contraction.

392.44 Expansion Splice Plates

Expansion splice plates for cable trays must be provided where necessary to compensate for thermal expansion and contraction.

Author's Comment:

▸ Thermal expansion is an issue without the installation of raceway expansion joints and is often overlooked. In order for the raceway to properly serve its function, it must be able to expand, as well as contract, and expansion joints provide the ability to do so.

▸ This *Code* section gives no guidance as to how to determine the need for an expansion splice plate but there is a National Electrical Manufacturer's Association (NEMA) document available as a free download that may assist. This document is titled; "NEMA VE2, Cable Tray Installation Guidelines."

392.46 Bushed Conduit and Tubing

This section was expanded to provide guidance for the protection of cables and conductors where they transition from the cable tray to raceways or into enclosures.

Analysis

EXPANDED This section was revised to include two new subsections and clarify that some long-standing installation practices are *Code* compliant. The previous language did not adequately address these installations.

The original language is now parent language for this section and has been expanded. The expansion clarifies that a box is not required where conductors or cables transition to a raceway, bushed conduit, or tubing from the tray. The parent text further specifies that cables and conductors are permitted to enter equipment per the requirements of subsections (A) or (B). In both cases the *NEC* uses the words multiconductor cables with "entirely nonmetallic sheaths." This is to clarify that these rules are not intended to apply to multiconductor cables with "metal jackets" such as Types AC or MC.

392.46 Bushed Conduit and Tubing

A box is not required where cables or conductors are installed in a bushed raceway used for support, for protection against physical damage or where conductors or cables transition to a raceway from the cable tray.

(A) Through Bushed Conduit or Tubing. Individual conductors or multiconductor cables with entirely nonmetallic sheaths, can enter enclosures where they are terminated through nonflexible bushed conduit or tubing installed for their protection, provided they are secured at the point of transition from the cable tray and the raceway is sealed at the outer end using an approved means so as to prevent debris from entering the equipment through the raceway.

(B) Flanged Connections. Individual conductors or multiconductor cables with entirely nonmetallic sheaths, can enter enclosures through openings associated with flanges from cable trays where the cable tray is attached to the flange and the flange is mounted directly to the equipment. The openings must be made such that the conductors are protected from abrasion and the openings must be sealed or covered to prevent debris from entering the enclosure through them.

Note: One method of preventing debris from entering the enclosure is to seal the outer end of the raceway or the opening with duct seal.

EQUIPMENT FOR GENERAL USE

Introduction to Chapter 4—Equipment for General Use

With the first three chapters of the *NEC* behind you, this fourth one is necessary for building a solid foundation in general equipment installations. It helps you apply the first three chapters to installations involving general equipment. You need to understand the first four chapters of the *Code* to properly apply the requirements to Chapters 5, 6, and 7, and at times to Chapter 8.

Chapter 4 is arranged in the following manner:

- **Article 400—Flexible Cords and Flexible Cables.** Article 400 covers the general requirements, applications, and construction specifications for flexible cords and flexible cables.

- **Article 402—Fixture Wires.** This article covers the general requirements and construction specifications for fixture wires.

- **Article 404—Switches.** The requirements of Article 404 apply to switches of all types. These include snap (toggle) switches, dimmer switches, fan switches, knife switches, circuit breakers, and automatic switches such as time clocks, timers, and switches and circuit breakers used as a disconnecting means.

- **Article 406—Receptacles and Attachment Plugs (Caps).** This article covers the rating, type, and installation of receptacles and attachment plugs (cord caps). It also covers flanged surface inlets.

- **Article 408—Switchboards and Panelboards.** Article 408 covers specific requirements for switchboards, panelboards, and distribution boards that supply lighting and power circuits.

Author's Comment:

▸ See Article 100 for the definitions of "Panelboard" and "Switchboard."

- **Article 410—Luminaires and Lamps.** This article contains the requirements for luminaires, lampholders, and lamps. Because of the many types and applications of luminaires, manufacturer's instructions are very important and helpful for proper installation. Underwriters Laboratories produces a pamphlet called the *Luminaire Marking Guide*, which provides information for properly installing common types of incandescent, fluorescent, and high-intensity discharge (HID) luminaires. Spaces dedicated to the cultivation and growth of agricultural products (such as "hot houses") that reproduce the natural effects of sunlight and seasonal temperatures may present unique conditions. Additional requirements are addressed in Part XVI, Special Provisions for Horticultural Lighting Equipment.

- **Article 411—Low-Voltage Lighting.** Article 411 covers lighting systems, and their associated components, that operate at no more than 30V alternating current, or 60V direct current.

- **Article 422—Appliances.** This article covers electric appliances used in any occupancy.

- **Article 424—Fixed Electric Space-Heating Equipment.** Article 424 covers fixed electric equipment used for space heating. For the purpose of this article, heating equipment includes heating cable, unit heaters, boilers, central systems, and other fixed electric space-heating equipment. Article 424 does not apply to process heating and room air-conditioning.

- **Article 430—Motors, Motor Circuits, and Controllers.** This article contains the specific requirements for conductor sizing, overcurrent protection, control circuit conductors, motor controllers, and disconnecting means. The installation requirements for motor control centers are covered in Article 430, Part VIII.

- **Article 440—Air-Conditioning and Refrigeration Equipment.** Article 440 applies to electrically driven air-conditioning and refrigeration equipment with a motorized hermetic refrigerant compressor. The requirements in this article are in addition to, or amend, the requirements in Article 430 and others.

- **Article 445—Generators.** Article 445 contains the electrical installation requirements for generators and other requirements, such as where they can be installed, nameplate markings, conductor ampacity, and disconnecting means.

- **Article 450—Transformers.** This article covers the installation of transformers.

- **Article 480—Storage Batteries.** Article 480 covers stationary installations of storage batteries.

FLEXIBLE CORDS AND FLEXIBLE CABLES

Introduction to Article 400—Flexible Cords and Flexible Cables

This article covers the general requirements, applications, and construction specifications for flexible cords and flexible cables. The *NEC* does not consider flexible cords to be a wiring method like those addressed in Chapter 3.

Always use a flexible cord (and fittings) identified for the application. Table 400.4 will help you in that regard. For example, use cords listed for a wet location if you are using them outdoors. The jacket material of any flexible cord is tested to maintain its insulation properties and other characteristics in the environments for which it has been listed. Tables 400.5(A)(1) and 400.5(A)(2) are also important tables to turn to when looking for the ampacity of flexible cords. Flexible cords and flexible cables may include the various types of wire which might be used for lamps, appliances, extension cords, drop and pendant lights, pool pumps, and so on.

400.12 Uses Not Permitted

This section was revised to clarify what types of cords and cables to which the "uses not permitted" applies. The exception to (5) was expanded to include power-supply cords (extension cords) as well as flexible cords and flexible cables.

Analysis

CLARIFIED This change attempts to clarify to what this section applies. In the previous *Code* it did not apply to flexible cords. It used the incorrect term of "flexible cord sets" which applies to extension cords, but not bulk flexible cord. The new language applies the uses not permitted to flexible cords, flexible cables, cord sets, and power-supply cords. These restrictions apply unless the cables and cords listed in the parent text here are specifically permitted to be used in the 400.10 Uses Permitted section.

EXPANDED **400.12(4) Where Attached to Building Surfaces, Exception.** This list item prohibits flexible cords and cables from being used where attached to building surfaces.

The exception to this prohibition was expanded to include installations made in accordance with 590.4. Sections 590.4(B) and (C) permit the use of cables and cords listed in Table 400.4 to be used for temporary feeders and branch circuits. Section 590.4(J) requires the feeders and branch circuits to be supported and such support requires attachment to the structure. This exception was probably not actually needed as 90.3 permits the rules in Article 590 to modify those in Article 400. The part of the exception that referred to 368.56(B) for the support of busway cables remains. Section 368.56(B) requires the busway cable to be supported from the building. This part of the exception is required as there is no provision that permits a Chapter 3 rule to modify one in Chapter 4.

EXPANDED **400.12(5) Where Concealed, Ex to (5).** Power-supply cords were added to this exception that permits cords and cables contained within an enclosure to be used in other spaces used for environmental air as permitted by 300.22(C). The substantiation was that power-supply cords are more commonly used in this exception than are flexible cords and flexible cables.

400.12 Uses Not Permitted

Unless specifically permitted in 400.10, flexible cords, flexible cables, cord sets (extension cords), and power-supply cords are not permitted for the following:

(1) Flexible cords, flexible cables, cord sets (extension cords), and power-supply cords are not permitted to be a substitute for the fixed wiring. ▶Figure 400–1

▶Figure 400–1

(2) Flexible cords, flexible cables, cord sets (extension cords), and power-supply cords are not permitted to be run through holes in walls, structural ceilings, suspended or dropped ceilings, or floors. ▶Figure 400–2

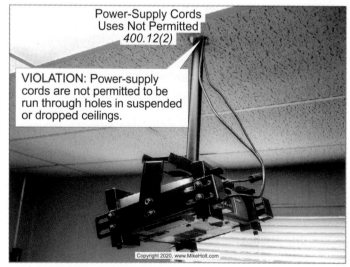

▶Figure 400–2

(3) Flexible cords, flexible cables, cord sets (extension cords), and power-supply cords are not permitted to be run through doorways, windows, or similar openings.

(4) Flexible cords, flexible cables, cord sets (extension cords), and power-supply cords are not permitted to be attached to building surfaces.

(5) Flexible cords, flexible cables, cord sets (extension cords), and power-supply cords are not permitted to be concealed by walls, floors, or ceilings, or located above suspended or dropped ceilings. ▶Figure 400–3

▶Figure 400–3

Ex to (5): Flexible cords, flexible cables, and power-supply cords are permitted if contained within an enclosure for use in other spaces used for environmental air as permitted by [300.22(C)(3)].

(6) Flexible cords, flexible cord sets (extension cords), and power-supply cords are not permitted to be installed in raceways, except as permitted by 400.17 for industrial establishments where the conditions of maintenance and supervision ensure that only qualified persons will service the installation.

(7) Flexible cords, flexible cord sets (extension cords), and power-supply cords are not permitted where they are subject to physical damage.

Author's Comment:

▶ It remains unclear how the uses not permitted can apply to cord sets and power-supply cords since they are not included in the scope of Article 400.

400.17 Protection from Damage

This rule was revised to replace "reduced" with "adjusted," as that is the correct *NEC* term. Cords are subject to the same ampacity adjustments as other wiring methods.

Analysis

CLARIFIED

The language of this requirement was revised to use the correct term of "adjusted" as applied to cases where there are more than three current-carrying conductors in a cord or cords installed in raceways. The previous *Code* required the ampacity to be reduced, and while that is exactly what happens when the adjustment factors are applied, "reduced" was not the correct *NEC* term. Note that list item (6) in 400.12 says you cannot install flexible cords and cables in raceways unless otherwise permitted in the *Code*. The provisions of the second paragraph in 400.17 is one of those permissions; flexible cords and cables are permitted to be installed in raceways in industrial establishments with qualified maintenance and supervision. The word "allowable," which preceded the word ampacity, was removed to correlate with the global *NEC Style Manual* change.

400.17 Protection from Damage

Flexible cords must be protected by bushings or fittings where passing through holes in covers, outlet boxes, or similar enclosures.

Author's Comment:

▸ Your guess is as good as mine as to why the ampacity adjustment rule is found in a section that deals with protecting the cord from damage.

Notes

ARTICLE
402

FIXTURE WIRES

Introduction to Article 402—Fixture Wires

This article covers the general requirements and construction specifications for fixture wires. One such requirement is that fixture wires can be no smaller than 18 AWG. Another is that they must be of a type listed in Table 402.3 which makes up the bulk of Article 402. Table 402.5 lists the ampacity for fixture wires.

402.3 (Fixture Wire) Types

A new type of fixture wire has been recognized by the product standards and was added to this table.

Analysis:

EXPANDED

Table 402.3 (Fixture Wires) Types. Type FFHH-2 fixture wire is new. It has a rubber or cross-linked synthetic polymer insulation and, like all wire types containing "HH," it is a 90°C conductor. The "-2" in the fixture wire types is just part of the type and does not have a meaning like it does with the types found in 310.4.

402.3 Types

Fixture wires must be of a type contained in Table 402.3. (See the *NEC* for the Table.)

ARTICLE
404

SWITCHES

Introduction to Article 404—Switches

The requirements of Article 404 address switches of all types, including snap (toggle) switches, dimmer switches, fan switches, knife switches, circuit breakers, and automatic switches, such as time clocks and timers.

404.2 Switch Connections

This rule was revised to better clarify the locations where light switches are required to have a neutral conductor run to the switch box.

Analysis

CLARIFIED   **404.2(C) Switches Controlling Lighting Loads.** The wording in this rule was changed from "or rooms suitable for human habitation or occupancy" to "habitable rooms and occupiable spaces" to clarify that both dwelling and nondwelling occupancies require a neutral conductor at the light switch location.

EXPANDED   **404.2(C)(5) Ex.** The exception that permits a replacement electronic lighting control switch to use the equipment grounding conductor (EGC) as a neutral was expanded to include other types of electronic control switches. There are switching devices that control loads other than lighting that have used the equipment grounding conductor as a neutral and present the same hazard as a lighting control switch.

In recognition of this the word "lighting" was deleted, making the device requirements apply to all "electronic control" switches that use the equipment grounding conductor as the neutral for the electronics. In the past, it had been permitted to use the equipment grounding conductor as the neutral for the electronics in the switches, creating a safety hazard for the unsuspecting electrician who opens the equipment grounding conductor and is shocked.

404.2 Switch Connections

(C) Switches Controlling Lighting Loads. Switches controlling line-to-neutral lighting loads must have a neutral conductor installed at all switches serving bathroom areas, hallways, stairways, and habitable rooms or occupiable spaces as defined in the building code. ▶Figure 404–1

Where 3-way and 4-way switches are visible in a room, only one of the switches requires a neutral conductor. ▶Figure 404–2 and ▶Figure 404–3

A neutral conductor is not required to be installed at lighting switch locations under any of the following conditions:

(1) Where conductors enter the box enclosing the switch through a raceway with sufficient cross-sectional area to accommodate a neutral conductor. ▶Figure 404–4

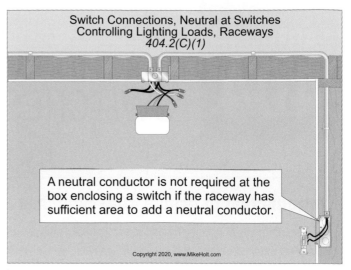

▶Figure 404–1

Switch Connections, Switches Controlling Lighting Loads
404.2(C)

Switches controlling line-to-neutral lighting loads must have a neutral installed at all switches serving bathrooms, hallways, stairways, <u>and habitable rooms or occupiable spaces</u> as defined in the building code.

Copyright 2020, www.MikeHolt.com

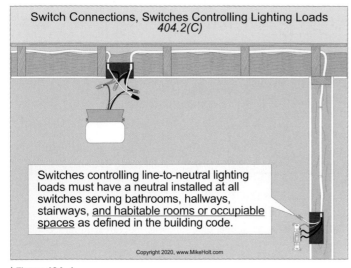

▶Figure 404–2

3- and 4-Way Switches Controlling Lighting Loads
<u>Habitable Rooms or Occupiable Spaces</u>
404.2(C)

Where 3-way and 4-way switches are visible in a room, only one of the switches requires a neutral conductor.

Copyright 2020, www.MikeHolt.com

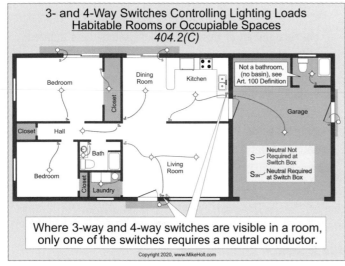

▶Figure 404–3

3- and 4-Way Switches Controlling Lighting Loads
<u>Habitable Rooms or Occupiable Spaces</u>
404.2(C)

Where 3-way and 4-way switches are visible in a room, only one of the switches requires a neutral conductor.

Copyright 2020, www.MikeHolt.com

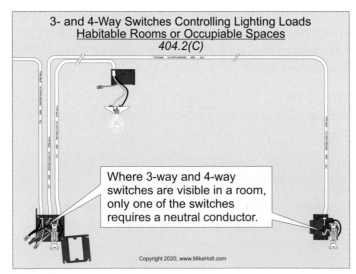

Switch Connections, Neutral at Switches
Controlling Lighting Loads, Raceways
404.2(C)(1)

A neutral conductor is not required at the box enclosing a switch if the raceway has sufficient area to add a neutral conductor.

Copyright 2020, www.MikeHolt.com

▶Figure 404–4

(2) Where the box enclosing a switch can be accessed to add or replace a cable without damaging the building finish. ▶Figure 404–5

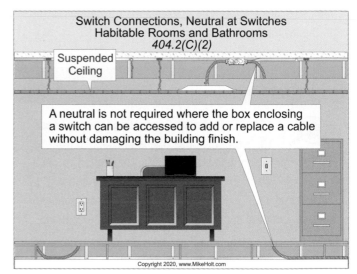

Switch Connections, Neutral at Switches
Habitable Rooms and Bathrooms
404.2(C)(2)

Suspended Ceiling

A neutral is not required where the box enclosing a switch can be accessed to add or replace a cable without damaging the building finish.

Copyright 2020, www.MikeHolt.com

▶Figure 404–5

(3) Where snap switches with integral enclosures comply with 300.15(E).

(4) Where the lighting is controlled by automatic means.

(5) Where switches control receptacles. ▶Figure 404–6

If not already present, a neutral conductor must be installed for any replacement switch that requires line-to-neutral voltage [404.22] to operate the electronics of the switch in the standby mode. ▶Figure 404–7

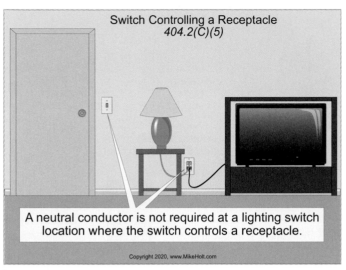

Figure 404–6

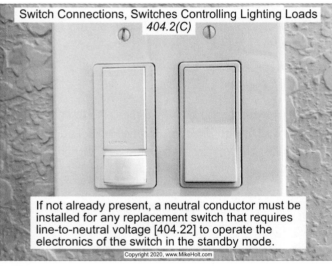

If not already present, a neutral conductor must be installed for any replacement switch that requires line-to-neutral voltage [404.22] to operate the electronics of the switch in the standby mode.

Figure 404–7

Ex: A neutral conductor is not required for replacement switches installed in locations wired prior to the adoption of 404.2(C) where the neutral conductor cannot be extended without removing finish materials. The number of electronic lighting control switches without a neutral conductor on a branch circuit are not permitted to exceed five switches, and the number connected to any feeder are not permitted to exceed 25 switches.

Author's Comment:

▸ The purpose of the neutral conductor at a switch is to complete a circuit path for electronic lighting control devices that require a neutral conductor.

404.4 Damp or Wet Locations

This section was edited to prohibit switches from being installed in tub spaces; the previous language only prohibited them from being installed within the tub itself.

Analysis

404.4(C) Switches in Tub or Shower Spaces. CLARIFIED Subsection (C) was revised to correct an unintentional change from the 2011 *Code* cycle. The language in the 2017 *NEC* said that switches may not be installed within tubs or shower spaces. With that language the rule does not prohibit the installation of a switch within in the "tub space" but only within the actual tub. The word "tubs" was replaced with "tub" to make it clear the prohibition against switches is within tub and shower "spaces" which includes the tub or shower itself, as well as the space directly above the footprint of the tub or shower.

404.4 Damp or Wet Locations

(C) Switches Within Tub or Shower Spaces. Switches can be located next to but not within a bathtub, hydromassage bathtub, or shower space. ▸Figure 404–8

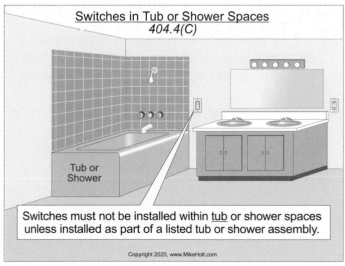

Switches must not be installed within <u>tub</u> or shower spaces unless installed as part of a listed tub or shower assembly.

Figure 404–8

404.7 Indicating

Changes to this rule clarify that the on/off indication for a switch or circuit breaker must be visible when accessing the external operating means.

Analysis

CLARIFIED The revision here added a requirement for the on/off indication for switches or circuit breakers to be in a location that is visible when accessing the external operating means. It also deleted the term "clearly" that previously preceded "indicate" because it is a subjective term that should not be used.

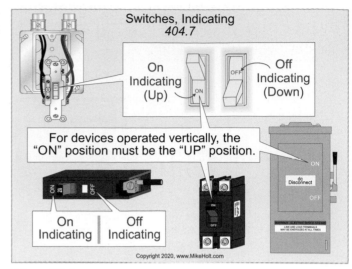

▸Figure 404–9

404.7 Indicating

Switches and circuit breakers must be marked to indicate <u>in a location that is visible when accessing the external operating means</u>, whether they are in the "on" or "off" position.

Author's Comment:

▸ This is typically accomplished by marking on the toggle of the switch itself or by indicative labeling. If you find a switch not so marked, chances are it is a 3-way or 4-way switch which can be on or off in either the up or down position.

▸ It is permitted, that When the operating handle is behind a cover that must be opened to access the handle, it is permissible for the on/off indication to be visible only at that time

When the switch is operated vertically, it must be installed so the "up" position is the "on" position [240.81]. ▸Figure 404–9

Ex 1: Double-throw switches, such as 3-way and 4-way switches, are not required to be marked "on" or "off."

Author's Comment:

▸ Circuit breakers used to switch fluorescent lighting must be listed and marked "SWD" or "HID," and those used to switch high-intensity discharge lighting must be listed and must be marked "HID" [240.83(D)]. ▸Figure 404–10

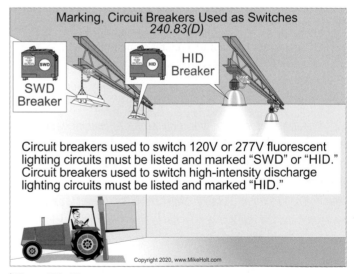

Circuit breakers used to switch 120V or 277V fluorescent lighting circuits must be listed and marked "SWD" or "HID." Circuit breakers used to switch high-intensity discharge lighting circuits must be listed and marked "HID."

▸Figure 404–10

404.9 General-Use Snap Switches, Dimmers, and Control Switches

This section was expanded to include dimmers and control switches, and (A) and (B) were expanded and clarified along with two of the three exceptions following (B).

Analysis

EXPANDED This section and its subsections were expanded to include requirements for other than "general-use snap switches." The previous heading made these requirements specific to "snap switches" but the rules also needed to apply to other types of switching or control devices that are in the same environment.

EXPANDED **404.9(A) Faceplates.** Faceplates are required to completely cover the opening in which a switch or control device has been installed and, where the device is flush mounted, the faceplate must seat against the finished surface.

EXPANDED **404.9(B) Grounding.** The requirement for metal face plates to be "grounded" was revised to require metal faceplates to be bonded to the equipment grounding conductor. In addition, the subsection was expanded to include dimmers and control switches as well as snap switches. The revised language specifies that snap switches, dimmers, control switches, and metal faceplates must be connected to an EGC using either of the two list items.

There is a strong move towards the use of "control devices" other than snap switches, and the same installation requirements should apply to those other devices. This change will accomplish that.

EXPANDED **DELETED** **404.9(B) Ex 1 Grounding.** The term "snap switch" was deleted from Exception 1. Since this is an exception to (B), it applies to the same devices as does (B); that is "snap switches, dimmers, and control switches." This exception permits the installation of a replacement switch in an enclosure that does not have an equipment grounding conductor without requiring an equipment grounding conductor connection.

EXPANDED **404.9(B) Ex 2 Grounding, Ex 2.** This exception permits listed kits or assemblies not to be connected and bonded to an equipment grounding conductor under four specified conditions. The replacement of the word "connected" with "bonding" is more technically correct. The only change was to condition (1) where the device is required to be provided with a nonmetallic faceplate and be designed so that no metallic faceplate can replace the nonmetallic one provided. The previous language was such that a manufacturer could provide a nonmetallic faceplate, but that did not prevent the switch design from accepting a metallic one. These assemblies are not connected to an equipment grounding conductor and there would be no means to bond a metallic faceplate to the equipment grounding conductor.

404.9 General-Use Snap Switches, Dimmers, and Control Switches

(A) Faceplates. Mounting for switches, <u>dimmers, and control switches</u> must completely cover the outlet box opening and, where flush mounted, the faceplate must seat against the wall surface.

(B) Grounding. The metal mounting yokes for switches, dimmers, and control switches must be connected to an equipment grounding conductor and <u>metal faceplates must be bonded to the equipment grounding conductor. Snap switches, dimmers, control switches, and metal faceplates are considered connected to an equipment grounding conductor using either of the following methods:</u>

(1) Metal Boxes. The switch is mounted with metal screws to a metal box or a metal cover that is connected to an equipment grounding conductor in accordance with 250.148. ▸Figure 404–11 and ▸Figure 404–12

Author's Comment:

▸ Direct metal-to-metal contact between the device yoke of a switch and the box is not required. The switch is connected to the effective ground-fault current path when the yoke is mounted with metal screws to a metal box. ▸Figure 404–13

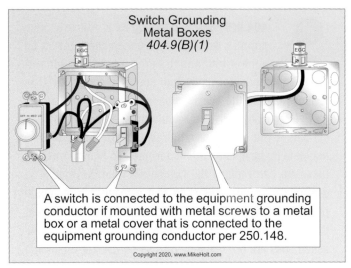

Figure 404–11

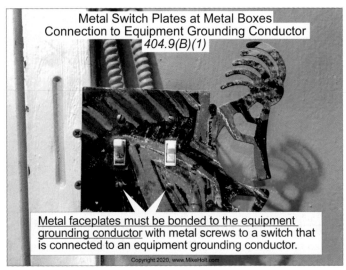

Figure 404–12

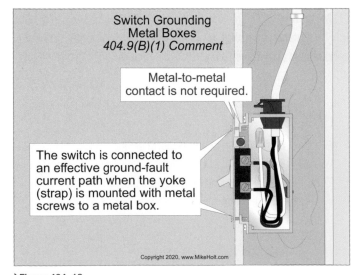

Figure 404–13

(2) Nonmetallic Boxes. The grounding terminal of the switch yoke must be connected to the circuit equipment grounding conductor. ▸Figure 404–14

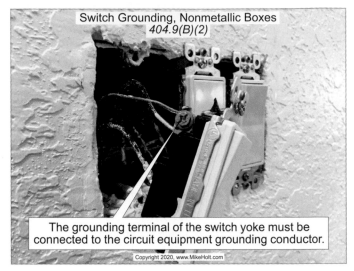

Figure 404–14

Ex 1: Where no means exists within the box for bonding to an equipment grounding conductor or if the wiring method at the existing switch does not contain an equipment grounding conductor, a switch without such a connection to the equipment grounding conductor is permitted for replacement purposes only. A switch installed under this exception must have a faceplate that is nonmetallic with nonmetallic screws, or the replacement switch must be GFCI protected.

Ex 2: Listed assemblies are not required to be bonded to an equipment grounding conductor if all of the following conditions are met:

(1) The device is provided with a nonmetallic faceplate and the device is designed such that no metallic faceplate replaces the one provided,

(2) The device does not have a mounting means to accept other configurations of faceplates,

(3) The device is equipped with a nonmetallic yoke, and

(4) Parts of the device that are accessible after installation of the faceplate are manufactured of nonmetallic material.

Ex 3: An equipment grounding conductor is not required for bonding a snap switch with an integral nonmetallic enclosure complying with 300.15(E).

404.10 Mounting of General-Use Snap Switches, Dimmers, and Control Switches

Switches must now be mounted flush to the box or finished surface and their cover plates must completely cover the wall opening.

Analysis

EXPANDED This section was expanded to specify that snap switches, dimmers, control switches, and metal faceplates must be connected to an equipment grounding conductor.

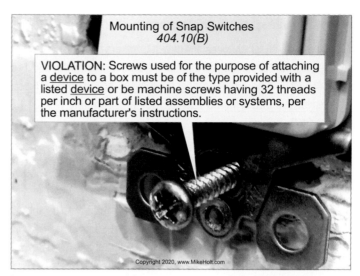

Mounting of Snap Switches
404.10(B)

VIOLATION: Screws used for the purpose of attaching a device to a box must be of the type provided with a listed device or be machine screws having 32 threads per inch or part of listed assemblies or systems, per the manufacturer's instructions.

Copyright 2020, www.MikeHolt.com

▶Figure 404–16

404.10 Mounting of Snap Switches, Dimmers, and Control Switches

(B) Box Mounted. General-use snap switches, dimmers, and control switches mounted in boxes that are set back from the finished surface must be installed so that the extension plaster ears are seated against the surface. ▶Figure 404–15

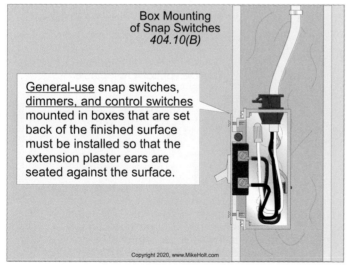

Box Mounting
of Snap Switches
404.10(B)

General-use snap switches, dimmers, and control switches mounted in boxes that are set back of the finished surface must be installed so that the extension plaster ears are seated against the surface.

Copyright 2020, www.MikeHolt.com

▶Figure 404–15

Screws used for the purpose of attaching a device to a box must be of the type provided with a listed device or be machine screws having 32 threads per in. or part of listed assemblies or systems, in accordance with the manufacturer's instructions. ▶Figure 404–16

Author's Comment:

▸ In walls or ceilings of noncombustible material, such as drywall, boxes are not permitted to be set back more than ¼ in. from the finished surface. In combustible walls or ceilings, boxes must be flush with, or project slightly from, the finished surface [314.20]. There must not be any gaps more than ⅛ in. at the edge of the box [314.21].

404.12 Grounding of Enclosures

The final sentence of this rule was changed to add a direct reference to the exceptions in 314.3.

Analysis

CLARIFIED There is now added text which references the exceptions to 314.3 and is meant to simplify the application of this rule. The grounding of metal boxes and the bonding of what is mounted to them may be straight forward but, "What about plastic boxes"? This new reference provides guidance for what might be required when plastic boxes are used.

404.12 Grounding of Enclosures

Metal enclosures for switches and circuit breakers must be connected to an equipment grounding conductor of a type recognized in 250.118 [250.4(A)(3)]. <u>Where nonmetallic enclosures are used with metal raceways or metal-armored cables, they must comply with 314.3 Ex 1 or Ex 2.</u>

404.14 Rating and Use of Switches

Switches must now be listed devices as indicated in the parent text. In addition, (A) was edited and (E) was expanded.

Analysis

EXPANDED While it is a given that most switches are already required to be listed, as we have seen in previous editions of the *NEC*, there is an ongoing move to require all equipment to be listed. The revision to this section requires switches to be listed. The substantiation indicated that the construction requirements in Part II of Article 404 only address a small portion of the requirements found in the UL standards for the various types of switching devices, and that it would be very difficult for an AHJ to verify that a nonlisted switch complies with the listing standard requirements. Other additional changes were made to subsections (A) and (E).

REORGANIZED **404.14 (A) Alternating-Current General-Use Snap Switches.** This subsection contains the permitted uses of general-use ac snap switches. These are switches that are rated for use with alternating current only. The former list item (3) for motor loads not exceeding 80 percent of the ampere rating of the switch at its rated voltage was renumbered as list item (4). The second added item is list item (5) that addresses electronic ballasts, self-ballasted lamps, compact fluorescent lamps, and LED driver lamp loads up to 20A but not exceeding the ampere rating of the switch at its rated voltage.

EXPANDED **404.14(E) Dimmer and Electronic Control Switches.** This subsection was expanded to include "electronic control switches" which often have remote control or other advanced features not available with traditional switches and are becoming widely used as an alternative to general-use switches.

This new language permits the use of "other" electronic control switches, such as timing switches and occupancy sensors, for the control of permanently connected loads. They are required to be marked by the manufacturer with their current and voltage ratings and used for loads that do not exceed these specifications.

404.14 Rating and Use of Snap Switches

General-Use Snap Switches. General-use snap switches <u>must be listed</u> and used within their ratings as indicated.

(A) Alternating-Current General-Use Snap Switches. General-use snap switches are permitted to control:

<u>(4)</u> Motor loads not exceeding 80 percent of the ampere rating of the switch [430.109(C)].

<u>(5) Electronic ballasts, self-ballasted lamps, compact fluorescent lamps, and LED lamp loads with their associated drivers, not exceeding 20A and not exceeding the ampere rating of the switch at the voltage applied.</u>

(E) Dimmers <u>and Electronic Control Switches</u>. General-use dimmer switches are only permitted to control permanently installed incandescent luminaires, unless listed for control of other loads. ▶Figure 404–17

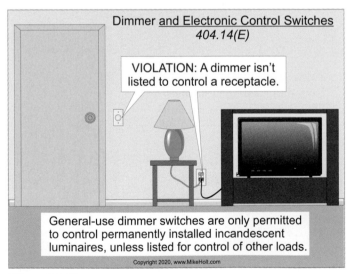

Dimmer <u>and Electronic Control Switches</u>
404.14(E)

VIOLATION: A dimmer isn't listed to control a receptacle.

General-use dimmer switches are only permitted to control permanently installed incandescent luminaires, unless listed for control of other loads.

Copyright 2020, www.MikeHolt.com

▶Figure 404–17

<u>Other electronic control switches, such as timing switches and occupancy sensors, can only be used to control permanently connected loads. Such switches must be marked by the manufacturer with their current and voltage ratings and used for loads that do not exceed their ampere rating at the voltage applied.</u>

ARTICLE 406

RECEPTACLES AND ATTACHMENT PLUGS (CAPS)

Introduction to Article 406—Receptacles and Attachment Plugs (Caps)

This article covers the rating, type, and installation of receptacles and attachment plugs (cord caps). It also covers flanged surface inlets.

406.2 Definitions

New parent text is a part of the global reorganization of definitions throughout the *Code.*

Analysis

NEW This is an example of a definition that is specific to the article in which it appears and is not anywhere else. If it were it would have to be in Article 100.

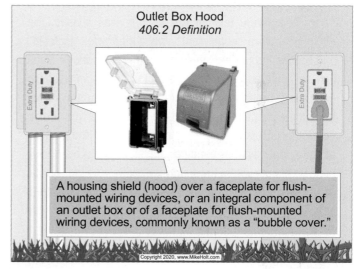

Outlet Box Hood
406.2 Definition

A housing shield (hood) over a faceplate for flush-mounted wiring devices, or an integral component of an outlet box or of a faceplate for flush-mounted wiring devices, commonly known as a "bubble cover."

Copyright 2020, www.MikeHolt.com

▶Figure 406–1

406.2 Definitions

The definitions in this section apply only within this article.

Child Care Facility. A building or portions thereof used for educational, supervision, or personal care services for five or more children seven years in age or less.

Outlet Box Hood. A housing shield (hood) over a faceplate for flush-mounted wiring devices, or an integral component of an outlet box or of a faceplate for flush-mounted wiring devices, commonly known as a "while in use" or "bubble" cover. ▶Figure 406–1

406.3 Receptacle Rating and Type

Language was added to prohibit the use of reconditioned receptacles, the text in (D) was clarified, and (D)(2) now says there must be a provision to connect a metal faceplate to the equipment grounding conductor.

Analysis

EXPANDED

406.3(A) Receptacles. Language has been added in several *Code* sections indicating that some types of equipment are not suitable for reconditioning. Some receptacles, such as pin and sleeve receptacles and single-pole locking-type connectors, are capable of being serviced in the field using replacement parts available as part of a listed kit. Such repair falls outside the scope of the Article 100 definition of "Reconditioned" and is permitted.

The same change was made in 406.7, Attachment Plugs, Cord Connectors, and Flanged Surface Devices.

CLARIFIED

406.3(D) Isolated Ground Receptacles. The parent text for this section was revised. The word "equipment" was added after "isolated" and before "grounding" to clarify that the conductor is not just an "isolated grounding conductor" but is an "isolated equipment grounding conductor." This conductor serves the same purpose as any other equipment grounding conductor but is electrically isolated back to the location of the supply system bonding jumper. It could be a main bonding jumper where the supply is directly from the service, or a system bonding jumper where the supply is from a separately derived system (transformer). Many of these systems have not been correctly installed creating a dangerous condition with no effective ground fault current path.

A second change was made clarifying that the purpose of this isolated EGC is to reduce electromagnetic interference for sensitive electronic equipment. The previous *NEC* said, "for the reduction of electrical noise" (electromagnetic interference) but the words "electrical noise" were deleted in favor of the more correct term of "electromagnetic interference."

CLARIFIED

406.3(D)(2) Ex Installation in Nonmetallic Boxes. The main text in (D)(2) requires that where a receptacle with an isolated equipment grounding conductor is installed at a nonmetallic box, the faceplate must be nonmetallic. The previous language was revised to require that the faceplate have a connection to the equipment grounding conductor.

This could be the isolated equipment grounding conductor that is used for the receptacle, or it could be a standard equipment grounding conductor. The intent is to ensure there is an effective ground-fault current path for any accidental phase conductor contact with the metal faceplate.

406.3 Receptacle Rating and Type

(A) Receptacles. Receptacles must be listed and marked with the manufacturer's name or identification and voltage and ampere ratings. Receptacles are not permitted to be reconditioned.

(D) Isolated Ground Receptacles. Receptacles of the isolated equipment grounding conductor type must be identified by an orange triangle marking on the face of the receptacle. ▶Figure 406–2

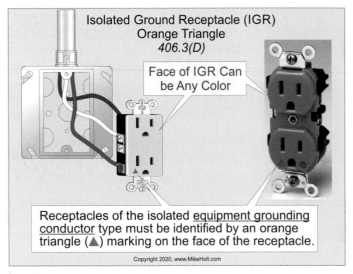

Isolated Ground Receptacle (IGR)
Orange Triangle
406.3(D)

Face of IGR Can be Any Color

Receptacles of the isolated equipment grounding conductor type must be identified by an orange triangle (▲) marking on the face of the receptacle.

Copyright 2020, www.MikeHolt.com

▶Figure 406–2

(1) Isolated ground receptacles must have the grounding contact of the receptacle connected to an insulated equipment grounding conductor installed with the circuit conductors, in accordance with 250.146(D). ▶Figure 406–3

Author's Comment:

▶ The word "isolated" might lead some to believe that this conductor does not need to be connected to the electrical grounding system. In fact, there have been many cases where people have just driven a ground rod locally thinking that attachment to it would isolate the ground! Maybe the addition of the word "equipment" will help correct these installation issues.

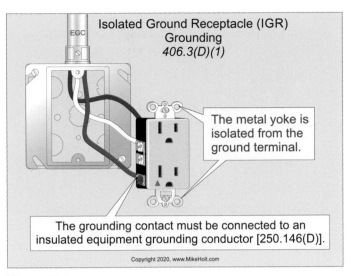

Isolated Ground Receptacle (IGR)
Grounding
406.3(D)(1)

The metal yoke is isolated from the ground terminal.

The grounding contact must be connected to an insulated equipment grounding conductor [250.146(D)].

Copyright 2020, www.MikeHolt.com

▶Figure 406–3

406.4 General Installation Requirements

Section 406.4(A) was revised to correlate with the rules in Article 210 and a new list item was added in (D).

Analysis

CLARIFIED

406.4(A) Grounding Type. The previous language could be read as conflicting with the rules in Article 210. It specified that all receptacles installed on 15A or 20A branch circuits be of the grounding type and only be installed on circuits of the voltage class and current for which they are rated. The rule in 210.21(B)(1) permits single receptacles with an ampere rating not less than that of the branch circuit.

This language effectively permits a single receptacle with an ampere rating greater than that of the branch circuit to be installed and conflicts with the language in this section that requires the branch circuit and receptacle ampere rating to be the same. To correct this issue, references to 210.21(B)(1) and to Tables 210.21(B)(2) and (B)(3) were added to this section.

NEW

406.4(D) Replacements. The new list item is for "Controlled Receptacles." This requires that where an automatically controlled receptacle is replaced it must be replaced with an "equivalently controlled receptacle."

Where automatic control is no longer required, the receptacle must be replaced with one that is not marked as required by 406.3(E). The intent here is that only receptacles controlled by an automatic means have this marking to avoid confusion to the user of the receptacles.

406.4 General Installation Requirements

(A) Grounding Type. Receptacles installed on 15A and 20A branch circuits must be of the grounding type, except as permitted for two-wire receptacle replacements as permitted in 406.4(D)(2). ▶Figure 406–4

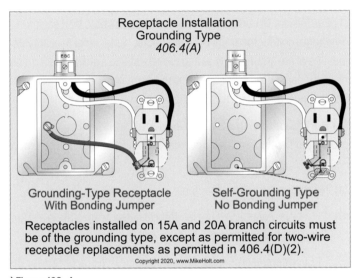

Receptacle Installation
Grounding Type
406.4(A)

Grounding-Type Receptacle
With Bonding Jumper

Self-Grounding Type
No Bonding Jumper

Receptacles installed on 15A and 20A branch circuits must be of the grounding type, except as permitted for two-wire receptacle replacements as permitted in 406.4(D)(2).

Copyright 2020, www.MikeHolt.com

▶Figure 406–4

Receptacles must be installed on circuits rated in accordance with Table 210.21(B)(2) for single receptacles and Table 210.21(B)(3) for two or more receptacles.

Table 210.21(B)(3) Receptacle Ratings	
Circuit Rating	**Receptacle Rating**
15A	15A
20A	15A or 20A
30A	30A
40A	40A or 50A
50A	50A

(C) Methods of Grounding. The equipment grounding conductor contacts of receptacles and cord connectors must be connected to the equipment grounding conductor of the circuit supplying the receptacle or cord connector.

Note: For installation requirements for the reduction of electromagnetic interference, see 250.146(D).

The branch-circuit wiring method must include or provide an equipment grounding conductor to which the equipment grounding conductor contacts of the receptacle or cord connector are connected.

Note No. 1: See 250.118 for acceptable grounding means.

Note No. 2: For extensions of existing branch circuits, see 250.130.

(D) Receptacle Replacement. If the receptacle to be replaced is in a location that requires AFCI and/or GFCI type receptacles, they must be installed at a readily accessible location.

(1) Equipment Grounding Conductor in Outlet Box. If an equipment grounding conductor exists in an outlet box, replacement receptacles must be of the grounding type and the receptacle's grounding terminal must be connected to the circuit equipment grounding conductor in accordance with 406.11.

(2) No Equipment Grounding Conductor in Box. If an equipment grounding conductor does not exist in the outlet box, replacement receptacles can be a:

(a) Nongrounding-type receptacle.

(b) GFCI-type receptacle if the receptacle or the cover plate is marked "No Equipment Ground." ▶Figure 406–5

(c) GFCI-protected grounding-type receptacle if the receptacle or the cover plate is marked "GFCI Protected" and "No Equipment Ground." ▶Figure 406–6

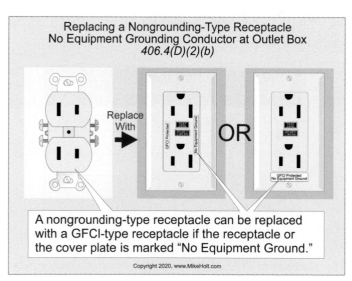

Replacing a Nongrounding-Type Receptacle
No Equipment Grounding Conductor at Outlet Box
406.4(D)(2)(b)

A nongrounding-type receptacle can be replaced with a GFCI-type receptacle if the receptacle or the cover plate is marked "No Equipment Ground."

Copyright 2020, www.MikeHolt.com

▶Figure 406–5

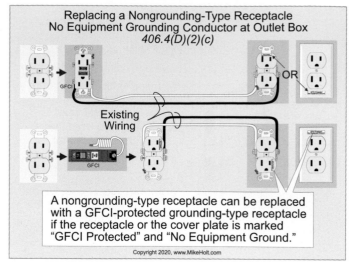

Replacing a Nongrounding-Type Receptacle
No Equipment Grounding Conductor at Outlet Box
406.4(D)(2)(c)

Existing Wiring

A nongrounding-type receptacle can be replaced with a GFCI-protected grounding-type receptacle if the receptacle or the cover plate is marked "GFCI Protected" and "No Equipment Ground."

Copyright 2020, www.MikeHolt.com

▶Figure 406–6

Author's Comment:

▶ GFCI protection functions properly on a 2-wire circuit without an equipment grounding conductor because the circuit's equipment grounding conductor serves no role in the operation of a GFCI device. See the Article 100 definition of "Ground-Fault Circuit Interrupter" in this textbook for more information. ▶Figure 406–7

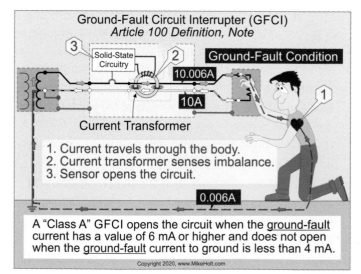

Ground-Fault Circuit Interrupter (GFCI)
Article 100 Definition, Note

Solid-State Circuitry

Ground-Fault Condition

10.006A
10A

Current Transformer

1. Current travels through the body.
2. Current transformer senses imbalance.
3. Sensor opens the circuit.

0.006A

A "Class A" GFCI opens the circuit when the ground-fault current has a value of 6 mA or higher and does not open when the ground-fault current to ground is less than 4 mA.

Copyright 2020, www.MikeHolt.com

▶Figure 406–7

> **⚠ Caution**
>
> The permission to replace nongrounding-type receptacles with GFCI-protected grounding-type receptacles does not apply to new receptacle outlets that extend from an existing outlet box that is not connected to an equipment grounding conductor. ▶Figure 406–8

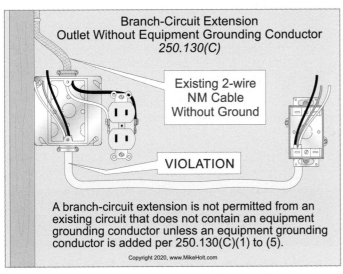

Branch-Circuit Extension
Outlet Without Equipment Grounding Conductor
250.130(C)

Existing 2-wire NM Cable Without Ground

VIOLATION

A branch-circuit extension is not permitted from an existing circuit that does not contain an equipment grounding conductor unless an equipment grounding conductor is added per 250.130(C)(1) to (5).

Copyright 2020, www.MikeHolt.com

▶Figure 406–8

Note 1: Some equipment or appliance manufacturers require the branch circuit to the equipment or appliance include an equipment grounding conductor.

Note 2 : See 250.114 for a list of cord-and-plug-connected equipment or appliances that require an equipment grounding conductor.

(3) GFCI Protection Required. When existing receptacles are replaced in locations where GFCI protection is required, the replacement receptacles must be GFCI protected.

Ex: Where the outlet box size will not permit the installation of the GFCI receptacle, a GFCI-protected grounding-type receptacle marked "GFCI Protected" and "No Equipment Ground" in accordance with 406.4(D) is permitted.

Author's Comment:

▸ See 210.8 for specific locations requiring GFCI-protection requirements.

▸ Where an *NEC* rule requires GFCI protection, it can be provided by either a GFCI circuit breaker, GFCI receptacle, or downstream of a feed-thru type GFCI receptacle.

(4) Arc-Fault Circuit Interrupters. When existing receptacle are replaced in locations where AFCI protection is required [210.12], the replacement receptacle(s) must be one of the following:

(1) A listed AFCI receptacle.

(2) A receptacle protected by a listed AFCI receptacle.

(3) A receptacle protected by an AFCI circuit breaker.

(5) Tamper-Resistant Receptacles. When existing receptacles are replaced in locations where tamper resistance is required [406.12], the replacement receptacle(s) must be listed tamper resistant.

(6) Weather-Resistant Receptacles. When existing receptacles are replaced in locations where weather resistance is required, replacement receptacles must be weather resistant in accordance with 406.9(A) and (B).

(7) Controlled Receptacles. Automatically controlled receptacles must be replaced with an equivalently controlled receptacle. If automatic control of the receptacle is no longer required, the replacement receptacle must not be marked in accordance with 406.3(E).

Author's Comment:

▸ Prior to the *Code* adding "replacement" rules, it stood to reason that any repair or replacement work would have to comply with the current *Code* rules. Now with specific rules, it appears that, that may no longer be the case.

406.5 Receptacle Mounting

Section 406.5(G) was revised into a two-item list format and new language in list item (2) was added.

Analysis

REORGANIZED **406.5(G)(1) Countertop and Work Surfaces.** List item (1) prohibits receptacles from being installed in a face-up position in or on countertop surfaces or work surfaces unless listed for those applications. This requirement was in the previous *NEC*.

406.5(G)(2) Under Sinks. List item (2) is new and is titled, "Under Sinks." This new language prohibits receptacles from being installed in a face-up position where they are installed under a sink. The area under the sink is subject to leaks that could result in a safety hazard, and the receptacle could be damaged by the debris that is also common in that area. In some cases, face-up receptacles were being installed in the bottom of the cabinet to serve dishwashers or disposals.

NEW

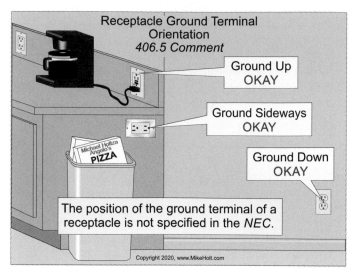

▶Figure 406–10

406.5 Receptacle Mounting

(G) Receptacle Orientation

(1) Countertop and Work Surfaces. Receptacles are not permitted to be installed in a face-up position in or on countertop surfaces or work surfaces unless listed for countertop surface or work surface applications. ▶Figure 406–9

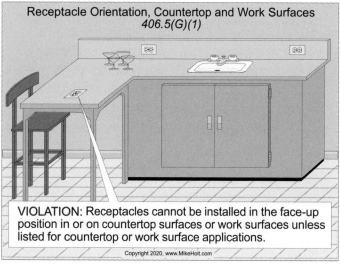

VIOLATION: Receptacles cannot be installed in the face-up position in or on countertop surfaces or work surfaces unless listed for countertop or work surface applications.

Copyright 2020, www.MikeHolt.com

▶Figure 406–9

(2) Under Sinks. Receptacles are not permitted to be installed in a face-up position in the area below a sink.

Author's Comment:

▶ The position of the ground terminal of a receptacle is not specified in the *NEC*. The ground terminal can be up, down, or to the side. Proposals to specify the mounting position of the ground terminal have been rejected throughout many *Code* revision cycles. ▶Figure 406–10

406.7 Attachment Plugs, Cord Connectors and Flanged Surface Devices

Additional language was added to say that reconditioned attachment plugs, cord connectors, and flanged surface devices are not permitted.

Analysis

EXPANDED Additional language has been added in several *Code* sections indicating that some types of equipment are not suitable for reconditioning. Some attachment plugs, cord connectors, and flanged surface devices may be capable of being serviced in the field using replacement parts available as part of a listed kit. Such repair falls outside the scope of the Article 100 definition of reconditioned and is permitted. This change was also made in 406.3 for receptacles.

406.7 Attachment Plugs and Flanged Surface Devices

Attachment plugs and flange inlets must be listed for the purpose and marked with the manufacturer's name or identification and voltage and ampere ratings.

(B) No Energized Parts. Attachment plugs must be installed so their prongs, blades, or pins are not energized unless inserted into an energized receptacle or flexible cord connector. ▶Figure 406–11

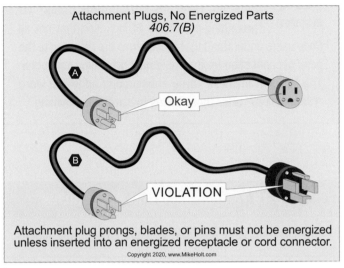

Attachment Plugs, No Energized Parts
406.7(B)

Okay

VIOLATION

Attachment plug prongs, blades, or pins must not be energized unless inserted into an energized receptacle or cord connector.

Copyright 2020, www.MikeHolt.com

▶Figure 406–11

(D) Flanged Surface Inlet. A flanged surface inlet must be installed so the prongs, blades, or pins are not permitted to be energized unless an energized flexible cord connector is inserted into it. ▶Figure 406–12

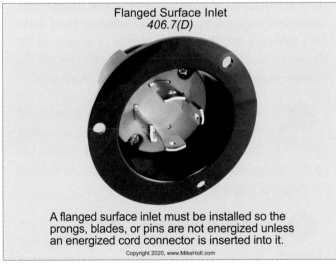

Flanged Surface Inlet
406.7(D)

A flanged surface inlet must be installed so the prongs, blades, or pins are not energized unless an energized cord connector is inserted into it.

Copyright 2020, www.MikeHolt.com

▶Figure 406–12

406.9 Receptacles in Damp or Wet Locations

The prohibited locations for receptacles in bathrooms were expanded and a new exception was added.

Analysis

EXPANDED **406.9(C) Bathtub and Shower Space.** The language in this section was revised to be much more specific and restrictive as to the permitted locations of receptacles in bathtub and shower spaces and prohibits receptacles from being installed within 3 ft horizontally and 8 ft vertically from the top of the bathtub rim or shower stall threshold. This distance matches that in 410.10(D) for luminaires in those spaces. The previous language only said that the receptacle could not be within or directly over a bathtub or shower stall. This now requires a specific distance from the tub or shower.

NEW **406.9(C) Ex Bathtub and Shower Space.** The exception recognizes that some bathrooms are just too small to be able to locate the receptacle 3 ft horizontally from the bathtub rim or shower stall threshold. It permits a receptacle to be located opposite the tub or shower on the farthest wall within the room, even where that location is less than 3 ft from the tub rim or shower stall threshold.

406.9 Receptacles in Damp or Wet Locations

Scan this QR code for a video of Mike explaining this topic; it's a sample from the videos that accompany this textbook.

(C) Bathtub and Shower Space. Receptacles are not permitted to be installed within a zone measured 3 ft horizontally and 8 ft vertically from the top of the bathtub rim or shower stall threshold. The zone is all-encompassing and includes the space directly over the tub or shower stall. ▶Figure 406–13

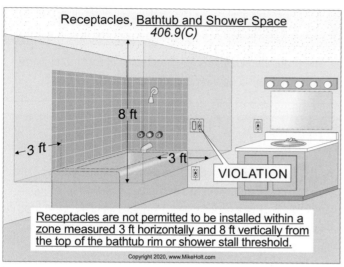

Receptacles, Bathtub and Shower Space
406.9(C)

8 ft

3 ft

3 ft

VIOLATION

Receptacles are not permitted to be installed within a zone measured 3 ft horizontally and 8 ft vertically from the top of the bathtub rim or shower stall threshold.

Copyright 2020, www.MikeHolt.com

▶Figure 406–13

Ex to (C): Ex to (C): In bathrooms with less than the required zone, a receptacle is permitted on the furthest wall opposite the bathtub rim or shower stall threshold. ▶Figure 406–14

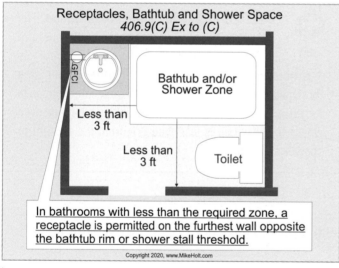

Receptacles, Bathtub and Shower Space
406.9(C) Ex to (C)

GFCI

Bathtub and/or
Shower Zone

Less than
3 ft

Less than
3 ft

Toilet

In bathrooms with less than the required zone, a receptacle is permitted on the furthest wall opposite the bathtub rim or shower stall threshold.

Copyright 2020, www.MikeHolt.com

▶Figure 406–14

406.10 Grounding-Type Receptacles, Adapters, Cord Connectors, and Attachment Plugs

Three subsection titles were revised.

Analysis

CLARIFIED **406.10(A), (B), and (D).** These three subsections all refer to "grounding poles" or "grounding-pole." The PI indicated that not all *Code* users understand that these terms are referring to the point of connection for the equipment grounding conductor. The revision in these three subsections adds the word "(Connection)" after those terms to clarify the meaning.

406.12 Tamper-Resistant Receptacles

Four list items were modified, and one list item was added.

Analysis

EXPANDED **406.12(1) Dwelling Units.** Additional language was added to this list item that applies to dwelling units to clarify that tamper resistant receptacles are required in attached or detached garages and accessory buildings, as well as in the dwelling unit itself. The reference to 210.52 was intended to require the TR receptacles in these areas, but many *Code* users did not understand that, so specific language was added here.

EXPANDED **406.12(2) Guestrooms.** The requirement for TR in hotels and motels was expanded to include the common areas of hotels and motels. The previous requirement only applied to the receptacles installed in the guest rooms or guest suites.

EXPANDED **406.12(4) Preschools.** The tamper resistant requirement for educational facilities was expanded. The previous rule required tamper-resistant receptacles in preschool and elementary educational facilities. The word "elementary" was deleted. The deletion of that word now makes the tamper resistant requirement apply to high schools, colleges, and universities as well as elementary educational facilities. The substantiation said, "With many facilities being built and used as 'multi-use,' it is difficult to determine what age group of student will be utilizing the space.

The language would be easier to enforce and not be a debatable issue." This requirement now applies to all 15A and 20A, 125V and 250V receptacles installed in all locations in all educational facilities.

 EDITED **406.12(7) Dormitory Units.** The change in this list item was just from the term "dormitories" to the defined term of "dormitory units." There is no change in the actual requirements.

NEW **406.12(8) Assisted Living Facilities.** This new requirement specifies that tamper-resistant receptacles must be installed in assisted living facilities. This was added because children may be present at these locations visiting grandparents.

▶Figure 406–15

406.12 Tamper-Resistant Receptacles

Scan this QR code for a video of Mike explaining this topic; it's a sample from the videos that accompany this textbook.

Nonlocking-type 15A and 20A receptacles in the following areas must be tamper resistant "TR":

Author's Comment:

▸ Inserting an object into one slot of a tamper-resistant receptacle does not open the internal shutter mechanism. Simultaneous pressure applied to the polarized slots is required to insert the plug. ▶Figure 406–15

(1) Dwelling units, including attached and detached garages and accessory buildings, and common areas of multifamily dwellings specified in 210.52. ▶Figure 406–16

(2) Hotel and motel guest rooms and guest suites, and their common areas.

(3) Childcare facilities.

Author's Comment:

▸ A childcare facility is a building or portions thereof used for educational, supervision, or personal care services for five or more children seven years in age or less [406.2].

(4) Preschools and education facilities.

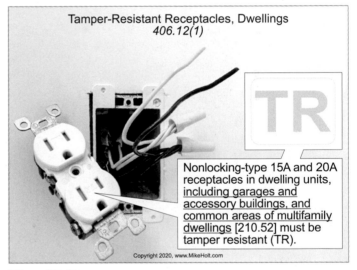
▶Figure 406–16

Author's Comment:

▸ In response to a Public Comment to restore the word "elementary" to this section, the CMP said: "Elementary was removed in the first revision due to the ambiguity as to what age group of children will occupy the space. High school and college facilities also warrant this protection."

(5) Business offices, corridors, waiting rooms and the like in clinics, medical and dental offices, and outpatient facilities.

(6) Places of awaiting transportation, gymnasiums, skating rinks, and auditoriums.

(7) Dormitory units.

(8) Assisted living facilities.

Ex: Receptacles in the following locations are not required to be tamper resistant:

    (1) Receptacles located more than 5½ ft above the floor.

    (2) Receptacles that are part of a luminaire or appliance.

    (3) A receptacle located within dedicated space for an appliance that in normal use is not easily moved.

    (4) Where nongrounding receptacles are installed as permitted in 406.4(D)(2)(a)8.

SWITCHBOARDS AND PANELBOARDS

Introduction to Article 408—Switchboards and Panelboards

Article 408 covers the specific requirements for switchboards and panelboards that control power and lighting circuits. As you study this article, keep these key points in mind:

▸ Perhaps the most important objective of Article 408 is to ensure that the installation will prevent contact between current-carrying conductors and people or equipment.

▸ The circuit directory of a panelboard must clearly identify the purpose or use of each circuit that originates in the panelboard.

▸ You must understand the detailed grounding and overcurrent protection requirements for panelboards.

408.3 Arrangement of Busbars and Conductors

The revisions to this section were minor and included no technical changes.

The access to load terminals without being exposed to energized live parts is only an issue with switchboards and switchgear so panelboards were removed from this rule. The prescriptive requirement in this section was deleted and a reference to a new subsection (C) in 408.18 took its place.

Analysis

 CLARIFIED **408.3(A)(2) Conductors and Busbars, Same Vertical Section.** This rule was relocated to 230.62(C) and expanded because there are other types of equipment that are used as service equipment, such as disconnects and MCCs, that have the same hazard as found on the service equipment covered by Article 408.

 CLARIFIED **408.3(D) Terminals.** This section was revised and now excludes panelboards from the requirement, and a reference to the new subsection 408.18(C) was added to address required rear and/or side access for switchboards and panelboards. The rule prohibited the design of the equipment from requiring an installer to reach across an uninsulated bus to make neutral or equipment grounding conductor connections.

408.4 Field Identification

A change in subsection (A) now permits the required circuit directory to be located adjacent to the panel.

Analysis

 CLARIFIED **408.4(A) Circuit Directory or Circuit Identification.** This section requires that each circuit be clearly identified with enough detail that it can be distinguished from all other circuits. The level of detail required to accomplish this often requires more space than is available in or on the panel itself, as required by the 2017 *NEC*.

408.4 Field Identification

(A) Circuit Directory or Circuit Identification. Circuits and circuit modifications must be legibly identified as to their clear, evident, and specific purpose. ▶Figure 408–1

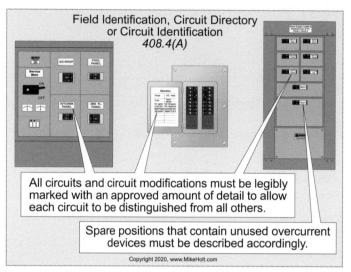

▶Figure 408–1

Identification must include an approved amount of detail to allow each circuit to be distinguished from all others, and the identification must be on a circuit directory located on the face or inside of, <u>or in an approved location adjacent to,</u> the door of the panelboard. See 110.22. ▶Figure 408–2

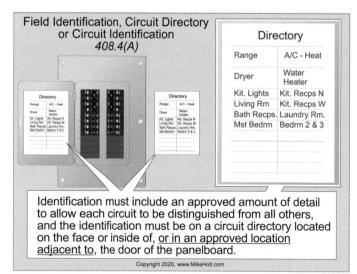

▶Figure 408–2

Circuit identification must not be based on transient conditions of occupancy, such as "Dad's Office." ▶Figure 408–3

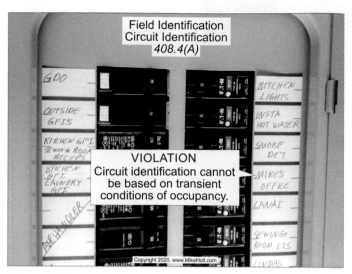

▶Figure 408–3

Author's Comment:

▶ This revision permits the directory to be located at an approved location adjacent to the panel. "Approved" makes the location up to the AHJ, but the intent is that a directory that, (for whatever reason), is not in or on the panel, be located close enough that it is obvious that it is the directory for that panel.

408.6 Short-Circuit Current Rating

This new rule requires switchboards, switchgear, and panelboards to have a short-current rating not less than the available fault current, and the available fault current must be field marked on the enclosure at the point of supply.

Analysis

NEW This new section has two requirements. First it requires that the switchboard, switchgear, or panelboard have a short-circuit current rating not less than the fault current. This is not really a new requirement as it is required by 110.9 and 110.10, but in the past few *Code* cycles it has been repeated in various *NEC* articles. The second requirement is that the available fault current and the date of calculation be field marked on the enclosure at the point of supply and that the marking comply with 110.21(B)(3).

408.6 Short-Circuit Current Rating

Switchboards and panelboards must have a short-circuit current rating of not less than the available fault current. In other than one and two-family dwellings, the available fault current and the date the calculation was performed must be field marked on the enclosure at the point of supply. The marking must be of sufficient durability to withstand the environment involved in accordance with 110.21(B)(3).

Author's Comment:

▸ The available fault current marking requirement of this rule does not apply to equipment in one- and two-family dwellings.

408.8 Reconditioning of Equipment

This new section addresses the reconditioning of panelboards, switchboards, and switchgear.

Analysis

NEW This recognizes that panelboards, switchboards, and switchgear can be successfully reconditioned and returned to service under restrictive conditions. It requires the use of design qualified parts that are verified under the product standards and the work must be in accordance with any instructions provided by the manufacturer. It also requires that equipment that has been damaged by fire, products of combustion (smoke), or water must be specifically evaluated by its manufacturer or a qualified testing laboratory prior to being returned to service.

NEW **408.8(A) Panelboards.** This new rule indicates that a panelboard may not be reconditioned, but it can be replaced within an existing enclosure if it is listed for that specific enclosure. If the available fault current is greater than 10,000A and the panelboard is not listed for the enclosure, it must be field labeled and existing listing marks that pertain to the panelboard must be removed.

This will permit the replacement of many obsolete dwelling unit and small commercial unit panelboards with one that is not identical to the original.

NEW **408.8(B) Switchboards and Switchgear.** Reconditioned switchboards or switchgear must be listed, or field labeled, as reconditioned. Any previously applied listing marks within the portions that have been reconditioned must be removed.

NEW **408.8(C) Connections Reconditioning of Equipment.** This new subsection addresses side and rear access requirements where needed. Since this requirement is in Part II of the article, it only applies to switchboards and switchgear.

Part III contains the requirements for panelboards. The parent text requires each section of equipment requiring side or rear access to make field connections be so marked by the manufacturer. Side and/or rear access, if required, must comply with 110.26. In addition, load terminals must comply with 408.18(C)(1), (C)(2) or (C)(3) as follows:

NEW **408.8(C)(1) Equipment Grounding Conductors.** Load terminals for field wiring of equipment grounding conductors are required to be located so it is not necessary to reach across uninsulated ungrounded conductors to make the connection.

NEW **408.8(C)(2) Grounded Circuit Conductors.** This subsection has two paragraphs. The first addresses the case where there are multiple branch or feeder grounded circuit conductors grouped together in a single location. This part of the rule requires these terminations to be located so it is not necessary to reach across an uninsulated ungrounded bus, energized or not, to make the grounded conductor connection. The second paragraph is for where there is only one branch or feeder grounded conductor load terminal grouped with its associated ungrounded load terminals. This requires the grounded conductor terminal to be located so one does not have to reach across any uninsulated bus, including another branch or feeder bus, to make the connection.

NEW **408.8(C)(3) Ungrounded Conductors.** The load terminals for ungrounded conductors must be located so it is unnecessary to reach across an uninsulated bus to make the connections. The rule specifies that a bus on the line side of service, branch, or feeder disconnects is considered energized with respect to the load side.

• • •

This change is really to provide access to the sides and the back of switchboards and switchgear where such access is necessary to safely make wiring connections. CMP-9 was made aware of equipment designs that required installers to reach across busbars to make some connections, including to equipment grounding conductors, where side or rear access to the equipment was not provided. Such equipment did not comply with the requirements that were in 408.3(D) in the 2017 *NEC*. The change makes such equipment compliant by requiring side or rear access for the terminations where such is required in order to make the wiring connections without reaching across energized parts.

408.8 Reconditioning of Equipment

The reconditioning process must use design qualified parts verified under applicable standards and be performed in accordance with any instructions provided by the manufacturer. If equipment has been damaged by fire, products of combustion, or water, it must be specifically evaluated by its manufacturer or a qualified testing laboratory prior to being returned to service.

(A) Panelboards. Panelboards are not permitted to be reconditioned, but replacement of a panelboard within an enclosure is permitted. In the event the replacement panelboard has not been listed for the specific enclosure and the available fault current is greater than 10,000A, the completed work must be field labeled, and previously applied listing marks on the cabinet must be removed.

(B) Switchboards. Switchboards, or sections of switchboards can be reconditioned. Reconditioned switchboards must be listed, or field labeled as reconditioned, and previously applied listing marks must be removed.

Author's Comment:

▶ The language "field labeled" as used in these subsections, should be replaced with "field evaluated and labeled" as was done in most other rules for field evaluation.

▶ The panelboard is only what is often called in the field the "guts." Switchboards and switchgear are standalone equipment which are permitted to be serviced and or maintained on site.

408.18 Clearances

A new subsection was added, along with two new list items that address side and rear access requirements to switchgear and panelboards.

Analysis

NEW

408.18(C) Connections. Since this requirement is in Part II of the article, it only applies to switchboards and switchgear. Part III contains the requirements for panelboards.

The parent text requires that each section of equipment requiring side or rear access to make field connections be so marked by the manufacturer. Side and/or rear access, if required, must comply with 110.26. In addition, load terminals must comply with 408.18(C)(1), (C)(2) or (C)(3).

Some equipment designs where side or rear access to the equipment is not provided, requires installers to reach across busbars to make some connections, including those to equipment grounding conductors. Such equipment did not comply with the requirements that were in 408.3(D) in the 2017 *Code*. This change makes such equipment compliant by requiring side or rear access for making the terminations without having to reach across energized parts.

408.18 Clearances

(C) Connections. Each section of equipment that requires rear or side access to make field connections must be so marked by the manufacturer on the front of the equipment. Section openings requiring rear or side access must comply with the workspace and access to workspace requirements of 110.26.

Author's Comment:

▶ The addition of this section goes a long way to providing much safer access to the sides and the back of switchboards and switchgear where such access may be necessary to make wiring connections. This addition exemplifies the NFPA's intent and continued efforts to reduce exposure and risk to unnecessary hazards to keep electrical workers safe.

408.23 Power Monitoring and Energy Management Equipment

This new section references the requirements of 312.8(B).

Analysis

NEW This new section indicates that the requirements of 312.8(B) apply to the installation of power monitoring and energy management equipment in a panelboard cabinet. However, the same issues exist with switchboards and switchgear when installing power monitoring or energy management equipment in that equipment.

408.36 Overcurrent Protection

The exception to this rule that permitted panelboards not to have individual protection where used as service equipment with multiple service disconnects was deleted.

Analysis

DELETED 408.36 Overcurrent Protection, Exceptions. This deletion correlates this section with the changes made in 230.71. The change there no longer permits multiple service disconnects within a single enclosure. The exception is no longer needed as it permits something that 230.71 now prohibits. The two remaining exceptions (that were exceptions 2 and 3) were renumbered as 1 and 2.

The renumbered Exception No. 1 for isolated equipment grounding conductors, was revised to clarify that isolated equipment grounding conductors for feeders or branch circuits are permitted to pass through the panelboard without a connection to the equipment grounding terminal bar in the panel.

408.43 Panelboard Orientation

This new section prohibits a panelboard from being installed in a face-up position.

Analysis

NEW Installation of a panelboard in the face-up position increases the likelihood that contaminants will accumulate on the breakers and the panelboard bussing thereby creating a hazard. Such an installation also creates an issue with the application of the rules of 110.26 as they weren't written to cover a panelboard installed in the face-up position.

408.43 Panelboard Orientation

Panelboards are not permitted to be installed in the face-up position.

Author's Comment:

▸ The Code-Making Panel stated that this new limitation does not prohibit "mounting the panelboard in a horizontal face-down position." Interesting! However, 240.33 requires that enclosures for overcurrent devices be installed in the vertical position.

LUMINAIRES, LAMPHOLDERS, AND LAMPS

Introduction to Article 410—Luminaires, Lampholders, and Lamps

This article covers luminaires, lamps, decorative lighting products, and lighting for temporary seasonal and holiday use. Even though Article 410 is highly detailed, it is broken down into 16 parts. The first five are sequential, and apply to all luminaires, and lamps:

- Part I. General
- Part II. Locations
- Part III. Outlet Boxes and Covers
- Part IV. Supports
- Part V. Equipment Grounding Conductors

The first five parts contain mostly mechanical information and are not hard to follow or absorb. Part VI, Wiring, ends the sequence. The seventh, ninth, and tenth parts provide requirements for manufacturers to follow—use only equipment that conforms to these requirements. Part VIII provides requirements for installing lampholders. The rest of Article 410 addresses specific types of lighting. Spaces dedicated to the cultivation and growth of agricultural products, ("hot houses" etc.), that reproduce the natural effects of sunlight and seasonal temperature may present unique conditions. Additional requirements are addressed in the Horticultural Part XVI.

Author's Comment:

▸ Article 411 addresses "Low-Voltage Lighting" which are lighting systems and their associated components that operate at no more than 30V alternating current, or 60V direct current.

410.2 Definitions

The name of this definition was changed from "closet storage space" to "clothes closet storage space."

Analysis

CLARIFIED

Clothes Closet Storage Space. The definition and its accompanying figure were revised to specify that the definition only applies to clothes closets. The substantiation indicated that the field data that resulted in 410.16 only involved clothes closets. The panel also stated that this revision could necessitate research into other types of closet space. This is not a change in any installation requirement as the rules in this section only apply to clothes closets; it just makes the definition and the figure match the title.

410.2 Definitions

Clothes Closet Storage Space. This is defined as a volume bounded by the sides and back closet walls, extending from the closet floor vertically to a height of 6 ft or the highest clothes-hanging rod at a horizontal distance of 2 ft from the sides and back of the closet walls. Clothes closet storage space continues vertically to the closet ceiling for a distance of 1 ft or the width of the shelf, whichever is greater. ▶Figure 410–1

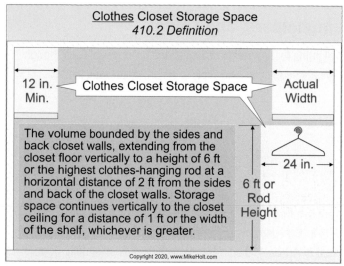

▶Figure 410–1

Author's Comment:

▸ There are countless instances where a space labeled "closet" is used for anything but clothes and is of sufficient size to offer the required working space about the equipment. The fact that a space has the word "closet" in its name, ("Utility Closet" for example), doesn't preclude it from containing electrical equipment.

▸ In case you didn't notice the absence of punctuation, this definition consists of approximately 125 words in one sentence, perhaps the longest sentence in the *Code*. Take a breath and do not get lost when reading it!

410.7 Reconditioned Equipment

This new rule prohibits the use of reconditioned luminaires, lampholders, and retrofit kits.

Analysis

 NEW Based on the definition of "reconditioned," the replacement of parts such as the lampholder or a ballast is not considered reconditioning and such repairs are permitted. The language in this new section also says that installing a retrofit kit in a luminaire is not to be considered as reconditioning that luminaire.

410.7 Reconditioned Equipment

Luminaires, lampholders, and retrofit kits are permitted to be reconditioned. If a retrofit kit is installed in a luminaire in accordance with the installation instructions, the retrofitted luminaire is not considered reconditioned.

410.10 Luminaires in Specific Locations

Subsection (D) was revised into a list format with parent text. No technical changes were made, but the requirements for luminaires in the shower area were clarified.

Analysis

 CLARIFIED **410.10(D) Bathtub and Shower Areas.** This section indicates that luminaires installed in a bathtub or shower area must meet all the requirements of the section, and that a luminaire subject to shower spray must be marked as suitable for wet locations.

410.10 Luminaires in Specific Locations

(D) Bathtub and Shower Areas. A luminaire installed in a bathtub or shower area must meet all of the following requirements:

(1) No part of chain-, cable-, or cord-suspended luminaires, track luminaires, or ceiling paddle fans can be located within 3 ft horizontally and 8 ft vertically from the top of the bathtub rim or shower stall threshold. ▶Figure 410–2

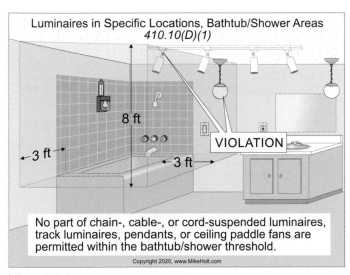

Luminaires in Specific Locations, Bathtub/Shower Areas
410.10(D)(1)

8 ft

3 ft

3 ft

VIOLATION

No part of chain-, cable-, or cord-suspended luminaires, track luminaires, pendants, or ceiling paddle fans are permitted within the bathtub/shower threshold.

Copyright 2020, www.MikeHolt.com

▶Figure 410–2

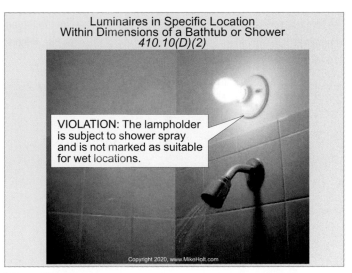

Luminaires in Specific Location
Within Dimensions of a Bathtub or Shower
410.10(D)(2)

VIOLATION: The lampholder is subject to shower spray and is not marked as suitable for wet locations.

Copyright 2020, www.MikeHolt.com

▶Figure 410–4

(2) Luminaires located within the outside dimensions of a bathtub or shower to a height of 8 ft from the top of the bathtub rim or shower threshold must be marked for damp locations or marked <u>suitable</u> for wet locations. Where subject to shower spray, the luminaires must be marked <u>suitable</u> for wet locations. ▶Figure 410–3 and ▶Figure 410–4

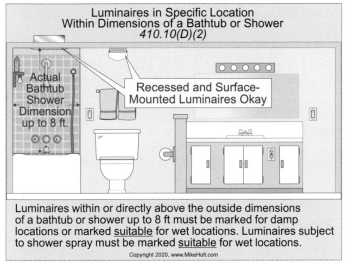

Luminaires in Specific Location
Within Dimensions of a Bathtub or Shower
410.10(D)(2)

Actual Bathtub Shower Dimension up to 8 ft.

Recessed and Surface-Mounted Luminaires Okay

Luminaires within or directly above the outside dimensions of a bathtub or shower up to 8 ft must be marked for damp locations or marked <u>suitable</u> for wet locations. Luminaires subject to shower spray must be marked <u>suitable</u> for wet locations.

Copyright 2020, www.MikeHolt.com

▶Figure 410–3

Author's Comment:

▶ The previous *Code* language actually required that the luminaire be marked "wet locations where subject to shower spray." There is no such marking on any luminaire.

410.16 Luminaires in Clothes Closets

The word "closet" was changed to "clothes closet" throughout this section.

Analysis

CLARIFIED The title already included the word "clothes," but to avoid confusion it was added in all locations in the section. This makes it clear that these rules for the location and type of luminaires in closets, apply only where that closet is primarily used for the storage of clothes.

410.16 Luminaires in Clothes Closets

(A) Luminaire Types Permitted. Only the following types of luminaires are permitted in a <u>clothes</u> closet:

(1) Surface or recessed incandescent or LED luminaires with an enclosed light source.

(2) Surface or recessed fluorescent luminaires.

(3) Surface-mounted or recessed LED luminaires identified for use within the <u>clothes</u> closet storage space.

(B) Luminaire Types Not Permitted. Incandescent and pendant-type luminaires <u>or</u> lampholders are not permitted in a <u>clothes</u> closet. ▶Figure 410–5

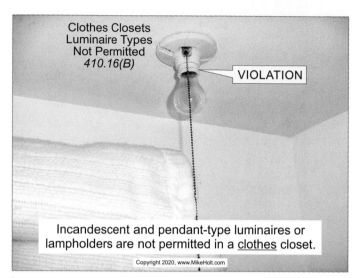

▶Figure 410–5

(C) Installation of Luminaires. Luminaires must maintain a minimum clearance from the <u>clothes</u> closet storage space as follows:

(1) 12 in. for surface-mounted incandescent or LED luminaires with an enclosed light source. ▶Figure 410–6

(2) 6 in. for surface-mounted fluorescent luminaires.

(3) 6 in. for recessed incandescent or LED luminaires with an enclosed light source. ▶Figure 410–7

(4) 6 in. for recessed fluorescent luminaires.

(5) Surface-mounted fluorescent or LED luminaires are permitted within the <u>clothes</u> closet storage space if identified for this use. ▶Figure 410–8

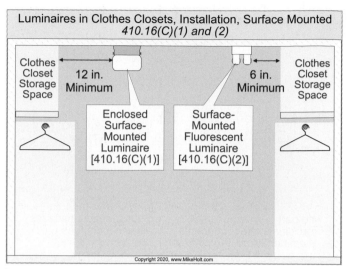

▶Figure 410–6

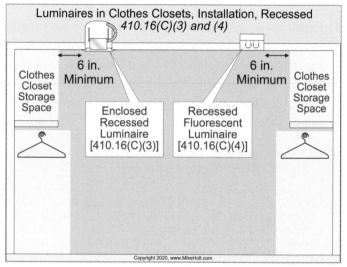

▶Figure 410–7

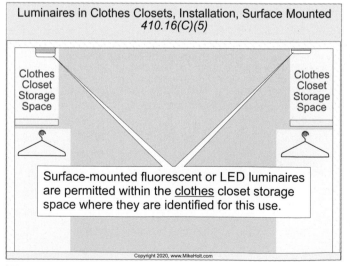

▶Figure 410–8

410.22 Outlet Boxes to Be Covered

Additional wording clarifies that the entire opening around a lighting outlet box must be covered.

Analysis

CLARIFIED The previous *Code* specified that an outlet box must be provided with a cover, unless covered by means of a canopy, lampholder, receptacle, or similar device. The following words were added, "that covers the box or is provided with a faceplate." This recognizes that receptacles alone, without a faceplate, are not enough to cover the outlet box opening and acts to require a faceplate.

410.22 Outlet Boxes to be Covered

Outlet boxes for luminaires must be covered with a luminaire or lampholder <u>that covers the box or is provided with a faceplate.</u> See 314.25. ▶Figure 410–9

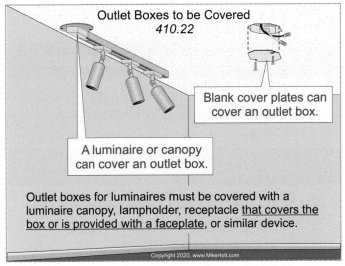

Outlet Boxes to be Covered
410.22

Blank cover plates can cover an outlet box.

A luminaire or canopy can cover an outlet box.

Outlet boxes for luminaires must be covered with a luminaire canopy, lampholder, receptacle <u>that covers the box or is provided with a faceplate</u>, or similar device.

Copyright 2020, www.MikeHolt.com

▶Figure 410–9

410.36 Means of Support

The title of this section was revised, the rule was reorganized into a list format, and a reference to 314.27(E) was added.

Analysis

EXPANDED **410.36(A) Luminaires Supported by Outlet Boxes.** The charging text in (A), and the first list item are unchanged from the previous *NEC*. The second list item was needed to permit luminaires to be supported by a separable attachment fitting as covered in 314.27(E). That is a new device that was added in the 2017 *Code*, and this change permits such a device to provide the required support for a luminaire.

The third list item was added to specify that outlets boxes complying with 314.27(E) must be considered as lighting outlets and are permitted to be used to satisfy the requirements of 210.70(A), (B), and (C). The separable attachment fitting is a receptacle outlet based on the language in 314.27(E) and this new language makes it clear that these devices are permitted to be installed as lighting outlets.

410.36 Means of Support

(A) Luminaires Supported by Outlet Boxes. <u>Luminaires are permitted to be supported by outlet boxes or fittings installed as required by 314.23 and must comply with:</u>

(1) <u>The outlet boxes or fittings must comply with 314.27(A).</u>

(2) <u>Luminaires can be supported in accordance with 314.27(E).</u>

(3) <u>Outlet boxes complying with 314.27(E) are considered lighting outlets as required by 210.70(A), (B), and (C).</u>

410.40 General

Revisions were made to require lighting and lighting equipment to be grounded by being connected to an equipment grounding conductor.

**Luminaires
Equipment Grounding Conductor
410.44**

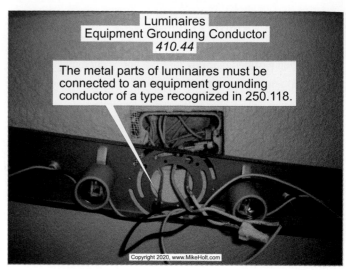

The metal parts of luminaires must be connected to an equipment grounding conductor of a type recognized in 250.118.

▶Figure 410–10

Analysis

CLARIFIED

The intent of this rule is to provide an effective ground-fault current path which is accomplished by a connection to an equipment grounding conductor. This type of correction is being made in many sections of the *Code* as part of an ongoing process.

410.40 General

Luminaires and lighting equipment must be <u>connected to the circuit equipment grounding conductor</u> as required in Article 250 and Part V of this article.

410.44 Methods of Grounding, Exceptions

An exception was deleted and the remaining two were revised.

Analysis

CLARIFIED

This new language simplifies the requirements for protection against electric shock injury associated with luminaires having accessible conductive surfaces. Exception No.1 was deleted since there is obviously no need for a requirement for a luminaire with no accessible conductive parts, or "made of insulating material" to be grounded so there is no reason to exempt it from grounding. The same reasoning is what prompted the revision of Exception No. 2. to indicate that replacement luminaires may be connected to an equipment grounding conductor in the same manner as replacement receptacles. Exception No. 3 was also revised to permit replacement luminaires not to have a connection to an equipment grounding conductor if there are no "exposed conductive parts."

410.44 Equipment Grounding Conductor

The metal parts of luminaires must be connected to an equipment grounding conductor of a type recognized in 250.118. ▶Figure 410–10

Ex 2: 1: Replacement luminaires are permitted to connect an equipment grounding conductor in the same manner as replacement receptacles in compliance with 250.130(C). The luminaire must then comply with 410.42.

Ex 2: Where no equipment grounding conductor exists at the outlet, replacement luminaires that are GFCI protected <u>or do not have exposed conductive parts</u> are not required to be connected to an equipment grounding conductor.

410.116 Clearance and Installation

A new subsection (C) was added to cover the installation and clearances of luminaires in fire-resistant construction.

Analysis

NEW

410.116(C) Installation in Fire-Resistive Construction. The new subsection covers the requirements for installing luminaires in fire-resistive construction. The parent text prohibits luminaires marked "for use in nonfire-rated installations" from being used in fire-rated installations. It also requires that luminaires recessed in fire-resistant materials must comply with one of the three list items.

410.116 Clearance and Installation

(C) <u>Installation in Fire-Resistant Construction.</u> Luminaires marked "FOR USE IN NON-FIRE-RATED INSTALLATIONS" must not be used in fire-rated installations. Where a luminaire is recessed in fire-resistant material in a building of fire-resistant construction, the recessed luminaire must satisfy one of the following:

(1) <u>The recessed luminaire must be listed for use in a fire resistance-rated construction.</u>

(2) <u>The recessed luminaire must be installed in or used with a luminaire enclosure that is listed for use in a fire resistance-rated construction.</u>

(3) <u>The recessed luminaire must be listed and installed in accordance with a tested fire resistance-rated assembly.</u>

<u>When a tested fire resistance–rated assembly allows the installation of a recessed fluorescent luminaire, a recessed LED luminaire of comparable construction is permitted.</u>

410.118 Access to Other Boxes

This new section prohibits the use of luminaires recessed in ceilings, floors, or walls as the access point for outlet, pull, or junction boxes or conduit bodies, unless the box is an integral part of the listed luminaire.

Analysis

NEW This is to prevent the luminaire from having to be removed to access boxes or conduit bodies. As written, it even applies to the box that supplies the luminaire unless the box is an actual part of the luminaire. While can lights often have integral boxes, other types of luminaires installed in "hard ceilings" might not. One example is a troffer type luminaire installed in a plaster or drywall ceiling. These are typically installed with a flexible connection from a junction box within reach from the opening when the luminaire is removed. That practice is prohibited by this new rule.

410.118 Access to Other Boxes

Luminaires recessed in ceilings, floors, or walls must not be used to access outlet, pull, or junction boxes or conduit bodies, unless the box or conduit body is an integral part of the listed luminaire.

Part XVI Special Provisions for Horticultural Lighting Equipment

A new "Part XVI" was added to specifically address the unique requirements for horticultural lighting equipment.

Analysis

NEW Indoor growing facilities have been around for a very long time. Perhaps better known as "hot houses," they have always made freshly grown produce available regardless of seasonal climate changes. This new part to the *NEC* was added to address the increasing numbers of indoor plant growing facilities and some of the unique requirements for the specialized types of lighting that may be required.

Part XVI. Special Provisions for Horticultural Lighting Equipment

410.170 General

Luminaires complying with Parts I, II, III, IV, V, VI, VII, IX, X, XI, and XII of this article are permitted to be used for horticultural lighting. Part XVI additionally applies to lighting equipment specifically identified for horticultural use.

Note: Lighting equipment identified for horticultural use is designed to provide a spectral characteristic needed for the growth of plants and can also provide supplemental general illumination within the growing environment.

410.172 Listing

Lighting equipment identified for horticultural use must be listed.

410.174 Installation and Use

Lighting equipment identified for horticultural use must be installed and used in accordance with the manufacturer's installation instructions and installation markings on the equipment.

410.176 Locations Not Permitted

(A) General Lighting. Lighting equipment identified for horticultural use is not permitted for general illumination unless such use is indicated in the manufacturer's instructions.

(B) Installed Location. Lighting equipment identified for horticultural use is not permitted to be installed where it is likely to be subject to physical damage or where concealed.

410.178 Flexible Cord

Flexible cord is only permitted when provided as part of listed lighting equipment identified for horticultural use for any of the following applications:

(1) Connecting a horticultural lighting luminaire directly to a branch-circuit outlet

(2) Interconnecting horticultural lighting luminaires

(3) Connecting a horticultural lighting luminaire to a remote power source

Note: Remote power sources include LED drivers, fluorescent ballasts, and HID ballasts.

410.180 Fittings and Connectors

Fittings and connectors attached to flexible cords must be provided as part of a listed horticultural lighting equipment device or system and be installed in accordance with the instructions provided as part of that listing.

410.182 Grounding

to the circuit equipment grounding conductor as required in Article 250 and Part V of this article.

410.184 Ground-Fault Circuit-Interrupter Protection

Lighting equipment identified for horticultural use employing flexible cord(s) must be supplied by GFCI-protected lighting outlets.

410.186 Support

Special fittings identified for support of horticultural lighting equipment must be installed and must be used in accordance with the installation instructions provided and be securely fastened.

ARTICLE 411

LOW-VOLTAGE LIGHTING

Introduction to Article 411—Low-Voltage Lighting

Article 411 provides the requirements for indoor or outdoor low-voltage lighting systems and their components. They are often found in such applications as landscaping, kitchen under cabinet lighting, commercial display lighting, and museums. Do not let the half-page size of Article 411 give you the impression that low-voltage lighting is not something you need to be concerned about. These systems are limited in their voltage, but the current rating can be as high as 25A, which means they are still a potential source of fire and electrical shock. Installation of these systems is widespread and becoming more so.

411.4 Listing Required

The parent text was expanded to prohibit the reconditioning of listed low-voltage lighting systems, or a low-voltage lighting system assembled from listed parts. In addition, the language in (B) was revised.

Analysis

EXPANDED

411.4 Listing Required. As with luminaires in Article 410, low-voltage lighting equipment is not permitted to be reconditioned. That does not prohibit the repair of such lighting systems with OEM parts.

CLARIFIED

411.4(B) Assembly of Listed Parts. Listed parts for low-voltage lighting equipment must be used in accordance with their listing. It is possible to create an assembly of listed parts that is not safe if the listed parts are not suitable for the application. The addition of the words "identified for the use" clarifies that the parts must not only be listed but identified as suitable for the use.

411.4 Listing Required

Low-voltage lighting systems must comply with (A) or (B).

(A) Listed System. A listed low-voltage lighting system, including the power supply and luminaires.

(B) Assembly of Listed Parts. A low-voltage lighting system assembled from the following listed parts:

(1) Low-voltage luminaires identified for the use.

(2) Power supply identified for the use.

(3) Low-voltage luminaire fittings identified for the use.

(4) Cable suitable for the application or conductors installed within a Chapter 3 wiring method.

ARTICLE

422

APPLIANCES

Introduction to Article 422—Appliances

Article 422 covers electric appliances that are fastened in place, permanently connected, or cord-and-plug-connected. The core content of this article is contained in Parts II and III. Parts IV and V are primarily for manufacturers, but you should examine appliances for compliance before installing them.

422.5 GFCI Protection

GFCI protection for appliances were relocated to this section, editorial revisions were made, and two new list items were added as was a new Informational Note.

Analysis

EXPANDED
422.5(A) General. The parent text in this subsection was revised to apply to appliances that operate at 150V or less to ground and at 60A or less, either single or three-phase removing the previous reference to 250V. The language was also clarified to require the use of Class A GFCI devices.

EDITED
422.5(A)(1). Automotive vacuum machines were changed to reflect that the shock hazard is with the appliances and their use, and not specific to who may be using or operating the appliance.

EXPANDED
422.5(A)(2). Drinking water coolers was expanded to include bottle fill stations. This equipment is sometimes integral with, or installed adjacent to, drinking water coolers and have a similar risk of electric shock hazard as do water coolers.

EDITED
422.5(A)(4). Tire inflation machines were changed to reflect that the shock hazard is with the appliances and their use, and not specific to who may be using or operating the appliance.

NEW
422.5(A)(6). "Sump Pumps" is new to Article 422 for the 2020 *NEC*. There was no specific sump pump GFCI requirement in the 2017 *Code*. This new requirement applies GFCI protection no matter where the sump pump is installed and applies to both cord-and-plug-connected and hard-wired sump pumps.

NEW
422.5(A)(7). "Dishwashers" is also new to Article 422 for the 2020 *NEC*. Prior *Code* language required that the outlet supplying the dishwasher in a dwelling unit have GFCI protection. The change here will greatly expand the number of dishwashers that require GFCI protection as this rule now applies to all occupancies and to equipment that operates at 60A or less, and 150V or less to ground.

NEW
422.5(A) Informational Note. This note referencing the GFCI protection requirements in 210.8 was added at the end of the section during the second revision to the *NEC*.

422.5 GFCI Protection

(A) General. The following appliances rated 150 volts-to-ground or less and 60A or less must be GFCI protected by Class "A" protective device(s), [422.5(B)].

(1) Automotive vacuum machines. ▶Figure 422–1

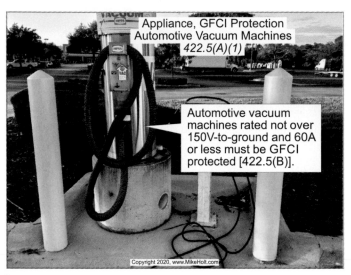

Appliance, GFCI Protection
Automotive Vacuum Machines
422.5(A)(1)

Automotive vacuum machines rated not over 150V-to-ground and 60A or less must be GFCI protected [422.5(B)].

▶Figure 422–1

(2) Drinking water coolers <u>and bottle fill stations</u>. ▶Figure 422–2

Appliances, GFCI Protection
Drinking Water Coolers and Bottle Fill Stations
422.5(A)(2)

Drinking water coolers (not drinking water dispensers) and bottle fill stations rated not over 150V- to-ground and 60A or less require GFCI protection [422.5(B)].

▶Figure 422–2

(3) <u>Cord-and-plug-connected high-pressure spray washing machines.</u>

(4) Tire inflation machines. ▶Figure 422–3

(5) Vending machines.

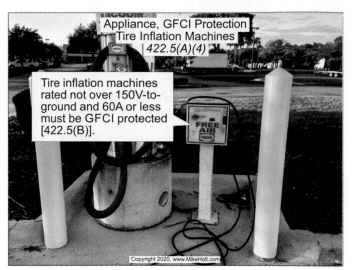

Appliance, GFCI Protection
Tire Inflation Machines
422.5(A)(4)

Tire inflation machines rated not over 150V-to-ground and 60A or less must be GFCI protected [422.5(B)].

▶Figure 422–3

(6) Sump pumps. ▶Figure 422–4

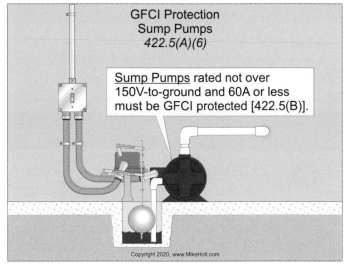

GFCI Protection
Sump Pumps
422.5(A)(6)

Sump Pumps rated not over 150V-to-ground and 60A or less must be GFCI protected [422.5(B)].

▶Figure 422–4

(7) Dishwashers.

Note: Section 210.8 specifies requirements for GFCI protection for the receptacle outlets where the location warrants such protection.

(B) Type and Location. The GFCI must be readily accessible and located in one or more of the following locations:

(1) A GFCI circuit breaker,

(2) A GFCI device or receptacle,

(3) A GFCI integral with the attachment plug,

(4) A GFCI within the supply cord not more than 12 in. from the attachment plug, or

(5) A factory installed GFCI within the appliance.

Author's Comment:

▸ The additional reference to Class A GFCIs seems to be redundant as Article 100 defines a GFCI stating that the device must comply with the time current trip requirements that have been established for a Class A device. As a result of that definition, anytime the *NEC* requires GFCI protection, it must be provided by a Class A GFCI.

422.6 Listing Required

The listing requirement was clarified so it applies to appliances supplied at 50V or higher.

Analysis

CLARIFIED This requirement was new in the 2017 *Code* and was revised only slightly for the 2020 cycle. It now requires all appliances supplied by 50V or higher to be listed as there is a distinction between the supply voltage and the operating voltage for many of them. "50 volts or more" was replaced by "50 volts or higher" to be consistent with the usage throughout the *NEC*.

422.6 Listing Required

Appliances supplied by 50V or higher must be listed.

422.10 Branch Circuits

The title and the scope of this section was revised and (A) was clarified.

Analysis

CLARIFIED The requirements in the subsections cover more than just the rating of the branch circuit. The parent text says that this section "specifies the requirements for branch circuits." While the title change makes it clear that the section is talking about branch circuits that supply appliances, the text of subsection **(A)** for individual branch circuits added the word "conductors" making it apparent the section is talking about the ampacity of the branch-circuit conductors.

422.10 Branch Circuits

(A) Individual Branch Circuits. The ampacities of branch-circuit conductors for an individual appliance are not permitted to be less than the branch-circuit rating marked on the appliance.

Author's Comment:

▸ Listed appliances come with installation instructions from the manufacturer, and sometimes the minimum overcurrent protection and or conductor size are marked on the appliance.

Branch-circuit conductors for household ranges and cooking appliances are sized in accordance with Table 220.55 and 210.19(A)(3).

(B) Branch Circuits Supplying Two or More Loads. Branch circuits supplying appliances in addition to other loads must be sized in accordance with 210.23(A) as follows:

▸ Cord-and-plug-connected equipment is not permitted to be rated more than 80 percent of the branch-circuit ampere rating [210.23(A)(1)].

▸ Equipment fastened in place is not permitted to be rated more than 50 percent of the branch-circuit ampere rating, if the circuit supplies both luminaires and receptacles [210.23(A)(2)].

422.13 Storage-Type Water-Heaters

The language in this section was revised to clarify that the branch-circuit conductors and branch-circuit overcurrent protective device that supplies storage type water heaters with a capacity of 120 gallons or less must be rated at not less than 125 percent of the load.

Analysis

CLARIFIED While the previous language requiring the branch circuit to be considered a continuous load should have been enough for the installer to size the conductors and OCPD at a minimum of 125 percent of the load, the new language makes it absolutely clear they must be sized that way. This change also clarifies that the 125 percent is not required to be carried through the load calculations as the previous language said that this branch circuit is to be considered a continuous load for the purposes of sizing only the branch circuits.

422.13 Storage Water Heaters

The branch-circuit overcurrent device and conductors for fixed storage-type water heaters that have a capacity of 120 gallons or less must be sized not smaller than 125 percent of the rating of the water heater. ▶Figure 422–5

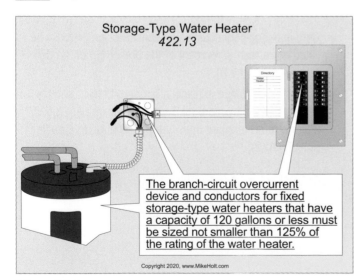

Storage-Type Water Heater
422.13

The branch-circuit overcurrent device and conductors for fixed storage-type water heaters that have a capacity of 120 gallons or less must be sized not smaller than 125% of the rating of the water heater.

Copyright 2020, www.MikeHolt.com

▶Figure 422–5

▶ **Example**

Question: *What size conductor and overcurrent protection are required for a 4,500W, 240V water heater, having a wiring method or Type NM cable?* ▶Figure 422–6

(a) 20A/12 AWG   (b) 25 or 30A/10 AWG
(c) 40A/8 AWG   (d) 50A/6 AWG

Answer: *(b) 30A/10 AWG*

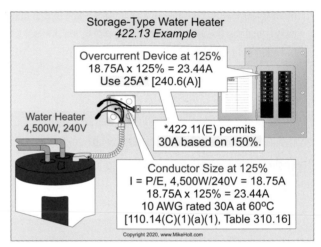

Storage-Type Water Heater
422.13 Example

Overcurrent Device at 125%
18.75A x 125% = 23.44A
Use 25A* [240.6(A)]

Water Heater
4,500W, 240V

*422.11(E) permits
30A based on 150%.

Conductor Size at 125%
I = P/E, 4,500W/240V = 18.75A
18.75A x 125% = 23.44A
10 AWG rated 30A at 60°C
[110.14(C)(1)(a)(1), Table 310.16]

Copyright 2020, www.MikeHolt.com

▶Figure 422–6

Solution:

Step 1: *Determine the branch-circuit rating [210.19(A)(1) and 422.13].*

Circuit Current = 4,500W/240V
Circuit Current = 18.75A

Circuit Rating = 18.75A × 125%
Circuit Rating = 23.44A

Circuit Conductor = 10 AWG rated 30A at 60°C [110.14(C) (1)(a)(2), 334.80, and Table 310.16]

Step 2: *Determine the overcurrent protection rating [210.20 and 422.13].*

Circuit Current = 4,500W/240V
Circuit Current = 18.75A

Circuit Protection = 18.75A × 125%
Circuit Protection = 23.44A, use next size up: 25A [240.6(A)]

Note: *422.11(E) permits the overcurrent protective device to be sized up to 150% of the appliance rating.*

Circuit Protection = 18.75A × 150%
Circuit Protection = 28.75A, use next size up: 30A [240.6(A)]

▸ This clarification seems long overdue as many mistakenly felt it necessary to treat the water heater load as continuous for the purpose of service demand calculations. Treating this load as continuous was simply meant to adequately size the branch circuit. The correct application of this rule does not place any additional demand on the service or feeder.

422.16 Flexible Cords

Subsection (A) was split into two list items and the list items in (B) were reorganized.

Analysis

REORGANIZED

422.16(A) General. These requirements were split into two list items for ease of use. These list items specify where flexible cord is permitted to be used with appliances.

REORGANIZED

422.16(B) Specific Appliances. List items for specific appliances (1) through (4) were reorganized, clarified, and/or expanded with no technical changes other than a requirement for a grommet or bushing where cords pass through bored or cut openings, and an exception regarding grounding-type attachment plugs.

CLARIFIED

422.16(B)(1) Electrically Operated In-Sink Disposers. The requirement for the flexible cord to be terminated in a grounding-type attachment plug was relocated to be the last list item and clarified to require that not only is the cord to be terminated in a grounding-type attachment plug, but it must actually have an equipment grounding conductor in the cord.

CLARIFIED

422.16(B)(2) Built-In Dishwashers and Trash Compactors. The rule now requires that where the cord passes through an opening it must be protected from damage by using a bushing, grommet, or other approved means.

The rule requires the dishwasher receptacle to be in the space adjacent to the dishwasher itself and that often means it passes through a cabinet divider. This change provides protection for the cord where it passes through that divider.

CLARIFIED

422.16(B)(3) Wall-mounted Ovens and Counter Mounted Cooking Units. This change requires the appliance manufacturer to specify the type of cord that may be used to connect the appliances. This will ensure the cord type is suitable for the application, including the temperature at the termination point. The language that only permitted the use of a flexible cord for "ease in servicing or installation" was deleted as unenforceable. The choice to hardwire or cord connect these appliances is a simple one to be made by the designer or installer. The *NEC* does not intend to specify one over the other.

CLARIFIED

422.16(B)(4) Range Hoods and Microwave Oven/Range Hood Combinations. This subsection was revised to include combination microwave range hoods as well as just a range hood. As we saw in the other specific appliance sections, the cord for the appliance must not only terminate in a grounding-type attachment plug, there must be an equipment grounding conductor in the cord to connect to the grounding terminal in the plug. This was always the intent, but it is physically possible to install a grounding-type attachment plug on a cord that does not contain an equipment grounding conductor.

422.16 Flexible Cords

(A) General. Flexible cords are permitted for appliances when needed to:

(1) Facilitate frequent interchange, or to prevent the transmission of noise and vibration [400.10(A)(6) and 400.10(A)(7)].

(2) Facilitate the removal of appliances fastened in place, where the fastening means and mechanical connections are specifically designed to permit ready removal [400.12(A)(8)].

▸ Flexible cords are not permitted for the connection of water heaters, furnaces, and other appliances fastened in place, unless the appliances are specifically identified to be used with a flexible cord. ▸Figure 422–7

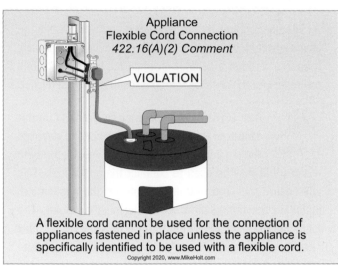

A flexible cord cannot be used for the connection of appliances fastened in place unless the appliance is specifically identified to be used with a flexible cord.

Copyright 2020, www.MikeHolt.com

▶Figure 422–7

(B) Specific Appliances.

(1) In-Sink Waste Disposal. A flexible cord is permitted for an in-sink waste disposal if: ▶Figure 422–8

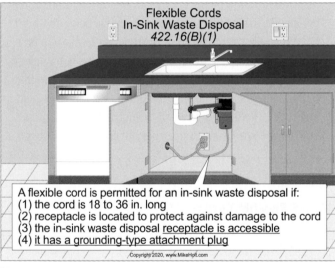

A flexible cord is permitted for an in-sink waste disposal if:
(1) the cord is 18 to 36 in. long
(2) receptacle is located to protect against damage to the cord
(3) the in-sink waste disposal <u>receptacle is accessible</u>
(4) <u>it has a grounding-type attachment plug</u>

Copyright 2020, www.MikeHolt.com

▶Figure 422–8

(1) The flexible cord is at least 18 in. in length and no longer than 3 ft

(2) The receptacle is located so as to protect the flexible cord from damage.

(3) The receptacle is accessible.

Author's Comment:

▸ Note that the term, (where used), regarding the location of the receptacle(s) is "accessible" and not "readily accessible." The common locations of receptacles are accessible but may not be readily accessible.

(4) The flexible cord has an equipment grounding conductor and is terminated with a grounding-type attachment plug.

Ex: A listed appliance distinctly marked to identify it as protected by a system of double insulation is not required to be terminated with a grounding-type attachment plug.

Author's Comment:

▸ If the appliance is hard wired, then the appliance disconnect must be located within sight from the appliance or circuit breaker for the appliance and must be lockable with provisions for locking to remain in place whether the lock is installed or not [422.31(B)].

422.19 Space for Conductors

This rule was clarified to say that the volume of the canopy and the outlet box must be combined when determining the amount of wiring space.

Analysis

CLARIFIED

The language in this section was revised for clarity and to align this text with that found in 314.16 for box fill.

The new text says that the volume provided by the canopies of ceiling-suspended fans and outlet boxes added together must provide enough space so the conductors and connecting devices are capable of being installed in accordance with 314.16.

422.19 Space for Conductors

The combined volume of the canopy of ceiling-suspended (paddle) fans and outlet box must provide sufficient space so that conductors and their connecting devices are capable of being installed in accordance with 314.16.

Author's Comment:

▸ Regardless of the type of equipment, sufficient wiring space or "volume," must be provided to make electrical connections. Wherein ceiling fans are concerned, you might gain additional volume with the space provided by the canopy covering the outlet opening. Ceiling fan boxes are often secured to the bottom face of a ceiling joist in a box no deeper that the finished surface material so this additional space might be just enough to remain *Code* compliant. This was clarified to say that you combine the volume of the canopy and the outlet box for wiring space.

422.22 Utilizing Separable Attachment Fittings

This new section specifically permits the use of separable attachment fittings to support appliances.

Analysis

NEW This is a new section, and the previous 422.22 was renumbered as 422.23 without change. The language in what is now 422.23 required the AHJ to grant special permission to use the separable attachment fittings to support appliances as they were an "installation method" that was not covered in Article 422. These are the safety quick lighting (SQL) devices, primarily for lighting and ceiling fan applications, that were added to the *Code* in the 2017 cycle.

Specific permission is provided for the use of listed locking support and mounting receptacles in combination with compatible attachment fittings to support appliances where used within their ratings and in accordance with 314.27(E).

422.31 Permanently Connected Appliance Disconnects

Sections 422.31(A) and (B) were revised to be consistent with other lockable disconnect rules in the *NEC*.

Analysis

EDITED **Subsections (A) and (B)** permit the branch-circuit switch or circuit breaker to be used as the disconnecting means where the switch or circuit breaker is within sight from the appliance, or where it is "capable of being locked in the open position in compliance" with 110.25. The text in quotes is new text for both (A) and (B) and is consistent with other lockable disconnect rules in the *Code*.

422.31 Permanently Connected Appliance Disconnects

(A) Appliances Rated Not Over 300 VA. For permanently connected appliances rated at not over 300 VA or 1/8 hp, the branch-circuit overcurrent device is permitted to serve as the disconnecting means where the switch or circuit breaker is within sight from the appliance or is capable of being locked in the open position in accordance with 110.25.

Author's Comment:

▸ If an appliance is hard wired, then an appliance disconnect must be located within sight from the appliance or the circuit breaker for the appliance must be provided with a lockable means that remains in place whether a lock is installed or not [422.31(B)].

▸ According to Article 100, "Within Sight" means that it is visible and not more than 50 ft from the location of the equipment.

▸ Notice that both (A) and (B) read exactly the same as far as the disconnection requirements. I can see no reason for separate subsections.

FIXED ELECTRIC SPACE-HEATING EQUIPMENT

Introduction to Article 424—Fixed Electric Space-Heating Equipment

Many people are surprised to see how many pages Article 424 has. This is a nine-part article on fixed electric space heaters. Why so much text for what seems to be a simple application? The answer is that Article 424 covers a variety of applications—heaters come in various configurations for various uses. Not all of these parts are for the electrician in the field—the requirements in Part IV are for manufacturers.

Fixed space heaters (wall-mounted, ceiling-mounted, or free-standing) are common in many utility buildings and other small structures, as well as in some larger structures. When used to heat floors, space-heating cables address the thermal layering problem typical of forced-air systems—so it is likely you will encounter them. Duct heaters are very common in large office and educational buildings. These provide a distributed heating scheme. Locating the heater in the ductwork, but close to the occupied space, eliminates the waste of transporting heated air through sheet metal routed in unheated spaces, so it is likely you will encounter those as well.

424.1 Scope

The scope statement was changed to reference "central heating systems" rather than "central systems" and was editorially revised for compliance with the *NEC Style Manual*.

Analysis

CLARIFIED There are central systems that are not heating systems, and the requirements of this article only apply to heating systems. The addition of the word "heating" between "central" and "systems" clarifies the scope. This section was also editorially revised to remove the mandatory terms "shall" and "shall not." since the *NEC Style Manual* does not permit the use of those terms in a scope statement.

424.1 Scope

Article 424 contains the installation requirements for fixed electrical equipment used for space heating, such as heating cables, unit heaters, boilers (such as those used for radiant heating), <u>central heating systems,</u> or fixed electric space-heating equipment. ▶Figure 424–1

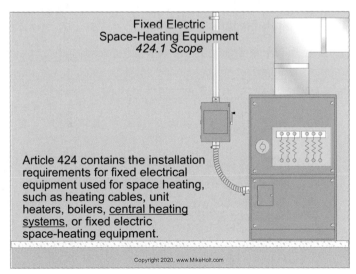

Fixed Electric Space-Heating Equipment
424.1 Scope

Article 424 contains the installation requirements for fixed electrical equipment used for space heating, such as heating cables, unit heaters, boilers, <u>central heating systems,</u> or fixed electric space-heating equipment.

Copyright 2020, www.MikeHolt.com

▶Figure 424–1

424.4 Branch Circuits, Branch-Circuit Requirements

This section was revised to clarify reference is being made to individual branch circuits that serve "fixed" heating equipment.

Analysis

CLARIFIED **424.4(A) Branch-Circuit Requirements.** This is an editorial clarification. The use of the word "they" as a reference to "the branch circuit" is ambiguous. The new language in clarifies the text.

CLARIFIED **424.4(B) Branch-Circuit Sizing.** This requirement was clarified by specifying that the motors to which this section applies, are those that are associated with the fixed electric space-heating equipment. For example, the blower motor in an electric furnace would be an associated motor. The "continuous load" language which was intended to trigger a 125 percent requirement for the branch-circuit conductors and OCPD was replaced with language that specifically requires the branch-circuit conductors and OCPD to have ratings not less than 125 percent of the electric space-heating load.

424.4 Branch Circuits

(B) Branch-Circuit Sizing. The branch-circuit conductors for fixed electric space-heating equipment and any associated motors must be sized not smaller than 125 percent of the load. ▶Figure 424–2

Author's Comment:

▸ The branch-circuit conductors and overcurrent protection for fixed electric space-heating equipment must have an ampacity not less than 125 percent of the total heating load [210.19(A)(1) and 210.20(A)].

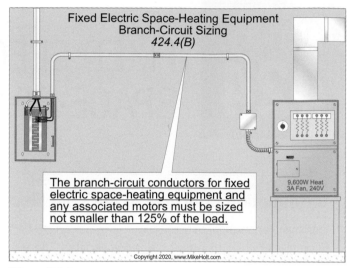

Fixed Electric Space-Heating Equipment
Branch-Circuit Sizing
424.4(B)

The branch-circuit conductors for fixed electric space-heating equipment and any associated motors must be sized not smaller than 125% of the load.

9,600W Heat
3A Fan, 240V

Copyright 2020, www.MikeHolt.com

▶Figure 424–2

▸ **Example**

Question: What size NM cable and overcurrent protection are required for a 9,600W, 240V fixed electric space heater that has a 3A, 240V blower motor? ▶Figure 424–3

(a) 10 AWG/30A   (b) 8 AWG/40A
(c) 6 AWG/50A   (d) 6 AWG/60A

Answer: (d) 6 AWG/60A

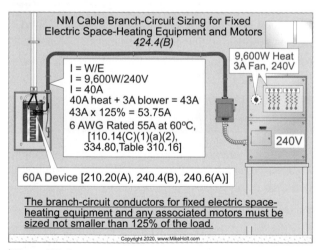

NM Cable Branch-Circuit Sizing for Fixed
Electric Space-Heating Equipment and Motors
424.4(B)

9,600W Heat
3A Fan, 240V

I = W/E
I = 9,600W/240V
I = 40A
40A heat + 3A blower = 43A
43A x 125% = 53.75A
6 AWG Rated 55A at 60°C,
[110.14(C)(1)(a)(2),
334.80,Table 310.16]

240V

60A Device [210.20(A), 240.4(B), 240.6(A)]

The branch-circuit conductors for fixed electric space-heating equipment and any associated motors must be sized not smaller than 125% of the load.

Copyright 2020, www.MikeHolt.com

▶Figure 424–3

Solution:

Step 1: Determine the total load.

I = Watts/Volts
I = 9,600W/240V
I = 40A

Total Amperes = 40A (heat) + 3A (blower)
Total Amperes = 43A

Step 2: *Size the conductors at 125 percent of the total current load [210.19(A)(1)].*

Conductor = 43A × 125%
Conductor = 53.75A, use 6 AWG rated 55A at 60°C 1
[10.14(C)(1)(a)(2), 334.80, and Table 310.16]

Step 3: *Size the overcurrent protection at 125 percent of the total current load [210.20(A), 240.4(B), and 240.6(A)].*

Overcurrent Protection = 43A × 125%
Overcurrent Protection = 53.75A, use next size up: 60A

Author's Comment:

▸ The "continuous load" language which was intended to trigger an 125% requirement for the branch circuit conductors and OCPD, was replaced with language that specifically requires the branch circuit conductors and OCPD to have ratings not less than 125% of the electric space-heating load in accordance with [210.19(A)(1) and 210.20(A)]

424.19 Disconnecting Means

The language was editorially revised to be consistent with 110.25 and other lockable disconnect rules in the *Code*.

Analysis

EDITED This rule is in Part III, Control and Protection of Fixed Electric Space-Heating Equipment. There was no actual change in the requirements, but *Code* usability is improved where rules that are identical in meaning use the same language throughout the *NEC*. There were also slight editorial language revisions in 424.19(A)(1) and (A)(2) (heaters without or with motor(s) over ⅛ horsepower) to reference the parent text in the section and to avoid redundancy.

424.19 Disconnecting Means

Heating equipment must have a means to simultaneously disconnect all circuit phase conductors.

(B) Heating Equipment Without Supplementary Overcurrent Protection. The disconnect for fixed heating equipment must be located within sight from the fixed heating equipment or it must be capable of being locked in the open position with provisions for locking to remain in place whether the lock is installed or not in accordance with 110.25. ▸Figure 424–4

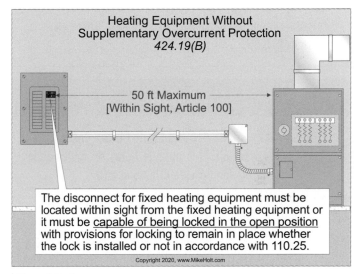

Heating Equipment Without
Supplementary Overcurrent Protection
424.19(B)

50 ft Maximum
[Within Sight, Article 100]

The disconnect for fixed heating equipment must be located within sight from the fixed heating equipment or it must be capable of being locked in the open position with provisions for locking to remain in place whether the lock is installed or not in accordance with 110.25.

Copyright 2020, www.MikeHolt.com

▸Figure 424–4

(C) Unit Switch as Disconnecting Means. A unit switch on fixed electric heating equipment with a marked "off" position can serve as the required disconnect. ▸Figure 424–5

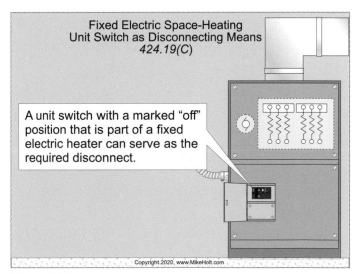

Fixed Electric Space-Heating
Unit Switch as Disconnecting Means
424.19(C)

A unit switch with a marked "off" position that is part of a fixed electric heater can serve as the required disconnect.

Copyright 2020, www.MikeHolt.com

▸Figure 424–5

Author's Comment:

▸ The same language change as in the parent text of 424.19, is also made in 424.19(B)(1) for consistency.

424.44 Electric Heating Cables in Concrete or Masonry Floors

The language in (E) was revised to clarify that the GFCI protection required in this rule is in addition to any requirements in 210.8.

Analysis

CLARIFIED

424.44(E) Ground-Fault Circuit-Interrupter Protection. This change helps to improve the correlation between this and 210.8.

424.44 Electric Heating Cables in Concrete or Masonry Floors

(E) GFCI Protection. In addition to the requirements in 210.8, GFCI protection is required for electric space-heating cables embedded in concrete or masonry floors of bathroom areas, kitchens, and hydromassage bathtub locations. ▸Figure 424–6

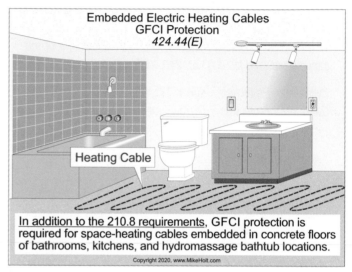

Embedded Electric Heating Cables
GFCI Protection
424.44(E)

Heating Cable

In addition to the 210.8 requirements, GFCI protection is required for space-heating cables embedded in concrete floors of bathrooms, kitchens, and hydromassage bathtub locations.

Copyright 2020, www.MikeHolt.com

▸Figure 424–6

Author's Comment:

▸ The text, "in addition to the requirements in 210.8," appears in quite a number of Articles throughout the 2020 *NEC*. There have been instances where, before such language was added, it may have been incorrectly assumed that, if an Article referred to any type of GFCI protection, that was all that was required and the requirements in 210.8 didn't apply. This was especially the case in Chapters 5 through 8 because of their ability to modify general rules in Chapters 1 through 4. This new language should put to rest any misinterpretation of 90.3 to at least the extent of GFCI protection.

ARTICLE 430

MOTORS, MOTOR CIRCUITS, AND CONTROLLERS

Introduction to Article 430—Motors, Motor Circuits, and Controllers

Article 430 contains the specific rules for conductor sizing, overcurrent protection, control circuit conductors, controllers, and disconnects for electric motors. The installation requirements for motor control centers are covered in Part VIII, and air-conditioning and refrigeration equipment are covered in Article 440.

This is one of the longest articles in the *NEC*. It is also one of the most complex, but motors are complex equipment. They are electrical and mechanical devices, but what makes motor applications complex is the fact that they are inductive loads with a high-current demand at start-up that is typically six, or more, times the running current. This makes overcurrent protection for motor applications necessarily different from the overcurrent protection employed for other types of equipment. So, do not confuse general overcurrent protection with motor protection—you must calculate and apply them differently using the rules in Article 430.

You might be uncomfortable with the allowances for overcurrent protection, such as protecting a 10 AWG conductor with a 60A overcurrent protective device, found in this article. As you progress through this article, you will learn to understand how motor overcurrent protection works and realize just why these allowances are not only safe, but necessary.

430.2 Definitions

A new definition of "Electronically Protected (as applied to motors)" was added.

Analysis

NEW **Electronically Protected (as applied to motors).** Electronically protected motors are beginning to be used as stand-alone motors and needed to be added to the *NEC*. The definition says that an "electronically protected" motor is one that has an electronic control as an integral part of the motor and protects it against dangerous overheating due to the failure of the electronic control, overload, and failure to start.

430.2 Definitions

Controller. Any switch or device used to start and stop a motor by making and breaking the motor circuit current. ▶Figure 430–1

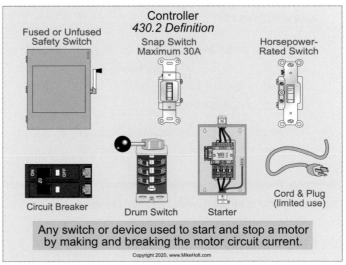

▶Figure 430–1

Author's Comment:

▶ A controller can be a horsepower-rated switch, snap switch, or circuit breaker. A pushbutton that operates an electromechanical relay is not a controller because it does not meet the controller rating requirements of 430.83. Devices such as start-stop stations and pressure switches are control devices, not motor controllers. ▶Figure 430–2

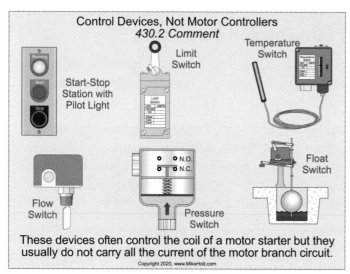

Control Devices, Not Motor Controllers
430.2 Comment

These devices often control the coil of a motor starter but they usually do not carry all the current of the motor branch circuit.

Copyright 2020, www.MikeHolt.com

▶Figure 430–2

___

Electronically Protected (as applied to motors). A motor that is provided with electronic control that is an integral part of the motor and protects the motor against dangerous overheating due to failure of the electronic control, overload, and failure to start.

Author's Comment:

▶ This type of motor will be identified by the words "electronically protected" or "E.P." on the nameplate, just like the motors with internal thermal protection have the words "thermally protected" on the nameplate.

▶ A reference to this type of protection was added to 430.32(A)(2) that previously only covered thermal protection.

Thermally Protected (as applied to motors). A motor or motor-compressor that is provided with a thermal protector.

Author's Comment:

▶ The definition for "Thermally Protected" appears in Article 100 but is included here for the reader's convenience.

430.32 Continuous-Duty Motors

The requirements of 430.32(A)(2) and (B)(2) were expanded to include electronically protected motors as well as thermally protected motors.

Analysis

EXPANDED This section requires motors to be protected from overloads and recognizes that the branch-circuit short-circuit and ground-fault protective device is not sufficient to provide the overload protection. The second list item in (A) for motors more than 1 hp, and in (B) for motors that are automatically started and are 1 hp or less, were both expanded to include internal electronic protection as a permitted overload protection method. The listing standard requirements for an electronic protection device include all the requirements that apply to a thermal protective device, so the electronic devices were added to the existing thermal protective device rules.

430.99 Available Fault Current

Documentation of the available short-circuit current calculations must now be made readily available to those who install and maintain motor control center equipment as well as those who inspect the equipment.

Analysis

CLARIFIED This is Part VIII, Motor Control Centers and requires the available fault current and the date the calculation was performed be made available to those authorized to inspect, <u>install, or maintain</u> the installation. The change recognizes that those who install and maintain the equipment, as well as those who inspect it, must have the fault current data available. The *Code* does not specify the method of making the information available, but the simplest method would work.

430.122 Conductor Sizing

A new Informational Note was added to (A), and new subsections (B) and (D) were added as well.

Analysis

NEW **430.122(A) Branch/Feeder Circuit Conductors, Informational Note No. 2.** The output waveform from an adjustable-speed drive (VFD) system can potentially cause damage to the output conductor insulation. This is determined by several factors including the output voltage, frequency, current, length of the conductors, the spacing between the conductors, and the dielectric strength of the conductor insulation. The note does not specify methods to prevent this as there are several methods that may be used.

NEW **430.122(B) Output Conductors.** The ampacity of the conductors between the output of the adjustable-speed drive and the motor was not addressed in the previous *Code*. This change and its associated exception correct that oversight. The rule requires these conductors to have an ampacity equal to or greater than 125 percent of the full-load current as determined by 430.6(A) or (B). The exception provides the minimum size of these conductors where the power conversion equipment is listed and marked as "suitable for output motor conductor protection."

NEW **430.122(D) Several Motors or a Motor and Other Loads.** This new subsection was added to clarify that where several drives are supplied by a single branch circuit, the ampacity is in accordance with 430.24 and the rated input current of the drives is used for the purposes of calculating the conductor ampacity. This matches up with the required conductor size for a single motor as found in 430.122(A).

430.122 Conductor Sizing

(A) Branch/Feeder Circuit Conductors. Circuit conductors for an adjustable-speed drive system must have an ampacity of not less than 125 percent of the rated input current of the adjustable-speed drive system. ▸Figure 430–3

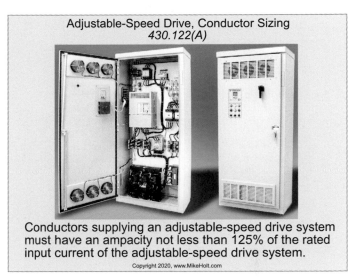

Adjustable-Speed Drive, Conductor Sizing
430.122(A)

Conductors supplying an adjustable-speed drive system must have an ampacity not less than 125% of the rated input current of the adjustable-speed drive system.

Copyright 2020, www.MikeHolt.com

▸Figure 430–3

Conductor Sizing [430.122(A)]

Circuit conductors supplying an adjustable-speed drive system must have an ampacity not less than 125 percent of the rated input current to the power conversion equipment [430.122(A)].

Motor Branch-Circuit Conductors for Adjustable-Speed Drive Systems [430.122]

▶ **Motor Branch-Circuit for Adjustable Speed Drive Example**

Question: *What size branch-circuit conductors are required for an adjustable-speed drive system with a rated input of 25A and terminals rated 75°C?* ▶**Figure 430–4**

(a) 14 AWG   *(b) 12 AWG*   *(c) 10 AWG*   *(d) 8 AWG*

Answer: *(c) 10 AWG*

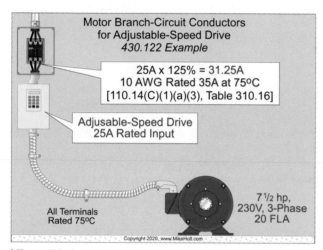

**Motor Branch-Circuit Conductors
for Adjustable-Speed Drive
430.122 Example**

25A x 125% = 31.25A
10 AWG Rated 35A at 75°C
[110.14(C)(1)(a)(3), Table 310.16]

Adjusable-Speed Drive
25A Rated Input

All Terminals
Rated 75°C

7 ½ hp,
230V, 3-Phase
20 FLA

Copyright 2020, www.MikeHolt.com

▶Figure 430–4

Solution:

Rated Input from Adjustable-Speed Drive = 25A

Branch Circuit Conductor = 25A × 125%
Branch Circuit Conductor = 31.25A

Use 10 AWG rated 35A at 75°C [Table 310.16 and 110.14(C)(1)(a)(3)].

Note 1: *Adjustable-speed drive systems can have multiple power ratings and corresponding input currents.*

Note 2: *Circuit conductors on the output of an adjustable-speed drive system are susceptible to breakdown under certain conditions due to the characteristics of the output waveform of the drive. Factors affecting the conductors include but are not limited to the output voltage, frequency, and current, the length of the conductors, the spacing between the conductors, and the dielectric strength of the conductor insulation. Methods to mitigate breakdown include consideration of one or more of these factors.*

(B) Output Conductors. The conductors <u>between</u> the power conversion equipment and the motor must have an ampacity <u>equal to or greater than</u> 125 percent of the motor's full-load current (FLC) as listed in Tables 430.248 and 430.250.

Ex: If the power conversion equipment is listed and marked as "Suitable for Output Motor Conductor Protection," the conductor between the power conversion equipment and the motor must have an ampacity equal to or greater than the larger of:

(1) 125 percent of the motor's full-load current (FLC) as listed in Tables 430.248 and 430.250

(2) The ampacity of the minimum conductor size marked on the power conversion equipment

> **Author's Comment:**

▶ This exception may require conductors that are larger than 125% of the motor full load current. This may occur where the drive that supplies the motor has a horsepower rating greater than the horsepower of the motor.

Note: The minimum ampacity required of output conductors is often different than that of the conductors supplying the power conversion equipment. See 430.130 and 430.131 for branch-circuit protection requirements.

(D) Several Motors or a Motor and Other Loads. Conductors supplying several motors or a motor and other loads, including power conversion equipment, must have ampacity in accordance with 430.24, using the rated input current of the power conversion equipment for purposes of calculating ampacity.

> **Author's Comment:**

▶ 430.24 Requires that the ampacity of the feeder conductors, not be less the sum of each of the following:

   1) 125% of highest motor load or the power conversion equipment (drive) rated input current

   2) Sum of remaining full-load motor current (drive input current)

   3) 100% of non-continuous non-motor loads

   4) 125% of continuous non-motor loads

430.130 Branch-Circuit Short-Circuit and Ground-Fault Protection

A new exception and Informational Note were added to 430.130(A)(1).

Analysis

NEW **430.130(A)(1) Ex Circuits Containing an Adjustable-Speed Drive System.** This section applies to the required branch-circuit short-circuit and ground-fault protection for the branch circuit that supplies the power conversion equipment (drive). This exception permits the use of the power conversion unit rated input current for the selection of the branch circuit protective device, where the power conversion equipment is listed and marked as "suitable for output motor conductor protection."

NEW **430.130(A)(1) Note 2 Circuits Containing an Adjustable-Speed Drive System.** This Informational Note was added to say that the motor branch circuit for power conversion equipment starts at the upstream OCPD and includes the power conversion input conductors, the power conversion equipment, and the power conversion output conductors.

430.130 Branch-Circuit Short-Circuit and Ground-Fault Protection

(A) Circuits Containing an Adjustable-Speed Drive System. Circuits containing power conversion equipment must be protected by a branch-circuit short-circuit and ground-fault protective device in accordance with all of the following:

(1) The rating and type of protection must be determined by 430.52(C)(1), (C)(3), (C)(5), or (C)(6), using the motor's full-load current (FLC) as listed in Tables 430.248 and 430.250.

Ex: The rating and type of protection is determined by Table 430.52 using the power conversion equipment's rated input current where the power conversion equipment is listed and marked "Suitable for Output Motor Conductor Protection."

Note 1: Motor conductor branch-circuit short-circuit and ground-fault protection from the power conversion equipment to the motor is provided by power conversion equipment that is listed and marked "Suitable for Output Motor Conductor Protection."

Note No. 2: A motor branch circuit using power conversion equipment, including equipment listed and marked "Suitable for Output Motor Conductor Protection," includes the input circuit to the power conversion equipment.

(2) The maximum branch-circuit short-circuit and ground-fault protective ratings must be in accordance with the manufacturer's instructions.

AIR-CONDITIONING AND REFRIGERATION EQUIPMENT

Introduction to Article 440—Air-Conditioning and Refrigeration Equipment

This article applies to electrically driven air-conditioning and refrigeration equipment. Each equipment manufacturer has the motor for a given air-conditioning unit built to its own specifications. Cooling and other characteristics are different from those of non-hermetic motors. For each motor, the manufacturer has worked out all the details and typically identifies the conductor and protection size, and other information, on the nameplate. So, when wiring an air conditioner, trust the information on the nameplate and do not try to over-complicate the situation. The math for sizing the overcurrent protection and conductor minimum ampacity has already been done for you.

440.9 Grounding and Bonding

This section was revised for clarity.

Analysis

CLARIFIED The intent of this rule is to now apply to all air-conditioning and refrigerating equipment located on a roof. It was also revised to apply to metallic raceways that use "compression type" fittings. This change reflects the intent of the previous *NEC* to require the wire type equipment grounding conductor where the raceway itself is not threaded. The language in the previous *Codes* said the equipment grounding conductor was required where "non-threaded fittings" were used. The issue with that is that a compression fitting has threads, just not the type of threads the panel had in mind when the section was approved for the 2017 *NEC*. The use of the term "compression fitting" makes the intent of the section very clear.

440.9 Grounding and Bonding

Where air-conditioning or refrigeration equipment is installed on the roof and connected with a metallic raceway, an equipment grounding conductor of the wire type must be installed within metallic raceway systems that use compression-type fittings. ▶Figure 440–1

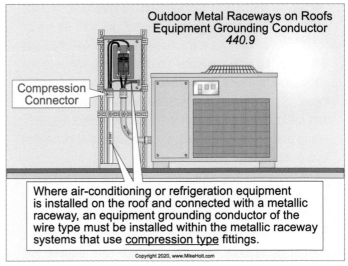

Outdoor Metal Raceways on Roofs
Equipment Grounding Conductor
440.9

Compression Connector

Where air-conditioning or refrigeration equipment is installed on the roof and connected with a metallic raceway, an equipment grounding conductor of the wire type must be installed within the metallic raceway systems that use compression type fittings.

Copyright 2020, www.MikeHolt.com

▶Figure 440–1

Author's Comment:

▶ When the wiring method for rooftop units is not a threaded type system, you cannot rely on the raceway to serve as the equipment grounding conductor as permitted by 250.118 and must install an appropriately sized wire-type equipment grounding conductor instead.

▶ When a raceway is being used as an equipment grounding conductor (EGC) it is imperative that the integrity of conduit connections are maintained. Threadless fittings are prone to damage and structural degradation preventing an effective ground path during abnormal fault conditions.

440.10 Short-Circuit Current Rating

Subsections (A) and (B) were revised. The available fault current calculation was expanded and now applies to industrial control panels as well as motor controllers used with air-conditioning and refrigerating equipment.

Analysis

EXPANDED

440.10(A) Installation. Revisions to include "industrial control panels" as well as motor controllers were made. Sections 440.4(B) and 440.10(B) include industrial control panels. Without the addition of that term this subsection would not require the industrial control panel that is associated with air-conditioning and refrigeration equipment to have a short-circuit current rating that equals or exceeds the available fault current at that point on the circuit.

EXPANDED

440.10(B) Documentation. This was expanded to require those who install and maintain the equipment have access to the available fault current calculations. The previous *Code* only required this information to be available to the inspectors.

440.32 Single Motor-Compressor

This section was editorially revised to clarify the requirement for conductor sizing.

Analysis

EDITED

The parent text was revised to include two list items to clarify that the minimum branch-circuit conductor ampacity is the greater of 125 percent of the motor compressor load current or 125 percent of the branch-circuit selection current.

440.32 Conductor Size for Single Motor-Compressors

Branch-circuit conductors to a single motor-compressor for air-conditioning and refrigeration equipment must have an ampacity not less than the greater of:

(1) 125 percent of the motor-compressor rated-load current.

(2) 125 percent of the branch-circuit selection current.

Author's Comment:

▶ Branch-circuit conductors for a single motor-compressor must have short-circuit and ground-fault protection sized between 175 percent and 225 percent of the rated-load current [440.22(A)].

▶ **Conductor Size Example**

Question: What size conductor and overcurrent device are required for an 18A motor-compressor for air-conditioning equipment? ▶Figure 440–2

(a) 10 AWG, 30A   (b) 10 AWG, 50A
(c) a or b   (d) 10 AWG, 60A

Answer: (a) 10 AWG, 30A

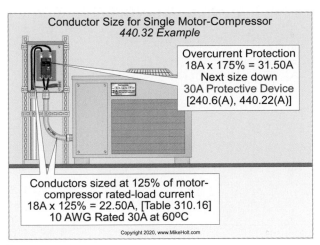

▶Figure 440–2

Solution:

Step 1: *Determine the branch-circuit conductor [440.32 and Table 310.16].*

Branch-Circuit Conductor = 18A × 125%
Branch-Circuit Conductor = 22.50A

Use 10 AWG rated 30A at 60°C [110.14(C)(1)(a)(2), Table 310.16]

Step 2: *Determine the branch-circuit overcurrent protection [240.6(A) and 440.22(A)]:*

Branch-Circuit Over Current Protection = 18A × 175%
Branch-Circuit Over Current Protection = 31.50A, use next size down: 30A

If the 30A short-circuit and ground-fault protective device is not capable of carrying the starting current, then the protective device can be sized up to 225 percent of the equipment load current rating.

Branch-Circuit Over Current Protection = 18A × 225%
Branch-Circuit Over Current Protection = 40.50A, use next size down: 40A

Author's Comment:

▸ A 30A or 40A overcurrent device can protect a 12 AWG conductor for an air-conditioning circuit. See 240.4(G) for details.

▸ The branch circuit selection current is not required to be marked on the nameplate unless the internal overload equipment permits continuous operation at a current that exceeds 156% of rate-load current. The minimum circuit ampacity that is found on the equipment nameplate is 125% of the rated load current and the conductor selection can be made directly from that value as shown on the nameplate.

ARTICLE
445

GENERATORS

Introduction to Article 445—Generators

This article contains the electrical installation, and other requirements, for generators. These rules include such things as where generators can be installed, nameplate markings, conductor ampacity, transference of power, and disconnect requirements.

445.6 Listing

A new subsection was added requiring stationary generators operating at 600V or less to comply with this section.

Analysis

NEW This is another addition to equipment that is required to be listed. The language only applies to stationary generators 600V or below. The term "stationary" makes it clear this listing requirement does not apply to portable generators. There is an exception that permits "one of a kind" or custom manufactured generators to be field labeled by a field evaluation body.

445.6 Listing

Stationary generators rated 600V and less must be listed.

Exception: One-of-a-kind or custom manufactured generators are permitted to be field labeled by a field evaluation body.

445.18 Disconnecting Means and Emergency Shutdown

The title change clarifies that this section applies to both the disconnection of the emergency generator and the emergency shutdown of the generator; (A), (C), and (D) were also revised to clarify the intent of this section.

Analysis

CLARIFIED **445.18(A) Disconnecting Means.** This subsection was revised for clarity with the common language for disconnects that are required to be lockable. The language previously said the generator disconnect must be "lockable in the open position." It was changed to "lockable open" to be consistent with 110.25.

CLARIFIED **445.18(C) Remote Emergency Shutdown.** This information was given its own subsection and the phrase "additional requirement to shut down the prime mover" was replaced with "a remote emergency stop switch." This clarifies the function of this shutdown requirement. As in the previous *Code*, the device must be located outside of the equipment room or generator enclosure.

NEW

445.18(D) Emergency Shutdown Means in One- and Two-Family Dwelling Units. The concern behind subsection (D) is that if a firefighter must shut down the utility power the generator may automatically start and put the first responders in danger unless they have a readily accessible means to shut it down too. The *NEC* language does not require the emergency shutdown device to be in a specific location, only that it be outside at a readily accessible location. If the device required by 445.18(B) is located outside at a readily accessible location, that device would be permitted to serve as the shutdown device required by this section.

445.18 Disconnecting Means and Emergency Shutdown

(A) Disconnecting Means. Generators, other than cord-and-plug-connected portable generators, must have one or more disconnecting means. Each disconnecting means must simultaneously open all associated phase conductors. Each disconnecting means must be lockable in the open position in accordance with 110.25.

(B) Emergency Shutdown of Prime Mover. Generators must have provisions to shut down the prime mover. The means of shutdown must comply with all the following:

(1) Be equipped with provisions to disable all prime mover start control circuits to render the prime mover incapable of starting

(2) Initiate a shutdown mechanism that requires a mechanical reset

The provisions to shut down the prime mover are permitted to satisfy the requirements of 445.18(A) where it is capable of being locked in the open position in accordance with 110.25.

(C) Remote Emergency Shutdown. Generators with a greater than 15 kW rating must be provided with a remote emergency stop switch to shut down the prime mover. The remote emergency stop switch must be located outside the equipment room or generator enclosure and must also meet the requirements of 445.18(B)(1) and (B)(2).

(D) Emergency Shutdown in One- and Two-Family Dwelling Units. For other than cord-and-plug-connected portable generators, an emergency shutdown device must be located outside the dwelling unit at a readily accessible location.

Introduction to Article 450—Transformers

Article 450 opens by saying, "This article covers the installation of all transformers." Then it lists eight exceptions. So, what does it really cover? Essentially, Article 450 covers transformers supplying power and lighting loads. So for the purposes of this article only, a transformer is, an individual power transformer, single or poly-phase, identified by a single nameplate unless otherwise indicated.

A major concern with transformers is preventing overheating. The *Code* does not completely address this issue. Article 90 explains that the *NEC* is not a design manual, and it assumes that anyone using the *Code* has a certain level of expertise. Proper transformer selection is an important part of preventing it from overheating. The *NEC* assumes you have already selected a transformer suitable to the load characteristics. For the *Code* to tell you how to do that would push it into the realm of a design manual. Article 450 then takes you to the next logical step—providing overcurrent protection and the proper connections. But this article does not stop there; 450.9 provides ventilation requirements, and 450.13 contains accessibility requirements.

Part I contains the general requirements such as guarding, marking, and accessibility; Part II contains the requirements for different types of transformers; and Part III covers transformer vaults.

450.9 Ventilation

This section was expanded to include a requirement for top horizontal surfaces of transformers to be marked to prohibit storage.

Analysis

EXPANDED Transformers must be installed so the ventilating openings are not blocked by walls or obstructions. It also says that the required clearances from obstructions must be clearly marked on the transformer. A new marking requirement was added for this *NEC* cycle. It requires that where the top surface of a transformer is horizontal and readily accessible the transformer must be marked to prohibit storage on the top of the transformer. No specific language for the marking was included for this new rule.

450.9 Ventilation

Transformers must be installed in accordance with the manufacturer's instructions, and their ventilating openings are not permitted to be blocked [110.3(B)].

Transformer top surfaces that are horizontal and readily accessible must be marked to prohibit storage.

Author's Comment:

▸ Since this rule only applies to readily accessible transformers, it is expected that this will require an "approved" field applied marking much like the requirements similar to generic arc flash labels for panels which are typically supplied by the manufacturer, but field installed.

▸ The internal temperature rise of a transformer is often specified as 239°F (115°C) over a 104°F (40°C) ambient, it is not unreasonable to expect that the top surface of the transformer to reach 170°F, especially where things like paper that have an insulating effect are stored on top of the transformer.

450.14 Disconnecting Means

The revision to this rule clarifies that a remote disconnecting means must be lockable in the open position.

Analysis

CLARIFIED

As we have seen in other disconnect rules, the language was changed to "lockable open" to be consistent with 110.25.

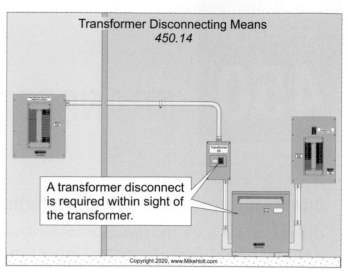

Transformer Disconnecting Means
450.14

A transformer disconnect is required within sight of the transformer.

Copyright 2020, www.MikeHolt.com

▶Figure 450–1

450.14 Disconnecting Means

A transformer disconnect within sight of the transformer is required, unless the location of the disconnect is field marked on the transformer and the disconnect is capable of being locked in the <u>open</u> position with provisions for locking to remain in place whether the lock is installed or not [110.25]. ▶Figure 450–1 and ▶Figure 450–2

Author's Comment:

▸ "Within Sight" means that it is visible and not more than 50 ft from the location of the equipment [Article 100].

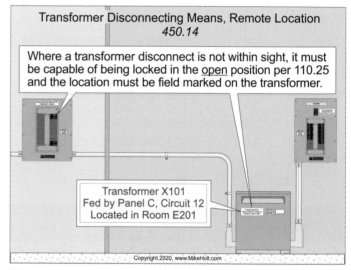

Transformer Disconnecting Means, Remote Location
450.14

Where a transformer disconnect is not within sight, it must be capable of being locked in the <u>open</u> position per 110.25 and the location must be field marked on the transformer.

Transformer X101
Fed by Panel C, Circuit 12
Located in Room E201

Copyright 2020, www.MikeHolt.com

▶Figure 450–2

ARTICLE
480

STORAGE BATTERIES

Introduction to Article 480—Storage Batteries

The stationary battery is the heart of any uninterruptible power supply. Article 480 addresses stationary batteries for commercial and industrial grade power supplies, not the small, "point of use," UPS boxes.

Stationary batteries are also used in other applications, such as emergency power systems. Regardless of the application, if it uses stationary batteries, Article 480 applies.

Lead-acid stationary batteries fall into two general categories; flooded, and valve regulated (VRLA). These differ markedly in such ways as maintainability, total cost of ownership, and scalability. The *NEC* doesn't address these differences, as they are engineering issues and not fire safety or electrical safety matters [90.1].

The *Code* does not address such design issues as optimum tier height, distance between tiers, determination of charging voltage, or string configuration. Nor does it address battery testing, monitoring, or maintenance. All of these involve highly specialized areas of knowledge and are required for optimizing operational efficiency. Standards other than the *NEC* address these topics.

What the *Code* does address, in Article 480, are issues related to preventing electrocution and the ignition of the gases that all stationary batteries (even "sealed" ones) emit.

480.2 Definitions

The definition of "Storage Battery" was revised.

Analysis

CLARIFIED

Storage Battery (Battery). These changes were primarily the result of the previously defined term "Battery" being deleted from this section. It was decided that having only one definition for "Storage Battery" was enough and would prevent any confusion with any other type of battery.

The changes from the previous text now recognize that this article can apply to storage battery equipment, with one or more cells connected together electrically as needed to provide the required operating voltage and current levels. The previous text was revised to define a storage battery as "A single cell, or a group of cells connected together electrically in series, in parallel, or a combination of both." This change was made to align the definition of "battery" in the *NEC* with the one in NFPA 855, *Standard for the Installation of Stationary Energy Storage Systems*. The word "battery" was added in parenthesis following "storage battery" to clarify that those two terms are interchangeable within this article.

480.2 Definitions

The definitions in this section apply only within this article.

Storage Battery. A single or group of rechargeable cells connected together electrically in series, in parallel, or a combination of both, and comprised of lead-acid, nickel-cadmium, or other rechargeable electrochemical types.

480.4 Battery and Cell Terminations

A new subsection (D) was relocated from 706.33 and added here without change.

Analysis

RELOCATED

480.4(D) Accessibility. A new subsection (D) was added for this *Code* cycle and was part of the work of the Energy Storage Task Group that was put together to correlate Article 706, Energy Storage Systems (ESS) and Article 480, Batteries. The group found redundant requirements between the two articles. It was decided to move any requirements that apply to batteries out of Article 706 and place them in Article 480.

480.4 Battery and Cell Terminations

(D) Accessibility. The terminals of all cells or multicell units must be readily accessible for readings, inspections, and cleaning where required by the equipment design. One side of transparent battery containers must be readily accessible for inspection of the internal components.

480.7 DC Disconnect Methods

Subsection 480.7(B) was added. Information in subsection (C) was relocated from 706.30(B) and editorial changes were made. Section 480.7(F)(3) was expanded and subsection (G) with two list items was added.

Analysis

REORGANIZED

480.7(B) Emergency Disconnect. As we have seen in other sections, this subsection was modified to require an external disconnecting means or remote control located at an exterior readily accessible location at one- and two-family dwelling units. This change resulted from a Public Input (PI) to address ongoing concerns expressed by the fire service and other first responders on the need to secure on-site power sources during emergencies. The disconnect must be labeled "EMERGENCY DISCONNECT." Existing subsections (B) through (E) are revised to (C) through (G) to accommodate the new (B) for Emergency Disconnects. The language in the first sentence of (A) tells us that a disconnect is not required where phase conductors derived from a stationary battery system have a voltage of 60V dc or less. The dwelling unit emergency disconnect is now a stand-alone subsection, and it appears this emergency disconnect is required no matter what the battery system voltage is. The marking requirement in (F) was expanded to require an arc flash label and (G), Identification of Power Sources, is a new subsection with two list items requiring identification of battery systems.

RELOCATED

480.7(C) Disconnection of Series Batteries Circuits. Information was relocated from 706.30(B) and added here in subsection (C) as it only applies to batteries. There were editorial changes in the language, but no technical change.

EXPANDED

480.7(F) Notification. This subsection requires the battery disconnect to have specific voltage, fault current, arc flash, and calculation(s) date information markings applied in the field. There is one new list item, one was deleted, and one that was modified. An exception was also added to not require arc flash labels for storage batteries in one- and two-family dwellings.

NEW

480.7(G)(1) Identification of Power Sources. The rule in this new section requires plaques or directories to be installed in accordance with 705.10 and 712.10. Article 705 is Interconnected Electric Power Production Sources and Article 712 is Direct Current Microgrids.

These directory requirements are intended to lend guidance to firefighters so all electric power sources that serve a building or structure can be located and controlled.

The exception to 480.7(G)(1) states that the requirements do not apply if the battery system voltage is 60V or less [480.7(A)].

 NEW **480.7(G)(2) Facilities with Stand-Alone Systems.** These also require a directory denoting the locations of each power source disconnecting means in accordance with 710.10. Some power sources previously required identification, but some did not. Additionally, the different placards or directories could be in different locations.

480.7 Direct-Current Disconnect Methods

(A) Disconnecting Means. A disconnect is required to open all phase conductors derived from a stationary battery system with a voltage over 60V dc. The disconnecting means must be readily accessible and located within sight of the battery system.

> **Author's Comment:**
>
> ▸ OSHA and NFPA 70E both recognize anything above 50 volts to be an electrical shock hazard and appropriate safety related work practices must be employed while working on batteries.

(B) Emergency Disconnect. For one-family and two-family dwellings, a disconnecting means or its remote control for a stationary battery system must be located at a readily accessible location outside the building for emergency use. The disconnect must be labeled "**EMERGENCY DISCONNECT.**"

(D) Remote Actuation. Where a disconnecting means, located in accordance with 480.7(A), is provided with remote controls to activate the disconnecting means, and the controls for the disconnecting means are not located within sight of the stationary battery system, the disconnecting means must be capable of being locked in the open position, in accordance with 110.25, and the location of the controls must be field marked on the disconnecting means.

(F) Notification. The disconnecting means must be legibly marked in the field. A label with the marking must be placed in a conspicuous location near the battery if a disconnecting means is not provided. The marking must be of sufficient durability to withstand the environment involved and must include the following:

(1) Nominal battery voltage

(2) Available fault current derived from the stationary battery system

Note: Battery equipment suppliers can provide information about available fault current on any particular battery model.

(3) An arc flash label in accordance with acceptable industry practice

Note: NFPA 70E, *Standard for Electrical Safety in the Workplace*, aids in determining the severity of potential exposure, planning safe work practices, arc flash labelling, and selecting personal protective equipment.

(4) Date the available fault current calculation was performed

Ex: List items (2), (3), and (4) do not apply to one and two-family dwellings.

(G) Identification of Power Sources. Battery systems must be indicated by 480.7(G)(1) and (G)(2).

(1) Facilities with Utility Services and Battery Systems. Plaques or directories must be installed in accordance with 705.10 and 712.10(A).

Ex: This requirement does not apply where a disconnect in 480.7(A) is not required.

(2) Facilities with Stand-Alone Systems. A permanent plaque or directory must be installed in accordance with 710.10.

Ex: This requirement does not apply where a disconnect in 480.7(A) is not required.

480.10 Battery Locations

This rule was clarified to permit the use of listed fire exit hardware.

Analysis

CLARIFIED

480.10(E) Egress. Both panic and fire exit hardware permit the door to open without requiring the use of one's hands and both are acceptable for the application. Both types of hardware are evaluated to UL 305, *Standard for Panic Hardware*.

480.10 Battery Locations

(E) Egress. Personnel doors intended for entrance to, and egress from, rooms designated as battery rooms must open in the direction of egress and be equipped with listed panic <u>or listed fire exit</u> hardware.

480.12 Battery Interconnections

The rules for the interconnecting of storage batteries were moved from 706.32 to this location.

Analysis

RELOCATED

This section permits the use of flexible cables as identified in Article 400 (in sizes 2/0 AWG and larger) to be used within the battery enclosure, and from the battery to a nearby junction box where they must be connected to an approved wiring method. It previously required the cables to be listed and identified as moisture resistant. The requirement was replaced with one saying the cables must be listed and identified for the environmental conditions.

This use of flexible cable does not appear to meet any of the general uses permitted in 400.10(A), but the reference in this section complies with list item (10) in that subsection "where specifically permitted elsewhere in this *Code*."

480.12 Battery Interconnections

Flexible cables, as identified in Article 400, in sizes 2/0 AWG and larger are permitted within the battery enclosure from battery terminals to a nearby junction box where they must be connected to an approved wiring method. Flexible battery cables are also permitted between batteries and cells within the battery enclosure. Such cables must be listed and identified <u>for the environmental conditions</u>. Flexible, fine-stranded cables may only be used with terminals, lugs, devices, or connectors in accordance with 110.14.

480.13 Ground-Fault Detection

This section was revised and relocated from 706.30(D), and the title was changed.

Analysis

RELOCATED

The title was "Storage Systems of More than 100V," but did not reflect the requirement in the section which is to provide ground-fault detection, and that is the new title.

The section permits battery circuits exceeding 100V between conductors, or to ground, to operate with phase conductors, provided a ground-fault detector and indicator is installed to monitor for ground faults.

480.13 Ground-Fault Detection

<u>Battery circuits</u> exceeding 100 volts between the conductors or to ground are permitted to operate with ungrounded conductors, provided a ground-fault detector and indicator is installed to monitor for ground faults.

SPECIAL OCCUPANCIES

Introduction to Chapter 5—Special Occupancies

Chapter 5, which covers special occupancies, is the first of four *NEC* chapters that deal with special topics. Chapters 6 and 7 cover special equipment and special conditions, respectively. Remember, the first four chapters of the *Code* are sequential and form a foundation for each of the subsequent three and may at times modify or reference those foundational rules.

Chapter 8 covers communications systems (twisted pair and coaxial cable) and is not subject to the requirements of Chapters 1 through 7 except where the requirements are specifically referenced in Chapter 8 [90.3].

What exactly is a "Special Occupancy"? It is a location where a facility, or its use, creates specific conditions that require additional measures to ensure the "practical safeguarding of people and property" purpose of the *NEC* as put forth in Article 90.

Many people struggle to understand the requirements for special occupancies (especially hazardous locations), mostly because of the narrowness of application. If you study the illustrations and explanations here, you will better understand them.

- **Article 500—Hazardous (Classified) Locations.** A hazardous (classified) location is an area where the possibility of fire or explosion exists due to the presence of flammable or combustible liquid-produced vapors, flammable gases, combustible dusts, or easily ignitable fibers/flyings.

- **Article 501—Class I Hazardous (Classified) Locations.** A Class I hazardous (classified) location is an area where flammable or combustible liquid-produced vapors or flammable gases may present the hazard of a fire or explosion.

- **Article 502—Class II Hazardous (Classified) Locations.** A Class II hazardous (classified) location is an area where the possibility of fire or explosion may exist due to the presence of combustible dust.

- **Article 503—Class III Hazardous (Classified) Locations.** Class III hazardous (classified) locations are hazardous because fire or explosion risks may exist due to easily ignitible fibers/flyings. These include materials such as cotton and rayon, which are found in textile mills and clothing manufacturing plants. They can also include establishments and industries such as sawmills and woodworking plants.

- **Article 511—Commercial Garages, Repair and Storage.** These occupancies include locations used for service and repair operations in connection with self-propelled vehicles (including, but not limited to, passenger automobiles, buses, trucks, and tractors) in which flammable liquids or flammable gases are used for fuel or power.

- **Article 514—Motor Fuel Dispensing Facilities.** Article 514 covers gasoline dispensing and service stations where gasoline or other volatile liquids are transferred to the fuel tanks of self-propelled vehicles. Wiring and equipment in the area of service and repair rooms of service stations must comply with the installation requirements in Article 511.

- **Article 517—Health Care Facilities.** This article applies to electrical wiring in human health care facilities such as hospitals, nursing homes, limited care facilities, clinics, medical and dental offices, and ambulatory care, whether permanent or movable. It does not apply to animal veterinary facilities.

- **Article 518—Assembly Occupancies.** Article 518 covers buildings or portions of buildings specifically designed or intended for the assembly of 100 or more persons.

- **Article 525—Carnivals, Circuses, Fairs, and Similar Events.** This article covers the installation of portable wiring and equipment for temporary carnivals, circuses, exhibitions, fairs, traveling attractions, and similar functions, including wiring in or on structures.

- **Article 547—Agricultural Buildings.** Article 547 covers agricultural buildings or those parts of buildings or adjacent areas where excessive dust or dust with water may accumulate, or where a corrosive atmosphere exists.

- **Article 550—Mobile Homes, Manufactured Homes, and Mobile Home Parks.** Article 550 covers electrical conductors and equipment within or on mobile and manufactured homes, conductors that connect mobile and manufactured homes to the electrical supply, and the installation of electrical wiring, luminaires, and electrical equipment in or on mobile and manufactured homes.

- **Article 555—Marinas, Boatyards, and Commercial and Noncommercial Docking Facilities.** This article covers the installation of wiring and equipment in the areas that comprise fixed or floating piers, wharves, docks, and other areas in marinas, boatyards, boat basins, boathouses, and similar locations used, or intended to be used, for the repair, berthing, launching, storing, or fueling of small craft, and the mooring of floating buildings.

- **Article 590—Temporary Installations.** Article 590 covers temporary power and lighting for construction, remodeling, maintenance, repair, demolitions, and decorative lighting.

ARTICLE 500

HAZARDOUS (CLASSIFIED) LOCATIONS

Introduction to Article 500—Hazardous (Classified) Locations

A hazardous (classified) location is an area where the possibility of fire or explosion can be created by the presence of flammable or combustible gases or vapors, combustible dusts, or easily ignitable fibers/flyings. Electric arcs, sparks, and/or heated surfaces can serve as a source of ignition in such environments.

Article 500 provides a foundation for applying Article 501 (Class I Locations), Article 502 (Class II Locations), and Article 503 (Class III Locations)—all of which immediately follow Article 500. This article also provides a foundation for using Articles 510 through 516.

Before you apply any of the articles just mentioned, you must understand and use Article 500 which is fairly long and detailed. You'll notice when studying this article that there are many Informational Notes which you should review. Although Informational Notes are not *NEC* requirements [90.5(C)], they contain information that helps *Code* users better understand the related *NEC* rules.

A Fire Triangle (fuel, oxygen, and energy source) helps illustrate the concept of how combustion occurs. ▶Figure 500–1

- ▸ *Fuel.* Flammable gases or vapors, combustible dusts, and easily ignitable fibers/flyings.
- ▸ *Oxygen.* Air and oxidizing atmospheres.
- ▸ *Ignition Source (Heat).* Electric arcs or sparks, heat-producing equipment such as luminaires and motors, failure of transformers, coils, or solenoids, as well as sparks caused by metal tools dropping on metal surfaces.

Many of the graphics contained in Chapter 5 use two shades of red to identify a Division location (darker red for Division 1 and lighter red to identify Division 2). In some cases, these color schemes are used as a background color to help you tell if the graphic applies to Division 1, Division 2, or both (split color background).

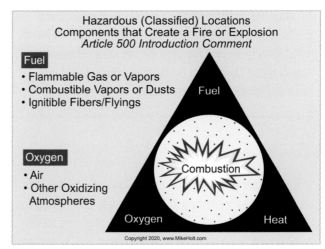

Hazardous (Classified) Locations
Components that Create a Fire or Explosion
Article 500 Introduction Comment

Fuel
- Flammable Gas or Vapors
- Combustible Vapors or Dusts
- Ignitible Fibers/Flyings

Oxygen
- Air
- Other Oxidizing Atmospheres

Combustion

Fuel

Oxygen   Heat

Copyright 2020, www.MikeHolt.com

▶Figure 500–1

500.1 Scope—Articles 500 Through 503 Informational Notes

The Informational Note that preceded this section was relocated without change to follow 500.1 as Informational Note No. 4.

Analysis

RELOCATED Informational Notes call attention to the fact that information has been extracted from other NFPA documents. The document number and section are shown in brackets following the extracted information. These types of rules are under the purview of the other document and cannot be changed by the Code-making process. In the case of this article, the two documents being referenced are:

NFPA 497, *Recommended Practice for the Classification of Flammable Liquids, Gasses, or Vapors and of Hazardous (Classified) Locations for Electrical Installations in Chemical Process Areas*, and NFPA 499, *Recommended Practice for the Classification of Combustible Dusts and Hazardous (Classified) Locations in Chemical Process Areas*.

Author's Comment:

▸ It is important to understand that, in general, the *NEC* tells us how to wire something only after it has been classified using other documents such as NFPA 497. There are specific occupancies, such as those in 511 through 516, where the *NEC* does define the classified areas, but in general other documents must be used to define the area. For chemical process plants, the people involved in the determination of the classified area boundaries would typically include process and mechanical engineers along with the electrical engineer.

500.4 Documentation

The title of this section was change from "General" to "Documentation" and a new Informational Note was added.

Analysis

CLARIFIED The title now matches the requirements of the section which is that hazardous (classified) locations must be properly documented and the documentation made available to those who design, install, inspect, maintain, or operate electrical equipment at those locations.

500.4 Documentation

All areas designated as hazardous (classified) locations must be properly documented. The documentation must be available to those who are authorized to design, install, inspect, maintain, or operate the electrical equipment.

Author's Comment:

▸ Proper documentation of hazardous areas assists the designer, installer, and authority having jurisdiction in ensuring adherence to the stringent requirements contained in Articles 501 through 517 of the *Code*.

▸ To assist in compliance with the above requirements, some authorities having jurisdiction require drawings that indicate hazardous (classified) location areas and their classification(s).

▸ The *NEC* does not classify specific hazardous (classified) locations in Articles 511 through 517, unless identified as such in the articles. Determining the classification of a specific hazardous area is the responsibility of those who understand the dangers of the products being used, such as the fire marshal, plant facility engineer, or insurance underwriter. It is not the responsibility of the electrical designer, electrical contractor, or electrical inspector. Before performing any wiring in or near a hazardous (classified) location, contact the plant facility and design engineer to ensure that proper installation methods and materials are used. Be sure to review 500.4(B) for additional standards that might need to be consulted.

Other Reference Standards. Important information related to topics covered in Chapter 5 may be found in other publications.

Note 1: For further information on the classification of locations, see:

▸ *Recommended Practice for the Classification of Flammable Liquids, Gases, or Vapors and of Hazardous (Classified) Locations for Electrical Installations in Chemical Process Areas,* NFPA 497

▸ *Standard for Dipping and Coating Processes Using Flammable or Combustible Liquids,* NFPA 34

▸ *Area Classification in Hazardous (Classified) Dust Locations,* ISA 12.10

▸ *Flammable and Combustible Liquids Code,* NFPA 30

▸ *Recommended Practice for Classification of Locations of Electrical Installations at Petroleum Facilities Classified as Class I, Division 1 and Division 2,* ANSI/API RP 500

▸ *Standard for Spray Application Using Flammable or Combustible Materials,* NFPA 33

▸ *Liquefied Petroleum Gas Code,* NFPA 58

▸ *Standard for Fire Overcurrent Protection in Wastewater Treatment and Collection Facilities,* NFPA 820

Note 2: For further information on protection against static electricity and lightning hazards in hazardous (classified) locations, see:

▸ *Standard for the Installation of Lightning Protection Systems,* NFPA 780

▸ *Recommended Practice on Static Electricity,* NFPA 77

▸ *Protection Against Ignitions Arising Out of Static Lightning and Stray Currents,* API RP 2003

500.5 Classifications of Hazardous Locations

Wording was added in 500.5(C)(1) to clarify the class and division of Group E combustible dusts.

Analysis

CLARIFIED **500.5(C) Class II Locations, (1) Class II, Division 1 Location.** There are no Division 2 locations where Group "E" products are handled. This was the intent of the previous language but was not completely clear. The new wording says, "in normal or abnormal operating conditions." With other combustible dusts, the Division 1 location is where there is combustible dust in ignitable quantities under normal operating conditions, and Division 2 is where the ignitable quantities exist under only abnormal operating conditions. The revision clarifies that (for combustible metal dusts) if there is an ignitable quantity of metal dust, the location is Division 1 regardless of the operating condition.

500.5 Classifications of Hazardous Locations

(C) Identification of a Class II Location. Class II locations are hazardous because of the presence of combustible dust. ▸Figure 500–2

Identification of a Class II Location
500.5(C)

Class II locations are hazardous because of the presence of combustible dust.

Copyright 2020, www.MikeHolt.com

▸Figure 500–2

(1) Class II, Division 1 Location. A Class II, Division 1 location is an area where combustible dust may exist under any of the following conditions:

(1) Nonconductive combustible dust is continuously or periodically suspended in the air in sufficient quantities to produce mixtures that will ignite or explode, or

---

(2) If faulty equipment releases ignitible mixtures of dust and the equipment becomes a source of ignition.

(3) In which Group E combustible dusts may be present in quantities sufficient to be hazardous in normal or abnormal operating conditions.

Note: Dusts containing magnesium or aluminum are particularly hazardous, and the use of extreme precaution is necessary to avoid ignition and explosion.

500.7 Protection Techniques

An editorial change in the parent text clarifies the various protection methods permitted for the different hazardous location classes where electrical and electronic equipment might be installed.

Analysis

CLARIFIED

The parent text was updated to include subsections (A) through (P) as they are all Division approved protection techniques.

500.7 Protection Techniques

Electrical and electronic equipment in hazardous (classified) locations must be protected by one or more of the following techniques:

(A) Explosionproof Equipment. Explosionproof equipment is permitted in any Class 1 location for which it is identified. ▶Figure 500–3

> **Author's Comment:**
>
> ▶ Explosionproof equipment is designed to be capable of withstanding and containing the force of an internal explosion, and the hot gases within the enclosure cool as they escape [Article 100]. ▶Figure 500–4

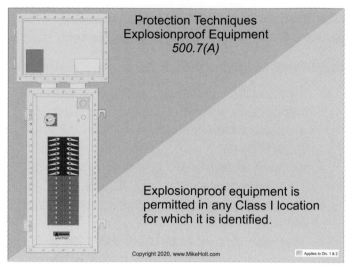

Protection Techniques
Explosionproof Equipment
500.7(A)

Explosionproof equipment is permitted in any Class I location for which it is identified.

Copyright 2020, www.MikeHolt.com

Applies to Div. 1 & 2

▶Figure 500–3

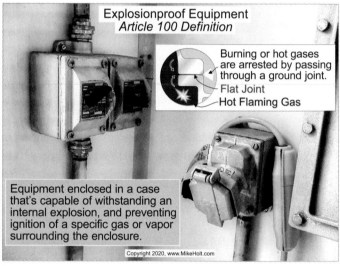

Explosionproof Equipment
Article 100 Definition

Burning or hot gases are arrested by passing through a ground joint.
Flat Joint
Hot Flaming Gas

Equipment enclosed in a case that's capable of withstanding an internal explosion, and preventing ignition of a specific gas or vapor surrounding the enclosure.

Copyright 2020, www.MikeHolt.com

▶Figure 500–4

(B) Dust-Ignitionproof Enclosures. Dust-ignitionproof enclosures are permitted in any Class II location. ▶Figure 500–5

> **Author's Comment:**
>
> ▶ Dust-ignitionproof enclosures are designed to exclude dusts and will not permit arcs, sparks, or heat within the enclosure to cause the ignition of exterior dust [Article 100].

(C) Dusttight Enclosures. Dusttight enclosures are permitted in Class II, Division 2 or any Class III location. ▶Figure 500–6

(D) Purged and Pressurized Systems. Purged and pressurized systems are permitted for equipment in any hazardous (classified) locations for which they are identified. ▶Figure 500–7

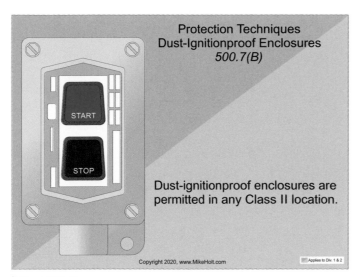

▶Figure 500–5

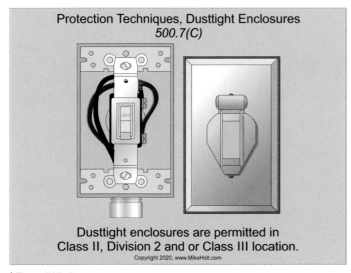

▶Figure 500–6

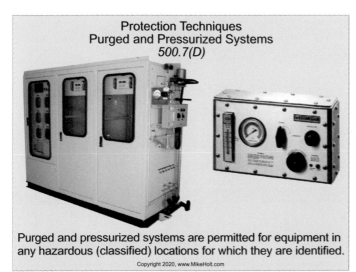

▶Figure 500–7

Author's Comment:

▸ "Purging" is supplying an enclosure with a safe gas at a flow and pressure to sufficiently reduce concentrations of flammable gases, flammable liquid-produced vapors, or combustible liquid-produced vapors to a safe level. "Pressurization" is supplying an enclosure with a safe gas, with or without a continuous flow, with enough pressure to prevent the entrance of combustible dust or ignitible fibers/flyings [Article 100].

(I) Oil-Immersed Contacts. Oil-immersed make-and-break contacts can be installed in a Class I, Division 2 location.

(J) Hermetically Sealed Contacts. Hermetically sealed contacts can be installed in Class I, Division 2; Class II, Division 2; or Class III, Division 1 and 2 Locations.

Author's Comment:

▸ "Hermetically Sealed" is when equipment is sealed against the entrance of an external atmosphere where the seal is made by methods such as soldering, brazing, welding, or the fusion of glass to metal [Article 100].

(P) Other Protection Techniques. Other protection techniques used in equipment identified for use in hazardous (classified) locations are permitted.

500.8 Equipment Involving Optical Radiation

A new subsection (G) addressing the risk of ignition from sources of optical radiation (such as laser or LED sources) was added.

Analysis

550.8(G) Equipment Involving Optical Radiation. The new protection techniques discussed in 500.7 now also provide methods to protect from optical radiation ignition of hazardous atmospheres. An exception says that the provisions of this new subsection do not apply to luminaires (including LEDs) that have "divergent" light sources.

NEW

CLASS I HAZARDOUS (CLASSIFIED) LOCATIONS

Introduction to Article 501—Class I Hazardous (Classified) Locations

If sufficient flammable or combustible gases, vapors, or liquids are, or may be, present to produce an explosive or ignitable mixture, you have a Class I location. Examples of such locations include some fuel storage areas, certain solvent storage areas, grain processing facilities (where hexane is used), plastic extrusion areas where oil removal is part of the process, refineries, and paint storage areas. Article 500 contained a general background on hazardous (classified) locations, and described the differences between Class I, II, and III locations and the differences between Division 1 and Division 2. Article 501 contains the actual Class I, Division 1 and Division 2 installation requirements, including wiring methods, seals, and specific equipment requirements.

501.10 Wiring Methods

The language throughout 501.10(B)(1) was changed to clarify that both threaded and threadless fittings can used with IMC and RMC in Class I, Division 2 locations. Others were revised and a new list item (9) was added.

Analysis

CLARIFIED
501.10(B)(1)(1) Class I, Division 2. The previous *Code* listed only threadless fittings as being permitted. In the 2014 *NEC*, list item (1) permitted all the wiring methods shown in 510.10(A) for Division 1 locations to be used in Division 2 locations. In 2017 that language was changed to permit IMC and RMC with listed threadless fittings to be used in Division 2 locations. Division 1 locations require threaded fittings and the change for 2017 was intended to permit both threaded and threadless fittings; however, the actual language permitted only those of the threadless type.

EXPANDED
501.10(B)(1)(3), (4), and (5). List items (3) for Power-Limited Tray Cable, (4) Instrument Tray Cable, and (5) that includes TC-ER cables, were revised to require an EGC in addition to the "drain wire." The product standard does not require an equipment grounding conductor (EGC) for these cables.

These cables are often shielded and the shield has a drain wire, but such a wire is not suitable for use as an EGC since it is frequently connected at one end of the cable only, and is smaller than what would be required for an EGC. This will not require a new product as these cables are currently available with EGCs.

REDUCED
501.10(B)(1)(6). List item (6) covers wiring methods in classified areas that are also corrosive areas. It expanded to specifically permit the use of PVC coated RMC and IMC conduits. While it has been generally accepted that coated IMC and RMC is still the same conduit, the change was made to avoid any confusion.

RTRC (fiberglass) was permitted for this application, but in the previous *Code* it was restricted to use in industrial establishments with restricted public access where the conditions of maintenance and supervision ensure that only qualified persons service the installation.

• • •

That restriction was removed and RTRC, as well as coated IMC and RMC, are permitted to be used without restriction in corrosive Class I, Division 2 applications.

Schedule 80 PVC conduit has the same restriction as did RTRC, but it was not removed. The Code-Making Panel does not see the Schedule 80 PVC as providing the same physical protection as the other conduits that may be used in corrosive locations and chose to retain the industrial restriction.

NEW **501.10(B)(1)(9).** This new list item now permits listed Type P cable to be used in Class I, Division 2 locations. Unlike Division 1, where only the metal armored type is permitted, Type P with or without metal braid armor is permitted for use in Division 2. It must be terminated with fittings listed for the location and installed in accordance with the requirements of Article 337.

501.10 Wiring Methods

(B) Class I, Division 2.

(1) General. All wiring methods included in Class 1, Division 1 locations [501.10(A)] and the following wiring methods are permitted within a Class I, Division 2 location.

(1) Rigid and intermediate metal conduit with listed threaded or threadless fittings. ▶Figure 501–1

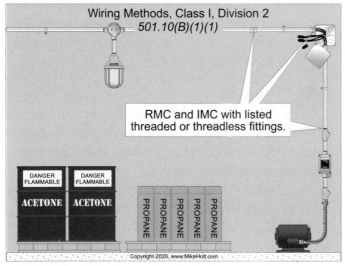

▶Figure 501–1

(2) Enclosed gasketed wireways.

(3) Types PLTC and PLTC-ER cable terminated in accordance with Parts II and III of Article 725. Type PLTC-ER cable must include an equipment grounding conductor in addition to any drain wire that might be present.

(4) Types ITC and ITC-ER cable as permitted in 727.4. Type ITC-ER cable must include an equipment grounding conductor in addition to a drain wire.

(5) Types MC, MV, TC, or TC-ER cable, including installation in cable tray systems. Type TC-ER cable must include an equipment grounding conductor in addition to any drain wire that might be present. All cable types must be terminated with listed fittings.

(6) Where metallic conduit does not provide sufficient corrosion resistance, any of the following wiring methods are permitted:

   a. Listed reinforced thermosetting resin conduit (RTRC), factory elbows, and associated fittings, all marked with the suffix "-XW,"

   b. PVC-coated rigid metal conduit (RMC), factory elbows, and associated fittings,

   c. PVC-coated intermediate metal conduit (IMC), factory elbows, and associated fittings, or

   d. In industrial establishments with restricted public access, where the conditions of maintenance and supervision ensure that only qualified persons service the installation, Schedule 80 PVC conduit, factory elbows, and associated fittings.

501.15 Raceway and Cable Seals

The language is this section was revised to clarify that standard conduit couplings are permitted between an enclosure that requires a seal and the sealing fitting.

Analysis

CLARIFIED **501.15(A)(1) Conduit Seals, Class I, Division 1.** The last paragraph of this section was revised to clarify that standard conduit couplings are permitted between an enclosure that is required to be sealed and the sealing fitting.

The previous language specified the use of an explosionproof coupling—something that simply does not exist. The revision in the language now just specifies threaded couplings. It also permits the use of explosionproof fittings such as unions, reducers, elbows, and capped elbows not larger than the trade size of the raceway. The same change was made in 501.15(D) where couplings are installed between a seal-off fitting and an enclosure that is required to be explosionproof.

501.15 Raceway and Cable Seals

Seals for raceway and cable systems must comply with 501.15(A) through (F).

Note 1: Raceway and cable seals must be installed to: ▶Figure 501–2

- ▶ Minimize the passage of gases and vapors from one portion of electrical equipment to another through the raceway or cable.
- ▶ Minimize the passage of flames from one portion of electrical equipment to another through the raceway or cable.
- ▶ Limit internal explosions to within the explosionproof enclosure.

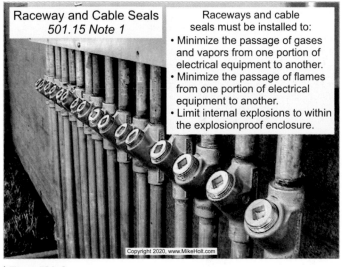

Raceway and Cable Seals
501.15 Note 1

Raceways and cable seals must be installed to:
• Minimize the passage of gases and vapors from one portion of electrical equipment to another.
• Minimize the passage of flames from one portion of electrical equipment to another.
• Limit internal explosions to within the explosionproof enclosure.

▶Figure 501–2

(A) Raceway Seal—Class I, Division 1. In Class I, Division 1 locations, raceway seals must be located as follows:

(1) Entering Enclosures. A raceway seal is required in each raceway that enters an explosionproof enclosure if either (1) or (2) apply:

(1) If the explosionproof enclosure contains make-and-break contacts. ▶Figure 501–3

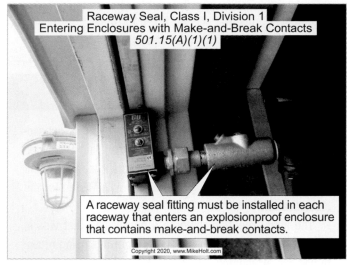

Raceway Seal, Class I, Division 1
Entering Enclosures with Make-and-Break Contacts
501.15(A)(1)(1)

A raceway seal fitting must be installed in each raceway that enters an explosionproof enclosure that contains make-and-break contacts.

▶Figure 501–3

Ex: A raceway seal is not required if the make-and-break contacts are:

(1) *Within a hermetically sealed chamber.* ▶Figure 501–4

(2) *Immersed in oil in accordance with 501.115(B)(1)(2).*

(3) *Contained within an enclosure that is marked "Leads Factory Sealed," "Factory Sealed," "Seal not Required," or the equivalent.*

Raceway Seal, Class I, Division 1
Entering Enclosures with Make-and-Break Contacts
501.15(A)(1)(1) Ex (1)

FACTORY SEALED
INTERNAL SEAL NOT REQUIRED

A raceway seal is not required if the make-and-break contacts are within a hermetically sealed chamber.

▶Figure 501–4

501.105 Meters, Instruments, and Relays

A new exception was added to permit the use of cord-and-plug connections that are not listed for Class I, Division 2 locations in industrial establishments.

Analysis

NEW

501.105(B)(6) Class I, Division 2. This subsection addresses the use of cord-and-plug-connected equipment in Class I, Division 2 locations and requires the cord-and-plug connection to be listed for the classification.

The new exception restores a permission that was in the 2014 *NEC*, but not in the 2017. It permits using receptacles and attachment plugs that are not listed for Class I, Division 2 locations where there is a label warning against plugging and unplugging while energized and the installation complies with 501.105(B)(6)(2) through (4). This exception is limited to industrial establishments where the conditions of maintenance and supervision ensure that only qualified persons service the installation.

The 2017 *Code* limited these Class I, Division 2 cord-and-plug-connections to circuits with a maximum current of 3A. That restriction was deleted as there is no current prohibition per the UL standard.

ARTICLE 502

CLASS II HAZARDOUS (CLASSIFIED) LOCATIONS

Introduction to Article 502—Class II Hazardous (Classified) Locations

If an area has combustible dust present, it is considered to be a Class II location. Examples of such locations include flour mills, grain silos, coal bins, wood pulp storage areas, and munitions plants.

Article 502 follows a logical arrangement similar to that of Article 501 and provides guidance in selecting equipment and wiring methods for Class II locations, including distinctions between Class II, Division 1 and Class II, Division 2 requirements.

502.10 Wiring Methods

Language was added to clarify 502.10(B) and a new subsection was added.

Analysis

NEW
502.10(A)(2) Class II, Division 1. While Type P is a very flexible wiring method, Type TC is often made using hard-drawn copper and is not as flexible. However, this change permits the use of both for flexible connections.

CLARIFIED
502.10(B)(1)(2) and (3) Class 2, Division 2. List item (2) permits the use of rigid metal conduit (RMC) with listed threaded or threadless fittings, and list item (3) is a relocation permitting the use of electrical metallic tubing (EMT) and dusttight raceways.

RELOCATED
502.10(B)(1)(4). This was (3) but became (4) when EMT and dusttight wireways were moved to (3). Type MI was deleted from this list item as it is permitted in Division 1 applications, and since (1) permits all Division 1 methods to be used in Division 2 it was redundant.

CLARIFIED
502.10(B)(1)(4), (5), and (6). List items (4) for power-limited tray cable, (5) for power-limited cable, and (6) for instrument tray cable that includes Type TC-ER cables, were revised to require an EGC in addition to the "drain wire." The product standard does not require an equipment grounding conductor (EGC) for these cables. They are often shielded and the shield has a drain wire, but such a wire is not suitable for use as an EGC since it is frequently connected at one end of the cable only, and is smaller than what would be required for an EGC. This will not require a new product as these cables are currently available with EGCs.

CLARIFIED
502.10(B)(1)(7). List item (7) applies where metal conduit does not have enough corrosion resistance was revised in both format and content.

502.10 Wiring Methods

(A) Class II, Division 1

(1) General. The following wiring methods can be installed in a Class II, Division 1 location: ▶Figure 502–1

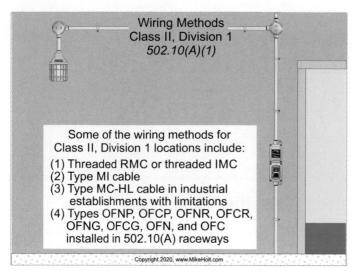

▸Figure 502–1

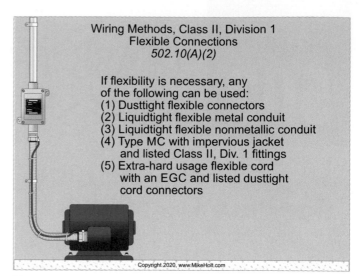

▸Figure 502–2

(1) Threaded rigid metal conduit (Type RMC) or threaded interme-diate metal conduit (Type IMC).

(2) Type MI cable terminated with fittings that are listed for the location.

(3) In industrial establishments with restricted public access where only qualified persons will service the installation, MC-HL cable listed for use in Class II, Division 1 locations with a gas/vapor-tight continuous corrugated metallic sheath, an overall jacket of suitable polymeric material, a separate equipment grounding conductor(s) sized in accordance with 250.122, based on the rating of the overcurrent protective device, and terminated with fittings that are listed for the location.

(4) Types OFNP, OFCP, OFNR, OFCR, OFNG, OFCG, OFN, and OFC optical fiber cable can be installed in raceways [502.10(A)] and must be sealed in accordance with 502.15.

(2) Flexible Connections. If flexibility is necessary, any of the following wiring methods are permitted in a Class II, Division 1 loca-tion: ▸Figure 502–2

(1) Dusttight flexible connectors.

(2) Liquidtight flexible metal conduit, (Type LFMC), with listed fittings.

(3) Liquidtight flexible nonmetallic conduit, (Type LFNC), with fittings that are listed.

(4) Interlocked armor Type MC cable with an impervious jacket and termination fittings that are listed for Class II, Division 1 locations.

(5) Flexible cords listed for extra-hard usage, containing an equip-ment grounding conductor and terminated with listed dusttight flexible cord connectors. The flexible cord must be installed in accordance with 502.140.

(3) Boxes and Fittings. Boxes and fittings must be provided with threaded bosses and must be dusttight. Boxes and fittings in which taps, joints, or terminal connections are made, or used in locations where dusts are of a combustible, electrically conductive nature [500.6(B)(1) Group E], must be identified for Class II locations. ▸Figure 502–3

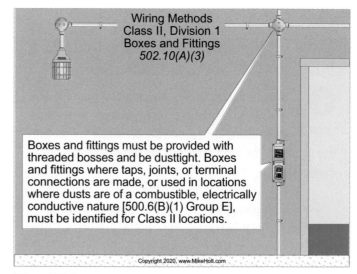

▸Figure 502–3

(B) Class II, Division 2

(1) General. In Class II, Division 2 locations, the following wiring methods are permitted: ▸Figure 502–4

(1) Any of the wiring methods in 502.10(A).

(2) Rigid metal conduit, (RMC), and intermediate metal conduit, (IMC), with listed threaded or threadless fittings.

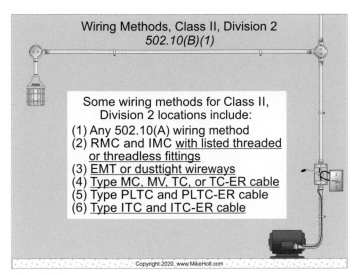

▶Figure 502–4

(3) Electrical metallic tubing, (EMT), or dusttight wireways

(4) Type MC, MV, TC, or TC-ER cable, including installation in cable tray systems. Type TC-ER cable must include an equipment grounding conductor in addition to any drain wire that might be present. The cable must be terminated with listed fittings.

(5) Type PLTC and PLTC-ER cable in accordance with Parts II and III of Article 725, including installation in cable tray systems. The cable must be terminated with listed fittings. Type PLTC-ER cable must include an equipment grounding conductor in addition to a drain wire that might be present.

(6) Type ITC and ITC-ER cable as permitted in 727.4 and terminated with listed fittings. Type ITC-ER cable must include an equipment grounding conductor in addition to a drain wire.

(7) Where metal conduit will not provide sufficient corrosion resistance, any of the following is permitted:

a. Listed reinforced thermosetting resin conduit (RTRC), factory elbows, and associated fittings, all marked with the suffix "-XW"

b. PVC-coated rigid metal conduit (RMC), factory elbows, and associated fittings.

c. PVC-coated intermediate metal conduit (IMC), factory elbows, and associated fittings.

d. In industrial establishments with restricted public access, where the conditions of maintenance and supervision ensure that only qualified persons service the installation, Schedule 80 PVC conduit, factory elbows, and associated fittings

(8) Types OFNP, OFCP, OFNR, OFCR, OFNG, OFCG, OFN, and OFC optical fiber cables can be installed in cable trays or raceways [502.10(B)] and must be sealed in accordance with 502.15. ▶Figure 502–5

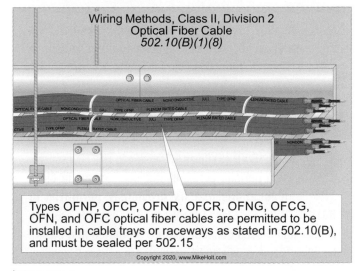

▶Figure 502–5

(2) Flexible Connections. If flexibility is required, wiring methods complying with 502.10(A)(2) are permitted in a Class II, Division 2 location.

(4) Boxes and Fittings. Boxes and fittings in Class II, Division 2 areas must be dusttight. ▶Figure 502–6

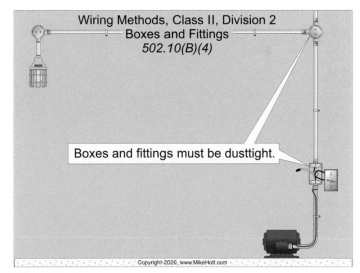

▶Figure 502–6

502.150 Signaling, Alarm, Remote-Control, and Communications Systems; Meters, Instruments, and Relays

Subsection 502.150(B)(5) was added which allows the use of cord-and-plug-connections under certain conditions in Class II, Division 2 locations.

Analysis

NEW

502.150(B)(5) Class II, Division 2. This new subsection permits cord-and-plug-connections in Class II locations just as previously permitted in 501.105(B)(6) for Class I locations. The hazards are very similar and if such connections are permitted in a Class I location, they should also be permitted in a Class II location.

ARTICLE 503

CLASS III HAZARDOUS (CLASSIFIED) LOCATIONS

Introduction to Article 503—Class III Hazardous (Classified) Locations

The Class III location scope can be a bit cumbersome, and some may have a hard time comprehending what it means. If you have easily ignitable fibers/flyings present, you may have a Class III location. Examples of such locations include sawmills, textile mills, and fiber processing plants. In many cases, the distinction between Class II and Class III locations may simply be the size of the particles. The definition of "Combustible Dust" in Article 100 defines it based on the size of the particles, so the same material (such as sawdust) may be subject to Article 503 if the predominant material is "larger" than the definition.

Author's Comment:

▸ Article 100 defines "Combustible Dust" as dust particles that are 500 microns in size or smaller. That is approximately 2/100ths of an inch!

503.10 Wiring Methods

While there were both editorial and technical changes made to this section, the primary revision here was to require cable tray systems to contain an equipment grounding conductor.

Analysis

EXPANDED **503.10(A)(1) Class III, Division 1.** List items (2), (3), and (4) contain the first technical revisions and are identical to those made in Articles 501 and 502. Types PLTC, PLTC-ER, ITC, ITC-ER, and TC-ER cables are now required to contain an EGC in addition to any drain wire.

These cables often have only a shield drain conductor that is not suitable for use as an EGC. Types MC and MI cables were deleted from list item (4) as they are already included in (1) so there is no reason to have the permission to use these two cables in both list items.

Language was added to clarify that the remaining cable types (MV, TC, and TC-ER) are permitted to be installed in cable tray systems. The previous language indicating cables that are installed in cable tray systems be installed in single layers with a spacing not less than the diameter of the larger adjacent cable was deleted. The panel comment indicated that a buildup of fibers or flyings is not likely and there is no need for the previously required spacing. With this change, the exception that followed this list item, which permitted MC cable installation without spacing required by 503.10(A)(1)(4), eliminates the need for the exception and was deleted.

503.10 Wiring Methods

The wiring methods permitted in Class III locations include:

(A) Class III, Division 1 Location

(1) General. The following wiring methods can be installed in a Class III, Division 1 location: ▸Figure 503–1

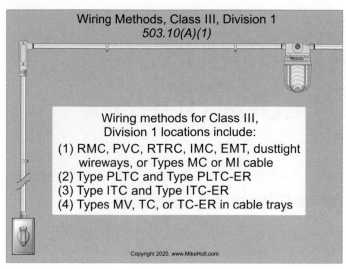

Wiring Methods, Class III, Division 1
503.10(A)(1)

Wiring methods for Class III,
Division 1 locations include:
(1) RMC, PVC, RTRC, IMC, EMT, dusttight
wireways, or Types MC or MI cable
(2) Type PLTC and Type PLTC-ER
(3) Type ITC and Type ITC-ER
(4) Types MV, TC, or TC-ER in cable trays

Copyright 2020, www.MikeHolt.com

▶Figure 503–1

(1) Rigid metal conduit, (Type RMC), PVC conduit, RTRC conduit, intermediate metal conduit, (Type IMC), electrical metallic tubing, dusttight wireways, or Types MC or MI cable terminated with fittings that are listed.

(2) Types PLTC and PLTC-ER cable terminated with listed fittings in accordance with Parts II and III of Article 725. Type PLTC-ER cable must include an equipment grounding conductor in addition to any drain wire that might be present.

(3) Type ITC and ITC-ER cable as permitted in 727.4 and terminated with listed fittings. Type ITC-ER cable must include an equipment grounding conductor in addition to a drain wire.

(4) Types MV, TC, or TC-ER cable including installation in cable tray systems. Type TC-ER cable must include an equipment grounding conductor in addition to any drain wire that might be present. The cable must be terminated with listed fittings.

ARTICLE 511

COMMERCIAL GARAGES, REPAIR AND STORAGE

Introduction to Article 511—Commercial Garages, Repair and Storage

Article 511 covers locations used for the service and repair of vehicles that use volatile flammable liquids or flammable gases for fuel.

First, it is essential to understand whether the facility is a major or minor repair garage. Pay careful attention to these definitions as you study this article. The next factor that makes a difference in the classification of a location is the presence or absence of a below-floor pit. Finally, mechanical ventilation is critical and can change the classification of a location. Read this material carefully, review the illustrations, and you will find that the Article 511 requirements are not that difficult.

511.1 Scope

The Informational Note referencing NFPA 30A, *Code for Motor Fuel Dispensing Facilities and Repair Garages* was relocated to follow the scope statement.

Analysis

RELOCATED As with other hazardous area articles, this one contains information that was extracted from other *NFPA* standards. In this case the standard is NFPA 30A, *Code for Motor Fuel Dispensing Facilities and Repair Garages*. Following any such extracted information is the section number brackets. While the actual text from the book may have editorial changes, no change in the technical requirements of the extracted language is permitted to be made by the Code-Making Panel (CMP). The technical information can be changed only by the CMP for NFPA 30A.

511.1 Scope

Article 511 applies to areas used for the service and repair operations of self-propelled vehicles including passenger automobiles, buses, trucks, tractors, and so on, in which volatile flammable liquids or flammable gases are used for fuel or power. ▶Figure 511–1

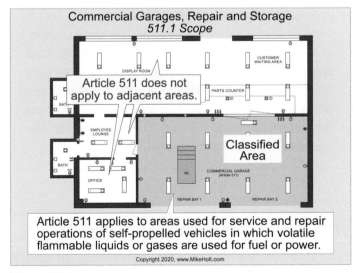

▶Figure 511–1

Author's Comment:

▸ Installations within the scope of Article 511 include automobile service/repair centers; service/repair garages for commercial vehicles such as trucks and tractors; service/repair garages for fleet vehicles such as cars, buses, and trucks; and shops that service motorcycles and all-terrain vehicles (ATVs).

▸ This article does not apply to garages used for diesel fueled or electric vehicle service.

▸ Definitions for this Article have been relocated to Part III of Article 100.

511.3 Area Classification, General

Additional language and a new Informational Note were added to this section.

Analysis

CLARIFIED The new language says that where the term "Class I" is used with respect to Zone classifications, it applies to Zones 0, 1, and 2. The new Informational Note explains that Zones 0, 1, and 2 apply to areas where the hazard is only flammable gasses, vapors, or liquids. The term "Class I" is no longer used with those zones as it is redundant. It will still appear in some *Code* sections that were extracted from other documents over which the technical committees for the *NEC* do not have the authority to make changes. The same revision was made in Articles 511 through 516.

511.3 Classification of Hazardous Areas

General. Where Class I liquids or gaseous fuels are stored, handled, or transferred, electrical wiring and electrical utilization equipment must be designed in accordance with the requirements for Class I, Division 1 or 2 hazardous (classified) locations.

511.8 Underground Wiring Below Class I Locations

The title was revised to clarify that the use of IMC and RMC threaded fittings applies to wiring installed below a Class I location only.

Analysis

CLARIFIED There was never an intent to require the use of threaded RMC or IMC conduit in underground installations when the aboveground area is not classified. The addition of the words "below Class I locations" in the title clarifies that the rule applies below only the classified locations. There is an exception that remains unchanged that permits the use of PVC, RTRC, and HDPE conduits below classified areas as long as these conduits have at least 2 ft of cover and RMC or IMC is used to emerge from below grade.

511.8 Underground Wiring Below Class I Locations

Wiring below a commercial garage must be threaded rigid metal conduit or intermediate metal conduit.

Ex: Type PVC conduit, Type RTRC conduit, and Type HDPE conduit can be installed below a commercial garage if buried under not less than 2 ft of cover. Threaded rigid metal conduit or threaded intermediate metal conduit must be used for the last 2 ft of the underground run. ▸Figure 511–2

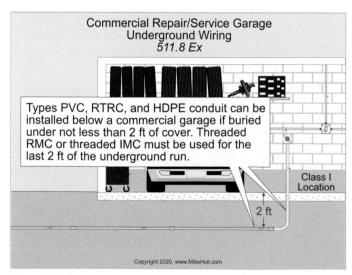

Commercial Repair/Service Garage
Underground Wiring
511.8 Ex

Types PVC, RTRC, and HDPE conduit can be installed below a commercial garage if buried under not less than 2 ft of cover. Threaded RMC or threaded IMC must be used for the last 2 ft of the underground run.

Class I Location

2 ft

Copyright 2020, www.MikeHolt.com

▸Figure 511–2

511.12 Ground-Fault Circuit-Interrupter Protection for Personal

This rule was expanded by referencing the requirements of 210.8(B).

Analysis

EXPANDED

In the previous *Code* this section required GFCI protection for only single-phase 15A and 20A receptacles located in areas where electrical diagnostic equipment, electric hand tools, or portable lighting equipment would be used. The revised language simply states that GFCI protection is required for occupancies covered by Article 511 in accordance with 210.8(B). This is a fairly major change in that 210.8(B) applies to receptacles on branch circuits with a voltage of 150V or less to ground, and where the single-phase current rating is 50A or less and 100A or less for three-phase circuits.

511.12 GFCI-Protected Receptacles

GFCI protection is required in accordance with 210.8(B).

Author's Comment:

▸ This change provides consistency of application between the GFCI requirements of 210.8(B) and the governing occupancy within Article 511.

ARTICLE 514

MOTOR FUEL DISPENSING FACILITIES

Introduction to Article 514—Motor Fuel Dispensing Facilities

The portion of a facility where fuel is stored and dispensed into the fuel tanks of motor vehicles and marine craft, or into approved containers, must comply with Article 514.

What is most striking is the large table that makes up about half of this article. It does not provide any electrical requirements, list any electrical specifications, or address any electrical equipment. What it does tell you is how to classify a motor fuel dispensing area. The rest of this article contains specific provisions and refers to other articles that must be applied.

Author's Comment:

▸ Diesel fuel is not a flammable liquid. Therefore, areas associated with diesel dispensing equipment and associated wiring are not required to comply with the hazardous (classified) location requirements of Article 514 [514.3(A)]. However, the other requirements in this article still apply.

514.1 Scope

The Informational Note referencing NFPA 30A, *Code for Motor Fuel Dispensing Facilities and Repair Garages* was relocated to follow the scope statement.

Analysis

RELOCATED The relocated Informational Note refers to extracted material from NFPA 30A, *Code for Motor Fuel Dispensing Facilities and Repair Garages*.

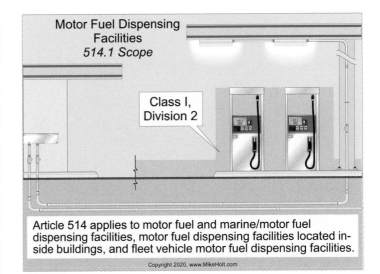

Motor Fuel Dispensing Facilities
514.1 Scope

Class I, Division 2

Article 514 applies to motor fuel and marine/motor fuel dispensing facilities, motor fuel dispensing facilities located inside buildings, and fleet vehicle motor fuel dispensing facilities.

Copyright 2020, www.MikeHolt.com

▸Figure 514–1

514.1 Scope

Article 514 applies to motor fuel dispensing facilities, marine/motor fuel dispensing facilities, motor fuel dispensing facilities located inside buildings, and fleet vehicle motor fuel dispensing facilities. ▸Figure 514–1

Author's Comment:

▸ Definitions for this Article have been relocated to Part III of Article 100

514.3 Classification of Locations

Additional language and a new Informational Note were added to this section.

Analysis

CLARIFIED The new language says that where the term "Class I" is used with respect to Zone classifications, it applies to Zones, 0, 1, and 2. The new Informational Note explains that Zones 0, 1, and 2 apply to areas where the hazard is only flammable gasses, vapors, or liquids.

Author's Comment:

▶ For an illustrated perspective of this new parent text, see Figure 514.3 in the *NEC*.

514.11 Emergency Electrical Disconnects

The requirement for the emergency disconnect to open the neutral as well as the phase conductors was restored.

Analysis

EXPANDED **514.11(A) Emergency Electrical Disconnects.** This section was revised in 2017 to conform to the language in NFPA 30A, *Code for Motor Fuel Dispensing Facilities and Repair Garages* [6.7] but that revision deleted a long-standing requirement (one that existed from 1959 through the 2014 in the NEC) that the disconnect open the neutral circuit conductor in addition to the phase conductors. The issue is that the NFPA 30A addresses the need for an "emergency disconnect." The disconnection of the neutral circuit conductor is not an important issue for an emergency disconnect; however, where service is being done on the dispensing equipment it is important that the neutral circuit conductor also be disconnected. There can be a small amount of voltage on the neutral circuit conductor and working with it where it remains connected to the electrical system could result in a spark and ignition of flammable products at the dispenser. The 2020 change adds language that goes beyond what is required for the emergency disconnect in NFPA 30A by requiring the disconnect to simultaneously disconnect all conductors from the source of supply, including the neutral conductor. Additional language requires that the EGC must remain connected.

HEALTH CARE FACILITIES

Introduction to Article 517—Health Care Facilities

Health care facilities differ from other types of buildings in many important ways. Article 517 is primarily concerned with those parts of health care facilities where patients are examined and treated. Whether those facilities are permanent or movable, they still fall under the scope of this article. However, Article 517 wiring and protection requirements do not apply to business offices or waiting rooms and they do not apply to animal veterinary facilities.

This article contains many specialized definitions that apply to only health care facilities. While you do not need to be able to quote these definitions, you should have a clear understanding of what the terms mean. As you study Parts II and III, keep in mind the special requirements of hospitals and why they exist. The requirements in Parts II and III are highly detailed and not intuitively obvious. These are two of the main objectives of Article 517, Parts II and III:

> ▸ Maximize the physical protection of wiring by requiring metal raceways.
> ▸ Minimize electrical hazards by keeping the voltage between patients' bodies and medical equipment low.

Part IV addresses gas anesthesia stations. The primary objective of Part IV is to prevent ignition. Part V addresses X-ray installations and really has two main objectives:

> ▸ Provide adequate ampacity and overcurrent protection for the branch circuits.
> ▸ Address the safety issues inherent in high-voltage equipment installations.

Part VI provides requirements for low-voltage communications systems such as fire alarms and intercoms. The primary objective here is to prevent compromising those systems with inductive couplings or other sources of interference. Part VII provides requirements for isolated power systems where the main objective is to keep them truly isolated.

Be aware that the *NEC* is just one of the standards that applies to health care facilities, and there may be additional requirements from other standards and special requirements for sophisticated equipment.

Article 517 Health Care Facilities	Analysis
The Informational Note referencing NFPA 99, *Health Care Facilities Code* was relocated to follow the scope statement.	**RELOCATED** This Informational Note No. 2 references material extracted from NFPA 99, *Health Care Facilities Code* and NFPA 101, *Life Safety Code*. As with the other articles, such extracted information will include the section from the other *Code(s)* shown in brackets.

517.2 Definitions

New parent text was added to say that the definitions in Article 517 apply only within that article, and additions and changes were made to some of the definitions.

Analysis

NEW

Dental Office. This new definition is specific to dental offices. In the 2017 *Code*, these offices were covered under the definition of "Medical Office (Dental Office)." The 2018 edition of NFPA 99, *Health Care Facilities Code* has a definition of dental office which was extracted from that document and added to the *NEC*. The actual requirements have not been changed from the 2017 *NEC*.

CLARIFIED

Health Care Facility's Governing Body. This change in the *Code* reflects a change in NFPA 99, *Health Care Facilities Code* in which the title was revised to be consistent with its other requirements and to clarify that the governing body in question is that body who has the authority over the health care facility. The actual definition was unchanged.

CLARIFIED

Limited Care Facility. The outdated term "mental retardation" was replaced with "intellectual disability." This reflects the change in terms as used in Federal Law and other documents.

CLARIFIED

Medical Office. All the references to dental treatment were deleted from this definition as there is a new stand-alone definition of "Dental Office." This definition now applies to a medical office only.

517.2 Definitions

The definitions in this section must apply only within this article.

Dental Office. A building or portion of a building in which the following occur:

(1) Examinations and minor treatments/procedures performed under the continuous supervision of a dental professional;

(2) Use of limited to minimal sedation and treatment or procedures that do not render the patient incapable of self-preservation under emergency conditions; and

(3) No overnight stays for patients or 24-hour operations.

Health Care Facilities. Buildings or portions of buildings, or mobile enclosures in which medical, dental, psychiatric, nursing, obstetrical, or surgical care is provided for humans.

Note: Examples of health care facilities include, but are not limited to, hospitals, nursing homes, limited care facilities, supervisory care facilities, clinics, medical and dental offices, and ambulatory care facilities.

Health Care Facility's Governing Body. The person or persons who have the overall legal responsibility for the operation of a health care facility.

Hospital. A building or an area of a building used for medical, psychiatric, obstetrical, or surgical care on a 24-hour basis of four or more inpatients.

Limited Care Facility. A building or an area of a building used for the housing, on a 24-hour basis, of four or more persons who are incapable of self-preservation because of age, physical limitations due to accident or illness, or limitations such as intellectual disability, developmental disability, mental illness, or chemical dependency.

Medical Office. A building or part thereof in which the following occur:

(1) Examinations and minor treatments/procedures are performed under the continuous supervision of a medical professional;

(2) The use of limited to minimal sedation and treatment or procedures that do not render the patient incapable of self-preservation under emergency conditions; and

(3) No overnight stays for patients or 24-hour operations.

517.10 Applicability

A new list item (3) was added to (B) to include additional areas not covered by the rules in Part II.

Analysis

 CLARIFIED **517.10(B)(3)(a) (b), (c), and (d) Not Covered.** There was a need to clarify where the more restrictive wiring methods required by Part II apply. Some inspection authorities were requiring the use of Part II wiring methods for locations where such wring methods are not required for the safety of the patient.

Subpart (a) was added to the areas used exclusively for a specific purpose to address the fact that many pharmacies provide "flu" or other immunization injections in their locations.

Subparts (b), (c), and (d) are areas where invasive procedures are not performed, and where electro-medical equipment is not connected to the body so there is no need for the redundant equipment grounding paths to reduce the shock hazard.

517.10 Applicability

(A) Applicability. Part II applies to patient care spaces.

(B) Not Covered. The requirements contained in Part II of Article 517 do not apply to:

(1) Business offices, corridors, waiting rooms, or similar areas in clinics, medical and dental offices, and outpatient facilities.

(2) Areas of nursing homes and limited care facilities used exclusively for patient sleeping and wired in accordance with Chapters 1 through 4.

(3) Areas used exclusively for any of the following purposes:

    a. Intramuscular injections (immunizations)

    b. Psychiatry and psychotherapy

    c. Alternative medicine

    d. Optometry

517.13 Equipment Grounding Conductor for Receptacles and Fixed Electrical Equipment in Patient Care Spaces

The title of this section was revised and a new list item, 517.13(B)(1)(4) specific to metal faceplates was created.

Analysis

 CLARIFIED The title of the section was revised to clarify that this section is talking about the equipment grounding conductor (EGC) for receptacles and fixed electrical equipment in patient care spaces. The use of just the word "grounding" did not convey the intent of the section.

 RELOCATED **517.13(B)(1)(4) Insulated Equipment Grounding Conductors and Insulated Equipment Bonding Jumpers.** This new list item specifies that a metal face plate secured to a metal yoke or strap of a receptacle, or to a metal outlet box using metal screws is connected to an EGC.

517.13 Equipment Grounding Conductor for Receptacles and Fixed Electrical Equipment in Patient Care Spaces

Wiring in patient care spaces must comply with (A) and (B):

Author's Comment:

▶ Patient care spaces, as designated by the facility administrator, include patient rooms as well as examining rooms, therapy areas, treatment rooms, and some patient corridors. They do not include business offices, corridors, lounges, day rooms, dining rooms, or similar areas not classified as patient care spaces [517.2].

▶ Equipment grounding requirements in patient care spaces are based on the concept of two different types of equipment grounding conductors so if there is an installation error, the effective ground-fault current paths are not lost. One effective ground-fault current path is "mechanical" (the wiring method), and the other is of the "wire type." Section 517.13(A) requires the wiring method to be a metal raceway or metal cable that qualifies as an equipment grounding conductor in accordance with 250.118 and 517.13(B) requires an insulated copper equipment grounding conductor of the wire type in accordance with 250.118.

(A) Wiring Methods. Branch-circuit conductors serving patient care spaces must be in a metal raceway or metal cable having a metal sheath that qualifies as an equipment grounding conductor in accordance with 250.118. ▶Figure 517-1

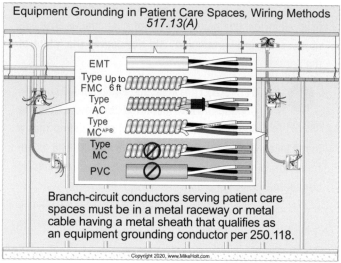

Equipment Grounding in Patient Care Spaces, Wiring Methods
517.13(A)

EMT
Type Up to
FMC 6 ft
Type AC
Type MC^AP®
Type MC
PVC

Branch-circuit conductors serving patient care spaces must be in a metal raceway or metal cable having a metal sheath that qualifies as an equipment grounding conductor per 250.118.

Copyright 2020, www.MikeHolt.com

▶Figure 517-1

Author's Comment:

▸ The metal sheath of traditional Type MC interlocked cable does not qualify as an equipment grounding conductor [250.118(10)(a)], therefore this wiring method is not permitted to be used for circuits in patient care spaces. ▶Figure 517-2

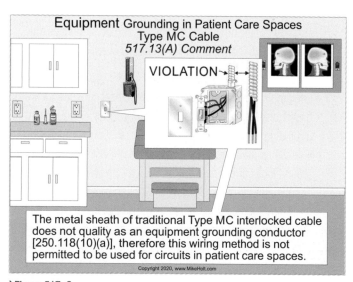

Equipment Grounding in Patient Care Spaces
Type MC Cable
517.13(A) Comment

VIOLATION→

The metal sheath of traditional Type MC interlocked cable does not quality as an equipment grounding conductor [250.118(10)(a)], therefore this wiring method is not permitted to be used for circuits in patient care spaces.

Copyright 2020, www.MikeHolt.com

▶Figure 517-2

Author's Comment:

▸ The metal sheath of Type AC cable is identified as an equipment grounding conductor in 250.118(8) because it contains an internal bonding strip that is in direct contact with the metal sheath of the interlock cable. ▶Figure 517-3

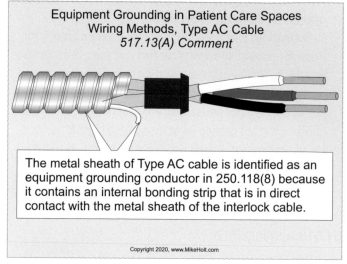

Equipment Grounding in Patient Care Spaces
Wiring Methods, Type AC Cable
517.13(A) Comment

The metal sheath of Type AC cable is identified as an equipment grounding conductor in 250.118(8) because it contains an internal bonding strip that is in direct contact with the metal sheath of the interlock cable.

Copyright 2020, www.MikeHolt.com

▶Figure 517-3

Author's Comment:

▸ The metal sheath of Type MC^AP cable (metal-clad all-purpose) is identified as an equipment grounding conductor in 250.118(10)(b) because it contains an internal bonding strip that is in direct contact with the metal sheath of the interlock cable. ▶Figure 517-4

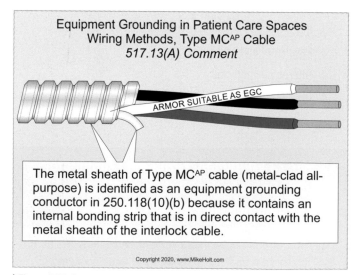

Equipment Grounding in Patient Care Spaces
Wiring Methods, Type MC^AP Cable
517.13(A) Comment

ARMOR SUITABLE AS EGC

The metal sheath of Type MC^AP cable (metal-clad all-purpose) is identified as an equipment grounding conductor in 250.118(10)(b) because it contains an internal bonding strip that is in direct contact with the metal sheath of the interlock cable.

Copyright 2020, www.MikeHolt.com

▶Figure 517-4

(B) Insulated Equipment Grounding Conductors.

(1) General. The following equipment must be directly connected to an insulated copper equipment grounding conductor that has green insulation along its entire length. Such conductors must be contained in a suitable wiring method as required in 517.13(A).

(1) The grounding contact of receptacles, other than isolated ground receptacles must be directly connected to a green insulated copper equipment grounding conductor. ▸Figure 517–5

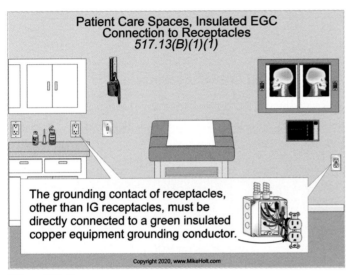

Patient Care Spaces, Insulated EGC Connection to Receptacles
517.13(B)(1)(1)

The grounding contact of receptacles, other than IG receptacles, must be directly connected to a green insulated copper equipment grounding conductor.

Copyright 2020, www.MikeHolt.com

▸Figure 517–5

(2) Metal enclosures containing circuit conductors must be directly connected to an insulated copper equipment grounding conductor that has green insulation. ▸Figure 517–6

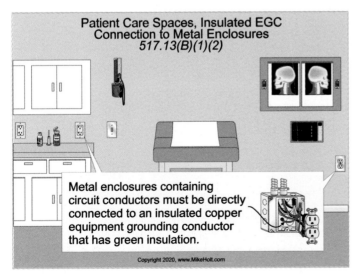

Patient Care Spaces, Insulated EGC Connection to Metal Enclosures
517.13(B)(1)(2)

Metal enclosures containing circuit conductors must be directly connected to an insulated copper equipment grounding conductor that has green insulation.

Copyright 2020, www.MikeHolt.com

▸Figure 517–6

(3) Non-current carrying metal parts of fixed electrical equipment must be directly connected to an insulated copper equipment grounding conductor. ▸Figure 517–7

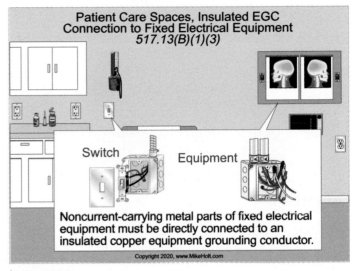

Patient Care Spaces, Insulated EGC Connection to Fixed Electrical Equipment
517.13(B)(1)(3)

Switch   Equipment

Noncurrent-carrying metal parts of fixed electrical equipment must be directly connected to an insulated copper equipment grounding conductor.

Copyright 2020, www.MikeHolt.com

▸Figure 517–7

(4) Metal faceplates must be connected to the circuit equipment grounding conductor by means of a metal mounting screw(s) securing the faceplate to a metal yoke or strap of a receptacle or to a metal outlet box. ▸Figure 517–8

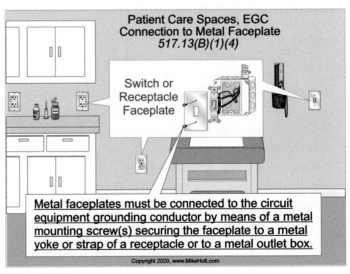

Patient Care Spaces, EGC Connection to Metal Faceplate
517.13(B)(1)(4)

Switch or Receptacle Faceplate

Metal faceplates must be connected to the circuit equipment grounding conductor by means of a metal mounting screw(s) securing the faceplate to a metal yoke or strap of a receptacle or to a metal outlet box.

Copyright 2020, www.MikeHolt.com

▸Figure 517–8

Ex 2: Circuits for luminaires located more than 7½ ft above the floor and switches located outside of the patient care vicinity must be installed in a wiring method in accordance with 517.13(A), however an equipment grounding conductor of the wire-type is not required within the wiring method. ▸Figure 517–9

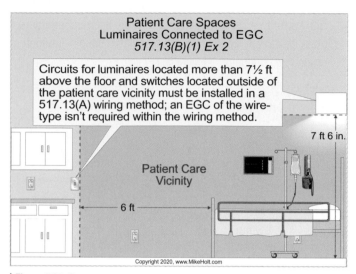

Patient Care Spaces
Luminaires Connected to EGC
517.13(B)(1) Ex 2

Circuits for luminaires located more than 7½ ft above the floor and switches located outside of the patient care vicinity must be installed in a 517.13(A) wiring method; an EGC of the wire-type isn't required within the wiring method.

7 ft 6 in.

Patient Care Vicinity

6 ft

Copyright 2020, www.MikeHolt.com

▶Figure 517–9

517.16 Use of Isolated Ground Receptacles

New parent text from NFPA 99, *Health Care Facilities Code* was added and (B)(1) and (2) were revised to improve clarity.

Analysis

CLARIFIED The new text specifies that where an isolated ground receptacle is used, it must not defeat the purposes of the safety features of the grounding system detailed in 517.13. Note that the provisions of 517.16(A) prohibit the use of an isolated ground receptacle inside the "patient care vicinity" which is the area within 6 ft horizontally and 7 ft 6 in. vertically from the normal location of the patient bed, chair, table, treadmill, or other device that supports the patient during examination and treatment. The grounding system required by 517.13 applies to the "patient care area" which includes areas beyond the "patient care vicinity."

CLARIFIED **517.16(B) Outside of a Patient Care Vicinity.** The language in (1) was revised to clarify that the "isolated" equipment grounding conductor is not required to be connected to the redundant equipment grounding path required by 517.13.

The previous language was written in a way that said the two EGC paths both had to be connected to the grounding terminal of the isolated ground receptacle. The word "equipment" was also added in front of "grounding" to clarify that we are talking about EGCs; of both the normal and isolated type.

In subsection (2), as in (1), the language was revised to make it clear we are talking about EGCs, by the addition of the word "equipment."

517.16 Isolated Ground Receptacles

An isolated ground receptacle, if used, must not defeat the purposes of the safety features of the grounding systems detailed in 517.13. ▶Figure 517–10

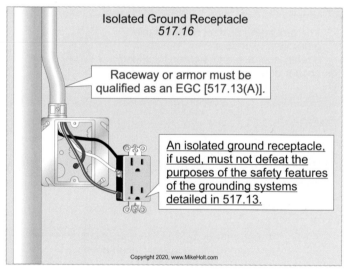

Isolated Ground Receptacle
517.16

Raceway or armor must be qualified as an EGC [517.13(A)].

An isolated ground receptacle, if used, must not defeat the purposes of the safety features of the grounding systems detailed in 517.13.

Copyright 2020, www.MikeHolt.com

▶Figure 517–10

(A) Inside of a Patient Care Vicinity. An isolated ground receptacle must not be installed within a patient care vicinity. ▶Figure 517–11

Author's Comment:

▶ The patient care vicinity is a space extending 6 ft beyond the normal location of the patient bed, chair, table, treadmill, or other device that supports the patient during examination and treatment and extends vertically to 7 ft 6 in. above the floor [517.2 Definition].

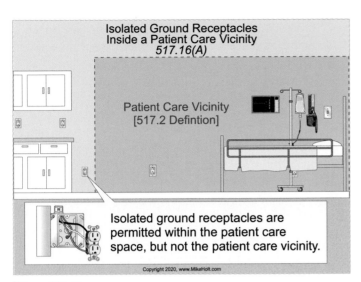

▶Figure 517–11

(B) Outside Patient Care Vicinity. Isolated ground receptacle(s) within the patient care space (as defined in 517.2) must comply with the following: ▶Figure 517–12

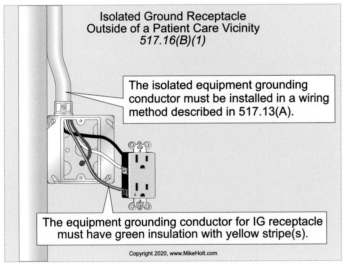

▶Figure 517–12

(1) The <u>equipment</u> grounding terminal of isolated grounding receptacles must be connected to an insulated equipment grounding conductor in accordance with 250.146(D) and <u>installed in a wiring method described in 517.13(A).</u>

The equipment grounding conductor connected to the <u>equipment</u> grounding terminals of the isolated grounding receptacle must have green insulation with one or more yellow stripes along its entire length.

(2) The insulated equipment grounding conductor required by 517.13(B)(1) must be connected to the metal enclosure containing the receptacle as required by 517.13(B)(1)(2).

Note 2: Care should be taken in specifying a system containing isolated ground receptacles, because the <u>impedance of the effective ground-fault current path is dependent upon the equipment grounding conductor(s)</u> and does not benefit from any conduit or building structure in parallel with the <u>equipment grounding conductor.</u>

ARTICLE
518

ASSEMBLY OCCUPANCIES

Introduction to Article 518—Assembly Occupancies

More commonly referred to as "Places of Occupancy," these are buildings specifically designed or intended for the assembly of 100 or more people and fall under Article 518. This article goes out of its way to eliminate any confusion about the types of occupancies to which it is intended to apply. (See 518.2 for a list of occupancies.)

518.6 Illumination

This new section address illumination for working spaces about fixed service equipment, switchboards, switchgear, panelboards, or motor control centers installed outdoors where this equipment serves assembly occupancies.

Analysis

NEW As with the rule in 110.26(D), control by only automatic means is not permitted. If enough illumination is supplied by adjacent light sources, additional lighting outlets are not required. This is because of the possible need for quickly locating and shutting off power to an outdoor assembly area in the case of an emergency. The substantiation indicates that the requirement in 110.26(D) applies only to indoor equipment. There is no *NEC* requirement for the illumination of outdoor service equipment for other types of occupancies.

518.6 Illumination

Illumination must be provided for all working spaces about fixed service equipment, switchboards, switchgear, panelboards, or motor control centers installed outdoors that serve assembly occupancies. Control by only automatic means is not permitted. Additional lighting outlets are not required where the workspace is illuminated by an adjacent light source.

CARNIVALS, CIRCUSES, FAIRS, AND SIMILAR EVENTS

Introduction to Article 525—Carnivals, Circuses, Fairs, and Similar Events

This article covers the installation of portable wiring and equipment for temporary carnivals, circuses, exhibitions, fairs, traveling attractions, and similar functions, including wiring in or on structures.

525.20 Wiring Methods

Subsection 525.20(G) was revised to require protective matting to be secured to the walkway surface.

Analysis

EXPANDED

525.20(G) Protection. This revision requires that where protective matting is installed over cords or cables, the matting must be secured to the walkway surface. Loose matting may become a tripping hazard and securing it to the surface will limit that hazard. The rule was also expanded to permit the use of other approved protection methods. One such method would be cable "crossovers" or "tunnels." The protective method must not constitute a greater tripping hazard than the uncovered cables.

525.20 Wiring Methods

(G) Protection. Flexible cords or flexible cables accessible to the public must be arranged to minimize the tripping hazard and they can be covered with nonconductive matting secured to the walkway surface or protected with another approved cable protection method, provided that the matting or other protection method does not constitute a greater tripping hazard than the uncovered cables. Burying cables is permitted and the burial depth requirements of 300.5 do not apply. ▶Figure 525–1

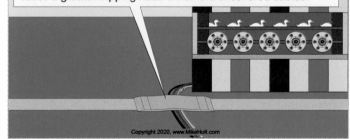

Carnivals, Circuses, and Fairs, Wiring Methods, Flexible Cords and Flexible Cables, Protection
525.20(G)

Flexible cords or flexible cables accessible to the public must be arranged to minimize tripping hazards and they can be covered with nonconductive matting secured to the walkway surface or protected with another approved cable protection method, provided that the matting or other protection method does not cause a greater tripping hazard than the uncovered cables.

Copyright 2020, www.MikeHolt.com

▶Figure 525–1

525.23 GFCI-Protection

Wording was added to 525.23(A) to reference the 210.8(B) requirements.

Analysis

EXPANDED

525.23(A) Where GFCI Protection is Required. This change applies all the GFCI requirements of 210.8(B) along with the more specific requirements of this article. It might appear to some that the rule in 525.23(B) is intended to act as an exception to the requirements of 210.8(B)(4), as that section would require GFCI protection for receptacles located outdoors and this is not the case.

525.23 GFCI-Protected Receptacles and Equipment

(A) GFCI Protection Required. In addition to the requirements of 210.8(B), GFCI protection must be provided for the following: ▶Figure 525-2

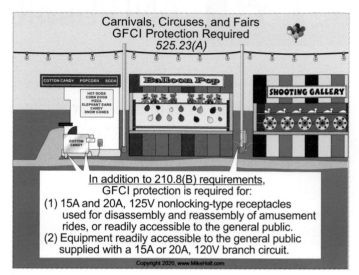

▶Figure 525-2

(1) 15A and 20A, 125V nonlocking-type receptacles used for disassembly and reassembly of amusement rides and attractions, or readily accessible to the general public.

(2) Equipment readily accessible to the general public if it is supplied from a 15A or 20A, 120V branch circuit.

GFCI protection can be integral with the attachment plug or located in the power-supply cord within 12 in. of the attachment plug, or listed cord set incorporating GFCI protection.

(B) GFCI Protection Not Required. GFCI protection is not required for locking-type receptacles not accessible from grade level.

ARTICLE 547

AGRICULTURAL BUILDINGS

Introduction to Article 547—Agricultural Buildings

Three factors, (dust, moisture, and an overall corrosive environment), have a tremendous influence on the lifespan of agricultural equipment. Dust gets into mechanisms and causes premature wear. Add electricity to the mix, and dust adds two additional dangers: fire and explosion. Dust from hay, grain, and fertilizer is highly flammable. Litter materials, such as straw, are also highly flammable.

Another factor to consider in agricultural buildings is moisture, which causes corrosion. Water is present for many reasons, including wash down. Excrement from farm animals may cause corrosive vapors that eat at mechanical equipment and wiring methods and can cause electrical equipment to fail. For these reasons, Article 547 includes requirements for dealing with dust, moisture, and corrosion.

This article also has other rules. For example, you must install equipotential planes in all concrete floor confinement areas of livestock buildings containing metallic equipment accessible to animals and likely to become energized. Livestock animals have a low tolerance to small voltage differences, which can cause loss of milk production and, at times, livestock fatality. As a result, the *NEC* contains specific requirements for an equipotential plane in buildings that house livestock.

547.2 Definitions

The new parent text is part of the *NEC Style Manual* global change for 2020 regarding definitions. Also, the definition of "Equipotential Plane" was revised to clarify it is very specific to agricultural buildings and applies only within this article.

Analysis

 NEW This is an example of a definition that is specific to the article in which it appears and does not appear exactly like this anywhere else (which would require it to be in Article 100) and is in keeping with the global reorganization of definitions throughout the *Code*. The new text reads,

"The definitions in this section apply only within this article."

Equipotential Plane (as applied to agricultural buildings). While there is a new definition of **CLARIFIED** "Equipotential Plane" in Article 100 that is somewhat generic, this definition specifies that the conductive parts are wire mesh or other conductive elements embedded in or under the concrete and connected to the electrical grounding system. This is intended to minimize voltage differences within the plane and between the plane, grounded equipment, and the Earth.

547.2 Definitions

Equipotential Plane, (as applied to agricultural buildings). An area where conductive elements are embedded in or placed under concrete and bonded to all metal structures and nonelectrical equipment that <u>could</u> become energized and connected to the electrical system to minimize voltage differences within the plane. ▸Figure 547–1

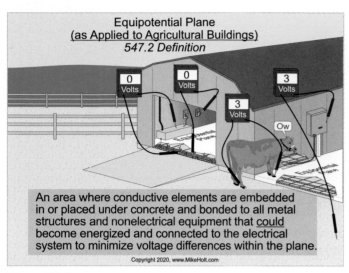

Equipotential Plane
(as Applied to Agricultural Buildings)
547.2 Definition

An area where conductive elements are embedded in or placed under concrete and bonded to all metal structures and nonelectrical equipment that <u>could</u> become energized and connected to the electrical system to minimize voltage differences within the plane.

Copyright 2020, www.MikeHolt.com

▶Figure 547–1

547.5 Wiring Methods

Section 547.5(F) was clarified, and new language was added to (G).

Analysis

CLARIFIED

547.5(F) Separate Equipment Grounding Conductor. This rule required that EGCs installed underground within an Article 547 application be insulated. It was modified to permit an uninsulated EGC that is part of a listed cable assembly to be uninsulated. For example, the EGC in Type UF cable is "covered" by the jacket but is not insulated. The change clarifies that the EGC within a listed cable assembly is not required to be insulated. The language now specifies that a separate EGC, that is not part of a listed cable assembly, must be insulated.

CLARIFIED

547.5(G) Receptacles. This rule starts out by saying that 210.8(B) applies to Article 547 applications, then goes on to clarify that GFCI protection is not required for other than 125V, 15A and 20A receptacles installed in specific areas. It appears that the second sentence completely overrides the first and that the only GFCI protection required is for 125V, 15A and 20A receptacles installed in the four specified locations.

547.5 Wiring Methods

(F) Separate Equipment Grounding Conductor. Where the equipment grounding conductor <u>is not part of a listed cable assembly</u>, it must be insulated when installed underground. ▶Figure 547–2

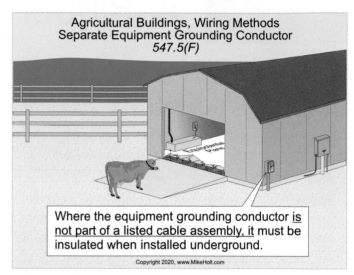

Agricultural Buildings, Wiring Methods
Separate Equipment Grounding Conductor
547.5(F)

Where the equipment grounding conductor <u>is not part of a listed cable assembly</u>, it must be insulated when installed underground.

Copyright 2020, www.MikeHolt.com

▶Figure 547–2

(G) Ground-Fault Circuit-Interrupter Protection. GFCI <u>protection must be provided as required in 210.8(B), GFCI protection is not required for other than 125-volt, 15- and 20-ampere receptacles installed within the following areas:</u> ▶Figure 547–3

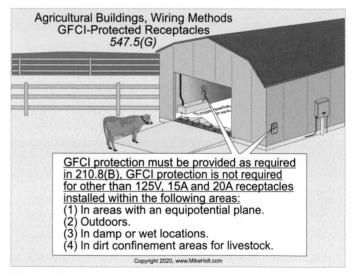

Agricultural Buildings, Wiring Methods
GFCI-Protected Receptacles
547.5(G)

GFCI protection must be provided as required in 210.8(B), GFCI protection is not required for other than 125V, 15A and 20A receptacles installed within the following areas:
(1) In areas with an equipotential plane.
(2) Outdoors.
(3) In damp or wet locations.
(4) In dirt confinement areas for livestock.

Copyright 2020, www.MikeHolt.com

▶Figure 547–3

(1) In areas having an equipotential plane in accordance with 547.10(A).

(2) Outdoors.

(3) In damp or wet locations.

(4) In dirt confinement areas for livestock.

547.9 Electrical Supply to Buildings or Structures from a Distribution Point

This rule was revised to improve clarity and to indicate there can be more than one electrical power distribution point.

Analysis

CLARIFIED The modification here requires that any agricultural building or structure for livestock must be supplied from a distribution point on the same premises. This section previously permitted, but did not require, any building or structure to be supplied from a distribution point. The change requires that buildings or structures for livestock be supplied from a distribution point. This assures that these structures are supplied by a system that contains an EGC to reduce "stray" voltages that may affect livestock. The rule also permits multiple distribution points on the same premises.

This rule also permits any existing buildings or structures for other than livestock, or buildings not under the scope of 547, to be supplied in accordance with 250.32(B)(1) Ex 1.

ARTICLE 550

MOBILE HOMES, MANUFACTURED HOMES, AND MOBILE HOME PARKS

Introduction to Article 550—Mobile Homes, Manufactured Homes, and Mobile Home Parks

Among dwelling types, mobile homes have the highest rate of fire. Article 550 addresses some of the causes of those fires with the intent of reducing these statistics. This article recognizes that the same mobile or manufactured homes used as dwellings are also used for nondwelling purposes, such as construction offices or clinics [550.4(A)].

Mobile homes and manufactured homes are not covered by the same building codes as are site-built homes. They are covered instead by HUD standards. According to HUD, both are referred to as manufactured homes and the term "mobile home" has not been used for many years. This disparity between the *NEC* and industry practices can cause confusion, so read the *Code* carefully as you apply this article.

550.13 Receptacle Outlets

New language was added in 550.13(B) addressing the GFCI protection required in 210.8(A); additional language limits those requirements.

Analysis

CLARIFIED

550.13(B) Ground Fault Circuit Interrupters. The first sentence makes the requirements of 210.8(A) apply to mobile homes. This would act to include areas like garages and accessory buildings associated with the mobile home. As we saw in 547.5(G), there is a confusing second sentence in the subsection that says GFCI protection for other than 125V, 15A and 20A receptacles are not required in certain areas. The last item for dishwashers sets up a bit of a conflict with the rule found in 422.5(A)(7) that requires dishwashers to have GFCI protection even where they are hard wired. This would seem to limit the required dishwasher protection to cord-and-plug-connected dishwashers.

The language in 550.13(B) would be a modification of that in 422.5 as permitted by 90.3. It appears (based on the Informational Note) the intent is that the requirement in 422.5(A)(7) for dishwashers applies, but it is not reflected in the actual *Code* language.

550.13 Receptacle Outlets

(B) GFCI-Protected Receptacles. Ground-fault circuit-interrupter protection must be provided as required in 210.8(A). GFCI protection is not required for other than 125V, 15A and 20A ampere receptacles installed within a mobile or manufactured home in the following areas:

(1) Compartments accessible from the outdoors.

(2) Bathroom areas.

(3) Kitchens, where receptacles are installed to serve countertop surfaces. ▶Figure 550–1

(4) Sinks, where within 6 ft from the top inside edge of the sink. ▶Figure 550–2

(5) Dishwasher outlets.

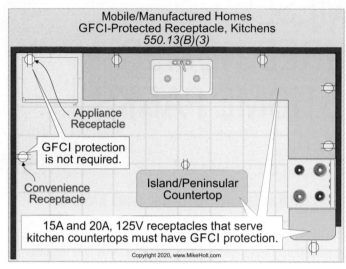

Mobile/Manufactured Homes
GFCI-Protected Receptacle, Kitchens
550.13(B)(3)

Appliance Receptacle

GFCI protection is not required.

Convenience Receptacle

Island/Peninsular Countertop

15A and 20A, 125V receptacles that serve kitchen countertops must have GFCI protection.

Copyright 2020, www.MikeHolt.com

▶Figure 550–1

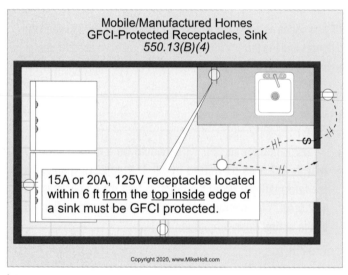

Mobile/Manufactured Homes
GFCI-Protected Receptacles, Sink
550.13(B)(4)

15A or 20A, 125V receptacles located within 6 ft <u>from</u> the <u>top inside</u> edge of a sink must be GFCI protected.

Copyright 2020, www.MikeHolt.com

▶Figure 550–2

Author's Comment:

▶ There doesn't seem to be a good reason to limit the protection required by 210.8(A). The hazards in and around a mobile home are no different from those in a standard dwelling unit.

550.15 Wiring Methods and Materials

The previous prohibition on the use of aluminum conductors for mobile home branch-circuit wiring was deleted and 550.15(D) was revised.

Analysis

EXPANDED This section previously prohibited the use of aluminum conductors, aluminum alloy conductors, and aluminum core conductors (such as copper-clad aluminum) from being used as branch-circuit conductors in mobile dwelling units covered by this article. The revision permits the use of those conductors where they are used with equipment terminations listed for aluminum conductors. The substantiation indicated that the *NEC* has long permitted the use of aluminum conductors for other occupancies and there is no reason to prohibit their use in the mobile dwelling units covered by this article.

CLARIFIED **550.15(D) Metal Faceplates.** The previous language required that metal faceplates be "grounded." That was modified and the revised language now requires that the installation of metal faceplates comply with 404.9(B) for switches, and with 406.6(B) for receptacles.

Author's Comment:

▶ Currently, there are no 15 or 20 amp aluminum conductors or cables being sold in the US. Larger size aluminum conductors are sold and used. Aside from main service and feeder conductors, the applications would be for only branch circuits rated 30 amps or greater such as clothes dryers, electric ranges, and heating and air conditioning equipment and so forth.

▶ Although branch circuits in pre-fabricated housing are typically installed by the manufacturer, electricians often times do make additions and modifications to the original wiring.

ARTICLE
555

MARINAS, BOATYARDS, COMMERCIAL AND NON-COMMERCIAL DOCKING FACILITIES

Introduction to Article 555—Marinas, Boatyards, and Docking Facilities

Water levels are not constant. Ocean tides rise and fall, while lakes and rivers vary in depth in response to rain. To provide power to a marina, boatyard, or docking facility, you must allow for these variations in water level between the point of use and the electric power source. Article 555 addresses this issue.

This article begins with the concept of the electrical datum plane. You might think of it as the border of a "demilitarized zone" for electrical equipment. Or, you can think of it as a line that marks the beginning of a "no man's land" where you simply do not place electrical equipment. Once you determine where this plane is, do not place transformers, connections, or receptacles below that line.

Article 555—Marinas, Boatyards, Floating Buildings, and Commercial and Noncommercial Docking Facilities

This article was reorganized, includes several technical changes, and was expanded to incorporate the rules for floating buildings that were in Article 553.

Analysis

REORGANIZED   This article was reorganized and slightly expanded to include floating buildings that were previously covered by Article 553. Both the title and scope were revised to reflect that the rules for floating buildings now reside here. This article is now divided into three parts and several sections were relocated from where they appeared in the 2017 *NEC*. Part I is the general information for the application throughout the article, Part II contains more specific information for electrical installations at marinas, boatyards, and docking facilities, and Part III is where the specific requirements for floating buildings are now located.

555.1 Scope

Informational Notes following the scope text were added and renumbered.

Analysis

REORGANIZED   The original Informational Note is now called Informational Note No. 1 and references NFPA 303, *Fire Protection Standard for Marinas and Boatyards* as a source of additional information for these types of installations. The change here was to update the reference from the 2011 edition to the 2016 edition.

➕ **NEW**   555.1 Note 2. This Informational Note calls attention to the fact that where boats, floating buildings, docks, and so forth are connected to a source of electric power, that hazardous voltages and currents may create serious safety concerns.

• • •

The substantiation indicates the concerns are with hazardous voltages and currents within the water, but there is no actual wording to that effect. The intent is to call attention to the possibility that the boats themselves, as well as the electrical infrastructure for the marina, can introduce the hazardous voltages and currents.

555.1 Note 3. Informational Note No. 3 references the extracted information used in Article 555 from NFPA 303, *Fire Protection Standard for Marinas and Boatyards* and NFPA 307, *Standard for the Construction and Fire Protection of Marine Terminals, Piers, and Wharves*. As with other extracted information in the *Code*, the reference to the section of NFPA 303 or 307 is shown in brackets following the extracted information.

NEW

555.2 Definitions

New definitions were added, and some were relocated to Article 100.

Analysis

NEW

Docking Facility. This definition was added because the GFPE requirements apply to feeder and branch circuits which supply docking facilities.

NEW

Shore Power. This is defined as the electrical equipment required to power a floating vessel including, but not limited to, the receptacle and the cords used to tap into this power source. This now places the cord, in addition to the supplying receptacle, under the auspices of the *NEC*.

555.2 Definitions

Author's Comment:

▸ Some of the definitions in this section of the text, appear in Article 100 of the *Code*. They are included here as well for context and illustrative purposes.

Docking Facility. A covered or open, fixed or floating structure that provides access to the water and to which boats are secured.

Electrical Datum Plane. A specified distance above a water level, (which may or may not be subject to tidal fluctuation), which electrical equipment can be installed and electrical connections can be made.

Marina. A facility, generally on the waterfront, that stores and services boats in berths, on moorings, and in dry storage or dry stack storage.

Marine Power Outlet. An enclosed assembly that can include equipment such as receptacles, circuit breakers, watt-hour meters, and panelboards approved for marine use. ▸Figure 555–1

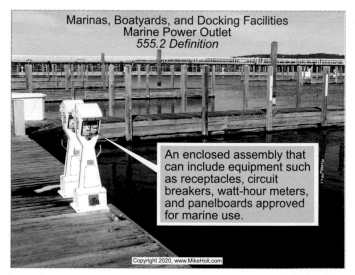

Marinas, Boatyards, and Docking Facilities
Marine Power Outlet
555.2 Definition

An enclosed assembly that can include equipment such as receptacles, circuit breakers, watt-hour meters, and panelboards approved for marine use.

Copyright 2020, www.MikeHolt.com

▸Figure 555–1

Pier. A structure extending over the water and supported on a fixed foundation (fixed pier), or on flotation (floating pier), that provides access to the water.

Pier, Fixed (Fixed Pier). A pier constructed on a permanent, fixed foundation, such as on piles, that permanently establishes the elevation of the structure deck with respect to land. ▸Figure 555–2

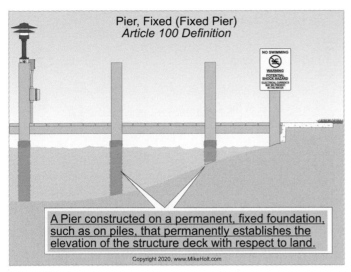

▶Figure 555–2

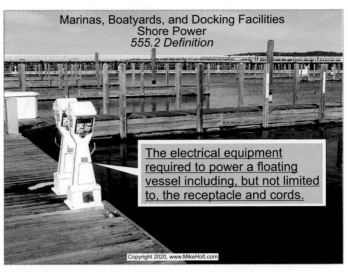

▶Figure 555–4

Pier, Floating (Floating Pier). A pier designed with inherent flotation capability that allows the structure to float on the water surface and rise and fall with water level changes. ▶Figure 555–3

Slip. A berthing space between or adjacent to piers, wharves, or docks; the water areas associated with boat occupation. ▶Figure 555–5

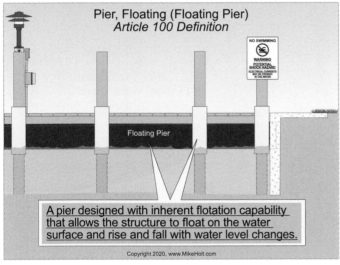

▶Figure 555–3

▶Figure 555–5

Shore Power. The electrical equipment required to power a floating vessel including, but not limited to, the receptacle and cords. ▶Figure 555–4

555.3 Electrical Datum Plane Distances

This new section provides electrical datum plane distance rules for floating piers, areas subject to tidal fluctuations, and areas not subject to tidal fluctuations.

Analysis

NEW There are three subsections in this new section that align with the three list items which were removed from the definition of "Electrical Datum Plane."

555.3 Electrical Datum Plane Distances

(A) Floating Piers. The electrical datum plane for floating piers and boat landing stages must be a horizontal plane 30 in. above the water level at the floating pier and a minimum of 12 in. above the level of the deck. ▸Figure 555–6

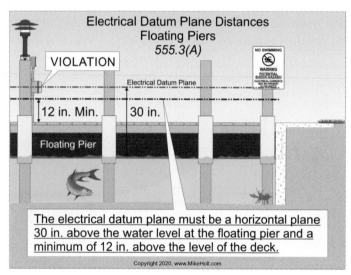

▸Figure 555–6

(B) Areas Subject to Tidal Fluctuations. In land areas subject to tidal fluctuation, the electrical datum plane must be a horizontal plane that is 2 ft above the highest tide level for the area occurring under normal circumstances, based on the highest high tide. ▸Figure 555–7

(C) Areas Not Subject to Tidal Fluctuations. In land areas not subject to tidal fluctuation, the electrical datum plane must be a horizontal plane that is 2 ft above the highest water level for the area occurring under normal circumstances. ▸Figure 555–8

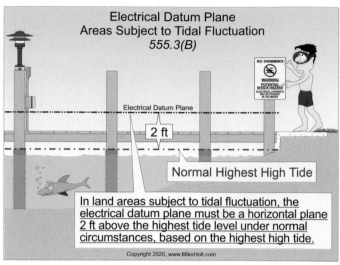

▸Figure 555–7

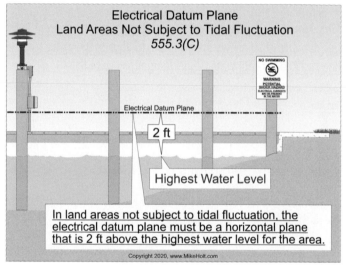

▸Figure 555–8

Author's Comment:

▸ The new subsections, (B) and (C), are not changes from the previous *Code* however, it is important to note they are based on highest "normal" water levels. They do not consider established flood levels.

555.4 Location of Service Equipment

This requirement was relocated from 555.7 and was revised to include an additional reference to floating buildings.

Analysis

RELOCATED This was 555.7 in the 2017 *NEC* and relocated here with revisions. The language was expanded to include floating buildings. It requires that the service equipment for floating buildings, docks, or a marina be located adjacent to the structure, but not on or in the structure itself, <u>or on or in any other floating structure</u>. The last part is new, as the previous *Code* could be read as permitting the service equipment for one floating structure to be in an adjacent floating structure. The intent has always been that the service equipment be on land and not on any floating structure. The additional language now makes that clear.

555.4 Location of Service Equipment

The service equipment for a dock or marina must be located adjacent to the structure, but not on or in, the structure itself.

555.5 Maximum Voltage

This rule was relocated from 555.4 and the maximum voltage for dock or marina service equipment was reduced.

Analysis

RELOCATED This was 555.4 and was relocated and re-titled with some editorial clarification. The title is now "Maximum Voltage" and that maximum voltage was reduced from the 1,000V volts in the 2017 *NEC* to 250V phase-to-phase. It goes on to permit pier power distribution systems where qualified personnel service the equipment under engineering supervision to exceed 250V, but with a maximum of 600V.

555.5 Maximum Voltage

<u>Pier power distribution systems must not exceed 250 volts phase to phase. Pier power distribution systems, where qualified personnel service the equipment under engineering supervision, are permitted to exceed 250 volts but these systems must not exceed 600 volts.</u>

555.7 Transformers

This section was formerly 555.5; it was expanded, separated into two subsections, and editorially revised.

Analysis

EXPANDED **555.7(A) General. This rule** requires that transformers and enclosures used for Article 555 applications be "identified for wet locations." The previous language was "specifically approved for the intended location." Section 110.2 requires all equipment to be "approved" and there was no need to have that language here. The requirement for the transformer to be "identified for wet locations" is more suitable for this section. The previous requirement that the bottom of the transformer must not be located below the electrical datum plane was retained.

NEW **555.7(B) Replacements.** This is a new rule and requires that where a transformer is replaced, the replacement transformer must be identified for wet locations.

555.7 Transformers

(A) General. Transformers must be <u>identified for wet locations</u> and the bottom of the transformer enclosure is not permitted to be located below the electrical datum plane. ▶Figure 555–9

(B) Replacement. Replacement transformers must be <u>identified for wet locations</u> and the bottom of the transformer enclosure is not permitted to be located below the electrical datum plane.

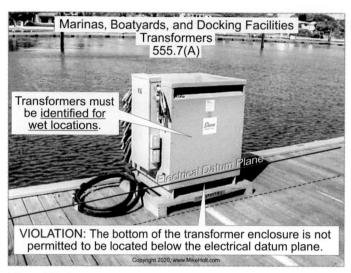

Marinas, Boatyards, and Docking Facilities
Transformers
555.7(A)

Transformers must be <u>identified for wet locations</u>.

Electrical Datum Plane

VIOLATION: The bottom of the transformer enclosure is not permitted to be located below the electrical datum plane.

Copyright 2020, www.MikeHolt.com

▶Figure 555–9

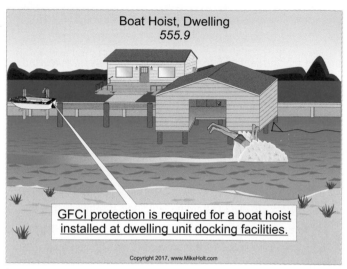

Boat Hoist, Dwelling
555.9

<u>GFCI protection is required for a boat hoist installed at dwelling unit docking facilities.</u>

Copyright 2017, www.MikeHolt.com

▶Figure 555–10

Author's Comment:

▸ The 2017 language said the transformer was to be "approved for the intended location." That would permit standard transformers to be installed in indoor locations. The new language appears to require that all Article 555 transformers be "identified for wet locations" even if they would be installed in a building on shore.

555.9 Boat Hoists

This new rule replaces the GFCI protection requirement for boat hoists that was previously found in 210.8(C).

Analysis

NEW

This is the same language that was in 210.8(C) and requires that GFCI protection be provided for outlets not exceeding 240V that supply a boat hoist installed at a dwelling unit docking facility. The panel statement indicates that it is more appropriately addressed in Article 555 rather than in Article 210. Its placement here improves the usability of this rule.

555.9 Boat Hoists

GFCI protection is required for a boat hoist installed at dwelling unit docking facilities. ▶Figure 555–10

555.13. Bonding of Noncurrent-Carrying Metal Parts

This rule was relocated here from 553.11 and requires all metal parts likely to become energized that are in contact with the water to be connected to the ground bus of the panelboard.

 Scan this QR code for a video of Mike explaining this topic; it's a sample from the videos that accompany this textbook.

Analysis

RELOCATED

The rules pertaining to floating buildings are more appropriately placed in Article 555 because they need to apply to more than just floating buildings which was the case in Part III. Locating these rules here in Part I, make them enforceable throughout the entire scope of Article 555.

Author's Comment:

▸ It seems that complying with this section would be very difficult because there are many independent metal parts in contact with the water.

Part II. Marinas, Boatyards, and Docking Facilities

This new Part II of Article 555 covers specific electrical installation rules for marinas, boatyards, and docking facilities.

Analysis

NEW The information in this part was relocated from other sections in the 2017 *NEC* and includes some technical changes. This new part was a result of merging of Articles 553 and 555. The new Part III will address the specific requirements of floating buildings.

555.30 Electrical Connections

This section was divided into subsections and the new 555.30(C) was added.

Analysis

NEW 555.30(C) Replacements. This section was divided into subsections and a new (C) was added to require that the rules in (A) and (B) apply to all replacement installations which essentially means that the existing installation be brought up to *Code*.

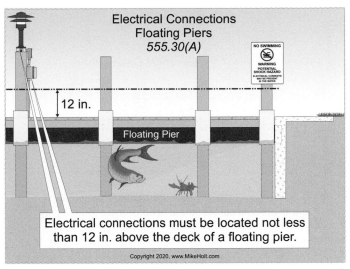

Electrical connections must be located not less than 12 in. above the deck of a floating pier.

▶Figure 555–11

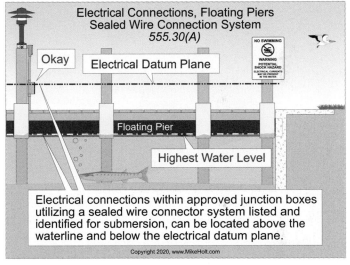

Electrical connections within approved junction boxes utilizing a sealed wire connector system listed and identified for submersion, can be located above the waterline and below the electrical datum plane.

▶Figure 555–12

(B) Fixed Piers. Electrical connections must be located at least 12 in. above the deck of a fixed pier and not below the electrical datum plane. ▶Figure 555–13 and ▶Figure 555–14

(C) Replacements. Replacement electrical connections for a floating pier must be located at least 12 in. above its deck. Conductor splices, within junction boxes identified for wet locations, utilizing sealed wire connector systems listed and identified for submersion are required where located above the waterline but below the electrical datum plane for floating piers.

Part II. Marinas, Boatyards, and Docking Facilities

555.30 Electrical Connections

(A) Floating Piers. Electrical connections must be located at least 12 in. above the deck of a floating pier. ▶Figure 555–11

Electrical connections within approved junction boxes utilizing a sealed wire connector system listed and identified for submersion, can be located above the waterline and below the electrical datum plane. ▶Figure 555–12

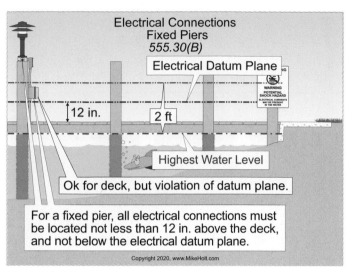

Electrical Connections
Fixed Piers
555.30(B)

Electrical Datum Plane

12 in. 2 ft

Highest Water Level

Ok for deck, but violation of datum plane.

For a fixed pier, all electrical connections must be located not less than 12 in. above the deck, and not below the electrical datum plane.

Copyright 2020, www.MikeHolt.com

▶Figure 555–13

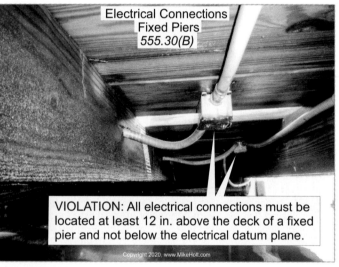

Electrical Connections
Fixed Piers
555.30(B)

VIOLATION: All electrical connections must be located at least 12 in. above the deck of a fixed pier and not below the electrical datum plane.

Copyright 2020, www.MikeHolt.com

▶Figure 555–14

555.33 Receptacles

A new subsection (C) is about replacing receptacles subject to the equipotential plane rules.

Analysis

555.33(C) Replacement Receptacles. Existing locations of electrical equipment installed before *NEC* revisions are not always "grand-fathered in." This is especially true if the need for replacement is caused by a recurring incident such as storm tides or flooding from excessive rainfall.

NEW

555.33 Receptacles

(C) **Replacement Receptacles.** Replacement receptacles must comply with 555.33.

555.34 Wiring Methods and Installation

Section 555.34(B)(2) was modified to require compliance with only Part I of Article 225.

Analysis

555.34(B)(2) Installation. The revised language permits multiple feeders and branch circuits. With the GFPE requirements there is concern with the leakage current on large feeders. The rules in Part I of Article 225 are the "general" outside wiring requirements. Those in Part II that no longer apply to this article are the requirements that cover buildings or structures that are supplied by feeders or branch circuits.

CLARIFIED

555.34 Wiring Methods and Installation

(B) Installation

(2) **Outdoor Branch Circuits and Feeders.** Multiple feeders and branch circuits are permitted and clearances for overhead branch-circuit and feeder wiring in locations of the boatyard other than those described in 555.34(B)(1) must be located not less than 18 ft above grade. Only Part I of Article 225 must apply to marina installations.

555.35 Ground-Fault Protection of Equipment (GFPE) and Ground-Fault Circuit-Interrupter (GFCI) Protection

This section was relocated from 550.3 and divided into two subsections. New Informational Notes were added to both.

Analysis

RELOCATED **To clarify the requirements for ground-fault protection, this section was divided into two subsections.** Subsection (A) addresses the shore power receptacles, as well as the feeders and branch circuits supplying the receptacles from shore and (B) covers a new requirement to be able to measure leakage current where more than three receptacles supply shore power to boats. The Informational Notes were added to address the concerns regarding vessel testing to alleviate potential leakage current which contributes to electrical shock drowning (ESD).

555.35 Ground-Fault Protection of Equipment (GFPE) and Ground-Fault Circuit-Interrupter (GFCI) Protection

(A) Ground-Fault Protection. For other than floating buildings, ground-fault protection for docking facilities must be provided in accordance with the following:

(1) GFPE Protection. Receptacles installed in accordance with 555.33(A) can have individual GFPEs set to open at currents not exceeding 30 mA.

(2) GFCI Protection. All 15A and 20A, 125V receptacles for other than shore power must be protected in accordance with 555.19(B)(1) and (B)(2).

(3) Feeder and Branch-Circuit Conductors with GFPE. Feeder and branch-circuit conductors that are installed on docking facilities must be provided with GFPEs set to open at currents not exceeding 100 mA.

Ex to (3): Transformer secondary conductors of a separately derived system that do not exceed 10 ft and are installed in a raceway are be permitted to be installed without ground-fault protection. This exception also applies to the supply terminals of the equipment supplied by the transformer secondary conductors.

(B) Leakage Current Measurement Device. Where more than three receptacles supply shore power to boats, a leakage current measurement device must be available and be used to determine leakage current from each boat that will utilize shore power.

 Scan this QR code for a video of Mike explaining this topic; it's a sample from the videos that accompany this textbook.

Note 1: Leakage current measurement will provide the capability to determine when an individual boat has defective wiring or other problems contributing to hazardous voltage and current. The use of this test device will allow the facility operator to identify a boat that is creating an electrical hazard. In some cases, a single boat may cause an upstream GFPE device protecting a feeder to trip even though multiple boats are supplied from the same feeder. The use of this test device will help the facility operator prevent a particular boat from contributing to hazardous voltage and current in the marina area.

Note 2: An annual test of each boat with the leakage current measurement device is a prudent step toward determining if a boat has defective wiring that may be contributing hazardous voltage and current. Where the leakage current measurement device reveals that a boat is contributing hazardous voltage and current, repairs should be made to the boat before it is permitted to utilize shore power.

Author's Comment:

▸ A review of reported ESD events shows that 50% of the ESD incidents may have been avoided by having the 30 mA protection at the shore power receptacles.

555.37 Equipment Grounding Conductor

This was relocated from 555.15. The title and 555.37(A) were both revised to improve clarity.

Analysis

RELOCATED This section was relocated from 555.15 and the term "grounding" was replace with the correct terms "Equipment Grounding Conductor" where appropriate.

CLARIFIED **555.37(A) Equipment to Be Connected to Equipment Grounding Conductor.** "Grounded" was not the correct term since the Article 100 definition is "connected to earth." This change certainly clarifies the intent of the rule.

There were no technical changes, just revisions so the titles now use the correct *Code* terms. Using terms as defined in Article 100 is critical to the correct application of the *NEC* rules.

555.37 Equipment Grounding Conductor

(A) Equipment to be <u>Connected to the Equipment Grounding Conductor.</u> The following items must be connected to an equipment grounding conductor run with the circuit conductors in the same raceway, cable, or trench:

(1) Metal boxes, metal cabinets, and all other metal enclosures.

(2) Metal frames of utilization equipment.

(3) Grounding terminals of grounding-type receptacles.

Part III Floating Buildings

This new Part III primarily consists of rules that were relocated from the now deleted Article 553 although a new one was added.

Analysis

NEW

555.53 Ground-Fault Protection. This is a new rule that requires the main overcurrent protective device (OCPD) that feeds a floating building to have GFPE that is set at not more than 100 mA.

The rule goes on to say that ground-fault protection of each individual branch or feeder breaker must be permitted as a suitable alternative. It does not specify the level of protection required where there are multiple feeders or branch circuits supplying the floating building.

Author's Comment:

▸ As long as the individual protection does not exceed 100 mA, it could be expected that most authorities would consider the installation compliant.

Introduction to Article 590—Temporary Installations

Article 590 addresses the practicality and execution issues that are inherent in temporary installations thereby making them less time consuming to install. While it might be a common misconception that temporary wiring represents a lower standard of wiring than permanent wiring, in truth it merely meets a different standard. The same rules of workmanship, ampacity, and overcurrent protection apply to temporary installations as to others. So, how is a temporary installation different? You must remove a temporary installation upon completion of the purpose for which it was installed. If the temporary installation is for holiday displays, it cannot last more than 90 days.

590.4 General

The language in 590.4(F) was revised to improve clarity and two new exceptions were added to (G).

Analysis

CLARIFIED **590.4(F) Lamp Protection.** The last sentence of this subsection relating to lampholders was revised. The rule required that where brass shell, paper lined sockets, or other metal cased sockets are used, the outer shell must be grounded. This was revised to require the outer shell to be connected to the circuit equipment grounding conductor.

NEW **590.4(G) Splices Ex 1.** The mark-ups for the 2020 *Code* do not show Exception No. 1 as a change. The tentative interim amendment (TIA) had been incorporated into the draft that the Code-Making Panel worked with. The TIA was needed because the original text in the 2017 *NEC* permitted open splices in temporary wiring in all locations where temporary wiring is used and the TIA restricted open splices to being used only on construction sites.

NEW **590.4(G) Splices Ex 2.** This exception acts to permit the use of branch-circuit wiring installed as permanent wiring in framed walls and ceilings to supply temporary wiring or power without the boxes having covers, provided the branch circuit has GFCI protection.

590.4 General

(F) Lamp Protection. Lamps (bulbs) must be protected from accidental contact by a suitable luminaire or lampholder with a guard. ▶Figure 590–1

(G) Splices. A box, conduit body, or other enclosure, with a cover installed, is required for all splices.

Ex 1: On construction sites a box is not required if the conductors being spliced, are from nonmetallic sheathed cables or cords, or metal sheathed cable assemblies so long as the grounding continuity can be maintained without the box.

   (1) The circuit conductors being spliced are all from nonmetallic multiconductor cord or cable assemblies, provided that the equipment grounding continuity is maintained with or without the box.

   (2) The circuit conductors being spliced are all from metal-sheathed cable assemblies terminated in listed fittings that mechanically secure the cable sheath to maintain effective electrical continuity.

Temporary Installations
Lamp Protection
590.4(F)

Lamps (bulbs) must be protected from accidental contact by a suitable luminaire or a lampholder with a guard.

Copyright 2020, www.MikeHolt.com

▶Figure 590–1

Ex 2: On construction sites a box is not required for GFCI-protected branch circuits that are permanently installed in framed walls and ceilings and are used to supply temporary power or lighting.

(1) A box cover is not required for splices installed completely inside of junction boxes with plaster rings.

(2) Listed pigtail-type lampholders can be installed in ceiling-mounted junction boxes with plaster rings.

(3) Finger safe devices are permitted for supplying and connecting devices.

590.6 GFCI Protection for Personnel

The title of 590.6(B) was revised for clarity.

Analysis

CLARIFIED

590.6(B) Other Receptacle Outlets. This rule required these other receptacle outlets to be protected with GFCIs, SPGFCIs (special purpose ground fault circuit interrupter for personnel), or the assured equipment grounding conductor program. List item (2) for the SPGFCI was deleted and list item (3) for the assured equipment grounding conductor program was renumbered as (2).

590.6 GFCI Protection for Personnel

(B) Other <u>Receptacle</u> Outlets. Receptacles other than those covered by 590.6(A)(1) through (A)(3) that supply temporary power used by personnel during construction, remodeling, maintenance, repair, or demolition of buildings, structures, equipment, or similar activities must be GFCI protected.

590.8 Overcurrent Protective Devices

This section was added to provide guidance for AHJs in the reuse of equipment for temporary applications.

Analysis

NEW

Equipment that has been previously installed may have been subjected to environments, uses, and conditions that may not be visibly obvious. Approval of that equipment is often difficult and under the purview of the inspecting AHJ.

590.8 Overcurrent Protective Devices

(A) Where Reused. Where overcurrent protective devices that have been previously used are installed in a temporary installation, they must be examined to ensure the devices have been properly installed, properly maintained, and there is no evidence of impending failure.

Note: The phrase "evidence of impending failure" means that there is evidence such as arcing, overheating, loose parts, bound equipment parts, visible damage, or deterioration. The phrase "properly maintained" means that the equipment has been maintained in accordance with the manufacturers' recommendations and applicable industry codes and standards.

References for manufacturers' recommendations and applicable industry codes and standards include but are not limited to NEMA AB 4, *Guidelines for Inspection and Preventative Maintenance of Molded-Case Circuit Breakers Used in Commercial and Industrial Applications*, NFPA 70B, *Recommended Practice for Electrical Equipment Maintenance*; NEMA GD, *Evaluating Water-Damaged Electrical Equipment*; and IEEE 1458, *IEEE Recommended Practice for the Selection, Field Testing, and Life Expectancy of Molded-Case Circuit Breakers for Industrial Applications*.

(B) Service Overcurrent Protective Devices. Overcurrent protective devices for 277/480V services must be of the current limiting type.

SPECIAL EQUIPMENT

Introduction to Chapter 6—Special Equipment

Chapter 6, which covers special equipment, is the second of the four *NEC* chapters that deal with special topics. Chapters 5 and 7 focus on special occupancies, and special conditions respectively, while Chapter 8 covers communications systems. Remember, the first four chapters of the *Code* are sequential and form a foundation for each of the subsequent four.

What exactly is "Special Equipment"? It is equipment that, by the nature of its use, construction, or by its unique nature creates a need for additional measures to ensure the "safeguarding of people and property" mission of the *NEC*, as stated in Article 90. The *Code* groups the articles in this chapter logically, as you might expect.

- **Article 600—Electric Signs and Outline Lighting.** This article covers the installation of conductors and equipment for electric signs and outline lighting as defined in Article 100. They include all products and installations that utilize neon tubing, such as signs, decorative elements, skeleton tubing, or art forms.

- **Article 620—Elevators, Escalators, and Moving Walks.** This article covers electrical equipment and wiring used in connection with elevators, dumbwaiters, escalators, moving walks, wheelchair lifts, and stairway chair lifts.

- **Article 625—Electric Vehicle Charging System.** An electrically-powered vehicle needs a dedicated charging circuit. And that is where Article 625 comes in. It provides the requirements for the electrical equipment needed to charge automotive-type electric and hybrid vehicles, including cars, bikes, and buses.

- **Article 630—Electric Welders.** Electric welding equipment does its job either by creating an electric arc between two surfaces or by heating a rod that melts from overcurrent. Either way results in a hefty momentary current draw. Welding machines come in many shapes and sizes. This article covers electric arc welding and resistance welding apparatus, and other similar welding equipment connected to an electric supply system.

- **Article 645—Information Technology Equipment.** This article applies to equipment, power-supply wiring, equipment interconnecting wiring, and grounding of information technology equipment and systems, including terminal units in an information technology equipment room.

- **Article 680—Swimming Pools, Spas, Hot Tubs, Fountains, and Similar Installations.** Article 680 covers the installation of electric wiring and equipment that supplies swimming, wading, therapeutic and decorative pools, fountains, hot tubs, spas, and hydromassage bathtubs, whether permanently installed or storable.

- **Article 690—Solar Photovoltaic (PV) Systems.** This article focuses on reducing the electrical hazards that may arise from installing and operating a solar PV system, to the point where it can be considered safe for property and people. The requirements of the *NEC* Chapters 1 through 4 apply to these installations, except as specifically modified here.

- **Article 691—Large-Scale Solar Photovoltaic (PV) Electric Power Production Facility.** Article 691 covers large-scale PV power production facilities with a generating capacity of 5,000 kW or more and not under exclusive utility control.

- **Article 694—Wind Electric Systems.** Article 694 entails wind turbine alternative energy systems. It covers their alternators, generators, and all associated equipment necessary to make available, electricity generated by this alternative source.

- **Article 695—Fire Pumps.** This article covers the electric power sources and inter-connecting circuits for electric motor-driven fire pumps. It also covers switching and control equipment dedicated to fire pump drivers. Article 695 does not apply to sprinkler system pumps in one- and two-family dwellings or to pressure maintenance (jockey) pumps.

ELECTRIC SIGNS AND OUTLINE LIGHTING

Introduction to Article 600—Electric Signs and Outline Lighting

One of the first things you will notice when entering a strip mall is that there is a sign for every store. Every commercial occupancy that provides entrances meant for public access needs a form of identification, and the standard method is the electric sign. It is for this reason that section, 600.5 requires a sign outlet at the entrance of each tenant location. Article 600 requires a disconnect within sight of a sign which can be located on the sign itself or able to be locked in the open position if located remotely.

Author's Comment:

▸ Article 100 defines an electric sign as any "fixed, stationary, or portable self-contained, electrically illuminated utilization equipment with words or symbols designed to convey information or attract attention."

Freestanding signs, such as those that might be erected in a parking lot, must be located at least 14 ft above vehicle areas unless they are protected from physical damage. Neon art forms or decorative elements are subsets of electric signs and outline lighting. If installed and not attached to an enclosure or sign body, they are considered skeleton tubing for the purpose of applying the requirements of Article 600. However, if that neon tubing is attached to an enclosure or sign body, which may be a simple support frame, it is considered a sign or outline lighting subject to all the provisions that apply to signs and outline lighting, such as 600.3, which requires the product to be listed.

600.2 Definitions

New definitions for "Host Sign," "Retrofit Kit, General Use," "Retrofit Kit, Sign Specific," and "Subassembly" were added to this section.

Analysis

NEW

Host Sign. This is a sign that was already installed in the field and designated for a conversion on location of the illumination system with a retrofit kit. Signs, unlike luminaires, are often custom made. For a retrofit kit that consists of a "complete subassembly of parts and devices," it must be identified for use with that specific sign or host sign.

UL 879A, *Standard for Safety for LED Sign and Sign Retrofit Kits* requires a sign undergoing field conversion to be identified in the retrofit kit instructions. The instructions must also include:

a) A kit parts list
b) Identification and preparation of the host sign
c) Identification of which parts are to be removed

NEW

Retrofit Kit, General Use. This is a kit that contains only the primary parts necessary for retrofitting which contains a list of required parts and instructions to complete the process in the field. This type of kit is not designed for use in a specific sign but is more generic in that it provides major components and might not contain all the parts and pieces required to complete the retrofit.

Retrofit Kit, Sign Specific. The Article 100 definition of "Retrofit Kit" requires a complete subassembly of parts and devices that would often be supplied by the original sign manufacturer for specific signs.

NEW

Note that the definitions in this article apply within this article only and modify the definition in Article 100 in accordance with the permission in 90.3 for a Chapter 6 article to modify a Chapter 1 article.

Subassembly. This term describes the components of a subassembly.

NEW

600.2 Definitions

The definitions in this section apply only within this article.

Neon Tubing. Electric-discharge luminous tubing, including cold cathode luminous tubing, that is made into shapes to illuminate signs, form letters, parts of letters, skeleton tubing, outline lighting, or other decorative elements, or art forms and filled with various inert gases.

Photovoltaic (PV) Powered Sign. A sign powered by a solar PV system. ▶Figure 600–1

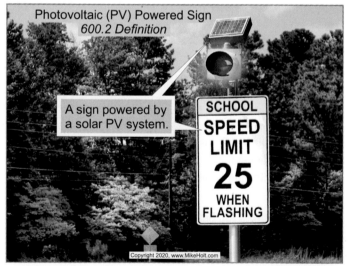

Photovoltaic (PV) Powered Sign
600.2 Definition

A sign powered by a solar PV system.

SCHOOL
SPEED
LIMIT
25
WHEN
FLASHING

Copyright 2020, www.MikeHolt.com

▶Figure 600–1

Host Sign. A sign or outline lighting system already installed in the field that is designated for field conversion of the illumination system with a retrofit kit.

Retrofit Kit, General Use. A kit consisting of primary parts, which does not include all the parts for a complete subassembly but includes a list of required parts and installation instructions to complete the subassembly in the field.

Retrofit Kit, Sign Specific. A kit consisting of the necessary parts and hardware to allow for field installation in a host sign, based on the included installation instructions.

Subassembly. Component parts or a segment of a sign, retrofit kit, or outline lighting system that, when assembled, forms a complete unit or product.

Author's Comment:

▸ Of the two "retrofit kit" definitions, the general use retrofit kit will likely be the most commonly used kit.

▸ These three new definitions are needed because of the custom nature of most signs. They are not of a standard design as are many luminaires.

600.3 Listing

The parent text in this section was revised to require both listing and labeling.

Analysis

CLARIFIED The words "and labeled" were added immediately following "listed." The rule requires fixed or portable electric signs, section signs, outline lighting, photovoltaic (PV) powered signs, and retrofit kits (regardless of voltage) to be both listed and labeled. It is important for the AHJ to be able to identify that the equipment is listed, and is most easily accomplished by looking at a listing "label" on the product. The change in language reflects the requirements of the listing agencies, as they require listed equipment to be labeled identifying it as such.

600.3 Listing

Fixed, mobile, or portable electric signs, section signs, outline lighting, PV powered signs, and retrofit kits, must be listed <u>and labeled,</u> and installed in accordance with their installation instructions.

600.4 Markings

The rule in (D) was modified to permit the markings required by 600.4(A) to be installed in a location not visible to the public.

Analysis

 600.4(D) Visibility. This subsection requires the listing labels to be visible and permanently **CLARIFIED** applied in a location that will be visible prior to servicing the equipment. The new language clarifies that the marking is permitted to be installed in a location that is not visible to the public. Labels visible to the public are unnecessary for safety and often detract from the aesthetic appearance of the sign. This change permits the label to be installed behind a cover that would be opened or removed to access and service the electrical parts making the label visible prior to servicing the equipment.

600.4 Markings

(D) Marking Visibility. The markings required in 600.4(A) and listing labels must be visible after installation and be permanently applied in a location visible <u>prior to</u> servicing. <u>The marking is permitted to be installed in a location not viewed by the public.</u>

The marking and listing labels required in 600.4(A) are not required to be visible after installation but must be visible during servicing.

600.5 Branch Circuits

Section 600.5(A) was clarified and subsection (B) requiring the disconnecting means to be marked to identify the equipment it disconnects was added.

Analysis

 600.5(A) Required Branch Circuit. This subsection requires each commercial occupancy and **CLARIFIED** building accessible to pedestrians to be provided with at least one outlet, in an accessible location, at each public entrance to each tenant space. It requires a dedicated 20A branch circuit to supply the outlet. The language for service locations was modified for clarification. The intent is to clarify that entrances not used by the customers, such as a delivery entrance, are not required to have a sign outlet. Subsection (D)(2) was revised to make it clear the sign body itself cannot be used as a pull or junction box.

 600.5(B) Marking. This new subsection requires a disconnecting means for a sign, outline lighting **NEW** system, or controller be marked to identify the sign, outline lighting system, or controller it controls. An exception says that an external disconnect mounted on the sign body, sign enclosure, sign pole, or controller is not required to be so identified.

The mandatory identification will make it easier for emergency responders to disconnect the power if such disconnection is necessary. The exception excludes disconnects mounted on the equipment as that mounting location makes it clear what the disconnect controls.

 600.5(D)(2) Wiring Methods. This rule was revised to permit transformer enclosures to be **CLARIFIED** used as pull or junction boxes for conductors supplying other adjacent signs, outline lighting systems, or floodlights that are part of a sign—provided the sign disconnecting means de-energizes all current-carrying conductors in these enclosures.

The words "signs or" were removed this now permits only the transformer enclosure to be used as a junction or pull box for conductors supplying other adjacent signs, outline lighting systems, or floodlights. Additional language requires the sign disconnecting means to de-energize all current-carrying conductors that pass through the enclosure.

600.5 Branch Circuits

(A) Required Branch Circuit. Each commercial building or occupancy accessible to pedestrians must have at least one outlet located at the entrance of each tenant space that is supplied by an individual branch circuit rated at least 20A. ▶Figure 600–2

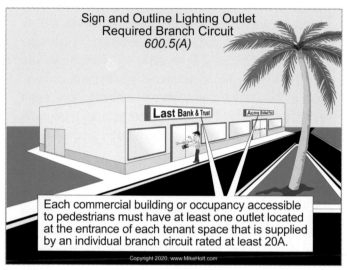

▶Figure 600–2

A sign or outline lighting outlet is not required at entrances for deliveries, service corridors, or service hallways that are intended to be used only by service personnel or employees. ▶Figure 600–3

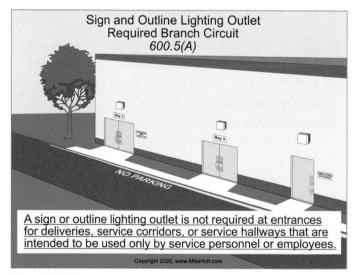

▶Figure 600–3

▸ Essentially, what this means is that each commercial building and each commercial occupancy accessible to pedestrians requires a minimum of one 20A branch circuit for the sign outlet. This requirement applies whether or not a sign will be installed. If it is supplying a neon sign, that branch circuit can be rated up to 30A.

(B) Marking. A disconnecting means for a sign, outline lighting system, or controller must be marked to identity the sign, outline lighting system, or controller it controls.

Ex: An external disconnecting means that is mounted on the sign body, sign enclosure, sign pole, or controller is not required to identify the sign or outline lighting system it controls.

(C) Rating. Branch circuits that supply signs are considered continuous loads. ▶Figure 600–4

▶Figure 600–4

(D) Wiring Methods. Wiring methods used to supply signs must comply with 600.5(D)(1), (D)(2), and (D)(3).

(1) Supply. The wiring method used to supply signs and outline lighting systems must terminate within a sign, an outline lighting system enclosure, a suitable box, a conduit body, or panelboard.

(2) Enclosures as Pull Boxes. Transformer enclosures is permitted to be used as pull or junction boxes for conductors supplying other adjacent signs, outline lighting systems, or floodlights that are part of a sign and is permitted to contain both branch and secondary circuit conductors, provided the sign disconnecting means de-energizes all current-carrying conductors in these enclosures.

(3) Metal or Nonmetallic Poles. Metal or nonmetallic poles used to support signs are permitted to enclose supply conductors, provided the poles and conductors are installed in accordance with 410.30(B).

600.6 Disconnecting Means

This rule was revised to say that conductors passing through a sign, and not disconnected by the sign disconnect, must be inaccessible to service personnel. Subsection (A)(4) requires that there be first responder access to sign disconnects located remotely from the sign.

Analysis

CLARIFIED

600.6(A)(1) Ex 1 and 2 Disconnect Location. These exceptions were revised to clarify that the sign disconnect is not required to disconnect feeder or branch-circuit conductors installed in a Chapter 3 wiring method where those conductors are not accessible. This change is intended to address the problem of accessible energized conductors within sign after the sign disconnect has been placed in the off position. A new subsection (A)(4) requires a remote sign disconnect to be installed in a location that is readily accessible to firefighters and clearly marked to identify what the disconnect controls.

NEW

600.6(A)(4) Remote Location. This new subsection addresses firefighter access to remotely located disconnects. The disconnecting means is permitted to be located at the sign or controller, or remotely as long as local control by first responders is provided.

600.6 Disconnecting Means

The circuit conductors to a sign, outline lighting system, or skeleton tubing must be controlled by an externally-operable switch or circuit breaker that will open all phase conductors. ▶Figure 600–5

Note: The location of the disconnect is intended to allow service or maintenance personnel <u>and first responders,</u> complete and local control of the disconnect.

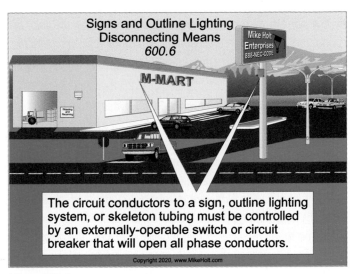

▶Figure 600–5

▸ The disconnect for the sign is permitted to be located next to the sign [404.8(A) Ex 2]. In many cases, the sign disconnect is an integral part of the sign itself or simply field installed and conveniently secured to the outside of the sign.

(A) Disconnect Location. The sign disconnect is permitted to be located as follows:

(1) At the Point of Entrance to a Sign. The sign disconnect must be located where the conductors enter a sign enclosure, sign body, or pole. ▶Figure 600–6

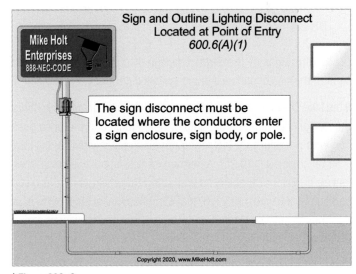

▶Figure 600–6

Ex 1: A sign disconnect is not required to be located at the point the conductors enter a sign enclosure or sign body for conductors that pass through a sign where <u>not accessible and</u> enclosed in a Chapter 3 raceway or metal-jacketed cable.

Ex 2: A sign disconnect is not required to be located at the point the conductors enter a sign enclosure or sign body for a feeder that supplies a panelboard located within the sign under the following conditions: The feeder conductors must be enclosed <u>where not accessible</u> in a Chapter 3 raceway or metal-jacketed cable, a permanent field-applied warning label having sufficient durability to withstand the environment involved, complying with 110.21(B), and visible during servicing is applied to the raceway or metal cable at or near the point of the feeder circuit conductor's entry into the sign enclosure or sign body and the warning label reads:

DANGER. THIS RACEWAY CONTAINS
ENERGIZED CONDUCTORS

The warning label must identify the location of the sign disconnect and the it must be capable of being locked in the open position with provisions for locking to remain in place whether the lock is installed or not [110.25].

Author's Comment:

▸ This rule now requires that any pass through conductors not controlled by the sign disconnect, be enclosed in an approved wiring method that does not include accessible points such as conduit bodies or junction boxes. Conductors ran in conduit bodies and junction boxes are considered to be accessible.

(2) Within Sight of the Sign. The sign disconnect must be within sight of the sign or outline lighting system it controls. ▸Figure 600–7

If the sign disconnect is not within sight of the sign or outline lighting, the disconnect must be capable of being locked in the open position with provisions for locking to remain in place whether the lock is installed or not [110.25]. A permanent field-applied warning label, having sufficient durability to withstand the environment involved and complying with 110.21(B) that identifies the location of the sign disconnect, must be located on the sign where it will be visible during servicing. ▸Figure 600–8

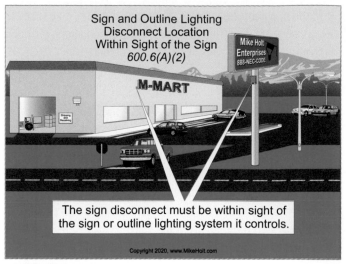

▸Figure 600–7

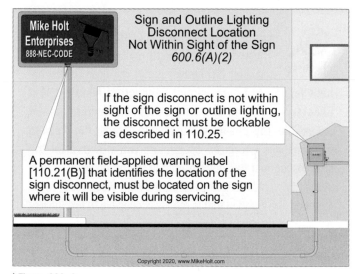

▸Figure 600–8

Author's Comment:

▸ According to Article 100, "Within Sight" means that it is visible and not more than 50 ft from the location of the equipment.

(3) Controller Disconnect as Sign Disconnect. Signs or outline lighting systems operated by controllers located external to the sign or outline lighting system must have a disconnect for the sign controller in accordance with the following:

(1) The controller disconnect must be located within sight of or within the controller enclosure.

(2) The controller disconnect must disconnect the sign or outline lighting and the controller from all phase conductors. ▸Figure 600–9

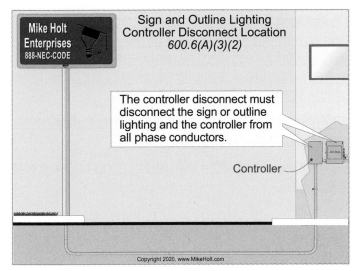

Sign and Outline Lighting
Controller Disconnect Location
600.6(A)(3)(2)

The controller disconnect must disconnect the sign or outline lighting and the controller from all phase conductors.

Controller

Copyright 2020, www.MikeHolt.com

▶Figure 600–9

(3) The controller disconnect must be capable of being locked in the open position with provisions for locking to remain in place whether the lock is installed or not [110.25].

Ex: Where the controller disconnect is not within sight of the controller, a permanent field-applied warning label, having sufficient durability to withstand the environment involved and in accordance with 110.21(B) that identifies the location of the sign disconnect, must be located on the sign where it can be visible during servicing.

(4) Remote Location. The disconnecting means, if located remote from the sign, sign body, or pole, must be mounted at an accessible location available to first responders and service personnel. The location of the disconnect must be marked with a label at the sign location and marked as the disconnect for the sign or outline lighting system. The label must be permanent, field-applied, have sufficient durability to withstand the environment involved, and be in accordance with 110.21(B).

600.35 Retrofit Kits

This new section provides the installation requirements for retrofit kits.

Analysis

600.35(A) General. This says that general use or sign specific retrofit kits for a sign or outline lighting system must include instructions and requirements for the field conversion of a host sign. It also requires the retrofit kit to be listed and labeled. There was no need to specify that the retrofit kit be listed in this subsection as it is already required by 600.3.

600.35(B) Installation. The retrofit kit must be installed in accordance with the manufacturer's installation instructions and be listed and labeled. Four new list items are as follows:

(B)(1) Wiring Methods. This specifies the use of approved wiring methods for the installation of the retrofit kit, with an exception for kits powered by a Class 2 source. Where powered from such a source, the wiring methods must in accordance with 600.12(C)(1)(2), 600.24, and 600.33.

(B)(2) Damaged Parts. This requires all the parts not being replaced by parts from the retrofit kit to be inspected for damage. Any damaged parts must be replaced or repaired to maintain the sign or outline lighting system's dry, damp, or wet location rating. In general, this applies to the mechanical parts as the retrofit kit replaces most (if not all) of the electrical parts of the host sign.

(B)(3) Workmanship. This requires the installation to comply with 110.12. General requirements automatically apply to Chapter 6, so a specific reference here appears to be just a reminder as there was no modification to the rule.

(B)(4) Marking. The retrofitted sign must be marked in accordance with 600.4(B). This requires a marking that the illumination system has been replaced and must include the kit provider's and installer's name, logo, or unique identifier. If the sign has been equipped with tubular LED lamps powered by the existing sign sockets, a label indicating this must be installed.

600.35 Retrofit Kits

(A) General. A general-use or sign-specific retrofit kit for a sign or outline lighting system must include installation instructions and requirements for field conversion of a host sign. The retrofit kit must be listed and labeled.

(B) Installation. The retrofit kit must be installed in accordance with the installation instructions.

(1) Wiring Methods. Wiring methods must be in accordance with Chapter 3.

Ex: If powered from a Class 2 source, wiring methods must be in accordance with 600.12(C)(1)(2) and (C) (2) , 600.24, and 600.33.

(2) Damaged Parts. All parts that are not replaced by a retrofit kit must be inspected for damage. Any part found to be damaged or damaged during conversion of the sign must be replaced or repaired to maintain the sign or outline lighting system's dry, damp, or wet location rating.

(3) Workmanship. Field conversion workmanship must be in accordance with 110.12.

(4) Marking. The retrofitted sign must be marked in accordance with 600.4(B).

ELEVATORS, ESCALATORS, AND MOVING WALKS, PLATFORM LIFTS, AND STAIRWAY CHAIR LIFTS

Introduction to Article 620—Elevators, Escalators, and Moving Walks, Platform Lifts, and Stairway Chair Lifts

Except for dumbwaiters, the equipment covered by Article 620 moves people. Thus, a major concept in this article is that of keeping people separated from electrical power. That is why, for example, 620.3 requires live parts to be enclosed. This article consists of 10 parts:

- **Part I. General.** This part provides the scope of the article, definitions, and voltage limitations.
- **Part II. Conductors.** The single-line diagram of Figure 620.13 in the *NEC* illustrates how the requirements of Part II work together.
- **Part III. Wiring.** This addresses wiring methods and branch-circuit requirements for different equipment.
- **Part IV. Installation of Conductors.** Part IV covers conductor fill, supports, and related items.
- **Part V. Traveling Cables.** Installation, suspension, location, and protection of cables that move with the motion of the elevator or lift are all covered.
- **Part VI. Disconnecting Means and Control.** The requirements vary with the application.
- **Part VII. Overcurrent Protection.** While most of this part refers to Article 430, it does include additional requirements, such as providing selective coordination.
- **Part VIII. Machine and Control Rooms and Spaces.** The primary goal here is the prevention of unauthorized access.
- **Part IX. Equipment Grounding Conductor.** While most of this part refers to Article 250, it includes additional requirements as well. For example, 15A and 20A, 125V receptacles in certain locations must be GFCI protected.
- **Part X. Emergency and Standby Systems.** This deals with regenerative power and with the need for a disconnecting means that can disconnect an elevator from both the normal power system and the emergency or standby system.

620.6 GFCI Protection for Personnel

This rule was moved from 620.85 to this location.

Analysis

RELOCATED This was relocated from 620.85 and revised to require machinery spaces and sump pump receptacles to be GFCI protected. You would think machinery spaces would be considered "equipment requiring servicing" and covered by the 210.8 requirement for GFCI protection which addresses such equipment now referenced in 210.63; but nonetheless, that requirement is made perfectly clear in this rule. Ground level elevator pits are typically below grade and prone to water accumulation, so they are required to have a sump pump on a dedicated circuit. • • •

This circuit was in addition to the required pit service receptacle that was already required to be GFCI protected, and the sump pump was exempt since it was a dedicated circuit so long as a single receptacle was installed for the pump. This change makes it clear this is no longer the case and the sump pump is required to be GFCI protected unless it is permanently wired ("hardwired").

620.6 GFCI-Protected Receptacles

Receptacles rated 15A and 20A, 125V located in pits, hoistways, on the cars of elevators, and in escalator and moving walk wellways must be of the GFCI type. ▶Figure 620–1

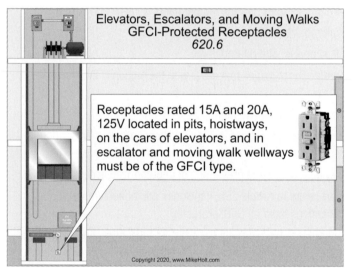

Elevators, Escalators, and Moving Walks
GFCI-Protected Receptacles
620.6

Receptacles rated 15A and 20A, 125V located in pits, hoistways, on the cars of elevators, and in escalator and moving walk wellways must be of the GFCI type.

Copyright 2020, www.MikeHolt.com

▶Figure 620–1

Receptacles rated 15A and 20A, 125V installed in machine rooms, control spaces, <u>machinery spaces,</u> and control rooms must be GFCI protected. ▶Figure 620–2

<u>A permanently installed sump pump must be permanently wired or be supplied by a single receptacle that is GFCI protected.</u>

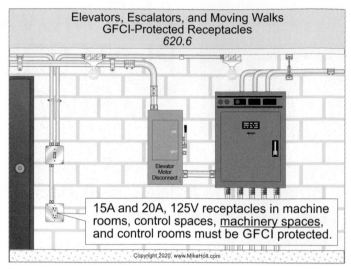

Elevators, Escalators, and Moving Walks
GFCI-Protected Receptacles
620.6

15A and 20A, 125V receptacles in machine rooms, control spaces, <u>machinery spaces,</u> and control rooms must be GFCI protected.

Copyright 2020, www.MikeHolt.com

▶Figure 620–2

620.22 Branch Circuits for Elevator Car(s)

Section 620.22(A) was revised to clarify which types of equipment can be supplied by the lighting circuit, and to specify the location of the overcurrent protective device if there is no machine room or machine space.

Analysis

CLARIFIED **620.22(A) Car Light Receptacles, Auxiliary Lighting, and Ventilation.** The title of this subsection was revised to more completely reflect the content of the rule. It was revised to clarify that while the separate branch circuit is permitted to also supply receptacle(s), accessory equipment (alarm devices/bells or monitoring devices not part of the control system), auxiliary lighting, and ventilation on each elevator car it is not required to supply all of those items. The previous language appeared to require this branch circuit to do so.

This revised permissive language permits single or multiple circuits to supply those items. The rule requires the overcurrent protective device that protects this branch circuit to be in the elevator machine room or control room/machinery space. Additional wording says that where these specified spaces do not exist, the OCPD must be located outside of the hoistway and accessible to qualified persons.

620.22 Branch Circuits for Elevator Car(s)

(A) Car Light, Receptacles, Auxiliary Lighting and Ventilation. A separate branch circuit must supply the car lights. The car lights branch circuit is permitted to supply receptacles, accessory equipment (alarm devices, alarm bells, monitoring devices not part of the control system), auxiliary lighting power source, and ventilation on each elevator car or inside the operation controller.

Where there is no machine room, control room, machinery space, or control space outside the hoistway, the overcurrent device must be located outside the hoistway and accessible to qualified persons only.

620.51 Disconnecting Means

A revision in (A) now requires disconnects to be lockable only in the open position.

Analysis

CLARIFIED

620.51(A) Type (of disconnect). The language here was modified and is different from all other "lockable" disconnect rules. This rule requires the disconnecting means to be lockable in only the open (off) position. The Public Input (PI) cites the issue of not being able to shut the elevator power off if the disconnect were permitted to be lockable in the on (closed) position.

620.51 Disconnecting Means

A disconnect must be provided for each elevator, escalator, or moving walk. The disconnect for the main power supply conductors is not permitted to disconnect power to the branch circuits required in 620.22, 620.23, and 620.24.

(A) Type. The disconnect must be an enclosed externally operable fused motor-circuit switch or circuit breaker that is lockable only in the open position with provisions for locking to remain in place whether the lock is installed or not [110.25]. ▶Figure 620–3

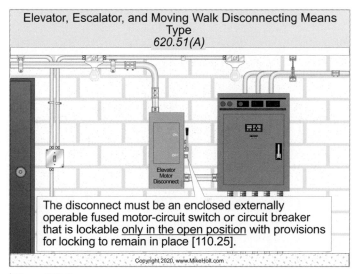

Elevator, Escalator, and Moving Walk Disconnecting Means Type
620.51(A)

The disconnect must be an enclosed externally operable fused motor-circuit switch or circuit breaker that is lockable <u>only in the open position</u> with provisions for locking to remain in place [110.25].

Copyright 2020, www.MikeHolt.com

▶Figure 620–3

Note: See ASME A17.1/CSA B44, *Safety Code for Elevators and Escalators,* for additional information for the disconnect.

Author's Comment:

▸ Commonly used lockable disconnect devices can be locked in either position. This will require that the installer pay close attention to the type of disconnect that is installed.

ARTICLE
625

ELECTRIC VEHICLE POWER TRANSFER SYSTEM

Introduction to Article 625—Electric Vehicle Power Transfer System

Electric vehicles have been around for a long time. Anyone who has worked in a factory or warehouse has probably encountered an electric lift truck. And, of course, we are all familiar with golf carts. These and other off-road vehicles have charging requirements that are easily accommodated by small charging systems.

But today, a new challenge has emerged and is becoming increasingly common. That challenge is the electrically-powered passenger vehicle, bus, truck, and motorcycle. Such vehicles, especially an electric car or bus, can weigh considerably more than a golf cart and just moving one takes a proportionately larger motor. In fact, many designs use multiple drive motors.

Those motors are powered by batteries. Adding to the battery sizing requirement are other demands. For example, these vehicles:

▸ Must be able to travel at highway speeds over distances roughly comparable to those traveled by their internal combustion engine counterparts.

▸ Have powered accessories that you typically will not find on a golf cart, such as air conditioning, electric windows, stereo systems, windshield wipers, security systems, and window defrosters.

▸ Are expected to start in summer heat and in brutal winter cold.

The battery system for an electrically-powered passenger vehicle is considerably larger than for a golf cart or other typical off-road electric vehicle. Consequently, the charging system must have the capability of delivering far more power than the one for a typical off-road electric vehicle.

An electrically-powered passenger vehicle needs a dedicated charging circuit. Article 625 defines the requirements for the installation of the electrical equipment needed to charge automotive-type electric and hybrid vehicles including cars, motorcycles, and buses.

This article consists of three parts:

- **Part I. General.** This includes the scope of the article, definitions, voltages, and listing/labeling requirements.
- **Part II. Equipment Construction.** Most of this applies to the manufacturer, but there are a few requirements you need to know.
- **Part III. Installation.** This part covers overcurrent protection and the disconnect in addition to the different requirements for indoor and outdoor locations.

625.1 Scope

The scope was changed to include systems which permit bidirectional current flow.

Analysis

EXPANDED Several other changes in Article 625 permit the use of equipment with bidirectional current flow. That is to say that the batteries in a vehicle can be either charged from, or supply power to, the building electrical system. This article covers the electrical conductors and equipment that connect to premises wiring for the purposes of charging, power export, or bidirectional current flow.

625.1 Scope

Article 625 covers the installation of conductors and equipment connecting an electric vehicle to premises wiring <u>for the purposes of charging, power export, or bidirectional current flow.</u> ▶Figure 625–1

Electric Vehicle Power Transfer System
625.1 Scope

Article 625 covers the installation of conductors and equipment connecting an electric vehicle to premises wiring <u>for the purposes of charging, power export, or bidirectional current flow.</u>

Copyright 2020, www.MikeHolt.com

▶Figure 625–1

625.2 Definitions

A definition for "Electric Vehicle Power Export Equipment (EVPE)" was added and the one for "Electric Vehicle Supply Equipment (EVSE)" was clarified.

Analysis

NEW **Electric Vehicle Power Export Equipment (EVPE).** This is the equipment, including the outlet, on the vehicle used to provide electrical power to external loads using the vehicle as the source of supply. The electrical export voltages are limited and may not exceed 30V ac or 60V dc. An Informational Note was added to indicate the EVPE equipment and the electric vehicle supply equipment may be contained in a single piece of equipment that is sometimes called "bidirectional EVSE" (Electric Vehicle Supply Equipment).

CLARIFIED **Electric Vehicle Supply Equipment (EVSE).** The acronym EVSE was added to the term title and the definition was revised. The acronym is used in the text of the article but was not shown in this definition in the previous *Code*. The revision says the EVSE includes a personal protection system installed specifically for the purpose of transferring energy between the premises wiring system and the electric vehicle. Items include, but are not limited to, neutral, phase, equipment grounding conductors, electric vehicle connectors, other fittings, devices, power outlets, and/or apparatus of the EVSE required by 625.22. An Informational Note was added that says electric vehicle power export equipment and electric vehicle supply equipment are sometimes contained in one piece of equipment and may be referred to as bidirectional EVSE.

625.2 Definitions

The following definitions only apply within this article.

Electric Vehicle Power Export Equipment (EVPE). The equipment, including the outlet on the vehicle, that is used to provide electrical power at voltages greater than 30V ac or 60V dc to loads external to the vehicle as the source of supply.

Note: Electric vehicle power export equipment and electric vehicle supply equipment are sometimes contained in one piece of equipment, referred to as a bidirectional EVSE.

Electric Vehicle Supply (EVSE) Equipment. Conductors, electric vehicle connectors, attachment plugs, personnel protection system, devices, and power outlets installed for the purpose of transferring energy between the premises wiring and the electric vehicle. ▶Figure 625–2

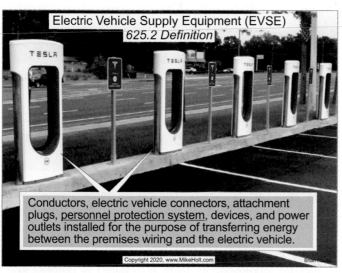

Conductors, electric vehicle connectors, attachment plugs, personnel protection system, devices, and power outlets installed for the purpose of transferring energy between the premises wiring and the electric vehicle.

Copyright 2020, www.MikeHolt.com

▶Figure 625–2

Note: Electric vehicle power export equipment and electric vehicle supply equipment are sometimes contained in one piece of equipment, sometimes referred to as a bidirectional EVSE.

Wireless Power Transfer Equipment (WPTE). Equipment consisting of a charger power converter and a primary pad. The two devices are either separate units or they are contained within a single enclosure. ▶Figure 625–3

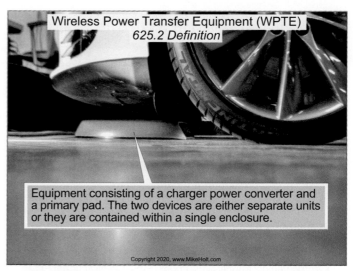

Wireless Power Transfer Equipment (WPTE)
625.2 Definition

Equipment consisting of a charger power converter and a primary pad. The two devices are either separate units or they are contained within a single enclosure.

Copyright 2020, www.MikeHolt.com

▶Figure 625–3

625.5 Listed

Equipment covered by the scope of this article must now be listed.

Analysis

EXPANDED The previous requirement required electric vehicle supply equipment (EVSE) and wireless power transfer equipment (WPTE) to be listed. This now expands the listing requirement to include electric vehicle power export (EVPE) equipment as well as the other equipment installed under the scope of this article.

625.5 Listed

All electric vehicle power transfer equipment covered by this article must be listed.

625.41 Overcurrent Protection

This section was expanded to include bidirectional electric vehicle supply equipment (EVSE) and wireless power transfer equipment (WPTE).

Analysis

EXPANDED This is part of the expansion of this rule to include electric vehicle supply equipment that has the ability to export power. It requires the overcurrent device for feeders and branch circuits used for electric vehicle supply equipment (EVSE), bidirectional EVSE, and wireless power transfer equipment (WPTE) to be sized for continuous duty and have a rating of not less than 125 percent of the maximum equipment load. Where there are noncontinuous loads supplied by the same feeder, the overcurrent protective device (OCPD) must be rated not less than the sum of the noncontinuous loads plus 125 percent of the continuous loads.

625.41 Overcurrent Protection

Overcurrent protection for circuits supplying <u>electric vehicle supply equipment (EVSE), including bidirectional EVSE, (EVPE), and wireless equipment (WPTE)</u>, must be sized no less than 125 percent of the maximum load of the electric vehicle supply equipment. ▶Figure 625–4

Author's Comment:

▸ Since the charging load for electric vehicle supply equipment is required to be sized no less than 125 percent of the load, then the conductors must be sized to be protected by the circuit overcurrent protective device in accordance with 240.4, including 110.14(C)(1) considerations, as well as 310.16.

Electric Vehicle Supply Equipment
Overcurrent Protection
625.41

Overcurrent protection for circuits supplying <u>electric vehicle supply equipment (EVSE), including bidirectional EVSE, (EVPE), and wireless equipment (WPTE)</u>, must be sized no less than 125 percent of the maximum load of the electric vehicle supply equipment.

▶Figure 625–4

625.42 Rating

This section was expanded to address equipment designs with adjustable input settings.

Analysis

EXPANDED   NEW New language addresses the use of EVSE systems with adjustable settings and permits the equipment to be installed, adjusted, and used at a current level that is less than the maximum. The lower setting may be required by the available power supply. The adjustments are permitted for equipment requiring only tools to move, as opposed to equipment fastened in place that would not require tools to move. Where the adjustments have an impact on the equipment labeling, the label must be marked to show the new rating. Where the access to the adjustments is limited, the ampere rating of the equipment and supply is permitted to be based on the adjusted rating. The lower input setting eliminates the need to rewire the user's connection to utilize the EVSE. This works only when the user cannot access the adjusting means, therefore restricted access is required.

625.42 Rating

The power transfer equipment must have sufficient rating to supply the load served. Electric vehicle charging loads are considered to be continuous loads for the purposes of this article. Services and feeders must be sized in accordance with the product ratings. Where an automatic load management system is used, the maximum equipment load on a service and feeder is the maximum load permitted by the automatic load management system.

Adjustable settings are allowed only on fixed-in-place equipment only. If adjustments have an impact on the rating label, those changes must be in accordance with manufacturer's instructions, and the adjusted rating must appear with sufficient durability to withstand the environment involved on the rating label.

Electric vehicle supply equipment with restricted access to an ampere adjusting means are permitted to have an ampere rating(s) that is ratings that are equal to the adjusted current setting. Sizing the service and feeder to match the adjusting means is allowed.

Restricted access must prevent the user from gaining access to the adjusting means. Examples of restricted access are as follows Restricted access must be accomplished by at least one of the following:

(1) A cover or door that requires the use of a tool to open.

(2) Bolted equipment enclosure doors.

(3) Locked doors accessible only to qualified personnel.

(4) Password protected commissioning software accessible only to qualified personnel.

625.48 Interactive Systems

The term "electric vehicle supply equipment" was removed and replaced with the acronym EVSE.

Analysis

CLARIFIED The term "electric vehicle supply equipment" was replaced with EVSE as was done in other instances within Article 625. A new sentence was added at the end of the paragraph to indicate the receptacle in the vehicle that is considered part of a power export system needs to comply with the new requirements for those receptacles as indicated.

625.48 Interactive Systems

Electric vehicle supply equipment (EVSE) that incorporates a power export function and is part of an interactive system that serves as an optional standby system, an electric power production source, or a bidirectional power feed must be listed and marked as suitable for that purpose. When used as an optional standby system, the requirements of Article 702 apply; when used as an electric power production source, the requirements of Article 705 apply.

Electric vehicle power export equipment (EVPE) that consists of a receptacle outlet only must be in accordance with 625.60.

625.54 GFCI Protection for Personnel

The GFCI requirement was expanded to apply to all receptacles installed for the connection of electric vehicle charging equipment.

Analysis

EXPANDED In the previous *NEC*, the GFCI requirement applied to only single-phase receptacles rated 150V to ground or less and 50A or less. This language change requires GFCI protection for any receptacle that supplies electric vehicle charging equipment, regardless of the current and voltage ratings. Additional wording was added to say this GFCI requirement is in addition to those in 210.8.

625.54 Ground-Fault Circuit-Interrupter Protection for Personnel

In addition to the GFCI protection requirements contained in 210.8, all receptacles installed for the connection of electric vehicle supply equipment must be GFCI protected.

Author's Comment:

▸ GFCI breakers or receptacles typically used in dwelling units are not suitable for back feeding. That would prohibit their use for bidirectional EVSE. This GFCI requirement only applies to cord and plug connected EVSE, making hard wired EVSE the only type that would be suitable for bidirectional use.

625.60 AC Receptacle Outlets Used for EVPE

This new section covers alternating-current receptacles installed in electric vehicles intended to allow for the connection of off-board utilization equipment.

Analysis

NEW There are four requirements for the receptacle outlets used for electric vehicle power export (EVPE) equipment covered in subsections (A) through (D) including listing, rating, overcurrent, and GFCI protection.

625.60 AC Electric Vehicle Power Export, (EVPE), Receptacles

AC receptacles installed in electric vehicles and intended to allow for connection of off-board utilization equipment must comply with:

(A) Type. The receptacle must be listed.

(B) Rating. The receptacle outlet must be rated a maximum, 250 volts single phase 50A.

(C) Overcurrent Protection. The overcurrent protection must be integral to the power export system.

(D) GFCI Protection for Personnel. Ground-fault protection for personnel must be provided for all receptacles.

Note: There are various methods available to achieve GFCI protection.

Author's Comment:

▸ This probably should be a listing standard construction requirement. Other construction requirements in Part II of the article were deleted but yet this was added. It also appears to be outside the scope of the *NEC* per 90.2(B)(1). If it were to be within the scope of the *NEC*, would the adopting unit of government have legal authority to enforce this requirement?

INFORMATION TECHNOLOGY EQUIPMENT (ITE)

Introduction to Article 645—Information Technology Equipment (ITE)

One of the unique things about Article 645 is the requirement for a shutoff switch for information technology equipment rooms [645.10]. This requirement seems to be wrong on its face because it allows someone to shut power to the IT room off from a single point. So, despite having a UPS and taking every precaution against a power outage, the IT system is still vulnerable to a shutdown from a readily accessible switch. It's important to understand, that this disconnect is only required if you want to use the lesser wiring methods permitted by this article and that Article 645 is not a requirement.

What about the rest of Article 645? The major goal is to reduce the spread of fire and smoke. The raised floors common in IT rooms pose additional challenges to achieving this goal, so this article devotes a fair percentage of its text to raised floor requirements. Fire-resistant walls, separate HVAC systems, and other requirements further help to achieve this goal.

645.5 Supply Circuits and Interconnecting Cables

Revisions were made in this section to eliminate conflicts between the *NEC* and NFPA 75, *Standard for the Fire Protection of Information Technology Equipment*.

Analysis

CLARIFIED

645.5(E)(2) Under Raised Floors. The list items were revised and a new list item 5 was added. These changes were made to remove a conflict between the *NEC* and NFPA 75, *Standard for the Fire Protection of Information Technology Equipment*.

ARTICLE 680

SWIMMING POOLS, SPAS, HOT TUBS, FOUNTAINS, AND SIMILAR INSTALLATIONS

Introduction to Article 680—Swimming Pools, Spas, Hot Tubs, Fountains, and Similar Installations

The requirements contained in Article 680 apply to the installation of electrical wiring and equipment for swimming pools, spas, hot tubs, fountains, and hydromassage bathtubs. The overriding concern of this article is to keep people and electricity separated.

Article 680 is divided into seven parts. The various parts apply to certain types of installations, so be careful to determine which parts of this article apply to what and where. For instance, Part I and Part II apply to spas and hot tubs installed outdoors, except as modified in Part IV. In contrast, hydromassage bathtubs are only covered by Part VII. Read the details of this article carefully so you will be able to provide a safe installation.

- Part I. General.
- Part II. Permanently Installed Pools. Installations at permanently installed pools must comply with both Parts I and II of this article.
- Part III. Storable Swimming Pools, Storable Spas, and Storable Hot Tubs. Installations of storable pools, storable spas, and storable hot tubs must comply with Parts I and III of Article 680.
- Part IV. Spas and Hot Tubs. Spas and hot tubs must comply with Parts I and IV of this article; outdoor spas and hot tubs must also comply with Part II in accordance with 680.42.
- Part V. Fountains. Parts I and II apply to permanently installed fountains. If they have water in common with a pool, Part II also applies. Self-contained, portable fountains are covered by Article 422, Parts II and III.
- Part VI. Pools and Tubs for Therapeutic Use. Parts I and VI apply to pools and tubs for therapeutic use in health care facilities, gymnasiums, athletic training rooms and similar installations. If they are portable appliances, then Article 422, Parts II and III apply.
- Part VII. Hydromassage Bathtubs. Part VII applies to hydromassage bathtubs, but no other parts of Article 680 do.

680.2 Definitions

The definition of "Fountain" was revised and the term "Immersion Pool" was added.

Analysis

RELOCATED

Corrosive Environment. This was previously defined in 680.14(A) and is new to 680.2. It was relocated with clarifications and a new Informational Note providing additional information about corrosion hazards and corrosive environments. The previous text was considered overly broad in scope.

• • •

Sanitation chemicals and pool water are considered to pose a risk of corrosion due to the presence of oxidizers. The note lists three sources where additional information may be found.

EXPANDED **Fountain.** The term fountain now also includes "splash pads." A splash pad is a special type of fountain and there is a new definition for that term as well.

NEW **Immersion Pool.** This new definition is being added to clarify what an immersion pool is for the application of two new sections; 680.35 for storable immersion pools and 680.45 for permanently installed immersion pools. It is simply a pool used for ceremonial or ritual immersion of users and is designed and intended to have its contents drained or discharged. There are potential safety hazards related to electricity with immersion pools just as there are with bathtubs or pools.

NEW **Splash Pad.** The term "splash pad" was added to the definition of fountain so all the requirements for fountains also apply to splash pads. The definition does not include showers intended for hygienic rinsing prior to the use of a water feature. Splash pads are a common feature in many public areas, and this will help ensure that the electrical systems for them are safely installed.

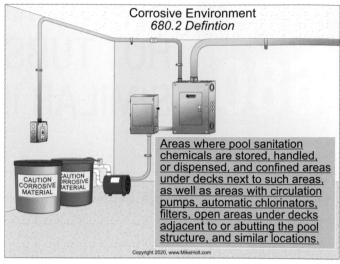

Corrosive Environment
680.2 Definition

Areas where pool sanitation chemicals are stored, handled, or dispensed, and confined areas under decks next to such areas, as well as areas with circulation pumps, automatic chlorinators, filters, open areas under decks adjacent to or abutting the pool structure, and similar locations.

Copyright 2020, www.MikeHolt.com

▶Figure 680–1

1Note: Sanitation chemicals and pool water are considered to pose a risk of corrosion (gradually damaging or destroying materials) due to the presence of oxidizers (for example, calcium hypochlorite, sodium hypochlorite, bromine, and chlorinated isocyanurates) and chlorinating agents that release chlorine when dissolved in water. More information about swimming pool chemicals can be found on or in the following:

(1) Environmental Protection Agency website

(2) NFPA 400, *Code for the Storage of Liquid and Solid Oxidizers*

(3) Advisory: Swimming Pool Chemicals: Chlorine, OSWER 90-008.1, available from the *EPA National Service Center for Environmental Publications* (NSCEP)

Author's Comment:

▶ This seems overly broad, especially to require areas where these chemicals are stored in their dry form and away from water sources, to be considered a corrosive environment.

Fountain. An ornamental structure or recreational water feature from which one or more jets or streams of water are discharged into the air, including splash pads, ornamental pools, display pools, and reflection pools. The definition does not include drinking water fountains or water coolers. ▶Figure 680–2

Immersion Pool. A pool for ceremonial or ritual immersion of users, which is designed and intended to have its contents drained or discharged. ▶Figure 680–3

680.2 Definitions

The definitions in this section apply only within this article.

Corrosive Environment. Areas where pool sanitation chemicals are stored, handled, or dispensed, and confined areas under decks adjacent to such areas, as well as areas with circulation pumps, automatic chlorinators, filters, open areas under decks adjacent to or abutting the pool structure, and similar locations. ▶Figure 680–1

An ornamental structure or recreational water feature from which one or more jets or streams of water are discharged into the air, including splash pads, ornamental pools, display pools, and reflection pools. The definition does not include drinking water fountains or water coolers.

▶Figure 680–2

A fountain with a pool depth 1 in. or less, intended for recreational use by pedestrians. This definition does not include showers intended for hygienic rinsing prior to the use of a pool, spa, or other water feature.

▶Figure 680–4

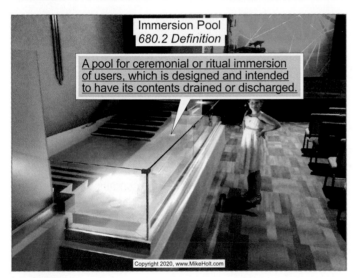

A pool for ceremonial or ritual immersion of users, which is designed and intended to have its contents drained or discharged.

▶Figure 680–3

Splash Pad. A fountain with a pool depth 1 in. or less, intended for recreational use by pedestrians. This definition does not include showers intended for hygienic rinsing prior to use of a pool, spa, or other water feature. ▶Figure 680–4

680.3 Approval of Equipment

Revisions to this section clarify that all electrical equipment and products covered by Article 680 must be listed and installed in compliance with this article.

Analysis

RELOCATED This rule was in 680.4 in the previous *Code* and was renumbered as 680.3 for this edition to accommodate a new rule. The previous language was poorly written and required electrical equipment installed in the water, walls, or decks of pools, fountains, and similar installations to comply with the requirements of this article and to be listed. That was never the intent of the language, but it was what was said.

680.3 Approval of Equipment

Electrical equipment and products covered by this article are required to be listed and must be installed in compliance with this article.

Author's Comment:

▸ This rule might just as easily state, that "all electrical equipment and products covered by this article are to be listed." Is it really necessary to state that the installation of equipment and products is required to comply with the rules in this article? Isn't that the purpose of the article in the first place? The current language seems unnecessary and could lead some to believe that these installations only require compliance with the rule in Article 680 and not those found in other *Code* articles.

▸ It is important to understand that, Chapters 1 through 4 are the foundation of the *NEC*. As a general rule all applications start by using these foundation of requirements, and only when Chapters 5 through 7 are applied can they modify or enhance the previous requirements based on the "special" nature of the installation.

680.4 Inspections After Installation

The authority having jurisdiction can now require periodic inspection and testing of the pool system after installation.

Analysis

NEW

This is intended to provide the AHJ with the opportunity to address hazards associated with aging pool installations. Even installations in compliance with the *Code* will deteriorate over time, especially the parts of the system that are exposed to the corrosive effects of the pool water and treatment chemicals. Failure of the equipment grounding conductor system or the bonding system could result in fatalities.

The panel member who represents the United States Association of Pool and Spa Professionals voted no on this change with the comment that it has no enforceable language. He is strongly in favor of the inspections but does not see this change as being effective. He recommended that the rule be in NFPA 70B, *Recommended Practice for Electrical Equipment Maintenance* and not in the *NEC*.

680.4 Inspections After Installation

The authority having jurisdiction is permitted to require periodic inspection and testing.

Author's Comment:

▸ The Correlating Committee (CC) comment in the First Revision, directed that the Code-Making Panel revise this and specify if this applies to public or private pools or to both, but that is not reflected in the Second Draft ballot report.

680.5 Ground-Fault Circuit Interrupters

Additional wording clarifies that the GFCI requirements in Article 680 (unless otherwise noted) are in addition to those found in 210.8.

Analysis

CLARIFIED

This just clarifies that the requirements found in Article 680 and 210.8 both apply to the pool installation. Article 680 contains the specific requirements for the pool equipment and pool area, and 210.8 covers the general GFCI protection requirements.

680.5 Ground-Fault Circuit Interrupters

The GFCI requirements in Article 680, unless otherwise noted, are in addition to the requirements in 210.8.

680.6 Bonding and Equipment Grounding

Revisions to this rule clarify that this section covers the requirements for bonding in addition to grounding electrical equipment.

Analysis

CLARIFIED The title was "Grounding" in the 2017 *Code*, but that did not reflect the content of the section. In the parent text the term "grounded" was replaced by the correct term of "bonded." The rule requires bonding to be in accordance with Part V, Bonding of Article 250, and the equipment grounding must be in accordance with Part VI, Equipment Grounding and Equipment Grounding Conductors and Part VII, Methods of Equipment Grounding. The seven list items that require bonding or equipment grounding remain unchanged from the 2017 *NEC*.

680.6 Bonding and Equipment Grounding

Electrical equipment must be bonded in accordance with Part V of Article 250 and must meet the requirements of Parts VI and VII of Article 250. The equipment must be connected by the wiring methods in Chapter 3 unless modified by this article. Equipment subject to these requirements include:

(1) Through-wall lighting assemblies and underwater luminaires except for listed low-voltage lighting.

(2) All electrical equipment within 5 ft. of the inside wall of the specified body of water.

(3) All electrical equipment associated with the water recirculating system.

(4) Junction boxes.

(5) Transformer and power supply enclosures.

(6) Ground-fault circuit interrupters.

(7) Sub-panels that supply associated equipment.

680.7 Bonding and Equipment Grounding Terminals

Revisions to the section title and text clarified the intent of this rule.

Analysis

CLARIFIED The language requires terminals used for bonding and equipment grounding to be identified for use in wet and corrosive environments. It goes on to says that field installed terminals in a damp, wet, or corrosive environment must be composed of copper, copper alloy, or stainless steel and requires them to be listed for direct burial use. Terminals listed for direct burial use are evaluated for use in corrosive conditions.

680.7 Bonding and Equipment Grounding Terminals

Terminals used for bonding and equipment grounding must be identified as suitable for use in wet and corrosive environments and be listed for direct burial use. ▶Figure 680–5

Pools, Spas, Hot Tubs, or Fountains Bonding and Equipment Grounding Terminals *680.7*

Terminals used for bonding and equipment grounding must be identified as suitable for use in wet and corrosive environments and be listed for direct burial use.

▶Figure 680–5

680.11 Underground Wiring

This section was editorially revised to improve clarity and readability with only a minor technical change.

Analysis

REORGANIZED Long, hard to read and understand paragraphs in several *Code* sections have been split into multiple subsections. This section now includes charging text and three subsections which simplify and sort the requirements.

CLARIFIED **680.11(A) Underground Wiring Methods.** This subsection has parent text and lists seven wiring methods considered suitable for the location. There was no change, just an editorial relocation.

RELOCATED **680.11(B) Wiring Under Pools.** In the 2017 *NEC* this was the second to the last sentence in 680.11. It prohibits underground wiring under the pool unless necessary to support pool equipment. There was no technical change to the rule, but it was relocated to its own subsection (B).

RELOCATED **680.11(C) Minimum Cover Requirements.** As with (B), this is not a *Code* rule change but an editorial relocation into a new subsection. It provides a reference to the requirements in 300.5 for the minimum cover of underground wring methods in pool areas.

680.11 Underground Wiring

(A) Underground Wiring. Underground wiring located within 5 ft horizontally from the inside wall of the pool must be of the following wiring methods. ▶Figure 680–6

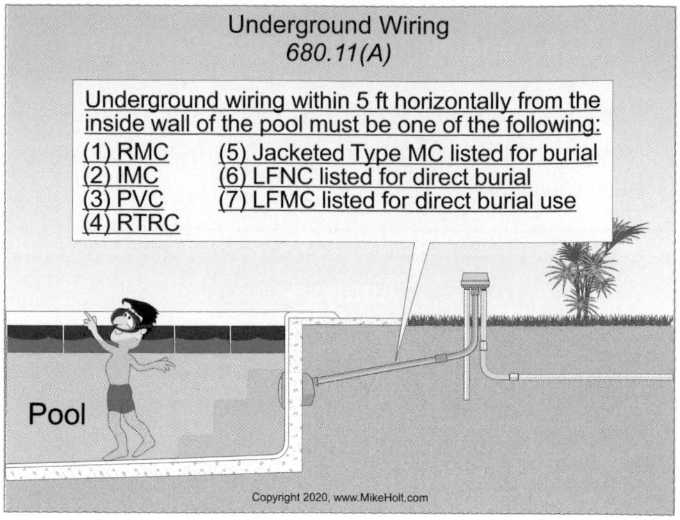

> Underground Wiring
> *680.11(A)*
>
> Underground wiring within 5 ft horizontally from the inside wall of the pool must be one of the following:
> (1) RMC   (5) Jacketed Type MC listed for burial
> (2) IMC   (6) LFNC listed for direct burial
> (3) PVC   (7) LFMC listed for direct burial use
> (4) RTRC
>
> Pool
>
> Copyright 2020, www.MikeHolt.com

▶Figure 680–6

(1) Rigid metal conduit

(2) Intermediate metal conduit

(3) Rigid polyvinyl chloride conduit

(4) Reinforced thermosetting resin conduit

(5) Jacketed Type MC cable that is listed for direct burial use

(6) Liquidtight flexible nonmetallic conduit listed for direct burial use

(7) Liquidtight flexible metal conduit listed for direct burial use

(B) Wiring Under Pools. Underground wiring beneath pools is permitted for the supply of pool equipment permitted by this article.

(C) Minimum Cover Requirements. Minimum cover depths contained in 300.5 apply.

680.14 Wiring Methods in Corrosive Environment

The definition of a corrosive environment was removed from this so only the requirements for the wiring methods permitted in a corrosive location remain.

Analysis

RELOCATED Subsection (A) in the 2017 *NEC*, which contained the definition of a corrosive environment, was revised and relocated to 680.2. Without the definition there is no need for subsections so the language from (B) Wiring Methods has become the complete rule. This section specifies the wiring methods that are to be used in corrosive environments and "Wiring Methods in" were added to the title to reflect that.

The rule now simply requires wiring methods used in a corrosive environment to be listed and identified for use in such an area. It lists four specific wiring methods considered to be resistant to corrosive environments; RMC, IMC, PVC, and RTRC. This is the same language as was in 680.14(B) for the 2017 *Code*.

680.14 Wiring Methods in Corrosive Environment

Wiring methods (boxes and enclosures) in corrosive environments must be rigid metal conduit, intermediate metal conduit, rigid polyvinyl chloride conduit, or reinforced thermosetting resin conduit. ▶Figure 680–7

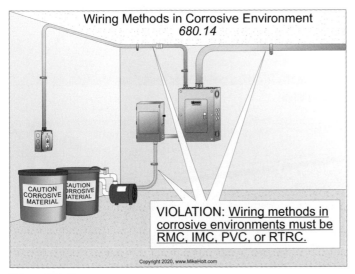

Wiring Methods in Corrosive Environment
680.14

VIOLATION: <u>Wiring methods in corrosive environments must be RMC, IMC, PVC, or RTRC.</u>

Copyright 2020, www.MikeHolt.com

▶Figure 680–7

680.21 Motors (for permanently installed pools)

The GFCI protection of motors was expanded and a new subsection requires GFCI protection to be provided for existing pump receptacles when replacing a pool pump motor.

Analysis

EXPANDED **680.21(A)(1) Wiring Methods.** Pool pumps are installed in a corrosive location in accordance with the definition of such locations in 680.2. Type MC with a PVC jacket has been a long-standing wiring method for pool pumps. The additional language here permits the continued use of that wiring method for pool pump motors.

CLARIFIED **680.21(C) GFCI Protection.** This requirement was clarified to indicate that it applies to outlets supplied by branch circuits with a voltage of 150V or less to ground. The 2017 *NEC* said it applied to pumps connected to single-phase 120V through 240V branch circuits. A 240V line-to-line branch circuit could be supplied by a 4-wire high-leg delta system (a rare but available application for a pool), where one leg has a voltage of 208V to ground; GFCI protection is designed for circuits with a maximum voltage of 150V to ground.

The rule was also expanded to apply to both single- and three-phase pool pumps. The 2017 *Code* did not set an ampere rating where GFCI protection was required. The change requires the GFCI protection for circuits rated 60A amperes or less. The requirement for the "outlet" supplying the pool pump to have GFCI protection acts to require upstream protection where the pool pump is hardwired. This could be an upstream feed-through device or a GFCI breaker.

CLARIFIED **680.21(C) Ex.** The previous language required GFCI protection for circuits rated 120V through 240V. That exempted a low-voltage pump from the GFCI requirement. The new language specifies all outlets on a circuit with a voltage of 150V or less to have GFCI protection. That would include these low-voltage pumps.

• • •

To correct this issue, a new exception was added to say that listed low-voltage motors not requiring grounding, having a rating not exceeding the low-voltage contact limit, and complying with 680.23(A)(2) are permitted to be installed without GFCI protection.

NEW **680.21(D) Pool Pump Motor Replacement.** When a pump that does not have the GFCI protection required in 680.21(C) is replaced, such protection must be added as part of the pump replacement. Older installations may not have the GFCI protection required by the current *Code* and this will ensure such protection is added when a pool pump is replaced.

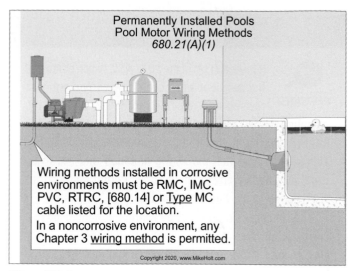

Wiring methods installed in corrosive environments must be RMC, IMC, PVC, RTRC, [680.14] or Type MC cable listed for the location.
In a noncorrosive environment, any Chapter 3 wiring method is permitted.

Copyright 2020, www.MikeHolt.com

▶Figure 680–8

680.21 Pool Motors

(A) Wiring Methods. The wiring to a pool-associated motor must comply with 680.21(A)(1) unless modified by (A)(2) or (A)(3).

(1) General. Branch-circuit wiring for pool-associated motors installed in corrosive locations must be rigid metal conduit, intermediate metal conduit, rigid polyvinyl chloride conduit, reinforced thermosetting resin conduit [680.14], or Type MC cable listed for the location. ▶Figure 680–8

The wiring methods must contain an insulated copper equipment grounding conductor sized in accordance with 250.122, but in no case can the equipment grounding conductor be sized smaller than 12 AWG.

Where installed in noncorrosive environments, any Chapter 3 wiring method is permitted.

(2) Flexible Connections. Liquidtight flexible metal or liquidtight flexible nonmetallic conduit are permitted.

(C) GFCI Protection. GFCI protection is required for all pool motors rated 60A or less, at not over 150V to ground, whether by receptacle or by direct connection. ▶Figure 680–9

Ex: Listed low-voltage motors not requiring grounding, with ratings not exceeding the low-voltage contact limit supplied by transformers or power supplies that comply with 680.23(A)(2), may be installed without GFCI protection.

(D) Pool Pump Motor Replacement. Where a pool pump motor is replaced, the replacement pump motor must be provided with GFCI protection. Figure 680–10

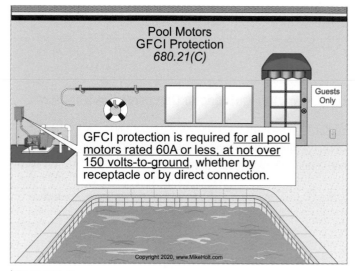

Pool Motors
GFCI Protection
680.21(C)

Guests Only

GFCI protection is required for all pool motors rated 60A or less, at not over 150 volts-to-ground, whether by receptacle or by direct connection.

Copyright 2020, www.MikeHolt.com

▶Figure 680–9

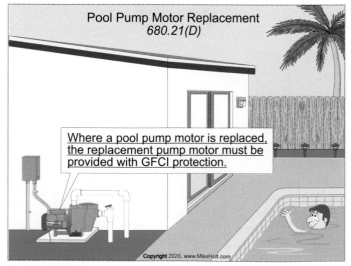

Pool Pump Motor Replacement
680.21(D)

Where a pool pump motor is replaced, the replacement pump motor must be provided with GFCI protection.

Copyright 2020, www.MikeHolt.com

▶Figure 680–10

680.22 Lighting, Receptacles, and Equipment

Revisions were made to clarify this rule and new subsections were added.

Analysis

680.22(A)(4) Receptacles. This referenced a new subsection (5) for pool equipment rooms and it specifies that the GFCI protection must be of the Class A type. Note that this rule requires only 15A and 20A, single-phase, 125V receptacles located within 20 ft of the pool wall to have GFCI protection; however, the revision to 680.5 says the rules in 210.8 also apply, so receptacles of the ratings specified in 210.8 and installed in areas covered by 210.8 will also require GFCI protection. For indoor pools, 210.8 will not likely trigger a requirement for other receptacles have GFCI protection, but it may for those outside.

CLARIFIED

680.22(A)(5) Pool Equipment Room. This new requirement was added to ensure that there is a GFCI-protected 15A or 20A, 125V receptacle on a general-purpose branch circuit in the pool equipment room for the use of service personnel. It additionally requires all receptacles within the pool room that are supplied by a branch circuit with a voltage of 150V or less to ground to have GFCI protection. Without this rule the receptacles in a pool equipment room may not be required to have protection.

NEW

There is no upper current limit on the branch-circuit rating that supplies receptacles in the pool equipment room like there is in 210.8. This rule applies to all single- or three-phase receptacles supplied from a branch circuit with a voltage to ground of 150V or less regardless of the branch circuit's ampere rating.

680.22(B)(8) Luminaires, Lighting Outlets, and Ceiling-Suspended (Paddle) Fans. As with the measurements specified in other *Code* sections, this measurement is the shortest path an imaginary cord connected to the luminaire would follow without piercing a floor, wall, ceiling, doorway with a hinged or sliding door, window opening, or other effective permanent barrier. This requirement matches up with the one in 680.22(A)(6) for receptacles in the pool area that has been in the *NEC* for several cycles.

CLARIFIED

680.22(C) Switching Devices. This rule was clarified to ensure the "reach distance" between the inside wall of the pool and a switch location is at least 5' unless the switch is listed for that purpose. The intent here is to ensure someone cannot be in contact with the water and the switch at the same time. The determining factor is the "reach distance" and this revision makes that clear. The section permits switches listed for the application to be installed within the 5-ft reach distance.

CLARIFIED

680.22(E) Other Equipment. The 2017 *NEC* had no restrictions on locating electric power production equipment (such as generators, PV systems, wind systems, and others) near a pool. Such equipment may constitute a shock hazard if not a reasonably safe distance from the pool. The new rule requires this "other equipment" with ratings exceeding the low-voltage contact limit, to be located at least 5 ft horizontally from the inside walls of a pool unless separated from the pool by a solid fence, wall, or other permanent barrier. This new subsection does not address installations in a pump room.

NEW

680.22 Receptacles, Luminaires, and Switches

(A) Receptacles.

(4) GFCI Protection. 15A and 20A, single-phase, 125V receptacles located within 20 ft of the inside walls of a pool must be GFCI protected. ▶Figure 680–11

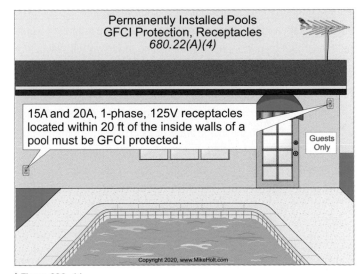

Permanently Installed Pools
GFCI Protection, Receptacles
680.22(A)(4)

15A and 20A, 1-phase, 125V receptacles located within 20 ft of the inside walls of a pool must be GFCI protected.

Guests Only

Copyright 2020, www.MikeHolt.com

▶Figure 680–11

▸ A "Class A" ground-fault circuit interrupting device is designed to trip at between 4 - 6 mA of detected current imbalance for the protection of human life. (See UL 943, Standard for Ground-Fault Circuit Interrupters.)

(5) Pool Equipment Room. At least one GCFI-protected 15A or 20A, 125V receptacle must be located within a pool equipment room. Receptacles rated 150V or less to ground within the pool equipment room must be GFCI protected. ▸Figure 680–12

▸Figure 680–12

(B) Luminaires and Ceiling Fans.

(8) Measurements. In determining the dimensions in this section addressing luminaires, the distance to be measured must be the shortest path an imaginary cord connected to the luminaire would follow without piercing a floor, wall, ceiling, doorway with hinged or sliding door, window opening, or other effective permanent barrier.

(C) Switching Devices. Circuit breakers, time clocks, pool light switches, and other switching devices must be located not less than 5 ft horizontally from the inside walls of a permanently installed pool unless separated by a solid fence, wall, or other permanent barrier that provides at least a 5 ft. reach distance. ▸Figure 680–13

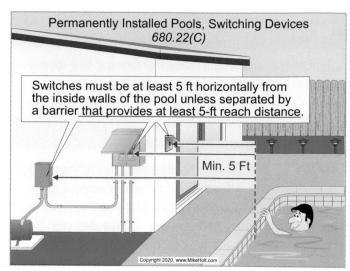

▸Figure 680–13

(E) Other Equipment. Other equipment with ratings exceeding the low-voltage contact limit must be located at least 5 ft horizontally from the inside walls of a pool unless separated from the pool by a solid fence, wall, or other permanent barrier. ▸Figure 680–14

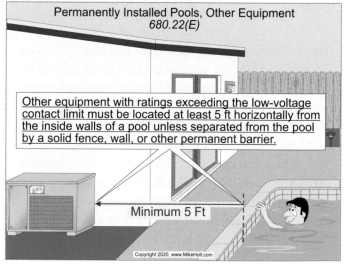

▸Figure 680–14

▸ Reach distance is not a defined term and this section may be better served by specifying a method of measurement as is done in 210.8 and 680.22(B)(8).

680.23 Underwater Pool Luminaires

This section was editorially revised to clarify existing *Code* requirements regarding underwater wet-niche luminaires.

Analysis

680.23(B)(2)(a) Wet-Niche Luminaires. Previously, brass or other approved corrosion-resistant material was permitted. The rule was revised to require the use of either red brass or stainless steel conduit to the forming shell where metal conduit is used. These are the only metal conduit materials that can withstand the corrosive conditions of a wet-niche luminaire installation.

CLARIFIED

The previous language using the term "approved" was deleted. The new language now limits the conduit types to the two that have been proven to suitably resist continuous exposure to pool water.

680.23(B)(3) Equipment Grounding Provisions for Cords and (4) Luminaire Grounding Terminations. The term "grounding conductor" is no longer defined and is being replaced throughout the *Code* with the "equipment grounding conductor."

CLARIFIED

680.23(B)(6) Servicing. The requirement for serving spa wet-niche luminaires was revised to say that where a spa can be drained to make the spa bench dry, that luminaire is required to have only enough cord to permit the fixture to be placed on the bench. This applies to the provisions of the servicing of wet-niche luminaires. The rule had required all such luminaires to have a cord long enough to permit the luminaire to be placed on the deck or other dry location for servicing. A modification was made for wet-niche luminaires installed low in the footwell of a spa.

CLARIFIED

680.23(F)(1) Branch Circuit Wiring. Liquidtight flexible nonmetallic conduit (LFNC) was added as it is a wiring method with a long-standing application in corrosive environments. Before this revision, the rule required the wiring method to be in accordance with 680.14.

EXPANDED

680.23(F)(2) Ex Equipment Grounding. The exception in (F)(2) applies to the secondary of a transformer that supplies a pool luminaire and is needed so the branch-circuit equipment grounding conductor is not required to be extended to the luminaire itself as required by 680.23(F)(2). The branch-circuit equipment grounding conductor will end at the transformer enclosure and an equipment grounding conductor based on the secondary overcurrent protective device will be extended to the luminaire. This exception does not require the minimum size of the equipment grounding conductor to be 12 AWG as does the main rule.

CLARIFIED

680.23 Underwater Pool Luminaires

(B) Wet-Niche Luminaires.

(2) Wiring to the Forming Shell.

(a) Metal Conduit. Metal conduit must be <u>listed and identified as red brass or stainless steel</u>.

> **Author's Comment:**
>
> ▸ According to 680.2, a "Wet-Niche Luminaire" is a luminaire intended to be installed in a forming shell where it will be completely surrounded by water. ▸**Figure 680–15**
> ▸ According to Article 680.2, a "Forming Shell" is a structure mounted in a pool or fountain to support a wet-niche luminaire. ▸**Figure 680–16**

(6) Luminaire Servicing.

Pool. The location of the forming shell and length of flexible cord for wet-niche pool luminaires must allow for personnel to place the luminaire on the deck or other dry location for maintenance. The luminaire maintenance location must be accessible without entering or going into the pool water.

Spa. <u>In spa locations where wet-niche luminaires are installed in the foot well of the spa, the location of the forming shell and length of flexible cord for the underwater spa luminaire must allow for personnel to place the luminaire on the bench where the spa can be drained to make the bench location dry.</u> ▸**Figure 680–17**

Wet-Niche Luminaire
680.2 Definition

A luminaire intended to be installed in a forming shell where the luminaire will be completely surrounded by water.

Copyright 2020, www.MikeHolt.com

▶Figure 680–15

Forming Shell
680.2 Definition

A structure designed to support a wet-niche luminaire.

Copyright 2020, www.MikeHolt.com

▶Figure 680–16

Wet-Niche Luminaires, Servicing, Spas
680.23(B)(6)

Where wet-niche luminaires are installed in the foot well of the spa, the location of the forming shell and length of flexible cord for the underwater spa luminaire must allow for personnel to place the luminaire on the bench where the spa can be drained to make the bench location dry.

Copyright 2020, www.MikeHolt.com

▶Figure 680–17

(F) Branch-Circuit Wiring.

(1) General. Branch-circuit wiring installed in corrosive locations, must be in rigid metal conduit, intermediate metal conduit, rigid polyvinyl chloride conduit, reinforced thermosetting resin conduit [680.14], or liquidtight flexible nonmetallic conduit. ▶Figure 680–18

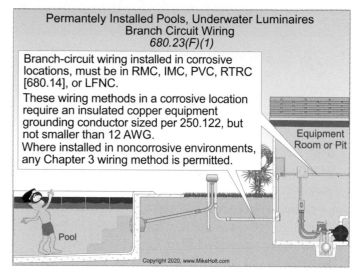

Permantely Installed Pools, Underwater Luminaires
Branch Circuit Wiring
680.23(F)(1)

Branch-circuit wiring installed in corrosive locations, must be in RMC, IMC, PVC, RTRC [680.14], or LFNC.

These wiring methods in a corrosive location require an insulated copper equipment grounding conductor sized per 250.122, but not smaller than 12 AWG.

Where installed in noncorrosive environments, any Chapter 3 wiring method is permitted.

Equipment Room or Pit

Pool

Copyright 2020, www.MikeHolt.com

▶Figure 680–18

The wiring methods in corrosive environments must contain an insulated copper equipment grounding conductor sized in accordance with 250.122, but not smaller than 12 AWG.

Where installed in noncorrosive environments, any Chapter 3 wiring method is permitted.

(2) Branch-Circuit Equipment Grounding Conductor. Branch-circuit conductors for all through-wall underwater pool luminaires must have insulated copper equipment grounding conductors, (without joint or splice except as permitted in 680.23(F)(2)(a) and (b) sized in accordance with 250.122, but not smaller than 12 AWG. ▶Figure 680–19

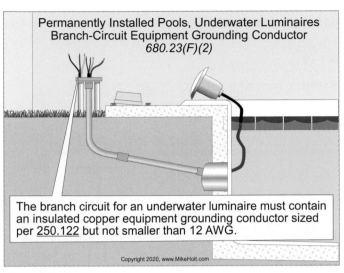

Permanently Installed Pools, Underwater Luminaires
Branch-Circuit Equipment Grounding Conductor
680.23(F)(2)

The branch circuit for an underwater luminaire must contain an insulated copper equipment grounding conductor sized per 250.122 but not smaller than 12 AWG.

Copyright 2020, www.MikeHolt.com

▶Figure 680–19

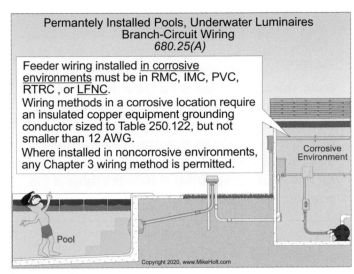

Permantely Installed Pools, Underwater Luminaires
Branch-Circuit Wiring
680.25(A)

Feeder wiring installed in corrosive environments must be in RMC, IMC, PVC, RTRC , or LFNC.
Wiring methods in a corrosive location require an insulated copper equipment grounding conductor sized to Table 250.122, but not smaller than 12 AWG.
Where installed in noncorrosive environments, any Chapter 3 wiring method is permitted.

Corrosive Environment

Pool

Copyright 2020, www.MikeHolt.com

▶Figure 680–20

680.25 Feeders

A change in (A) now permits the use of LFNC as a wring method for feeders installed in a corrosive environment.

Analysis

EXPANDED

680.25(A) Feeders. Liquidtight flexible nonmetallic conduit (LFNC) has excellent corrosion-resistant properties and there is no reason to prohibit its use as a wiring method for feeders installed in a corrosive environment as defined in 680.2.

680.25 Feeders

(A) Wiring Methods. Where feeder wiring is installed in corrosive environments, the wiring methods must be rigid metal conduit, intermediate metal conduit, rigid polyvinyl chloride conduit, reinforced thermosetting resin conduit, and liquidtight flexible nonmetallic conduit.

The wiring methods in corrosive environments must have insulated copper equipment grounding conductors sized in accordance with Table 250.122, but not smaller than 12 AWG. ▶Figure 680–20

Where installed in noncorrosive environments, any Chapter 3 wiring method is permitted.

680.26 Equipotential Bonding

Two revisions in the perimeter bonding requirements were made.

Analysis

CLARIFIED

680.26(B)(2)(b) Bonded Parts. This subsection requires a copper ring to be used where the steel reinforcing does not exist or cannot be used for the required bonding; but, there is also a (c) that requires a "copper grid" to be used where the steel cannot. Both subsections use the words "shall be utilized." These are vastly different bonding methods, and this creates a conflict in the application of the *NEC*.

NEW

680.26(B)(2)(c) Copper Grid. The language in 680.26(B)(2)(b) and (c) use the words "shall be utilized." That creates a *Code* conflict as it acts to require the use of both (b) and (c). It appears the intent is to use one or the other; however, far superior protect is provided by the use of a copper grid in method (c).

CLARIFIED

690.26(B)(5) Metal Fittings. There was an expansion of requirements for the use of pool safety covers to prevent drowning in unattended pools. These covers require the use of metallic anchors that are typically too small to attach a bonding conductor to. A new sentence was added saying that metallic pool cover anchors in concrete or masonry deck surfaces less than 1 in. in any dimension or less than 2 in. in length, and anchors in wood or composite decks with a flange of 2 in. or less do not require bonding.

680.26 Equipotential Bonding

(B) Bonded Parts. The parts of a permanently installed pool listed in (B)(1) through (B)(7) must be bonded together with a solid copper conductor not smaller than 8 AWG with a listed pressure connector, terminal bar, or other listed means in accordance with 250.8(A). ▶Figure 680–21

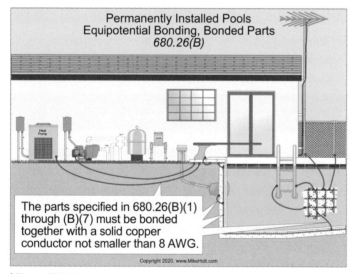

Permanently Installed Pools
Equipotential Bonding, Bonded Parts
680.26(B)

The parts specified in 680.26(B)(1) through (B)(7) must be bonded together with a solid copper conductor not smaller than 8 AWG.

Copyright 2020, www.MikeHolt.com

▶Figure 680–21

Equipotential bonding is not required to extend to or be attached to any panelboard, service disconnect, or grounding electrode.

(1) Conductive Pool Shells. Cast-in-place concrete, pneumatically applied or sprayed concrete, and concrete block with painted or plastered coatings are considered to be conductive materials due to water permeability and porosity. Vinyl liners and fiberglass composite shells are considered to be nonconductive materials.

Reconstructed pool shells must also comply with this section.

(a) Structural Reinforcing Steel. Unencapsulated structural reinforcing steel bonded together by steel tie wires or the equivalent. ▶Figure 680–22

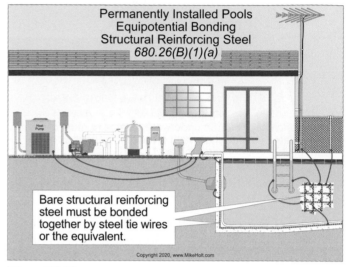

Permanently Installed Pools
Equipotential Bonding
Structural Reinforcing Steel
680.26(B)(1)(a)

Bare structural reinforcing steel must be bonded together by steel tie wires or the equivalent.

Copyright 2020, www.MikeHolt.com

▶Figure 680–22

Where structural reinforcing steel is encapsulated in a nonconductive compound, a copper conductor grid must be installed in accordance with 680.26(B)(1)(b).

(b) Copper Conductor Grid. A copper conductor grid must comply with all of the following: ▶Figure 680–23

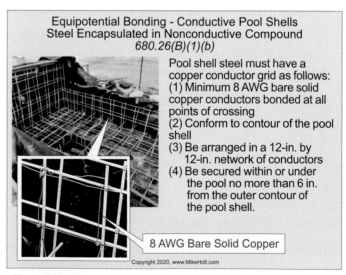

Equipotential Bonding - Conductive Pool Shells
Steel Encapsulated in Nonconductive Compound
680.26(B)(1)(b)

Pool shell steel must have a copper conductor grid as follows:
(1) Minimum 8 AWG bare solid copper conductors bonded at all points of crossing
(2) Conform to contour of the pool shell
(3) Be arranged in a 12-in. by 12-in. network of conductors
(4) Be secured within or under the pool no more than 6 in. from the outer contour of the pool shell.

8 AWG Bare Solid Copper

Copyright 2020, www.MikeHolt.com

▶Figure 680–23

(1) Be constructed of minimum 8 AWG bare solid copper conductors bonded to each other at all points of crossing in accordance with 250.8 or other approved means.

(2) Conform to the contour of the pool.

(3) Be arranged in a 12-in. by 12-in. network of conductors in a uniformly spaced perpendicular grid pattern with a tolerance of 4 in.

(4) Be secured within or under the pool no more than 6 in. from the outer contour of the pool shell.

(2) Perimeter Surfaces. Equipotential perimeter bonding must extend a minimum of 3 ft horizontally from the inside walls of a pool where not separated by a building or permanent wall 5 ft in height. ▶Figure 680-24 and ▶Figure 680-25

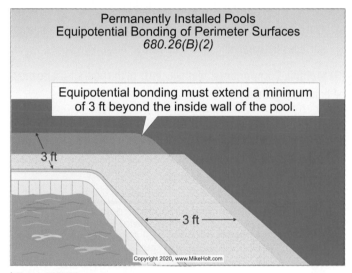

▶Figure 680-24

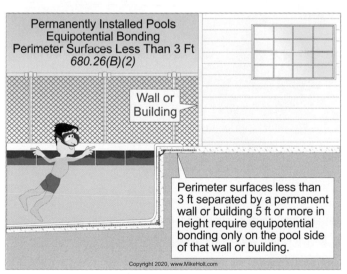

▶Figure 680-25

Equipotential bonding for perimeter surfaces must be in accordance with 680.26(B)(2)(a), (B)(2)(b), or (B)(2)(c) and be attached to the concrete pool reinforcing steel at a minimum of four (4) points uniformly spaced around the perimeter of the pool. ▶Figure 680-26

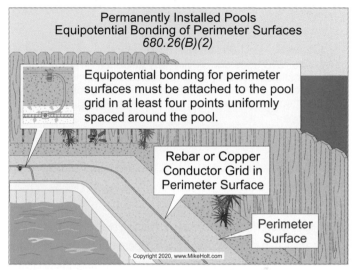

▶Figure 680-26

For nonconductive pool shells, bonding at four points is not required.

(a) Structural Reinforcing Steel. Bare structural reinforcing steel bonded together by steel tie wires in accordance with 680.26(B)(1)(a). ▶Figure 680-27

▶Figure 680-27

Author's Comment:

▶ The *NEC* does not provide any guidance on the installation requirements for structural reinforcing steel when used as a perimeter equipotential bonding method. ▶**Figure 680-28**

▸Figure 680–28

(b) Copper Ring. Where structural reinforcing steel is not available or it is encapsulated in a nonconductive compound, a copper conductor can be used for equipotential perimeter bonding where the following requirements are met: ▸Figure 680–29

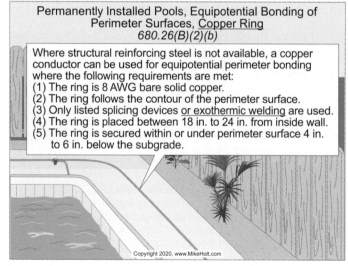

▸Figure 680–29

(1) The copper ring is constructed of 8 AWG bare solid copper.

(2) The copper ring conductor follows the contour of the perimeter surface.

(3) Only listed splicing devices or exothermic welding are used.

(4) The copper ring conductor is placed between 18 in. and 24 in. from the inside walls of the pool.

(5) The copper ring conductor is secured within or under the perimeter surface 4 in. to 6 in. below the subgrade.

(c) Copper Grid. Where structural reinforcing steel is not available or it is encapsulated in a nonconductive compound, a copper grid can be used for perimeter bonding where all of the following requirements are met:

(1) The copper grid is constructed of 8 AWG solid bare copper and arranged in a 12-in. by 12-in. network of conductors in a uniformly spaced perpendicular grid pattern with a tolerance of 4 in. in accordance with 680.26(B)(1)(b)(3).

(2) The copper grid follows the contour of the perimeter surface extending 3 ft horizontally beyond the inside walls of the pool.

(3) Only listed splicing devices or exothermic welding are used.

(4) The copper grid is be secured within or under the deck or unpaved surfaces between 4 in. and 6 in. below the subgrade.

(3) Metallic Components. Metallic parts of the pool structure must be bonded together.

(5) Metal Fittings. Metal fittings sized over 4 in. in any direction and located within or attached to the pool structure, such as ladders and handrails, must be connected to the swimming pool equipotential bonding means. ▸Figure 680–30

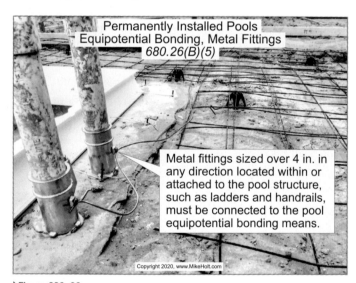

▸Figure 680–30

Metallic pool cover anchors 1 in. or less in any dimension and 2 in. or less in length are not required to be bonded to the equipotential bonding means.

Author's Comment:

▸ The title of Part III was revised to reflect the addition of new section 680.35 for the electrical installation of storable immersion pools.

Part III Storable Pools, Storable Spas, Storable Hot Tubs, and Storable Immersion Pools

"Storable Immersion Pools" was added to the title.

Analysis

EXPANDED The title of Part III was revised to reflect the addition of the new section 680.35 for the electrical installation of a storable immersion pool.

680.31 Pumps

Section 680.31 was revised to clarify that the required grounding conductor is intended to be the equipment grounding conductor.

Analysis

EDITED This section was revised to replace the more generic term of "grounding" with "equipment grounding conductor." Anything referring to the term "grounding conductor" where the intent was "equipment grounding conductor" has seen this modification throughout the 2020 revision.

680.31 Pumps

A cord-connected pool filter pump must incorporate an approved system of double insulation or its equivalent and be provided with means for the termination of an equipment grounding conductor for the noncurrent-carrying metal parts of the pump.

An equipment grounding conductor must be run with the power-supply conductors in the flexible cord.

Cord-connected pool filter pumps must be provided with GFCI protection that is an integral part of the attachment plug or located in the power-supply cord within 12 in. of the attachment plug.

Author's Comment:

▸ 680.35 is a new section that covers the electrical installation for storable and portable immersion pools.

680.35 Storable and Portable Immersion Pools

This new section covers the electrical installation requirements for storable and portable immersion pools.

Analysis

NEW The charging text of this new section advises that there are seven subsections, from (A) to (G), which address the electrical requirements for storable and portable immersion pools.

680.35 Storable and Portable Immersion Pools

Storable and Portable Immersion Pools must comply with the additional requirements specified in 680.35(A) through (G) of the *Code*.

680.45 Permanently Installed Immersion Pools

The electrical installation requirements for permanently installed immersion pools are covered by this new section.

Analysis

NEW The charging text of this new section requires electrical installations for permanently installed immersion pools to comply with the requirements of Parts I, II, and IV of Article 680, except as modified by this section. It further requires the use of Chapter 3 wiring methods.

NEW **680.45 Permanently Installed Immersion Pools.** Electrical installations at permanently installed immersion pools, whether installed indoors or outdoors, must comply with Part I, Part II, and Part IV of this article except as modified by section 680.45 and must be connected by the wiring methods of Chapter 3 of the *Code*. With regard to provisions in Part IV of this article, an immersion pool is considered to be a spa or hot tub.

NEW Ex. No.1 States that the equipotential bonding requirements of 680.26(B) do not apply where there is not any permanently installed or connected electrical equipment and the immersion pool is located on or above floor level. Ex. No. 2 Goes on to say that, the equipotential bonding requirements of 680.26(B) for perimeter surfaces do not apply to nonconductive perimeter surfaces such as steps, treads, and walking surfaces made of fiber glass composite.

NEW **680.45(A) Cord-and-Plug Connections.** This section permits the use of cord-and-plug connections for the removal or disconnection of the units for maintenance, storage, and repair of self-contained portable packaged immersion pools. The cord must not be shorter than 6 ft or longer than 15 ft and must be GFCI protected.

NEW **680.45(B) Storable and Portable Pumps.** This permits the use of cord-connected storable or portable pumps with a permanently installed immersion pool to be identified for swimming pool and spa use with a system of double insulation.

NEW **680.45(C) Heaters.** This new rule requires heaters used with immersion pools to be identified for use with swimming pools or spas, supplied by branch circuits of 150 volts or less to ground, and have GFCI protection. Where they're rated 120 volts and 20 amperes or less or 250 volts and 30 amperes or less, single phase, they are permitted to be cord and plug connected.

NEW **680.45 (D) Audio Equipment.** Audio equipment must not be installed on or in a permanently installed immersion pool. Audio equipment operating above the low-voltage contact limit and within 6 ft of the immersion pool must be connected to the equipment grounding conductor and GFCI protected.

680.45 Permanently Installed Immersion Pools

Electrical installations at permanently installed immersion pools, whether installed indoors or outdoors, must comply with Part I, Part II, and Part IV of this article except as modified by section 680.45 and must be connected by the wiring methods of Chapter 3 of the *Code*. With regard to provisions in Part IV of this article, an immersion pool is considered to be a spa or hot tub.

Part V. Fountains

680.50 General

This general requirement was expanded to include "fountains intended for recreational use by pedestrians, including splash pads."

Analysis

  EXPANDED **NEW** Fountains in general must comply with Parts I and V of this article. Fountains that have water common with a pool and the newly added "splash pads" must also comply with the requirements of Part II. Splash pads have many of the same safety issues as pools and the reference to Part II will trigger all the pool bonding requirements for splash pads.

680.50 General

The general installation requirements contained in Part I apply to fountains intended for recreational use by pedestrians, including splash pads, in addition to those contained in Part V.

> **Author's Comment:**
>
> ▸ According to 680.2, a "Fountain" is defined as an ornamental structure or recreational water feature from which one or more jets or streams of water are discharged into the air, including splash pads, ornamental pools, display pools, and reflection pools.

680.54 Grounding and Bonding

The titles and sections for bonding and grounding fountains were combined, expanded, clarified, and relocated to include bonding as well as grounding.

Analysis

EXPANDED This section was renamed and expanded to include both bonding and grounding. The grounding requirements are in the new subsection (A) and those for bonding are in (B) which contains the relocated and expanded requirements for bonding that were previously in 680.53.

CLARIFIED 680.54(A) Grounding. Combining the bonding requirements from 680.53 with the grounding requirements of 680.54 required the creation of new subsections; (A) for grounding and (B) for bonding. The language was revised to require the equipment to be connected to the equipment grounding conductor.

RELOCATED 680.54(B) Bonding. This replaces and expands on the bonding requirements for metal piping systems associated with fountains that was in 680.53. That section deleted and relocated here along with additional fountain bonding requirements. There are six list items that are all required to be bonded together and connected to the equipment grounding conductor associated with the branch circuit that supplies the fountain.

680.54 Connection to an Equipment Grounding Conductor

(A) Connection to Equipment Grounding Conductor. The following equipment must be connected to the circuit equipment grounding conductor:

(1) Other than listed low-voltage luminaires not requiring grounding, all electrical equipment located within the fountain or within 5 ft of the inside wall of the fountain.

(2) All electrical equipment associated with the recirculating system of the fountain.

(3) Panelboards that are not part of the service equipment and that supply any electrical equipment associated with the fountain.

Note: See 250.122 for sizing of these conductors.

(B) Bonding. The following parts must be bonded together and connected to an equipment grounding conductor of the branch circuit supplying the fountain:

(1) All metal piping systems associated with the fountain

(2) All metal fittings within or attached to the fountain

(3) Metal parts of electrical equipment associated with the fountain water-circulating system, including pump motors

(4) Metal raceways within 5 ft of the inside wall or perimeter of the fountain and not separated from the fountain by a permanent barrier

(5) All metal surfaces within 5 ft of the inside wall or perimeter of the fountain and not separated from the fountain by a permanent barrier

(6) Electrical devices and controls that are not associated with the fountain and are located less than 5 ft of the inside wall or perimeter of the fountain

680.59 GFCI Protection for Permanently Installed Nonsubmersible Pumps

GFCI protection is now required for outlets that supply permanently installed nonsubmersible fountain pump motors.

Analysis

NEW

Submersible fountain pumps are already required to be GFCI protected by the requirements of 680.51(A). This new rule requires GFCI protection for all permanently installed nonsubmersible pump motors rated 250V or less and 60A or less, single- or three-phase.

680.59 GFCI Protection for Permanently Installed Nonsubmersible Pumps

Outlets supplying permanently installed nonsubmersible pump motors rated 250 volts or less and 60 amperes or less must be GFCI protected.

Author's Comment:

▸ This language was not corrected, like other GFCI requirements, to make it apply only to pumps supplied by branch circuits of 150 volts or less to ground.

Part VIII. Electrically Powered Pool Lifts

680.80 General

This section was revised to require electrically powered pool lifts to comply with only Part VIII of this article, except where requirements in other parts are specifically referenced.

Analysis

CLARIFIED

The previous language that said pool lift installations did not have to comply with other parts of this article was deleted. The panel statement said the deleted language could have permitted receptacles to be located within 5 ft of the pool and that would be an unacceptable shock risk.

680.80 General

Electrically powered pool lifts as defined in 680.2 must comply with Part VIII of this article. Part VIII is not subject to the requirements of other parts of this article except where the requirements are specifically referenced. ▸Figure 680-31

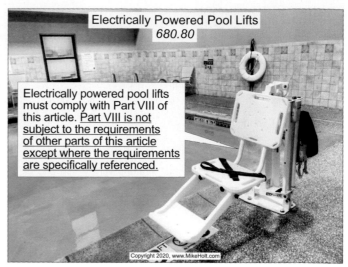

Electrically Powered Pool Lifts
680.80

Electrically powered pool lifts must comply with Part VIII of this article. Part VIII is not subject to the requirements of other parts of this article except where the requirements are specifically referenced.

Copyright 2020, www.MikeHolt.com

▸Figure 680-31

680.84 Switching Devices and Receptacles

This section was expanded to require receptacles for electrically powered pool lifts that operate above the low-voltage contact limit to comply with the requirements of 680.22(A)(3) and (A)(4).

Analysis

EXPANDED

This section previously applied to switches for only electrically powered pools lifts and they had to comply with 680.22(C), which required them to be at least 5 ft away from the pool or be listed for use within 5 ft of the pool. The rule was expanded to include receptacles and to require them to comply with 680.22(A)(3) and (A)(4). Section 680.22(A)(3) requires the receptacle to be at least 6 ft from the inside walls of the pool and (A)(4) says it must have GFCI protection.

680.84 Switching Devices and Receptacles

Switches and switching devices that operate above the low-voltage contact limit must comply with 680.22(C). Receptacles for electrically powered pool lifts that are operated above the low-voltage contact limit must comply with 680.22(A)(3) and (4).

ARTICLE 690

SOLAR PHOTOVOLTAIC (PV) SYSTEMS

Introduction to Article 690—Solar Photovoltaic (PV) Systems

You have seen, or maybe own, devices powered by photovoltaic cells, such as night lights, car coolers, and toys. These generally consist of a small solar module powering a small device running on less than 10V direct current and drawing only a fraction of an ampere. A solar PV system that powers a building or interconnects with an electric utility to offset a building's energy consumption operates on the same principals but on a much larger scale.

Solar PV systems that provide electrical power to an electrical system are large, heavy, and complex. There are mechanical and site selection issues that require expert knowledge as well as complex structural and architectural concerns that must be addressed. The purpose of the *NEC* is to safeguard persons and property from the hazards arising from the use of electricity [90.1(A)]. Article 690 keeps that theme by focusing on reducing the electrical hazards that may arise from installing and operating a PV system, to a point where it can be considered safe for people and property.

This article consists of eight Parts and the general *Code* requirements of Chapters 1 through 4 apply to these installations, except as specifically modified by Article 690.

690.2 Definitions

Some definitions were moved to Article 100 and references to "PV" were removed, and others were deleted altogether.

Analysis

NEW

AC Module System. This new definition supports new language in 690.6 related to the installation of ac module systems.

Manufacturers of PV systems are increasingly incorporating multiple array components into functional systems. These systems often need assembly in the field but are restricted to specific configurations and equipment.

CLARIFIED

Array. The revised language says that an array is "A mechanically and electrically integrated grouping of modules with support structure, including any attached system components such as inverter(s) or dc-to-dc converter(s) and attached associated wiring." The PI indicates that a clear understanding of a PV array boundary is critical for the application of the rapid shutdown rule in 690.12. This updated definition clarifies that those parts that serve both a mechanical and electrical function should be considered part of a PV array.

CLARIFIED

DC-to-DC Converter Output Circuit. The previous language was unclear as to how much of the dc distribution system would be included in these circuits. Direct-current utilization loads, feeders, or branch circuits are not part of the PV system. The previous definition could have been interpreted to include those conductors and loads.

• • •

The revised definition clarifies that the converter output circuit starts at any dc combiner equipment and stops where it becomes a different circuit (for example at an inverter input terminal or the dc PV system disconnecting means).

Direct Current (dc) Combiner. This definition was revised for clarity and is simply a piece of equipment that includes an enclosure used to connect two or more PV system dc circuits in parallel providing one or more dc circuit output(s). The inclusion of the term "enclosure" was added to differentiate this equipment from other devices such as a connector used to connect multiple circuit conductors together.

CLARIFIED

Electronic Power Converter. This new definition is intended to clarify that many inverters and dc-to-dc converters are electronic power converters, and the conductor sizing for these devices should be based on the ratings of the power conversion device. Although they do not function as overcurrent protective devices, they do have limited current capabilities based on their listed ratings. For instance, it is possible to connect an array to an inverter where the maximum array current is greater than the output current of the inverter. If the conductors are sized on the rated electronic power converter input current, as opposed to maximum current, an overcurrent protective device will be necessary to protect the conductors under fault conditions.

NEW

Grounded, Functionally. This definition was revised for conformance with the *NEC Style Manual*. The Informational Note was also revised and says that examples of operational reasons for a functionally grounded system include ground-fault detection and performance related issues for some power supplies.

EDITED

PV Output Circuit. The wording was revised to clarify that this circuit is the dc conductors from two or more connected PV source circuits to their point of termination. This more clearly defines the beginning and ending points of the PV output circuit.

CLARIFIED

PV Source Circuit. This was revised to indicate where this circuit ends and should help with the application of other rules in this article. The previous *Code* had this circuit ending at "the common connection points of the dc system." That was revised to be more specific and now the ending point is the "dc combiners, electronic power converters, or the dc PV system disconnecting means."

CLARIFIED

In addition to the relocation of terms that are used in multiple articles and appear in Article 100, some definitions were deleted from this article as the terms are no longer used here. Those terms are as follows:

Diversion Charge Controller. This definition was deleted from this article, but the term still resides in Articles 694 and 706.

DELETED

Electrical Power Production and Distribution Network. This term was deleted as there is an almost identical term in Article 100 (Electric Power Production and Distribution Network) which serves the purpose throughout the *NEC*.

DELETED

Interactive System. Once again, an almost identical term and definition exists in Article 100. The difference between the term here and the one in Article 100 is the specific PV reference in the Article 690 definition. Without the reference to "PV" the term works throughout the *Code* where power production sources are operating in parallel with an electric power production and distribution network.

DELETED

Interactive Inverter Output Circuit. The substantiation for this deletion said,

DELETED

"This term is self-defined. The usage of this term in 690 is clear without the definition. The definition section of 690 is still too long and needs to be curtailed to those terms that must be defined for clarity in using the *NEC*."

DELETED

Panel. This term was deleted as it is rarely used as defined. The substantiation said,

"The term "Panel" according to its original NFPA 70 definition is rarely, if ever, used in this context by product manufacturers or other industry literature, and instead replaced with the word "String" (i.e. "string inverter"). In contrast, the term "Panel" is more often associated with the NFPA 70 definition of "Module" by both technical and non-technical professionals alike, as well as the general public. For example, "solar panel" generally refers to a single solar module. This term is even referenced inconsistently and/or ambiguously in other NFPA publications such as Chapter 12 of NFPA 780."

DELETED

Stand-Alone System. This term already exists in Article 100 and there is no need to duplicate it here. Like other definitions that appeared in both locations, the difference in this case was that the Article 690 definition had a specific reference to PV. The definition is appropriate where it is used throughout the *Code* without the "PV" reference.

DELETED

Subarray. This term was deleted as not being necessary and because the actual term used in Article 690 is monopole subarray.

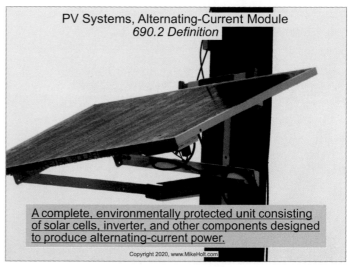

PV Systems, Alternating-Current Module
690.2 Definition

A complete, environmentally protected unit consisting of solar cells, inverter, and other components designed to produce alternating-current power.

Copyright 2020, www.MikeHolt.com

▶Figure 690–1

Author's Comment:

▶ Alternating-current modules are connected in parallel with each other and in parallel with the electric utility in an interactive mode. Operating interactively means that the ac output current from the alternating-current module will cease exporting power upon sensing the loss of voltage from the electric utility.

▶ Manufacturer instructions for alternating-current modules will specify the size of the dedicated branch circuit on which they are to be connected and the maximum number of alternating-current modules permitted on the branch circuit.

690.2 Definitions

The definitions in this section only apply within this article.

Alternating-Current Module System. An assembly of alternating-current modules, wiring methods, materials, and subassemblies that are evaluated, identified, and defined as a system.

Alternating-Current Module. An alternating-current module is a complete, environmentally protected unit consisting of solar cells, inverter, and other components designed to produce alternating-current power. ▶Figure 690–1

Array. An array is a mechanically and electrically integrated grouping of modules, inverter(s), dc-to-dc converter(s), and associated wiring on a support structure. ▶Figure 690–2

Bipolar Circuit. A bipolar circuit is a direct-current circuit that is comprised of two monopole circuits, each monopole circuit having opposite polarity and having one conductor of each monopole circuit connected to a common reference point.

DC-to-DC Converter Output Circuit. A dc-to-dc converter output circuit is the two direct-current circuit conductors connected to the output of direct-current combiner containing multiple dc-to-dc converter source circuits.

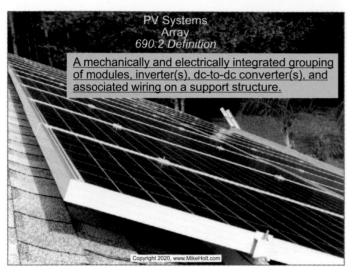

▶Figure 690–2

Author's Comment:

▸ According to Article 100, a "DC-to-DC Converter" is a device that can provide an output dc voltage and current at a higher or lower value than the input dc voltage and current. ▶**Figure 690–3**

▸ DC-to-DC converters are intended to maximize the output of independent modules and reduce losses due to variances between the modules' outputs. They are directly wired to each module and are bolted to the module frame or the PV rack.

▸ A dc-to-dc converter enables the inverter to automatically maintain a fixed circuit voltage, at the optimal point for direct current/alternating current conversion by the inverter, regardless of the circuit length and individual module performance.

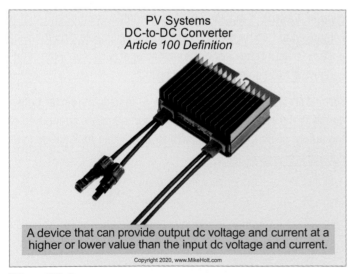

▶Figure 690–3

Direct-Current Combiner. A direct-current combiner is an enclosure that includes devices for the parallel connection of two or more PV system direct-current circuits. ▶Figure 690–4

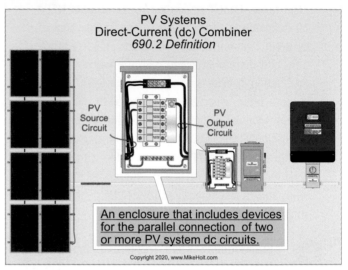

▶Figure 690–4

Author's Comment:

▸ A direct-current combiner connects multiple PV source circuits and dc-to-dc converter source circuits in parallel with each other with a two-wire PV output or dc-to-dc converter output circuit. Direct-current combiners can also recombine multiple PV output circuits and dc-to-dc converter output circuits with a larger two-wire PV output or dc-to-dc converter output circuit.

Electronic Power Converter. An electronic power converter is a device that uses electronics to convert one form of electrical power into another form of electrical power.

Note: Examples of electronic power converters include, but are not limited to, inverters, dc-to-dc converters, and electronic charge controllers. These devices have limited current capabilities based on the device ratings at continuous rated power.

Grounded, Functionally. A functionally grounded PV system is one that has an electrical ground reference for operational purposes. Functionally grounded PV systems are not solidly grounded. ▶Figure 690–5

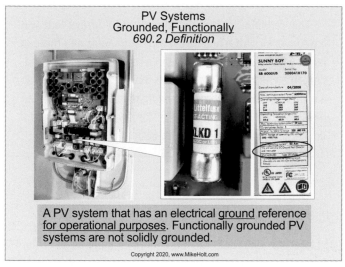

▶Figure 690–5

Note: A functionally grounded PV system is connected to ground through an electronic means that is internal to an inverter. Purposes for functionally grounded systems include ground-fault detection and protection, as well as performance-related issues for some power sources.

Module. A PV module is a unit of environmentally protected solar cells and components designed to produce direct-current power. ▶Figure 690–6

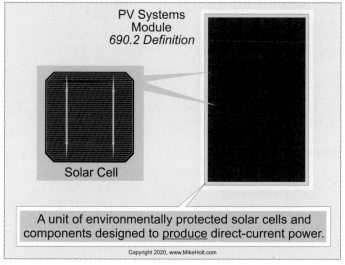

▶Figure 690–6

Author's Comment:

▸ PV modules use sunlight to generate direct-current dc electricity by using light (photons) to move electrons in a semi-conductor. This is known as the "photovoltaic effect."

Monopole Circuit. A PV monopole circuit has two direct-current circuit conductors; one positive (+) and one negative (−).

PV Output Circuit. A PV output circuit consists of two direct-current circuit conductors connected to the output of a direct-current combiner containing two or more PV source circuits. ▶Figure 690–7

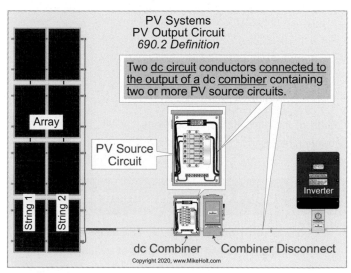

▶Figure 690–7

PV Source Circuit. The PV source circuit consists of the two direct-current circuit conductors between modules and from modules to direct-current combiners, inverters, dc-to-dc converters, charge controllers, or the PV system disconnecting means. ▶Figure 690–8

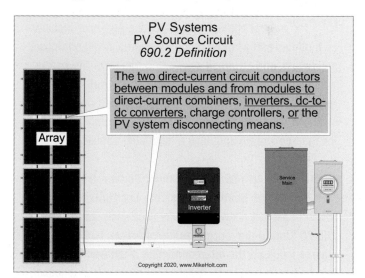

▶Figure 690–8

Author's Comment:

▸ A number of terms that previously appeared in 690.2 have been relocated to Article 100 as they are used in two or more *Code* articles. Those terms are:

- ◆ DC-to-DC Converter
- ◆ Generating Capacity, Inverter
- ◆ Inverter
- ◆ Inverter Input Circuit
- ◆ Inverter Output Circuit
- ◆ Multimode Inverter

As part of the relocation of these terms, specific references to PV have been removed.

690.4 General Requirements

Section 690.4(B) was expanded to add three items to the list of equipment required to be listed or evaluated for the application, and new language in (F) addresses electronic power converters mounted in not readily accessible locations.

Analysis

EXPANDED

690.4(B) Equipment. The list of equipment required to be listed or evaluated and a field label applied was expanded and now includes ac modules and ac input module systems, rapid shutdown equipment, and dc circuit controllers. The term "PV panels" was removed from this rule because its definition was removed and leaving an undefined term would cause confusion. The term "field labeled" was replaced with "evaluated for the application and have a field label applied."

NEW

690.4(F) Electronic Power Converters Mounted in Not Readily Accessible Locations. This was always allowed but was previously addressed in 705.70. During the reorganization of Article 705 to provide clearer focus on the interconnection of different systems, this text was moved to Article 690 where its application will be more common.

This reflects the fact that there are PV arrays that will have inverters attached below the PV modules and there is no way those inverters can be in a readily accessible location. In some cases, just the fact that they are installed on a rooftop prevents them from being readily accessible. The new language also requires that the disconnecting means be installed in accordance with 690.15.

690.4 General Requirements.

(B) Listed or Field-Labeled Equipment. Components of the PV system, including inverters, PV modules, alternating-current modules, alternating-current module systems, direct-current combiners, dc-to-dc converters, rapid shutdown equipment, direct-current circuit controllers, and charge controllers must be listed or be evaluated for the application and have a field label applied. ▸Figure 690–9

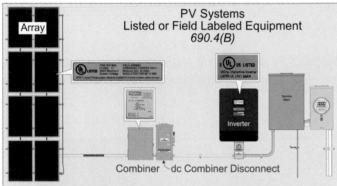

Components of the PV system, including inverters, PV modules, ac modules, ac module systems, dc combiners, dc-to-dc converters, rapid shutdown equipment, dc circuit controllers, and charge controllers must be listed or be evaluated for the application and have a field label applied.

Copyright 2020, www.MikeHolt.com

▸Figure 690–9

Author's Comment:

▸ "Listing" means the equipment is in a list published by a testing laboratory acceptable to the authority having jurisdiction [Article 100].

▸ "Field Labeled" means the equipment or materials which have a label, symbol, or other identifying mark of a field evaluation body (FEB) indicates the equipment or material was evaluated and found to comply with the requirements described in the field body evaluation report [Article 100].

(F) Electronic Power Converters Not Readily Accessible. Electronic power converters (inverters and dc-to-dc converters) are not required to be readily accessible.

Author's Comment:

▸ This *Code* language does not address the requirement in 690.13(A) that the photovoltaic system disconnecting means be located at a readily accessible location, however the panel statement says this new first level subsection does not eliminate the requirements of 690.13. Just looking at accessibility here.

690.6 Alternating-Current Modules and Systems

This section was expanded to include ac systems as well as ac modules, and to clarify that the wiring for these modules and systems are internal components and not subject to the requirements of Article 690.

Analysis

CLARIFIED

This change in subsections (A) and (B) is to clarify that where ac modules and module systems are installed the PV system dc circuits, conductors and inverters are considered internal components of the ac module or ac module system.

This revision removes these components from the application of the rules in the *NEC* and makes them subject to only the manufacturer's instructions. All ac and dc wiring up to the system termination point, as defined in the system instructions, should be considered internal to the system. The considerations for ampacity, disconnection, and other requirements that generally apply to the interconnection of multiple ac modules will have been addressed in the pre-engineering of the system. Since 690.4(B) requires all ac modules and systems to be listed, the listing agency will have addressed all *Code* calculations, much like as is done for the nameplates on HVAC condenser units.

These systems may utilize cable types that are not otherwise covered in the *NEC* so new rules were added to 690.31(C) to cover specific requirements for the installation of these wiring methods where such installation requirements are not clearly defined in the ac module system installation instructions.

690.6 Alternating-Current Modules and Systems

(A) PV Source Circuits. The requirements of Article 690 do not apply to the PV source circuits for an alternating-current module or alternating-current module system. ▸Figure 690–10

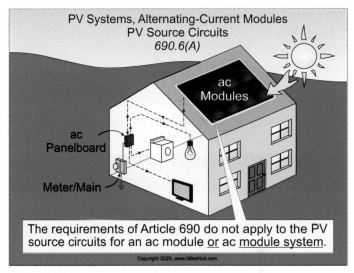

PV Systems, Alternating-Current Modules
PV Source Circuits
690.6(A)

ac Modules

ac Panelboard

Meter/Main

The requirements of Article 690 do not apply to the PV source circuits for an ac module or ac module system.

Copyright 2020, www.MikeHolt.com

▸Figure 690–10

Author's Comment:

▸ PV source circuits for alternating-current modules or alternating-current module systems are covered by the listing of the product. Listed factory-installed internal wiring of equipment that has been processed by a qualified testing laboratory does not need inspecting for *NEC* compliance [90.7].

(B) Output Circuit. The alternating-current output conductors for an alternating-current module or alternating-current module system is considered to be the "Inverter Output Circuit" as defined in Article 100. ▸Figure 690–11

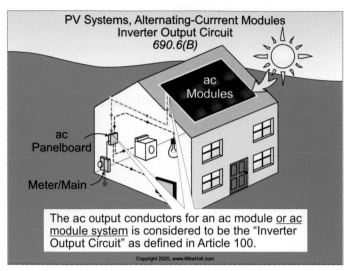

▶Figure 690–11

690.7 Maximum Voltage

This revisions in this section were editorial in nature.

Analysis

CLARIFIED There is the chance for confusion when applying voltage and voltage-to-ground requirements throughout the *Code* as it relates to dc PV system circuits. To clarify how voltage is to be used, the statement in the sentence at the end of 690.7(A) was moved to the initial charging paragraph as examples of how maximum voltage is to be applied. Added to the previous list is "working space" to clarify this use for 110.26.

The changes in 690.7(B) were organizational in nature and without technical change.

690.7 Maximum PV System Direct-Current Circuit Voltage

For the purpose of Article 690, the maximum voltage of a circuit is defined as the highest voltage between any two conductors of a circuit or any conductor to ground.

The maximum voltage of a circuit value is used when selecting conductors, cables, equipment, determining working space, and other applications where circuit voltage ratings are used.

The maximum PV system direct-current circuit voltage for a one- or two-family dwelling is not permitted to exceed 600V. ▶Figure 690–12

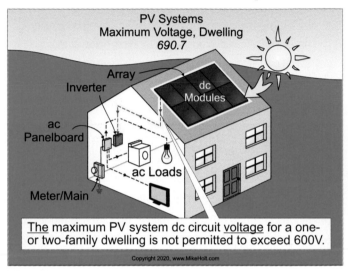

▶Figure 690–12

For other types of buildings, the maximum PV system direct-current circuit voltage is not permitted to exceed 1,000V. Where PV systems are not located on or in buildings, the maximum PV system direct-current circuit voltage is not permitted to exceed 1,500V. ▶Figure 690–13

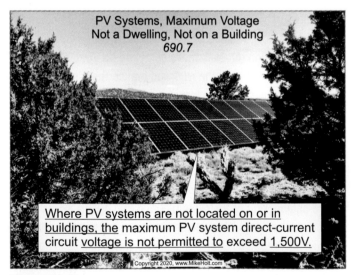

▶Figure 690–13

PV systems having a maximum PV system direct-current circuit voltage over 1,000V are not required to comply with Parts II and III of Article 490.

Author's Comment:

▸ The PV system direct-current circuit consists of PV source circuits, PV output circuits, dc-to-dc converter source circuits, and dc-to-dc converter output circuits [690.2].

690.8 Circuit Sizing and Current

Section 690.8(A)(2) specifying calculation of the maximum permitted input circuit currents to electronic power converters was added, and editorial changes were made in (B).

Analysis

NEW

690.8(A) Calculation of Maximum Circuit Current. This new rule in (A)(2) specifies that where a circuit is protected by an overcurrent protective device not exceeding the conductor ampacity, the maximum current is permitted to be the rated input current of the electronic power converter to which it is connected.

EDITED

690.8(B) Conductor Ampacity. As in 210.19(A)(1) for branch circuits and 215.2(A)(1) for feeders, there are two conductor ampacity selection requirements, and as in those cases the larger of the two methods is required to be used. There were editorial revisions made in the two ampacity calculation methods, (B)(1) and (2), but there are no technical changes. In addition, subsection (3) was removed.

690.8 Circuit Current and Conductor Sizing

(A) Calculate PV Circuit Current. The maximum PV system current is calculated in one the methods in 690.8(A)(1) or (2):

(1) PV System Circuit Current. The maximum PV system dc circuit current is calculated in accordance with one of the five following methods, 690.8(A)(1)(a) through (e).

(a) PV Source Circuit Currents. The maximum PV source circuit current is calculated in accordance with either of the following:

(1) PV System Rated Less Than 100 kW. The maximum PV source circuit current is equal to the short-circuit current ratings marked on the modules connected in parallel, multiplied by 125 percent. ▸Figure 690–14

PV System Rated Less Than 100 kW
Maximum PV Source Circuit Current (Isc)
690.8(A)(1)(a)(1)

ELECTRICAL CHARACTERISTICS	
Maximum Power (Pmax)*	250W
Tolerance of Pmax	+5%/-0%
PTC Rating	223.60W
Type of Cell	Polycrystalline silicon
Cell Configuration	60 in series
Open Circuit Voltage (Voc)	38.30V
Maximum Power Voltage (Vpm)	29.80V
Short Circuit Current (Isc)	8.90A
Maximum Power Current (Ipm)	8.40A
Module Efficiency (%)	15.30%
Maximum System (dc) Voltage	600V (UL)/1000V (IEC)
Series Fuse Rating	15A
NOCT	47.50°C
Temperature Coefficient (Pmax)	-0.485%/°C
Temperature Coefficient (Voc)	-0.36%/°C
Temperature Coefficient (Isc)	0.053%/°C

*Illumination of 1 kW/m² (1 sun) at spectral distribution of AM 1.5 (ASTM E892 global spectral irradiance) at a cell temperature of 25°C.

The maximum PV source circuit current is equal to the short-circuit current ratings marked on the modules connected in parallel, multiplied by 125%.

Copyright 2020, www.MikeHolt.com

▸Figure 690–14

Author's Comment:

▸ The PV source circuit is defined as the two direct-current circuit conductors between modules, direct-current circuit conductors from the modules to dc-to-dc converters, direct-current circuit conductors from modules to direct-current combiners, and direct-current circuit conductors from modules to inverters [690.2].

▸ A module can produce more than the rated current when the intensity of the sunlight is greater than the standard used to determine the module's short-circuit rating. This happens when sunlight intensity is affected by altitude, reflection due to snow, refraction through clouds, or the dryness of the air. For this reason, the PV system circuit current is calculated at 125 percent of the module short-circuit current rating marked on the module's nameplate.

▸ **Maximum PV Source Circuit Current Example**

Question: What is the maximum PV source circuit current for 12 series-connected direct-current modules having a nameplate short-circuit current (Isc) of 10A? ▸Figure 690–15

(a) 12.50A   *(b) 15A*   *(c) 20A*   *(d) 25A*

Answer: (a) 12.50A

Solution:

Source Circuit Current = Module Isc × 1.25
Source Circuit Current = 10A × 1.25
Source Circuit Current = 12.50A

• • •

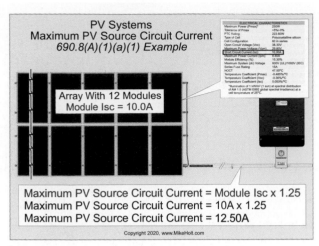

▶Figure 690–15

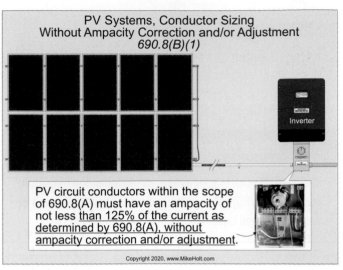

▶Figure 690–16

(2) PV System Rated 100 kW or Greater. The maximum PV source circuit current calculations for PV systems with an inverter generating capacity of 100 kW or greater is permitted to be determined by a licensed professional electrical engineer providing documented and stamped PV system design using an industry standard method.

The maximum PV source circuit current value is based on the highest 3-hour current average resulting from the simulated local irradiance on the array accounting for elevation and orientation. In no case is the maximum PV source circuit current permitted to be less than 70 percent of the maximum PV source circuit current as calculated in 690.8(A)(1)(a)(1).

Note: One industry standard method for calculating the maximum PV source current is available from Sandia National Laboratories, reference SAND 2004-3535, *Photovoltaic Array Performance Model*. This model is used by the System Advisor Model simulation program provided by the National Renewable Energy Laboratory.

(B) Conductor Sizing. PV circuit conductors must be sized to carry the larger of 690.8(B)(1) or 690.8(B)(2).

(1) Conductor Sizing, Without Ampacity Correction and/or Adjustment. PV circuit conductors within the scope of 690.8(A) must have an ampacity of not less than 125 percent of the current as determined by 690.8(A), without ampacity correction and/or adjustment. ▶Figure 690–16

▶ **PV Source Circuit Without Ampacity Correction and/ or Adjustment Example**

Question: What is the minimum direct-current source circuit conductor ampacity, without the application of conductor correction or adjustment, for source circuit conductors having a short-circuit current rating of 10A? ▶**Figure 690–17**

(a) 12.50A   (b) 15.62A   (c) 20.41A   (d) 25.56A

Answer: (b) 15.62A

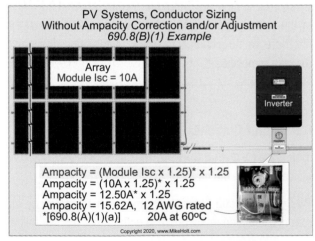

▶Figure 690–17

Solution:

Conductor Ampacity = (Module Isc × 1.25)* × 1.25

Conductor Ampacity = (10A × 1.25)* × 1.25

Conductor Ampacity = (12.50A)* × 1.25

Conductor Ampacity = 15.62A

Use 12 AWG rated 20A at 60°C [110.14(C)(1) and Table 310.16].
*[690.8(A)(1)(a)]

▶ **PV Output Circuit Ampacity Without Correction and Adjustment Example 1**

Question: What is the minimum direct-current PV output circuit conductor ampacity, without the application of conductor correction or adjustment, supplied by four source circuits each with a short-circuit current rating of 10A where the terminals are rated 75°C? ▶**Figure 690–18**

(a) 33A   (b) 32A   (c) 43A   (d) 63A

Answer: (d) 63A

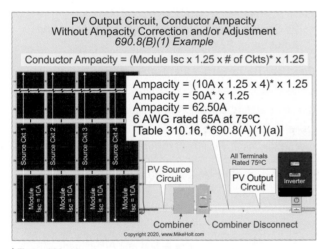

PV Output Circuit, Conductor Ampacity
Without Ampacity Correction and/or Adjustment
690.8(B)(1) Example

Conductor Ampacity = (Module Isc x 1.25 x # of Ckts)* x 1.25

Ampacity = (10A x 1.25 x 4)* x 1.25
Ampacity = 50A* x 1.25
Ampacity = 62.50A
6 AWG rated 65A at 75°C
[Table 310.16, *690.8(A)(1)(a)]

▶Figure 690–18

Solution:

Conductor Ampacity = (Module Isc × 1.25 × Number of Source Circuits)* × 1.25

Conductor Ampacity = (10A × 1.25 × 4 circuits)* × 1.25

Conductor Ampacity = 50A* × 1.25

Conductor Ampacity = 62.50A

Use 6 AWG rated 65A at 75°C [110.14(C)(1) and Table 310.16].
*[690.8(A)(1)(a)]

▶ **Inverter Output Circuit Ampacity Without Correction and Adjustment Example 2**

Question: What is the minimum inverter alternating-current output circuit conductor ampacity, without the application of conductor ampacity correction and/or adjustment factors, if the maximum continuous nameplate rating of the inverter is 24A? ▶**Figure 690–19**

(a) 20A   (b) 25A   (c) 30A   (d) 35A

Answer: (c) 30A

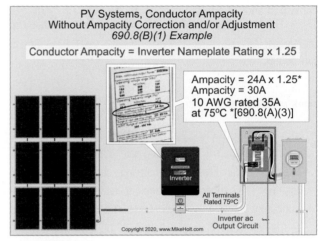

PV Systems, Conductor Ampacity
Without Ampacity Correction and/or Adjustment
690.8(B)(1) Example

Conductor Ampacity = Inverter Nameplate Rating x 1.25

Ampacity = 24A x 1.25*
Ampacity = 30A
10 AWG rated 35A
at 75°C *[690.8(A)(3)]

▶Figure 690–19

Solution:

Conductor Ampacity = Inverter Nameplate Rating [690.8(A)(3)] × 1.25

Conductor Ampacity = 24A × 1.25

Conductor Ampacity = 30A

Use 10 AWG rated 35A at 75°C [310.16].

Ex 1: Where the assembly, including the overcurrent devices protecting the feeder(s), is listed for operation at 100 percent of its rating, the ampere rating of the overcurrent device can be sized to 100 percent of the continuous and noncontinuous loads.

(2) Conductor Sizing, With Ampacity Correction and/or Adjustment. PV circuit conductors within the scope of 690.8(A) must have an ampacity of not less than 100 percent of the current as determined by 690.8(A) after the application of conductor ampacity correction and adjustment in accordance with Table 310.15(B)(1) and Table 310.15(C)(1). ▶**Figure 690–20**

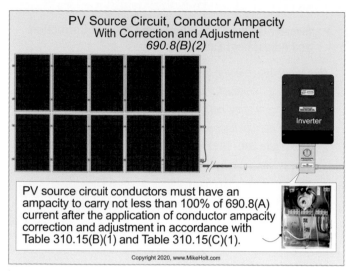

PV Source Circuit, Conductor Ampacity
With Correction and Adjustment
690.8(B)(2)

Inverter

PV source circuit conductors must have an ampacity to carry not less than 100% of 690.8(A) current after the application of conductor ampacity correction and adjustment in accordance with Table 310.15(B)(1) and Table 310.15(C)(1).

Copyright 2020, www.MikeHolt.com

▶Figure 690–20

Author's Comment:

▶ The Table 310.16 ampacity must be corrected when the ambient temperature is less than 77°F or greater than 86°F and adjusted when more than three current-carrying conductors are bundled together. The temperature correction [Table 310.15(B)(1)] and conductor bundle adjustment [Table 310.15(C)(1)] are applied to the conductor ampacity, based on the temperature rating of the conductor insulation as contained in Table 310.16, typically in the 90°C column [310.15].

▶ PV Source Circuit Ampacity with Correction and Adjustment Example 1

Question: What is the conductor ampacity with temperature correction for two current-carrying 12 AWG USE-2 or PV conductors rated 90°C within a raceway or cable located 1 in. above the roof, where the ambient temperature is 94°F in accordance with 310.15(B)(3)(c)? The modules have an Isc rating of 10A.
▶Figure 690–21

(a) 19A   (b) 29A   (c) 39A   (d) 49A

Answer: (b) 29A

Solution:

Conductor Ampacity = Table 310.16 Ampacity at 90°C Column x Temperature Correction.

Temperature Correction = 0.96 based on a 94°F ambient temperature [Table 310.15(B)(1)].

12 AWG rated 30A at 90°C [Table 310.16]

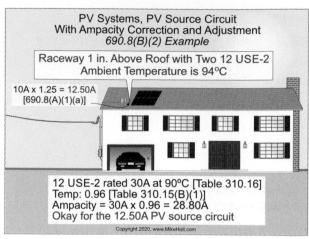

PV Systems, PV Source Circuit
With Ampacity Correction and Adjustment
690.8(B)(2) Example

Raceway 1 in. Above Roof with Two 12 USE-2
Ambient Temperature is 94°C

10A x 1.25 = 12.50A
[690.8(A)(1)(a)]

12 USE-2 rated 30A at 90°C [Table 310.16]
Temp: 0.96 [Table 310.15(B)(1)]
Ampacity = 30A x 0.96 = 28.80A
Okay for the 12.50A PV source circuit

Copyright 2020, www.MikeHolt.com

▶Figure 690–21

Conductor Corrected Ampacity = 30A x 96%
Conductor Corrected Ampacity = 28.80A

12 AWG with ampacity correction has sufficient ampacity to supply the source circuit current of 12.50A, (10A x 1.25) [690.8(A)(1)(a)].

▶ PV Source Circuit Ampacity with Correction and Adjustment Example 2

Question: For an array with modules having a nameplate Isc rating of 10A for each circuit; what is the conductor ampacity with temperature correction and adjustment for four current-carrying 12 AWG USE-2 conductors located 1 in. above the roof, where the ambient temperature is 94°F? ▶Figure 690–22

(a) 23A   (b) 29A   (c) 39A   (d) 49A

Answer: (a) 23A

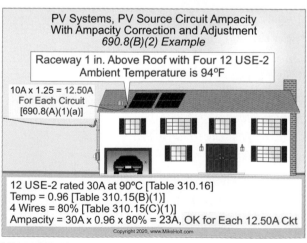

PV Systems, PV Source Circuit Ampacity
With Ampacity Correction and Adjustment
690.8(B)(2) Example

Raceway 1 in. Above Roof with Four 12 USE-2
Ambient Temperature is 94°F

10A x 1.25 = 12.50A
For Each Circuit
[690.8(A)(1)(a)]

12 USE-2 rated 30A at 90°C [Table 310.16]
Temp = 0.96 [Table 310.15(B)(1)]
4 Wires = 80% [Table 310.15(C)(1)]
Ampacity = 30A x 0.96 x 80% = 23A, OK for Each 12.50A Ckt

Copyright 2020, www.MikeHolt.com

▶Figure 690–22

Solution:

Conductor Ampacity = Table 310.16 Ampacity at 90°C Column x Temperature Correction x Bundle Adjustment

Temperature Correction = 0.96 based on a 94°F ambient temperature [Table 310.15(B)(1)].

Bundle Adjustment = 80% based on four current-carrying conductors [Table 310.15(C)(1)].

12 AWG rated 30A at 90°C [Table 310.16].

Conductor Corrected/Adjusted Ampacity = 30A x 0.96 x 80%
Conductor Corrected/Adjusted Ampacity = 23A

Note: 12 AWG has sufficient ampacity with correction and adjustment to supply the dc source circuits, each with a current of 12.50A [10A x 1.25, 690.8(A)(1)(a)].

▶ **PV Output Circuit Ampacity with Correction Example**

Question: What is the direct-current PV output circuit conductor ampacity with conductor temperature correction for two 6 AWG USE-2 PV output circuit conductors, with a PV output circuit current of 40A, at an ambient temperature of 94°F? ▶**Figure 690–23**

(a) 59A   (b) 69A   (c) 72A   (d) 89A

Answer: (c) 72A

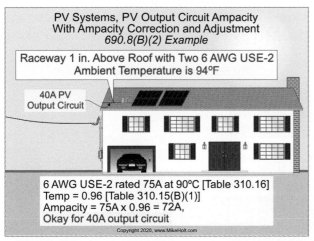

PV Systems, PV Output Circuit Ampacity
With Ampacity Correction and Adjustment
690.8(B)(2) Example

Raceway 1 in. Above Roof with Two 6 AWG USE-2
Ambient Temperature is 94°F

40A PV
Output Circuit

6 AWG USE-2 rated 75A at 90°C [Table 310.16]
Temp = 0.96 [Table 310.15(B)(1)]
Ampacity = 75A x 0.96 = 72A,
Okay for 40A output circuit
Copyright 2020, www.MikeHolt.com

▶Figure 690–23

Solution:

Conductor Ampacity = Table 310.16 Ampacity at 90°C Column x Temperature Correction

Temperature Correction = 0.96 based on 94°F ambient temperature [Table 310.15(B)(1)].

6 AWG rated 75A at 90°C [Table 310.16].

Conductor Corrected Ampacity = 75A x 96%
Conductor Corrected Ampacity = 72A

Note: 6 AWG with correction has sufficient ampacity to supply the PV output circuit current of 40A.

▶ **Inverter Output Circuit Ampacity with Correction and Adjustment Example**

Question: What is the conductor ampacity with temperature correction for two current-carrying 10 AWG RHH/RHW-2/USE-2 or PV conductors rated 90°C supplying a 24A inverter output circuit and installed in a location where the ambient temperature is 94°F? ▶**Figure 690–24**

(a) 18.40A   (b) 29.40A   (c) 38.40A   (d) 49.40A

Answer: (c) 38.40A

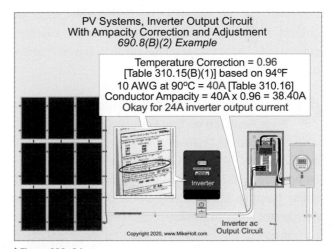

PV Systems, Inverter Output Circuit
With Ampacity Correction and Adjustment
690.8(B)(2) Example

Temperature Correction = 0.96
[Table 310.15(B)(1)] based on 94°F
10 AWG at 90°C = 40A [Table 310.16]
Conductor Ampacity = 40A x 0.96 = 38.40A
Okay for 24A inverter output current

Inverter

Inverter ac
Output Circuit
Copyright 2020, www.MikeHolt.com

▶Figure 690–24

Solution:

Conductor Ampacity = Ampacity at 90°C Column [Table 310.16] x Temperature Correction.

Temperature Correction = 0.96 based on a 94°F ambient temperature [Table 310.15(B)(1)].

10 AWG rated 40A at 90°C [Table 310.16].

Conductor Ampacity = 40A x 96%
Conductor Ampacity = 38.40A

Note: 10 AWG has sufficient ampacity with correction to supply the inverter output circuit current of 24A [690.8(A)(3)].

690.9 Overcurrent Protection

The parent text in (B) was expanded to include electronic devices that are listed to prevent backfeed, and the Informational Note following (B)(2) was revised.

Analysis

REORGANIZED **690.9(A)(1) Circuits and Equipment.** This replaces the deleted exception with positive text and with a technical change. The language of the exception did not require overcurrent protection where there were no external sources such as parallel-connected source circuits, batteries, or backfeed from inverters, or where the short-circuit currents from all sources did not exceed the conductor ampacity. The new subsection does not require overcurrent protection where the conditions are met. With the previous language the circuits could have enough ampacity, but the available current could have exceeded the rating of the overcurrent protective device for the module.

EDITED **690.9(A)(2) Circuits Where Overcurrent Protection is Required on One End.** This rule requires that where the circuit is connected to a current-limited supply such as PV modules or electronic power converters on one end, and to a source having higher current availability (such as utility power) on the other end, that the overcurrent protective device must be located at the higher current source connection. It provides for the proper circuit protection for the conductors that run between the two sources.

CLARIFIED **690.9(A)(3) Other Circuits.** This subsection addresses circuits that are not covered by either (A)(1) or (A)(2) and specifies the required protection of these circuits. These circuits will be more commonly found in larger PV systems, particularly those not attached to buildings. Section 690.9(A)(1) covers cases where the ampacity of the circuit exceeds the maximum circuit current; (A)(2) applies where the circuit is connected to a power-limited source on one end. Sections 690.9(A)(3)(1) through (4) apply where the power source on each end is not power limited and could supply more current than that for which the circuit is rated.

EXPANDED **690.9(B) Device Ratings.** The title was changed to generically deal with all device ratings related to overcurrent protection. The section title is "Overcurrent Protection" and it did not need to be repeated here.

New parent text language was added to permit electronic devices listed to prevent backfeed current in PV system dc circuits to be used to protect the conductors on the PV array side of the device from overcurrent. The parent text also permits the overcurrent protective device to be rounded up to the next standard size in accordance with 240.4(B).

The Informational Note that follows list item (2) was revised to provide some information on electronic protective devices.

With PV systems, the current from the array is limited by the array itself and it cannot produce enough current to overload properly sized conductors. The source of damaging current to those conductors would be a backfeed. A protective device that prevents backfeed will protect the conductors. Such a device would need to have a listing specific to its use in PV systems.

690.9 Overcurrent Protection

(A) General. PV system direct-current circuit conductors sized in accordance with 690.8(A)(2) are required to be protected against overcurrent by one the following three methods. ▶Figure 690–25

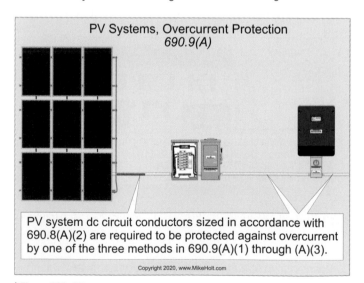

PV system dc circuit conductors sized in accordance with 690.8(A)(2) are required to be protected against overcurrent by one of the three methods in 690.9(A)(1) through (A)(3).

Copyright 2020, www.MikeHolt.com

▶Figure 690–25

(1) Circuits Without Overcurrent Protection. Overcurrent protection is not required where both of the following conditions are met:

(1) The PV system direct-current circuit conductors have an ampacity equal to or greater than the maximum circuit current calculated in 690.8(A).

(2) Where the currents from all PV sources do not exceed the maximum overcurrent protective device rating specified by the manufacturer for the PV module or electronic power converters (inverters and dc-to-dc converters, and charger controllers). ▶Figure 690–26

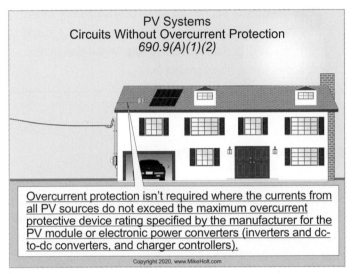

PV Systems
Circuits Without Overcurrent Protection
690.9(A)(1)(2)

Overcurrent protection isn't required where the currents from all PV sources do not exceed the maximum overcurrent protective device rating specified by the manufacturer for the PV module or electronic power converters (inverters and dc-to-dc converters, and charger controllers).

Copyright 2020, www.MikeHolt.com

▶Figure 690–26

(2) Overcurrent Protection Required on One End. Circuit overcurrent protection is required at the point of connection to the higher current source for a circuit conductor connected at one end to a current-limited supply (for example; PV modules, inverters, and dc-to-dc converters), and also connected to sources having an available maximum circuit current greater than the ampacity of the conductor.

Note: PV system direct-current circuits and electronic power converter (inverters, dc-to-dc converters, and charge controllers) outputs powered by these circuits are current-limited and in some cases do not need overcurrent protection. When these circuits are connected to higher current sources, such as parallel-connected PV system direct-current circuits or energy storage systems, the overcurrent device is often installed at the higher current source end of the circuit conductor.

(3) Other Circuits. PV system direct-current circuits that do not comply with 690.9(A)(1) or (A)(2) must be protected in one of the three following methods:

(1) PV system direct-current circuit conductors on, but not within, a building must not be longer than 10 ft in length and have overcurrent protection at one end of the circuit.

(2) PV system direct-current circuit conductors within a building must not be longer than 10 ft in length, must be installed within a raceway or metal cable, and have overcurrent protection at on one end of the circuit.

(3) Conductors protected from overcurrent on both ends.

(4) PV system direct-current circuit conductors not installed on or within buildings having overcurrent protection at one end of the circuit must comply with all of the following four conditions:

   a. The PV system direct-circuit circuit conductors are installed in metal raceways, metal-clad cables, enclosed metal cable trays, underground, or pad-mounted enclosures.

   b. The PV system direct-circuit circuit conductors must terminate to a single circuit breaker or a single set of fuses that limit the current to the ampacity of the conductors.

   c. The overcurrent device for the conductors is integral with the disconnecting means.

   d. The disconnect containing the overcurrent protection is located outside the building, or at a readily accessible location nearest the point of entrance of the conductors inside the building. PV system direct-circuit circuit conductors are considered outside of a building where they are encased or installed under not less than 2 in. of concrete or brick [230.6].

(B) Overcurrent Device Ratings. Overcurrent devices for PV system direct-circuit circuits must be listed for PV systems. ▶Figure 690–27

Electronic devices that are listed to prevent backfeed in PV system direct-circuit circuits are permitted to prevent overcurrent of conductors on the PV array side of the device.

Overcurrent protective devices required by 690.9(A)(2) must comply with one of the following; the next higher standard size in accordance with 240.4(B) is permitted.

(1) The overcurrent protective device must have a rating of not less than 125 percent of the maximum currents calculated in 690.8(A). ▶Figure 690–28

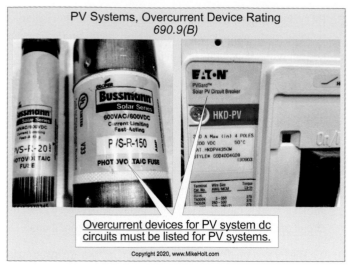

PV Systems, Overcurrent Device Rating
690.9(B)

Overcurrent devices for PV system dc circuits must be listed for PV systems.

Copyright 2020, www.MikeHolt.com

▶Figure 690–27

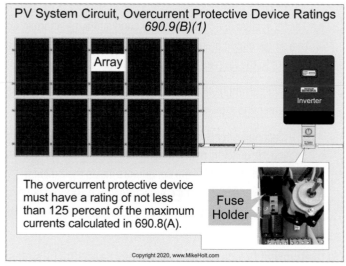

PV System Circuit, Overcurrent Protective Device Ratings
690.9(B)(1)

Array

Inverter

The overcurrent protective device must have a rating of not less than 125 percent of the maximum currents calculated in 690.8(A).

Fuse Holder

Copyright 2020, www.MikeHolt.com

▶Figure 690–28

(2) Where the assembly, together with its overcurrent device(s), is listed for continuous operation at 100 percent of its rating, it is permitted to be sized at 100 percent of the maximum currents calculated in 690.8(A).

Note: Some electronic devices prevent backfeed current, which in some cases is the only source of overcurrent in PV system direct-current circuits.

690.11 Arc-Fault Circuit Protection (Direct Current)

Changes were made to the exception to allow additional wiring methods to exempt PV output circuits from arc-fault circuit protection.

Analysis

EXPANDED **690.11 Ex.** The exception now allows any wiring method installed underground to not require AFCI protection. Additionally, "metal-clad cables" was added to the aboveground list.

690.11 Arc-Fault Circuit Protection

PV system direct-current circuits operating at 80V dc or greater between any two circuit conductors must be protected by a listed PV arc-fault circuit interrupter or other component listed to provide equivalent protection. The PV direct-current AFCI system must detect and interrupt arcing faults from a failure in the continuity of the conductor, connection, module, or other direct-current system component.

Note: Annex A includes the reference for the Photovoltaic DC Arc-Fault Circuit Protection product standard.

Ex: PV direct-current AFCI protection is not required for PV circuits within metal raceways, metal-clad cables, enclosed cable trays, or underground, or for PV circuits installed in a detached building whose only purpose is to house the PV system equipment.

690.12 Rapid Shutdown of PV Systems on Buildings

Subsection (A) was revised to clarify that where an ac inverter output circuit originates within the array, it must be shut down by the rapid shutdown system. Subsections (B) and (C) were clarified.

Analysis

690.12(A) Controlled Conductors. This subsection was modified to clarify that where ac inverter output circuits originate at the array, those circuits must also be shut down by the rapid shutdown system. To accomplish this, the rule was broken down into charging text and two list items.

CLARIFIED

690.12(A) Note. An Informational Note was added to help *Code* users understand the function of the rapid shutdown system by explaining that it reduces the risk of electrical shock that dc circuits in a PV system may pose to firefighters since those circuit are energized independent of other sources, such as a utility.

NEW

690.12(B)(3) Controlled Limits. Although there were several changes made to the text in this section, the technical requirements did not fundamentally change. List item (1) and its Informational Note language was revised to better align with the progress made in the development of the new PV hazard control standard in UL 3741. List item (2) removed some language that was considered duplicative since these limits are already provided in 690.12(B)(1).

CLARIFIED

List item (3) describes an alternate construction for a PV array that could comply with the 690.12(B)(2) requirements and was revised for clarity. Where the PV array has no exposed wiring methods or conductive parts and is installed more than 8 ft from any exposed grounded conductive parts or ground, no additional circuit control is required within the array. Note that conductors leaving the array would still require control in accordance with 690.12(B)(1).

690.12(C) Initiation Device. The language in this section was clarified to address situations where multiple rapid shutdown (RS) initiation devices might be present for a single PV system. There may be cases where this is desirable, even if not required. In those cases, any one of the initiation devices would have to shut down the system. A system could not require multiple switch operations.

CLARIFIED

690.12 Rapid Shutdown

PV system conductor on or in a building must be controlled by a rapid shutdown system to reduce shock hazard for firefighters. ▶Figure 690–29

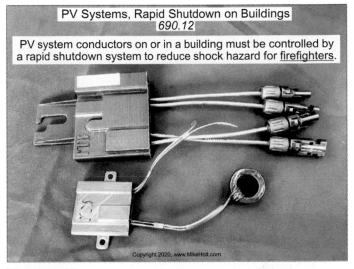

PV Systems, Rapid Shutdown on Buildings
690.12

PV system conductors on or in a building must be controlled by a rapid shutdown system to reduce shock hazard for firefighters.

Copyright 2020, www.MikeHolt.com

▶Figure 690–29

Ex: A rapid shutdown system is not required for ground-mounted PV system conductors that enter buildings whose sole purpose is to house PV system equipment.

(A) Controlled Conductors. The PV system conductors that are required to be controlled by the rapid shutdown system include:

(1) PV system direct-current circuit conductors.

(2) Inverter output alternating-current circuits originating from inverters located within the array boundary.

Note: The rapid shutdown function reduces the risk of electrical shock that direct-current circuits in a PV system could pose for firefighters. The alternating-current output conductors from PV systems that include inverters will either be de-energized after shutdown initiation or will remain energized by other sources such as a utility service. To prevent PV arrays with attached inverters from having energized alternating-current conductors within the PV array(s), those circuits must also be controlled after shutdown initiation.

(B) Controlled Limits. For the purpose of 690.12, the array boundary is defined as the area 1 ft outside the PV array in all directions.

(1) Outside the Array Boundary. PV system direct-current circuit conductors and inverter output alternating-current circuit conductors [690.12(A)] located outside the PV array boundary, or more than 3 ft from the point of entry inside a building, must be limited to 30V within 30 seconds of rapid shutdown initiation.

(2) Inside the Array Boundary. The PV system rapid shutdown system must comply with one of the following three methods:

(1) A PV hazard control system listed for the purpose must be installed in accordance with the instructions included with the listing or field labeling. Where a hazard control system requires initiation to transition to a controlled state, the rapid shutdown initiation device required in 690.12(C) must perform this initiation.

Note: A listed or field labeled hazard PV control system is comprised of either an individual piece of equipment that fulfills the necessary functions, or multiple pieces of equipment coordinated to perform the functions as described in the installation instructions to reduce the risk of electric shock hazard within a damaged PV array for fire fighters.

(2) PV system direct-current circuit conductors and inverter output alternating-current circuit conductors [690.12(A)] located inside the PV array boundary must be limited to 80V within 30 seconds of rapid shutdown initiation.

(3) PV arrays must have no exposed wiring methods, no exposed conductive parts, and be installed more than 8 ft from exposed conductive parts are not required to have a PV hazard control system [690.12(B)(2)].

(C) Initiation Device. A rapid shutdown initiation device is required to initiate the rapid shutdown function of the PV system.

When the rapid shutdown initiation device is placed in the "off" position, this indicates that the rapid shutdown function has been initiated.

For one-family and two-family dwellings, the rapid shutdown initiation device must be located outside the building at a readily accessible location.

For a single PV system, the rapid shutdown initiation must occur by the operation of any single device that must be at least one of the three following types:

(1) The service disconnect.

(2) The PV system disconnect. ▶Figure 690–30

(3) A readily accessible switch that plainly indicates whether it is in the "off" or "on" position.

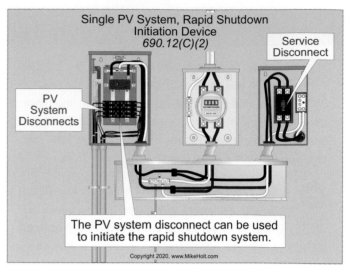

Single PV System, Rapid Shutdown
Initiation Device
690.12(C)(2)

Service Disconnect

PV System Disconnects

The PV system disconnect can be used to initiate the rapid shutdown system.

Copyright 2020, www.MikeHolt.com

▶Figure 690–30

Note: An example of where a rapid shutdown initiation device that complies with 690.12(C)(3) would be located is where a PV system is connected to an optional standby or stand-alone system.

Where multiple PV systems are on a single service, the rapid shutdown initiation device(s) for the multiple PV systems must consist of not more than six switches or six sets of circuit breakers, or a combination of not more than six switches and sets of circuit breakers.

690.13 Photovoltaic System Disconnecting Means

This section was expanded and clarified, and (C) was moved to Article 705.

Analysis

EXPANDED

690.13(A) Location. This subsection requires the disconnecting means to be in a readily accessible location. It was modified to mandate that where the system operates above 30V, and where the disconnecting means is readily accessible to unqualified persons, that any enclosure door or hinged cover that exposes live parts when open must be locked or require a tool to open. The operating handle of the disconnect, and not the internal parts, is what is required to be readily accessible.

Having the interior parts accessible by only the use of a tool does not influence the disconnect meeting the definition of readily accessible. Such a situation might occur when using certain general-duty switches.

DELETED **690.13(C) Suitable for Use.** This relocated subsection requiring a PV system disconnect connected to the supply side of the utility service to be listed as suitable for use as service equipment is covered in Article 705, Interconnected Electric Power Production Sources; the suitability of the PV disconnect for such a system is located in 705.11. The requirement is not necessary in both locations and was deleted here.

CLARIFIED **690.13(E) Type of Disconnect.** This was (F) in the previous *NEC* but became (E) as a result of the deletion of (C). It was rewritten into parent text and five list items to improve clarity and usability.

The parent text specifies that the PV system must simultaneously disconnect the PV system conductors that are not solidly grounded from all conductors of other systems. The rule was revised to say that the disconnecting means or its remote operating device, or the enclosure providing access to the disconnecting means must be capable of being locked in accordance with 110.25. A new Informational Note was added following the list items. This note advises the *Code* user that circuit breakers marked "line" and "load" may not be suitable for backfeed or reverse current. Breakers marked "line" and "load" are typically not evaluated to be used in backfeed or reverse current applications, but some could be.

This was previously addressed this as a rule in 690.13(F)(2) and prohibited the use of breakers marked "line" and "load" in backfeed or reverse current applications. The new language alerts the reader of this fact while providing an allowance for any device listed or approved for this application.

690.13 PV System Disconnect

Means must be provided to disconnect the PV system conductors from all wiring systems, including power systems, energy storage systems, utilization equipment, and associated premises wiring. ▶Figure 690–31

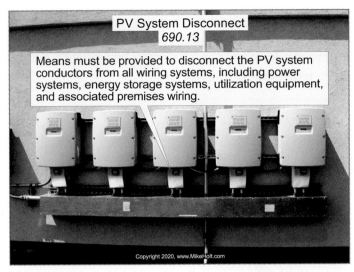

▶Figure 690–31

(A) Location. The PV system disconnect must be readily accessible and be at a readily accessible location. ▶Figure 690–32

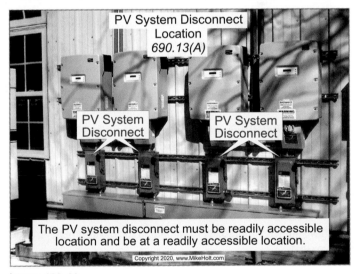

▶Figure 690–32

Where disconnecting means of systems above 30V are readily accessible to unqualified persons, any enclosure door or hinged cover that exposes live parts when open must be locked or require a tool to open.

Note: Rapid shutdown systems installed in accordance with 690.12 address the concerns related to energized conductors entering a building.

(B) Marking. Each PV system disconnect must indicate if it is in the open (off) or closed (on) position and the PV system disconnect must be permanently marked "**PV SYSTEM DISCONNECT**" or equivalent. ▸Figure 690–33

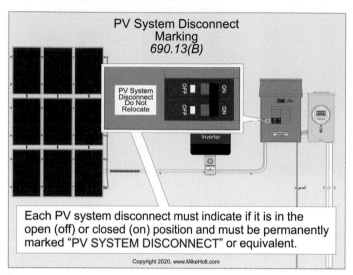

▸Figure 690–33

Where the line and load terminals of the PV system disconnect may be energized when the disconnect is in the open (off) position, the disconnect must be marked with the following words or equivalent:

**WARNING—ELECTRIC SHOCK HAZARD
TERMINALS ON THE LINE AND LOAD SIDES
MAY BE ENERGIZED IN THE OPEN POSITION**

The warning markings on the disconnect must be permanently affixed and have sufficient durability to withstand the environment involved [110.21(B)].

(C) Maximum Number of Disconnects. Each PV system must have a disconnect consisting of not more than six switches or six sets of circuit breakers, or a combination of not more than six switches and sets of circuit breakers. ▸Figure 690–34

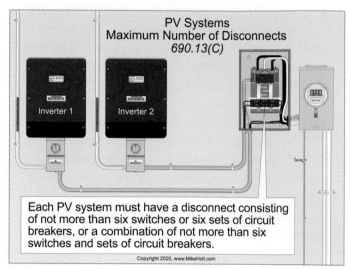

▸Figure 690–34

A single PV system disconnect is permitted for the combined alternating-current output of one or more inverters or alternating-current modules in an interactive system.

Note: This maximum of six disconnect requirement does not limit the number of PV systems connected to a service as permitted in 690.4(D). For PV systems where all power is converted through interactive inverters, a dedicated circuit breaker, in accordance with 705.12(A), is an example of a single PV system disconnect.

(D) Ratings. The PV system disconnect must have a rating sufficient for the maximum circuit current, the available fault current, and the voltage that is available at the terminals of the PV system disconnect.

(E) Type of Disconnect. The PV system disconnect must simultaneously disconnect all ungrounded PV system circuit conductors. The PV system disconnect, its remote operating device, or the enclosure providing access to the disconnect must be capable of being locked. The provisions for locking must remain in place whether the lock is installed or not [110.25].

The PV system disconnect must be one of the five following types:

(1) A manually operable switch or circuit breaker.

(2) A connector meeting the requirements of 690.33(D)(1) or (D)(3).

(3) A load-break rated pull-out switch with sufficient short-circuit current rating.

(4) A remote-controlled switch or circuit breaker that is capable of being operable manually and can be opened automatically when control power is interrupted.

Author's Comment:

▸ Shunt trip breakers typically require the application of power to the shunt trip coil to open the breaker and would not be suitable for this application as the rule requires the device to open on loss of control power unless special provisions have been provided.

(5) A device listed or approved for the intended application.

Note: Circuit breakers marked "line" and "load" are not be suitable for backfeed or reverse current, therefore they are not permitted to serve as the PV system disconnect.

690.15 Disconnecting Means for Isolating Photovoltaic Equipment

The title and parent text were revised to improve clarify, and new language regarding isolating disconnects operating at over 30V was added.

Analysis

CLARIFIED The title change reflects the intent of this section, it does not apply to disconnects that are required for the safe operation of the system. It does apply to disconnects used to "isolate" the systems or parts thereof to permit safe and convenient replacement or service of specific PV equipment without exposure to energized parts. Language related to requirements for isolating disconnects (which was (B) in the 2017 *Code*) used where the current exceeds 30A was removed from the parent text of this section and relocated to the new subsection (C).

EXPANDED **690.15(A) Location.** The isolating disconnect is not required to be in a readily accessible location but is required to be within the equipment, or within sight and within 10 ft of the equipment. It also permits remote isolating equipment where it can be operated remotely from within 10 ft of the equipment. The change for this cycle is to limit access to energized parts by unqualified persons. This is to be accomplished by having covers requiring the use of a tool to open or covers that are locked. This is the same change that was made in 690.13(A) for the required system disconnect.

RELOCATED **690.15(B) Isolating Device.** The rating requirements of the former (B) were relocated. The isolation rating requirements are now in this subsection that sets the requirements for an isolating device. The interrupting rating requirements are now found in (D) Equipment Disconnecting Means. The parent text now contains language that was at the end of the subsection and requires that where the isolating device is not rated for interrupting the circuit, it must be so marked. There is a safety issue in opening a disconnect that is not designed to interrupt a load to which this language calls attention, and the parent text language makes it clear that a single isolating device is not required to simultaneously disconnect all current-carrying conductors of the circuit. The equipment disconnect required in 690.13 must do this, but the isolating disconnects required here are not. However, there may be applications where one disconnect would serve both purposes, and if so, it would have to meet the more stringent requirements found in 690.13. Section 690.15(B) continues with four list items showing the acceptable types of isolating devices.

CLARIFIED **690.15(C) Equipment Disconnecting Means.** This was (D) in the 2017 *NEC* but became (C) with the relocation of the text from (C) into (B) for this *Code* cycle. Wording was added to clarify that these devices must have ratings suitable for the operating current and voltage, and for the available fault current. The requirement for all disconnects to be lockable in the open position was relaxed. It now just requires that disconnects, their remote operating means, or the enclosure providing access to the disconnecting means not within sight of and within 10 ft of the equipment be capable of being locked in accordance with 110.25.

The four list items showing the permitted types of disconnect were deleted with a simple reference to 690.13(E) as the types required for both these applications are identical.

CLARIFIED **690.15(D) Type of Disconnecting Means.** This subsection specifies the types of disconnects used to isolate equipment with the requirements in list items (1) or (2).

690.15 PV Disconnecting Means to Isolate PV Equipment

A disconnecting means of the type required in 690.15(D) must be provided to disconnect alternating-current PV modules, fuses, dc-to-dc converters, inverters, and charge controllers from all conductors. ▶Figure 690–35

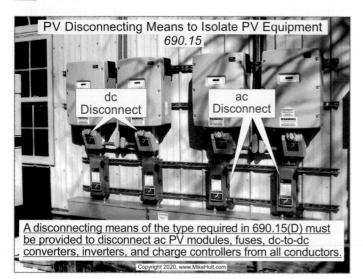

▶Figure 690–35

Author's Comment:

▶ The purpose of a disconnect is to ensure the safe and convenient replacement or maintenance of PV equipment without exposing qualified persons to energized conductors.

(A) Location. Isolating devices or disconnecting means must be placed either within the equipment or within sight and within 10 ft of the equipment. The PV equipment disconnect can be remote from the equipment where the PV disconnect can be remotely operated from within 10 ft of the equipment. ▶Figure 690–36

Where a PV equipment disconnect for equipment operating above 30V is readily accessible to unqualified persons, any enclosure door or hinged cover that exposes live parts when open must be locked or require a tool to open.

(B) Isolating Device. An isolating device is not required to have an interrupting rating. Where an isolating device is not rated for interrupting the circuit current, it must be marked "Do Not Disconnect Under Load" or "Not for Current Interrupting." Isolating devices are not required to simultaneously disconnect all ungrounded circuit conductors and they must be one of the four following types:

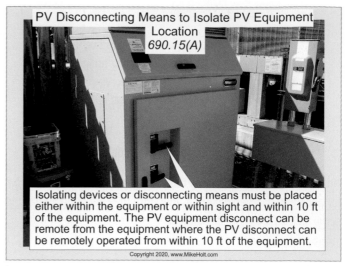

▶Figure 690–36

(1) A mating connector meeting the requirements of 690.33 and listed and identified for use with specific equipment.

(2) A finger-safe fuse holder. ▶Figure 690–37

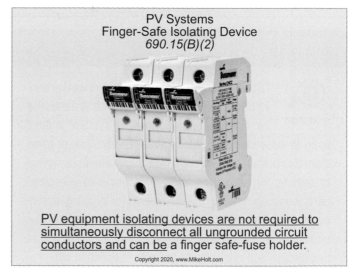

▶Figure 690–37

(3) An isolating device that requires a tool to place in the open (off) position.

(4) An isolating device listed for the intended application.

(C) Equipment Disconnecting Means. The equipment disconnecting means must have a rating sufficient for the maximum circuit current, available fault current, and the voltage that is available at the terminals of the disconnect. The equipment disconnecting means must simultaneously disconnect all ungrounded circuit conductors to which it is connected, must be externally operable without exposing the operator to contact with energized parts, and indicate whether in the open (off) or closed (on) position. Where not within sight and within 10 ft of the equipment, the equipment disconnect or its remote operating device or enclosure providing access to the disconnecting means must be capable of being locked. The provisions for locking must remain in place whether the lock is installed or not [110.25]. The equipment disconnecting means must be of the same type as required in 690.13(E). ▶Figure 690–38

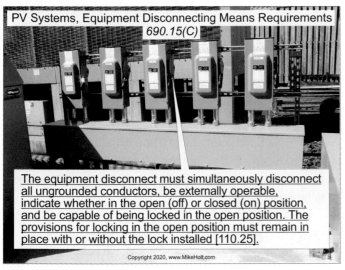

PV Systems, Equipment Disconnecting Means Requirements 690.15(C)

The equipment disconnect must simultaneously disconnect all ungrounded conductors, be externally operable, indicate whether in the open (off) or closed (on) position, and be capable of being locked in the open position. The provisions for locking in the open position must remain in place with or without the lock installed [110.25].

Copyright 2020, www.MikeHolt.com

▶Figure 690–38

An equipment disconnecting means, other than those complying with 690.33, must be marked in accordance with the warning in 690.13(B) if the line and load terminals can be energized in the open position.

Author's Comment:

▶ According to 690.13(B), each PV system disconnect must indicate if it is in the open (off) or closed (on) position and the disconnect must be permanently marked "PV SYSTEM DISCONNECT" or equivalent.

Where the line and load terminals of the PV system disconnect may be energized when the disconnect is in the open (off) position, the disconnect must be marked with the following words or equivalent:

**WARNING—ELECTRIC SHOCK HAZARD
TERMINALS ON THE LINE AND LOAD SIDES
MAY BE ENERGIZED IN THE OPEN POSITION**

The warning markings on the disconnect must be permanently affixed and have sufficient durability to withstand the environment involved [110.21(B)].

Note: A common installation practice is to terminate PV system direct-current circuit conductors on the line side of a disconnect. This practice is more likely to de-energize load-side terminals, blades, and fuses when the disconnect is in the open position and no energized sources are connected to the load side of the disconnect.

(D) Type of Disconnecting Means. Where disconnects are required to isolate equipment, the disconnecting means must be one of the two following types.

(1) A disconnecting means in accordance with 690.15(C) for direct-current circuits having a maximum PV dc current over 30A.

(2) An isolating device in accordance with 690.15(B) for direct-current circuits having a maximum PV dc current not over 30A.

Part IV Wiring Methods and Materials

The title of this part was expanded to include both wiring methods and materials.

Analysis

EXPANDED

Some of the subject matter in this part covers materials as well as wiring methods. This change also aligns this section title with the title of Chapter 3.

690.31 Wiring Methods

There were several changes in this section including clarifications, editorial restructuring and relocation, and modified guidance for the adjustments of conductor ampacities.

Analysis

690.31(A) Wiring Systems. While there are high temperature conductor ampacity tables in Article 310, 105°C and 125°C aren't addressed there for conductors 2,000V volts or less. Revisions to this section and the associated tables clarify the requirements for temperature correction of conductors that may be used in PV systems.

EXPANDED

Table 690.31(A)(a) Correction Factors. The temperature correction factor table now contains only correction factors for 105°C and 125°C conductors. Those correction factors are not available elsewhere in this *Code*. The correction factors for conductors rated 60° C, 75° C, and 90°C were deleted as they are available in Table 310.15(B)(1).

EXPANDED

Table 690.31(A)(b) Ampacities of Insulated Conductors. This new table provides the ampacities of conductors rated 105°C and 125°C. There is a new Informational Note that follows this new table. The note directs the reader to 110.14(C) for conductor temperature limitations due to the termination provisions. The rule in 110.14(C) requires the equipment to be listed and marked for conductor ampacities other than those found in Table 310.16 and is an important consideration for the installer.

NEW

690.31(B) Identification and Grouping. The terms "PV source" and "PV output circuits" were replaced by the inclusive term of "PV system dc circuits." New language permits PV system dc circuits and their associated Class 1 control circuits to be in the same wiring enclosure, cable, or raceway. The last sentence of this subsection requires the PV system circuit conductors to be identified and grouped as required by 690.31(B)(1) and (B)(2).

CLARIFIED

690.31(B) Ex. This exception permits PV circuits that utilize multiconductor jacketed cable, metal clad cable assemblies, or listed wiring harnesses identified for the purpose to occupy the same wiring method as inverter output circuits or other non-PV systems without being separated by a barrier as required in the rule itself.

NEW

690.31(B)(1) Identification. This new language aligns with that found in applicable product safety standards such as those for PV connectors. In order to prevent overvoltage of equipment, or abnormal current flow, it is critical for installers maintain the correct polarity at connections when connecting multiple PV dc circuits in parallel. The rule requires the PV system dc circuit conductors to be identified for their polarity at all termination, connection, and splice points. The permitted means of identification are color coding, marking tape, tagging, or other approved means and language was added to address the identification requirements.

EXPANDED

690.31(C) Cables. The title was changed to match the rules in the section; it said "Single-Conductor Cable" but list item (3) covers multiconductor cables. The new language now requires PV wire or cable, and Type distributed generation (DG) cable to be listed products.

EXPANDED

690.31(C)(1) Single-Conductor Cable. The use of USE-2 remains in the list of permitted cable types; however, it now must also be marked type RHW-2 and sunlight resistant in order to comply with this rule. The supporting and securement requirements were expanded in this *Code* cycle and now require a reduced maximum distance of 24 in. between supports. In previous cycles, up to 4½ ft was allowed. The last change here was a new sentence that says PV wire or cable is permitted in all locations where RHW-2 is permitted. This clarifies that, due to their similar construction, these insulations are suitable to be used in locations such as raceways, both outdoors and indoors.

CLARIFIED

690.31(C)(2) Cable Tray. This rule permits PV system circuits using single-conductor PV wire or cable, or DG cable of any size, with or without a cable tray rating, to be installed in cable tray. It acts as a modification to the rules in 392.10(A) and (B) which restrict the types of cables that can be installed in cable tray and prohibits the installation of single conductors in cable tray in other than industrial occupancies. This modification of the cable tray rules as found in Article 392 is permitted by 90.3.

EXPANDED

690.31(C)(3) Multiconductor Jacketed Cables. This was previously 690.31(D) and was relocated and modified. The title was revised to indicate that the cables to which this subsection applies are jacketed cables. DG cable is a cable that is closely related to TC-ER, but better suited for renewable energy and DG applications.

CLARIFIED

690.31(C)(5) Flexible, Fine-Stranded Cables. This relocated rule calls attention to the requirements in 110.14 for conductors and cables that have stranding other than Types B and C. The rule previously appeared in 690.33(H).

RELOCATED

690.31(D) Direct-Current Circuits on or in Buildings. The title of this subsection which was previously (G), was changed from "Photovoltaic System" to "Direct-Current Circuits on or in Buildings" so it reflects the content of the rule. PV system dc circuits operating at greater than 30V or 8A, run inside of buildings must be contained in metal raceways, in MC cable that complies with 250.118(10), or in a metal enclosure.

RELOCATED

There is a new exception that permits a portion of the conductors used with a PV hazard control system installed in accordance with 690.12(B)(2)(1) to use nonmetallic raceways and enclosures. The substantiation for this exception says that some PV hazard control systems rely on PV array isolation from ground to reduce the shock hazard for firefighters. The high heat from a roof fire could break down the conductor insulation and create a ground fault to metallic wiring methods. Such a ground fault would reduce the effectiveness of the PV hazard control system. The previous 690.31(G)(1), Embedded in Building Surfaces was deleted as it relates to a marking requirement for a wiring method that is no longer used and was needed prior to requirements in 690.12.

690.31(F) Wiring Methods and Mounting Systems. Section 110.13(A) requires electrical equipment to be firmly secured to the surface. PV arrays are often secured to structures that are held in place by "ballast." This is a practical and effective means to reduce roof membrane penetrations. The building and seismic *codes* permit this type of securement limited movement. This revision is a modification of the rule in 110.13 to permit this method. This rule is also intended to make the installer take this movement into account with the selection and installation of the wiring methods used for ballasted systems.

NEW

Part IV. Wiring Methods

690.31 Wiring Methods

(A) Wiring Systems. Wiring methods permitted for PV systems include Chapter 3 wiring methods, wiring systems and fittings listed for use on PV arrays, and wiring that is part of a listed PV system. ▶Figure 690–39

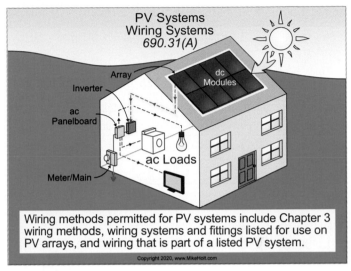

Wiring methods permitted for PV systems include Chapter 3 wiring methods, wiring systems and fittings listed for use on PV arrays, and wiring that is part of a listed PV system.

Copyright 2020, www.MikeHolt.com

▶Figure 690–39

Author's Comment:

▶ An example of a wiring method that is part of a listed system includes the wiring harness of PV micro or mini inverters.

Where PV system direct-current circuit conductors operating at over 30V are readily accessible, the circuit conductors must be guarded, or installed within a raceway or Type MC cable. ▶Figure 690–40

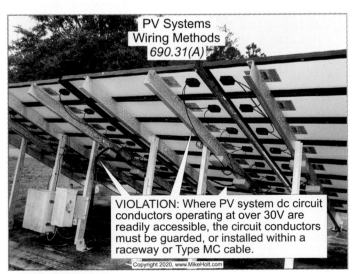

VIOLATION: Where PV system dc circuit conductors operating at over 30V are readily accessible, the circuit conductors must be guarded, or installed within a raceway or Type MC cable.

Copyright 2020, www.MikeHolt.com

▶Figure 690–40

For ambient temperatures greater than 30°C (86°F), temperature corrections for PV circuit conductors operating above 30V must be determined by Table 690.31(A)(a). Conductors with insulation rated at 105°C (221°F) and 125°C (257°F), are permitted to use Table 690.31(A)(b).

Table 690.31(A)(a) Correction Factors

Ambient Temperature (°C)	Temperature Rating of Conductor		Ambient Temperature (°F)
	105°C (221°F)	125°C (257°F)	
31–35	0.97	0.97	87–95
36–40	0.93	0.95	96–104
41–45	0.89	0.92	105–113
46–50	0.86	0.89	114–122
51–55	0.82	0.86	123–131
56–60	0.77	0.83	132–140
61–65	0.73	0.79	141–149
66–70	0.68	0.76	150–158
71–75	0.63	0.73	159–167
76–80	0.58	0.69	168–176
81–85	0.52	0.65	177–185
86–90	0.45	0.61	186–194
91–95	0.37	0.56	195–203
96–100	0.26	0.51	204–212
101–105	–	0.46	213–221
106–110	–	0.4	222–230
111–115	–	0.32	231–239
116–120	–	0.23	240–248

Table 690.31(A)(b) Ampacities of Insulated Conductors Rated up to and Including 2,000V, 105°C Through 125°C (221°F Through 257°F), not More Than Three Current-Carrying Conductors in Raceway, Cable, or Earth (Directly Buried), Based on Ambient Temperature of 30°C (86°F)

Wire Size AWG	PVC, CPE, XLPE 105°C	XLPE, EPDM 125°C
18	15	16
16	19	20
14	29	31
12	36	39
10	46	50
8	64	69
6	81	87
4	109	118
3	129	139
2	143	154
1	168	181
1/0	193	208
2/0	229	247
3/0	263	284
4/0	301	325

Note: See 110.14(C) for conductor temperature limitations due to termination provisions.

(B) Identification and Grouping. PV system direct-current circuits are permitted to occupy the same enclosure, cable, or raceway with Class 1 remote-control circuits of a PV system.

PV system direct-current circuits are not permitted to occupy the same enclosure, cable, or raceway with non-PV system direct-current circuits or inverter output circuits, unless separated by a partition. ▶Figure 690–41

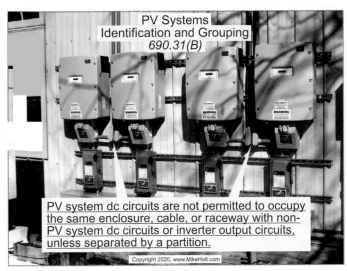

▶Figure 690–41

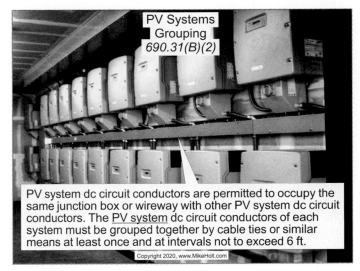

▶Figure 690–42

Exception: PV system direct-current circuits utilizing multiconductor jacketed cable, Type MC cable, or listed wiring harnesses identified for the application are permitted to occupy the same enclosure, cable, or raceway as inverter output circuits and other non-PV system circuits. All conductors, harnesses, or assemblies must have an insulation rating equal to at least the maximum circuit voltage applied to any conductor within the enclosure, cable, or raceway.

PV system direct-current circuits must be identified and grouped as required by 690.31(B)(1) and (B)(2).

(1) Identification. PV system direct-current circuit conductors must have all termination, connection, and splice points permanently marked for polarity by color coding, marking tape, tagging, or other approved means. Conductors relying on other than color coding for polarity identification must be identified by an approved permanent marking means such as labeling, sleeving, or shrink-tubing that is suitable for the conductor size.

The marking must also include the positive sign (+) or the word "POSITIVE" or "POS" for the positive conductor and the negative sign (−) or the word "NEGATIVE" or "NEG" for the negative conductor. Marking must be durable and, in a color, other than green, white, gray, or red.

Exception: Identification is not required where the identification of the conductors is evident by spacing or arrangement.

(2) Grouping. PV system direct-current circuit conductors are permitted to occupy the same junction box or wireway with other PV system direct-current circuit conductors. The PV system direct-current circuit conductors of each system must be grouped together by the use of cable ties or similar means at least once and at intervals not to exceed 6 ft. ▶Figure 690–42

Exception: Grouping is not required if the direct-current circuit enters from a cable or raceway unique to the circuit that makes the grouping obvious.

(C) Cables. Type PV wire, Type PV cable, and Type DG cable must be listed.

(1) Single-Conductor Cable. Single-conductor cable within the PV array must be one of the two following types: ▶Figure 690–43

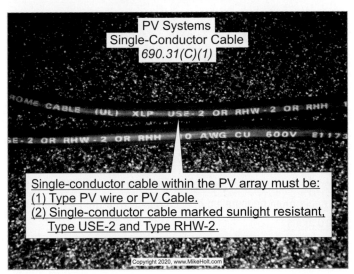

▶Figure 690–43

(1) Type PV wire or PV Cable.

(2) Single-conductor cable marked sunlight resistant, Type USE-2, and Type RHW-2.

Exposed cables must be supported and secured at intervals not to exceed 24 in. by cable ties, straps, hangers, or similar fittings listed and identified for securement and support in outdoor locations.

PV wire or PV cable can be installed in all locations where RHW-2 is permitted.

(2) Cable Tray. Single-conductor Type PV wire, PV cable, or Type DG cable can be installed in cable trays in outdoor locations, provided the cables are supported at intervals not to exceed 12 in. and secured at intervals not to exceed 4½ ft.

Note: Type PV wire, Type PV cable, and Type DC cable have a nonstandard outer diameter. Chapter 9, Table 1 contains the allowable percent of cross section of conduit and tubing for conductors and cables. ▸Figure 690–44

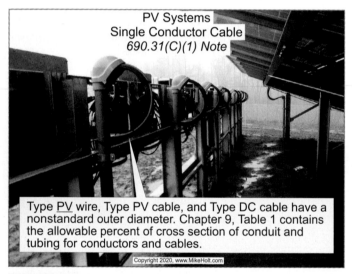

Type PV wire, Type PV cable, and Type DC cable have a nonstandard outer diameter. Chapter 9, Table 1 contains the allowable percent of cross section of conduit and tubing for conductors and cables.

▸Figure 690–44

(3) Multiconductor Jacketed Cable.

Where a multiconductor jacketed cable is part of a listed PV assembly, the cable must be installed in accordance with the manufacturer's instructions.

Multiconductor jacketed cable that is not part of a listed assembly or not covered in this *Code* must be installed in accordance with the product listing.

Multiconductor jacketed cable must be installed in accordance with the two following requirements.

(1) Multiconductor jacketed cable is permitted in raceways located on or in buildings; a raceway is not required for cables installed on rooftops.

(2) Where multiconductor jacketed cable is not installed within a raceway, the cable must be:

(a) Marked "Sunlight Resistant" when in exposed outdoor locations.

(b) Be protected or guarded where subject to physical damage.

(c) Closely follow the surface of support structures.

(d) Be secured at intervals not exceeding 6 ft.

(e) Be secured within 24 in. of mating connectors or entering enclosures.

(f) Marked "Direct Burial" where buried in the earth.

(4) Flexible Cords for Tracking PV Arrays. Flexible cords connected to moving parts of tracking PV arrays must be installed in accordance with Article 400, be identified as hard service cord or portable power cable, be suitable for extra-hard usage, and be listed for outdoor use, water resistant, and sunlight resistant.

Stranded copper PV wire can be used for moving parts of tracking PV arrays if they comply with the minimum number of strands specified in Table 690.31(C)(4).

Table 690.31(C)(4) Minimum PV Wire Strands	
PV Wire AWG	Minimum Strands
18	17
16–10	19
8–4	49
2	130
1 AWG–1,000MCM	259

(5) Flexible, Fine-Stranded Cables. Flexible, fine-stranded cables must terminate on terminals, lugs, devices, or connectors identified for the use of finely stranded conductors in accordance with 110.14. ▸Figure 690–45

(6) Small-Conductor Cables. Single-conductor cables listed for outdoor use that are sunlight resistant and moisture resistant in sizes 16 AWG and 18 AWG are permitted for module interconnections where the cables meet the ampacity requirements of 690.9.

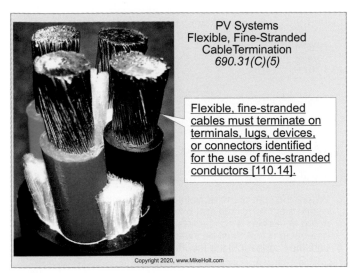

PV Systems
Flexible, Fine-Stranded
Cable Termination
690.31(C)(5)

Flexible, fine-stranded cables must terminate on terminals, lugs, devices, or connectors identified for the use of fine-stranded conductors [110.14].

Copyright 2020, www.MikeHolt.com

▶Figure 690–45

(D) PV System Direct-Current Circuits on or in a Buildings. When the PV system direct-current circuit is located inside a building and the current exceeds 30V or 8A, the PV system direct-current circuit conductors must be installed in a metal raceway, Type MC cable where the armor sheath is listed as an equipment grounding conductor in accordance with 250.118(10), or a metal enclosure. ▶Figure 690–46

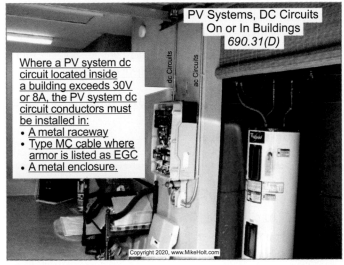

PV Systems, DC Circuits
On or In Buildings
690.31(D)

Where a PV system dc circuit located inside a building exceeds 30V or 8A, the PV system dc circuit conductors must be installed in:
• A metal raceway
• Type MC cable where armor is listed as EGC
• A metal enclosure.

dc Circuits
ac Circuits

Copyright 2020, www.MikeHolt.com

▶Figure 690–46

Exception: PV hazard control system conductors for rapid shutdown application in accordance with 690.12(B)(2)(1) can be provided with listed for use with nonmetallic enclosure(s), nonmetallic raceway(s), and cable of a permitted type other than Type MC, at the point of penetration of the building to the PV hazard control actuator.

Wiring methods for PV system direct-current circuits on or in buildings must comply with the following two additional requirements:

(1) Flexible Wiring Methods. Where flexible metal conduit smaller than trade size ¾ or Type MC cable smaller than 1 in. in diameter containing PV system direct-current circuit conductors are run across ceilings or floor joists, the flexible metal conduit or Type MC cable must be protected by substantial guard strips that are at least as high as the flexible metal conduit or Type MC cable.

Where flexible metal conduit or Type MC cable containing PV system direct-current circuit conductors are run exposed further than 6 ft of their connection to equipment, the flexible metal conduit or Type MC cable must closely follow the building surface or be protected from physical damage by an approved means.

(2) Marking and Labeling. Unless located and arranged so the purpose is evident, the wiring methods and enclosures identified in (1), (2), and (3) containing PV system direct-current circuit conductors must be marked with a permanent label containing the words "**PHOTOVOLTAIC POWER SOURCE**" or "**SOLAR PV DC CIRCUIT**." ▶Figure 690–47

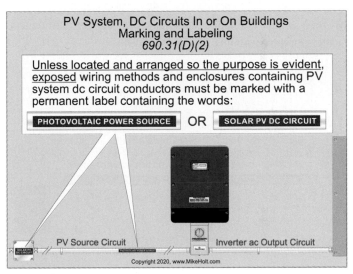

PV System, DC Circuits In or On Buildings
Marking and Labeling
690.31(D)(2)

Unless located and arranged so the purpose is evident, exposed wiring methods and enclosures containing PV system dc circuit conductors must be marked with a permanent label containing the words:

PHOTOVOLTAIC POWER SOURCE   OR   SOLAR PV DC CIRCUIT

PV Source Circuit   Inverter ac Output Circuit

Copyright 2020, www.MikeHolt.com

▶Figure 690–47

(1) Exposed raceways, cable trays, and other wiring methods.

(2) Covers or enclosures of pull boxes and junction boxes.

(3) Conduit bodies having conduit unused openings.

The label must be visible after installation and all letters must be capitalized and be a minimum height of ⅜ in. in white on a red background. ▶Figure 690–48

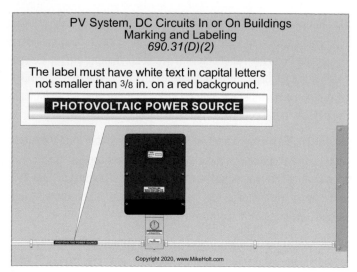

▶Figure 690–48

Labels must appear on every section of the wiring system that is separated by enclosures, walls, partitions, ceilings, or floors. Spacing between labels must not be more than 10 ft, and the label must be suitable for the environment. ▶Figure 690–49

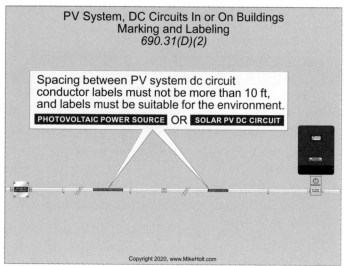

▶Figure 690–49

(E) Bipolar Circuits. Where the sum of the maximum PV direct-current voltages of two monopole circuits connected in a manner to create a bipolar circuit exceeds the maximum voltage rating of the circuit conductors, the two conductors of each monopole circuit must be installed in separate raceways until they connect to the inverter. ▶Figure 690–50

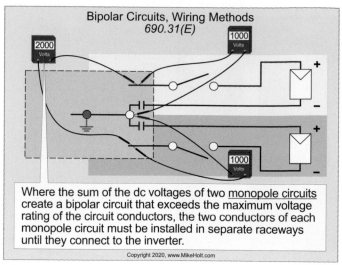

▶Figure 690–50

The disconnect and overcurrent protective devices for each monopole circuit of a bipolar circuit must be in separate enclosures.

Exception: Listed switchgear rated for the maximum voltage between circuits and containing a physical barrier separating the disconnect for each monopole circuit is permitted instead of two separate disconnect enclosures.

(F) Wiring Methods and Mounting Systems. Roof-mounted PV array mounting systems are permitted to be held in place with an approved means other than those required by 110.13 and must utilize wiring methods that allow any expected movement of the array.

Note: Expected movement of unattached PV arrays is often included in structural calculations.

690.33 Connectors

This rule was expanded to include mating connectors as an additional method of circuit interruption, and a new Informational Note follows new list item (3).

Analysis

EXPANDED

690.33(D) Interruption of Circuit. This was (E) in the 2017 *NEC* but was moved as a result of the deletion of the previous (D). In addition to the two interruption methods in the 2017 *Code*, a third method was added.

That method covers connectors supplied as part of listed equipment and used in accordance with the provided instructions. This allows for the use of connectors that are not included in the first two list items. The new Informational Note informs the reader that some listed equipment, such as microinverters, are evaluated to make use of connectors as disconnect devices, even though the connectors are marked "Do Not Disconnect Under Load" or "Not for Current Interrupting."

Note: Some listed equipment, such as micro inverters, are evaluated to make use of mating connectors as disconnect devices even though the mating connectors are marked as "Do Not Disconnect Under Load" or "Not for Current Interrupting."

Author's Comment:

▸ How would anyone other than the original installer, know this information in the note unless he or she has access to and has read the equipment instructions?

690.33 Connectors

(D) Interruption of Circuit. <u>Mating</u> <u>connectors</u> must comply with one of the three following requirements. ▸Figure 690–51

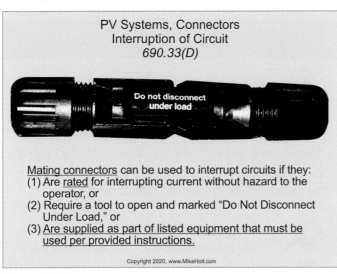

PV Systems, Connectors
Interruption of Circuit
690.33(D)

Mating connectors can be used to interrupt circuits if they:
(1) Are <u>rated</u> for interrupting current without hazard to the operator, or
(2) Require a tool to open and marked "Do Not Disconnect Under Load," or
(3) <u>Are supplied as part of listed equipment that must be used per provided instructions.</u>

Copyright 2020, www.MikeHolt.com

▸Figure 690–51

(1) Mating connectors must be <u>rated</u> to interrupt current without hazard to the operator.

(2) A tool must be required to open the mating connector and the mating connectors must have a marking "Do Not Disconnect Under Load" or "Not for Current Interrupting."

(3) <u>Mating connectors supplied as part of listed equipment must be used in accordance with instructions provided with the listed connected equipment.</u>

690.41 System Grounding

Ground-fault protection for systems that operate at 30V or less, or 8A or less is no longer required, and (B)(3) was added to require visible indication of ground faults.

Analysis

REDUCED

690.41(B) Ground-Fault Protection. The purpose of ground-fault protection is to reduce the fire hazard from PV systems. Small systems do not pose a serious fire hazard, so the requirement to provide ground-fault protection for systems that operate at 30V or less and at 70W or less was removed. A new Informational Note to this rule advises the user that not all inverters, charge controllers, or dc-to-dc converters include ground-fault protection. Equipment that does not have such protection will have a statement in the manual telling the installer the unit is not provided with a ground-fault protection device.

CLARIFIED

690.41(B)(1) Ground-Fault Detection. A new sentence was added to address dc-to-dc converters that are not listed as providing ground-fault protection. The new sentence requires such equipment to have listed ground-fault protection equipment installed and requires the ground fault equipment to be identified for use with the dc-to-dc equipment.

A new Informational Note advises that some dc-to-dc converters that do not have integral ground-fault protection on their input side, may prevent other ground-fault protective equipment from functioning properly on portions of PV system dc circuits.

NEW

690.41(B)(3) Indication of Faults. This new subsection requires that where the equipment performing ground-fault protection is mounted in not readily accessible locations an indication of a ground fault at a readily accessible location must be provided. Quite often the device that provides the ground-fault protection is placed in areas that are not readily visible, and remote indication is required. A new Informational Note gives examples of types of remote indications. Those may be, but are not limited to, remote indicator lights, display monitors, signal to a monitored alarm system, or notification by web-based services.

690.41 System Grounding

(B) Ground-Fault Protection. PV system direct-current circuits that exceed 30V or 8A must be provided with ground-fault protection meeting the following two requirements.

Note: Not all inverters, charge controllers, or dc-to-dc converters include ground-fault protection. Equipment that does not have ground-fault protection often includes the following statement in the instruction manual: "Warning: This unit is not provided with a GFCI device."

(1) Ground-Fault Detection. A ground-fault protection device is required to be listed to detect ground fault(s) in the PV system direct-current circuit conductors.

Where ground-fault protection is required for dc-to-dc converter circuits and the dc-to-dc converter is not listed as providing ground-fault protection, listed ground-fault protection equipment identified for the dc-to-dc converter and the ground-fault protective device must be installed.

Note: Some dc-to-dc converters without integral ground-fault protection on their input side can prevent other ground-fault protection equipment from properly functioning on portions of PV system direct-current circuits.

(2) Faulted Circuits. A PV system direct-current circuit having a ground fault must have the fault controlled by one of the three following methods.

(1) The PV system direct-current circuit having the ground fault must be automatically disconnected.

(2) A PV system direct-current circuit having the ground fault must cause the ground-fault protection devices to automatically cease to supply power to output circuits. For functionally grounded PV

systems, the ground-fault protection device must interrupt the faulted PV system direct-current circuits from the ground reference.

(3) Indication of Faults. Ground-fault protection devices must provide an indication of a ground fault at a readily accessible location.

Note: Examples of indication include, but are not limited, to remote indicator light, display, monitor, signal to a monitored alarm system, or receipt of notification by web-based services.

690.43 Equipment Grounding and Bonding

The term "grounded" was replaced with language that requires the equipment to be connected to an equipment grounding conductor, and a new subsection (D) addresses the bonding methods for PV systems over 250V to ground.

Analysis

CLARIFIED

This section required exposed noncurrent-carrying metal parts of PV module frames, electrical equipment, and conductor enclosures be "grounded." The word "grounded" was replaced with "connected to an equipment grounding conductor." This is part of the ongoing process to use the correct *Code* language for grounding and bonding throughout the *NEC*.

NEW

690.43(D) Bonding for Over 250V. If the voltage is over 250V the rule in 250.97 applies and sends you to the service bonding requirement of 250.82(B). This is because of the higher energy levels typically associated with the higher voltage circuits.

This new rule says that these bonding requirements apply to only solidly grounded PV system circuits operating at over 250V to ground. The PV systems that are not solidly grounded are current limited and have limited fault current to ground as a result of the required ground-fault protection. Because of functional grounding, where there may be a measured voltage to ground, the ground-fault current lower than a utility supply and the control of this fault current is located within the ground-fault protection equipment, not the operation of a large circuit protector closer to the source. This lower fault current permits standard bonding connections and does not require the more robust connections required by 250.97.

690.43 Equipment Grounding and Bonding

Exposed metal parts of PV module frames, electrical equipment, and any enclosure containing PV system conductors <u>must be connected to the</u> PV system <u>circuit equipment grounding conductor</u> in accordance with 250.134. ▸Figure 690–52

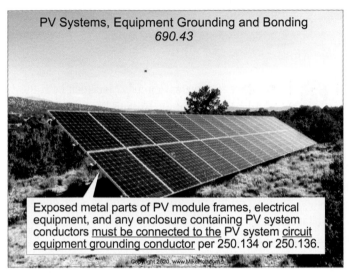

▸Figure 690–52

▸ According to 250.134, metal parts of equipment, raceways, and enclosures must be connected to an equipment grounding conductor by connecting to one of the equipment grounding conductor types identified in 250.118(2) through (14), or the equipment grounding conductor of the wire type <u>contained within the same wiring method with</u> the circuit conductors. However, the equipment grounding conductor for a direct-current circuit can be run separately from the circuit conductors when within the array [250.134 Ex 2, 690.31(C), and 690.46].

(A) Photovoltaic Module Mounting Systems and Devices. Devices listed, labeled, and identified for bonding PV modules can be used to secure PV module frames to metal support structures, to bond PV module frames to the metal support structure, and to bond PV modules to adjacent PV modules. ▸Figure 690–53 and ▸Figure 690–54

(B) Equipment Secured to Grounded Metal Support Structure. Metallic support structures listed, labeled, and identified for bonding and grounding the metal parts of PV systems can be used to bond PV equipment to the metal support structure that has been connected to the PV circuit <u>equipment grounding conductor.</u>

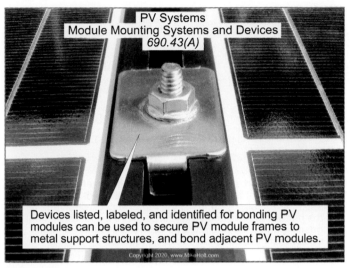

▸Figure 690–53

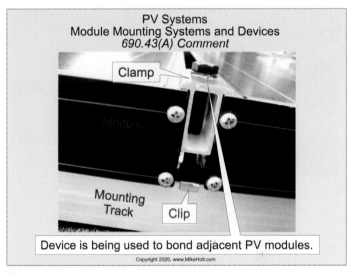

▸Figure 690–54

Metallic support structures used as an equipment grounding conductor must have identified bonding jumpers between separate metallic sections of the metal support structure, or the metal support structure must be identified for equipment bonding purposes and must be connected to the PV circuit <u>equipment grounding conductor</u> as required by 690.43. ▸Figure 690–55

(C) With Circuit Conductors. When PV system circuit conductors leave the vicinity of the PV array, the equipment grounding conductors for the PV system and metal support structure must be contained within the same raceway, cable, or otherwise run with the PV circuit conductor. ▸Figure 690–56

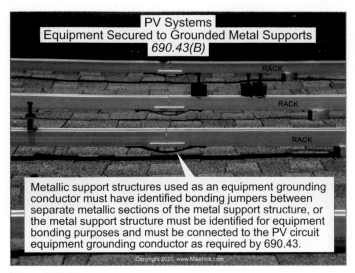

▸Figure 690–55

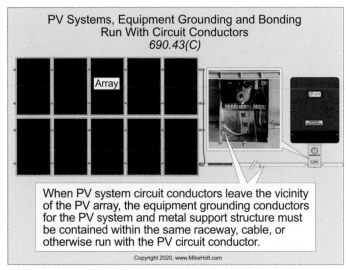

▸Figure 690–56

(D) Bonding Over 250V. The bonding requirements contained in 250.97 apply only to solidly grounded PV system circuits operating over 250V to ground. According to 310.3(C), conductors 8 AWG and larger installed in a raceway must be stranded. According to 250.120(C), exposed equipment grounding conductors 8 AWG (solid or stranded) and smaller for direct-current circuits [250.134(B) Ex.2], such as required by 690.45 for solar PV systems are permitted to be run separately from the circuit conductors. Where the 8 AWG (solid or stranded) or smaller exposed equipment grounding conductor is subject to physical damage, it must be installed within a raceway or cable.

690.45 Size of Equipment Grounding Conductors

Equipment grounding conductors for PV system circuits are no longer required to be increased in size due to voltage-drop considerations.

Analysis

EDITED The term "PV system circuits" includes both PV source and PV output circuits, including those utilizing dc-to-dc converters, so those two terms were replaced by "PV system circuits." The rule requires the equipment grounding conductor to be sized in accordance with 250.122 and is not subject to being increased in size when supply conductors are increased in size due to voltage drop.

690.45 Size of Equipment Grounding Conductors

Equipment grounding conductors for PV system circuits must be sized in accordance with 250.122, based on the circuit overcurrent protection ampere rating. ▸Figure 690–57

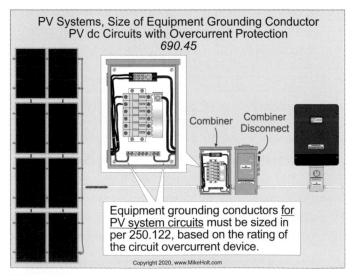

▸Figure 690–57

Where no overcurrent protective device is used in the PV system direct-current circuit, the equipment grounding conductor for the PV system direct-current circuit must be sized in accordance with Table 250.122 based on an assumed overcurrent device sized in accordance with 690.9(B) for the PV system direct-current circuit.

Equipment grounding conductors are not required to be increased in size to address voltage-drop considerations. ▶Figure 690–58

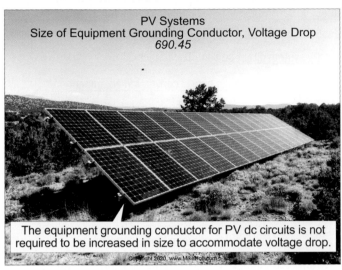

▶Figure 690–58

690.47 Grounding Electrode System

The word "Auxiliary" was deleted from the title of subsection (B).

Analysis

EDITED **690.47(B) Grounding Electrodes and Grounding Electrode Conductors.** This revision was to permit the subsection to apply to all grounding electrodes associated with the PV system. It now simply provides guidance as to how to apply several rules from Article 250 to equipment specific to a PV system. There are editorial changes and the structural steel reference was corrected to reflect changes made in Article 250 in the 2017 *Code* cycle.

690.47 Grounding Electrode System

(B) Grounding Electrodes and Grounding Electrode Conductors. Additional grounding electrodes are permitted to be installed in accordance with 250.52 or 250.54 and they are permitted to be connected directly to the PV frames or support structure. The conductor used for this purpose must be sized in accordance with 250.66. ▶Figure 690–59

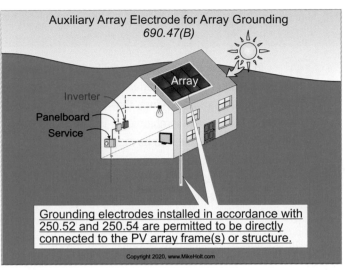

▶Figure 690–59

A support structure for a ground-mounted PV array can be considered a grounding electrode if it meets the requirements of 250.52. ▶Figure 690–60

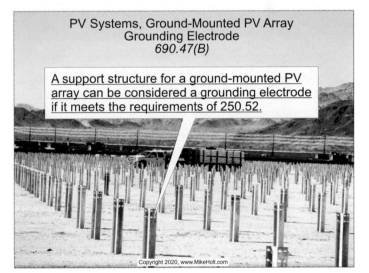

▶Figure 690–60

PV arrays mounted on buildings are permitted to use the metal structural frame of the building if the requirements of 250.68(C)(2) are met.

690.51 Modules and Alternating-Current Modules

Sections 690.51 and 690.52 were combined and simplified to remove marking requirements that are found in the listing standard.

Analysis

CLARIFIED In the previous *NEC*, 690.51 applied to dc modules and 690.52 to ac modules; both contained a laundry list of markings that were required on the modules. This revision combines the two sections into one and simply requires them to be marked in accordance with the listing. This eliminates rules the installer does not need and permits the listing standard to change the marking requirements without necessitating a *Code* change.

690.51 Modules and Alternating-Current Modules

Modules and alternating-current modules must be marked in accordance with their listing.

690.53 DC PV Circuits

This section was editorially simplified and retitled to reflect the current *NEC* term of "PV" instead of "Photovoltaic," and was also revised to say that the required voltage label be both permanent and readily visible.

Analysis

CLARIFIED The voltage label in the previous *Code* was required only to be permanent. This revision requires it to be both permanent and readily visible. It could be permanent but not visible, and this change requires it be both. Coupled with this change is an allowance to provide this label at any suitable location, not at every disconnect in the system regardless of location. Since some PV systems could have multiple voltages present within equipment, the highest maximum dc voltage is the only one required on this label. The voltage label is required as there are multiple system configurations that can affect the maximum system dc voltage. This information is needed by workers for the proper selection of the PPE and tools needed when servicing the equipment so it needs to be clearly and effectively communicated.

690.53 Direct-Current PV Circuit Label

A permanent readily visible label indicating the maximum PV system direct-current voltage [690.7] must be installed at one of the three following locations. ▶Figure 690–61

(1) PV system direct-current disconnect

(2) PV system electronic power conversion equipment

(3) Distribution equipment associated with the PV system

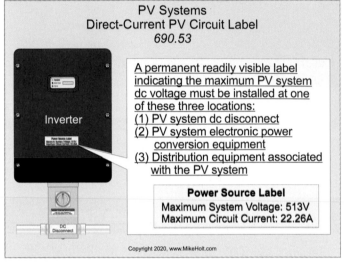

PV Systems
Direct-Current PV Circuit Label
690.53

A permanent readily visible label indicating the maximum PV system dc voltage must be installed at one of these three locations:
(1) PV system dc disconnect
(2) PV system electronic power conversion equipment
(3) Distribution equipment associated with the PV system

Power Source Label
Maximum System Voltage: 513V
Maximum Circuit Current: 22.26A

Copyright 2020, www.MikeHolt.com

▶Figure 690–61

690.56 Identification of Power Sources

The rules for the identification of power sources for stand-alone systems were revised to reference the identification requirements found in Chapter 7 of the *Code*.

Analysis

EDITED **690.56(A) Facilities with Stand-Alone Systems.** This section previously specified the requirements for plaques or directories for stand-alone PV systems. Article 710 addresses those systems, so this rule was modified to direct the user to 710.10 for the requirement to install plaques and directories.

690.56(B) Facilities with Utility Services and Photovoltaic Systems. This rule expanded the requirement for plaques or directories to include identification requirements for PV systems connected to dc microgrids as well as to other interconnected electric power production sources. Since PV systems may also be connected to dc microgrids, a reference to 712.10 was added for the plaques or directories that are required in that case.

This additional reference is in addition to the previous reference to 705.10 for interconnected electric power production sources and the removal of prescription language in favor of pointers to other sections was part of a broad effort across multiple articles to standardize any placard or directory requirements related to the presence of any onsite power sources. Previously, some power sources required identification, but some did not. Additionally, the different placards or directories could be placed in different locations. Keeping all requirements in 710 and 712 should prevent diversion of requirements in future cycles.

690.56(C) Buildings with Rapid Shutdown. This section was revised to list the locations where the rapid shutdown label is required. The rule requires buildings that have a PV system to have a label located at each service equipment location to which the PV systems are connected, or at an approved readily visible location. This label must indicate the location of all identified rapid shutdown initiation devices if they are not in the same place.

The figure that was in 690.56(C)(1) and a mandatory requirement in the 2017 *NEC* is now Informational Figure 690.56(C). It is intended to be an example of a label that would be suitable, but it is not required to look exactly like the figure. An allowance is still provided for cases where existing PV systems might be present that were installed prior to these requirements.

690.56 Identification of Power Sources

(A) Stand-Alone Systems. A building with a stand-alone PV system must have a permanent <u>plaque or directory installed in accordance with 710.10</u>. ▸Figure 690–62

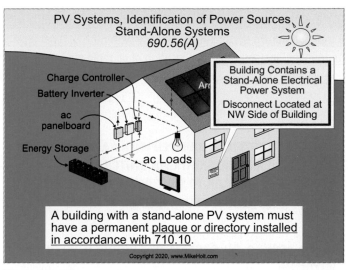

▸Figure 690–62

Author's Comment:

▸ A permanent plaque or directory must be installed at a building supplied by a stand-alone system at each service equipment location or at an approved readily visible location [710.10].

(B) Building with Utility Power and PV Systems. A building having both utility power and an interactive PV system(s) must have a plaque or directory installed in accordance with 705.10 <u>and 712.10</u>. ▸Figure 690–63

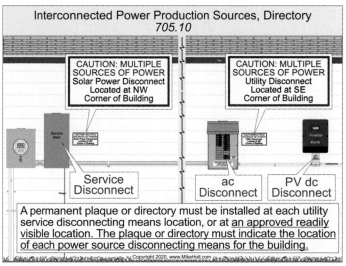

▸Figure 690–63

(C) Building with Rapid Shutdown System(s). A building with a rapid shutdown system in accordance with 690.12 must have a permanent label indicating the location of all rapid shutdown initiation devices. The label must be located at each service location or at an approved readily visible location and it must include a diagram of a building with a roof with the following words:

SOLAR PV SYSTEM IS EQUIPPED WITH RAPID SHUTDOWN
TURN RAPID SHUTDOWN SWITCH TO THE
"OFF" POSITION TO SHUT DOWN PV SYSTEM
AND REDUCE SHOCK HAZARD IN ARRAY

The title "**SOLAR PV SYSTEM IS EQUIPPED WITH RAPID SHUTDOWN**" must have capitalized characters with a minimum height of ⅜ in. in black on a yellow background. The words "**TURN RAPID SHUTDOWN SWITCH TO THE "OFF" POSITION TO SHUT DOWN PV SYSTEM AND REDUCE SHOCK HAZARD IN ARRAY**" must be capitalized with a minimum height of ³⁄₁₆ in. in black on a white background. ▶Figure 690–64

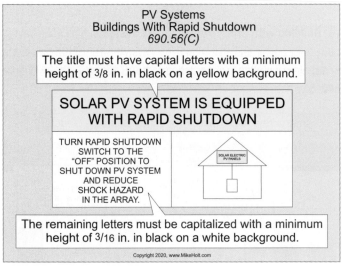

▶Figure 690–64

Note: See Informational Note Figure 690.56(C).

(1) Buildings with More Than One Rapid Shutdown Type. A building having more than one rapid shutdown system or a building without a rapid shutdown system must have a label with a detailed plan view diagram of the roof showing each PV system with a dotted line around areas that remain energized after the rapid shutdown has been initiated.

(2) Rapid Shutdown Switch. A rapid shutdown switch must have a label that includes the following wording located on or no more than 3 ft from the switch: "**RAPID SHUTDOWN SWITCH FOR SOLAR PV SYSTEM.**"

The rapid shutdown label must be reflective with all letters capitalized and having a minimum height of 3⁄8 in. in white on a red background.

ARTICLE 691

LARGE-SCALE PHOTOVOLTAIC (PV) ELECTRIC SUPPLY STATIONS

Introduction to Article 691—Large-Scale Photovoltaic (PV) Electric Supply Stations

The general requirements for solar photovoltaic (PV) systems are covered by Article 690. That is, until such installations become large enough to be called a large-scale PV electric supply station. If they are not under exclusive utility control, they are covered by Article 691.

A PV system is considered a large-scale PV electric supply station when its production capacity is 5,000 kW or greater. When systems have this much energy available, they pose a much greater hazard than, for example, the small-scale systems you find in single-residence applications.

Because of the extra hazard, a documented review of the electrical portion of the engineered design by a licensed professional engineer is necessary to ensure their safe operation. That review is part of what Article 691 requires beyond simply meeting the Article 690 requirements.

This article specifies several items the documented review must include, such as the grounding details for fencing and compliance with the engineered design.

The title of the article was changed. The term "power production facility" was only used in the article title and in the scope of the article. The term "supply station" is used throughout the rest of the article and better aligns the *NEC* and the *NESC* which is describing the same equipment in both *Codes*. Given the size of these installations, there is a lot of overlap with the *National Electric Safety Code*, *NESC*, which is used by the utilities and this change will help avoid any confusion between the two *Codes*.

691.1 Scope

This article now applies to the installation of large-scale PV electric supply stations with an inverter generating capacity of no less than 5,000 kW and not under an electric utility's control.

Analysis

CLARIFIED The term "supply station" is already used in the *Code* but the term "power production facility" was used in only the former title of 691 and in its scope statement. The term "supply station" better correlates the *NEC* and the NESC.

Informational Note 3 was added which directs the reader to the new Informational Note Figure 691.1. This figure shows a single line drawing of a large-scale PV electric supply station. Notes in the drawing indicate that custom designs are used, some components are optional, that the drawing is for informational purposes only, and it is not representative of all potential configurations.

691.1 Scope

This article covers the installation of large-scale PV electric <u>supply stations with an inverter</u> generating capacity of not less than 5,000 kW and not under the electric utility control. ▶Figure 691–1

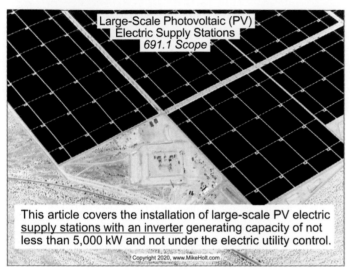

Large-Scale Photovoltaic (PV)
Electric Supply Stations
691.1 Scope

This article covers the installation of large-scale PV electric <u>supply stations with an inverter</u> generating capacity of not less than 5,000 kW and not under the electric utility control.

Copyright 2020, www.MikeHolt.com

▶Figure 691–1

Note 1: Facilities covered by this article have specific design and safety features unique to large-scale PV facilities and are operated for the sole purpose of providing electric supply to a system operated by a regulated utility for the transfer of electric energy.

Note 2: Section 90.2(B)(5) includes information about utility-owned properties not covered under this *Code*. For additional information on electric supply stations, see ANSI/IEEE C2, *National Electrical Safety Code*.

Note 3: <u>See Figure 691.1 Identification of Large-Scale PV Electric Supply Station Components in the *NEC*.</u>

Author's Comment:

▸ The term Generating Capacity that previously appeared in 691.2 has been relocated to Article 100 and combined with a similar term from Article 690 into Inverter Generating Capacity. This move now allows this same term to be used in other Articles in future cycles without creating divergent definitions and is a small piece of the global restricting of definitions throughout the *Code*.

691.9 Disconnecting Means for Isolating Photovoltaic Equipment

The language in this section and its title were revised to clarify that the purpose of the PV disconnecting equipment is isolation.

Analysis

CLARIFIED This requirement is to isolate the equipment so it can be worked on safely. The language as to the location of the isolating device was simplified; it is not required to be within sight of the equipment and may be remote from the equipment. The previous *Code* permitted this where written safety procedures and conditions of maintenance and supervision ensured that only qualified people would service the equipment. Given the requirement in 691.4(2) to restrict access, it is unlikely unqualified people would even have access to the large-scale PV equipment. A new last sentence was added to say the engineering design required by 691.6 must document disconnection procedures and means for isolating the equipment. This new language replaces the previous requirement requiring written safety procedures. The engineering design documents are now required to provide those written procedures.

691.9 Disconnect for Isolating Photovoltaic Equipment

<u>Isolating devices are not required to be located within sight of equipment and they may be located remotely from equipment.</u>

<u>The engineered design required by 691.6 must document disconnection procedures and means of isolating equipment.</u>

Note: <u>For information on electrical system maintenance, see NFPA 70B, *Recommended Practice for Electrical Equipment Maintenance*. For information on written procedures and conditions of maintenance, including lockout/tagout procedures, see NFPA 70E, *Standard for Electrical Safety in the Workplace*.</u>

Buildings whose sole purpose is to house and protect supply station equipment are not required to include a rapid shutdown function to reduce shock hazard <u>for firefighters</u> [690.12]. Written standard operating procedures must be available at the site detailing necessary shutdown procedures in the event of an emergency.

691.11 Fence Bonding and Grounding

This title change recognizes that any metal fencing in proximity to the large-scale energy system may require bonding and not grounding.

Analysis

CLARIFIED A new Informational Note references 250.194 for the bonding and grounding requirements for the fence that encloses the substation portions of an electric supply station. These areas have the possibility of very high step and touch potentials under fault conditions. The second part of the note tells the *Code* user that fencing enclosing other parts of the PV installation should be assessed as to the associated step and touch potential based on the proximity of the fence to overhead lines, generation, and distribution.

The previous language was being interpreted as requiring all the PV system fencing to be bonded and grounded in accordance with the requirements of 250.194. That is not necessary; it is required only where the step and touch potential is unreasonably high.

The fence must be bonded and grounded in accordance with the engineered design required by 691.6.

691.11 Fence Bonding and Grounding

Fence grounding requirements and details must be included in the documentation required in 691.6.

Note: See 250.194 for fence bonding and grounding requirements operating at more than 1,000V. Grounding requirements for other portions of electric supply station fencing are assessed based on the presence of overhead conductors, proximity to generation and distribution equipment, and associated step and touch potential.

WIND ELECTRIC SYSTEMS

Introduction to Article 694—Wind Electric Systems

The practice of converting the force of the wind into energy to perform work, is a concept that has been around for millennia. Wind turbines come in a variety of shapes and sizes and up to hundreds of feet in height. They are sometimes installed on top of existing structures or as stand-alone independent units on land and offshore as part of a lake or ocean "wind farm." They can contain one or more generators and have equipment just like other types of alternative energy (AE) sources, (such as PV systems), which may include, alternators, generators, inverters, combiners, controllers, automatic transfer switches and so forth. As such, many of the *NEC* rules and requirements for other forms of alternative energy, are the same for wind turbine systems. We've included the article scope and a few definitions but there were no changes to these.

694.1 Scope

Article 694 applies to wind turbine electric systems that may consist of one or more wind electric generators and their related equipment such as, alternators, generators, inverters, controllers, and other associated equipment.

694.2 Definitions

The definitions in this section apply only within this article.

Diversion Charge Controller. Equipment that regulates the charging process of a battery or other energy storage device by diverting power from energy storage to dc or ac loads, or to an interconnected utility service.

Diversion Load. A load connected to a diversion charge controller or diversion load controller, also known as a "dump load."

Nacelle. An enclosure housing the alternator and other parts of a wind turbine.

694.22 Additional Provisions

New language (C) to specifies that the wind electric system disconnect, or manual shutdown button be located at a readily accessible exterior location for one- and two-family dwellings.

Analysis

CLARIFIED

694.22(C)(1) Requirements for Disconnecting Means. A new last sentence requires that one- and two-family dwellings having a wind system, have a disconnecting means or a manual shutdown switch located at a readily accessible location outside the building. There was already a requirement for a readily accessible shutdown switch for larger turbines in 694.23. As with disconnection and shutdown requirements for other onsite sources in other articles, this requirement to make a means of shutdown or disconnection accessible on the outside of a one- or two-family dwelling is intended to provide first responders with the ability to reduce the risk of electric shock from any live conductors within these buildings in case of an emergency.

694.54 Identification of Power Sources

This section was editorially revised to reference the identification requirements found in other articles instead of duplicating the information here.

Analysis

EDITED This had language that specified the details of the power source identification requirements in the 2017 *NEC*. Since those requirements are spelled out in other articles, this section was revised to reference them. The long paragraphs were changed to a reference to the other articles in order to keep identification of all onsite power sources the same.

New parent text says that wind systems must be identified according to 694.54(A) through (C).

The requirement in (C) was not in the 2017 *Code*, but wind systems can be installed as stand-alone systems, so that information was added.

ARTICLE
695

FIRE PUMPS

Introduction to Article 695—Fire Pumps

The general philosophy behind most *Code* requirements is to provide circuit overcurrent protection that will shut down equipment before allowing the supply conductors to overheat and become damaged from overload. Article 695 departs from this philosophy. The idea is that the fire pump motor must keep running no matter what! It supplies water to a facility's fire protection piping, which in turn supplies water to the sprinkler system and fire hoses so the philosophy is that it is better to sacrifice the fire pump rather than the entire structure. This article contains many requirements to make certain an uninterrupted supply of water is maintained.

Some of these requirements are obvious. For example, locating the pump where its exposure to fire is minimized, which is usually in a separate space with fire rated construction. It is important that the source of power is maintained for both the fire pump and its jockey (pressure maintenance) pump. Also, fire pump wiring must remain independent of all other wiring. Some of the requirements of Article 695 seem wrong at first glance, until you remember why that fire pump is there in the first place. For example, the disconnect must be designed to be lockable in the closed position. You would normally expect it to be lockable in the open position because other articles require that for the safety of maintenance personnel. But the fire pump runs to ensure the safety of an entire facility and everyone within. For the same reason, fire pump power circuits cannot have automatic overcurrent protection against overloads.

Remember, the fire pump must be kept in service, even if doing so damages or destroys the pump. It is better to sacrifice the pump, than to save the fire pump and lose the facility. The intent of this article is to allow enough time for building occupants to escape and, if possible, to save the facility.

695.3 Power Source(s) for Electric Motor-Driven Fire Pumps

The exception to (B)(1) and (2) was revised to permit a redundant electric fire pump with an independent source of power in lieu of redundant power sources and an automatic transfer switch. Changes to (C)(3) provide more specific requirements for the selective coordination of fire pump power supplies among other things.

Analysis

CLARIFIED

695.3(B)(2) Ex Individual Source and On-Site Standby Generator. The exception to (1) and (2) was modified to match the requirements of NPFA 20, *Standard for the Installation of Stationary Pumps for Fire Protection*. That standard governs the operational and functional requirements, and the *NEC* governs only the electrical installation required to meet those operational and functional requirements.

CLARIFIED **695.3(C)(3) Selective Coordination.** The language of this section is identical to that of 645.47. The words "disconnecting means" were deleted as, on campus type systems, the selective coordination may be provided by protective relays. This language change clarifies the system must be selectively coordinated regardless of the type of device used.

The requirement is now for the overcurrent protective device to be rated to carry indefinitely the sum of the locked-rotor current of the largest fire pump motor, and the full load-current of all other pump motors and accessory equipment.

695.3 Electric Power Source(s)

(B) Multiple Sources. If reliable power cannot be obtained from a source described in 695.3(A), power must be supplied by any of the following:

(1) Individual Sources. A combination of two or more of the sources from 695.3(A) approved by the authority having jurisdiction.

(2) Individual Source and On-Site Standby Generator. A combination of one of the sources in 695.3(A) and a generator complying with 695.3(D) and approved by the authority having jurisdiction.

Ex to (1) and (2): An alternate source of power is not required where a back-up, engine, steam turbine or electric motor driven fire pump with an independent power source in accordance with 695.3(A) or (C) is installed.

695.4 Continuity of Power

Section 695.4(B) now requires the use of the pressure maintenance (jockey) pump's full-load current instead of its locked-rotor current when selecting the proper overcurrent protective device(s).

Analysis

REDUCED **695.4(B)(2) Connection Through Disconnecting Means and Overcurrent Device.** The requirement for the locked-rotor current of the pressure maintenance (jockey) pump to be included was removed. NFPA 20, *Standard for the Installation of Stationary Pumps for Fire Protection* requires the inclusion of the full-load current of that pump; not the locked-rotor current.

695.4 Continuity of Power

(B) Connection Through Disconnect and Overcurrent Device.

(1) Number of Disconnecting Means

(a) A single means of disconnect is permitted to be installed between the fire pump electric supply and:

(1) A listed controller,

(2) A listed power transfer switch, or

(3) A combination controller/power transfer switch.

(2) Overcurrent Device Selection.

(a) Individual Sources. Overcurrent protection for individual must comply with the following:

(1) The overcurrent protective device(s) must be selected or set to carry indefinitely the sum of the locked-rotor current of the largest fire pump motor and <u>100 percent of the full-load current of the other pump motors</u> and fire pump's accessory equipment. ▶Figure 695–1

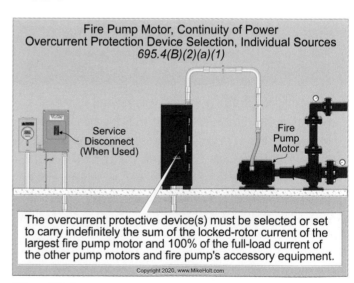

Fire Pump Motor, Continuity of Power
Overcurrent Protection Device Selection, Individual Sources
695.4(B)(2)(a)(1)

Service Disconnect (When Used)

Fire Pump Motor

The overcurrent protective device(s) must be selected or set to carry indefinitely the sum of the locked-rotor current of the largest fire pump motor and 100% of the full-load current of the other pump motors and fire pump's accessory equipment.

Copyright 2020, www.MikeHolt.com

▶Figure 695–1

▶ **Fire Pump Overcurrent Size Example**

Question: What size overcurrent protective device and conductor is required for a 25 hp, 460V, three-phase fire pump motor that has a lock rotor current rating of 183A? ▶Figure 695–2

(a) 100A, 8 AWG   *(b) 200A, 8 AWG*

(c) 400A, 8 AWG   *(d) 450A, 8 AWG*

Answer: (b) 200A, 8 AWG

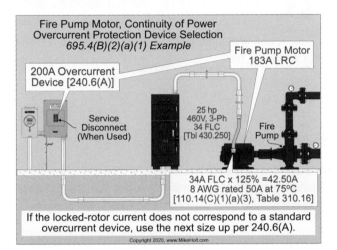

▶Figure 695–2

Solution:

Locked Rotor Current = 183A
Protection Size = 200A [240.6(A) and 695.4(B)(2)(a)(1)]

Determine the branch-circuit conductor at 125 percent of the motor's FLC [Table 310.16, 430.22, and Table 430.250].

Branch-Circuit Conductor = 34A × 125%
Branch-Circuit Conductor = 42.50A

Use an 8 AWG conductor rated 50A at 75°C [110.14)(C)(1)(a) (3) and Table 310.16].

Author's Comment:

▶ This rule only covers the selection of the overcurrent protection device and does not affect the selection of the conductor sizing. The conductor is sized like other motor conductors at 125% of the motor current as found in the Article 430 full load current tables, and adjusted as required by 695.7 for voltage drop.

695.6 Power Wiring

A new exception and Informational Note were added, and (J) was revised to recognize that both cables and raceways are used for fire pump system connections.

Analysis

695.6(A)(1) Services and On-Site Power Production Facilities. This rule requires these conductors to be physically routed outside of the building and installed as service-entrance conductors in compliance with 230.6, 230.9, and Parts III and IV of Article 230.

NEW

695.6(A)(1) Ex. Because a fire pump room is required to be 2-hour fire rated, an exception was added to clarify that supply conductors within the fire pump room are not required to be installed in accordance with 230.6.

NEW

695.6(A)(1) Informational Note. The fire pump controller is often service equipment, and the fire pump is a three-phase load that does not require a neutral conductor. The rule in 250.24(C) requiring the neutral conductor to be run to the service equipment was being missed by some designers and installers. This note calls attention to that requirement.

NEW

694.6(J) Terminations. The wiring methods permitted by 695.6(D) and NFPA 20, *Standard for the Installation of Stationary Pumps for Fire Protection* [9.4.4.1] did not align with the requirement to use conduit hubs for the raceway terminations. This change clarifies that listed cable fittings, as well as conduit hubs, are permitted for the wiring method termination at the fire pump controller. All the other requirements remain the same. Prior to this change, the term "conduit hubs" limited the wiring methods to IMC and RMC.

CLARIFIED

695.6 Power Wiring

(A) Supply Conductors.

(1) Services and On-Site Power Production Facilities. Service conductors and conductors supplied by on-site power production facilities must be physically routed outside buildings. Where supply conductors are run inside the building, they must be encased in 2 in. of concrete or brick [230.6].

Ex: Supply conductors within the fire pump room are not required to be encased in 2 in. of concrete or brick as required by 230.6(1) or (2).

(2) Feeder Conductors. Fire pump supply conductors must comply with all of the following:

(1) Independent Routing. The conductors must be kept entirely independent of all other wiring.

(2) Associated Fire Pump Loads. Conductors must only supply loads directly associated with the fire pump system.

(3) Overcurrent Protection from Potential Damage. Conductors must be protected from potential damage by fire, structural failure, or operational accident.

(4) Inside a Building. Fire pump conductors routed through a building must be protected from fire for two hours using any of the following methods:

(a) Encasing the cable or raceway in at least 2 in. of concrete.

(b) Using cable or a raceway that is a listed fire resistive cable system.

(c) Using cable or a raceway that is a listed electrical circuit protective system.

(J) Terminations. Where raceways or <u>cables</u> terminated to at a fire pump controller, the following requirements apply:

(1) <u>Raceway</u> or cable fittings must be <u>listed and identified for use in wet locations</u>.

(2) The <u>enclosure type</u> rating of the raceway <u>or cable fittings</u> must be at least equal to that of the fire pump controller.

(3) The installation instructions of the manufacturer of the fire pump controller must be followed.

(4) Alterations to the fire pump controller, other than <u>raceway or cable terminations</u>, must be approved by the authority having jurisdiction.

695.10 Listed Equipment

This section was revised to prohibit the reconditioning of fire pump controllers and transfer switches.

Analysis

EXPANDED As we have seen in other requirements, where the equipment provides critical safety functions, it is not permitted to be reconditioned. It is just not worth the risk!

695.10 Listed Equipment

Diesel engine fire pump controllers, electric fire pump controllers, electric motors, fire pump power transfer switches, foam pump controllers, and limited service controllers must be listed for fire pump service.

<u>Fire pump controllers and transfer switches are not be permitted to be reconditioned.</u>

CHAPTER 7

SPECIAL CONDITIONS

Introduction to Chapter 7—Special Conditions

Chapter 7, which covers special conditions, is the third of the *NEC* chapters that deal with special topics. Chapters 5 and 6 cover special occupancies, and special equipment, respectively. Remember, the first four chapters of the *Code* are sequential and form a foundation for each of the subsequent three. Chapter 8 covers communications systems (twisted pair and coaxial cable) and is not subject to the requirements of Chapters 1 through 7 except where the requirements are specifically referenced there.

What exactly is a "Special Condition"? It is a situation that does not fall under the category of special occupancies or special equipment but creates a need for additional measures to ensure the "safeguarding of people and property" mission of the *NEC*, as stated in 90.1(A).

- **Article 700—Emergency Systems.** The requirements of Article 700 apply only to the wiring methods for "Emergency Systems" that are essential for safety to human life and required by federal, state, municipal, or other regulatory codes. When normal power is lost, emergency systems must be capable of supplying emergency power in 10 seconds or less.

- **Article 701—Legally Required Standby Systems.** Legally required standby systems provide electrical power to aid in fire-fighting, rescue operations, control of health hazards, and similar operations, and are required by federal, state, municipal, or other regulatory codes. When normal power is lost, legally required standby systems must be capable of automatically supplying standby power in 60 seconds or less, instead of the 10 seconds or less required of emergency systems.

- **Article 702—Optional Standby Systems.** Optional standby systems are intended to protect public or private facilities or property where life safety does not depend on the performance of the system. These systems are typically installed to provide an alternate source of electrical power for such facilities as industrial and commercial buildings, farms, and residences, and to serve loads that, when stopped during any power outage, can cause discomfort, serious interruption of a process, or damage to a product or process. Optional standby systems are intended to supply on-site generated power to loads selected by the customer, either automatically or manually.

- **Article 705—Interconnected Electric Power Production Sources.** It used to be that a premises having more than one electric power source was a unique situation, but as more and more facilities supplement their utility electric supply with alternate sources of energy it's become more commonplace. Alternate power sources such as solar or wind turbine that run in parallel with a primary utility source require particular consideration and requirements. Article 705 provides the guidance necessary to ensure a safe installation.

- **Article 706—Energy Storage Systems.** Energy storage systems can be (and usually are) connected to other energy sources, such as the local utility distribution system. There can be more than one source of power connected to an ESS and the connection to other energy sources is required to comply with the requirements of Article 705 which covers installation of one or more electric power production sources operating in parallel with a utility source of electricity. It might also be a good idea to be mindful of how this article correlates with other articles in the *Code* such as Articles 480, 690, 692, and 694.

- **Article 710—Stand Alone Systems.** A "stand alone system" is an electrical system that is self-sufficient and a completely "off the grid" source of electrical energy such as solar or wind. However, it still may be connected to a utility supply as part of an interconnected system but the fact that it can be self-sustaining is why Article 710 specifically addresses these systems.

- **Article 712—Direct Current Microgrids.** A "Direct Current Microgrid" (DC Microgrid) is a (dc) power grid that has more than one dc power source capable of supplying dc-dc converters, dc loads, and ac loads which are powered by dc to ac inverters.

- **Article 725—Remote-Control, Signaling, and Power-Limited Circuits.** Article 725 contains the requirements for remote-control, signaling, and power-limited circuits that are not an integral part of a device or appliance.

  ▸ *Remote-Control Circuit.* A circuit that controls others through a relay or solid-state device. For example, a circuit that controls the coil of a motor starter or lighting contactor is one type of remote-control circuit.

  ▸ *Signaling Circuit.* A circuit that supplies energy to an appliance or device that gives a visual and/or audible signal. Circuits for doorbells, buzzers, code-calling systems, signal lights, annunciators, burglar alarms, and other indication or alarm devices are examples of signaling circuits.

- **Article 760—Fire Alarm Systems.** This article covers the installation of wiring and equipment for fire alarm systems. They include fire detection and alarm notification, voice communications, guard's tour, sprinkler waterflow, and sprinkler supervisory systems.

- **Article 770—Optical Fiber Cables and Raceways.** Article 770 covers the installation of optical fiber cables, which transmit signals using light for control, signaling, and communications. It also contains the installation requirements for raceways that contain optical fiber cables, and rules for composite cables (often called "hybrid" cables in the field) that combine optical fibers with current-carrying metallic conductors.

EMERGENCY SYSTEMS

Introduction to Article 700—Emergency Systems

Emergency systems are often required as a condition of an operating permit for a given facility. According to NFPA 101, *Life Safety Code*, emergency power systems are generally installed where artificial illumination is required for safe exiting and for panic control in buildings subject to occupancy by large numbers of people, such as hotels, theaters, sports arenas, health care facilities, and similar structures.

The authority having jurisdiction makes the determination as to whether such a system is necessary for a given facility and what it must entail. Sometimes, it simply provides power for exit lighting and exit signs upon loss of the main power or in the case of fire. Its purpose is not to provide power for normal business operations, but rather to provide lighting and controls essential for human life safety.

The general goal is to keep the emergency operation as reliable as possible. The emergency system must be able to supply all emergency loads simultaneously. When the emergency supply also supplies power for other nonemergency loads, the emergency loads take priority over the others, and those other loads must be subject to automatic load pickup and load shedding to support the emergency loads if the emergency system does not have adequate capacity and rating for all loads simultaneously.

As you study Article 700, keep in mind that emergency systems are essentially lifelines for people. The entire article is based on keeping those lifelines from breaking.

700.2 Definitions

The word "Emergency" was added to this term to clarify the luminaires to which this definition applies, and the definition was revised.

Analysis

CLARIFIED

Emergency Luminaire, Directly Controlled. There are directly controlled luminaires other than those used as emergency lighting. The addition of the term "emergency" makes it clear that this definition applies to directly controlled luminaires used in only the emergency lighting. These are luminaires where the brightness can be controlled for normal use; but, in the 2017 *Code*, were required to return to "full" brightness level upon the loss of normal power. The revision for 2020 requires that they return to "the required illumination level" upon the loss of normal power. The change recognizes that there are listed, directly controlled luminaires, that are intelligent and allow the control input to drive the luminaire to a brightness level sufficient to provide the required emergency illumination level even where that level is less than the full brightness of the luminaire.

700.4 Capacity and Rating

The title of this section was changed to clarify it covers both the capacity and the rating of the emergency system, and subsections were revised or added.

700.5 Transfer Equipment

Subsection (A) was modified to remove redundant language and to prohibit the use of meter-mounted transfer switches, and (C) was also revised.

Analysis

REORGANIZED

700.4(A) Rating. This section was split into two subsections for the 2020 *Code* with (B) covering the capacity of the system; (A) now addresses the rating of the equipment and requires that the emergency system equipment be suitable for the "available fault current" at its terminals.

This change deletes the term "maximum" that preceded "available fault current" in 2017. The defined term "available fault current" is the largest amount of current that can be delivered at that point on the system and "maximum" has become redundant as a result of the revised definition. This is already required by 110.9, and 110.10 and 90.3 make those requirements apply throughout the *NEC*; however, the CMPs seem to feel it is necessary to place additional requirements throughout the *Code*.

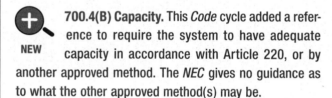
NEW

700.4(B) Capacity. This *Code* cycle added a reference to require the system to have adequate capacity in accordance with Article 220, or by another approved method. The *NEC* gives no guidance as to what the other approved method(s) may be.

Analysis

EXPANDED

The rule that the transfer equipment be "identified" in the 2017 *NEC* was replaced with a requirement that the transfer equipment be "listed and marked" for emergency use. This is not new as it previously appeared in (C) and was deleted. A new last sentence was added to prohibit the use of "meter-mounted" transfer switches for emergency systems. This is consistent with the listing standard for meter-mounted transfer switches which limits the use of that type of transfer switch to Article 702, Optional Standby Systems. As we have seen in other *Code* sections, critical safety equipment is not permitted to be reconditioned and a new last line was added to (C) to reflect this.

700.5 Transfer Equipment

(A) General. Transfer equipment must be automatic, <u>listed and marked</u> for emergency use, and approved. The equipment must be automatic to prevent the inadvertent interconnection of emergency and other power systems. <u>Meter-mounted transfer switches are not permitted for emergency system use.</u>

(C) Automatic Transfer Switches. Automatic transfer switches must be able to be electrically operated and mechanically held.

<u>Automatic transfer switches are not permitted to be reconditioned.</u>

700.4 Capacity and Rating

(A) Rating. An emergency power system must be suitable for the available fault current at its terminals.

(B) Capacity. <u>An emergency power system must have adequate capacity in accordance with Article 220 or by another approved method.</u>

700.6 Signals

Revisions were made to require indication that the emergency source, not just a battery, is carrying load; and the system bonding jumper for multiple paralleled emergency sources is now permitted to be installed at an alternate location.

Analysis

CLARIFIED

700.6(B) Carrying Load. The previous language in (B) required indication when the battery is carrying load. The change recognizes that there are multiple emergency sources, not just batteries. Generators and fuel cells are other sources that are permitted to supply emergency systems. This correlates the language of Article 700 with that of 701 for legally required standby systems. In both cases the intent is for there to be an indication that the alternate supply is carrying load.

EXPANDED

700.6(D) Ground Fault. In the 2017 *NEC*, (D) permitted the ground-fault sensor to be located at an alternate location where there are multiple emergency sources connected to a parallel bus. For the ground-fault sensing equipment to work at an alternate location, the "system bonding jumper" must also be located at the alternate location. This change is meant to meet the objective of preventing the flow of objectionable current. The previous *Code* could be read as requiring multiple main or system bonding jumpers where multiple emergency sources are used and that would result in objectionable current.

700.6 Signals

Audible and visual signal devices must be installed where practicable to indicate:

(A) Malfunction. A malfunction of the emergency source of power.

(B) Carrying Load. That the emergency source is carrying a load.

(C) Charger Not Functioning. That the battery charger is not functioning.

(D) Ground Fault. To indicate a ground fault in solidly grounded wye emergency systems. Instructions on the course of action to be taken in event of indicated ground fault is required to be located at or near the sensor location ground fault.

700.12 General Requirements

The multi-paragraph parent text for this section was shortened by moving portions of the information to two new subsections.

Analysis

CLARIFIED

700.12(B) Equipment Design and Location. This information was relocated to its own subsection and revised for clarity. The term "fire suppression" was replaced with "fire protection" as is the case in other articles and sections referencing the same term. The fire rating of the space that protects the emergency equipment was changed from a 1-hour rating to a 2-hour fire rating. The 2017 *NEC* required the space to have only a 1-hour fire rating, but the other requirements in this article require 2-hour protection. Consistent language provides clarity helping to ensure a *Code*-compliant application. In addition, the reference to "health care occupancies" was deleted as was done in 700.10(D)(1).

REORGANIZED

700.12(D)(2) Internal Combustion Engines as Prime Movers. This subsection was further broken down and the requirements from (D) (3) were incorporated into (D)3)(a) and (b). Both requirements apply to systems where internal combustion engines are used as prime movers for an emergency system. This is an editorial reorganization without technical change.

NEW

700.12(H) DC Microgrid Systems. This new subsection adds dc microgrid systems as a permitted source of power for an emergency system. A dc microgrid used as an emergency system supply must be capable of being isolated from all nonemergency sources and must be able to supply the total emergency load for not less than 2 hours. Where it serves as the normal supply for the building or group of buildings, it must not be the sole source of emergency power.

REORGANIZED

700.12(I)(2)(3) Unit Equipment. This was formerly subsection (F) but was re-lettered because the parent text was broken down into two subsections and (H) was added to cover dc microgrids. Most of the unit equipment rule remains unchanged except list item (3) that addresses the power supply to the unit equipment and is broken down into (a) and (b).

700.12 General Requirements

In the event of failure of the normal supply to the building, emergency power must be available within 10 seconds. Emergency equipment must be designed and located to minimize the hazards that might cause complete failure due to flooding, fires, icing, and vandalism. The emergency power supply must be any of the following:

(A) Power Source Considerations. In selecting an emergency source of power, consideration must be given to the occupancy and the type of service to be rendered, whether of minimum duration, as for evacuation of a theater, or longer duration, as for supplying emergency power and lighting due to an indefinite period of current failure from trouble either inside or outside the building.

(B) Equipment Design and Location. Equipment must be designed and located so as to minimize the hazards that might cause complete failure due to flooding, fires, icing, and vandalism.

(C) Storage Battery. Storage batteries are permitted as the emergency power source if of suitable rating and capacity to supply and maintain the total load for a period of at least 1½ hours, without the voltage applied to the load falling below 87½ percent of normal. Automotive-type batteries are not permitted for this purpose.

(D) Generator Set.

(1) Prime Mover-Driven. A generator approved by the authority having jurisdiction and sized in accordance with 700.4 is permitted as the emergency power source if it has means to automatically start the prime mover when the normal service fails.

(2) Internal Combustion Engines as Prime Movers.

(a) On-Site Fuel Supply. Where internal combustion engines are used as the prime mover, an on-site fuel supply must be provided with an on-premises fuel supply sufficient for not less than 2 hours operation of the system.

(b) Fuel Transfer Pumps. Where power is needed for the operation of the fuel transfer pumps to deliver fuel to a generator set day tank, this pump must be connected to the emergency power system.

(c) Public Gas System, Municipal Water Supply. Prime movers must not be solely dependent on a public utility gas system for their fuel supply or municipal water supply for their cooling systems.

Ex: Where approved by the authority having jurisdiction, the use of other than on-site fuels is permitted where there is a low probability of a simultaneous failure of both the off-site fuel delivery system and power from the outside electrical utility company.

(d) Automatic Fuel Transfer. Where dual fuel supplies are used, means must be provided for automatically transferring from one fuel supply to another.

(E) Uninterruptible Power Supplies. Uninterruptible power supplies are permitted as the emergency power source if they comply with the applicable requirements of 700.12(B) and (C).

(F) Separate Service. An additional service is permitted as the emergency power source where approved by the authority having jurisdiction and the following: ▶Figure 700–1

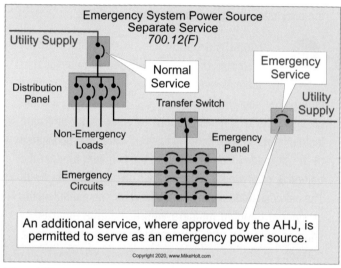

▶Figure 700–1

(1) Separate service conductors are installed from the utility.

(2) The emergency service conductors are electrically and physically remote from nonemergency service conductors to minimize the possibility of simultaneous interruption of supply.

Author's Comment:

▶ To minimize the possibility of simultaneous interruption, the service disconnect for the emergency system must be located remotely away from the other power system's service disconnect [230.72(B)].

(H) Direct-Current Microgrid Systems. Sources connected to a direct-current microgrid system are permitted where the system is capable of being isolated from all nonemergency sources. Direct-current microgrid systems used as a source of power for emergency systems must be of suitable rating and capacity to supply and maintain the total emergency load for not less than 2 hours of full-demand operation. Where a direct-current microgrid system source serves as the normal supply for the building or group of buildings concerned, it must not serve as the sole source of power for the emergency standby system.

(I) Emergency Battery Pack Unit Equipment.

(1) Components of Unit Equipment. Individual emergency lighting battery pack unit equipment is permitted as the emergency power source.

(2) The branch-circuit wiring that supplies emergency battery pack equipment must be one the following:

a. The same branch-circuit serving the normal lighting in the area, with a connection ahead of any local switches. ▶Figure 700–2

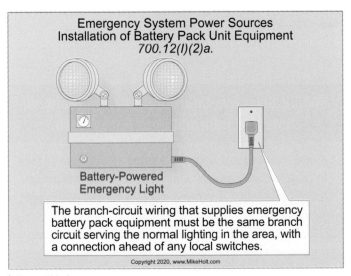

Emergency System Power Sources
Installation of Battery Pack Unit Equipment
700.12(I)(2)a.

Battery-Powered
Emergency Light

The branch-circuit wiring that supplies emergency battery pack equipment must be the same branch circuit serving the normal lighting in the area, with a connection ahead of any local switches.

Copyright 2020, www.MikeHolt.com

▶Figure 700–2

Author's Comment:

▶ There are two reasons why the emergency battery pack unit equipment must be connected ahead of the switch controlling the normal area lighting: (1) in the event of a power loss to the lighting circuit, the emergency battery lighting packs will activate and provide emergency lighting for people to exit the building, and (2) the emergency lighting battery packs will not turn on when the switch controlling normal lighting is turned off.

b. Where the normal lighting circuit is served by one or more branch circuits, a separate branch circuit, provided with a lock-on feature, that originates from the same panelboard as the normal lighting circuits. The branch-circuit disconnecting means for this branch circuit must be provided with a lock-on feature.

700.16 Emergency Illumination

Each paragraph of this rule was assigned a subsection letter and a title to make it easier to understand.

Analysis

REORGANIZED

700.16(A) General. This is the language from the first paragraph in the 2017 *NEC*. As a part of the reorganization it has become its own subsection and there was no change in the requirements from the previous *Code*.

REORGANIZED

700.16(B) System Reliability. This became a subsection with a title as part of the reorganization of the section and is the former second paragraph from 700.16. The previous text made it clear that the failure of a "single element" cannot leave a space in darkness, but the example of the "single element" (such as a burned out lamp) does not adequately cover the intent for assured reliability of a modern emergency lighting system. These systems may now contain complex data network switches, intelligent luminaires, automatic load control relays, branch-circuit emergency lighting transfer switches, and others—all of which may be in the chain of control required to energize emergency lighting. The revision states that the failure of any "illumination source" cannot leave an area in total darkness, no matter what causes the failure. This associated equipment must also be reliable so the emergency lighting can do its job. To help ensure that reliability, new language was added to require the control devices used for the emergency lighting to be specifically listed for that use. Listed unit equipment may be considered as meeting this requirement.

REORGANIZED

700.16(C) Discharge Lighting and (D) Disconnecting Means. These are the former third and fourth paragraphs of 700.16 and were given their own subsections and titles for *Code* usability; there was no change in the *NEC* text.

700.16 Emergency Illumination

(A) General. Emergency illumination must include means of egress lighting, illuminated exit signs, and all other luminaires specified as necessary to provide the required illumination.

(B) System Reliability. Emergency lighting systems must be designed and installed so that the failure of any <u>illumination source</u> will not leave in total darkness any space that requires emergency illumination. ▶Figure 700–3

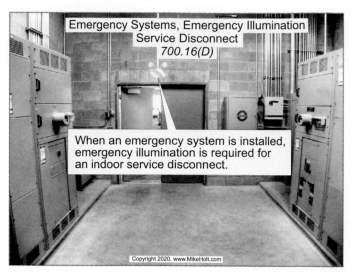

Emergency Systems, Emergency Illumination
Service Disconnect
700.16(D)

When an emergency system is installed, emergency illumination is required for an indoor service disconnect.

Copyright 2020, www.MikeHolt.com

▶Figure 700–4

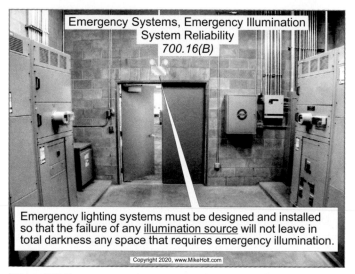

Emergency Systems, Emergency Illumination
System Reliability
700.16(B)

Emergency lighting systems must be designed and installed so that the failure of any <u>illumination source</u> will not leave in total darkness any space that requires emergency illumination.

Copyright 2020, www.MikeHolt.com

▶Figure 700–3

700.32 Selective Coordination, Informational Note and Informational Note Figure

A new Informational Note and related Figure were added to provide clarity on how emergency system overcurrent protective devices selectively coordinate with all supply-side OCPDs.

Author's Comment:

▶ This means that a single remote head is never sufficient for an area. A minimum of two lighting heads is always required. This is the reason individual emergency battery pack unit equipment (sometimes called "lunchboxes" in the field) always has two lighting heads.

(D) Disconnecting Means. When an emergency system is installed, emergency illumination is required for an indoor service disconnect. ▶Figure 700–4

Analysis

NEW

Selective coordination means that the overcurrent protective device (OCPD) protecting only the faulted circuit opens to clear the fault. This, in turn, limits the outage to just that circuit. Informational Note Figure 700.32 shows OCPDs on both the supply side and the load side of the transfer switch, and the notes make it clear that the selective coordination is for all supply-side OCPDs whether they are on the normal or the emergency side of the system.

700.32 Selective Coordination

Overcurrent devices for emergency power systems must be selectively coordinated with all supply-side overcurrent protective devices. The design must be made by an engineer or similarly qualified person and it must be documented and made available to those authorized to design, install, inspect, maintain, and operate the system.

Author's Comment:

▸ According to Article 100, "Selective Coordination" means the overcurrent protection scheme confines the interruption to a specific area rather than to the whole system. For example, if a short circuit or ground fault occurs with selective coordination, the only breaker/fuse that will open is the one protecting just the branch circuit involved. Without selective coordination, an entire floor of a building can go dark.

Note: See Figure 700.32 Informational Note for an example of how emergency system overcurrent protective devices (OCPDs) selectively coordinate with all supply-side OCPDs.

▸ OCPD D selectively coordinates with OCPDs C, F, E, B, and A.
▸ OCPD C selectively coordinates with OCPDs F, E, B, and A.
▸ OCPD F selectively coordinates with OCPD E.
▸ OCPD B is not required to selectively coordinate with OCPD A because OCPD B is not an emergency system OCPD.

ARTICLE
701

LEGALLY REQUIRED STANDBY SYSTEMS

Introduction to Article 701—Legally Required Standby Systems

In the hierarchy of electrical systems, Article 700 Emergency Systems receives top priority. Taking the number two spot is Legally Required Standby Systems, which fall under Article 701. Legally required standby systems must supply standby power in 60 seconds or less after a power loss, instead of the 10 seconds or less required for emergency power systems. Article 700 basically applies to systems or equipment required to protect people who are in an emergency and trying to get out, while Article 701 addresses systems or equipment needed to help people responding to <u>the emergency</u>.

701.4 Capacity and Rating

This section was reorganized into three subsections.

Analysis

REORGANIZED

701.4(A) Rating. This now addresses only the rating of the equipment and requires the emergency system equipment to be suitable for the "available fault current" at its terminals. The change here deletes the term "maximum" that preceded "available fault current" in 2017. The defined term "available fault current" is the largest amount of current that can be delivered at that point on the system and "maximum" has become redundant as a result. This is already required by 110.9, and 110.10 and 90.3 make those requirements apply throughout the *NEC*, however the CMPs seem to believe it is necessary to add additional requirements throughout the *Code*.

NEW

701.4(B) Capacity. Subsection (B) underwent the same change as did 700.4(B) by becoming its own subsection and added a reference to require the system to have adequate capacity in accordance with Article 220 or by another approved method although the *NEC* gives no guidance as to what the other approved method(s) may be.

701.4 Capacity and Rating

(A) Rating. <u>Equipment for a legally required standby system must be suitable for the available fault current at its terminals. The legally required standby alternate power supply can supply legally required standby and optional standby system loads if:</u>

(B) Capacity. The alternate power supply has adequate capacity <u>in accordance with Article 220 or by another approved method</u>.

(C) Load Pickup, Load Shedding, and Peak Load Shaving. <u>There is adequate capacity or where automatic selective load pickup and load shedding are provided that will ensure adequate power to the legally required standby system circuits.</u>

701.5 Transfer Equipment

Transfer equipment must now be listed, the use of meter-mounted transfer switches is now prohibited, and a requirement regarding reconditioned equipment was added.

701.5 Transfer Equipment

(A) General. Automatic transfer equipment must be automatic, <u>listed</u>, and <u>marked for emergency system or legally required</u> standby system use, and approved by the authority having jurisdiction. Transfer equipment must prevent the inadvertent interconnection of legally required standby and other power systems.

<u>Meter-mounted transfer switches are not permitted for legally required standby system use.</u>

(C) Automatic Transfer Switch. Automatic transfer switches must able to be electrically operated and mechanically held. Automatic transfer switches are not permitted to be reconditioned.

(D) Documentation. The short-circuit current rating of the transfer equipment must be field marked on the exterior of the transfer equipment.

701.12 General Requirements

If the normal supply fails, legally required standby power must be available within 60 seconds. The supply system for the legally required standby power supply is permitted to be one or more of the following:

(A) Power Source Considerations. In selecting a legally required standby source of power, consideration must be given to the type of service to be rendered, whether of short-time duration or long duration.

(B) Equipment Design and Location. Consideration must be given to the location or design, or both, of all equipment to minimize the hazards that might cause complete failure due to floods, fires, icing, and vandalism.

Note: For further information, see ANSI/IEEE 493, *Recommended Practice for the Design of Reliable Industrial and Commercial Power Systems.*

(C) Storage Battery. Storage batteries must be of suitable rating and capacity to supply and maintain the total load for a minimum period of 1½ hours without the voltage applied to the load falling below 87½ percent of normal. Automotive-type batteries are not permitted.

(D) Generator Set.

(1) Prime Mover-Driven. A generator approved by the authority having jurisdiction and sized in accordance with 701.4 is permitted as the legally required power source if it has the means to automatically start the prime mover on failure of the normal service.

(E) Uninterruptible Power Supplies. Uninterruptible power supplies are permitted as the legally required power source and must comply with 701.12(B) and (C).

(F) Separate Service. An additional service is permitted as the legally required power source where approved by the authority having jurisdiction and separate service conductors are installed from the utility. ▶Figure 701–1

The legally required service conductors must be electrically and physically remote from other service conductors to minimize the possibility of simultaneous interruption of supply.

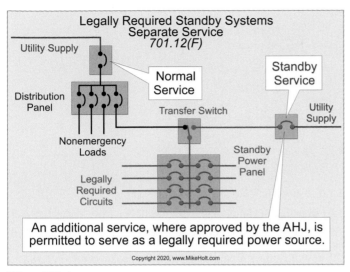

Figure 701–1

Author's Comment:

▶ To minimize the possibility of simultaneous interruption, the service disconnect for the legally required power system must be located remotely away from the other power system's service disconnect [230.72(B)].

(G) Connection Ahead of Service Disconnecting Means. If approved by the authority having jurisdiction, connection ahead of, but not within, the same cabinet, enclosure, or vertical switchboard or switchgear section are permitted as the legally required power source. ▶Figure 701–2

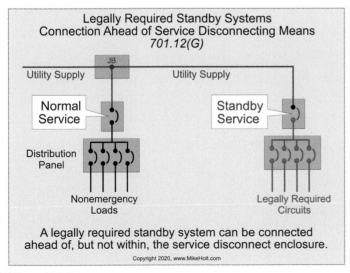

Figure 701–2

To minimize the possibility of simultaneous interruption, the disconnect for the legally required power system must be located remotely from other power system service disconnects.

Part IV Overcurrent Protection

Three sections in Part IV were renumbered to match the numbering sequence in Article 700, and a new Informational Note and related Figure were added to what is now 701.32.

Analysis

NEW The use of parallel numbering makes the *Code* much more user friendly. Several sections were relocated with no technical change as follows:

Section 701.25 in 2017 is 701.30 in the 2020 edition
Section 701.26 in 2017 is 701.31 in the 2020 edition
Section 701.27 in 2017 is 701.32 in the 2020 edition

NEW This new note and figure in 701.32 clarify that coordination is required with all supply-side OCDPs on both the normal supply and on the emergency supply. See comments at 700.32.

701.30 Accessibility

The branch-circuit overcurrent devices for legally required standby circuits must be accessible to authorized persons only.

701.32 Selective Coordination

Overcurrent devices for legally required standby systems must be selectively coordinated with all supply-side overcurrent protective devices. The design must be made by an engineer or similarly qualified person and it must be documented and made available to those authorized to design, install, inspect, maintain, and operate the system.

Author's Comment:

▸ According to Article 100, "Selective Coordination" means the overcurrent protection scheme confines the interruption to a specific area rather than to the whole system. For example, if a short circuit or ground fault occurs with selective coordination, the only breaker/fuse that will open is the one protecting just the branch circuit involved. Without selective coordination, an entire floor of a building can go dark.

Note: See Figure 701.32 Informational Note for an example of how emergency system overcurrent protective devices (OCPDs) selectively coordinate with all supply-side OCPDs.

▸ OCPD D selectively coordinates with OCPDs C, F, E, B, and A.
▸ OCPD C selectively coordinates with OCPDs F, E, B, and A.
▸ OCPD F selectively coordinates with OCPD E.
▸ OCPD B is not required to selectively coordinate with OCPD A because OCPD B is not an emergency system OCPD.

ARTICLE
702
OPTIONAL STANDBY SYSTEMS

Introduction to Article 702—Optional Standby Systems

Taking third priority after Emergency and Legally Required Systems, Optional Standby Systems protect public or private facilities or property where life safety does not depend on the performance of the system. These systems are not required for rescue operations.

Suppose a glass plant loses power. Once glass hardens in the equipment—which it will do when process heat is lost—the plant is going to suffer a great deal of downtime and expense before it can resume operations. An optional standby system can prevent this loss.

You will see these systems in facilities where loss of power can cause economic loss or business interruptions. Data centers can lose millions of dollars from a single minute of lost power. A chemical or pharmaceutical plant can lose an entire batch from a single momentary power glitch. In many cases, the lost revenue cannot be recouped.

This article also applies to the installation of optional standby generators in homes, farms, small businesses, and many other applications where standby power is not legally required.

702.2 Definition

The definition for "Optional Standby Systems" was revised to include stored power as well as on-site generated power.

Analysis

EXPANDED Optional Standby Systems. Batteries are an example of stored power as well as flywheel storage systems.

702.2 Definition

The definition in this section applies within this article and throughout the *Code*.

Optional Standby Systems. Optional standby systems are intended to supply power to public or private facilities, or to property where life safety does not depend on the performance of the system. These systems are intended to supply on-site generated or stored power to selected loads either automatically or manually. ▶Figure 702–1

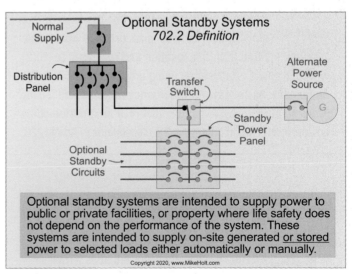

▶Figure 702–1

Note: Optional standby systems are typically installed to provide an alternate source of electric power for such facilities as industrial and commercial buildings, farms, and residences, and to serve loads such as heating and refrigeration systems, data processing and communications systems (twisted pair and coaxial cable), and industrial processes that, when stopped during any power outage, can cause discomfort, economic loss, serious interruption of the process, damage to the product or process, or the like.

702.4 Capacity and Rating

The title of subsection (A) was changed and (B) was revised to clarify that load calculations are an approved method of determining if an optional standby system can supply the load.

Analysis

702.4(A) Fault Current. Available fault current has replaced short-circuit current throughout the *Code*. **EDITED** The title was changed to match the Article 100 term, and the word "maximum" was deleted as the term "available fault current" is the maximum current available at that point on the system. This section also permits the load to be determined by another approved method.

702.4(B) System Capacity. The parent text that required load calculations for the load on the standby source to be in accordance with Article 220 was deleted from this location and relocated to (B)(2) **CLARIFIED** where it applies to systems using only automatic transfer equipment. As we saw for emergency systems and legally required standby systems, the load may be determined by an approved method other than the calculations in Article 220.

702.4 Capacity and Rating

(A) Available __Fault__ Current. Optional standby system equipment must be suitable for the available __fault__ current at its terminals.

(B) System Capacity.

(1) Manual Transfer Equipment. Where manual transfer equipment is used, an optional standby system must be capable of supplying all of the equipment intended to be operated at one time. The user of the optional standby system is permitted to select the load connected to the system.

Author's Comment:

▸ When a manual transfer switch is used, the user of the optional standby system selects the loads to be connected to the system, which determines the system's kVA/kW rating.

(2) The calculated load on the standby source must be in accordance with Article 220 __or by another approved method__.

(a) Full Load. The standby source must be capable of supplying the full load upon automatic transfer.

(b) Load Management. Where an automatic load management system is employed, the standby system must be capable of supplying the full load that will be connected.

Author's Comment:

▸ For existing facilities, the maximum demand data for one year or the average power demand for a 15-minute period over a minimum of 30 days can be used to size the electric power source [220.87]. ▸Figure 702–2

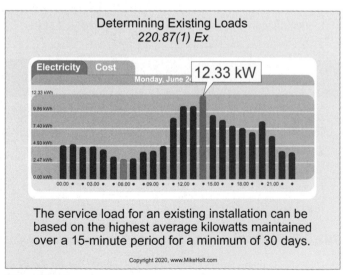

The service load for an existing installation can be based on the highest average kilowatts maintained over a 15-minute period for a minimum of 30 days.

Copyright 2020, www.MikeHolt.com

▸Figure 702–2

702.5 Transfer Equipment

This section was broken down into four subsections, one of which is a new rule added to permit the use of meter-mounted transfer switches.

Analysis

REORGANIZED

702.5(A) General. This is the relocation of the last paragraph and its exception to its own subsection with added language that prohibits transfer switches from being reconditioned. The use of transfer equipment ensures that the normal supply source will not be backfed from the standby source. Backfeeding can create a very dangerous condition for utility workers trying to restore power. The exception that permits the temporary connection of a portable generator without transfer equipment was relocated to this new subsection without change. The exception applies where the conditions of maintenance and supervision ensure that only qualified persons work on the system, and that the normal supply be physically isolated by a lockable disconnecting means or where the normal supply conductors have been disconnected from the equipment. New language prohibits the reconditioning of transfer switches. This prohibition applies to automatic transfer switches in only 700 and 701, but it applies to all transfer switches in this article.

NEW

702.5(B) Meter-Mounted Transfer Switches. This paragraph was added to address the use of meter-mounted transfer switches and unlike 700 and 701 where the use of such transfer switches is prohibited, they are permitted for use for optional standby systems. These switches are required to be manual transfer switches unless they meet the requirements for automatic transfer switches found in 702.4(B)(2). The listing standard, UL1008M, provides for either manual or automatic transfer switches. The manual type is typically designed for a cord connection between the meter-mounted transfer switch and the generator. In many cases these devices will be installed and owned by the utility and the customer will see a monthly rental charge on their electric bill for the meter-mounted transfer switch. This device greatly simplifies the installation of a dwelling unit optional standby system.

REORGANIZED

702.5(C) Documentation. This was the last paragraph and is now its own subsection. The requirement for field marking of the short-circuit current rating based on the specific overcurrent protective device type and settings was modified to not require such marking for dwelling unit transfer equipment.

REORGANIZED

702.5(D) Inadvertent Interconnection. This revision now requires optional standby transfer equipment to be listed. The previous requirements saying that the equipment must be suitable for the intended use and installed so as to prevent the inadvertent interconnection of all sources remain.

702.5 Transfer Equipment

(A) General. Transfer equipment, (manual or automatic), is required for all standby systems and are subject to the requirements of this article and for which an electric utility supply is either the normal or standby source. Transfer switches are not permitted to be reconditioned.

Ex: Temporary connection of a portable generator without transfer equipment is permitted where conditions of maintenance and supervision ensure that only qualified persons will service the installation, and where the normal supply is physically isolated by a lockable disconnect or by the disconnection of the normal supply conductors.

(B) Meter-Mounted Transfer Switches. A transfer switch installed between the utility meter and the meter enclosure must be a listed meter-mounted transfer switch. Meter-mounted transfer switches must be of the manual type unless rated in accordance with 702.4(B)(2). ▸Figure 702–3

(C) Documentation. In other than dwelling units, the short-circuit current rating of the transfer equipment must be field marked on the exterior of the transfer equipment.

(D) Inadvertent Interconnection. Transfer equipment must be suitable for the intended use and listed, designed, and installed so as to prevent the inadvertent interconnection of all sources of supply in any operation of the transfer equipment. ▸Figure 702–4

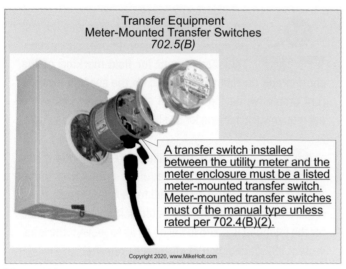

Transfer Equipment
Meter-Mounted Transfer Switches
702.5(B)

A transfer switch installed between the utility meter and the meter enclosure must be a listed meter-mounted transfer switch. Meter-mounted transfer switches must of the manual type unless rated per 702.4(B)(2).

Copyright 2020, www.MikeHolt.com

▶Figure 702–3

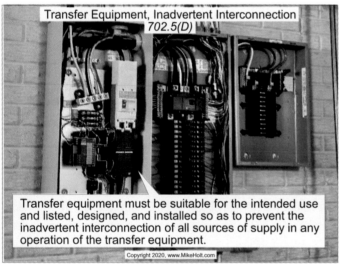

Transfer Equipment, Inadvertent Interconnection
702.5(D)

Transfer equipment must be suitable for the intended use and listed, designed, and installed so as to prevent the inadvertent interconnection of all sources of supply in any operation of the transfer equipment.

Copyright 2020, www.MikeHolt.com

▶Figure 702–4

Author's Comment:

▸ While there are listed breaker interlock kits, verifying that these are listed as transfer equipment is another story. This new listing requirement will require an interlock kit to be listed as transfer equipment. It is evident that the panel's intent is to prohibit the use of ordinary breaker interlock kits, (as they can be defeated by the removal of the panel cover), to avoid the danger of both the optional standby breaker and the normal supply breaker being placed in the on position. While the *Code* text does not say anything about the removal of covers defeating the transfer equipment interlock, breaker interlocks listed as "transfer equipment" satisfies the Code-Making Panel's (CMP) intent.

702.7 Signs

Subsection (A) was revised to coordinate with the new dwelling unit emergency disconnect required by 230.85.

Analysis

CLARIFIED

702.7(A) Standby Power Sources. This rule required that a sign be placed at the service equipment to indicate the type and location of all on-site optional standby power sources. That language now applies to only commercial and industrial installations. Language was added requiring signage to be located at the disconnecting means required by 230.85 for one- and two-family dwelling units. The change in 230.85 for standby power sources recognizes a need to be identified as to being on the premises. This serves to alert firefighters to the inherent risk of additional electrical hazards other than the normal utility fed source they would be counting on to disconnect the entire building from electrical energy.

702.7 Signs

(A) Standby Power Sources. A sign is required at service equipment for commercial and industrial installations that indicates the type and location of each on-site optional standby power source. ▶Figure 702–5

For one- and two-family dwelling units, a sign is required at the emergency disconnect switch mandated in 230.85 that indicates the location of each permanently installed on-site optional standby power source disconnect or means to shut down the prime mover as required in 445.18(D).

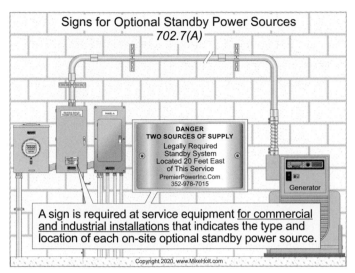

Signs for Optional Standby Power Sources
702.7(A)

DANGER
TWO SOURCES OF SUPPLY
Legally Required
Standby System
Located 20 Feet East
of This Service
PremierPowerInc.Com
352-978-7015

Generator

A sign is required at service equipment <u>for commercial</u> <u>and industrial installations</u> that indicates the type and location of each on-site optional standby power source.

Copyright 2020, www.MikeHolt.com

▶Figure 702–5

INTERCONNECTED ELECTRIC POWER PRODUCTION SOURCES

Introduction to Article 705—Interconnected Electric Power Production Sources

Anytime there is more than one source of power production at the same building, safety issues arise. In cases where a power production source such as a generator is used strictly for backup power, the *NEC* requires transfer switches and other safety considerations as covered in Articles 700, 701, or 702 depending on whether the backup power is an emergency system, a legally required system, or an optional standby system. When interactive electrical power production sources, such as wind powered generators, solar PV systems, or fuel cells are present, there usually is not a transfer switch. In fact, it can be expected that there will be multiple sources of electrical supply connected simultaneously. This requires careful planning to maintain a satisfactory level of safety when more than one electric power source is present. Article 705 covers the connection of electric power sources that operate in parallel with a primary source. The primary source is typically the electric utility power source, but it can be an on-site source instead.

Author's Comment:

▸ There was a significant amount of rewriting of Article 705 this cycle to better organize the requirements for all sources that may be interconnected together into a single set of harmonized requirements. This has reduced the structure of this Article from the previous four parts, to just two. Any language that applied to a specific power source was moved to the relevant Article wherever possible.

The definitions in this section apply within this article and throughout the *Code*.

Note: The definitions for Multimode Inverter and Power Production Equipment were moved from this section into Article 100 since they were used in other articles.

705.2 Definitions

This definition was added to clarify that the conductors between power production equipment or a power source, and the service equipment or distribution equipment are not feeder conductors.

Analysis

NEW **Power Source Output Circuit.** In previous *Code* versions there was no term to describe these circuit conductors. Since the power source terminates at its system disconnect, the conductors from that disconnect to their connection to other equipment, including feeders, did not have a unified term. This will make it clear that these conductors are subject to the rules and requirements of Article 705 and not the ones in Chapter 2 applying to the installation of these conductors. There are special considerations for these conductors that are addressed in this article.

705.2 Definitions

The definitions in this section apply within this article and throughout the *Code*.

Power Source Output Circuit. The conductors between power production equipment and distribution equipment or the utility service disconnect. ▸Figure 705–1

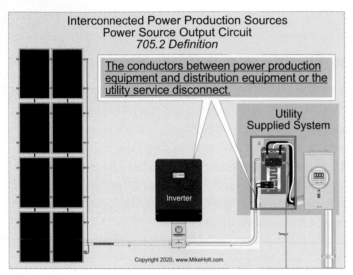

Interconnected Power Production Sources
Power Source Output Circuit
705.2 Definition

The conductors between power production equipment and distribution equipment or the utility service disconnect.

Utility Supplied System

Inverter

Copyright 2020, www.MikeHolt.com

▸Figure 705–1

705.10 Identification of Power Sources

The title of this section was changed to more directly inform the reader of the section content, and now requires a plaque or directory that is not installed at the service equipment to be at an approved readily visible location.

Analysis

CLARIFIED The new language now permits multiple plaques or directories at a common location; the previous rule required a single plaque or directory that denoted the location of all electric power source disconnecting means. With the possibility of multiple power production systems, plaques or directories for each such system at a common location will provide the required information. Since some service equipment could be located indoors, an allowance for a different approved location allows the local AHJ to determine if they want this notification in an alternate location, such as outdoors.

705.6 Equipment Approval

This was revised to clarify that where a field label is provided, it must be evaluated for interactive function.

Analysis

CLARIFIED The language was revised to clarify that the interactive equipment must be listed for interactive function or evaluated for interactive function and field labeled.

705.6 Equipment Approval

Interactive equipment must be approved for interactive function and be listed or be evaluated for interactive function and have a field label applied, or both.

705.10 Identification of Power Sources

A permanent plaque or directory must be installed at each utility service disconnecting means location, or at an approved readily visible location. The plaque or directory must indicate the location of each power source disconnecting means for the building and the it must be grouped with other plaques or directories for other on-site sources of power. ▸Figure 705–2

The plaque or directory for the power source disconnecting means must be marked with the wording;

"CAUTION: MULTIPLE SOURCES OF POWER"

Any posted diagrams must be correctly oriented with respect to the diagram's location.

The marking must be permanently affixed and have sufficient durability to withstand the environment involved [110.21(B)].

Ex: Plaques or directories for installations having multiple co-located power production sources are permitted to be identified as a group(s). A plaque or directory is not required for each power source.

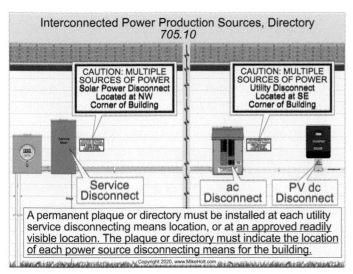

▶Figure 705-2

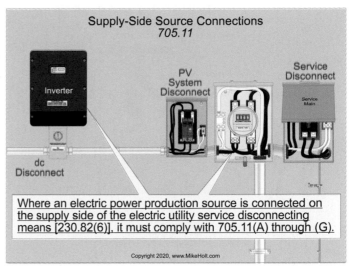

▶Figure 705-3

705.11 Supply-Side Source Connections

This new section addresses the requirements pertaining to the connection of electric power production sources to the supply side of the service disconnecting means as permitted by 230.82(6).

Analysis

NEW This new section was added so the rules for the connection of an electric power production source on the supply side of the service disconnect can be found in one location without requiring the *Code* user to locate relevant sections of Articles 705 and 230 on their own. The requirements largely parallel those of service equipment and service conductors but are unique since this equipment receives power from multiple sources.

705.11 Supply Side Source Connections

An electric power production source, where connected on the supply side of the electric utility service disconnecting means as permitted in 230.82(6), must comply with the following seven requirements, (A) through (G) : ▶Figure 705-3

(A) Output Rating. The sum of the power source continuous current output ratings, other than those controlled by a power control system in accordance with 705.13, is not permitted to exceed the ampacity of the service conductors connected to the electric utility supply. ▶Figure 705-4

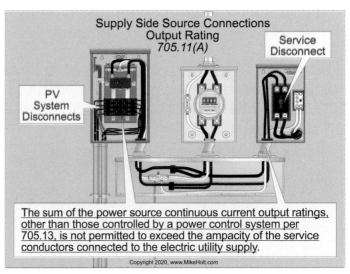

The sum of the power source continuous current output ratings, other than those controlled by a power control system per 705.13, is not permitted to exceed the ampacity of the service conductors connected to the electric utility supply.

▶Figure 705-4

Note: See Article 100 for the definition of "Service Conductors."

Author's Comment:

▶ Service conductors are the conductors on the load side of the electric utility service point to the service disconnect. ▶**Figure 705-5**

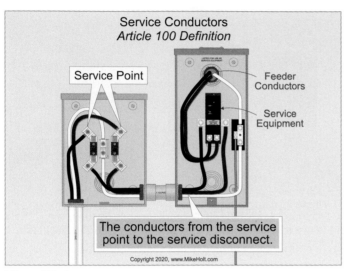
▶Figure 705–5

Author's Comment:

▸ Service conductors (load side of service point) include overhead service conductors, overhead service-entrance conductors, and underground service conductors. These conductors are not under the exclusive control of the serving electric utility, which means they are owned by the customer and fall within the requirements of Article 230.

(B) Conductors. The power source output circuit conductors to the terminating overcurrent protective device must be sized in accordance with 705.28, but in no case are the conductors permitted to be sized smaller than 6 AWG copper or 4 AWG aluminum. ▶Figure 705–6

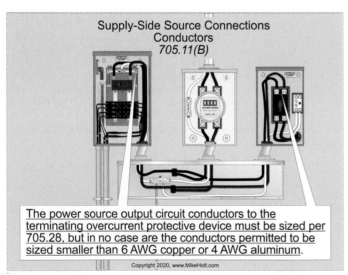
▶Figure 705–6

Underground power source output circuit conductors must be within a wiring method in accordance with 230.30 or for other installation, in accordance with 230.43.

(C) Overcurrent Protection. The power source output circuit conductors must be protected from overcurrent in accordance with 705.30.

Where the power source output circuit conductors make their connection to the utility service conductors outside a building, the overcurrent protective device for the power source output circuit conductors must be placed in a readily accessible location outside the building or at the first readily accessible location where the power source output circuit conductors enter the building.

Where the power source output circuit conductors make their connection to the utility service conductors inside a building, the power source output circuit conductors must be protected with one of the two following methods:

(1) For dwelling units, overcurrent protection is required within 10 ft of conductor length from the point of connection to the electrical service. For other than dwelling units, overcurrent protection is required within 16.50 ft of conductor length from the point of connection to the electrical service. ▶Figure 705–7

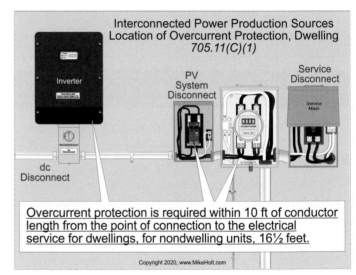
▶Figure 705–7

(2) For other than dwelling units, overcurrent protection is required within 71 ft of conductor length from the point of connection to the electrical service, provided that cable limiters are located within 16.50 ft of conductor length from the point of connection to the electrical service.

(D) Connections. Connection of power source output circuit conductors to utility service conductors must be made with listed connectors that comply with 110.14.

Modifications to equipment to accommodate the power source output circuit connection to the service conductors must be made in accordance with manufacturer's instructions or the modification to the equipment must be evaluated for the application and have a field label applied.

Power source output circuit connections within enclosures under the exclusive control of the electric utility are permitted where approved by the electric utility.

(E) Ground-Fault Protection. Ground-fault protection of equipment meeting the requirements of 230.95 must be provided for power source output circuit current rated 1,000A or more from a solidly grounded wye system, where the voltage-to-ground exceeds 150V and the phase-to-phase voltage does not exceed 1,000V.

705.12 Load-Side Source Connections

The title and rules of 705.12 were revised to address only load-side connection requirements and reorganized for ease of use.

Analysis

REORGANIZED The parent text for this section remains unchanged except that the reference to supply-side connections was deleted as they are now covered in 705.11, and a new requirement covering where a power system controller (PSC) is used and connected to other equipment which says that the setting of the PSC is to be considered the power source output current when applying the rules in 705.12.

REORGANIZED **705.12(A) Dedicated Overcurrent and Disconnect.** This is the requirement from (B)(2) in the 2017 *Code* and was relocated to its own subsection without change.

REORGANIZED **705.12(B) Bus or Conductor Ampere Rating.** This is the former 705.12(B)(2) and was relocated here with several editorial revisions and three technical changes. The parent text requires 125 percent of the power source output current to be used in the ampacity calculations for all the conductors used for load-side power source output.

CLARIFIED **705.12(B)(1) Feeders.** This was (B)(2)(1) in the 2017 *NEC*. The language was revised to clarify that where the power source output connection is made to the feeder at the end opposite the feeder primary source OCPD, the feeder must have an ampacity that is equal to or greater than 125 percent of the power source output circuit current. The two provisions for where the connection to the feeder is made other than at the end opposite the primary source were relocated without any technical change.

EDITED **705.12(B)(2) Taps.** This was 705.12(B)(2)(2) in the 2017 *Code* and is relocated language with minor editorial changes. The rule requires that where power source output connections are made at feeders, all taps must be sized based on the sum of 125 percent of the power source output circuit current(s) and the rating of the OCPD protecting the feeder; the tap rules in 240.21(B) apply.

RELOCATED **705.12(B)(3) Busbars.** This was (B)(2)(3) in the 2017 *NEC* and was relocated here with one change. In the 2017 *Code* this language applied to the ratings of busbars in only panelboards. The term "panelboards" was deleted to clarify that the rule applies to busbars that are in equipment other than panelboards.

REORGANIZED **705.12(B)(3)(4).** This fourth list item contains revised language to permit power source output circuits to be connected to both ends of a center-fed panelboard in dwelling units. This is permitted where 125 percent of the power source output current and the rating of the OCPD that protects the busbar does not exceed 120 percent of the current rating of the busbar. The change treats the busbar on each side of the center mounted OCPD as separate busbars and permits two power source output connections. The power source output connections are required to be installed at the ends of the busbars.

705.12(B)(3)(5). This rule was revised for clarity by replacing "multiple ampacity busbars" with the specific language "switchgear, switchboards, and panelboards in configurations other than those permitted in 705.12(B)(3)(1) through (4)" under engineering supervision.

CLARIFIED

705.12(B)(3)(6). This new list item permits connections to be made on the busbars of panelboards that supply feed-through conductors. While this was not outlawed in previous cycles, clearer guidance is now provided.

NEW

705.12(D) Suitable for Backfeed. The language from the Informational Note referring to backfed fusible disconnects was moved from the note into the actual *NEC* text. That makes it clear that the fused disconnect is permitted to be backfed. As a result, the note was deleted. The last sentence says that circuit breakers marked "line" and "load" are considered suitable for backfeed or reverse current if specifically rated.

RELOCATED

705.12 Load-Side Source Connections

Electric power source circuit conductors are permitted to be connected to feeders and distribution equipment on the load side of the service disconnect.

Where distribution equipment or feeders are capable of supplying branch circuits and/or feeders or are fed simultaneously by a primary source of electricity and other power sources, the interconnection of power source equipment to the primary source of electricity must be in accordance with one of the five following methods.

(A) Dedicated Overcurrent and Disconnect. The interconnection of each power source must be to a dedicated circuit breaker or fusible disconnect.

(B) Bus or Conductor Ampere Rating. The interconnection of each power source to a bus or conductor, multiplied by 125 percent, must be in accordance with one of the three following methods.

(1) Feeders. Where a power source connection is made to a feeder at the opposite end of the feeder primary source overcurrent device, the feeder conductor must have an ampacity no less than 125 percent of the source output circuit current.

Where a power source connection is made to a feeder at a location that is not at the opposite end of the feeder primary source overcurrent device, the feeder on the load side of the power source output connection must be protected by one of the two following methods.

(a) The feeder ampacity must not be less than the sum of the primary source overcurrent device and 125 percent of the power source output circuit current. ▶Figure 705–8

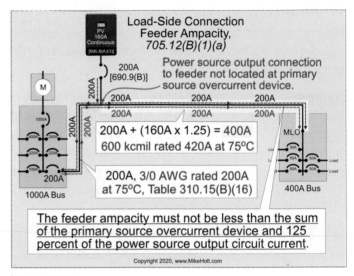

▶Figure 705–8

(b) An overcurrent device at the load side of the power source connection point must have a rating not greater than the ampacity of the feeder conductor. ▶Figure 705–9

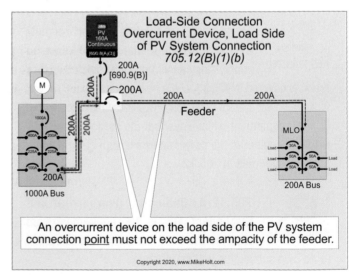

▶Figure 705–9

(2) Taps. Where a power source tap connection is made to a feeder in accordance with the feeder tap rules contained 240.21(B), the power source tap conductors must have an ampacity no less than 125 percent of all power source output circuit current(s) plus the rating of the overcurrent device protecting the feeder conductors, but in no case can the power source tap conductor ampacity be less than calculated in 240.21(B).

> **Author's Comment:**

▸ The feeder tap calculations are as follows:

◆ *10-Foot Tap.* PV system taps not longer than 10 ft must have an ampacity not less than ten percent of the sum of the feeder protection device plus 125 percent of the PV system rated output circuit current, but in no case less than the rating of the terminating overcurrent device, in accordance with 240.21(B)(1).

◆ *25-Foot Tap.* PV system taps not longer than 25 ft must have an ampacity not less than 33 percent of the sum of the feeder protection device plus 125 percent of the PV system rated output circuit current, but in no case less than the rating of the terminating overcurrent protective device, in accordance with 240.21(B)(2).

▸ **Feeder Tap—10-Foot Rule Example**

Question: What size feeder tap conductor (not longer than 10 ft) will be required for a tap to a 100A overcurrent protective device made between a feeder overcurrent protective device rated 200A and an inverter with ac output current rated 160A? ▸**Figure 705–10**

(a) 3 AWG   (b) 2 AWG   (c) 1 AWG   (d) 3/0 AWG

Answer: (a) 3 AWG

Solution:

PV system taps not longer than 10 ft must have an ampacity not less than ten percent of the sum of the feeder protection device (200) plus 125 percent of the PV system rated output circuit current (160A), but in no case less than the rating of the terminating overcurrent device (100A), in accordance with 240.21(B)(1).

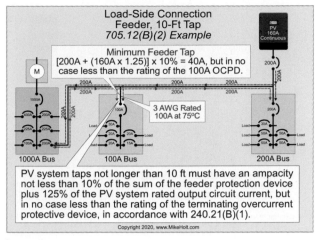

▸Figure 705–10

Feeder Tap Conductor Ampacity = > [200A + (160A x 125%)] x 10%, but no less than 100A

Feeder Tap Conductor Ampacity = > [200A + 200A] x 10%, but no less than 100A

Feeder Tap Conductor Ampacity = > [400A] x 10%, but no less than 100A

Feeder Tap Conductor Ampacity = > 40A, but no less than 100A

Feeder Contactor Size = 3 AWG rated 100A at 75°C, Table 310.16

▸ **Feeder Tap—25-Foot Rule Example**

Question: What size feeder tap conductor (longer than 10 ft but not over 25 ft) will be required for a tap to a 100A overcurrent protective device made between a feeder overcurrent protective device rated 200A and an inverter with ac output current rated 160A? ▸**Figure 705–11**

(a) 3 AWG   (b) 2 AWG   (c) 1 AWG   (d) 1/0 AWG

Answer: (d) 1/0 AWG
Solution:

PV system taps not longer than 25 ft must have an ampacity not less than 33 percent of the sum of the feeder protection device (200A) plus 125 percent of the PV system rated output circuit current (160A), but in no case less than the rating of the terminating overcurrent protective device (100A), in accordance with 240.21(B)(2).

● ● ●

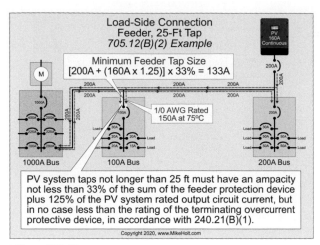

▶Figure 705–11

Feeder Tap Conductor Ampacity => [200A + (160A x 125%)] x 33%, but no less than 100A

Feeder Tap Conductor Ampacity => [200A + 200A] x 33%, but no less than 100A

Feeder Tap Conductor Ampacity => [400A] x 33%, but no less than 100A

Feeder Tap Conductor Ampacity => 133A, but no less than 100A

Feeder Contactor Size = 1/0 AWG rated 150A at 75°C, Table 310.16

(3) Busbars. Power source connections are permitted to panelboard busbars where they have an ampere rating determined by one of the six following methods.

(1) One-Hundred Twenty-Five Percent Rule. Termination of power source conductors to an overcurrent protective device placed at any point of the panelboard requires the busbar to have an ampacity rating of no less than 125 percent of the power source(s) output circuit current, plus the rating of the overcurrent protective device protecting the panelboard busbar. ▶Figure 705–12

Note: This general rule assumes no limitation in the number of the loads or sources applied to busbars or their locations.

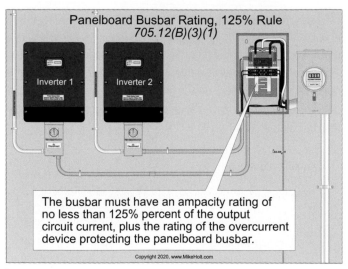

▶Figure 705–12

▶ **Panelboard Busbar Ampere Rating—Not Opposite Feeder Termination Example**

Question: *What is the minimum busbar ampere rating for a panelboard protected by a 200A overcurrent protective device if supplied by two inverters each having an output ac current rating of 24A, when not located opposite the feeder termination?* ▶Figure 705–13

(a) 200A   (b) 240A   (c) 260A   (d) none of these

Answer: *(c) 260A*

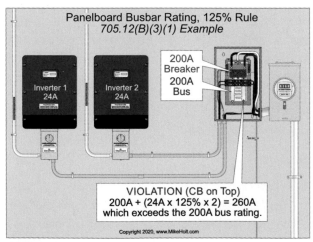

▶Figure 705–13

Solution:

Minimum Busbar Ampere Rating = > (24A x 125% x 2) + 200A
Minimum Busbar Ampere Rating = > 60A + 200A
Minimum Busbar Ampere Rating = > 260A

(2) One-Hundred Twenty Percent Rule. Where two sources, one a primary power source and the other another power source, are located at opposite ends of a panelboard that contains loads, the busbar must have an ampacity rating of no less than 125 percent of the power source(s) output circuit current, plus the rating of the overcurrent protective device protecting the panelboard busbar, and this value does not exceed 120 percent of the panelboard busbar ampacity. ▶Figure 705–14

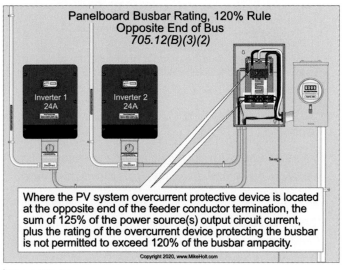

Where the PV system overcurrent protective device is located at the opposite end of the feeder conductor termination, the sum of 125% of the power source(s) output circuit current, plus the rating of the overcurrent device protecting the busbar is not permitted to exceed 120% of the busbar ampacity.

Copyright 2020, www.MikeHolt.com

▶Figure 705–14

▶ **Panelboard Busbar Ampere Rating—Opposite Feeder Termination Example**

Question: Can a panelboard having a 200A rated busbar, protected by a 175A overcurrent device be supplied by two inverters each having an output ac current rating of 24A when located opposite the feeder termination? ▶Figure 705–15

(a) Yes   *(b) No*

Answer: *(a) Yes*

Solution:

125 percent of the power source(s) output circuit current, plus the rating of the overcurrent protective device protecting the panelboard busbar is not permitted to exceed 120 percent of the panelboard busbar ampacity.

175A + (24A x 125% x 2) = < 200A Busbar x 120%
175A + (60A) = < 240A
235A = <240A

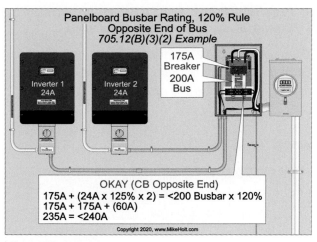

OKAY (CB Opposite End)
175A + (24A x 125% x 2) = <200 Busbar x 120%
175A + 175A + (60A)
235A = <240A

Copyright 2020, www.MikeHolt.com

▶Figure 705–15

A permanently affixed warning label that has sufficient durability to withstand the environment involved [110.21(B)] must be applied to the distribution equipment adjacent to the back-fed breaker from the power source to read:

WARNING:
POWER SOURCE OUTPUT CONNECTION.
DO NOT RELOCATE THIS OVERCURRENT DEVICE.

(3) One-Hundred Percent Rule. Termination of power source conductors to an overcurrent protective device placed at any point of the panelboard requires the panelboard busbar ampacity to be equal to or greater than sum of the ampere ratings of all overcurrent protective devices on the panelboard busbar. ▶Figure 705–16

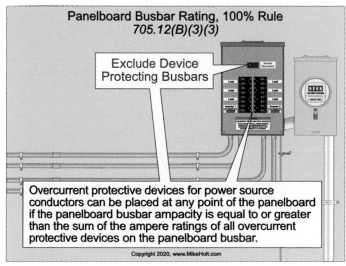

Overcurrent protective devices for power source conductors can be placed at any point of the panelboard if the panelboard busbar ampacity is equal to or greater than the sum of the ampere ratings of all overcurrent protective devices on the panelboard busbar.

Copyright 2020, www.MikeHolt.com

▶Figure 705–16

▶ **Panelboard Busbar Ampere Rating—Breakers not to Exceed Busbar Ampere Rating Example 1**

Question: What is the minimum busbar ampere rating for a panelboard containing two 30A, 240V, two-pole circuit breakers and six 20A, 240V, two-pole circuit breakers. ▶Figure 705–17

(a) 120A   (b) 150A   (c) 180A   (d) 200A

Answer: (c) 180A

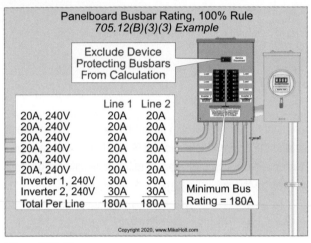

▶Figure 705–17

Solution:

The panelboard busbar ampacity to be equal to or greater than sum of the ampere ratings of all overcurrent protective devices on the panelboard busbar.

Panelboard Busbar => (30A x 2) + (20A x 6)
Panelboard Busbar => 60A + 120A
Panelboard Busbar = 180A

▶ **Panelboard Busbar Ampere Rating—Breakers Not to Exceed Busbar Ampere Rating Example 2**

Question: What is the minimum busbar ampere rating for a panelboard containing six 30A, 240V, two-pole circuit breakers and one 20A, 120V, one-pole circuit breaker? ▶Figure 705–18

(a) 120A   (b) 180A   (c) 200A   (d) 300A

Answer: (c) 200A

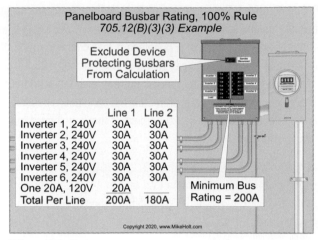

▶Figure 705–18

Solution:

The panelboard busbar ampacity to be equal to or greater than sum of the ampere ratings of all overcurrent protective devices on the panelboard busbar.

Panelboard Busbar = > (30A x 6) + (20A x 1)
Panelboard Busbar = > 180A + 20A
Panelboard Busbar = 200A

A permanently affixed warning label that and has sufficient durability to withstand the environment involved [110.21(B)] must be applied to the distribution equipment and read: ▶Figure 705–19

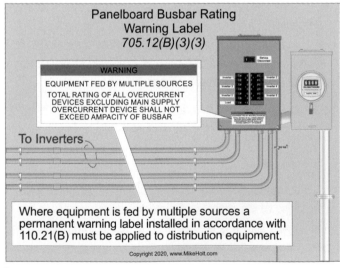

▶Figure 705–19

WARNING: THIS EQUIPMENT FED BY MULTIPLE SOURCES. TOTAL RATING OF ALL OVERCURRENT DEVICES EXCLUDING MAIN SUPPLY OVERCURRENT DEVICE MUST NOT EXCEED AMPACITY OF BUSBAR.

(4) Center-Fed Panelboard. A power source connection is permitted at either end of a dwelling unit center-fed panelboard where the panelboard busbar has an ampacity of no less than 125 percent of the power source(s) output circuit current, plus the rating of the overcurrent protective device protecting the panelboard busbar, and this value does not exceed 120 percent of the panelboard busbar ampacity. ▶Figure 705–20

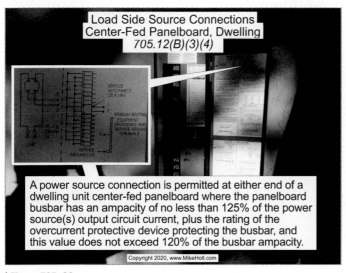

A power source connection is permitted at either end of a dwelling unit center-fed panelboard where the panelboard busbar has an ampacity of no less than 125% of the power source(s) output circuit current, plus the rating of the overcurrent protective device protecting the busbar, and this value does not exceed 120% of the busbar ampacity.

▶Figure 705–20

(5) Switchgear, switchboards, and panelboards can be designed under engineering supervision that includes available fault current and busbar load calculations for a power source connection.

(6) Power source connections are permitted on panelboard busbars connected to feed-through conductors. The feed-through conductors must be sized in accordance with 705.12(B)(1). Where an overcurrent device is installed at the supply end of the feed-through conductors, the busbar in the supplying panelboard is permitted to be sized in accordance with 705.12(B)(3).

(C) Marking. Panelboards containing multiple power source circuits must be field marked to indicate the presence of all sources of all power. ▶Figure 705–21

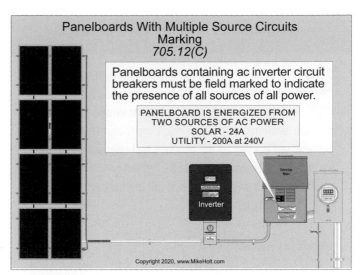

Panelboards With Multiple Source Circuits Marking
705.12(C)

Panelboards containing ac inverter circuit breakers must be field marked to indicate the presence of all sources of all power.

PANELBOARD IS ENERGIZED FROM
TWO SOURCES OF AC POWER
SOLAR - 24A
UTILITY - 200A at 240V

▶Figure 705–21

(D) Suitable for Backfeed. Fused disconnects, unless otherwise marked, are suitable for backfeed. Circuit breakers not marked "line" and "load" are suitable for backfeed, but circuit breakers marked "line" and "load" are only suitable for backfeed or reverse current if specifically rated for this application. ▶Figure 705–22

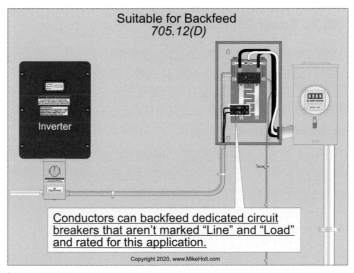

Suitable for Backfeed
705.12(D)

Conductors can backfeed dedicated circuit breakers that aren't marked "Line" and "Load" and rated for this application.

▶Figure 705–22

705.13 Power Control Systems

This new section addresses "multiple energy source situations" that can consist of utility, solar, generator, wind turbine, battery storage, and so forth.

Analysis

NEW

A "power control system" (PCS) is equipment that is listed and evaluated to control the output of one or more power production sources, energy storage systems, and other equipment and must limit the current and loading on the busbars and conductors supplied by the PCS. The current must be limited to the ampacity of the conductors or the ratings of the busbars in accordance with 705.13(A) though (E).

Author's Comment:

▸ With the increase in the application of microgrids for energy security, even within a single-family home, multiple sources connected in parallel will be encountered more frequently. Without any means of controlling currents from these sources, distribution equipment would become excessively oversized to prevent "worst-case" scenarios for overcurrent.

705.13 Power Control Systems

Power control systems must be listed and evaluated to control the output of power production sources, energy storage systems, and other equipment. The power control system must limit the current to the ampacity of the conductors or the ratings of the busbars to which it is connected in accordance with 705.13(A) through (E).

(A) Monitoring. The power control system controller must monitor all currents within the power control system. For any busbar or conductor on the load side of the service disconnect that is not monitored by the power control system, the busbar or conductors must be sized in accordance with 705.12.

Where the power control system is connected to the supply-side of service equipment as permitted by 705.11, the power control system must monitor the service conductors and prevent overload of these conductors.

(B) Settings. The sum of power control system currents plus all monitored currents from other sources of supply must not exceed the ampacity of any busbar or conductor ampacity supplied by the power production sources.

Where the power control system is connected to an overcurrent device protecting busbars or conductors not monitored by the power control system, the setting of the power control system must be set to the ratings of that overcurrent device.

(C) Overcurrent Protection. The power control system must provide overcurrent protection either by overcurrent devices or a power control system listed to provide overcurrent protection.

Note: Some power control systems are listed to provide overcurrent protection.

(D) Single Power Source Rating. The rating of the overcurrent device for any single power source controlled by the power control system is not permitted to exceed the rating of the busbar or the ampacity of the conductors to which it is connected.

(E) Access to Settings. The access to settings of the power control system must be restricted to qualified personnel in accordance with the requirements of 240.6(C).

Author's Comment:

▸ According to 240.6(C), restricted access is achieved by one of the following methods:

  (1) Locating behind removable and sealable covers over the adjusting means.

  (2) Locating behind bolted equipment enclosure doors.

  (3) Locating behind locked doors accessible only to qualified personnel.

  (4) Password protection, with the password accessible only to qualified personnel.

705.20 Disconnecting Means, Source

The title was changed from "Disconnecting Means, Sources" to "Disconnecting Means, Source," and in the parent text the term "ungrounded conductors" was replaced with "conductors that are not solidly grounded."

Analysis

RELOCATED The title was changed as the term is "source disconnecting means," not "sources disconnecting means." The term "ungrounded conductors" was replaced with the term "conductors that are not solidly grounded." This makes it clear that functionally grounded conductors must be disconnected. The disconnecting means requirements were relocated from 705.22 and incorporated into this section that covers all the requirements which are in eight list items as follows:

EXPANDED 705.20(1). This expands and clarifies the previous requirement as to the types of disconnects permitted.

RELOCATED 705.20(2). Simultaneous disconnection of the phase conductors was relocated from 705.22(6).

RELOCATED 705.20(3). Accessibility to disconnect equipment was relocated from 705.22(1).

EDITED 705.20(4). This was relocated from 705.22(2) and simplified. The requirement remains the same in that the disconnecting device can be operated without exposing the operator to energized parts.

NEW 705.20(5). Disconnecting means enclosure considerations is a new requirement to provide additional protection for unqualified persons.

RELOCATED 705.20(6). Indication of when the disconnect is "on" or "off" was relocated from 705.22(3).

RELOCATED 705.20(7). Rating requirements were relocated from 705.22(4).

RELOCATED 705.20(8). Capability of the line and load conductors being energized while the disconnect is in the opened or "off" position was relocated from 705.22(5) with a requirement that this must be so indicated, and the Informational Note following this item was edited.

705.20 Disconnect

Means must be provided to disconnect <u>power source output circuit</u> conductors from conductors <u>of other systems</u>. The power source disconnecting means must comply with the following:

(1) The power source disconnect must <u>be one of the four following types:</u>

(a) <u>A manually operable switch or circuit breaker.</u>

(b) <u>A load-break-rated pull-out switch.</u>

(c) <u>A remote-controlled switch or circuit breaker that is capable of being operated manually and can be opened automatically when control power is interrupted.</u>

(d) <u>A device listed or approved for the intended application.</u>

(2) The power source disconnect must simultaneously disconnect all phase conductors of the circuit.

(3) The power source disconnect must be readily accessible and be at a readily accessible location.

(4) The power source disconnect must be externally operable without <u>exposed</u> live parts.

(5) <u>Enclosures with doors or hinged covers with exposed live parts when open that require a tool to open or are lockable where readily accessible to unqualified persons.</u>

Author's Comment:

▸ Typically, safety switches are interlocked so the hinged door will not open without the use of a tool to defeat the door safety interlock. However, the door will open with the switch in the off position and with interconnected power sources where both sides of the switch are energized, an unqualified person could be exposed to energized parts where the switch is in the off position and the door is open.

(6) The power source disconnect must indicate if it is in the open (off) or closed (on) position.

(7) The power source disconnect must have a rating that is sufficient for the maximum circuit current, available fault current, and voltage that is available at the terminals.

(8) Be marked in accordance with the warning in 690.13(B), where the line and load terminals are capable of being energized in the open position.

WARNING—ELECTRIC SHOCK HAZARD
TERMINALS ON THE LINE AND LOAD SIDES
MAY BE ENERGIZED IN THE OPEN POSITION

The warning markings on the power source disconnect must be permanently affixed and have sufficient durability to withstand the environment involved [110.21(B)].

Note: With interconnected power sources, some equipment, including switches and fuses, is likely to be energized from both directions. See 240.40.

705.25 Wiring Methods

This new section specifies the permitted wiring methods for interconnected electric power production sources.

Analysis

This section is divided into subsections as follows:

 705.25(A) General. The permitted wiring methods for interconnected electric power production sources are specified here.
NEW

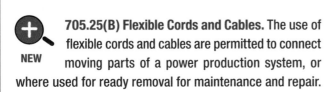 **705.25(B) Flexible Cords and Cables.** The use of flexible cords and cables are permitted to connect moving parts of a power production system, or where used for ready removal for maintenance and repair.
NEW

705.25(C) Multiconductor Cable Assemblies. This is designed to permit the use of manufactured "wiring harnesses" which are multiconductor cable assemblies where they are used in accordance with their listing requirements.
NEW

An Informational Note follows (C) and advises that an "ac module harness" is one example of a multiconductor cable assembly.

705.25 Wiring Methods

(A) General. All raceway and cable wiring methods included in Chapter 3 of this *Code* and other wiring systems and fittings specifically listed, intended, and identified for use with power production equipment are permitted.

(B) Flexible Cords and Cables. Flexible cords and cables used to connect moving parts of a power production system or where used for ready removal for maintenance and repair must be in accordance with Article 400. The flexible cord or cable must be listed and identified as Type DG cable, hard service cord or portable power cable, be suitable for extra-hard usage, listed for outdoor use, and water resistant. Cables exposed to sunlight must be sunlight resistant. Flexible, fine-stranded cables must terminate on terminals, lugs, devices, or connectors identified for the use of finely stranded conductors in accordance with 110.14(A).

(C) Multiconductor Cable Assemblies. Multiconductor cable assemblies used in accordance with their listings are permitted.

Note: An alternating-current module harness is one example of a multiconductor cable assembly.

705.28 Circuit Sizing and Current

The information in this new section was previously found in 705.60 and 705.95. The rules were relocated so they will apply throughout Article 705.

Analysis

Additional items that were relocated are as follows:

 705.28(A) Calculation of Maximum Circuit Current. This was 705.60 and moved to this location in Part I so it applies throughout this article. It was also revised to say that where not required or permitted elsewhere in this *Code*, the maximum current must be the continuous output rating of the power production equipment. In the 2017 *NEC*, this section referred to the maximum current of only the inverter. This article includes power production sources that do not require an inverter.
RELOCATED

705.28(B) Conductor Ampacity. This was relocated from 705.60 and reorganized; there were no technical changes.

705.28(C) Ampacity of Neutral Conductor. This subsection was relocated from 705.95(A) and (B) without technical change.

705.28(C)(1) Single-Phase Line-to-Neutral Power Sources. The requirements for the condition where a 2-wire power source is connected to a single-phase 3-wire system or to a 3-phase, 4-wire, wye system are provided here.

705.28(C)(2) Neutral Conductor Used Solely for Instrumentation, Voltage, Detection, or Phase Detection. This subsection covers the required ampacity where the neutral conductor is used for instrumentation, voltage detection, or phase detection. This conductor does not carry load current and is permitted to have an ampacity less than that of the current-carrying conductors.

705.28 Circuit Sizing and Current

(A) Calculation of Maximum Circuit Current. Where not elsewhere required or permitted in the *Code*, the maximum power source output circuit current is equal to the continuous output current rating of the power production equipment.

(B) Conductor Ampacity. Circuit conductors must be sized to the largest of the following:

(1) 125 percent of the maximum continuous output current rating of the power production equipment [705.28(A)] without conductor ampacity correction and/or adjustment.

(2) 100 percent of the maximum continuous output current rating of the power production equipment [705.28(A)] after conductor ampacity correction and/or adjustment.

(3) Where circuit conductors are tapped to feeders, the tap conductors must have an ampacity in accordance with 240.21(B).

(C) Neutral Conductors. Neutral conductors may be sized in accordance with either of the following:

(1) Single-Phase Line-to-Neutral Power Sources. Where not elsewhere required or permitted in this *Code*, the ampacity of a neutral conductor to which a single-phase line-to-neutral power source is connected cannot be smaller than the ampacity in 705.28(B).

(2) Neutral Conductor for Instrumentation, Voltage Detection, or Phase Detection. A neutral conductor to power production equipment that is used solely for instrumentation, voltage detection, or phase detection is permitted to be sized in accordance with Table 250.102(C)(1).

705.30 Overcurrent Protection

This section was revised to incorporate requirements that were in 705.65.

Analysis

The requirements in 705.30(A), (C), and (D) in the 2017 *NEC* were deleted as they did not add any additional rules. Those subsections addressed the overcurrent protection for solar PV systems, fuel cell systems, and interactive inverters but they simply referenced the overcurrent protection rules in the articles that address those systems.

Those rules automatically apply where that type of system is installed, and the additional reference here added no value to *Code* users. Those subsections were replaced with new ones to address Article 705's overcurrent protection requirements and designated (A), (B), (C), and (D) as follows:

705.30(A) Circuits and Equipment. This rule was relocated from 705.65(A) and simplified although the actual requirements remain unchanged from 2017. The power source output circuits and equipment must be provided with overcurrent protection. The 2017 *Code* referenced Article 240, but full article references are not permitted by the *NEC Style Manual*. The words "be provided with overcurrent protection" accomplishes the same thing as the overcurrent protection rules found in Article 240.

705.30(B) Overcurrent Device Ratings. This was relocated from 705.60(B) and revised to apply to all power production source output circuits other than generators. This rule applied to only inverters in the 2017 *Code* and did not require the OCPD to be sized at 125 percent of the maximum current as calculated in 705.28(A). There is also a new exception that says circuits that contain an assembly together with its OCPD that is listed for continuous operation at 100 percent of its rating is permitted to be utilized at 100 percent of its rating.

RELOCATED

705.30(C) Power Transformers. This is a relocation of the overcurrent protection rules for transformers from 705.30(B) with clarification as to the required transformer protection. The revised language specifies that the primary is the side connected to the largest source of available fault current. For most (if not all) utility-interactive systems, this would be the utility side.

RELOCATED

705.30(D) Generators. This was previously (E) and now re-designated (D) as a result of the other deletions. It previously required the generator protection to be in accordance with 705.130. That section was deleted and the rule in (D) now references 445.12 which specifies the overcurrent protection required for generators.

RELOCATED

705.30 Overcurrent Protection

(A) Circuits and Equipment. Power source output circuit conductors and equipment must be provided with overcurrent protection. Circuits connected to more than one electrical source must have overcurrent protection located so as to provide overcurrent protection from all sources of power.

(B) Overcurrent Device Ratings. The overcurrent protective device must have an ampere rating of not less than 125 percent of the maximum currents calculated in 705.28(A).

Ex: Where the assembly, together with its overcurrent device(s) is listed for continuous operation at 100 percent of its rating, the overcurrent device is permitted to be sized at 100 percent of the maximum currents calculated in 705.28(A).

(C) Power Transformers. Overcurrent protection for a transformer, within the scope of Article 450, having a power source on each side of the transformer is required to have overcurrent protection in accordance with 450.3(B). Each side of the transformer is to be considered the primary for this application.

Overcurrent protection is not required on the side of the transformer where the transformer current rating is equal to or greater than the sum of the rated power source output circuit currents connected to that side of the transformer.

705.32 Ground Fault Protection

This now applies to GFPE devices installed in accordance with only 230.95.

Analysis

This section was revised so it addresses ground-fault protection that is installed in accordance with only 230.95. At first glance this rule may appear to apply to only service ground-fault protection; however, the rules that require ground-fault protection of equipment for branch circuits (210.13) and for feeders (215.10) both specify that the GFPE be installed in accordance with 230.95. The language makes this rule apply even where the equipment ground-fault protection is installed on branch circuits or feeders.

CLARIFIED

705.32 Ground-Fault Protection

Where a ground-fault protection of equipment (GFPE) device is installed in accordance with 230.95, the output of an interactive system must be connected to the supply side of the GFPE device.

Ex: The output connection of an interactive system is permitted to be made to the load side of the ground-fault protection of equipment device, if ground-fault protection for equipment from all ground-fault current sources is provided.

705.40 Loss of Primary Source

The rules from 705.42 were combined with this section so a single rule applies to the loss of the primary supply regardless of its type.

Analysis

REORGANIZED This rule was combined with the one in 705.42 that applied to three-phase primary source loss. The revisions were to make the section apply to all types of electrical systems and the loss of any phase in an alternating-current system. There were no technical changes made with this revision.

705.40 Loss of Utility Power

The output of electric power production equipment must automatically disconnect from all phase conductors of the interconnected systems when one or more of the primary source phases opens. The electric power production equipment is not permitted to reconnected to the primary source of power until all the phases of the interconnected system have been restored.

This requirement does not apply to electric power production equipment providing power to an emergency or legally required standby system.

Ex: A listed interactive inverter is permitted to automatically disconnect when one or more phase conductors from the primary source opens and it is permitted to automatically or manually resume exporting power to the interconnected system once all phases of the source to which it is connected are restored. ▶Figure 705–23

If the utility (primary source) loses power, an interactive inverter stops exporting power back to the utility. During the power loss, the load side of the circuit breaker remains de-energized until the utility power is restored. ▶Figure 705–24

Note 1: Risks to personnel and equipment associated with the primary source could occur if an interactive electric power production source operates as an intentional island.

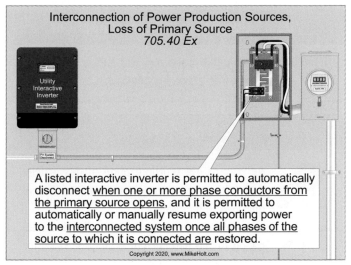

Interconnection of Power Production Sources, Loss of Primary Source
705.40 Ex

A listed interactive inverter is permitted to automatically disconnect when one or more phase conductors from the primary source opens, and it is permitted to automatically or manually resume exporting power to the interconnected system once all phases of the source to which it is connected are restored.

Copyright 2020, www.MikeHolt.com

▶Figure 705–23

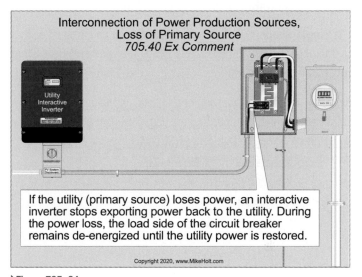

Interconnection of Power Production Sources, Loss of Primary Source
705.40 Ex Comment

If the utility (primary source) loses power, an interactive inverter stops exporting power back to the utility. During the power loss, the load side of the circuit breaker remains de-energized until the utility power is restored.

Copyright 2020, www.MikeHolt.com

▶Figure 705–24

Special detection methods are required to determine that a primary source supply system outage has occurred and whether there should be automatic disconnection. When the primary source supply system is restored, special detection methods are typically required to limit exposure of power production sources to out-of-phase reconnection.

Note 2: Induction-generating equipment connected on systems with significant capacitance can become self-excited upon loss of the primary source and experience severe overvoltage as a result.

Interactive power production equipment is permitted to operate in island mode to supply loads that have been disconnected from the electric power production and distribution network.

705.45 Unbalanced Interconnections

This rule was relocated from 705.100 and is specific to single-phase and three-phase installations.

Analysis

RELOCATED

As part of the reorganization of this article, 705.100 was relocated with no technical changes to its content.

705.45 Unbalanced Interconnections

(A) Single-Phase. Single-phase inverters must be arranged so that unbalanced system voltage at the utility service disconnect is not more than three percent.

Note: For interactive power sources, unbalanced voltages can be minimized by the same methods that are used for single-phase loads on a three-phase power system. See ANSI/C84.1, *Electric Power Systems and Equipment—Voltage Ratings (60 Hertz)*.

Author's Comment:

▸ An example of an unbalanced interconnection is connecting two single-phase inverters to a three-phase system.

▸ ANSI C84.1 recommends that "electric supply systems should be designed to limit the maximum voltage unbalance to three percent when measured at the electric-utility revenue meter under no-load conditions." Improperly connecting single-phase inverters to a three-phase system can result in a significant increase in unbalanced system voltage. Three-phase motors will run hotter using unbalanced voltage because the unbalanced magnetic fields created by the windings work against each other. The formula to determine maximum unbalanced voltage is: **Maximum Unbalanced Voltage = 100 x Maximum Deviation from Average Voltage/Average Voltage**.

▸ **Existing Installation Example**

Question: If two single-phase PV systems are connected to lines B–C and this causes the B–C voltage to increase from 200V to 202V because of a decrease in loading, the maximum unbalanced system voltage for the following line voltages: A–B 206V, B–C 202V, and A–C 204V will be _____ percent.

(a) 1   (b) 1.50   (c) 2.04   (d) 3

Answer: (a) 1

Solution:

Maximum Unbalanced Voltage = Maximum Deviation Volts from Average Voltage/Average Voltage x 100 (for Percent)

Average Voltage = (206V + 202V + 204V)/3 lines
Average Voltage = 204V

Maximum Deviation from Average = 206V–204
Maximum Deviation from Average = 2V

Maximum Unbalanced Voltage = 2V/204V x 100%
Maximum Unbalanced Voltage = 1%

▸ **Unbalanced System Voltage—Two Inverters Example 1**

Question: If two single-phase PV systems are connected to lines B–C and this results in B–C voltage to rise from 200V to 201V because of a decrease in loading, the maximum unbalanced system voltage for the following line voltages: A–B 206V, B–C 201V, and A–C 204V will be _____ percent.

(a) 1   (b) 1.15   (c) 1.50   (d) 2.06

Answer: (b) 1.15

Solution:

Maximum Unbalanced Voltage = Maximum Deviation from Average Voltage/Average Voltage x 100 (for Percent).

Average Voltage = (206V + 201V + 204V)/3 lines
Average Voltage = 203.66V

Maximum Deviation from Average = 206V–203.66V
Maximum Deviation from Average = 2.34V

Maximum Unbalanced Voltage = 2.34V/203.66V x 100%
Maximum Unbalanced Voltage = 1.15%

► **Unbalanced System Voltage—Two Inverters Example 2**

Question: *If two single-phase PV systems are connected to lines A–B and this causes the A–B voltage to increase from 206V to 208V because of a decrease in loading, the maximum unbalanced system voltage for the following line voltages: A–B 208V, B–C 200V, and A–C 204V will be _____ percent.*

(a) 1   (b) 1.15   (c) 1.50   (d) 1.96

Answer: *(d) 1.96*

Solution:

Maximum Unbalanced Voltage = Maximum Deviation from Average Voltage/Average Voltage x 100 (for Percent).

Average Voltage = (208V + 200V + 204V)/3 lines
Average Voltage = 204V

Maximum Deviation from Average = 208V–204V
Maximum Deviation from Average = 4V

Maximum Unbalanced Voltage = 4V/204V x 100%
Maximum Unbalanced Voltage = 1.96

(B) Three-Phase. Three-phase inverters must have all phases automatically de-energized upon loss of, or unbalanced voltage in, one or more phases unless the interconnected system is designed so that significant unbalanced voltages will not result.

Parts II and III

Parts II and III were deleted as part of the restructuring of Article 705.

Analysis

REORGANIZED   DELETED

Sections were deleted or incorporated into other sections of Article 705.

Part II Microgrid Systems was Part IV but has become Part II as result of the deletion of the previous Parts II and III. The numbering was changed by subtracting 100 from the previous section number; section 705.150 became 705.50.

705.50 System Operation

This section was clarified by replacing the phrase "operate as a separate microgrid system" with "as an isolated microgrid operating in island mode."

Analysis

CLARIFIED

This section permits the microgrid system to disconnect from the primary or other interconnected electric power production source and operate in island mode. This removes the undefined term "as a separate microgrid" and replaces it with the term "islanded" to align with other standards and *NEC* articles. The new language more closely aligns with Article 710 and the wording in IEEE 1547 and 2030.

Part II. Microgrid Systems

705.50 System Operation

Microgrid systems are permitted to disconnect from the primary source of power or other interconnected electric power production sources and operate <u>as an isolated microgrid system operating in island mode</u>.

705.60 Primary Power Source Connection

New language was added to clarify that the power source conductors connected to a microgrid are considered power source output conductors.

Analysis

CLARIFIED

This section required the connections of the microgrid to the primary power source to comply with the requirements of 705.12. Since the rules for supply-side connections were moved out of 705.12, expanded, and placed into the new section 705.11, the language was revised to reference both sections. It was also expanded to reference 705.13 for cases where the conductors are connected to a power control system (PCS).

● ● ●

A new sentence was added to clarify that the power source conductors connecting to a microgrid system are power source output conductors. This is intended to address the increasing use of on-site energy sources being connected to serve premises distribution equipment in a microgrid application and to clarify that the conductors associated with the microgrid are not service conductors, but branch-circuit or feeder conductors and their installation should comply with the rules in 210 and 215, not those in 230. The substantiation indicated that this new language will help prevent confusion and aid in the proper application of long-established *NEC* requirements to these relatively new systems.

705.70 Microgrid Interconnect Devices (MID)

This was relocated from 705.170 and a list item was revised.

Analysis

RELOCATED This is same language change that was made in other *Code* sections where "field labeled" was replaced with "evaluated and have a field label applied." This makes it clear that it must be first evaluated for the application, and when found suitable, a field label indicating its suitability is applied to the equipment.

705.60 Primary Power Source Connection

Connections to primary power sources that are external to the microgrid system must comply with the requirements of 705.11, 705.12, or 705.13.

Power source conductors connecting to a microgrid system, including conductors supplying distribution equipment, are considered as power source output conductors.

705.70 Microgrid Interconnect Devices

Microgrid interconnect devices must comply with the following:

(1) Be required for any connection between a microgrid system and a primary power source.

(2) Be evaluated for the application and have a field label applied or be listed for the application.

(3) Have a sufficient number of overcurrent devices that provide overcurrent protection from all sources.

Note: Microgrid interconnect device functionality is often incorporated in an interactive or multimode inverter, energy storage system, or similar device identified for interactive operation.

Introduction to Article 706—Energy Storage Systems

Only introduced to the *Code* during the 2017 revision cycle, the addition of Article 706 was, and still is, the result of massive amounts of energy production from alternative sources such as wind and solar. The need to store this energy was and is a fortunate inevitability. In fact, the *NEC* Correlating Committee formed a 79-member Task Group along with input from many other sources to develop the requirements contained within this article.

It is important to understand what Article 706 applies to and what it does not apply to. The scope of Article 706 informs us that this information applies to all permanently installed energy storage systems (ESS) "having a capacity greater than 1 kWh." These may be stand-alone or interactive with other electric power production sources.

An energy storage system (ESS) is one or more components, when assembled together capable of storing energy for future use. An (ESS) might include (but is not limited to) batteries, capacitors, and kinetic energy devices (such as flywheels and compressed air). Some of these systems will have either ac or dc output available. They may also include inverters and converters to change stored energy into electrical energy.

Energy storage systems can be (and usually are) connected to other energy sources, such as the local utility distribution system. There can be more than one source of power connected to an energy storage system (ESS) and the connection to other energy sources is required to comply with the requirements of Article 705 which covers installation of one or more electric power production sources operating in parallel with a utility source of electricity. It might also be a good idea to be mindful of how this article correlates with other articles in the Code such as Articles 480, 690, 692, and 694.

706.1 Scope

The scope was expanded to include temporary as well as permanent energy storage systems, and the size of the system to which the article applies was clarified.

Analysis

EXPANDED The scope of this article was expanded to include both permanently installed and temporary energy storage systems (ESS). This was accomplished by deleting the words "permanently installed" from the scope statement. The panel statement on this change indicated ESS used for temporary applications such as concerts, fairs, festivals, or disaster relief, pose the same fire and shock hazards as do permanently installed systems.

• • •

The previous voltage limit that said this article applied to systems "operating at over 50V ac, or 60V dc" was replaced with "having a capacity greater than 1 kWh." The hazard is more directly related to the energy stored than to the voltage. The 1 kWh capacity also aligns the *NEC* with language in the fire and building *codes*.

A new last sentence was added to the scope to say that the ESSs covered by this article are primarily intended to store and provide energy during normal operating conditions. Two Informational Notes were also added; Informational Note No. 1 was added to explain how to convert the capacity of batteries rated in ampere hours to kWh, and the second was added to say that there can be a subtle distinction between a battery storing energy and an energy storage system.

706.1 Scope

This article applies to all energy storage systems <u>having a capacity greater than 1 kWh</u> that may be stand-alone or interactive with the electric utility supply. Energy storage systems <u>are primarily intended to store and provide energy during normal operating conditions</u>.

▸Figure 706–1

Energy Storage Systems
706.1 Scope

Article 706 applies to all energy storage systems <u>having a capacity greater than 1 kWh</u> that may be stand-alone or interactive with the electric utility supply.

Copyright 2020, www.MikeHolt.com

▸Figure 706–1

<u>Note 1:</u> For batteries rated in ampere hours, kWh is equal to the battery nominal rated voltage times the battery ampere-hour rating, divided by 1,000.

Author's Comment:

▸ To better understand ampere hours relative to kilo-watt hours think of your cellphone. Many cellphone batteries are rated at 3,000 mAh (milli-amp hours), which when divided by 1000 would be 3 ampere hours. Lithium-ion batteries, prominent in cell phones, have a voltage of 3.7V. Multiplied by 3 ampere hours would result in 11.1 watt-hours. As you probably now realize, calculating the amount of power available in a battery is simply an exercise in Ohm's Law but on a larger scale.

<u>Note 2: There can be a subtle distinction between a battery storing energy and an energy storage system. A battery storing energy is not necessarily an Energy Storage System, see Article 480. An Energy Storage System can be comprised of batteries storing energy, see Article 706.</u>

Author's Comment:

▸ As always, Informational Notes provide additional information related to the *Code* article or rule, or list other sources where additional information may be obtained. The fact that a standard is listed in a note does not make it part of the *Code* or require that the installer comply with the rules in the referenced standard.

706.2 Definitions

Definitions in this section were relocated and a new one added.

Analysis

RELOCATED **Energy Storage System (ESS).** This definition was revised to clarify that energy storage systems not only store energy but can also provide electrical energy into premises wiring systems or to an electric power production and distribution network. One example of where the power would be supplied to an electric power production and distribution network is where the ESS is part of a microgrid system.

The previous definition included language giving examples of types of energy storage systems and that information was relocated into new Informational Note No.1. The language in the note is a direct relocation of what was in the previous definition without any change.

(+) NEW Informational Note No. 2. This note is intended to differentiate between a UPS (commonly used for backup power for only IT and communications systems) from an ESS that can provide other functions in addition to backup power.

(−) DELETED Energy Storage System, Self-Contained; Energy Storage System, Pre-Engineered and Energy Storage System, Other. These terms were deleted from the definitions as they are not used in Article 706 and are not commonly used in other codes or product safety standards.

706.2 Definitions

The definitions in this section only apply to this article.

Diversion Charge Controller. Equipment that regulates the charging process of an energy storage system by diverting power from energy storage to direct-current or alternating-current loads or to an interconnected utility service.

Author's Comment:

▸ The definition for Diversion Charge Controller has seen no technical changes but is included here because it was deleted from Article 690, PV Systems. It still appears in Article 694 but as the new parent text for "Definitions" states, as used here, "the definition only applies to this article." Even though it may serve the same purpose in Article 694, there is the same guidance there as well.

Energy Storage System (ESS). One or more components assembled together capable of storing energy and providing electrical energy into the premises wiring system or the electric utility supply.

Note 1: Energy storage systems can include but are not limited to batteries, capacitors, and kinetic energy devices such as flywheels and compressed air. Energy storage systems can include inverters or converters to change voltage levels or to make a change between an alternating-current or a direct-current system.

Note 2: Energy storage systems differ from other storage systems such as a UPS system, which is a power supply that provides alternating-current power for loads for some period of time in the event of a power failure.

706.3 Qualified Personnel

References to other articles were deleted and new language requiring an ESS to be installed and maintained by qualified persons was added.

Analysis

(+) NEW In the previous *NEC* this section did not modify any other articles, so it was unnecessary. It did reference rules in Article 705, but they automatically apply as there is no modification of them in this article.

706.3 Qualified Personnel

The installation and maintenance of energy storage system equipment and all associated wiring and interconnections must be performed only by qualified persons.

Note: See Article 100 for the definition of "Qualified Person."

706.4 System Requirements

This section was changed from "System Classification" to "System Requirements" and was expanded to specify marking requirements.

Analysis

EXPANDED

The revised language specifies that the name-plate be plainly visible after installation and be marked with the information provided by the manufacturer, and the list now better aligns with the UL standard that is currently used to list ESS equipment. The only thing the electrician needs to do is to make sure the manufacturer's nameplate is clearly visible after the equipment has been installed.

Analysis

EXPANDED

This section now creates the requirement for any energy storage system to be listed as a system. Previous text did not specify this. While components were required to be listed, a system listing was optional. Although this is a significant change, it aligns with updates to fire and building codes common in the U.S. The list of items that required listing was also deleted as that list included ESS classifications that are no longer used.

706.4 System Requirements

Each energy storage system must have a nameplate plainly visible after installation and marked with the following:

(1) Manufacturer's name, trademark, or other descriptive marking by which the organization responsible for supplying the energy storage system can be identified.

(2) Rated frequency.

(3) Number of phases, if ac.

(4) Rating (kW or kVA).

(5) Available fault current derived by the energy storage system (energy storage system (ESS) at the output terminals.

(6) Maximum output and input current of the energy storage system (energy storage system (ESS) at the output terminals.

(7) Maximum output and input voltage of the energy storage system (energy storage system (ESS) at the output terminals.

(8) Utility-interactive capability if applicable.

706.5 Listing

The title was changed from "Equipment" to "Listing" to better reflect the requirements in this section.

706.5 Listing

Energy storage systems must be listed.

706.7 Maintenance

The requirements for disconnects that were in this section were moved to 706.15; this rule now specifies the maintenance requirements for energy storage systems.

Analysis

NEW

This new language covers the maintenance of ESS equipment. It requires the equipment to be maintained in a proper and safe operating condition and that it be maintained in accordance the manufacturer's requirements and industry standards. It also requires a written record of the maintenance to be kept and include reports of repairs and replacements.

A new Informational Note references NFPA 70B, *Recommended Practice for Electrical Equipment Maintenance* and NETA ATS, *Standard for Acceptance Testing Specifications for Electrical Power Equipment and Systems*.

706.7 Maintenance

Energy storage systems must be maintained in proper and safe operating condition. The required maintenance must be in accordance with the manufacturer's requirements and industry standards. A written record of the system maintenance must be kept and include records of repairs and replacements necessary to maintain the system in proper and safe operating condition.

Note: For information related to general electrical equipment maintenance and developing an effective electrical preventive maintenance (EPM) program, see NFPA 70B, *Recommended Practice for Electrical Equipment Maintenance,* or ANSI/NETA ATS, *Standard for Acceptance Testing Specifications for Electrical Power Equipment and Systems*.

Author's Comment:

▸ A panel member's comment on his affirmative vote said: "While there are some examples of maintenance requirements in the *NEC*, this panel member notes that there are issues related to enforcement and uniformity of application given the *NEC* scope." One of those issues is that the scope of the *Code* only includes installation and not maintenance of electrical systems.

706.9 Maximum Voltage

This new section is intended to address the maximum voltage of an energy storage system.

Analysis

NEW There are several references in Article 706 as to the voltage of an ESS. The new *Code* text says the maximum voltage of an ESS is its rated voltage as marked on its nameplate or system listing.

706.9 Maximum Voltage

The maximum voltage of an energy storage system (energy storage system (ESS) must be the rated energy storage system (energy storage system (ESS) input and output voltage(s) indicated on the energy storage system (energy storage system (ESS) nameplate(s) or system listing

Author's Comment:

▸ Notice that some ESS may have different input and output voltages. This could be a case where the ESS allows for the connection of a dc source, like a PV system, while also having an output connection to an ac grid.

▸ While it is clear that the maximum voltage of an ESS is determined through its listing, it is strange to see a maximum voltage requirement in the *Code* that does not specify any numerical voltages.

Part II. Disconnecting Means

The name of this Part was changed.

Analysis

RELOCATED **706.15 Disconnecting Means.** The requirements from 706.7 in the 2017 *NEC* were relocated, clarified, and expanded as this new section for the 2020 *Code*.

EXPANDED **706.15(A) ESS Disconnecting Means.** This rule was expanded to permit the disconnecting means to be integral to the ESS and to require the disconnecting means for one- and two-family dwelling unit ESS systems to be in a readily accessible exterior location.

The section was reorganized into charging text and three list items.

EXPANDED **706.15(C) Notification and Marking.** With the deletion of the busway rule, (D) became (C) and the title was changed to include marking requirements since they were added to this rule.

RELOCATED **706.15(D) Partitions Between Components.** This was (E), it was moved up to (D) and modified as the result of the deletion of the busway requirement. All the previous *Code* language in this subsection was deleted. In many cases the previous text created significant confusion and conflicted with other requirements. The new language is intended to address cases where the parts of the ESS are separated from each other by walls, floors, or ceilings. In those cases, additional disconnecting means with the storage component of the system (such as a battery that is placed in a separate room from an inverter) will be required.

706.15 Disconnect

(A) Disconnect. A disconnecting means must be provided for all phase conductors derived from an energy storage system (energy storage system (ESS) and is permitted to be integral to listed energy storage system (energy storage system (ESS) equipment. The disconnecting means must be readily accessible and located within sight of the energy storage system (ESS). The disconnecting means must comply with all of the following:

(1) The disconnecting means must be readily accessible.

(2) The disconnecting means must be located within sight of the energy storage system (ESS). Where it is impractical to install the disconnecting means within sight of the energy storage system (ESS), the disconnect is permitted to be installed as close as practicable, and the location of the disconnecting means must be field marked on or immediately adjacent to the energy storage system (ESS). The marking must be of sufficient durability to withstand the environment involved and must not be handwritten.

(3) The disconnecting means must be lockable open in accordance with 110.25.

(B) Remote Actuation. Where controls to activate the disconnect of an energy storage system are not located within sight of the system, the location of the controls must be field marked on the disconnect.

(C) Notification and Marking. Each energy storage system disconnect must plainly indicate whether it is in the open (off) or closed (on) position and be permanently marked:

ENERGY STORAGE SYSTEM DISCONNECT

The disconnect must be legibly marked in the field to indicate the following:

(1) The nominal energy storage system alternating-current voltage and maximum energy storage system direct-current voltage.

(2) The available fault current derived from the energy storage system.

(3) An arc-flash label applied in accordance with acceptable industry practice.

(4) The date the arc flash calculation was performed.

Ex: List items (2), (3), and (4) do not apply to one and two-family dwellings.

Note 1: Industry practices for equipment labeling are described in NFPA 70E, *Standard for Electrical Safety in the Workplace*. This standard provides specific criteria for developing arc-flash labels for equipment that provides nominal system voltage, incident energy levels, arc-flash boundaries, minimum required levels of personal protective equipment, and so forth.

Note 2: Battery equipment suppliers can provide available fault current on any particular battery model.

Where the line and load terminals within the energy storage system disconnect may be energized in the open position, the disconnect must be marked with the following words or equivalent:

**WARNING ELECTRIC SHOCK HAZARD
TERMINALS ON THE LINE AND LOAD
SIDES MAY BE ENERGIZED IN THE OPEN POSITION**

The notification(s) and marking(s) must be permanently affixed and have sufficient durability to withstand the environment involved [110.21(B)].

(D) Partitions Between Components. Where circuits from the input or output terminals of energy storage components pass through a wall, floor, or ceiling, a readily accessible disconnect must be provided within sight of the energy storage component. Fused disconnects or circuit breakers are permitted to serve as the required disconnect.

706.16 Connection to Energy Sources

The rules in this section were relocated from 706.8 and clarified.

Analysis

RELOCATED The title was changed to delete the word "other" as was the parent text requirement for the connection to other sources to be in accordance with 705.12. The compliance with 705.12 is now required by (E) while the parent text now requires compliance with subsections (A) though (F).

706.16 Connection to Other Sources

The connection of an energy storage system to other sources of power must comply with the following:

(A) Source Disconnect. A disconnect that has multiple sources of power must disconnect all energy sources when in the off position.

(B) Identified Interactive Equipment. Energy storage systems that operate in parallel with other alternating-current sources must use inverters that are listed and identified as interactive.

(C) Loss of Interactive System Power. Upon loss of electric utility supply, an energy storage system with a utility-interactive inverter must comply with 705.40.

(D) Unbalanced Interconnections. Unbalanced alternating-current connections between an energy storage system and other than the electric utility supply must be in accordance with 705.45.

(E) Connection to Other Energy Sources. The connection of an energy storage system to the electric utility supply must be in accordance with 705.12 and Parts III and VI of Article 712.

(F) Stand-Alone Operation. Where the output of an energy storage system is capable of operating in stand-alone mode, the requirements of 710.15 apply.

Part III Installation Requirements

Part III was renamed and is intended to better group the installation requirements of this article.

Analysis

REORGANIZED **706.20(B) Dwelling Units.** This change is relocated from 706.10(B), deletes the reference to 110.27 for guarding of live parts as that automatically applies throughout the *Code*, and relocates and clarifies the dwelling unit maximum voltage requirement. The rule now contains information that was moved from 706.30(A). The language was also revised to specify that the voltage being addressed is the dc voltage of the system and the references to clearances around batteries were deleted as the rules in Article 480 "Storage Batteries" address those requirements.

A new exception addressing dwelling units was added to say that where live parts are not accessible during routine ESS maintenance, a maximum ESS voltage of 600V dc is permitted.

REORGANIZED **706.20(C) Spaces About ESS Components.** This subsection was separated from a long paragraph into two subsections along with some technical changes.

Subsections (D) and (E) were removed.

Part III. Installation Requirements

706.20 General

(A) Ventilation. Provisions appropriate to the energy storage technology must be made for sufficient diffusion and ventilation of any possible gases from the storage device, if present, to prevent the accumulation of an explosive mixture. A pre-engineered or self-contained energy storage system is permitted to provide ventilation in accordance with the manufacturer's recommendations and listing for the system.

Note 1: See NFPA 1, *Fire Code*, Chapter 52, for ventilation considerations for specific battery chemistries.

Note 2: Some storage technologies do not require ventilation.

Note 3: A source for design of ventilation of battery systems is IEEE 1635-2012/ASHRAE Guideline 21, *Guide for the Ventilation and Thermal Management of Batteries for Stationary Applications*, and the UBC.

Note 4: Fire protection considerations are addressed in NFPA 1, *Fire Code*.

(B) Dwelling Units. Energy storage systems for one and two-family dwelling units are not permitted to have a direct-current voltage greater than 100V between conductors or to ground.

Ex: Where live parts are not accessible during routine energy storage system maintenance, a maximum energy storage system voltage of 600V dc is permitted.

(C) Spaces About Energy Storage System Components.

(1) General. Working spaces for energy storage system must be in accordance with 110.26.

(2) Space Between Components. Energy storage systems are permitted to have space between components in accordance with the manufacturer's instructions and listing.

Note: Additional space may be needed to accommodate energy storage system hoisting equipment, tray removal, or spill containment.

706.21 Directory (Identification of Power Sources)

Directory and identification of power sources labeling and marking requirements for energy storage and stand-alone systems were relocated, retitled, and modified.

Analysis

RELOCATED The references to 706.11(A) and (B) were deleted from the parent language as that information is now covered by 705.10 and 712.10. The parent text now specifies that the "ESS must be indicated by markings or labels that must be in accordance with 110.21(B)."

CLARIFIED **706.21(A) Facilities with Utility Services and ESS.** The previous language specifying the required information on the plaque or directory was replaced with references to 705.10 and 712.10 for the plaque or directory requirements.

The exception that followed this rule in the previous *Code* was deleted.

CLARIFIED **706.21(B) Facilities with Stand-Alone Systems.** The previous language was greatly simplified and requires facilities with stand-alone systems to have plaques or directories in accordance with 710.10.

706.21 Directory (Identification of Power Sources)

Energy storage systems must be identified by markings or labels that are permanently affixed with sufficient durability to withstand the environment involved [110.21(B)].

(A) Facilities with Utility Services and Energy Storage System. Plaques or directories must be installed in accordance with 705.10 and 712.10.

(B) Facilities with Stand-Alone Systems. In accordance with section 710.10, a permanent plaque or directory must be installed outside a building supplied by a stand-alone system at each service equipment location or at an approved readily visible location.

The plaque or directory must identify the location of each power source disconnect on or in the premises or be grouped with other plaques or directories for other on-site sources.

Any structure or building with an energy storage system must also have a permanent plaque or directory installed on the exterior of the building at an approved readily visible location. The plaque or directory must indicate the location of the energy storage system disconnect. Where multiple sources supply the building, the plaque or directory must be marked with the wording:

CAUTION: MULTIPLE SOURCES OF POWER.

The marking must comply with 110.21(B).

Ex: Multiple power production sources that are grouped can use a common designation on the directory.

Part IV. Circuit Requirements

This Part was renamed, and related sections were relocated.

706.30 Circuit Sizing and Current

Rules in this section were revised to clarify what the nameplate-rated circuit current is and that the inverter utilization output current is the continuous alternating-current output current rating.

Analysis

REORGANIZED **706.30(A)(1) Maximum Rated Current for a Specific Circuit.** The references to pre-engineered or self-contained systems of matched components were deleted as unnecessary. The rule now says the circuit current is the rated current indicated on the ESS nameplate or system listing. New language was added to address the cases where the same terminals on the ESS are used for both charging and discharging. These two current ratings may not be the same, and the new wording requires that for these dual-use terminals, the circuit current must be the greater of the two.

CLARIFIED **706.30(A)(4) Inverter Utilization Output Circuit Current.** The term "ac" was added to the term "inverter" to clarify the rule applies to the ac current. That should have been clear as the function of an inverter is to convert dc input to ac output. The language that addressed the rated power "at the lowest input voltage" was also deleted.

CLARIFIED **706.30(B) Conductor Ampacity.** The title was changed to make it match the rule. This subsection addresses only the conductor ampacity; not the overcurrent protective device (OCPD) ratings as those requirements are in 706.31.

Part IV. Circuit Requirements

706.30 Circuit Sizing and Current

(A) Maximum Rated Current for a Specific Circuit. The maximum current for a specific circuit must be calculated in accordance with 706.30(A)(1) through (A)(5).

(1) Nameplate-Rated Circuit Current. Circuit current must be the rated current indicated on the energy storage system nameplate(s) or system listing. Where the energy storage system has separate input (charge) and output (discharge) circuits or ratings, they must be considered individually. Where the same terminals on the energy storage system are used for charging and discharging, the rated current must be the greater of the two.

(2) Inverter Output Circuit Current. The maximum current must be the inverter continuous output current rating.

(3) Inverter Input Circuit Current. The maximum current must be the continuous inverter input current rating when the inverter is producing its rated power at the lowest input voltage.

(4) Inverter Utilization Output Circuit Current. The maximum current must be the continuous alternating-current output current rating of the inverter when the inverter is producing its rated power.

(5) DC-to-DC Converter Output Current. The maximum current must be the dc-to-dc converter's continuous output current rating.

(B) Conductor Ampacity. The ampacity of the feeder circuit conductors from the energy storage system(s) to the wiring system serving the loads to be serviced by the system must not be less than the greater of the (1) nameplate(s)-rated circuit current as determined in accordance with 706.30(A) or (2) the rating of the energy storage system's overcurrent protective device(s).

(C) Ampacity of Grounded or Neutral Conductor. If the output of a single-phase, 2-wire energy storage system output(s) is connected to the grounded or neutral conductor and a single phase conductor of a 3-wire system or of a three-phase, 4-wire, wye-connected system, the maximum unbalanced neutral load current plus the energy storage system(s) output rating must not exceed the ampacity of the grounded or neutral conductor.

706.31 Overcurrent Protection

A new exception was added to this section covering 100 percent rated overcurrent devices and the requirements were revised for overcurrent protection of ESS circuit conductors.

Analysis

706.31(B) Ex Overcurrent Device Ampere Ratings. A new exception covers OCPDs listed for operation at 100 percent of their ratings.

NEW

706.31(F) Location. The previous requirement that the OCPD be located not more than 5 ft from the equipment was deleted. The word "partition" was replaced with "floor or ceiling." This change correlates with the revision that was made to 706.15(D) requiring the disconnecting means to be within sight from the equipment. The language that required the OCPD to be within 5 ft of the equipment that applied where the circuits did not pass through a wall, floor, or ceiling was deleted.

CLARIFIED

706.31 Overcurrent Protection

(A) Circuits and Equipment. Energy storage system circuit conductors must be protected in accordance with the requirements of Article 240. Protection devices for energy storage system circuits must be in accordance with the requirements of 706.31(B) through (F), and circuits must be protected at the source from overcurrent.

(B) Overcurrent Device Ampere Ratings. Overcurrent protective devices, where required, must be rated in accordance with Article 240 and the rating provided on systems serving the energy storage system and must be not less than 125 percent of the maximum currents calculated in 706.30(A).

Ex: Where the assembly, including the overcurrent protective devices, is listed for operation at 100 percent of its rating, the ampere rating of the overcurrent devices are permitted to be not less than the maximum currents calculated in 706.30(B).

(C) Direct-Current Rating. Overcurrent protective devices, either fuses or circuit breakers, used in any direct-current portion of an energy storage system must be listed for direct current and have the appropriate voltage, current, and interrupting ratings for the application.

(D) Current Limiting. A listed and labeled current-limiting overcurrent protective device must be installed adjacent to the energy storage system for each direct-current output circuit.

Ex: Where current-limiting overcurrent protection is provided for the direct-current output circuits of a listed energy storage system, additional current-limiting overcurrent devices are not required.

(E) Fuses. Means must be provided to disconnect any fuses associated with energy storage system equipment and components when the fuse is energized from both directions and is accessible to other than qualified persons. Switches, pullouts, or similar devices that are rated for the application are permitted to serve as a means to disconnect fuses from all sources of supply.

(F) Location. Where circuits from the input or output terminals of energy storage components in an energy storage system pass through a wall, floor, or ceiling, overcurrent protection must be provided at the energy storage component of the circuit.

Author's Comment:

▸ It would appear that this rule (F) no longer seems to address the location of the OCPD where the circuit does not pass through a wall, floor or ceiling. Since all ESS are now required to be listed, one must assume that this issue would be addressed during the product's evaluation.

▸ As a result of the overall reorganization of Article 706:
  ◆ former Part IV is now Part V Flow Battery Energy Storage Systems
  ◆ former Part V is now Part VI Other Storage Technologies
  ◆ Neither having any technical changes.

STAND-ALONE SYSTEMS

Introduction to Article 710—Stand-Alone Systems

The requirements for stand-alone power production sources are covered here in Article 710. Stand-alone sources are what the name implies; they are not connected to the utility power grid or any other power production/distribution network.

These sources must also comply with Chapters 1 through 4 of the *NEC*. Depending on the purpose and design of a particular stand-alone source, it may also be covered by a Chapter 6 and/or another Chapter 7 article. For example, if it is a stand-alone fuel cell optional standby system, then it is also covered by Article 692 and Article 702.

Occupying about half a page, Article 710 is one of the shortest in the *Code*, but its brevity does not imply insignificance. In fact, this article will take on increasing significance as the growth in stand-alone system installations continues. Many of these are systems that use wind, solar, or other "alternative energy" sources, but fossil fuel sources are also in the mix.

The main point here is to relieve the designer from some of the constraints imposed on interconnected systems. For example, you can size the source smaller than the total calculated load, but not smaller than the largest single connected utilization equipment. There are also restrictions; for example, you cannot have backfed breakers. If you understand the requirements and what is permitted, you can design a safe system at a lower construction/installation cost.

710.1 Scope

The scope was revised to clarify that this article covers electric power production systems that operate in island mode and installations not connected to an electric power production and distribution network.

Analysis

CLARIFIED The term "stand-alone mode" was replaced with "island mode;" something that is being done throughout the *Code*. Additional wording clarifies that this article also applies to installations not connected to an electric power production and distribution network.

A new Informational Note following the scope provides some explanation of what a "stand-alone" system operating in "Island Mode" is.

710.1 Scope

This article covers electric power production systems that operate in island mode and are not connected to an electric utility supply. ▶Figure 710–1

Note: Stand-alone systems are capable of operating in island mode, independent from the electric utility, and include isolated microgrid systems or they can be interactive with other power sources. Stand-alone systems often include a single or a compatible interconnection of sources such as engine generators, solar PV, wind, an energy storage system, or batteries.

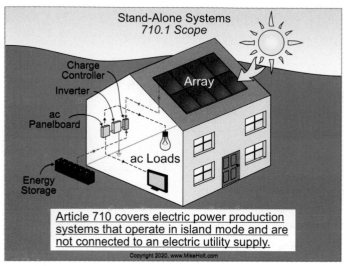

Stand-Alone Systems
710.1 Scope

Charge Controller

Inverter

ac Panelboard

Array

ac Loads

Energy Storage

Article 710 covers electric power production systems that operate in island mode and are not connected to an electric utility supply.

Copyright 2020, www.MikeHolt.com

▶Figure 710–1

Author's Comment:

▸ The definition for "Stand-Alone Mode" now resides in Article 100. A stand-alone system describes the system and how it is different from other systems but to differentiate from other operational modes such as utility-interactive, island mode is being used to better align with other standards. Especially since a stand-alone system could have a connection to another primary source such as a utility but differs from other systems through its ability to operate independent of that primary source.

Island Mode. The operational mode for stand-alone power production equipment or an isolated microgrid, or for a multimode inverter or an interconnected microgrid that is disconnected from the electric utility supply.

Note: Isolated microgrids are distinguished from interconnected microgrids, which are addressed in Article 705.

710.6 Equipment Approval

The field labeling requirement was clarified to include both evaluation and labeling.

Analysis

CLARIFIED This is a clarification on the field label process that has been done in several sections. The requirement is not just that a field label be applied, but that the equipment be evaluated for the application (and where found suitable) and a field label is applied to indicate that.

710.6 Equipment Approval

All equipment must be <u>approved</u> for the intended use in accordance with one of the following: ▶Figure 710–2

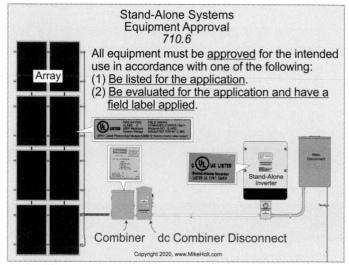

Stand-Alone Systems
Equipment Approval
710.6

All equipment must be <u>approved</u> for the intended use in accordance with one of the following:
(1) <u>Be listed for the application</u>.
(2) <u>Be evaluated for the application and have a field label applied</u>.

Array

Combiner   dc Combiner Disconnect

Stand-Alone Inverter

Main Disconnect

Copyright 2020, www.MikeHolt.com

▶Figure 710–2

(1) Be listed for the application.

(2) Be evaluated for the application and have a field label applied.

Note: Inverters identified as "multimode" and "stand-alone" are specifically identified and certified to operate in this application. Stand-alone inverters operate in island mode. Multimode inverters operate in either island mode (previously called "stand-alone mode") or interactive mode, if it has been installed with the optional utility grid connection. A multimode inverter will only operate in island mode if it is never connected to an electric utility supply. Stand-alone inverters are not evaluated, and are not intended, for connection to export power in parallel with an electric utility.

710.10 Identification of Power Sources

This new section requires a permanent plaque or directory to be installed at a building supplied by a stand-alone system.

Analysis

NEW This section requires a plaque or directory to be located at the service equipment or at an approved readily visible location. Since a service is optional for a stand-alone system, the AHJ will need to provide guidance for where this marking would be placed in those cases. The information on the required plaque or directory must note the location of each power source disconnecting means that can supply the building, and the marking must comply with 110.21(B). As with the plaque or directory requirements in other articles, there is an exception to permit multiple co-located power production sources to be identified by groups and not require the plaque to identify each power source in the group individually.

710.10 Identification of Power Sources

A permanent plaque or directory must be installed at a building supplied by a stand-alone system at each service equipment location or at an approved readily visible location. The plaque or directory must identify the location of each power source disconnect for the building or be grouped with other plaques or directories for other on-site sources.

Where multiple sources supply the building, the plaque or directory must be marked with the wording;

"CAUTION: MULTIPLE SOURCES OF POWER."

The marking must be permanently affixed with sufficient durability to withstand the environment involved [110.21(B)].

Ex: Installations with multiple co-located power production sources can be identified as a group(s). The plaque or directory is not required to identify each power source individually.

710.12 Stand-Alone Inverter Input Circuit Current

This rule specifies maximum current and was relocated from 690.8(A)(4).

Analysis

RELOCATED While new to this article, this is not a new rule. It was relocated from 690.8(A)(4) and belongs in 710 because, no matter what the power source is, if it is operating in stand-alone mode it is within the scope of Article 710. The rule specifies that the maximum current must be the stand-alone continuous inverter input current when the inverter is producing rated power at the lowest input voltage.

710.12 Stand-Alone Inverter Input Circuit Current

The maximum current must be the stand-alone continuous inverter input current rating when the inverter is producing its rated power at the lowest input voltage.

710.15 General

The permitted capacity of premises wiring systems supplied by stand-alone or isolated microgrid power sources was clarified and a new subsection (D) was added.

Analysis

CLARIFIED **710.15(A) Supply Output.** This was revised because the previous section was not clear that the power supply to the premises wiring system is permitted to have less capacity than the calculated load where supplied by only a stand-alone or isolated microgrid power source. • • •

The 2017 *Code* did not include any information about what sources are permitted to supply premises wiring systems at less than their calculated load. This recognizes that the stand-alone or isolated system may not have the capacity to support the total calculated loads. An Informational Note was also added to explain the system capacity calculations. Note that 710.15(G) still requires voltage and frequency control, so any concerns over the capacity of a stand-alone system to supply the loads are not completely ignored.

NEW

710.15(D) Three-phase Supply. This new information clarifies that three-phase stand-alone systems are available and used.

710.15 General

Premises wiring systems must be adequate to meet the requirements of this *Code* for similar installations supplied by a feeder or service. The wiring on the supply side of the building disconnect must comply with the requirements of the *NEC*, except as modified by 710.15(A) through (F).

(A) Supply Output. The power supply to premises wiring systems fed by stand-alone or isolated microgrid power sources is permitted to have less capacity than the calculated load. The capacity of the sum of all sources of the stand-alone supply must be equal to or greater than the load posed by the largest single utilization equipment connected to the system.

Note: For general-use loads, the system capacity can be calculated using the sum of the capacity of the firm sources, such as generators and energy storage system inverters. For specialty loads intended to be powered directly from a variable source, the capacity can be calculated using the sum of the variable sources, such as PV or wind inverters, or the combined capacity of both firm and variable sources.

(B) Sizing and Protection. The circuit conductors between a stand-alone source and a building disconnect must be sized based on the sum of the output ratings of the stand-alone source(s).

For three-phase interconnections, the phase loads must be controlled or balanced to be compatible with specifications of the sum of the power supply capacities.

(C) Single 120V Supply. Stand-alone and isolated microgrid systems can supply 120V to single-phase, 3-wire, 120/240V service disconnects of distribution panels if there are no 240V outlets and no multiwire circuits. The sum of the ratings of the power sources is not permitted to be greater than the neutral bus rating. This equipment must be marked with the following words or equivalent:

WARNING:
SINGLE 120-VOLT SUPPLY. DO NOT CONNECT.
MULTIWIRE BRANCH CIRCUITS!

(D) Three-phase Supply. Stand-alone and microgrid systems is permitted to supply three-phase, 3-wire or 4-wire systems.

Author's Comment:

▸ One has to wonder, "If I have a totally isolated system, does this mean that I don't have to comply with Article 220 when I design the isolated electrical supply system?"

ARTICLE 712

DIRECT CURRENT MICROGRIDS

Introduction to Article 712—Direct Current Microgrids

What exactly is a "Direct Current Microgrid" (DC Microgrid)? Simply stated it is a (dc) power grid that has more than one dc power source capable of supplying dc-dc converters, dc loads, and ac loads which are powered by dc to ac inverters.

DC microgrids are typically stand-alone systems that are not usually interconnected to a primary ac power source such as a utility but do sometimes interconnect through one or more dc-ac bidirectional converters or inverters.

712.2 Definitions

Parent text was added to say that these definitions apply only within this article and the word "Functionally" was added to the definition of "Grounded."

712.10 Directory

A source directory and a building directory listing the location and/or source of all power sources and disconnecting means are now both required.

Analysis

CLARIFIED **Grounded, Functionally.** The name of the term was changed, and the definition was revised to correlate with a similar definition in Article 690. The previous definition said this was a system with a high resistance connection between the current-carrying conductors and the equipment grounding system. That language was replaced with wording that says a system that is "grounded, functionally" is one that is not solidly grounded. The functional ground is for operational purposes and not for fault clearing purposes as in other types of electrical systems. A new Informational Note says that examples of operational reasons for using a functionally grounded system include ground-fault detection and performance-related issues for some power sources.

The term "resistively grounded" was replaced with "functionally grounded" in 712.52(B) and 712.55.

Analysis

EXPANDED This expansion resulted in the rule going from a single paragraph to subsections (A) and (B).

RELOCATED **712.10(A) Source Directory.** This is the language from 710.12 in the 2017 *NEC* without change. It requires a permanent directory denoting all dc electric power sources operating to supply the dc microgrid to be installed at each source location capable of acting as the primary dc source. The primary dc source is the source that supplies much of the dc load in the microgrid.

NEW

712.10(B) Building Directory. This new requirement for the 2020 *Code* is the same as the other building directory requirements for non-traditional power sources. It requires that a building supplied by a dc microgrid have a permanent plaque or directory installed outside the building at each service location or at an approved readily visible location. It must denote the location of each power source disconnecting means on or in the building or be grouped with other plaques or directories for other on-site sources.

As with other such rules there is an exception that does not require each individual power production source that is a part of a group of power production sources to be individually identified.

712.25 Identification of Circuit Conductors

Phase conductors 6 AWG or smaller can no longer be identified by marking tape, tagging, or other approved means.

Analysis

DELETED

712.25(B) Identification of Circuit Conductors. The language that was in the subsections was revised and relocated into the main rule.

712.34 DC Source Disconnecting Means

This rule was revised to reference 110.25.

Analysis

CLARIFIED

The previous *Code* required the disconnect to be "lockable in the open position." The revised language requires it to be "lockable open in accordance with 110.25."

712.65 Available DC Fault Current

The term "short-circuit current" was replaced with "fault current" and "maximum available short-circuit current" was replaced with "available fault current."

Analysis

CLARIFIED **NEW**

The new definition of "available fault current" in Article 100 defines it as the largest amount of current capable of being delivered at a point on the system during a short-circuit condition." This makes the use of "maximum" and "short-circuit" unnecessary when talking about faults.

The same term change was made in the text of 712.72.

ARTICLE 725

REMOTE-CONTROL, SIGNALING, AND POWER-LIMITED CIRCUITS

Introduction to Article 725—Remote-Control, Signaling, and Power-Limited Circuits

Circuits covered by Article 725 are remote-control, signaling, and power-limited circuits that are not an integral part of a device or appliance. This article includes circuits for burglar alarms, access control, sound, nurse call, intercoms, some computer networks, some lighting dimmer controls, and some low-voltage industrial controls. Here is a quick look at the types of circuits:

▸ A remote-control circuit controls other circuits through a relay or solid-state device, such as a motion-activated security lighting circuit.

▸ A signaling circuit provides output that is a signal or indicator, such as a buzzer, flashing light, or annunciator.

▸ A power-limited circuit is a circuit supplied by a transformer or other electric power source that limits the amount of power to provide safety from electrical shock and/or fire ignition.

The purpose of Article 725 is to allow for the fact that these circuits "are characterized by usage and power limitations that differentiate them from electrical power circuits" [725.1 Note]. This article provides alternative requirements for minimum conductor sizes, overcurrent protection, insulation requirements, wiring methods, and materials.

Article 725 consists of four parts. Part I provides general information, Part II pertains to Class 1 circuits, Part III addresses Class 2 circuits, and Part IV focuses on listing requirements. The key to understanding and applying each of these parts is in knowing the voltage and energy levels of the circuits, the wiring method involved, and the purpose(s) of the circuit.

725.2 Definitions

New parent text says the definitions in this article apply only within the article and some were moved to Article 100.

Analysis

NEW

Cable Bundle. Because 725.144 specifies differing cable ampacities based on the bundled configurations, a definition of what a bundle is was added to the *Code*.

The definition says that a group of cables that are tied together or in contact with one another in a closely packed configuration for at least 40 in. is a cable bundle. This is to account for the I²R heating in the conductors, but here it applies only where the cables are bundled for at least 40 in.

The substantiation indicates that without a definition, some will consider only cables that are passing through a sleeve or a slot in a floor or wall as bundled.

A new Informational Note was added to explain the reason and states that the random or loose installation of individual cables can result in less heating, and bundling can result in less heat dissipation and more signal interference as a result of "cross talk" between cables.

725.2 Definitions

Cable Bundle. A group of cables that are tied together or in contact with one another in a closely packed configuration for at least 40 in.
▶Figure 725–1

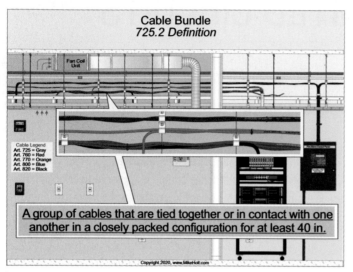

Cable Bundle
725.2 Definition

Cable Legend
Art. 725 = Gray
Art. 760 = Red
Art. 770 = Orange
Art. 800 = Blue
Art. 820 = Black

A group of cables that are tied together or in contact with one another in a closely packed configuration for at least 40 in.

Copyright 2020, www.MikeHolt.com

▶Figure 725–1

Note: Random or loose installation of individual cables can result in less heating. Combing of the cables can result in less heat dissipation and more signal cross talk between cables.

725.3 Other Articles

This section was revised to clarify that all the rules in Article 725 apply. It can be modified by only Article 300 and only if referenced in Article 725 as applied to Class 1, 2, and 3 circuits.

Analysis

CLARIFIED
This rule was modified in the parent text to clarify the intent. The previous language literally said that the rules in only 725.3 (A) through (N) applied. You were free to ignore the rest of the requirements in Article 725. Of course, this was never the intent and the section title told us that this rule specifies what requirements in articles other than 725 apply to Article 725 installations. The revision added the words "in addition to the requirements of this article" to clarify the intent.

CLARIFIED
725.3(D) Hazardous (Classified) Locations. In the previous *Code* this rule referenced complete articles, which is not permitted by the *NEC Style Manual*. It now requires that where Class 1, Class 2, or Class 3 circuits are installed in hazardous locations, the installation must comply with specific sections of Articles 501, 502, 503, 506, 511, 515, and 517.

This change replaces a blanket reference to Articles 500 through 516 with references to specific sections in those articles. A reference is required to be to a part of an article or to a specific section of an article.

CLARIFIED
725.3(E) Cable Trays. The reference was changed from the complete cable tray article (Article 392) to Parts I and II of Article 392. Part I is General, and Part II is Installation. Part III contains the construction requirements for the tray itself and is not referenced.

CLARIFIED
725.3(G) Instrumentation Tray Cable. The reference was changed from the complete article to sections 727.1 and 727.4 through 727.9. That makes all of Article 727 apply except for the definitions, the ".3" reference to other articles, and the minimum bending radius in 727.10.

NEW
725.3(O) Temperature Limitation of Class 2 and Class 3 Cables. This is a new rule requiring the temperature limitations found in 310.14(A)(3) to apply to cables used for Class 2 and Class 3 circuits. Cables have a maximum temperature rating, but the rule in 310 applies to only conductors and not to cables. This new language makes the temperature limitation of 310.14(A)(3) apply to Class 2 and Class 3 cables for installations covered by Article 725.

NEW
725.3(P) Identification of Equipment Grounding Conductors. This change permits signal conductors of Article 725 systems that operate at over 50V to use conductors with green insulation as other than equipment grounding conductors. Exception No. 1 to 250.119 already permits this for Class 2 and 3 circuits that operate as less than 50V to ground.

725.3 Other Articles

<u>In addition to the requirements of this article, circuits</u> and equipment must comply with the articles or sections listed in 725.3(A) through (P). Only those sections contained in Article 300 specifically referenced below apply to Class 1, 2, and 3 circuits.

Author's Comment:

▶ Boxes or other enclosures are not required for Class 2 splices or terminations because Article 725 does not reference 300.15, which contains those requirements. ▶Figure 725–2

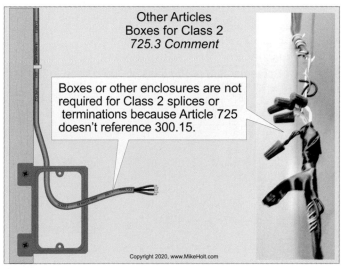

Other Articles
Boxes for Class 2
725.3 Comment

Boxes or other enclosures are not required for Class 2 splices or terminations because Article 725 doesn't reference 300.15.

Copyright 2020, www.MikeHolt.com

▶Figure 725–2

(A) Number and Size of Conductors in a Raceway. The number and size of conductors or cables within a raceway are limited in accordance with 300.17.

Author's Comment:

▶ Raceways must be large enough to permit the installation and removal of conductors without damaging conductor insulation [300.17].

▶ When all conductors within a raceway are the same size and insulation, the number of conductors permitted can be found in Annex C for the raceway type [Chapter 9, Table 1, Note 1].

▶ **Example**

Question: *How many 18 TFFN fixture wires can be installed in trade size ½ electrical metallic tubing?* ▶Figure 725–3

(a) 16   *(b) 18*   *(c) 22*   *(d) 38*

Answer: *(c) 22 [Annex C, Table C.1]*

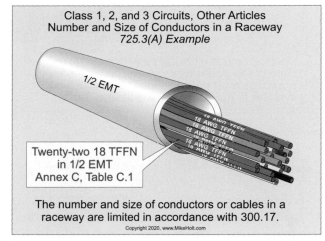

Class 1, 2, and 3 Circuits, Other Articles
Number and Size of Conductors in a Raceway
725.3(A) Example

1/2 EMT

Twenty-two 18 TFFN
in 1/2 EMT
Annex C, Table C.1

The number and size of conductors or cables in a raceway are limited in accordance with 300.17.

Copyright 2020, www.MikeHolt.com

▶Figure 725–3

(B) Spread of Fire or Products of Combustion. Installation of Class 1 and Class 2 circuits must comply with 300.21.

Author's Comment:

▶ Electrical circuits and equipment must be installed in such a way that the spread of fire or products of combustion will not be substantially increased. Openings into or through fire-resistive walls, floors, and ceilings for electrical equipment must be firestopped using methods approved by the authority having jurisdiction to maintain the fire-resistance rating of the fire-resistive assembly [300.21]. ▶Figure 725–4

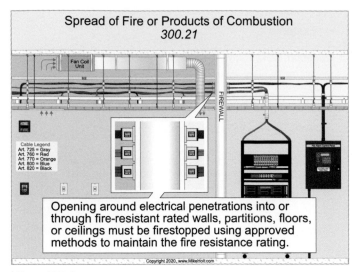

Spread of Fire or Products of Combustion
300.21

Opening around electrical penetrations into or through fire-resistant rated walls, partitions, floors, or ceilings must be firestopped using approved methods to maintain the fire resistance rating.

▶Figure 725–4

Author's Comment:

▸ Firestopping materials are listed for the specific types of wiring methods and the construction of the assembly they penetrate. ▶Figure 725–5

▸ Directories of electrical construction materials published by qualified testing laboratories contain listing and installation restrictions necessary to maintain the fire-resistive rating of assemblies. Building codes also have restrictions on penetrations on opposite sides of a fire-resistive wall. Outlet boxes must have a horizontal separation of not less than 24 in. when installed in a fire-resistive assembly, unless an outlet box is listed for closer spacing or protected by fire-resistant "putty pads" in accordance with manufacturer's instructions. ▶Figure 725–6 and ▶Figure 725–7

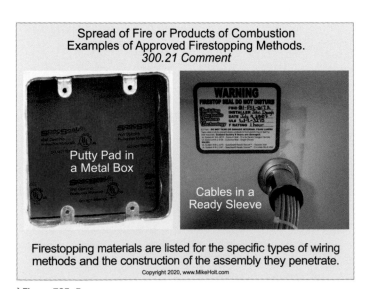

Spread of Fire or Products of Combustion
Examples of Approved Firestopping Methods.
300.21 Comment

Putty Pad in a Metal Box

Cables in a Ready Sleeve

Firestopping materials are listed for the specific types of wiring methods and the construction of the assembly they penetrate.

▶Figure 725–5

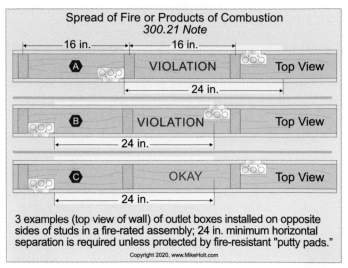

Spread of Fire or Products of Combustion
300.21 Note

16 in. — 16 in.
Ⓐ VIOLATION Top View
24 in.

Ⓑ VIOLATION Top View
24 in.

Ⓒ OKAY Top View
24 in.

3 examples (top view of wall) of outlet boxes installed on opposite sides of studs in a fire-rated assembly; 24 in. minimum horizontal separation is required unless protected by fire-resistant "putty pads."

▶Figure 725–6

Spread of Fire or Products of Combustion
300.21 Note

Outlet boxes installed on opposite sides of a fire-rated assembly must have a horizontal separation of not less than 24 in. unless listed for closer spacing or protected by fire-resistant "putty pads."

▶Figure 725–7

Author's Comment:

▸ Boxes installed in fire-resistive assemblies must be listed for the purpose. If steel boxes are used, they must be secured to the framing member, so cut-in type boxes are not permitted (UL White Book, *Guide Information for Electrical Equipment*).

(C) Ducts and Plenum Spaces. Class 1, Class 2, and Class 3 circuits installed in ducts or plenums must comply with 300.22. ▶Figure 725–8

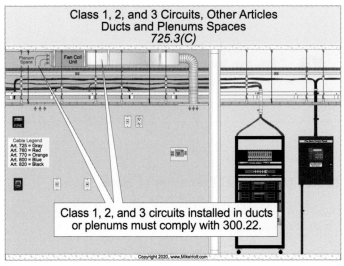

Class 1, 2, and 3 Circuits, Other Articles
Ducts and Plenums Spaces
725.3(C)

Class 1, 2, and 3 circuits installed in ducts or plenums must comply with 300.22.

▶Figure 725–8

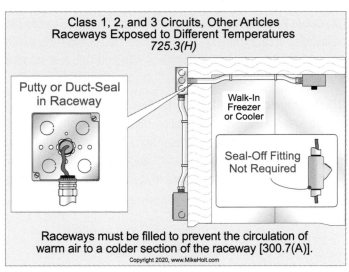

Class 1, 2, and 3 Circuits, Other Articles
Raceways Exposed to Different Temperatures
725.3(H)

Putty or Duct-Seal in Raceway

Walk-In Freezer or Cooler

Seal-Off Fitting Not Required

Raceways must be filled to prevent the circulation of warm air to a colder section of the raceway [300.7(A)].

▶Figure 725–9

Ex 1: Class 2 cables selected in accordance with Table 725.154 and installed in in accordance with 725.135(B) and 300.22(B) Ex, are permitted to be installed in ducts specifically fabricated for environmental air.

Ex 2: Class 2 cables selected in accordance with Table 725.154 and installed in accordance with 725.135(C) are permitted to be installed in plenum spaces.

(D) Hazardous Locations. Class 1, Class 2, and Class 3 circuits installed in hazardous (classified) locations must comply with 501.10(B)(1), 501.150, 502.10(B)(1), 502.150, 503.10(A)(1), 503.150, 506.15(A), 506.15(C), 511.7(B)(1), 515.7(A), and Article 517, Part IV.

(E) Cable Trays. Class 1, 2, and 3 circuits in cable trays must be installed in accordance with Parts I and II of Article 392.

(H) Raceways Exposed to Different Temperatures. If a raceway is subjected to different temperatures, and where condensation is known to be a problem, the raceway must be filled with a material approved by the authority having jurisdiction that will prevent the circulation of warm air to a colder section of the raceway. [300.7(A)]. ▶Figure 725–9

Author's Comment:

▶ This raceway seal is one that is approved by the authority having jurisdiction to prevent the circulation of warm air to a cooler section of the raceway and is not the same thing as an explosionproof seal.

(J) Bushing. When a raceway is used for the support or protection of cables, a fitting is required to reduce the potential for abrasion and must be placed at the location the cables enter the raceway in accordance with 300.15(C). ▶Figure 725–10

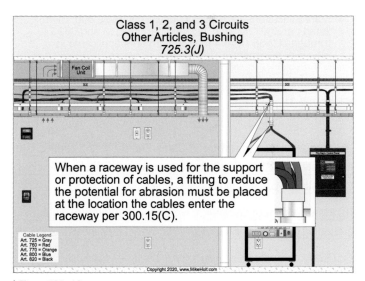

Class 1, 2, and 3 Circuits
Other Articles, Bushing
725.3(J)

When a raceway is used for the support or protection of cables, a fitting to reduce the potential for abrasion must be placed at the location the cables enter the raceway per 300.15(C).

▶Figure 725–10

(L) Corrosive, Damp, or Wet Locations. Where installed in corrosive, damp, or wet locations, Class 2 cables must be identified for the location in accordance with 110.11 and 310.10(G). Conductors and cables installed in underground raceways, or in raceways aboveground in wet locations, must also be identified for wet locations in accordance with 300.5(B). Where corrosion may occur, the requirements of 300.6 must be used.

(M) Cable Routing Assemblies. Class 2 and Type PLTC cables can be installed in cable routing assemblies selected in accordance with Table 800.154(b), listed in accordance with 800.182, and installed in accordance with 800.110(C) and 800.113.

(N) Communications Raceways. Class 2 and Type PLTC cables can be installed in communications raceways selected in accordance with Table 800.154(b), listed in accordance with 800.182, and installed in accordance with 800.113 and 362.24 through 362.56, where the requirements applicable to electrical nonmetallic tubing apply. ▸Figure 725–11

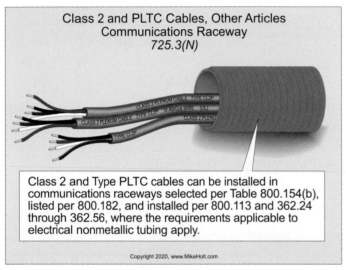

Class 2 and PLTC Cables, Other Articles
Communications Raceway
725.3(N)

Class 2 and Type PLTC cables can be installed in communications raceways selected per Table 800.154(b), listed per 800.182, and installed per 800.113 and 362.24 through 362.56, where the requirements applicable to electrical nonmetallic tubing apply.

Copyright 2020, www.MikeHolt.com

▸Figure 725–11

(O) Temperature Limitation of Class 2 and Class 3 Cables. The requirements of 310.14(A)(3) for the temperature limitation of conductors applies to Class 2 and Class 3 cables.

(P) Identification of Equipment Grounding Conductors. Equipment grounding conductors must be identified in accordance with 250.119.

Ex: Conductors with green insulation is permitted to be used as phase signal conductors for Types CL3P, CL2P, CL3R, CL2R, CL3, CL2, CL3X, CL2X, and substitute cables installed in accordance with 725.154(A).

725.24 Mechanical Execution of Work, Informational Note

A new Informational Note was added explaining the effects of foreign substances on cable assembly insulation.

Analysis

NEW

This new Informational Note lists some items that can adversely affect cable assemblies.

725.24 Mechanical Execution of Work

Equipment and cabling must be installed in a neat and workmanlike manner. ▸Figure 725–12

Class 1, 2, and 3 Circuits
Mechanical Execution of Work
725.24

VIOLATION
Equipment and cabling must be installed in a neat and workmanlike manner.

Copyright 2020, www.MikeHolt.com

▸Figure 725–12

Exposed cables must be supported by the structural components of the building so the cable will not be damaged by normal building use. Support must be by straps, staples, hangers, cable ties, or similar fittings designed and installed in a manner that will not damage the cable. The installation must comply with 300.4(D). ▸Figure 725–13

Note: Paint, plaster, cleaners, abrasives, corrosive residues, or other contaminants can result in an undetermined alteration of Class 1, Class 2, Class 3, and PLTC cable properties.

Author's Comment:

▸ Raceways and cables can be supported by independent support wires attached to the suspended ceiling in accordance with 300.11(B) [725.46 and 725.143].

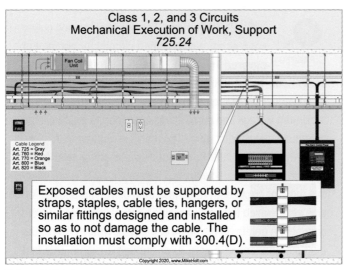

▶Figure 725–13

Cables installed through or parallel to framing members or furring strips must be protected, where they are likely to be penetrated by nails or screws, by installing the wiring method so it is not less than 1¼ in. from the nearest edge of the framing member or furring strips, or by protecting it with a ¹⁄₁₆ in. thick steel plate or equivalent [300.4(A)(1) and (D)]. ▶Figure 725–14

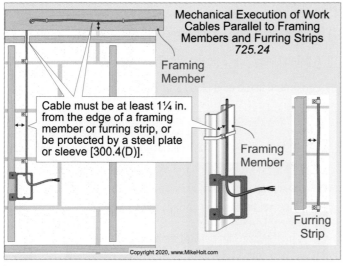

▶Figure 725–14

725.48 Conductors of Different Circuits in the Same Cable, Cable Tray, Enclosure, or Raceway

Class 1 circuits can now be installed with other circuits in a common enclosure (even if not functionally associated) if a barrier is installed to provide separation.

Analysis

725.48 (B)(1) Class 1 Circuits with Power-Supply Circuits. This new permission to install Class 1 circuits with power-supply circuits where separated by a barrier mirrors the permission in 725.136(B) for Class 2 circuits. If separation using a barrier is safe for Class 2 and 3 circuits, it is also safe for Class 1 circuits that are installed using Chapter 3 wiring methods.

NEW

725.48 Conductors of Different Circuits in Same Cable, Cable Tray, Enclosure, or Raceway

(A) Class 1 Circuits with Other Class 1 Circuits. Two or more Class 1 circuits can be installed in the same cable, enclosure, or raceway provided all conductors are insulated for the maximum voltage of any conductor.

(B) Class 1 Circuits with Power Circuits. Class 1 circuits are permitted to be installed with electrical power conductors under the following conditions:

(1) In a Cable, Enclosure, or Raceway. Class 1 circuits can be in the same cable, enclosure, or raceway with power-supply circuits, if the equipment powered is functionally associated with the Class 1 circuit. ▶Figure 725–15

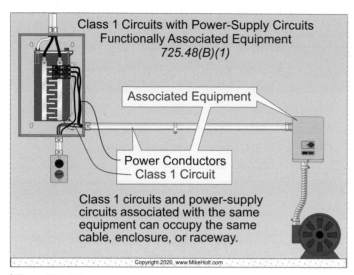

Class 1 Circuits with Power-Supply Circuits Functionally Associated Equipment
725.48(B)(1)

Associated Equipment

Power Conductors
Class 1 Circuit

Class 1 circuits and power-supply circuits associated with the same equipment can occupy the same cable, enclosure, or raceway.

Copyright 2020, www.MikeHolt.com

▶Figure 725–15

Class 1 circuits are also permitted to be installed together with the conductors of electric light, power, non-power-limited fire alarm, and medium power network-powered broadband communications circuits where separated by a barrier.

725.121 Power Sources for Class 2 and Class 3 Circuits

List item 5 was revised to specify a listed battery source or a battery source system identified as Class 2, and (C) was expanded and clarified.

Analysis

CLARIFIED

725.121(A) Power Source. The parent text was editorially revised to eliminate the specific list items. It now just says, "The power source for Class 2 and Class 3 circuits must be as follows." This permits the list to be changed without changing the parent text. In addition, list item 5 was revised because it referenced No. 6 carbon zinc cells, but they have not been manufactured for many years and there is no available information on what the capacity of those cells were. The revised language references a "listed battery source or battery source system identified as Class 2."

EXPANDED

725.121(C) Marking. This section requiring power sources for power-limited circuits for equipment covered by 725.121(A)(3) (listed audio/video equipment, listed information technology equipment, and listed industrial equipment) to have a label indicating the maximum voltage and current was expanded to include listed communications equipment. The marking requirements were also revised. The rule now requires the equipment to be marked with the "rated current." January 1, 2021 is the effective date for equipment rated less than 0.3A. This subsection was also revised to permit a single marking label for multiple connection points on the same equipment where each of the multiple connection points have the same rating. This last part was revised because of the use of Power over Ethernet (PoE) switches where the connection points are so close together it would not be possible to provide individual labels as required by the previous *Code*.

725.121 Power Sources for Class 2 and Class 3 Circuits

(A) Power Source. The power supply for a Class 2 or 3 circuit must be as follows:

(1) A listed Class 2 or 3 transformer. ▶Figure 725–16

(2) A listed Class 2 or 3 power supply.

(3) Equipment listed as a Class 2 or 3 power source.

Power Source for Class 2 and 3 Circuits
Transformer
725.121(A)(1)

AC/AC ADAPTOR
CLASS 2 TRANSFORMER
MODEL : MKA-410601000
INPUT :120V AC 60Hz 0.15A
OUTPUT :6V AC 1000mA

3G67
E149533

LISTED
0305

Class 2

16V 80 VA

Transformers used as a Class 2 or Class 3 power source must be listed.

Copyright 2020, www.MikeHolt.com

▶Figure 725–16

(4) Listed audio/video information technology equipment (computers), communications, and industrial equipment limited-power circuits. ▸Figure 725–17

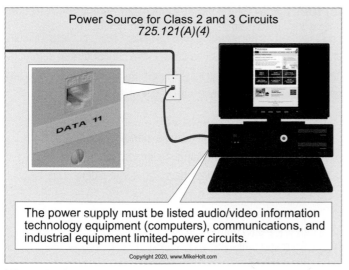

Power Source for Class 2 and 3 Circuits
725.121(A)(4)

DATA 11

The power supply must be listed audio/video information technology equipment (computers), communications, and industrial equipment limited-power circuits.

Copyright 2020, www.MikeHolt.com

▸Figure 725–17

Ex 2: Where a circuit has an energy level at or below the limits established in Chapter 9, Table 11(A) and 11(B), the equipment is not required to be listed as a Class 2 power transformer, power supply, or power source.

(5) A battery source or battery source system that is listed and identified as Class 2

(C) Marking. The power sources for power-limited circuits in 725.121(A)(3) and power-limited circuits for listed audio/video equipment, listed information technology equipment, listed communications equipment, and listed industrial equipment in 725.121(A)(4) must have a label indicating the maximum voltage and rated current output per conductor for each connection point on the power source. Where multiple connection points have the same rating, a single label is permitted to be used.

Note: The rated current for power sources covered in 725.144 is the output current per conductor the power source is designed to deliver to an operational load at normal operating conditions, as declared by the manufacturer.

725.135 Installation of Class 2 Cables

Subsection (B) was revised to permit only cables (and not wires) to be installed in ducts specifically fabricated for environmental air, and (E) was expanded to specifically permit the installation of innerduct within a metal raceway.

Analysis

725.135(B) Ducts Specifically Fabricated for Environmental Air. The language previously permitted both wires and cables to be installed in ducts specifically fabricated for environmental air. The most recent revision of NFPA 90A, *Standard for the Installation of Air-Conditioning and Ventilating Systems* does not have any provisions for the installation of wires in these ducts so they were removed from the *Code* for this application. Since that standard has purview over installations in ducts, the *NEC* must comply with its requirements so the word "wires" was removed.

CLARIFIED

Properly listed cables are still permitted. The only time cables are permitted in these ducts is when they are connecting to equipment necessary for the direct action upon, or sensing of, the contained air.

725.135(E) Risers—Cables and Innerducts in Metal Raceways. Innerducts are more typically associated with the installation of optical fiber but can be used for other cables. This change makes this section mirror those that were made to 770.113(E), 800.113(E), 820.113(E), and 830.113(E) in the 2017 *Code* cycle.

EXPANDED

725.135 Installation of Class 2 Cables

Installation of Class 2, and PLTC cables must comply with 725.135(A) through (M).

(A) Listing. Class 2 and PLTC cables installed in buildings must be listed.

(B) Ducts Specifically Fabricated for Environmental Air Spaces. Plenum rated Class 2 cables are permitted to be installed within ducts specifically fabricated for environmental air spaces in accordance with 725.3(B) Ex 1 if the cable is directly associated with the air distribution system and complies with (1) or (2): ▶Figure 725–18

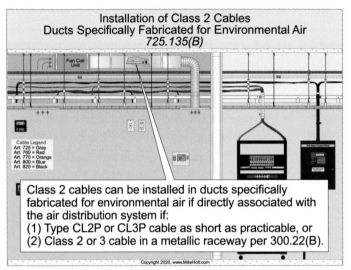

Installation of Class 2 Cables
Ducts Specifically Fabricated for Environmental Air
725.135(B)

Cable Legend
Art. 725 = Gray
Art. 760 = Red
Art. 770 = Orange
Art. 800 = Blue
Art. 820 = Black

Class 2 cables can be installed in ducts specifically fabricated for environmental air if directly associated with the air distribution system if:
(1) Type CL2P or CL3P cable as short as practicable, or
(2) Class 2 or 3 cable in a metallic raceway per 300.22(B).

Copyright 2020, www.MikeHolt.com

▶Figure 725–18

725.139 Conductors of Different Circuits in Same Cable, Enclosure, Cable Tray, Raceway, or Cable Routing Assembly

This was clarified to say that conductors of Class 2 or 3 circuits can be installed in the same cable with communications circuits if the cable is a listed communications cable.

Analysis

CLARIFIED

725.139(D) Class 2 and Class 3 Circuits with Communications Circuits. This subsection was revised for clarification and applies to conductors of a Class 2 or 3 circuit in the same cable as a communications circuit. It allows Class 2 or Class 3 circuits within the same cables with conductors of communications circuits if the cable is listed a communications cable that has been installed in accordance with Part V of Article 805.

725.139 Conductors of Different Circuits in the Same Cable, Enclosure, Cable Tray, Raceway, or Cable Routing Assembly

(D) Class 2 and Class 3 Circuits with Communications Circuits.

(1) Classified as Communications Circuits. Class 2 or Class 3 circuits are permitted within the same cables with conductors of communications circuits if <u>the cable is listed communications cable</u> that has been installed in accordance with <u>Part V of Article 805</u>.

Author's Comment:

▶ A common application of this requirement is when a single communications cable is used for both voice communications and data.

▶ Class 2 cables have an insulation rating of 150V [725.179(G)], whereas communications cables have a voltage rating of 300V [800.179].

725.144 Transmission of Power and Data

Editorial changes and three new Informational Notes help clarify these installations, the title of Table 724.144 was revised, and a new exception was added.

Analysis

EDITED

With more and more equipment (including lighting) being installed as PoE supplied equipment, this section will be of more importance over time. The parent text was clarified but there were no technical revisions.

NEW

725.144 Note 2. This Informational Note was revised and language was added telling the reader that the 8P8C (8 position, 8 conductors) connector in widespread use with powered communications systems has a current-carrying capacity per contact of 1.0A at 60°C; it was previously specified at 1.3A. Informational Notes 3 through 6 were added.

CLARIFIED

Table 725.144. The title of the table was revised to specify that its ampacities apply to only balanced twisted-pair cables. All the testing was based on that type of cabling and the results are valid for only that type of cabling. This should be no real-world issue as the "CAT" rated cables commonly used for these applications are balanced twisted-pair cables. It is also important to note that these ampacities apply to only cables having copper conductors. There are lower cost "CAT" cables that are copper-clad aluminum but they are not permitted for this application.

NEW

Table 724.144 Note 2. A new Informational Note No. 2 was added below the table which calls attention to the fact that the per-contact current rating of the connectors can limit the maximum allowable current below the ampacity shown in the table and is similar to the way 110.14(C) works for power conductors. The table itself was significantly revised to show the current to two decimal places and the previous column for a single cable was deleted. The single cable is now part of the column for "1-7" cables. There are three ampacities based on the same three temperature ratings that are used for power conductors rated 60°, 75°, and 90°C in all the columns.

All these revisions are driven by the steadily increasing power levels being permitted by the IEEE PoE standards. The original standard limited the power to 15W or 30W; the most recent proposed standard has that limit at 100W.

NEW

725.144(A) Ex Use of Class 2 or Class 3 Cables to Transmit Power and Data. A new exception was added to say that the Table 725.144 ampacities do not apply where the conductors in the cable are 24 AWG or larger and where the rated current in any conductor does not exceed 0.3A.

CLARIFIED

725.144(B) Use of Class 2-LP or Class 3-LP Cables to Transmit Power and Data. In the 2017 Code there was no reference to ampacity correction for LP cables. The revised language requires compliance with 310.15(B) where the ambient temperature exceeds 30°C. The substantiation points out that a cable rated 60°C has an ampacity of zero where installed in a 60°C ambient temperature as any temperature increase as a result of current flow would increase the conductor temperature above its rating.

725.144 Transmission of Power and Data

This section applies to Class 2 circuits that transmit power and data to a powered device. Section 300.11 and Parts I and III of Article 725 apply to Class 2 and Class 3 circuits that transmit power and data.

Conductors that carry power and data must be copper and the current is not permitted to exceed the current limitation of the connectors.

Note 1: An example of cables that transmit power and data include closed-circuit TV cameras (CCTV).

Note 2: The 8P8C connector is in widespread use with powered communications systems. IEC 60603-7, *Connectors for Electronic Equipment—Part 7-1* details specifications for 8-way, unshielded, free and fixed connectors, specifies these connectors to have a current-carrying capacity per contact of 1A maximum at 60°C (149°F). See IEC 60603-7 for more information on current-carrying capacity at higher and lower temperatures.

Note 3: The requirements of Table 725.144 were derived for carrying power and data over 4-pair copper balanced twisted-pair cabling. This type of cabling is described in ANSI/TIA 568-C.2, *Commercial Building Telecommunications Cabling Standard—Part 2: Balanced Twisted-Pair Telecommunications Cabling and Components.*

Note 4: See TIA-TSB-184-A, *Guidelines for Supporting Power Delivery Over Balanced Twisted-Pair Cabling,* for information on installation and management of balanced twisted-pair cabling supporting power delivery.

Note 5: See ANSI/NEMA C137.3, *American National Standard for Lighting Systems—Minimum Requirements for Installation of Energy Efficient Power over Ethernet (PoE) Lighting Systems,* for information on installation of cables for PoE lighting systems.

Note 6: The rated current for power sources covered in 725.144 is the output current per conductor the power source is designed to deliver to an operational load at normal operating conditions, as declared by the manufacturer. In the design of these systems, the actual current in a given conductor might vary from the rated current per conductor by as much as 20 percent. An increase in current in one conductor is offset by a corresponding decrease in current in one or more conductors of the same cable.

**Table 725.144 Copper Conductor Ampacity
in 4-Pair Class 2 Power/Data Cables with
All Conductors Carrying Current**

See *NEC* Table 725.144 for details.

Table 725.144 Note 1: For bundle sizes over 192 cables, or for conductor sizes smaller than 26 AWG, ampacities are permitted to be determined by qualified personnel under engineering supervision.

Table 725.144 Note 2: Where only half of the conductors in each cable are carrying current, the values in the table are permitted to be increased by a factor of 1.40.

Note 1 to Table 725.144: Elevated cable temperatures can reduce a cable's data transmission performance. For information on practices for 4-pair balanced twisted-pair cabling, see TIA-TSB-184-A and 6.4.7, 6.6.3, and Annex G of ANSI/TIA-568-C.2, which provide guidance on adjustments for operating temperatures between 20°C and 60°C.

Note 2 to Table 725.144: The per-contact current rating of connectors can limit the maximum current below the ampacity shown in Table 725.144.

(A) Use of Class 2 or Class 3 Cables to Transmit Power and Data. Where Types CL3P, CL2P, CL3R, CL2R, CL3, or CL2 transmit power and data, the rated current per conductor of the power source is not permitted to exceed the ampacities in Table 725.144 at an ambient temperature of 30°C. For ambient temperatures above 30°C, the correction factors in Table 310.15(B)(1) must be applied.

Ex: Compliance with Table 725.144 is not required for conductors 24 AWG or larger and the rated current per conductor of the power source does not exceed 0.30A.

Note: One example of the use of Class 2 cables is a network of closed-circuit TV cameras using 24 AWG, 60°C rated, Type CL2R, Category 5e balanced twisted-pair cabling.

(B) Use of Class 2-LP or Class 3-LP Cables to Transmit Power and Data. Cable Types CL3P-LP, CL2P-LP, CL3R-LP, CL2R-LP, CL3-LP, or CL2-LP are permitted to supply power to equipment from a power source with a rated current per conductor up to the marked current limit located immediately following the suffix "-LP" and are permitted to transmit data to the equipment. Where the number of bundled LP cables is 192 or less and the selected ampacity of the cables in accordance with Table 725.144 exceeds the marked current limit of the cable, the ampacity determined from the table is permitted to be used. For ambient temperatures above 30°C, the correction factors of Table 310.15(B)(1) or Equation 310.15(B)(2) must apply. The Class 2-LP and Class 3-LP cables must comply with the following, as applicable:

(1) Cables with the suffix "-LP" are permitted to be installed in bundles, raceways, cable trays, communications raceways, and cable routing assemblies.

(2) Cables with the suffix "-LP" and a marked current limit must follow the substitution hierarchy of Table 725.154 and Figure 725.154(A) in the *NEC* for the cable type without the suffix "-LP" and without the marked current limit.

(3) System design is permitted by qualified persons under engineering supervision.

Note: An example of a limited power (LP) cable is a cable marked Type CL2-LP (0.5A), 23 AWG.

FIRE ALARM SYSTEMS

Introduction to Article 760—Fire Alarm Systems

Article 760 covers the installation of wiring and equipment for fire alarm systems, including circuits controlled and powered by the fire alarm. These include fire detection and alarm notification, guard's tour, sprinkler waterflow, and sprinkler supervisory systems. NFPA 72, *National Fire Alarm and Signaling Code,* provides the requirements for the selection, installation, performance, use, testing, and maintenance of fire alarm systems.

760.3 Other Articles

Two new subsections were added.

Analysis

 760.3(N) Temperature Limitations of Power-Limited and Nonpower-Limited Fire Alarm Cables.
NEW This is a new subsection that makes the temperature limitations found in 310.14(A)(3) apply to fire alarm system cables. The change is needed because the temperature limitation rules in 310.14(A)(3) apply only to conductors. The rule in Article 310 states that the conductor, and with this change the cable, must not be used in a manner such that its operating temperature will exceed the rating of the conductor.

 760.3(O) Identification of Equipment Grounding Conductors. This new subsection requires EGCs
NEW to be identified in accordance with 250.119, and a new exception permits green insulated conductors that are part of power-limited fire alarm cables to be used as ungrounded signal conductors.

This is the same as in 725.3(O), but there is no existing exception to 250.119 to permit the use of green conductors in fire alarm cables for use as other than an EGC. This exception modifies the rule in 250.119.

760.3 Other Articles

Fire alarm circuits and equipment must comply with 760.3(A) through (O). Only those sections contained in Article 300 specifically referenced below apply to fire alarm systems.

(N) Temperature Limitations. The requirements of 310.14(A)(3) on the temperature limitation of conductors apply to power-limited fire alarm cables and non–power-limited fire alarms cables.

(O) Identification of Equipment Grounding Conductors. Equipment grounding conductors must be identified in accordance with 250.119.

Ex: Conductors with green insulation are permitted to be used as ungrounded signal conductors for Types FPLP, FPLR, FPL, and substitute cables installed in accordance with 760.154(A).

760.24 Mechanical Execution of Work

This section was expanded to require compliance with all of 300.4.

Analysis

EXPANDED

760.24(A) General. The previous language required protection only where the fire alarm cables were run in parallel to framing members. None of the other protections that are required for non-critical systems applied to fire alarms systems in the 2017 *Code*. The Public Input (PI) was submitted to require compliance with 300.4(E) Cables, Raceways, or Boxes Installed in or Under Roof Decking and 300.4(F) Cables and Raceways Installed in Shallow Grooves. The Code-Making Panel (CMP) expanded that Public Input to include all of 300.4. Since the text in 760.3 says that only those sections of Article 300 referenced in Article 760 apply to 760 installations, this change was needed to provide the protection for fire alarm system installations that is at least equal to the protection required for non-critical systems. As we saw in 725.24, a new Informational Note was added calling attention to the fact that contaminants may cause an undetermined alteration of the properties of PLFA and NPLFA cables.

760.24 Mechanical Execution of Work

(A) General. Equipment and cabling must be installed in a neat and workmanlike manner.

Exposed cables must be supported by the structural components of the building so the cable(s) will not be damaged by normal building use. Support must be by straps, staples, hangers, cable ties, or similar fittings designed and installed in a manner that will not damage the cable. The installation must comply with 300.4. ▶Figure 760–1

Note: Paint, plaster, cleaners, abrasives, corrosive residues, or other contaminants might result in an undetermined alteration of PLFA and NPLFA cable properties.

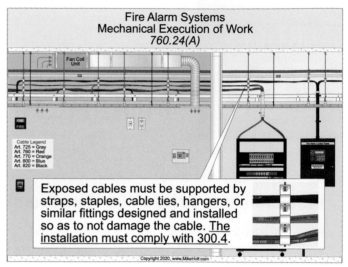

▶Figure 760–1

Author's Comment:

▶ Raceways and cables can be supported by independent support wires attached to the suspended ceiling in accordance with 300.11(B) [760.46 and 760.143]. ▶**Figure 760–2**

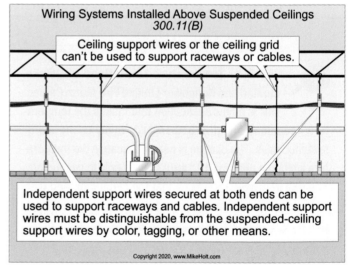

▶Figure 760–2

Cables installed through or parallel to framing members or furring strips must be protected, where they are likely to be penetrated by nails or screws, by installing the wiring method so it is not less than 1¼ in. from the nearest edge of the framing member or furring strips, or by protecting them with a ¹⁄₁₆ in. thick steel plate or the equivalent [300.4]. ▶Figure 760–3

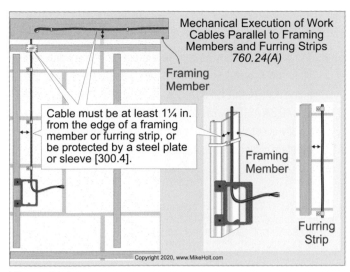

▶Figure 760–3

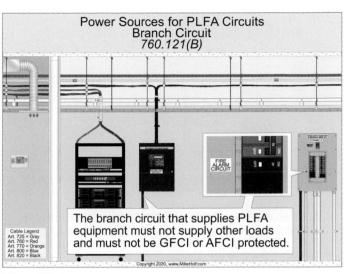

▶Figure 760–4

760.121 Power Sources for Power-Limited Fire Alarm Circuits

The fire alarm branch-circuit disconnecting means is now specifically permitted to be secured in the "on" position.

Analysis

CLARIFIED

760.121(B) Branch Circuit. The branch circuit disconnecting means for power-limited fire alarm systems is often secured or locked in the on position to prevent accidental disconnection of the fire alarm power supply; however, there was no language in this section that permitted that practice. This revision provides that language and correlates with 760.41 for nonpower-limited fire alarms. NPLFA alarm systems have had this provision beginning with the 2011 *Code*.

760.121 Power Sources for Power-Limited Fire Alarm Circuits

(B) Branch Circuit. Power-limited fire alarm equipment must be supplied by a branch circuit that supplies no other load and is not GFCI or AFCI protected. ▶Figure 760–4

The location of the branch-circuit overcurrent protective device for the power-limited fire alarm equipment must be permanently identified at the fire alarm control unit. ▶Figure 760–5

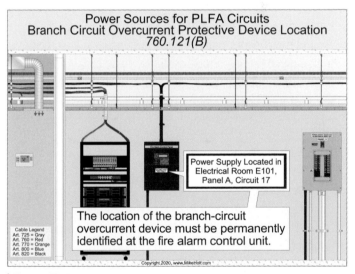

▶Figure 760–5

The branch-circuit overcurrent protective device must be identified in red, be accessible only to qualified personnel, and be identified as the "**FIRE ALARM CIRCUIT**." The red identification must not damage the overcurrent protective device or obscure any manufacturer's markings. The fire alarm branch-circuit disconnecting means is permitted to be secured in the closed (on) position. ▶Figure 760–6

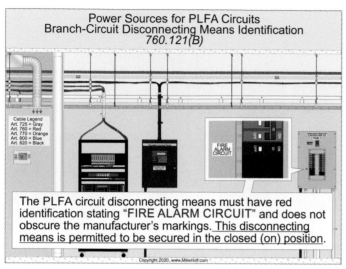

Power Sources for PLFA Circuits
Branch-Circuit Disconnecting Means Identification
760.121(B)

Cable Legend
Art. 725 = Gray
Art. 760 = Red
Art. 770 = Orange
Art. 800 = Blue
Art. 820 = Black

FIRE ALARM CIRCUIT

The PLFA circuit disconnecting means must have red identification stating "FIRE ALARM CIRCUIT" and does not obscure the manufacturer's markings. This disconnecting means is permitted to be secured in the closed (on) position.

Copyright 2020, www.MikeHolt.com

▶Figure 760-6

Author's Comment:

▸ Many "lock-on" devices require the use of a screwdriver or other tool to install and remove, which renders the fire alarm branch circuit OCPD no longer readily accessible as required by 240.24(A). This rule could be read as an exception to the readily accessible requirement in 240 but does not provide substantial language to support it.

ARTICLE 770

OPTICAL FIBER CABLES AND RACEWAYS

Introduction to Article 770—Optical Fiber Cables and Raceways

Article 770 provides the requirements for installing optical fiber cables and special raceways for optical fiber cables. It also contains the requirements for composite cables (often called "hybrid") that combine optical fibers with current-carrying conductors.

While we normally think of Article 300 in connection with wiring methods, you only need to use Article 770 for optical fiber cables, except where it makes specific references to Article 300 [770.3]. For instance, in 770.113, reference is made to 300.22, which applies when installing optical fiber cables and optical fiber raceways in ducts and plenum spaces.

Article 90 states that the *NEC* is not a design guide or installation manual. Thus, Article 770 does not deal with the performance of optical fiber systems. For example, it does not mention cable bending radii. It does not explain how to install and test cable safely either, but that does not mean you should look into an optical fiber cable, even if you cannot see any light coming through it. Light used in these circuits is usually not visible, but it can still damage your eyes.

Article 770 Informational Note

The Informational Note that followed the title of the article was deleted.

Analysis

DELETED Such "floating" notes are not permitted as they are required to be associated with an actual *Code* rule. This deleted note was replaced by new notes at 770.100(B)(1) and (B)(2).

Analysis

EXPANDED The 2017 *NEC* required compliance with only 300.4(D) through (G) which was intended to limit the possibility of damage to the optical fiber cable after it was installed. An additional change was made by adding a reference to 300.22(C) at the end of the section. The sentence to which this reference was added requires nonmetallic cable ties and other nonmetallic cable accessories used in other spaces for environmental air to be listed as having low smoke and heat release properties.

770.24 Mechanical Execution of Work

Equipment and cabling must be installed in a neat and workmanlike manner and comply with 300.4 and 300.11.

770.24 Mechanical Execution of Work

This section was expanded to require compliance with all of 300.4.

COMMUNICATIONS SYSTEMS

Introduction to Chapter 8—Communications Systems

Chapter 8 of the *National Electrical Code* covers the wiring requirements for communications systems such as telephones, radio and TV antennas, satellite dishes, closed-circuit television (CCTV), and coaxial cable systems. ▶Figure 800–1

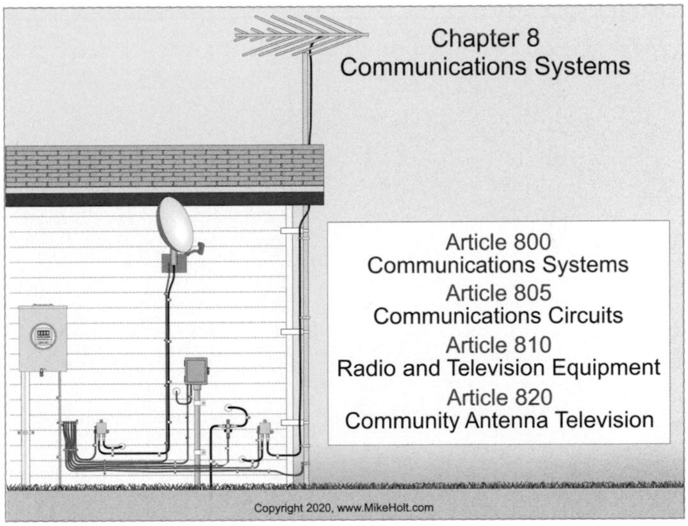

Communications systems are not subject to the general requirements contained in Chapters 1 through 4 or the special requirements of Chapters 5 through 7, except where a Chapter 8 rule specifically refers to one of those chapters [90.3]. Also, installations of communications equipment under the exclusive control of communications utilities located outdoors, or in building spaces used exclusively for such installations, are exempt from the *NEC* [90.2(B)(4)].

Chapter 8
Communications Systems

Article 800
Communications Systems
Article 805
Communications Circuits
Article 810
Radio and Television Equipment
Article 820
Community Antenna Television

▶Figure 800–1

- Article 800—General Requirements for Communications Systems. This article covers general requirements for the installation of communications circuits, community antenna television and radio distribution systems, network-powered broadband communications systems, and premises-powered broadband communications systems, unless modified by Articles 805 or 820.

- Article 805—Communications Circuits. Article 805 covers the installation requirements for circuits and equipment related to telephone wiring and other telecommunications purposes such as computer local area networks (LANs), and outside wiring for fire and burglar alarm systems connected to central monitoring stations.

- Article 810—Radio and Television Equipment. This article covers antenna systems for radio and television receiving equipment, amateur radio transmitting and receiving equipment, and certain features of transmitter safety. It also includes antennas such as multi-element, vertical rod and dish, and the wiring and cabling that connects them to the equipment.

- Article 820—Community Antenna Television (CATV) and Radio Distribution Systems (Coaxial Cable). Article 820 covers the installation of coaxial cables to distribute limited-energy high-frequency signals for television, cable TV, and closed-circuit television (CCTV), which is often used for security purposes. It also covers the premises wiring of satellite TV systems where the dish antenna is outside and covered by Article 810.

Introduction to the 2020 Changes in Chapter 8 Communications Systems

There was a major restructuring of Chapter 8 during the 2020 revision cycle. Article 800 is now "General Requirements for Communications Circuits." As the new title implies, it contains the general requirements for the other Chapter 8 articles. The only exception is Article 810 which stands completely on its own unless it specifically references *Code* rules in other articles.

The rules for "Communications Circuits" were relocated to the new Article 805. The general requirements that were in articles 805, 820, 830, and 840 were moved to Article 800 to make the *NEC* easier to use. Since the requirements were nearly identical in the four articles, the Code-Making Panel believed it would be more "user friendly" to have them in a single "general requirements" article.

You will now have to go to two different articles for a Chapter 8 installation; Article 800 for the general rules and one of the other four the more specific ones. The rules in this chapter are still separate from the rest of the *NEC*, unless there is a specific reference to a Chapter 1 through 7 rule in a Chapter 8 article.

ARTICLE 800

GENERAL REQUIREMENTS FOR COMMUNICATIONS SYSTEMS

Introduction to Article 800—General Requirements for Communications Systems

This article has its roots in telephone technology. Consequently, it addresses telephone and related systems that use twisted-pair wiring. This article contains the general rules for the installations of the systems covered by Articles 805, and 820. These general rules along with the more specific rules in the respective articles apply. Note that the scope of this article does not included Article 810, Radio and Television Equipment. That article remains standalone from the rest of the *Code*, including the Chapter 8 Articles. The specific rules in Articles 805, 820, 830 and 840 supplement or modify the requirements in Article 800. This is similar to the language in 90.3 that says the general rules in Chapters 1 through 4 may be modified by the specific rules in Chapters 5 through 7.

▸ Do not attach incoming communications cables to the service-entrance power mast.

▸ Keep the grounding electrode conductor for the primary protector as straight and as short as possible.

▸ If you locate communications cables above a suspended ceiling, route and support them to allow access via ceiling panel removal.

▸ Keep these cables separated from lightning protection circuits.

▸ If you install communications cables in a Chapter 3 raceway, you must do so in conformance with the *NEC* requirements for the raceway system.

▸ Special labeling and marking provisions apply—follow them carefully.

800.1 Scope

This article covers the general requirements for Chapter 8 installations.

Analysis

NEW This article contains the general rules for the installations of the systems covered by all of Chapter 8 except Article 810, Radio and Television Equipment which remains standalone from the rest of the *Code*, including the other Chapter 8 articles. The specific rules in Articles 805, 820, 830, and 840 supplement or modify the requirements in Article 800.

800.1 Scope

This article covers general requirements for communications systems. These general requirements apply to communications circuits, community antenna television, and radio distribution systems, and both network- and premises-powered broadband communications systems, unless modified by Articles 805, 820, 830 or 840. ▸Figure 800-2

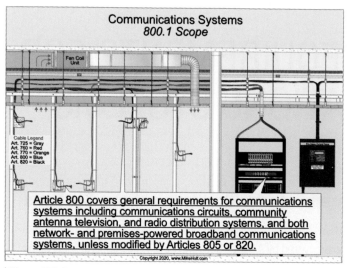

Communications Systems
800.1 Scope

Fan Coil
Unit

Cable Legend
Art. 725 = Gray
Art. 760 = Red
Art. 770 = Orange
Art. 800 = Blue
Art. 820 = Black

Article 800 covers general requirements for communications systems including communications circuits, community antenna television, and radio distribution systems, and both network- and premises-powered broadband communications systems, unless modified by Articles 805 or 820.

Copyright 2020, www.MikeHolt.com

▶Figure 800–2

800.2 Definitions

Definitions in Part I of Article 100 apply throughout Chapter 8 and those found in 800.2 apply only within Chapter 8.

Analysis

CLARIFIED

New language specifically references the definitions in Part I of Article 100 making them apply to all the Chapter 8 articles. It does not appear in any of the other chapters but is required here as (per 90.3) Chapter 8 stands alone and nothing in the previous seven chapters applies—unless specifically referenced in Chapter 8. The definitions in 800.2 are intended to apply to all the articles in Chapter 8; not just within Article 800. Most of the definitions were relocated without change, other than minor language edits to make the definitions apply to four of the five types of systems covered by this chapter. The articles are 805, Communications Systems; 820, Community Antenna Television and Radio Distribution Systems; 830, Network-Powered Broadband Communications Systems; and 840, Premises-Powered Broadband Communications Systems. Other modifications are as follows:

CLARIFIED

Abandoned Cable. This definition was simplified to say that cable that is not terminated or not identified for future use by a tag is abandoned. The types of terminations were removed for simplification; if the cable is terminated it is not abandoned. As before however, cables that are identified by a tag for future use are also not abandoned.

EXPANDED

Communications Circuit. The definition is now in the General Article 800 rather than in Article 805, Communications Circuits. There were four changes in this definition to more clearly reflect the intent of the *Code*. The term "communications utility or service provider" replaced "communications utility" because the latter was intended to apply to an entity that is defined and regulated by the State Public Service Commission and only applies to regulated telecommunications companies.

The second revision deleted the list of the types of services that are included and now just says, "the circuit that extends service from the communications utility or service provider up to and including the customer's communications equipment."

The third change was to remove the word "electrically" from this definition recognizing that in addition to "electrical" communications circuits there are also "optical" and "wireless" communications circuits.

The fourth revision removed the list of services that are communications circuits. The change clarified that not all circuits that use CM (Communications Multipurpose) cable are communications circuits. The substantiation for the removal of the list of services said this change was needed to clarify that Ethernet circuits are not covered by the communications circuit article. In addition, it said that the removal of the list would permit new technologies that are powered from the communications utility or service provider's central office. Note that in practice, communications cable generally is intended to mean network cable.

NEW

Communications Service Provider. This is a new definition for use in Chapter 8 and defines what a communications system provider is. Not all communications providers are utilities, so this definition was added to make the rules in this chapter apply no matter who provides communications service thereby covering providers who are utilities and well as those who are not.

800.2 Definitions

The definitions for more common items that appear in Article 100 and those that are contained here in 800.2 apply throughout Chapter 8.

Abandoned Cable. Cable that is not terminated to equipment or not identified for future use with a tag. ▸Figure 800–3

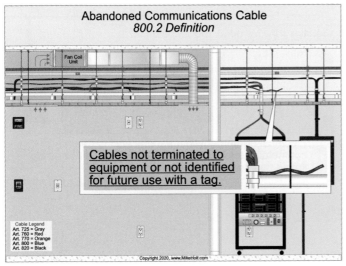

▸Figure 800–3

Communications Circuit. The circuit that extends service from the communications utility or service provider up to and including the customer's communications equipment. ▸Figure 800–4

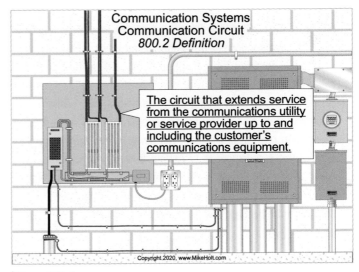

▸Figure 800–4

800.3 Other Articles

Common information from the "xxx.3" sections of the other Chapter 8 articles, except Article 810, is now located here.

Analysis

RELOCATED While it is interesting that the *Code* only references 300.22(A) Ducts for Dust, Loose Stock, or Vapor Removal, and 300.22(C) Other Spaces Used for Environmental Air (Plenums), it does not reference 300.22(B) Ducts Specifically Fabricated for Environmental Air. That was also the case in the previous *Code*. Section 800.3(D) makes the requirements in 110.3(B) apply to Articles 805, 820, 830, and 840 installations. All of those are just relocations of rules that were in the individual Chapter 8 articles in the 2017 *NEC*.

NEW **800.3(E) Optical Fiber Cable.** This new subsection was added to reference Article 770 for the installation of optical fiber cables used to provide communications circuits within a building. Without this reference the optical fiber rules in Article 770 would not apply to circuits installed to service the systems covered by the Chapter 8 articles.

NEW **800.3(F) Other Communications Systems.** A new subsection (F) was added as a result of the Chapter 8 restructuring. It requires that (in addition to the rules in Article 800) the requirements in the article appropriate for the system being installed also apply. While this information is also in the scope, scopes are not permitted to contain mandatory rules. This simply says that in addition to the requirements in Article 800, the requirements of Articles 805, 810, 820, 830, and 840 apply respectively to those systems. List item (2) is for Article 810, Radio and Television Equipment but that article is not within the scope of Article 800.

NEW **800.3(G) Reconditioned Equipment.** Some types of communications equipment covered in Chapter 8 may be reconditioned, but without this reference to the reconditioned marking requirements in Article 110, those rules would not apply. Reconditioned equipment must be marked with the name, trademark, or other descriptive marking that identifies the organization that reconditioned the equipment, along with the date of the reconditioning.

800.3 Other Articles

Only those sections of Chapters 1 through 7 referenced in Chapter 8 apply to Chapter 8. ▶Figure 800–5

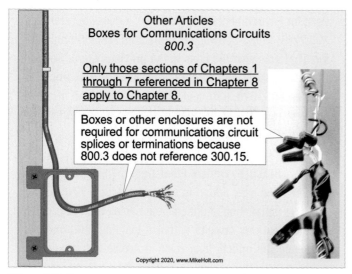

Other Articles
Boxes for Communications Circuits
800.3

Only those sections of Chapters 1 through 7 referenced in Chapter 8 apply to Chapter 8.

Boxes or other enclosures are not required for communications circuit splices or terminations because 800.3 does not reference 300.15.

Copyright 2020, www.MikeHolt.com

▶Figure 800–5

(A) Hazardous (Classified) Locations. Circuits and equipment installed in a location that is classified in accordance with 500.5 and 505.5, the applicable requirements of Chapter 5 apply.

(B) Wiring in Ducts for Dust, Loose Stock, or Vapor Removal. The requirements of 300.22(A) apply.

(C) Equipment in Plenum Spaces. Equipment installed in plenum spaces must comply with 300.22(C)(3).

> **Author's Comment:**
>
> ▸ According to 300.22(C)(3), electrical equipment with a metal enclosure or a nonmetallic enclosure listed for use in an air-handling space can be installed in a plenum space. ▶Figure 800–6

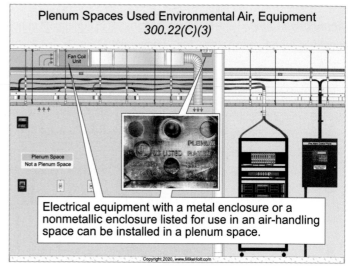

Plenum Spaces Used Environmental Air, Equipment
300.22(C)(3)

Fan Coil Unit

Plenum Space
Not a Plenum Space

Electrical equipment with a metal enclosure or a nonmetallic enclosure listed for use in an air-handling space can be installed in a plenum space.

Copyright 2020, www.MikeHolt.com

▶Figure 800–6

(D) Installation and Use. Communications equipment must be installed and used according to manufacturers' instructions in accordance with of 110.3(B).

(E) Optical Fiber Cable. Where optical fiber cable is used to provide a communications circuit within a building, Article 770 applies.

(F) Other Communications Systems. Communications systems must comply with the following requirements:

(1) Communications Circuits—Article 805

(2) Antennas—Article 810

(3) Coaxial Cable systems—Article 820

800.49 Metal Entrance Conduit Grounding

This rule was in 800, 820, and 840, was clarified, and relocated here.

Analysis

RELOCATED The clarification replaced "metallic conduit" with "metal conduit." The requirement is for a metal conduit containing a Chapter 8 entrance wire or cable to be connected via a bonding conductor or a grounding electrode conductor to the grounding electrode or the building grounding electrode in accordance with 800.10(B).

800.49 Metal Entrance Conduit Grounding

Metal raceways containing entrance cable must be bonded to a grounding electrode conductor, grounding electrode, or where present, the building grounding electrode system in accordance with 800.100(B). ▶Figure 800–7

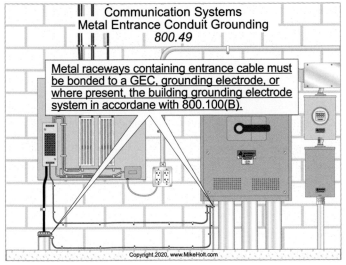

▶Figure 800–7

800.53 Separation from Lighting Conductors

The language was revised to clarify that communications cables and CATV cables must be separated from lightning conductors and not from each other, and two new Informational Notes were added.

Analysis

CLARIFIED Communications cables often have grounded shield conductors and there is a danger of a "side-flash" from the lighting protection system conductors to the communications conductors. The lighting conductors can be at a very high voltage when they are doing their job; a voltage high enough that there can be "mini" lightning bolts between the lightning protection system conductor and the communications cables. The 6-ft separation requirement helps prevent that. Informational Note No. 2 refers to NFPA 780, *Standard for the Installation of Lightning Protection Systems* for the method of calculating specific side-flash distances. (A "side-flash" is a lateral discharge from a conductive material carrying a substantial amount of current such as that from lightning and is basically a short-circuited lightning strike.)

800.53 Separation from Lightning Conductors

Where practicable, a separation of at least 6 ft must be maintained between communications circuits and lightning protection conductors.

800.100 Cable and Primary Protector Bonding and Grounding

Minor editorial changes were made and this rule now applies to the bonding and grounding of all Chapter 8 installations, except those covered by Article 810.

Analysis

RELOCATED

800.100(A)(1) through (6) Bonding Conductor or Grounding Electrode Conductor. These rules are identical to the requirements in the previous *Code*.

RELOCATED

800.100(B) Electrode. (1) through (3). This is identical language as appeared in 800.100(B), 820.100(B), and 830.100(B) in the 2017 *NEC*. It is a new requirement for Article 840 installations that would require bonding and/or grounding. The figures association with the Informational Note figures that were in the Communications System article following the scope statement were relocated to this section. The first of the two figures provide a graphic illustration of the communications system bonding conductor for the cases where the structure has an intersystem bonding termination and the second for cases where there is no intersystem bonding termination device.

RELOCATED

800.100 (C) Electrode Connection. This rule is identical to the one in the previous *Code* and requires that the connection to a grounding electrode to be accomplished in accordance with 250.70.

RELOCATED

800.100(D) Bonding of Electrodes. This is also the same as the previous *NEC* rules. It requires that where a separate grounding electrode has been installed for the Chapter 8 installation, it must be bonded to the electrical grounding electrode at the building or structure served. The two places that permit a separate grounding electrode are in the exception to 800.100(4) for one- and two-family dwellings, and in 800.100(B)(3) for buildings or structures that do not have grounding electrodes. Since there is no grounding electrode to which to bond a (B)(3) installation, this really applies only where the exception to 800.100(A)(4) has been applied.

800.100 Cable and Primary Protector Bonding and Grounding

(A) Bonding Conductor or Grounding Electrode Conductor.

(1) Insulation. The conductor must be listed and can be insulated, covered, or bare.

(2) Material. The conductor must be copper or other corrosion-resistant conductive material and can be stranded or solid.

(3) Size. The conductor is not permitted to be smaller than 14 AWG with a current-carrying capacity of not less than the grounded metallic sheath member(s) or protected conductor(s) of the communications cable or coaxial cable. The bonding conductor or grounding electrode conductor is not required to be larger than 6 AWG. ▶Figure 800–8

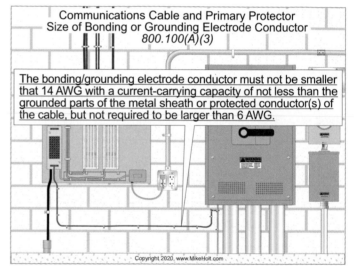

▶Figure 800–8

(4) Length. The bonding conductor or grounding electrode conductor must be as short as practicable. For one- and two-family dwellings, the bonding conductor or grounding electrode conductor is not permitted to exceed 20 ft in length. ▶Figure 800–9

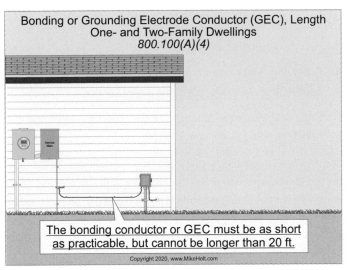

▶Figure 800-9

Note: Limiting the length of the bonding conductor or grounding electrode conductor helps limit induced voltage differences between the building's power and communications systems during lightning events.

Ex: If the bonding conductor or grounding electrode conductor is over 20 ft in length for one- and two-family dwellings, a separate ground rod not less than 5 ft long [800.100(B)(3)(2)] with fittings suitable for the application [800.100(C)] must be installed. The additional ground rod must be bonded to the power grounding electrode system with a minimum 6 AWG conductor [800.100(D)]. ▶Figure 800-10

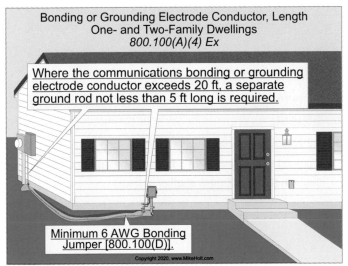

▶Figure 800-10

(5) Run in Straight Line. Run in as straight a line as practicable.

(6) Physical Protection. The bonding conductor and grounding electrode conductor are not permitted to be subject to physical damage. If installed in a metal raceway, both ends of the raceway must be bonded to the contained conductor or connected to the same terminal or electrode to which the bonding conductor or grounding electrode conductor is connected.

(B) Electrode. The bonding conductor or grounding electrode conductor must be connected in accordance with (B)(1), (B)(2), or (B)(3):

(1) Buildings with an Intersystem Bonding Termination. The bonding conductor must terminate to the intersystem bonding termination as required by 250.94. ▶Figure 800-11

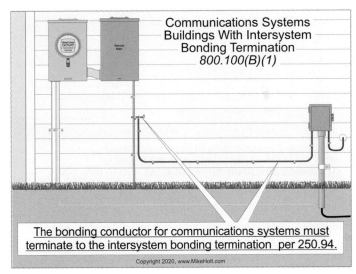

▶Figure 800-11

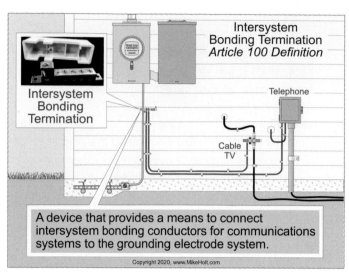

A device that provides a means to connect intersystem bonding conductors for communications systems to the grounding electrode system.

▶Figure 800-12

Note: Figure 800.100(B)(1) in the *NEC* illustrates the connection of the bonding conductor in buildings or structures equipped with an intersystem bonding termination.

(2) Building Without Intersystem Bonding Termination. The bonding conductor or grounding electrode conductor must terminate to the nearest accessible: ▶Figure 800–13

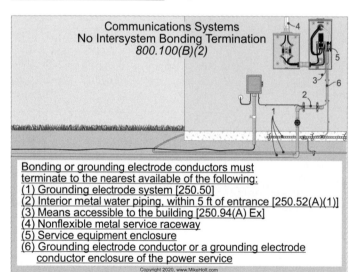

Bonding or grounding electrode conductors must terminate to the nearest available of the following:
(1) Grounding electrode system [250.50]
(2) Interior metal water piping, within 5 ft of entrance [250.52(A)(1)]
(3) Means accessible to the building [250.94(A) Ex]
(4) Nonflexible metal service raceway
(5) Service equipment enclosure
(6) Grounding electrode conductor or a grounding electrode conductor enclosure of the power service

▶Figure 800–13

(1) Building grounding electrode system [250.50].

(2) Interior metal water piping system, within 5 ft from its point of entrance [250.52(A)(1)].

(3) Means external to the building, using the options contained in 250.94(A) Ex.

(4) Nonflexible metal service raceway.

(5) Service disconnect enclosure.

(6) Grounding electrode conductor or the grounding electrode conductor metal enclosure of the power service.

(7) Grounding electrode conductor or the grounding electrode of a remote building disconnect [250.32].

The intersystem bonding termination must be mounted on the fixed part of an enclosure so it will not interfere with the opening of an enclosure door. A bonding device is not permitted to be mounted on a door or cover even if the door or cover is nonremovable.

For purposes of this section, mobile home service equipment or the mobile home disconnecting means located within 30 ft of the exterior wall of the mobile home it serves, or at a mobile home disconnecting means connected to an electrode by a grounding electrode conductor in accordance with 250.32 and located within 30 ft of the exterior wall of the mobile home it serves, is considered to meet the requirements of this section.

Note: Informational Note Figure 800.100(B)(2) illustrates the connection of the bonding conductor in buildings or structures equipped with an intersystem bonding termination or a terminal block providing access to the building grounding means.

(3) In Buildings Without Intersystem Bonding Termination or Grounding Means. If the building has no intersystem bonding termination, as described in 800.100(B)(2), the grounding electrode conductor must be connected to one of the following: ▶Figure 800–14

(1) Any individual grounding electrodes described in 250.52(A)(1), (A)(2), (A)(3), or (A)(4).

(2) Any individual grounding electrode described in 250.52(A)(5), (A)(7), and (A)(8).

(3) For communications circuits within the scope of Article 805, to a ground rod not less than 5 ft in length that is located no less than 6 ft from electrodes of other systems.

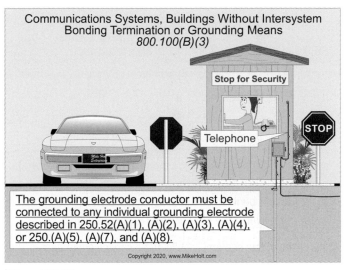

▶Figure 800–14

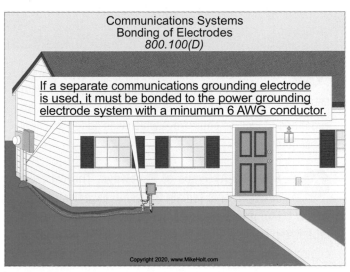

▶Figure 800–16

(C) Electrode Connection. Terminations at the grounding electrode must be by exothermic welding, listed lugs, listed pressure connectors, or listed clamps. Grounding fittings that are concrete-encased or buried in the earth must be listed for direct burial [250.70]. ▶Figure 800–15

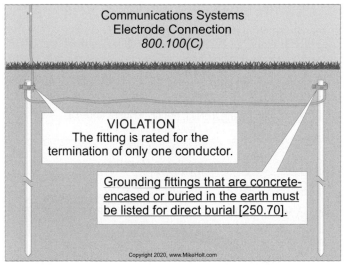

▶Figure 800–15

(D) Bonding of Electrodes. If a separate grounding electrode, such as a rod, is installed for a communications system, it must be bonded to the building's power grounding electrode system with a minimum 6 AWG conductor. ▶Figure 800–16

Note 2: The bonding of electrodes helps reduce induced voltage differences between the power and communications systems during lightning events. ▶Figure 800–17

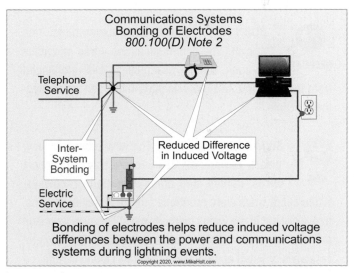

▶Figure 800–17

800.110 Raceways, Cable Routing Assemblies, and Cable Trays

This section now applies throughout Chapter 8 and so need not be repeated in each of its articles.

Analysis

RELOCATED The rules in subsections (A) through (D) were modified so they are appropriate for use with all the Chapter 8 articles. They were also expanded to include cable trays which was added in a new subsection (D).

EDITED **800.110(A) Types of Raceways.** The raceway requirements remain the same except a restriction prohibiting medium-power network-powered broadband communications cables from being installed in communications raceways as covered in 800.110(A)(2).

EDITED **800.110(B) Raceway Fill.** The fill requirements of Chapters 3 and 9 apply to only medium-powered network-powered broadband communications cables. The *Code* does not specify any raceway fill requirements for other communications cables; however, the project specifications will often have fill requirements.

RELOCATED **800.110(C) Cable Routing Assemblies.** This permits the communications wires or cables in cable routing assemblies. It is unchanged from the 2017 *NEC* but is now located in this general requirement article.

NEW **800.110(D) Cable Trays.** This new subsection now clearly permits the use of cable trays to support wires, cables, and communications raceways. While cable trays were mentioned in the installation rules, they were not in the wiring methods rules. This new language permits communications circuits to be installed in metal raceways or listed nonmetallic cable tray. Listing is required for the nonmetallic tray because of the potential fire and smoke issues with nonmetallic materials. Those issues are addressed in the product standard.

800.110 Raceways and Cable Routing Assemblies

(A) Types of Raceways.

(1) Chapter 3 Raceways. Communications cables can be installed in any Chapter 3 raceway in accordance with the requirements of Chapter 3. ▸Figure 800–18

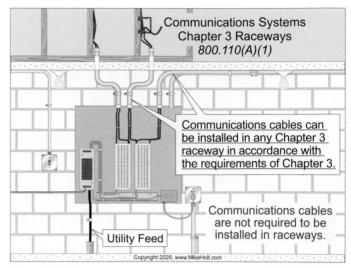

▸Figure 800–18

Author's Comment:

▸ Communications cable is not required to be installed in a Chapter 3 raceway, but when it is, it must be installed in accordance with the Chapter 3 requirements for that raceway.

(2) Communications Raceways. Communications cables can be installed in communications raceways selected using Table 800.154(b), listed in accordance with 800.182, and installed in accordance with 800.113 and 362.24 through 362.56 where the requirements to electrical nonmetallic tubing, (ENT), apply. ▸Figure 800–19

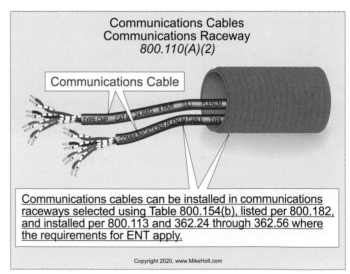

▸Figure 800–19

(3) Innerduct for Communications Wires and Cables, or Coaxial Cables. Listed plenum communications raceways, listed riser communications raceways, and listed general-purpose communications raceways selected in accordance with Table 800.154(b) are permitted to be installed as innerduct in any type of listed raceway permitted in Chapter 3.

(B) Raceway Fill for Communications Wires and Cables. The raceway fill limitations of 300.17 do not apply to communications cables installed within a raceway.

(C) Cable Routing Assemblies. Communications cables can be installed in cable routing assemblies selected in accordance with Table 800.154(c), listed in accordance with 800.182, and installed in accordance with 800.110(C)(1) and (C)(2) and 800.113.

(1) Horizontal Support. Where installed horizontally, cable routing assemblies must be supported every 3 ft, and at each end or joint, unless listed otherwise. The distance between supports can never exceed 10 ft.

(2) Vertical Support. Where installed vertically, cable routing assemblies must be supported every 4 ft, unless listed otherwise, and are not permitted to have more than one joint between supports.

800.113 Installation of Wires, Cables, Cable Routing Assemblies, and Communications Raceways

These provisions were relocated from the communications circuits article with only editorial revisions and no technical changes.

Analysis

RELOCATED

The rules have not changed from the 2017 *NEC*. The terms were editorially revised so this rule can be used throughout Chapter 8. For example, the term "CMP" (plenum rated multipurpose cable) was replaced with "plenum cables." This eliminates the need to list multiple plenum cable types.

800.113 Installation of Communications Wires, Cables, Raceways, and Cable Routing Assemblies

The installation of cables, cable routing assemblies, and communications raceways must comply with 800.110 and the following:

(A) Listing. Cables, cable routing assemblies, and communications raceways installed in buildings must be listed.

(B) Ducts Specifically Fabricated for Environmental Air. The following cables are permitted in ducts specifically fabricated for environmental air as described in 300.22(B) if they are directly associated with the air distribution system: ▶Figure 800-20

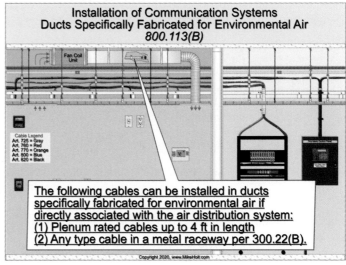

▶Figure 800-20

(1) Plenum rated cables up to 4 ft in length

(2) Any type cables in a metal raceway in accordance with 300.22(B)

Note: For information on fire protection of wiring installed in fabricated ducts, see NFPA 90A, *Standard for the Installation of Air-Conditioning and Ventilating Systems*.

(C) Plenum Spaces. The following cables, cable routing assemblies, and communications raceways can be installed in plenum spaces as described in 300.22(C): ▶Figure 800-21

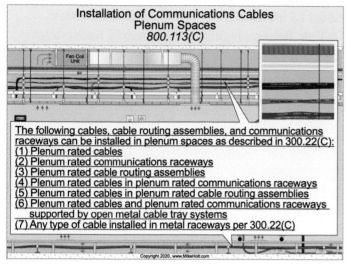

Installation of Communications Cables
Plenum Spaces
800.113(C)

The following cables, cable routing assemblies, and communications raceways can be installed in plenum spaces as described in 300.22(C):
(1) Plenum rated cables
(2) Plenum rated communications raceways
(3) Plenum rated cable routing assemblies
(4) Plenum rated cables in plenum rated communications raceways
(5) Plenum rated cables in plenum rated cable routing assemblies
(6) Plenum rated cables and plenum rated communications raceways supported by open metal cable tray systems
(7) Any type of cable installed in metal raceways per 300.22(C)

Copyright 2020, www.MikeHolt.com

▶Figure 800–21

(1) Plenum rated cables

(2) Plenum rated communications raceways

(3) Plenum rated cable routing assemblies

(4) Plenum rated cables installed in plenum rated communications raceways

(5) Plenum rated cables installed in plenum rated cable routing assemblies

(6) Plenum rated cables and plenum rated communications raceways supported by open metal cable tray systems

(7) Any type of cable installed in metal raceways in compliance with 300.22(C)

800.154 Applications of Listed Communications Wires, Cables, and Raceways, and Listed Cable Routing Assemblies

This section combines and relocates the permitted cable types for Articles 805, 820, 830, and 840 into a single section without technical change.

Analysis

RELOCATED The information was combined from the four articles into one general rule that applies to all of them. As a result, the tables were expanded to include cable types from the four articles, but there was no technical change. The specific cable types in the new Table 800.154(a) were replaced with general terms to encompass all the various types of cable that were previously included in each article. For example, CM and CMG cables were replaced with general-purpose cables, and CMX cables were replaced with limited-use cables. BM, BMR, and BMU cables are indicated specifically as these are medium-power cables. BMU and BLU cables are indicated specifically as they are underground cables. (CM and CMG are the most common commercial grade communications cables, CMX is for residential installs, and the "BM" types are various grades of coaxial cables.)

800.154 Applications of Listed Communications Wires, Cables, and Raceways, and Listed Cable Routing Assemblies

Permitted and nonpermitted applications of listed communications wires, cables, coaxial cables and raceways, and listed cable routing assemblies must be in accordance with one of the following:

(1) Listed communications wires and cables as indicated in Table 800.154(a)

(2) Listed communications raceways as indicated in Table 800.154(b)

(3) Listed cable routing assemblies as indicated in Table 800.154(c)

The permitted applications are subject to the installation requirements of 800.110 and 800.113.

800.179 Plenum, Riser, General-Purpose, and Limited Use Cables

The redundant requirements from 805.179, 820.179, and 830.179 were moved here as general requirements.

Analysis

RELOCATED This article requires that the cables listed in subsections (A) through (D) and named in the same order as in the section title, be installed in accordance with the requirements in their respective articles. The previous requirement that the wires and cables have a temperature rating of at least 60°C was also moved out of those articles and placed here.

800.179 Wires, Riser, General-Purpose, and Limited Use Cables

Plenum, riser, general-purpose, and limited-use cables must be listed in accordance with 800.179(A) through (D). The cable voltage rating must not be marked on the cable.

(A) Plenum Cables. Type CMP (communications plenum cables) and Type CATVP (community antenna television plenum coaxial cables must be listed as being suitable for use in ducts, plenums, and other spaces used for environmental air and also be listed as having adequate fire-resistant and low smoke-producing characteristics.

(C) General-Purpose Cables. Type CM (communications general-purpose cables) and Type CATV (community antenna television coaxial general-purpose cables) must be listed as being suitable for general-purpose use, with the exception of risers and plenums, and also be listed as being resistant to the spread of fire.

ARTICLE
805

COMMUNICATIONS CIRCUITS

Introduction to Article 805—Communications Circuits

The general rules for Chapter 8 installations, other than Article 810 installations, are contained within Article 800. The specific information for communications circuits are found here in Article 805. Many of the "common" requirements are consolidated in Article 800 General Requirements for Communications Systems. The specific rules here in Article 805, supplement or modify the requirements in Article 800. This is similar to the language in 90.3 that says the general rules in Chapters 1 through 4 may be modified by the specific rules in Chapters 5 through 7.

Article 805 has its roots in telephone technology. Consequently, it addresses telephone and related systems. Here are a few key points to remember about Article 805:

▸ Do not attach incoming communications cables to the service-entrance power mast.

▸ Keep the grounding electrode conductor for the primary protector as straight and as short as possible.

▸ If you locate communications cables above a suspended ceiling, route and support them to allow access via ceiling panel removal.

▸ Keep these cables separated from lightning protection circuits.

▸ If you install communications cables in a Chapter 3 raceway, you must do so in conformance with the *NEC* requirements for the raceway system.

Special labeling and marking provisions apply—follow them carefully

Author's Comment:

▸ The informational notes and figures that previously followed the article title have been relocated. They were "floating" notes and the *NEC Style Manual* does not permit "floating" notes.

▸ A "floating" note is one that is not located physically with the *Code* rule that the note applies to. These notes have been relocated to 800.100(B)(1) and (B)(2).

805.93 Grounding, Bonding, or Interruption of Non-Current-Carrying Metallic Sheath Members of Communications Cables

The section title and the language within the section was revised to add the words "bonding" or "bonded."

Analysis

CLARIFIED This revision coordinates with the requirements of 800.100 that uses both terms "bonding" and "grounding." In almost all cases the connection being made is a bonding connection and not a grounding connection.

805.93 Grounding, Bonding, or Interruption

(A) Entering Buildings. In installations where the communications cable enters a building, the metallic sheath members of the cable must be grounded or bonded as specified in 800.100 or interrupted by an insulating joint or equivalent device. The grounding, bonding, or interruption must be as close as practicable to the point of entrance.

(B) Terminating on the Outside of Buildings. In installations where the communications cable is terminated on the outside of the building, the metallic sheath members of the cable must be grounded or bonded as specified in 800.100 or interrupted by an insulating joint or equivalent device. The grounding, bonding, or interruption must be as close as practicable to the point of termination of the cable.

805.133 Installation of Communications Wires, Cables, and Equipment

This revision clarifies that where Class 2 and 3 circuits are in a communications cable, they remain classified as Class 2 or 3 circuits.

Analysis

CLARIFIED

Previous language for cables that contain both communications circuit conductors and Class 2 or 3 power circuit conductors required the power circuit to be classified as a communications circuit; however, it is a Class 2 or 3 power circuit. The new language permits both the communications and power circuit conductors to be in the same listed communications cable but does not require the reclassification of the power circuit as a communications circuit. The panel statement on this change said,

"This revision corrects a long-standing issue with reclassification of circuits within the same cable. A Class 2 or Class 3 power circuit is defined by its source and should not be reclassified based on the type of cable used."

805.133 Installation of Communications Wires, Cables, and Equipment

(A) Separation from Power Conductors.

(1) In Raceways, Cable Trays, Boxes, Enclosures, and Cable Routing Assemblies.

(a) With Other Circuits. Communications cables can be in the same raceway, cable tray, cable routing assembly, box, or enclosure with cables of any of the following: ▶Figure 805–1

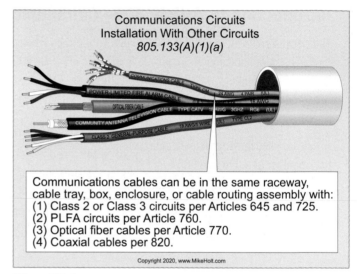

Communications Circuits
Installation With Other Circuits
805.133(A)(1)(a)

Communications cables can be in the same raceway, cable tray, box, enclosure, or cable routing assembly with:
(1) Class 2 or Class 3 circuits per Articles 645 and 725.
(2) PLFA circuits per Article 760.
(3) Optical fiber cables per Article 770.
(4) Coaxial cables per 820.

Copyright 2020, www.MikeHolt.com

▶Figure 805–1

(1) Class 2 and 3 circuits in accordance with Articles 645 and 725.

(2) Power-limited fire alarm circuits in accordance with Article 760.

(3) Optical fiber cables in accordance with Article 770.

(4) Coaxial cables in accordance with Article 820.

(b) Class 2 Circuits. Class 2 conductors can be within the same cable with communications conductors if the cable is communications rated [725.139(D)(1)]. ▶Figure 805–2

Author's Comment:

▶ A common application of this requirement is when a single cable is used for both voice communications and data.

▶ Listed Class 2 cables have a voltage rating of not less than 150V [725.179(G)], whereas communications cables have a voltage rating of at least 300V [800.179].

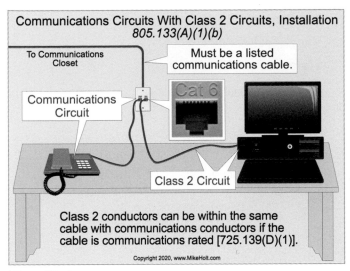

Communications Circuits With Class 2 Circuits, Installation
805.133(A)(1)(b)

To Communications Closet

Communications Circuit

Must be a listed communications cable.

Cat 6

Class 2 Circuit

Class 2 conductors can be within the same cable with communications conductors if the cable is communications rated [725.139(D)(1)].

Copyright 2020, www.MikeHolt.com

▶Figure 805-2

(c) With Power Conductors in Same Raceway or Enclosure. Communications conductors are not permitted to be placed in any raceway, compartment, outlet box, junction box, or similar fitting with conductors of electric power or Class 1 circuits.

(B) Support of Communications Cables. Communications cables are not permitted to be strapped, taped, or attached to the exterior of any raceway as a means of support. ▶Figure 805-3

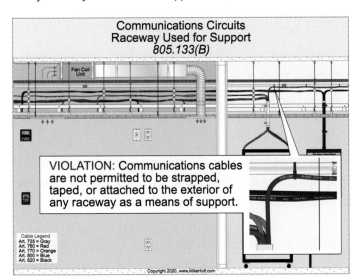

Communications Circuits
Raceway Used for Support
805.133(B)

Fan Coil Unit

VIOLATION: Communications cables are not permitted to be strapped, taped, or attached to the exterior of any raceway as a means of support.

Cable Legend
Art. 725 = Gray
Art. 760 = Red
Art. 770 = Orange
Art. 800 = Blue
Art. 820 = Black

Copyright 2020, www.MikeHolt.com

▶Figure 805-3

▶ Exposed cables must be supported by the structural components of the building so the cable will not be damaged by normal building use. The cables must be secured by straps, staples, cable ties, hangers, or similar fittings designed and installed in a manner that will not damage the cable [800.24].

805.154 Substitutions of Listed Communications Wires, Cables, and Raceways, and Listed Cable Routing Assemblies

This section now contains only the permitted substitutions of communications cables.

Analysis

REDUCED With the creation of the new general communications requirement article, all the application requirements specifying what type of cable or raceway can be used in the various locations (plenum, riser, and general) are found in 800.154. This rule now has only the cable substitution requirements. The parent text says that the substitutions for communications cables as listed in Table 805.154 and illustrated in Figure 805.154 of the *NEC* must be permitted.

805.154 Communications Cable(s) Substitutions

Cable substitutions are permitted provided that the substitute is of better fire resistance as indicated in the hierarchy in *NEC* figure 805.154.

RADIO AND TELEVISION SATELLITE EQUIPMENT

Introduction to Article 810—Radio and Television Satellite Equipment

Unlike other articles in this chapter, Article 810 is not covered by the general rules in Article 800, as a result, it stands completely alone in the *Code* unless a rule in 810 references a specific rule elsewhere in the *Code*.

This article covers transmitter and receiver (antenna) equipment, and the wiring and cabling associated with that equipment. Here are a few key points to remember about Article 810:

▸ Avoid contact with conductors of other systems.

▸ Do not attach antennas or other equipment to the service-entrance power mast.

▸ Keep the bonding conductor or grounding electrode conductor as straight as practicable and protect it from physical damage.

▸ If the mast is not bonded properly, you risk flashovers and possible electrocution.

▸ Keep in mind that the purpose of bonding is to prevent a difference of voltage between metallic objects and other conductive items, such as swimming pools.

▸ Clearances are critical, and Article 810 contains detailed clearance requirements. For example, it provides separate clearance requirements for indoor and outdoor locations.

Note: See Figure 800(a) and Figure 800(b) in the *NEC* for examples of bonding conductors and grounding electrode conductors.

810.21 Bonding Conductors and Grounding Electrode Conductors—Receiving Stations

Copper-clad aluminum was added to the list of permitted conductor types for bonding and grounding applications.

Analysis

EXPANDED

810.21(A) Material. The only technical change was here in 810.21(A) which addresses the materials permitted for bonding and grounding electrode conductors that are used with Radio and Television Systems. The list of permitted materials was expanded to include copper-clad aluminum. The other permitted materials for these conductors are copper, aluminum, copper-clad steel, bronze, or similar corrosion-resistant material. This change was necessary since the second sentence restricts the use of aluminum or copper-clad aluminum conductors within 18 in. of the earth, yet it was not one of the materials permitted for this application.

810.21 Bonding Conductor and Grounding Electrode Conductors

Bonding conductors and grounding electrode conductors must meet the requirements of 810.21(A) through 810.21(K).

(A) Material. The bonding conductor to the intersystem bonding termination or grounding electrode conductor to the grounding electrode [810.21(F)] must be copper, <u>copper-clad aluminum,</u> or other corrosion-resistant conductive material. ▶**Figure 810–1**

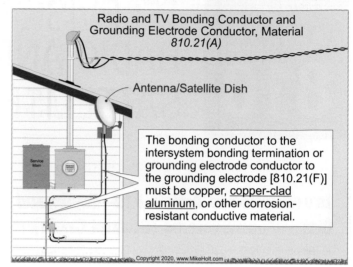

Radio and TV Bonding Conductor and Grounding Electrode Conductor, Material *810.21(A)*

Antenna/Satellite Dish

The bonding conductor to the intersystem bonding termination or grounding electrode conductor to the grounding electrode [810.21(F)] must be copper, <u>copper-clad aluminum,</u> or other corrosion-resistant conductive material.

Service Main

Copyright 2020, www.MikeHolt.com

▶Figure 810–1

ARTICLE 820

COMMUNITY ANTENNA TELEVISION (CATV) AND RADIO DISTRIBUTION SYSTEMS (COAXIAL CABLE)

Introduction to Article 820—Community Antenna Television (CATV) and Radio Distribution Systems (Coaxial Cable)

This article focuses on the distribution of television and radio signals within a facility or on a property via cable, rather than their transmission or reception via antenna. These signals are limited energy, but they are high frequency.

Article 800 defines the "point of entrance" for these circuits and the General requirements regarding installation methods of all types of communications wiring. Ground the incoming coaxial cable as close as practicable to the point of entrance. If coaxial cables are located above a suspended ceiling, route and support them to allow access via ceiling panel removal. Clearances are critical, and Article 800 contains detailed clearance requirements. For example, it requires at least 6 ft of clearance between coaxial cable and lightning conductors. The bonding conductor must be connected to the intersystem bonding termination if there is one in, or at, the building. If you use a separate grounding electrode, you must run a bonding jumper to the power grounding system.

Author's Comment:

▸ As with 810, the informational note that followed the title and had referenced Informational Notes and Figures 800(a) and 800(b) was deleted. With changes made in the *Code* since the 2014 edition, this note no longer serves any purpose.

820.3 Other Articles

General references made to other articles are now found in 800.3 as a part of Chapter 8's reorganization.

Analysis

REDUCED The general requirements for radio and television equipment are no longer found here in the parent text. Those references are now in 800.3. There are now only two references remaining in this section.

CLARIFIED **820.3(A) General Requirements.** This subsection applies the general requirements of Article 800 to this article.

CLARIFIED **820.3 (B) Alternate Wiring Methods.** This subsection permits the wiring methods in Article 830 to be a substitute for the wiring methods of this article.

820.44 Overhead (Aerial) Coaxial Cables

With the exception of 820.44(A) and (B), the requirements for overhead cables were relocated to 800.44.

Analysis

REDUCED

820.44(A) On Poles and In-Span, Above Roofs, on Masts, or Between Buildings. The charging text says that the overhead installation must comply with 820.44(A) or 800.44. Section 820.44(A) says that where coaxial cables are installed on poles and in-span, above roofs, on masts, or between buildings they must be installed in accordance with 800.44.

Author's Comment:

▸ You would think that 820.44(A) would have been deleted as 800.44 automatically applies to Article 820 installations.

RELOCATED

820.44(B) On Buildings. The rules for coaxial cables installed on buildings were not changed, just relocated from (E).

Author's Comment:

▸ The charging text in this section does not mention compliance with (B). It only species compliance with (A).

820.100 Cable Bonding and Grounding

Most of the cable bonding and grounding requirements are now found in 800.100.

Analysis

RELOCATED

All the requirements except one were relocated to 800.100. The two remaining subsections are:

CLARIFIED

820.100(A) General Requirements. The cable grounding and bonding is required to comply with 800.100.

REORGANIZED

820.100(B) Shield Protection Devices. This was (E) and is now (B) because the other requirements were relocated to Article 800. This permits the grounding of a coaxial drop cable shield by means of a protected device that does not interrupt the grounding system within the premises.

820.154 Substitutions of Listed CATV Cables

The application rules were relocated to 800.154, leaving just the cable substitution rules in this section.

Analysis

REDUCED

This section now contains only parent text referencing Table 820.154 and the *NEC*'s Figure 820.154 for the coaxial cable substitutions. The substitution rules in Article 805 permit substitution between the various multipurpose communications cable types. These rules for coaxial cables permit the use of CATV, CM, BM, and BL cable types.

2020 *NATIONAL ELECTRICAL CODE* CHANGES REVIEW QUIZ

Please use the 2020 *Code* book to answer the following questions.

1. Installations supplying _____ power to ships and watercraft in marinas and boatyards are covered by the *NEC*.

   (a) shore
   (b) primary
   (c) secondary
   (d) auxiliary

2. By definition, an attachment fitting is different from an attachment plug because no _____ is associated with the fitting.

   (a) cable
   (b) fixture wire
   (c) cord
   (d) wiring compartment

3. Fault current is the current delivered at a point on the electrical system during a _____ circuit condition.

   (a) short
   (b) excessive
   (c) induced
   (d) over

4. By definition, an equipment grounding conductor is considered to be a grounded conductor.

   (a) True
   (b) False

5. Reconditioned equipment shall be identified as

   (a) removed
   (b) updated
   (c) modified
   (d) preserved

6. As applied to electrical equipment, the term reconditioned may be interchangeable with the term_____.

   (a) rebuilt
   (b) refurbished
   (c) remanufactured
   (d) any of these

7. NFPA 70E, *Standard for Electrical Safety in the Workplace*, provides guidance for working space about electrical equipment, such as determining severity of potential exposure, planning safe work practices, arc-flash labeling, and selecting personal protective equipment.

   (a) True
   (b) False

8. Working space distances for enclosed live parts shall be measured from the _____ of equipment or apparatus, if the live parts are enclosed.

   (a) enclosure front
   (b) opening
   (c) mounting pad
   (d) footprint

9. For large equipment that contains service disconnecting means installed in accordance with 230.71 where the combined ampere rating is _____ amperes or more and over 6 ft wide, there shall be one entrance to and egress from the required working space not less than 24 in. wide and 6½ ft high at each end of the working space

    (a) 800A
    (b) 1000A
    (c) 1200A
    (d) 2000A

10. The term "rainproof" is typically used in conjunction with enclosure type(s) _____.

    (a) 3
    (b) 3R and 3RX
    (c) 4
    (d) 4R and 4RX

11. In existing installations where a voltage system(s) already exists and a different voltage system is being added, it shall be permissible to mark only the old system voltage.

    (a) True
    (b) False

12. Ground-fault circuit-interrupter protection for personnel shall be provided as required in 210.8(A) through (F). Additional GFCI requirements for specific circuits and equipment are contained in Chapters 4, 5, and 6.

    (a) True
    (b) False

13. All single-phase receptacles rated 150V to ground or less, 50A or less and three-phase receptacles rated 150V to ground or less, 100A or less installed _____ of commercial occupancies shall have GFCI protection.

    (a) in bathrooms
    (b) on rooftops
    (c) in kitchens
    (d) all of these

14. Where branch-circuit wiring in a dwelling unit is modified, replaced, or extended in any of the areas specified in 210.12(A), the branch circuit shall be protected by a _____.

    (a) listed combination AFCI circuit breaker or first receptacle in the branch circuit
    (b) listed combination AFCI circuit breaker only
    (c) GFCI circuit breaker
    (d) GFCI at first receptacle in the circuit

15. In a dwelling unit, lighting outlets for interior stairways controlled in accordance with 210.70(A)(2)(3) shall not be controlled by the use of dimmer switches unless they provide the full range of _____ at each location.

    (a) illumination
    (b) emergency lighting
    (c) dimming control
    (d) protection

16. For the purposes of 210.71, meeting rooms are typically designed or intended for the gathering of seated occupants for such purposes as conferences, deliberations, or similar purposes, where _____ electronic equipment such as computers, projectors, or similar equipment is likely to be used.

    (a) approved
    (b) portable
    (c) listed
    (d) permanently installed

17. For the purposes of 210.71, examples of rooms that are not meeting rooms include _____.

    (a) auditoriums
    (b) schoolrooms
    (c) coffee shops
    (d) all of these

18. Where the lighting load for a nondwelling building is designed and constructed to comply with an energy code adopted by the local authority, the lighting load shall be permitted to be calculated using the unit values specified in the _____.

    (a) energy code
    (b) manufacturer's instructions
    (c) *NEC*
    (d) lighting design manual

19. The requirement for maintaining a 3-foot vertical clearance from the edge of the roof shall not apply to the final feeder conductor span where the conductors are attached to _____.

    (a) a building pole
    (b) the side of a building
    (c) an antenna
    (d) the base of a building

20. A building or structure shall be supplied by a maximum of _____ feeder(s) or branch circuit(s), unless specifically permitted otherwise.

    (a) one
    (b) two
    (c) three
    (d) four

21. Meter sockets supplied by and under the exclusive control of an electric utility shall not be required to be _____ in accordance with 230.66.

    (a) approved
    (b) rated
    (c) listed
    (d) all of these

22. Where a method to reduce clearing time for fuses rated 1200A or greater is required in accordance with 240.67(B), the _____ reduction system shall be performance tested when first installed on site.

    (a) ground-fault
    (b) short-circuit
    (c) arc-fault
    (d) arc-energy

23. Type 1 surge protective devices, (SPDs), are permitted to be connected on the load side of the service disconnect overcurrent device.

    (a) True
    (b) False

24. When installed at services, Type 1 SPDs shall be connected to the _____.

    (a) grounded service conductor
    (b) grounding electrode conductor
    (c) equipment grounding terminal at the service equipment
    (d) any of these

25. Type 2 SPDs shall be connected at the building or structure anywhere on the load side of the _____.

    (a) first overcurrent device
    (b) service attachment point
    (c) meter socket
    (d) transformer

26. A grounded conductor shall not be connected to normally noncurrent-carrying metal parts of equipment on the _____ side of the system bonding jumper of a separately derived system except as otherwise permitted in Article 250.

    (a) supply
    (b) grounded
    (c) high-voltage
    (d) load

27. The building or structure grounding electrode system shall be used as the _____ electrode for the separately derived system.

    (a) grounding
    (b) bonding
    (c) grounded
    (d) bonded

28. The frame of a vehicle-mounted generator shall not be required to be connected to a(n) _____ if the generator only supplies equipment mounted on the vehicle or cord-and-plug-connected equipment, using receptacles mounted on the vehicle.

    (a) grounding electrode
    (b) grounded conductor
    (c) ungrounded conductor
    (d) equipment grounding conductor

29. Grounding electrode conductors that are not subject to physical damage can be run exposed along the surface of the building construction if securely fastened to the surface on which they are carried.

    (a) True
    (b) False

30. A(n) _____ AWG or larger copper or aluminum grounding electrode conductor exposed to physical damage shall be protected in rigid metal conduit, IMC, PVC conduit, reinforced thermosetting resin conduit Type XW (RTRC-XW), EMT, or cable armor.

    (a) 10
    (b) 8
    (c) 6
    (d) 4

31. Where a building or structure contains more than one service disconnect in separate enclosures, grounding electrode conductor connections shall be permitted to be _____.

    (a) multiple individual grounding electrode conductors
    (b) one grounding electrode conductor at a common location
    (c) a common grounding electrode conductor and taps
    (d) any of these

32. Ferrous metal raceways and enclosures for grounding electrode conductors shall be electrically continuous from the point of attachment to cabinets or equipment to the grounding electrode.

    (a) True
    (b) False

33. Ferrous metal raceways and enclosures for grounding electrode conductors shall be bonded at each end of the raceway or enclosure to the grounding electrode or grounding electrode conductor to create a(n) _____ parallel path.

    (a) mechanically
    (b) electrically
    (c) physically
    (d) effective

34. A rebar-type concrete-encased electrode installed in accordance with 250.52(A)(3) with an additional rebar section extended from its location within the concrete foundation or footing to an accessible location that is not subject to corrosion is permitted for connection of grounding electrode conductors and bonding jumpers providing _____.

    (a) the rebar is continuous or effectively connected to the grounding electrode rebar
    (b) the rebar extension is not in direct contact with the earth without corrosion protection
    (c) the rebar is not used as a conductor to interconnect the grounding electrode system
    (d) all of these

35. Metal water piping systems and structural metal that is interconnected to form a building frame shall be bonded to separately derived systems in accordance with 250.104(D)(1) through 250.104(D)(3).

    (a) True
    (b) False

36. Metal enclosures shall be permitted to be used to connect bonding jumpers and _____, or both, together to become a part of an effective ground-fault current path.

    (a) grounded conductors
    (b) neutral conductors
    (c) equipment grounding conductors.
    (d) grounded phase conductors

37. An equipment grounding conductor is not permitted to be used as a grounding electrode conductor under any circumstance(s).

    (a) True
    (b) False

38. Except as provided in 250.122(F)(2)(c) for raceway or cable tray installations, the equipment grounding conductor in each multiconductor cable shall be sized in accordance with 250.122 based on the _____.

    (a) largest circuit conductor
    (b) overcurrent protective device for the feeder or branch circuit
    (c) smallest branch-circuit conductor
    (d) overcurrent protective device for the service

39. Metal parts of cord-and-plug-connected equipment, if grounded, shall be connected to an equipment grounding conductor that terminates to a grounding-type attachment plug.

    (a) True
    (b) False

40. Where a metal box is surface mounted, the direct metal-to-metal contact between the receptacle yoke or strap to the box is permitted to provide the required effective ground-fault current path provided that _____.

    (a) at least one of the mounting screw retaining washers is removed
    (b) the device is attached to the box with at least two screws
    (c) the raised cover mounting holes are located on a flat portion of the cover
    (d) all of these

41. The arrangement of grounding connections shall ensure that the disconnection or the removal of a luminaire, receptacle, or other device fed from the box does not interrupt the electrical continuity of the _____ providing an effective ground-fault current path.

    (a) grounded conductor(s)
    (b) ungrounded conductor(s)
    (c) equipment grounding conductor(s)
    (d) all of these

42. The minimum size copper conductor permitted for voltage ratings up to 2000V _____ AWG.

    (a) 14
    (b) 12
    (c) 10
    (d) 8

43. When determining the number of current-carrying conductors, a grounding or bonding conductor shall not be counted when applying the provisions of 310.15(C)(1).

    (a) True
    (b) False

44. Nonmetallic-sheathed cables can enter the top of surface-mounted cabinets, cutout boxes, and meter socket enclosures through nonflexible raceways not less than 18 in. and not more than _____ in length if all of the required conditions are met.

    (a) 3 ft
    (b) 10 ft
    (c) 25 ft
    (d) 100 ft

45. Where the raceway is complete between boxes, conduit bodies, or both and encloses individual conductors or nonmetallic cable assemblies or both, the conductors or cable assemblies shall not be required to be additionally secured.

    (a) True
    (b) False

46. When Type AC cable is run across the top of a floor joist in an attic without permanent ladders or stairs, guard strips within _____ of the scuttle hole or attic entrance shall protect the cable.

    (a) 3 ft
    (b) 4 ft
    (c) 5 ft
    (d) 6 ft

47. Where Type TC-ER cable is used to connect a generator and associated equipment having terminals rated _____° C or higher, the cable shall not be limited in ampacity by 334.80 or 340.80.

    (a) 60
    (b) 75
    (c) 90
    (d) 100

48. Type SE cable shall be permitted to be used as _____.

    (a) branch circuits
    (b) feeders
    (c) underground service entrance conductors if in a raceway
    (d) branch circuits or feeders

49. For the purposes of the exceptions, _____ LFMC fittings shall be permitted as a means of securement and support.

    (a) identified
    (b) approved
    (c) listed
    (d) labeled

50. A multioutlet assembly shall not be installed _____.

    (a) in hoistways
    (b) where subject to severe physical damage
    (c) where subject to corrosive vapors
    (d) all of these

51. Weather-resistant receptacles _____ where replacements are made at receptacle outlets that are required to be so protected elsewhere in the *Code*.

    (a) shall be provided
    (b) are not required
    (c) are optional
    (d) are not allowed

52. Nonlocking-type 125V and 250V, 15A and 20A receptacles installed in _____ shall be listed as tamper resistant.

    (a) guest rooms and guest suites of hotels and motels
    (b) childcare facilities
    (c) preschools and elementary education facilities
    (d) all of these

53. If a retrofit kit is installed in a luminaire in accordance with the installation instructions, the retrofitted luminaire shall be considered reconditioned and field marked or labeled as such.

    (a) True
    (b) False

54. Luminaires and equipment shall be mechanically connected to an equipment grounding conductor as specified in 250.118 and shall be sized in accordance with _____.

    (a) Table 250.66
    (b) Table 250.102
    (c) Table 250.122
    (d) Table 310.16

55. A unit switch with a marked "_____" position that is part of a fixed space heater and disconnects all ungrounded conductors shall be permitted to serve as the required disconnecting means.

    (a) on
    (b) closed

56. Transformer top surfaces that are horizontal and readily accessible shall be marked _____.

    (a) to warn of high surface temperature(s)
    (b) for arc flash boundary
    (c) to prohibit storage
    (d) all of these

57. A storage battery is a single or group of _____ cells connected together electrically in series, in parallel, or a combination of both, and comprised of lead-acid, nickel-cadmium, or other rechargeable electrochemical types.

    (a) disposable
    (b) reusable
    (c) rechargeable
    (d) recyclable

58. Electrical and electronic equipment in hazardous (classified) locations shall be protected by a(an) _____ technique.

    (a) explosionproof
    (b) dust-ignitionproof
    (c) dusttight
    (d) any of these

59. A building or portion thereof used on a(an) _____ basis for the housing of four or more persons who are incapable of self-preservation because of age; physical limitation due to accident or illness; or limitations such as intellectual disability/developmental disability, mental illness, or chemical dependency.

    (a) occasional
    (b) 10-hour or less per day
    (c) 24-hour
    (d) temporary

60. Where overcurrent protective devices that have been previously used are installed in a temporary installation, these overcurrent protective devices shall be examined to ensure these devices _____.

    (a) have been properly installed
    (b) have been properly maintained
    (c) show no evidence of impending failure
    (d) all of these

61. The markings required by 600.4(A), for signs and outline lighting systems, and listing labels shall be visible after installation and shall be permanently applied in a location visible prior to servicing.

    (a) True
    (b) False

62. A field-applied permanent warning label that is visible during servicing shall be applied to the raceway at or near the point of entry into the sign enclosure or sign body; it shall comply with 110.21(B) and state the following: "Danger. This raceway contains energized conductors."

    (a) True
    (b) False

63. The marking for signs shall include the location of the disconnecting means for the energized conductor(s) and the disconnecting means shall be capable of being locked in the closed position in accordance with 110.25.

    (a) True
    (b) False

64. A permanent field-applied marking identifying the location of the disconnecting means shall be applied to the sign in a location visible during _____ and the warning label shall comply with 110.21(B).

    (a) installation
    (b) repair
    (c) retrofitting
    (d) servicing

65. All equipment covered by the scope of Article 625 shall be _____.

    (a) listed
    (b) labeled
    (c) identified
    (d) all of these

66. An ornamental structure or recreational water feature from which one or more jets or streams of water are discharged into the air, including splash pads, and _____ pools are defined as a fountain.

    (a) ornamental
    (b) wading
    (c) seasonal
    (d) permanently installed

67. The _____ shall be bonded together and connected to an equipment grounding conductor on a branch circuit supplying the fountain.

    (a) metal piping systems associated with the fountain
    (b) metal parts of electrical equipment associated with the fountain water-circulating system
    (c) metal raceways, metal surfaces, and electrical devices and controls located less than 5 ft of the inside wall or perimeter of the fountain
    (d) all of these

68. An _____ is a mechanically and electrically integrated grouping of modules with support structure including any attached system components such as inverter(s) or dc-to-dc converter(s) and attached associated wiring.

    (a) inverter
    (b) array
    (c) dc-to-dc converter
    (d) alternating-current photovoltaic module

69. The dc circuit conductors from two or more connected PV source circuits to their point of termination are part of the _____ circuit.

    (a) PV output
    (b) PV input
    (c) inverter input
    (d) inverter output

70. For other than one- and two-family dwellings, the maximum voltage for PV system dc circuits is limited to _____.

    (a) 30V
    (b) 50V
    (c) 600V
    (d) 1,000V

71. For PV systems, overcurrent devices, where required, shall be rated not less than _____ of the maximum currents calculated in 690.8(A).

    (a) 100%
    (b) 115%
    (c) 125%
    (d) 152%

72. For PV system rapid shutdown systems, controlled conductors located inside the array boundary shall be limited to not more than 80 volts within

    (a) 30 seconds
    (b) 45 seconds
    (c) 60 seconds
    (d) 90 seconds

73. The PV system disconnecting means shall be installed at a(n) _____ location.

    (a) guarded
    (b) accessible
    (c) protected
    (d) readily accessible

74. The PV system disconnecting means or the enclosure providing access to the disconnecting means shall be capable of being locked in accordance with 110.25.

    (a) True
    (b) False

75. Where PV source and output circuits operates at over 30V, single-conductor Type USE-2 or listed and identified PV wires installed in a readily accessible location shall be installed in _____ or guarded.

    (a) Type MC cable
    (b) any cable
    (c) any raceway
    (d) Type MC cable or any raceway

76. Single-conductor cable Type USE-2 and RHW-2 cable _____ sunlight resistant can be run exposed at outdoor locations for PV source circuits within the PV array.

    (a) approved
    (b) listed or labeled
    (c) marked
    (d) manufacturer certified

77. Equipment grounding conductors for PV circuits having overcurrent protection shall be sized in accordance with _____.

    (a) 250.66
    (b) 250.102(C)(1)
    (c) 250.122
    (d) Table 250.122

78. Facilities covered by Article 691 have specific design and safety features unique to large-scale _____ and are operated for the sole purpose of providing electric supply to a system operated by a regulated utility for the transfer of electric energy.

    (a) industrial facilities
    (b) electrical facilities
    (c) distribution facilities
    (d) PV facilities

79. Isolating devices for large scale PV electric supply stations are not be required to be located within sight of equipment and they may be located remotely from equipment.

    (a) True
    (b) False

80. A legally required standby system shall have adequate capacity in accordance with Article _____ or by another approved method.

    (a) 210
    (b) 220
    (c) 230
    (d) 700

81. Optional standby systems are typically installed to provide an alternate source of power for _____.

    (a) data processing and communication systems
    (b) emergency systems for health care facilities
    (c) emergency systems for hospitals
    (d) emergency systems for fire houses

82. A sign shall be placed at the service-entrance equipment for commercial and industrial installations indicating the _____ of each on-site optional standby power source.

    (a) type
    (b) date of installation
    (c) date of last testing
    (d) type and location

83. For _____ dwelling units, a sign shall be placed at the disconnecting means required in 230.85 that indicates the location of each permanently installed on-site optional standby power source disconnect or means to shut down the prime mover as required in 445.18(D).

    (a) apartment
    (b) guest suite
    (c) multi-family
    (d) one and two-family

84. For supply-side connected interconnected power production source(s), the sum of the interconnected power source continuous current output ratings on a service, other than those controlled in accordance with 705.13, shall not exceed the ampacity of the _____.

    (a) the service conductors
    (b) the power production source output current
    (c) the service disconnect rating
    (d) sum of all overcurrent protection devices

85. Where interconnected power production source output connections are made at busbars of a center-fed panelboard in a dwelling unit, the sum of 125 percent of the power source(s) output circuit current and the rating of the overcurrent device protecting the busbar does not exceed _____ of the current rating of the busbar.

    (a) 110%
    (b) 115%
    (c) 120%
    (d) 125%

86. In accordance with Article 705, the contribution of _____ currents from all interconnected power production source(s) shall not exceed the interrupting and short-circuit current ratings of equipment on interactive systems.

    (a) demand
    (b) load
    (c) monitored
    (d) limited

87. Any _____ raceway or cable type wiring methods in stalled in accordance with _____ shall be permitted to be used for interconnected power production systems.

    (a) Chapter 1
    (b) Chapter 2
    (c) Chapter 3
    (d) Article 705

88. Neutral conductor for interconnected power production systems used solely for instrumentation, voltage detection, or phase detection can be sized in accordance with _____.

    (a) 250.66
    (b) 250.102
    (c) 250.122
    (d) 310.16

89. Stand-alone system are capable of operating in _____ with other power sources.

    (a) in island mode, independent from the electric utility
    (b) isolated microgrid systems
    (c) interactive
    (d) all of these

90. Stand-alone and isolated microgrid systems can supply 120V to single-phase, 3-wire, 120/240V service disconnects of distribution panels if there are no 240V outlets and no multiwire circuits.

    (a) True
    (b) False

91. The requirements of 310.14(A)(3) on the temperature limitation of conductors shall apply to Class 1, Class 2, and Class 3 cables.

    (a) True
    (b) False

92. Class 1, Class 2, and Class 3 cables _____ conductors shall be identified in accordance with 250.119

    (a) ungrounded
    (b) grounded
    (c) equipment grounding
    (d) shielded

93. Class 1 circuits shall be permitted to be installed together with the conductors of _____ and medium power network-powered broadband communications circuits where separated by a barrier

    (a) electric light
    (b) power
    (c) non-power-limited fire alarm
    (d) all of these

94. The power source for a Class 2 circuit shall be _____.

    (a) a listed Class 2 transformer
    (b) a listed Class 2 power supply
    (c) other listed equipment marked to identify the Class 2 power source
    (d) any of these

95. Rated current for Class 2 and Class 3 power sources for conductors that transmit _____, is the output current per conductor the power source is designed to deliver to an operational load at normal operating conditions, as declared by the manufacturer.

    (a) power and data
    (b) emergency signaling
    (c) fire signaling
    (d) alarm signaling

96. The 8P8C connector is in widespread use with powered communications systems using Class 2 or Class 3 circuits and these connectors are typically rated at _____ maximum.

    (a) 0.50A
    (b) 1.00A
    (c) 1.20A
    (d) 1.30A

97. For communications circuit wiring in _____, the requirements of 300.22(C)(3) shall apply.

    (a) spaces for environmental air
    (b) ducts for dust
    (c) ducts for loose stock
    (d) ducts for vapor removal

98. In one- and two-family dwellings where it is not practicable to achieve an overall maximum primary protector grounding electrode conductor length of 20 ft, a separate communications ground rod not less than _____ ft shall be driven and it shall be connected to the power grounding electrode system with a 6 AWG conductor.

    (a) 5 ft
    (b) 8 ft
    (c) 10 ft
    (d) 20 ft

99. Communications systems _____ installed in buildings shall be listed.

    (a) wires and cables
    (b) cable routing assemblies
    (c) raceways
    (d) all of these

100. Communications systems wires, cables, cable routing assemblies, and communications raceways shall not be permitted in other spaces used for environmental air.

    (a) True
    (b) False

About the Author

Mike Holt—Author

Founder and President
Mike Holt Enterprises
Groveland, Florida

Mike Holt is an author, businessman, educator, speaker, publisher and *National Electrical Code* expert. He has written hundreds of electrical training books and articles, founded three successful businesses, and has taught thousands of electrical *Code* seminars across the US and internationally. His electrical training courses have set the standard for trade education, enabling electrical professionals across the country to take their careers to the next level.

Mike's approach to electrical training is based on his own experience as an electrician, contractor, inspector and teacher. Because of his struggles in his early education, he's never lost sight of how hard it can be for students who are intimidated by school, by their own feelings towards learning, or by the complexity of the *NEC*. As a result of that, he's mastered the art of explaining complicated concepts in a straightforward and direct style. He's always felt a responsibility to his students and to the electrical industry to provide education beyond the scope of just passing an exam. This commitment, coupled with the lessons he learned at the University of Miami's MBA program, have helped him build one of the largest electrical training and publishing companies in the United States.

Mike's one-of-a-kind presentation style and his ability to simplify and clarify technical concepts explain his unique position as one of the premier educators and *Code* experts in the country. In addition to the materials he's produced, and the extensive list of companies around the world for whom he's provided training, Mike has written articles that have been seen in numerous industry magazines including, *Electrical Construction & Maintenance (EC&M), CEE News, Electrical Design and Installation (EDI), Electrical Contractor (EC), International Association of Electrical Inspectors (IAEI News), The Electrical Distributor (TED), Power Quality (PQ),* and *Solar Pro.*

Mike's ultimate goal has always been to increase electrical safety and improve lives and he is always looking for the best ways for his students to learn and teach the *Code* and pass electrical exams. His passion for the electrical field continues to grow and today he is more committed than ever to serve this industry.

His commitment to pushing boundaries and setting high standards extends into his personal life. Mike's an eight-time Overall National Barefoot Waterski Champion with more than 20 gold medals, many national records, and he has competed in three World Barefoot Tournaments. In 2015, at the tender age of 64, he started a new adventure—competitive mountain bike racing. Every day he continues to find ways to motivate himself, both mentally and physically.

Mike and his wife, Linda, reside in New Mexico and Florida, and are the parents of seven children and six grandchildren. As his life has changed over the years, a few things have remained constant: his commitment to God, his love for his family, and doing what he can to change the lives of others through his products and seminars.

Special Acknowledgments

My Family. First, I want to thank God for my godly wife who's always by my side and also my children.

My Staff. A personal thank you goes to my team at Mike Holt Enterprises for all the work they do to help me with my mission of changing people's lives through education. They work tirelessly to ensure that in addition to our products meeting and exceeding the educational needs of our customers, we stay committed to building life-long relationships with them throughout their electrical careers.

The National Fire Protection Association. A special thank you must be given to the staff at the National Fire Protection Association (NFPA), publishers of the *NEC*—in particular, Jeff Sargent for his assistance in answering my many *Code* questions over the years. Jeff, you're a "first class" guy, and I admire your dedication and commitment to helping others understand the *NEC*. Other former NFPA staff members I would like to thank include John Caloggero, Joe Ross, and Dick Murray for their help in the past.

About the Illustrator

Mike Culbreath—Illustrator

Mike Culbreath
Graphic Illustrator
Alden, Michigan

Mike Culbreath has devoted his career to the electrical industry and worked his way up from apprentice electrician to master electrician. He began by doing residential and light commercial construction, and later did service work and custom electrical installations. While working as a journeyman electrician, he suffered a serious on-the-job knee injury. As part of his rehabilitation, Mike completed courses at Mike Holt Enterprises, and then passed the exam to receive his Master Electrician's license. In 1986, with a keen interest in continuing education for electricians, he joined the staff to update material and began illustrating Mike Holt's textbooks and magazine articles.

Mike started with simple hand-drawn diagrams and cut-and-paste graphics. Frustrated by the limitations of that style of illustrating, he took a company computer home to learn how to operate some basic computer graphics software. Realizing that computer graphics offered a lot of flexibility for creating illustrations, Mike took every computer graphics class and seminar he could to help develop his skills. He's worked as an illustrator and editor with the company for over 30 years and, as Mike Holt has proudly acknowledged, has helped to transform his words and visions into lifelike graphics.

Originally from south Florida, Mike now lives in northern lower Michigan where he enjoys hiking, kayaking, photography, gardening, and cooking; but his real passion is his horses. He also loves spending time with his children Dawn and Mac and his grandchildren Jonah, Kieley, and Scarlet.

Mike Culbreath-Special Acknowledgments

I would like to thank Eric Stromberg, an electrical engineer and super geek (and I mean that in the most complimentary manner, this guy is brilliant), for helping me keep our graphics as technically correct as possible. I would also like to thank all our students for the wonderful feedback to help improve our graphics.

A special thank you goes to Cathleen Kwas for making me look good with her outstanding layout design and typesetting skills; to Toni Culbreath who proofreads all of my material; and to Dawn Babbitt who has assisted me in the production and editing of our graphics. I would also like to acknowledge Belynda Holt Pinto, our Executive Vice-President, Brian House for his input (another really brilliant guy), and the rest of the outstanding staff at Mike Holt Enterprises, for all the hard work they do to help produce and distribute these outstanding products.

And last but not least, I need to give a special thank you to Mike Holt for not firing me over 30 years ago when I "borrowed" one of his computers and took it home to begin the process of learning how to do computer illustrations. He gave me the opportunity and time needed to develop my computer graphics skills. He's been an amazing friend and mentor since I met him as a student many years ago. Thanks for believing in me and allowing me to be part of the Mike Holt Enterprises family.

About the Mike Holt Team

Technical Writing

There are many people who played a role in the production of this textbook. Their efforts are reflected in the quality and organization of the information contained in this textbook, and in its technical accuracy, completeness, and usability.

Daniel Brian House

Brian House is Vice President of Digital and Technical Training at Mike Holt Enterprises and a permanent member of the video teams. He played a key role in editing this textbook, coordinating the content, and researching to assure the technical accuracy and flow of the information and illustrations presented. Brian also served as a member of the Video team for the videos that accompany this textbook.

Daniel Haruch

Dan Haruch has a skillset and general knowledge of the *NEC* that made him a natural as the newest member of our technical writing team. He sorted through and organized the first and second draft text and then verified it all against the final edition of the 2020 *NEC*. As a former electrical instructor, writing and editing the introductions and analyses shown throughout this textbook was almost second nature for Dan. His writing style helped to make the technical nature of the *Code* rules a bit easier to read and comprehend. His work ethic and ability to work with other members of the production team were a major part of the successful publication of this textbook.

Overall, Dan's contributions and efforts helped to keep the production of this book as fluid and seamless a process as possible.

Editorial and Production

A special thanks goes to **Toni Culbreath** for her outstanding contribution to this project. She worked tirelessly to proofread and edit this publication. Her attention to detail and her dedication is irreplaceable.

Many thanks to **Cathleen Kwas** who did the design, layout, and production of this textbook. Her desire to create the best possible product for our customers is greatly appreciated.

Also, thanks to **Paula Birchfield** who was the Production Coordinator for this product. She helped keep everything flowing and tied up all the loose ends. She and **Jeff Crandall** did a great job proofing the final files prior to printing.

Video Team

The following special people provided technical advice in the development of this textbook as they served on the video team along with author **Mike Holt** and graphic illustrator **Mike Culbreath**.

Vince Della Croce
Business Development Manager, Electrical Inspector
Port Saint Lucie, Florida

Vince Della Croce began his career in IBEW Local Union #3, New York City, as a helper and progressed to journeyman and foreman electrician before relocating to Florida. He's licensed by the State of Florida as a master electrician, electrical inspector and plans examiner.

He holds an Associate of Science degree in Electronic Engineering and Electrical Maintenance Technology from Penn Foster College and represents Siemens in the role of Business Development Manager with a focus on supporting electrical inspectors throughout the country.

Vince serves the IAEI Florida Chapter as Education Chairman and IAEI Southern Section as Assistant Secretary Treasurer. He was an alternate member of Code-Making Panels 7 and 12 for the 2017 *NEC* and is a principal technical committee member of NFPA 73, 78, 99 and 1078. He's also seated on a New York City electrical code revision technical committee which is tasked with moving the city from the 2008 to the 2014 *Code*.

Vince has two sons. The oldest is serving the community as a police detective and holds a master's degree in Business Administration. The youngest is pursuing a bachelor's degree in Marketing.

Daniel Brian House
Mike Holt Enterprises
Leesburg, Florida

Brian House is Vice President of Digital and Technical Training at Mike Holt Enterprises, and a Certified Mike Holt Instructor. He began teaching seminars in 2000 after joining the elite group of instructors who attended Mike Holt's Train the Trainer boot camp. Brian was personally selected for development by Mike Holt after being named as one of the top presenters in that class. He now travels around the country to teach Mike Holt seminars to groups that include electricians, instructors, the military, and engineers. His first-hand experience as an electrical contractor, along with Mike Holt's instructor training, gave him a teaching style that is practical, straightforward, and refreshing.

Brian is high-energy, with a passion for doing business the right way. He expresses his commitment to the industry and his love for its people whether he's teaching, working on books, or developing instructional programs. Brian also leads the Mike Holt Enterprises apprenticeship and digital products teams. They're creating cutting-edge training tools and partnering with apprenticeship programs nation-wide to help them take their curriculum to the next level.

Brian and his wife Carissa have shared the joy of their four children and many foster children during 22 years of marriage. When not mentoring youth at work or church, he can be found racing mountain bikes with his kids or fly fishing on Florida's Intracoastal Waterway. He's passionate about helping others and regularly engages with the youth of his community to motivate them into exploring their future.

Jennifer Martin
Master Electrician/Instructor
Richland, Washington

Jennifer Martin is a third-generation wireman, IBEW Local #112 member that brings enthusiasm and charisma to the formal instruction and application of Electrical Codes and Safety Standards. She has been a vital part of the Volpentest HAMMER training facility within the Department of Energy (DOE). She provides her extensive experience in electrical instruction and consultation to local industries and generation facilities for ElecTrain while currently acting as the Electrical Administrator for Federal Engineers & Constructors (FE&C). She manages this workload all the while attending to her amazing children (six to be exact) ranging from twenty to six months of age. It goes without saying she is an incredibly busy woman.

Jennifer is a master electrician with electrical contractors' licenses in multiple states, a certified electrical safety professional (CESCP) and IEEE member, adding to her unbridled dedication to the electrical industry. Some may ask what she prefers to read for enjoyment; she usually responds with "Electrical codes and safety standards" followed by a sincere smile and slight giggle. Through her various industry memberships and representation of building trades there is always an opportunity for learning and sharing her passion with others.

Jennifer was introduced to Mike Holt by Eric Stromberg who she has worked with at DOE supporting Energy Facility Contractors Group (EFCOG); Electrical Safety Task Group for DOE Complex wide consistency and best practices. She most humbly accepted the opportunity to work with this unbelievable group of individuals and looks forward to the future adventures to come.

Eric Stromberg, P.E.
Electrical Engineer/Instructor
Los Alamos, New Mexico

Eric Stromberg has a bachelor's degree in electrical engineering and is a professional engineer. He started in the electrical industry when he was a teenager helping the neighborhood electrician. After high school, and a year of college, Eric worked for a couple of different audio companies, installing sound systems in a variety of locations from small buildings to baseball stadiums. After returning to college he worked as a journeyman wireman for an electrical contractor.

After graduating from the University of Houston, Eric took a job as an electronic technician and installed and serviced life safety systems in high-rise buildings. After seven years he went to work for Dow Chemical as a power distribution engineer. His work with audio systems had made him very sensitive to grounding issues and he took this experience with him into power distribution. Because of this expertise, Eric became one of Dow's grounding subject matter experts. This is also how Eric met Mike Holt, as Mike was looking for grounding experts for his 2002 Grounding vs. Bonding video.

Eric taught the *National Electrical Code* for professional engineering exam preparation for over 20 years and has held continuing education teacher certificates for the states of Texas and New Mexico. He was on the electrical licensing and advisory board for the State of Texas, as well as on their electrician licensing exam board. Eric now works for a Department of Energy research laboratory in New Mexico, where he's responsible for the electrical standards as well as being a part of the laboratory's AHJ.

Eric's oldest daughter lives with her husband in Zurich, Switzerland, where she teaches for an international school. His son served in the Air Force, has a degree in Aviation logistics, and is a pilot and owner of an aerial photography business. His youngest daughter is a singer/songwriter in Los Angeles.

David Williams
Electrical Inspector and Instructor
Delta Township, Lansing, Michigan

David Williams is an electrical inspector for Delta Township, Lansing, Michigan and has been an Adjunct Associate Professor at Lansing Community College in the Electrical Technology Program since 1995. He began his electrical career as an apprentice in 1974 at U.S. Steel, started inspecting for the State of Michigan in 1988, and has been inspecting for Delta Township since 1994.

David is a Licensed Master Electrician, Registered Electrical Inspector, Plan Reviewer, and Instructor. He holds a Certified Electrical Inspector—Master, Electrical Inspector General, and Electrical Inspector 1-2 Family through the International Association of Electrical Inspectors, IAEI.

He's served on a Technical Committee for the *National Electrical Code* since 2007 and is currently serving on the *NEC* Correlating Committee for the 2020 *Code* and CMP-10 covering Articles 215, 225, 230, 240, and the new Article 242. He Chaired CMP-7 for the 2017 *NEC* and served on CMP-5 covering Grounding and Bonding for the 2008, 2011, and 2014 *Code* cycles.

David also serves on seven UL Standards Technical Panels; UL-111, Standard for Multi-Outlet Assemblies; UL-414, Meter Mounting Equipment; UL-1081, Swimming Pumps and Filters; UL-2200, Stationary Engine Generator Assemblies; UL-2201, Portable Engine Generators; UL-2743, Portable Power Packs; and UL-3001, Distributed Energy Generation and Storage Systems. He's served on the UL Electrical Council since 2010.

David is a Vice-President for the International Association of Electrical Inspectors, International Board of Directors. He's currently the IAEI Michigan Chapter Secretary and serves on the Western Section Board of Directors. He's Past President of the IAEI Michigan Chapter and Past President of the IAEI Western Section.

David and his wife Marie have two children, Christina and Aaron, and reside in Delta Township. He likes golfing and they enjoy spending time at their family cottage.

Mario Valdes, Jr.
Electrical Inspector, Plans Examiner
Pembroke Pines, Florida

Mario Valdes Jr. is an electrical inspector and plan examiner for an engineering firm that does private provider and municipal support services. He started his career at 16 years old with his father, who owns an electrical contracting company and worked himself up to a master electrician. Once he received his Florida state contractor's license, he ran his father's company as a project manager and estimator. Mario's passion for the *National Electrical Code* led him to obtain his inspector and plan review certifications to embark on a new journey as an electrical professional in the *Code*-compliance industry.

Mario is a goal setter and plans to become a certified instructor within a year. He's worked in very complex projects such as hospitals, casinos, hotels, and multi-family high-rise buildings bringing him diverse experience in the electrical field. He is a member of the IAEI, NFPA, & ICC and believes that by staying active in these organizations he'll be ahead of the game, with cutting-edge knowledge pertaining to safety codes. He enjoys participating in meetings and giving his input on certain topics.

When not immersed in the electrical world he enjoys fitness training because a healthy mind requires a healthy body.

Mario resides in Miami, Florida with his beautiful family which includes his wife and his two sons, and they enjoy family getaways to Disney World and other amusement parks.

Notes

Notes

Notes